THE ILLUSTRATED HISTORY OF
MANCHESTER UNITED

1878–2001

hamlyn

THE ILLUSTRATED HISTORY OF MANCHESTER UNITED

1878–2001

Tom Tyrrell and David Meek
Foreword by Sir Bobby Charlton

First published in Great Britain in 1988 under the title Manchester United, the Official
History by Hamlyn, a division of Octopus Publishing Group Limited, 2—4 Heron Quays,
Docklands, London, E14 4JP

Revised and reprinted 1992, 1996. Revised, enlarged and reprinted 1994, 1995, 1997,
1998, 1999, 2000, 2001

ISBN 0 600 60440 3

A catalogue record for this book is available from the British Library

Printed in Italy

Senior editor: **Trevor Davies**
Design: **Martin Topping**
Original design: **Birgit Eggers**
Production controller: **Edward Carter**

Photographic Acknowledgements

The publishers would like to thank those who contributed photographs for use in this book including the following:
Associated Sports Photography, Colorsport, Hulton Getty, David Meek, Octopus Picture Library,
Mirror Syndication International, and Tom Tyrell.

Every effort has been made to trace the copyright holders of all photographs used in this book.
We apologise for any omissions, which are unintentional, and would be pleased to include appropriate
acknowledgement in any subsequent edition.

FOREWORD BY SIR BOBBY CHARLTON

MANCHESTER UNITED seems to have been the focus of my sporting life for almost as long as I can remember.

When I think about it, I suppose it is really not so surprising considering that my association with the club now goes back some 45 years, even longer if you take into account my schooldays back home in Ashington in the north-east when Joe Armstrong, the United scout, first came round to our house. I shall always remember little Joe with the beaming smile because he was the first to take an interest, and later when there were a few more on the scene and I had to choose a club to go to, I thought I couldn't do better than stay with Joe. The fact that he represented Manchester United and Matt Busby came into it as well of course, but I think my first instincts were right.

I have had a most exciting and rewarding lifetime associated with Manchester United and the fact that I am now honoured to serve the club as a director has been the ultimate satisfaction. Outside my home and family, the club has been my life, and I guess there have even been times when Norma, my wife, has wondered whether football hasn't taken over at home as well. I have got to admit that the game fascinates me as much as ever, especially Manchester United, the club which gave me much of my education and most of my inspiration.

I was privileged to know and play alongside the Busby Babes, lucky to escape with my life when so many of those fine young players failed to survive that terrible crash at Munich. The experience perhaps left me a little more appreciative of the many good things which have happened to me since then, the successes and even the disappointments that make up a career.

Sir Matt Busby and Jimmy Murphy I hold in great affection and respect as the men who did so much to fashion me as a footballer and who led us to those achievements in Europe, to the League Championship and the FA Cup. I have so many memories of matches, friends and team-mates, not to mention opponents and the people I have met in my football travels. Now as I read this latest book on Manchester United my mind is refreshed as the events leap to life again, partly because I was there for 20 years as a player, but also because of the detailed touch of authority brought to a formidable task by Tom Tyrrell and David Meek.

For they were there as well! Tom reported for Piccadilly Radio and was writing about Old Trafford nearly 35 years ago. David was the *Manchester Evening News* representative who covered the club for more than 30 years.

There have been other fine books written about Manchester United, but not with quite the same insight and feel for the club and its many famous players. Even when they are writing about the early days I feel they have captured the essence and spirit of a club which so many of us hold so dear.

So it is with particular pleasure that I write this foreword to a book which I know will stand the test of time as a history of Manchester United.

No. 15.—THE NEWTON HEATH TEAM.

HENRYS.   CLEMENTS.

TIMMONS (*Trainer*).   COUPAR.   PERRINS.   STEWART.   ERRENTZ.   MITCHELL.

FARMAN.   HOOD.   DONALDSON.   FITZIMMONS.   COLVILLE.

CHAPTER
BIRTH OF A LEGEND

To give George Stephenson, the railway engineer, a part to play in the Manchester United story might seem the work of an overstretched imagination, but the man who had a leading role in the development of rail transport did indeed make a contribution. He came to Manchester in the late 1820s to build the first passenger railway from the city, to Liverpool. He chose for the Manchester terminal the site of Castlefield, the flat area on the outskirts of the city where the Roman legions had settled on their way north to combat the Picts and Scots and where they had built a fortress named Mancunium, which developed into the city of Manchester. It was the perfect spot for Stephenson, offering no unmanageable gradients to his famous 'Rocket' when it began its journeys to and from Liverpool Road Station, the first railway station in the world.

Stephenson's first passenger railway was the Manchester and Liverpool Railway, and as time passed and it became clear that the project was a success, other lines opened. One of these was a line operating in the opposite direction, the Manchester and Leeds Railway, setting off from Oldham Road, Newton Heath, and terminating in the Leeds area where its lines met with those of the North Midland Railway. Eventually the two companies combined, and formed the Lancashire and Yorkshire Railway Company, which had a branch at one end of its line, in Newton Heath.

This was in 1847 when the game of football was still going through a complicated phase of its progress towards becoming a major part of the lives of British working people. There were plenty of centres where the game was played, but no uniformity in its rules. Schools, colleges and universities had football as part of their recreational activities, but the game played at Cambridge, for example, differed from that of Eton.

The birth of football

It was not until 1863 that a group of football enthusiasts from the London area met in the Freemason's Tavern in Great Queen Street, London, and formed the Football Association, and eventually after much arguing and a walkout by certain representatives, drew up the first rules of association football.

In 1872 the Football Association introduced its first national competition. A trophy was bought for £20 and named the Football Association Cup, attracting entries from as far apart as the Queen's Park Club in Glasgow and Donnington in Lincolnshire, although the majority of teams were from the

The men of Newton Heath who played in the club's first season in the Football League. Goalkeepers Warner and Davies are missing, otherwise the players are those who appeared regularly throughout the season. Some records show that on 7 January 1893 Newton Heath played with only ten men, with Stewart (third from right, centre row) in goal. Could this be the day when the photographer called?

London area. Wanderers beat the Royal Engineers 1-0 at Kennington Oval in the first Cup final. Football had arrived as a public sport, with 2,000 having watched the game.

Newton Heath LYR

Six years later, when the railways of the country had grown into a gigantic network from the tiny acorn George Stephenson had planted in Manchester, the Dining Room Committee of the Lancashire and Yorkshire Railway Company responded to a request from men of the Carriage and Wagon Works for permission, and funds, to start their own football team.

The men chose the title 'Newton Heath LYR' for the team (the LYR being Lancashire and Yorkshire Railway), their nearest rivals being the men from the company's Motive Power Division (the engine drivers and maintenance men) whose team was 'Newton Heath Loco'(motive). Newton Heath LYR were given a pitch on a stretch of land in North Road, close to the railway yard. It was a bumpy, stony patch in summer, a muddy, heavy swamp in the rainy months. But the men of Newton Heath LYR didn't really care – football was a means of enjoyment and the mud would wash off.

There were many other clubs in the area and a Manchester Cup competition had been launched, so Newton Heath LYR entered in 1885 and reached the final. The following year they again competed, and this time won. The game was attracting a great deal of interest, and the success of the side was looked upon as bringing prestige to the Lancashire and Yorkshire Railway Company by the executives, who were quite prepared to make allowances for men to take time off work in order to prepare for important fixtures.

In 1887 Newton Heath LYR again reached the final of the Manchester Cup, only to lose, but the club was now ready for a major step in its history, as football itself took a massive stride forward. Meetings had taken place several times amongst representatives of many of the northern clubs to discuss the formation of a combination of teams who would take part in a new competition. Small leagues were in existence in various parts of the country, but the plans under consideration were for a league of a much grander nature. In 1888 the Football League was formed, its twelve members having a strong northern domination, but with others from the Midlands also involved.

The original twelve were Preston North End, Aston Villa, Wolverhampton Wanderers, Blackburn Rovers, Bolton Wanderers, West Bromwich Albion, Accrington Stanley, Everton, Burnley, Derby County, Notts County and Stoke City. All were based in industrial towns or cities, and each linked to the other by the railways.

In the first season Preston North End dominated the League, going through their 22 games without a single defeat, and for good measure they won the FA Cup as well, beating Wolves 3-0 at the Oval.

Newton Heath did not consider themselves strong enough to compete with the elite of the game, but they were growing in stature and it became obvious that the opposition being provided locally was not enough to test the mettle of the 'Heathens'. In 1888 they had the proud record of not losing a game at home until October, when a team of touring Canadians came to Manchester and beat them before 3,000 spectators in what was the first 'international' game played at North Road.

The club join the Football Alliance

By that time the idea of League football played between towns rather than within local boundaries, was catching on and in 1889, Newton Heath joined other clubs on the verge of the Football League to form the Football Alliance.

In their first season Newton Heath finished eighth, having played the eleven companions in their new league: Sunderland, Darwen, Crewe Alexandra, Bootle, Grimsby Town, Birmingham St George's, Walsall Town Swifts, Sheffield Wednesday, Small Heath, Nottingham Forest and Long Eaton.

They also played in the first round of the FA Cup, and had the misfortune to be drawn against Preston North End, the holders, who beat them 6-1 at Deepdale, the only consolation for Newton Heath being that they had scored against the 'Invincibles', which is more than many of their Football League 'superiors' had done the previous season.

In 1890 another major step came for Newton Heath. They began to sever their links with the railway company. The letters 'LYR' were dropped from their title. The club appointed its first full-time official, the secretary A H Albut, who arrived from Aston Villa and set up office in a terraced cottage close to North Road, at 33 Oldham Road, Newton Heath.

There was still a strong connection with the railways, even though the club was no longer supported by the social committee of the Lancashire and Yorkshire Railway. Most of the players worked for the railways, and it was this which had made the club successful in the first place. A job on the railways was considered a job for life, and being able to offer a talented footballer work in the Manchester area allowed the club to attract men from all parts of the country. Also, because they were 'staff' the players had concessionary travel, and the team was able to get from game to game without the added burden of transport to pay for.

Professionalism in football had started three years before the formation of the Football League and some of Newton Heath's players earned money by playing for the club. But their reward was small, helping only to boost their wages from their normal employment, and hardly putting them with high wage-earners.

International Players

Newton Heath had attracted some players who were highly rated in the game, Welshmen like the Doughty brothers, Jack and Roger, who found work in the railway depot and whose football skills earned them international honours. There were others in the side who had sound reputations, like goalkeeper Tom Hay, who moved to the area from Staveley close to the railway town of Crewe, and Pat McDonnell, a craggy Scot whose search for work led to him walking from Glasgow to Manchester, where he was given a job at Newton Heath and won his place in the side.

Jack Powell, the full-back, had a remarkable rise to fame. He was new to the game when the Welsh club Druids, in Ruabon, signed him but it was obvious that he had a bright future. After just three games he was selected to play for his country against England in 1879. In 1887 he registered as a professional with Newton Heath. Mitchell, Davies, Owen, Tait and Sam Black, skipper before Powell's arrival, had all played a part in the growth of the club from a works team to one good enough to represent the city of Manchester against clubs from other areas.

Sam Black always remained an amateur. He refused payment while those around him accepted the few shillings a week they could earn from their football. Black played with Newton Heath for most of the 1880s before returning to his native Burton on Trent and turning to refereeing.

Sunderland clear the way

At the end of the 1889-90 season Stoke City had finished bottom of the Football League, having won just three games in the entire season, and found life a struggle both on and off the field. They asked if they might stand down, and were replaced by Sunderland from the Alliance, who were highly successful. A link between the two leagues had been forged.

In their second season of Alliance football, Newton Heath did no better than in their first. They won seven games once again, five of them at North Road, their biggest victory being against Crewe, 6-3. Their biggest defeat was an 8-2 thrashing away to Nottingham Forest.

That summer Stoke City were allowed to re-enter the Football League, having proved too strong for the Alliance. The move was possible because the League's members decided that they would enlarge their numbers by two, and

1892-1949

they also accepted Darwen. Now there were fourteen clubs, and Sunderland had proved their worth by finishing in seventh place, only six points away from the Champions, Everton.

Sunderland's strength was further illustrated the following season when they won the title, and it was also a season of great significance for Newton Heath. With Darwen now out of the Alliance and Stoke back in the higher reaches, two new clubs filled their places, Ardwick FC from Manchester, and Lincoln City.

Ardwick eventually became Manchester City, and the first time the two great Manchester rivals met under senior league conditions was on Saturday, 10 October 1891, when Newton Heath won 3-1 at North Road, thanks to goals from Farman (2) and Donaldson. Strangely, the two sides had met the previous week in an FA Cup qualifying round, when Newton Heath won 5-1, so they had started favourites for that very first league 'derby' clash.

The Newton Heath team for the Alliance game was:

Slater, McFarlane, Clements, Sharpe, Stewart, Owen, Farman, Edge, Donaldson, Sneddon, Henrys

The win marked another milestone for the club, as it was the first time since joining the Alliance that the team had celebrated three successive victories.

By the end of the season they were undefeated at North Road, and had lost just three times: at Burton on Trent to the Swifts, at Muntz Street in Birmingham where Small Heath beat them 3-2, and at the Town Ground in Nottingham, where Forest showed their strength in a 3-0 victory. Forest won the Alliance, Newton Heath were runners up.

Newton Heath become a First Division side

Then in 1892 the Football League again decided to enlarge. It divided into two divisions, the League becoming the First Division, and growing to 16 clubs, whilst a Second Division was formed by others from the Alliance and clubs such as Northwich Victoria, Rotherham and London's first professional club, Woolwich Arsenal.

Nottingham Forest and Newton Heath were invited to join the First Division. So the club which had struggled for those first two seasons had reached a pinnacle just at the right moment, and was now one of football's elite.

Elite by status, but not one of the rich clubs by a long way.

Newton Heath seemed to stagger from financial problem to financial problem. Harry Renshaw, the first Newton Heath correspondent from the Manchester Evening News, wrote of the club's plight, and its operations from 33 Oldham Road:

The rent of the cottage was just six shillings a week [30 pence] and to increase the social side the club rented a schoolroom in Miles Platting as a place where supporters and players might meet. It was a place where they might spend time together in a common cause, and to add to the facilities a billiards table was purchased. But, sad to relate, the venture was not a success. Indeed at one meeting of directors the only light available was from three candles fixed in ginger beer bottles. The reason? The Corporation had cut off the gas supply, and served a summons on the club!

However, according to Renshaw's story, the summons was put to good use by the crafty Albut. He had his eye on a player with another club and knew that the man was unsettled and having problems getting his wages. So he met the player, lent him the summons and let him use it to threaten his club, telling them that he would 'serve it' if they didn't let him join Newton Heath. They did and his presence increased gate receipts by £10 for the next game.

The Heathens first season in the Football League was one of direct comparison with their performance off the field. They struggled, and yet survived.

The first game Newton Heath played in the First Division was against Blackburn Rovers, a formidable force. The town of Blackburn had provided football with its first 'super club'. In 1884

The Manchester County Football Asociation Cup, the first trophy to be won by Newton Heath. It was success in this competition which persuaded the club to reach for more distant horizons and which eventually led to League status. The trophy was unearthed in recent times and now stands in the club museum after many years in a bank vault

Rovers won the FA Cup, beating Queen's Park from Glasgow in the final. The following year they repeated the feat against the same opponents and then in 1886 beat West Bromwich Albion in a replayed final and were awarded a special trophy for their third successive cup win. In 1890 Blackburn beat Sheffield Wednesday 6-1 in the final, and the next season won the cup for the fifth time in eight years by beating Notts County 3-1.

A slow start

When the 1892-93 season began Newton Heath approached their first fixture against three-times Cup winners Rovers with some trepidation. The match was at Rovers' ground, and despite goals from Coupar, Donaldson and Farman, ended in a 4-3 defeat. Seven days later Manchester witnessed its first Football League game which ended in a 1-1 draw with Burnley, the Scot Robert Donaldson again scoring as he would do with regularity throughout that first season.

Newton Heath made a poor start, losing their next two games at Burnley and Everton, then followed this with a draw at West Bromwich and defeat by the Throstles at North Road. The Heathens had played six games in the first Division without a win, but when victory did arrive it came in true style. The club's first League win was in a game against Wolverhampton Wanderers, a club which would continue to be a rival until the days of the Busby Babes, and on Saturday 15 October 1892 Newton Heath won 10-1!

Nevertheless, the season was a long difficult road for the club, with victories few and far between, and when Blackburn knocked them out of the FA Cup in January 1893 it seemed a bleak journey for the 'Railwaymen'. When April came and the season ended with a 3-3 draw against Accrington Stanley, Newton Heath were 16th in the First Division, bottom of the table.

It is interesting to note here that in the 1986-87 season the League Management Committee caused a minor sensation when they introduced their proposals for end of season play-offs in an effort to trim down the First Division to twenty clubs. The bottom three clubs in the First Division were relegated, the top two from the Second Division promoted. The remaining place (in the first year the number of clubs was cut to 21, the final reduction being made in season 1987-88) was contested by a play-off series between the First Division club finishing fourth from the bottom, and the Second Division clubs in third, fourth and fifth places.

This 'new' method of securing or winning a position in the top division was a cause of great controversy. But it was not a new scheme – far from it.

The Football League in 1892 had decided that at the end of the season, the three bottom clubs in the new First Division would meet the first three of the Second Division for the right to play in the top section the following year.(see table)

Small Heath – later to become Birmingham City – were top of the Second Division, so on 22 April 1893, two weeks after the season officially ended, the clubs met at Stoke for the deciding 'Test Match'. It ended 1-1, with Farman's goal earning Newton Heath the right to fight once again in a replay. A crowd of over 6,000 crossed the Pennines to see Newton Heath win the replay at Bramall Lane, Sheffield, 5-2. Three goals from Farman, plus one each from Cassidy and Coupar were enough to secure their place in the First Division for the 1893-94 season.

END OF THE 1892/93 SEASON:

	P	W	D	L	F	A	Pts
Sunderland	30	22	4	4	100	36	48
Preston North End	30	17	3	10	57	39	37
Everton	30	16	4	10	74	51	36
Aston Villa	30	16	3	11	73	62	35
Bolton Wanderers	30	13	6	11	56	55	32
Burnley	30	13	4	13	51	44	30
Stoke City	30	12	5	13	58	48	29
West Bromwich Albion	30	12	5	13	58	69	29
Blackburn Rovers	30	8	13	9	47	56	29
Nottingham Forest	30	10	8	12	48	52	28
Wolverhampton Wdrs.	30	12	4	14	47	68	28
Sheffield Wednesday	30	12	3	15	55	65	27
Derby County	30	9	9	12	52	64	27
Notts County	30	10	4	16	53	61	24
Accrington Stanley	30	6	11	13	57	81	23
Newton Heath	30	6	6	18	50	85	18

A new ground

The club's ground at North Road was heavily criticised during the season not only by defeated opponents but by the local supporters and Newton Heath's own players. Secretary Albut had a mission: to find a new playing area. In 1893 the club left North Road, where on dry days stones and flints made life difficult for the players and on wet afternoons spectators had to squelch their way to and from the ground through ankle deep slime.

The new ground was in Bank Street, Clayton. Here the mud of North Road was replaced by the toxic fumes of a chemical works which ran alongside the pitch. There were those who claimed that if the Heathens were losing, the factory would belch out heavy smoke, on the premise that home players were accustomed to it, while it made life difficult for the visiting side. The registered office moved from Oldham Road to Bank Street, secretary Albut being quite prepared to share the wooden hut with the local newspaper which provided the telephone.

So the second season of League Football began and this was to have a significant effect on the future of the club. They won their first game at the new ground, beating Burnley 3-2, and by 23 September 1893 could look back on four games which had seen them winning twice, drawing once and losing 3-1 at West Bromwich.

It was the return fixture against the Midlands club which was to lead to a strange turn of events, and seriously affect Newton Heath's financial position. Football had now become very popular and newspapers assigned correspondents to cover games – readers pored over their words as the only means of following their favourites' progress. The newspaper was the bearer of facts, the bringer of truth, and when West Bromwich were beaten 4-1 on 14 October, readers of the *Birmingham Daily Gazette*, published on the Monday after the game, were stunned to read the words of 'Observer':

> *It wasn't football, it was simply brutality and if these are the tactics Newton Heath are compelled to adopt to win their matches, the sooner the Football Association deal severely with them the better it will be for the game generally.*

Newton Heath's officials were sent a cutting of the story, and were furious. This was criticism which they felt was unwarranted and decided to take the newspaper and its writer – William Jephcott – to court. They got the referee to back their claim, and he gave them ample support by writing to the *Manchester Guardian* that the game had not been the rough-house described in the Midlands newspaper, but had in his opinion been 'one of the best games he had ever controlled'. The referee, Mr. J R Strawson of Lincoln, wrote:

> *Not once was any decision that I gave questioned, the play of both sides was a credit to their clubs and a credit to the game.*

In March the following year, after a season of football that saw Newton Heath still fighting for survival, the Manchester Civil Court judge, Mr Justice Day, granted Newton Heath one farthing damages, and ordered both parties to pay their own costs. This was a body blow indeed for the club.

The first club to be relegated

From that game with West Bromwich, early in the season, until the last game of the 1893-94 campaign, only three League victories came Newton Heath's way, so it was no surprise to anyone when they found themselves involved in the play-off Test Match again.

Liverpool had topped the Second Division, eight points clear of Small Heath, and when Blackburn's ground at Ewood Park was chosen as the venue for the deciding game, Newton

John Henry Davies, first chairman of Manchester United and the man whose wealth created the club from the failing Newton Heath. Davies was managing director of Manchester Breweries and not only rescued the club from extinction when he became involved in 1901, but put up the £60,000 to build Old Trafford. The chance meeting of Davies and Harry Stafford was indeed a stroke of good fortune

Heath felt that the odds were stacked against them. The game ended in a 2-0 defeat, Liverpool were promoted from the Second Division, and Newton Heath became the first club ever to be relegated. They stayed in the Second Division for the next twelve seasons, but during that time the club was transformed, and perhaps that court case and its crippling outcome was fate playing a hand in the growth of Manchester United.

Newton Heath ended their first season in the Second Division in third place, again qualifying for the play-offs, but this time losing to Stoke, whose season had ended with them third from bottom in the First Division. Ironically, Liverpool were the only club to be relegated after losing their Test Match to Bury.

The play-off system was changed the following season to a mini-league among the qualifying clubs. Newton Heath, who finished in second place in the regular season, stayed down.

A season later the play-offs were abandoned in favour of automatic promotion and relegation of the top two and bottom two clubs. Burnley and Newcastle United moved up to replace Stoke and Blackburn, leaving the two Manchester clubs, City and Newton Heath in third and fourth places in the Second Division. By the turn of the century Newton Heath had missed promotion by two places for two successive seasons, and seen their financial position worsen. Players' demands were not high, but they did have the backing of the Players' Union, predecessor of the Professional Footballers' Association, formed in 1898 in Manchester, at the Spread Eagle Hotel in Corporation Street.

room. A hurried search revealed that the dog had broken loose and a fireman on duty in the hall saw two eyes staring at him in the darkness. He had no idea it was the dog and rushed out of the side entrance to the building. The St Bernard went out the same way.

What happened next has, over the years, become distorted somewhat, with parts added to give the story greater impact perhaps, but the *Manchester Evening News* of September 1906 (five years after the event, and 42 before Alf Clarke's recollections were published) told the story thus:

The animal was found by a friend of Mr James Taylor, and was seen by Mr J H Davies, who fancied it. The making of the bargain led to the meeting of Mr Davies and Stafford, and the latter, knowing the low water in which his club was in, asked Mr Davies for a contribution to its funds. This led to the club changing hands.

Harry Stafford was the club right-back and captain, and he and Taylor and Davies, a brewer, were to play a part in saving the club from extinction, so the role of the St Bernard can hardly be exaggerated.

Early in 1902 Newton Heath's creditors could wait no longer. The club had debts of £2,670 and was on the verge of bankruptcy, a fate which had already seen Bootle FC forced to quit the League and be replaced by Liverpool. Would Newton Heath also slip out of existence?

A creditors' meeting was held at New Islington Hall, but although secretary James West reported that there were no new tradesmen's debts outstanding since the date of the winding-up order, the club still needed £2,000 to make it solvent again. Harry Stafford then got to his feet and told the meeting that he knew where he could get hold of the money, massive amount though it was.

Stafford said he had met four businessmen who were each willing to invest £500, but who in turn would require a direct interest in running the club. The Newton Heath directors agreed, or were forced into agreement by the creditors, and the four men, J Brown of Denton, W Deakin of Manchester, together with James Taylor and John Henry Davies, eventually came forward with their proposals.

Saved by a St Bernard

Fate was to take a hand again. Newton Heath had ended the 1901 season in tenth place. Attendances for their Second Division games had dropped off, and the club needed cash. It was decided to organise a grand bazaar, in St James' Hall in Oxford Street, and here one man and his dog stepped into the creation of a legend. In his official history of 1948 Alf Clarke wrote:

A St Bernard dog, with a barrel fastened to its collar, was one of the attractions at the show. One night, after the place had closed (it was the third night of the four days of the bazaar) the dog apparently knocked over a part of a stall in the centre of the

The club's influential captain Charlie Roberts, who appeared on the scene in 1904 and played until the outbreak of the First World War in 1914. Roberts played three times for England in 1905 and skippered United to all their major successes in the early 1900s. Roberts caused a minor sensation by insisting on playing in shorts which were above knee length

Manchester United is born

On 28 April 1902 Newton Heath FC was no more. It was replaced by Manchester United Football Club.

The selection of the new title was not straightforward, though. While the 'uniting' of Davies's group and Stafford's club might have seemed an obvious inspiration for the name, others were tabled. Manchester Central was one suggestion, but this was rejected because it sounded too much like a rail-

1892-1949

way station. There was in fact a Central Station in Manchester (now the site of the G-MEX Exhibition Centre) which later served the Old Trafford area, and with Newton Heath's railway connections perhaps the name was not as ridiculous as it seems. Manchester Celtic was also put forward but turned down on the grounds that it might be felt that there was some link with Celtic organisations.

Eventually Louis Rocca, a man who would play a leading role on the club's scouting staff for the next 48 years, came forward with the name Manchester United and it was unanimously adopted. A new president was elected, Mr John Henry Davies, and Harry Stafford teamed up with James West to organise the day-to-day running of the club. Stafford was given the licence for one of Davies's public houses, and the St Bernard settled into its new home with the brewer's daughter! The curtain came down on Newton Heath as the club finished just four places from the foot of the Second Division.

The following season, as Manchester United, new spirit and new players took them to fifth from the top, but they were forced to look on with some envy as their rivals Manchester City were promoted.

Ernest Mangnall

The 1903-04 season began with a home draw against Bristol City, and defeats at the hands of Burnley and Port Vale, a start which led to a call for action from the supporters. Then in late September 1903 there arrived on the scene a man who was to play as important a part in the building of the Manchester United of today as any other . . . Ernest Mangnall.

Mangnall was the club's first **real** manager and a man who knew how to use the media to promote football, and to a certain extent himself. He was a well-known sportsman with a love of cycling, which saw him heavily involved with the National Cyclists Union, and Bolton Cycling Club and Bolton Harriers Athletic Club. He was involved at the turn of the century with the opening of Burnden Park, which was used for cycling and athletics as well as football, and eventually he was elected to Bolton Wanderers board of directors. In March 1900 he moved into management, taking over at Burnley from Harry Bradshaw, who moved south to manage Woolwich Arsenal. A football manager in the early years of the game was referred to as the club 'secretary' but he was responsible for selecting the team, deciding on the tactics to use, and conducting training sessions.

Mangnall was later to go on record as saying that he felt players should not use a ball too much during practice sessions, but should build up their physical fitness. 'A ball should only be used one day a week', he said, a true sign of the times.

Perhaps one of the most important events in the history of Manchester United was the fund-raising bazaar of 1901. The efforts of Newton Heath to stay afloat in football's formative years led to the event being staged. It was from St James's Hall that Harry Stafford's dog strayed to find its way to J H Davies

In a series of articles for the *Manchester Evening News* he wrote:

A great, intricate, almost delicate, and to the vast majority of the public an incomprehensible piece of machinery is the modern, up to date, football club. It is a creation peculiarly by itself. There is nothing like it and it is only when one takes an active and practical part in the manipulation of the strings that work such an organisation that one realises in the fullest sense what it all means.

The veriest layman need not be told that the greatest and first essential to success is the selection of a capable team, but it requires a deep rooted and special knowledge to know and to obtain the right stamp of men. How many clubs have lamentably failed and steered perilously near the rocks of irretrievable adversity by starting out with men with reputations; 'stars' as they are popularly called?

They are fickle, difficult to manage, and most times too supremely conscious of their own importance. 'Balloon headedness' is a disease which has ruined more promising players and brought greater disaster to clubs than anything else I know of. There must be a judicious blending of the young and old. A team may carry three or four men of small stature, but too many wee men, no matter how clever and artistic, will not do, for the reason that the strain of First Division football becomes more severe every season.

As they say in the world of fisticuffs, 'Nothing beats a good little'un like a good big'un!'

Ernest Mangnall's approach to football was the direct route, he knew where he was going and woe betide anyone who stood in his path. Manchester United was to be a successful club and he would see to that. At the end of his first season as manager United were third in the Second Division table, two places ahead of his old club Burnley. Manchester City were

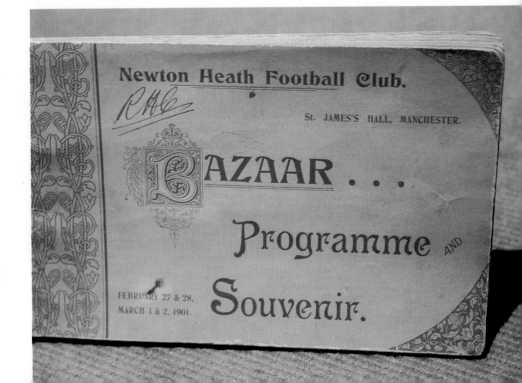

Newton Heath Football Club.
St. JAMES'S HALL, MANCHESTER.
BAZAAR . . .
Programme AND
Souvenir.
FEBRUARY 27 & 28, MARCH 1 & 2, 1901.

runners-up in the First Division. No fewer than 28 players had appeared in first team games that season as Mangnall searched for the right blend.

The 1904-05 season began well, in fact it took on record-breaking proportions, when after drawing with Port Vale in the opening fixture, then beating Bristol City a week later, United lost to Bolton on 17 September 1904, and then went on a run of games which saw them not lose another game until February 1905. Eighteen games without defeat, 16 of them wins.

United finished their second season in third place, missing promotion for the second year by one position. But the backbone of United's first successful side was being created by the manager.

In 1905-06, Ernest Mangnall's third full season in charge, United won promotion, finishing second, four points behind Bristol City, the pair changing places with Nottingham Forest and Wolves. Manchester United were a First Division team.

That year, too, they reached the quarter-finals of the FA Cup, stepping into unknown territory after victories over Staple Hill, Norwich City and Aston Villa. They were then beaten by Woolwich Arsenal 3-2. It was obvious to the thousands following the team that real success was sure to come soon.

In 1904, when Manchester City had finished runners-up to Sheffield Wednesday in the First Division, they had thrilled the people of Manchester (or at least half of them) by reaching the FA Cup final. In 1900 Bury had shown the way for local football by bringing the Cup to the area for the first time, beating Southampton 4-0, and three years later they did it again, this time thrashing Derby County by the final's biggest winning margin to date, 6-0. The 1904 final saw City winning 1-0 at Crystal Palace in a local 'derby' final against Bolton Wanderers.

It was the backbone of that City side which was to turn United into a footballing power after a shrewd piece of negotiation by Ernest Mangnall.

A year after that great victory one of City's star players, the legendary winger Billy Meredith, was suspended from the game for three years, firstly for trying to bribe an Aston Villa player to throw a game, and then for illegally trying to obtain payment from City while under suspension – when his punishment included a ban on even going to the ground. Even though the suspension prevented Meredith from playing until April 1908, in May 1906 Mangnall signed him for £500. It would turn out to be money well spent.

United started their first term in the First Division well enough, winning at Bristol City, drawing with Derby and Notts County, then beating Sheffield United at Bramall Lane, but Mangnall was constantly on the look-out for new players in an effort to compete with their rivals from across Manchester.

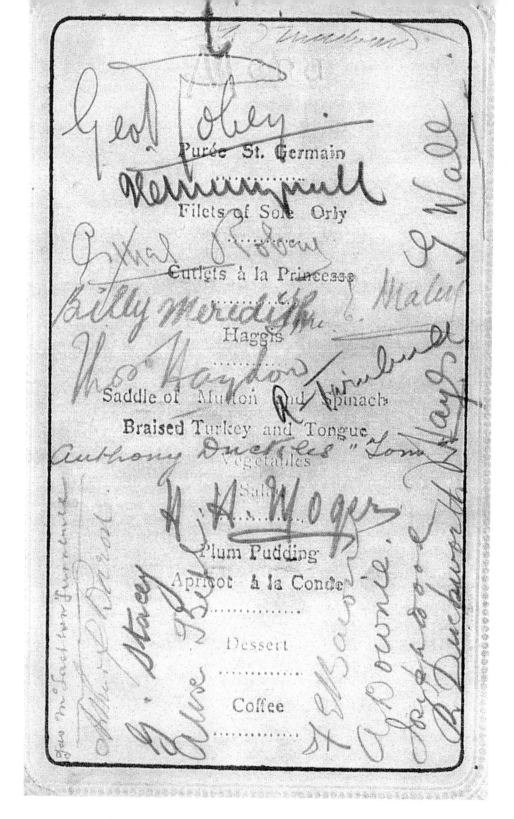

The menu from a celebration dinner signed by some guests. The signatures include those of entertainer George Robey, a close friend of Ernest Mangnall (whose autograph is below Robey's), and players Alex Bell, Dick Duckworth, Harry Moger, and Billy Meredith together with others who took part in the successful campaigns between 1908 and 1911

1892-1949

Mangnall buys City players

Then a bombshell, which proved disaster to City and boom-time for United, hit the game. A Football Association inquiry, which had been investigating the activities of many clubs, discovered that Manchester City had been making illegal payments to their players. There was an uproar and five City directors were forced to resign. That was perhaps the lesser of the two 'sentences' heaped upon the club by the FA for in the other, 17 players – the backbone of the Cup-winning side – were banned from playing for City for life. In a move unheard of before or since, City had to sell most of their playing staff or the club would not be allowed to continue in the Football League.

The news was greeted with disguised delight by other clubs. The vultures would swoop to pick the bones of the successful City side and improve their own chances.

With Meredith having already been signed by United, the spotlight turned on Herbert Burgess, thought to be the best full-back in the game. Everton, Newcastle United, Bolton, Celtic and Chelsea all wanted him but it was Ernest Mangnall who beat them to the punch.

The FA's sentence on the City players also suspended them from playing football at all until January 1907, and two months before the punishment was due to end, City announced a meeting at the Queens Hotel, in Manchester's Piccadilly. Clubs interested in their players were invited to attend . . . it was an auction of footballers!

Ernest Mangnall had no intentions of competing against rival clubs, many much richer than United, so he made arrangements to approach the players he wanted before the meeting started. The other clubs did not like it at all, and Everton made an official complaint to the FA about their loss of Burgess to United – who also signed inside-forward Alec 'Sandy' Turnbull and Jimmy Bannister, another striker.

Everton claimed that on 8 November 1906 they had agreed to exchange Percy Hill with City for Burgess, placing a valuation of £600 on their player. City had given them a transfer form which was completed in every way except for Burgess's signature, but they had not been able to find the player to get him to sign. The reason for this was obvious. He was with Ernest Mangnall, who was persuading him to join United, and as a Manchester man he didn't need much persuasion!

The *Manchester Evening Chronicle* of December 1906 told how Burgess had sent a telegram to City, saying he would not sign for Everton, and they had allowed United officially to approach him. The story also told of the distribution of the City players:

On inquiry at the Football Association offices in High Holborn today, our London correspondent learned that the following transfers of the suspended Manchester City players have been officially sanctioned and the registrations formally made.
A Turnbull to Manchester United; T Hynds to Woolwich

Part one of a photographic mystery. The players of 1908-09 pose with the English Cup after their victory at Crystal Palace. However a virtually identical picture exists showing the same players with the League Championship trophy of 1911. Both photographs have been published as authentic records of each event since 1909 but only one can have been taken at the exact time of the successes.

Arsenal; F Booth to Bury; J McMahon to Bury; James Bannister to Manchester United; J H Edmonson to Bolton Wanderers; G T Livingstone to Glasgow Rangers; H Burgess to Manchester United.

So far as the Football Association is concerned with the transfer of Burgess, he is a Manchester United player.

Meredith's suspension was adjusted to end along with his former City colleagues and on 1 January 1907 a crowd of over 40,000 turned up at Bank Street to see United's new quartet in action against Aston Villa. They weren't disappointed. Sandy Turnbull got the only goal of the game, and United went on to end the season in eighth place in the First Division.

Champions . . . and bother abroad

There were greater things on the horizon. The following season, 1907-08, Manchester United won the League Championship for the first time, a feat even the great City team had failed to achieve. They won in fine style, nine points ahead of Aston Villa and City, winning 23 of their 38 games and only letting their form slip away after the title had been secured.

That summer Manchester United played in Europe. The club decided to take its players on a summer tour to Hungary and Austria and were one of the first northern sides to play abroad. As English champions they were a great attraction, but even in 1908 there were signs of a disease which would spread into the game in later years. Earlier that season United's players had been pelted with mud and stones after they left Bradford City's ground, and there had been reports of similar outbreaks of hooliganism at Sheffield Wednesday. In Hungary their 'friendly' was anything but amicable.

The *Manchester Evening News* report of the game tells how: *It was by no means football weather when Manchester United arrived in Budapest from Vienna, for the sun had left its bronze impress even upon the face of Charlie Roberts.*

Having seen their side score twice against United, despite losing 6-2, the Hungarians came hoping to see at least a draw, for the Ferenczvaros Torna Club were the leaders of their league, and they had only conceded one goal all season.

Alas, such are the vagaries of the game, that before the local lads knew where they were, little Jimmy Bannister had opened the account, and Meredith added a second. A moment from the second kick-off Meredith caught the ball on his toe and running fully half the length of the field at top speed, scored another brilliant goal. There were now fully 11,000 spectators and the applause was deafening.

From this point the attitude of the crowd changed. The weakness of the local lads was apparent at every point, and, what was more painful, all could see it. Then followed a series of incidents which augmented the chagrin all Hungarians felt. Up to this point the referee had been passable, then the hostility of the crowd led to a series of adverse and pitiable decisions against the United. One cause of discontent was the removal of men who were stationed beside each goal as additional referees to inform the referee proper what happened on the line. These men shouted 'offside', 'touch' or 'goal' repeatedly, until play near goal became impossible. Finally they were removed.

On renewing the game, Wall broke away on the left and scored with a great shot. Five minutes later he was badly fouled by one of the opposing half-backs and after a lengthy appeal, awarded a penalty. This was taken by Moger (the United goalkeeper) who easily beat the Hungarian. By this act of one goalkeeper shooting at the other, the feelings of the crowd were again intensified and trouble brewed all round the ground.

Soon after the change of ends Picken got away and put in a beautiful ground shot which swerved into the net out of the reach of the custodian, 6-0. It was not long after this that a regrettable incident occurred.

Thomson was pulled up for fouling and he protested loudly against the decision. The game was stopped. Thompson thereupon – unable to speak the language – caught hold of the referee's hand to direct him to the spot to demonstrate how and what really had happened. This act was misunderstood by Gabrilovitch, the referee, and his hand rose threateningly. The referee being a very tall man, Duckworth rushed up to aid the centre half. Nobody understood each other and were ordered off. Both refused to go, and rightly so. For fully fifteen minutes arguments and gesticulation prevailed. Interpreters were requisitioned and eventually after an apology, the game was renewed, and Wall added another goal, the end coming in partial darkness with the score 7-0.

Crowd trouble

It was what happened next that made Ernest Mangnall vow: 'We will never go to Budapest again'. As the team left the field they were attacked by the crowd. Harry Renshaw, the *Manchester Evening News* reporter, wrote:

> Everybody made for the gateway through which the players must pass on their way to the dressing room . . . Harry Moger was struck across the shoulders by one of these [rioters] with a stick. Stacey was spat upon, Picken and Charlie Roberts struck, in fact nearly all the team were given a reminder. Then the police charged the rioters, and fully twenty were arrested and dragged into one of the club rooms which was utilised as a police station. Even in the dressing room the team were not safe and a shower of heavy stones let in more air and daylight.

The players left the ground under police escort and were on their way back to their hotel in a row of coaches when the rioters attacked again:

> Particular attention was paid to the last carriage and a huge stone knocked me down and cut my head. Then Alec Bell was hit behind the ear, and Picken received another. I was then hit on the head again. It was so sudden that the players had no time to raise the hoods of the carriages. Mr Mangnall was hit and Thomson caught it badly in the neck, with Wall and several others. Many arrests were made and the police were compelled to draw their swords.

United were glad to get back to England again and although the Hungarian incident made headline news for several weeks, it was quickly forgotten as rumour strengthened that the club was about to move from Bank Street to a new ground. As early as August 1907 'Wanderer' had written in the *Manchester Evening Chronicle*:

> The club is sure to remain at Clayton another season, but the intention is to move to a new ground as soon as possible, and it is just about a thousand to one that the home chosen will be at Old Trafford and that when erected it will compare with any ground in the kingdom.
> There can be no better site than Old Trafford where the City and Salford cars [trams] meet, the Sale and Altrincham service is tapped, and the cricket ground station would be available. The air would be purer for both the crowd and the players, and everything seems in favour of such a change and choice.

'Wanderer' also tipped United to do well that season, and, as noted, they obliged with the First Division title. The following

1908-09 season was not quite so successful in the League, but the FA Cup was a different story.

United up for the Cup

The Cup campaign began at Bank Street with a game against Brighton and Hove Albion who had little consolation for their long journey north. Facing a team determined to restore the faith of their supporters after a disappointing lapse of four defeats in their eight games before the first round of the Cup, Brighton had to defend in depth and United won by the only goal of the game.

The second round was played on 6 February, when Everton, who would finish second in the League, came to Clayton, and again it was a one-goal victory. In the third round Blackburn Rovers, who finished fourth in the League, were thrashed 6-1 when the third successive tie was played at Bank Street.

Then came the decisive game of the victorious run, when fate played a hand. United were drawn away to Burnley and were losing one-nil when the game was abandoned because of a blinding snowstorm, casually described in the *Weekly Dispatch* as 'conditions of a most rigorous character'. Four

Previous page: Louis Rocca suggested the name Manchester United as Newton Heath was wound up. In 1909 he rode in style to Manchester Central Station to join the official welcoming party for the first United cup homecoming. His decorated carriage was the centre of attraction. Twenty years later Rocca was appointed assistant manager as the club again struggled to survive

Below: Charlie Roberts holds the English Cup, predecessor of the FA Cup, as he stands with the United party on their arrival back in Manchester from the 1909 Cup Final. Chairman J H Davies is on his right, and next to him Ernest Mangnall, the club's secretary-manager. The players rode in carriages from Central Station to the town hall for a civic reception

days later, on 10 March 1909, United won the replayed game 3-2 and Ernest Mangnall was able to leave the ground of his former club with a feeling of satisfaction.

The semi-final was played at Bramall Lane with Newcastle United as the opposition. The Geordies were on their way to the League Championship, and many felt that they would win both competitions. But it was the year of United – Manchester United – and they reached the final for the first time, thanks to another one-goal success.

So to the final at Crystal Palace: Manchester United versus Bristol City, and United taking their first step into the last stage of the competition which had captured the imagination of the football following public, more so even than the Championship. Here, for one day, London belonged to the people of the north and the west. Trains carried supporters to the capital and a huge crowd gathered at the ground.

Before the final Ernest Mangnall had taken his players away from the distractions of Manchester, where supporters had caught 'Cup fever' for the first time. The Royal Forest Hotel at Chingford housed the players before their trip to the stadium, and they prepared for the game with training sessions, strolls in the nearby woodlands and games of golf.

1892-1949

With both United and Bristol being teams who played in red jerseys and white shorts, the Football Association made them select neutral colours. Bristol chose blue and white, while United proudly announced that they would play in 'an all white costume relieved with a thin red line at the neck and wrists, and with the red rose of Lancashire on the breast'. In order to obtain the best possible publicity for their Cup final build-up Ernest Mangnall arranged for music hall star George Robey to present the kit to the players – with the press on hand.

In the smart all-white strip, with its red V dropping from the shoulders to the centre of the chest United no doubt had the same effect on both spectators and opposition as did the first glimpse of Real Madrid almost 50 years later, when they earned themselves the title of 'the Spanish ghosts'. The spectres of Manchester certainly haunted Bristol City on the afternoon of Saturday, 24 April 1909.

The almost annual visit of northerners to the capital was something the London press appeared to enjoy. They wrote of the Lancashire supporter with his voice which seemed deeper than that of his southern counterpart as supplying a 'pulsating drone note in the fantasia of enthusiasm'. One paragraph ran:

The northern contingent pay great attention to the matter of commissariat. They bring stone jars of strong ale and sandwiches an inch thick, packed in little wicker baskets which are also used for conveying carrier pigeons.

Yes, Manchester was once again 'Up f' t' Cup' but this time it was the red and white of United taking over from the sky blue of City.

Billy Meredith

Like so many finals since, and probably some before, the game did not live up to its pre-match expectations. Sandy Turnbull scored the only goal and man of the match was Billy Meredith, adding another Cup winners' medal to the one he won with City in 1904.

Meredith was indeed an outstanding player noted for his casual approach to the game and his insistence on playing with a toothpick in his mouth. When play was in an area of the field away from him, Meredith would talk to the crowd, or put the toothpick to work, and he drew this description from Don Davies, the *Manchester Guardian* columnist 'Old International':

Meredith was the Lloyd George of Welsh football. The parallel is by no means perfect, but it was curious how many points of resemblance could be traced. Both men had a following not far short of the entire Welsh nation; both were hailed by friends as the highest product of Welsh genius and by opponents as the lowest form of Welsh cunning. Both found it necessary to leave Wales to find adequate scope for their talents, yet both

Inside-forward Alec 'Sandy' Turnbull leaves defenders in his wake on his route to goal. Turnbull formed an effective attacking partnership with Billy Meredith, which spearheaded the side that won the League Championship in 1908 and 1911 and the FA Cup in 1909, when Turnbull scored the only goal of the match. In 245 appearances, Turnbull scored 100 goals, though was sadly killed in action during World War One.

returned repeatedly in their hey-day to pay off debts in their heart-felt gratitude.

Round 1894 when Meredith was a youth, the newly formed Manchester City Football Club sent a deputation to Chirk, North Wales, with orders to bring him back. This mission was fulfilled but not without some hair-raising experiences. The angry townsfolk, roused by the thought of a local genius being sold for alien gold, seized one of the deputation and threw him into a nearby horse-trough. It is safe to assume that the sight of the stripling for whom he had suffered, did little to warm this gentleman's damp spirits on the journey home in the train! The Manchester United team in the final was: Moger, Stacey, Hayes, Duckworth, Roberts, Bell, Meredith, Halse, J Turnbull, A Turnbull, Wall.

The triumphant team returned home with the English Cup. Ernest Mangnall was the proudest man in the city as he strode from Central Station carrying the trophy in his right hand, grey jacket unbuttoned to reveal his waistcoat and watch chain. His bowler hat was cocked slightly but his face was expressionless as he watched his players board a horse-drawn open-topped bus for the journey through the streets, three days after that memorable game.

Manchester turned out in its masses. Cloth caps filled the streets in a woollen ocean stretching as far as the players were able to see . . .

The *Manchester Evening News* of Tuesday, 27 April 1909 described the 'wild scenes greeting United's homecoming':

An hour before the time the train was due to arrive at Central Station large crowds of people assembled outside the station and behind the barricades of the approach leading to the plat-

H. MOGER, J. PICKEN, W. CORBETT, R. HOLDEN, H. BURGESS, J. CLOUGH, W. MEREDITH, G. BOSWELL
G. WALL, A. TURNBULL, C. ROBERTS (Captain), T. COLEMAN, R. DUCKWORTH.

form at which the London train usually comes in. The great majority wore the United colours, and an ice cream merchant attracted considerable attention with his huge red and white umbrella and his similarly coloured barrow. Gutter merchants who did a good business with 'memory cards' of Bristol City came in for a good deal of good humoured badinage, while the United favours attached to a cardboard representation of the English Cup sold like hot cakes.

Five waggonettes, gaily decorated with red and white bannerettes and ribbon, were waiting, two containing members of the St Joseph's Industrial School Band. The arrival of Rocca's Brigade, gaudily dressed in the colours of the United Club, was the signal for an outburst of cheering.

The London train hove in sight, and amid a scene of wild enthusiasm Mr Mangnall emerged carrying the cup on high, followed by the players, their wives, and other people who had travelled from the Metropolis.

The band struck up 'See the Conquering Hero Comes' and there was a great scramble by the crowd, which had been permitted to enter the platform, to reach the players.

Some were carried shoulder high, and ultimately were comfortably seated in the third waggonette. Sticks were waved and hats were thrown in the air and the enthusiasm was

The United squad and Coleman of Everton form the 'Outcasts' line-up after being suspended for standing frim for their union rights. Only 24 hours before the 1909–1910 season was about to start the threatened strike by members of the Players' Union was called off

unbounded when Roberts, carrying the trophy, came into view.

So the conquering heroes made their journey to Manchester Town Hall in Albert Square, scene of so many homecomings in recent years, but this was United's first.

United had ended the 1908-09 season 13th in the League, but the Cup win meant success for Mangnall's men for the second time. Before the start of the next season football went through a major change, and the men of Manchester were largely responsible for it.

The team become outcasts

Although the Union of Professional Footballers had been formed in 1898 at that meeting in the Spread Eagle Hotel, ten years later players were still having difficulty in getting their employers to recognise their rights as trade unionists. There were constant battles for wage increases in smaller clubs, and with amateur and part-time players available, the role of the full-time professional was not as secure or as rewarding as it might later, in some cases, become.

In 1908 United had played a game against Newcastle United to raise funds for their union, and they did it against the wishes

1892-1949

of both the League and the Football Association. For the next twelve months the Players' Union sought affiliation to the Federation of Trades Unions and just before the 1909-10 season was due to start matters reached crisis point. The football authorities feared that, as Federation members, footballers might be drawn into arguments which were far removed from the game. If miners, cotton workers or railwaymen demanded a change in working conditions, would they ask for the support of other trade unionists? If they did, could they force the players to strike?

On 27 August 1909, five days before the start of the new season, representatives of the League clubs met in Birmingham and decided that any player admitting to being a member of the union should be suspended, have his wages stopped, and be banned from taking part in any game.

The move by the League and the Football Association was to try to prevent a strike. It almost caused one. Instead of persuading players that being part of a union would not be of any help to them, it convinced footballers all over the country that the only way for them to achieve their aims of better pay and conditions was to be part of such a body.

The next day Ernest Mangnall and the United board called the players to a mass meeting. Twenty-seven turned up, the exceptions being Harry Moger, who was attending a family funeral, and Jimmy Turnbull.

The players were told about the League directive, and under a headline 'Manchester United's Grave Position', the *Manchester Evening News* reported:

The various speakers pointed out to the men the very serious position the club was in, having three matches to play in the opening six days of the season. Some discussion followed and the players said they would like it to be understood that they had no grievance whatever with the club, but they were fighting for what they believed to be a just principle, and therefore they intended to retain their membership of the Players' Union.

After the players left the room the committee held a meeting and it was decided to wire the Bradford City club immediately, so as to cause no inconvenience, to the effect that, owing to the Manchester United players having determined to remain members of the Players' Union, the club had no players, and consequently the League fixture which should be played with Bradford City, at Clayton, on Wednesday next, could not be proceeded with.

Two days before the new season, most clubs claimed they had signed enough amateurs to get fixtures under way, but not United. The players joked about being the 'Outcasts' posing for a now famous photograph, but they stood firmly by their beliefs.

On 31 August, the eve of the new season, the authorities had a change of heart, and gave in. The Players' Union was recognised, the suspensions were removed, and the arrears of

The English Cup winners medal presented to Dick Duckworth in 1909 as United continued the successful run started a season earlier with their first Championship

pay were allowed. In the eyes of many, this was one of Manchester United's most important victories. Had they not stayed together their cause would have been lost.

It would have been a tragedy if the strike had gone ahead because United were on the verge of moving to their new ground. Immediately after the Cup final success John Henry Davies had once again shown that his heart, and his wealth, were deeply embedded in the club he had taken over by chance. He pledged to lend the massive sum of £60,000, which even from the head of a company like Manchester Breweries Ltd was a gigantic amount, worth millions by today's standards. The move to Old Trafford was finalised.

The strike threat over, work was able to continue, and the days at Bank Street were numbered. A large crowd turned up to see the game against Bradford City and gave the 'Outcasts' a warm reception. They replied with a 1-0 win.

The season went reasonably well, and always there was the move to the new ground to look forward to. On 22 January 1910, United played their last game at Bank Street in front of a modest 7,000 or so loyal supporters. They won 5-0, a fine way to say goodbye to a ground which held many memories for the play-

Manchester United Football Club, Ltd.,

WINNERS OF THE LEAGUE CHAMPIONSHIP, 1907-8.
WINNERS OF THE MANCHESTER CUP, 1908.
WINNERS OF THE FOOTBALL ASSOCIATION CHARITY SHIELD, 1908.
WINNERS OF THE ENGLISH CUP, 1909.

TELEPHONE 68, OPENSHAW.
TELEGRAMS:
"MANGNALL, CLAYTON, MANCHESTER."

SECRETARY:
J. E. MANGNALL.

BANK STREET, CLAYTON
MANCHESTER,

February 15th, 1910.

OPENING OF NEW GROUND,

Manchester United v. Liverpool,

FEBRUARY 19th, 1910.

Dear Sir,

The President (Mr. J. H. Davies) and Directors of the Manchester United Club ask your acceptance of enclosed, and extend a cordial invitation to attend the opening Match on Saturday next.

The ground is situate at Old Trafford near the County Cricket Ground, and can be reached by three tram routes—Deansgate, Piccadilly and St. Peter's Square.

The ground when completed will hold over 100,000 people. The present Stand will accomodate 12,000 people seated.

An early reply will greatly oblige.

Yours truly,

J. E. MANGNALL,
Secretary.

Guests of the club received this invitation to the official opening of Old Trafford and were thrilled by what they saw. The ground never reached its predicted capacity of 100,000 but has a record of 76,962 achieved at the 1939 FA Cup semi-final.

ers and the club's followers. Charlie Roberts scored twice, Connor and Hooper added two more, and Billy Meredith brought down the curtain. A week before that last League game at Bank Street, Burnley had taken revenge for the Cup defeat the previous season by knocking United out of the competition in the first round. United buckled down to a Championship attempt.

The move to Old Trafford

The move to Old Trafford took place in mid season, and preparations were made for the opening game against Liverpool, on 19 February 1910. A week before the event invitations were sent out to local dignitaries:

The President (Mr J H Davies) and Directors of the Manchester United Football Club ask your acceptance of enclosed, and extend a cordial invitation to attend the opening match on Saturday next.

The ground is situated at Old Trafford near the County Cricket Ground, and can be reached by three tram routes: Deansgate, Piccadilly and St Peter's Square.

The ground when completed will hold over 100,000 people. The present Stand will accommodate 12,000 people seated.

The formal opening of the ground took place during the week before the first match, after equipment had been moved into the new offices from the old ground at Clayton. And just in time. Two days before the Liverpool game fierce gales struck the Manchester area and the old wooden grandstand at Bank Street was blown down, wreckage spilling across into the roadway and badly damaging houses opposite. Had this happened during a game it would have been a terrible disaster. As it was no-one was injured.

So Old Trafford became the home of Manchester United and for the first game thousands walked the road in from Salford, others packed tramcars and carriages. The crowd inside looked in awe at the huge grandstand as it filled with well-known local faces, and tried to catch a glimpse of the celebrities present, including Ernest Mangnall's friend George Robey.

United had injury problems. Alan Bell was missing at left-half, Blott taking his place alongside Charlie Roberts, with Dick Duckworth in his familiar position at right-half. George Stacey and Vince Hayes were the full-backs in front of Harry Moger in goal, and the forward line was Meredith, Harold Halse, Homer, Sandy Turnbull and George Wall.

Sandy Turnbull scored the first of United's three goals, latching on to a centre from Meredith, but Liverpool were always in contention, closing the score to 2-1 before George Wall got United's third, then levelling at 3-3 through Goddard and Stewart, before the latter got his second of the afternoon.

So the Merseysiders spoiled the celebrations by winning 4-3.

But United were now able to compete in the status league as well as on the football field and Old Trafford became a show-piece ground, eventually staging the 1915 FA Cup final. In 1911 the replay between Bradford and Newcastle was played there, then in 1915 Sheffield United beat Chelsea 3-0 in Manchester.

United bring glory to Old Trafford

The 1909-10 season ended with United in fifth place but a year later they were champions once more. Under Ernest Mangnall's direction they had won the League Championship of 1907-08; became the first winners of the FA Charity Shield which was introduced in 1908, and the Manchester Cup the same year; then won the FA Cup in 1909. The Championship of 1910-11 would be their final peak under the man whose role in Manchester football is one of unquestionable importance.

New players came, familiar faces left Old Trafford, and the team that took the title by one point from Aston Villa was quite different from the one which earned the title three years earlier.

Enoch 'Knocker' West had been bought from Nottingham Forest. He was a centre-forward with a reputation for goal-scoring and lived up to it by netting 19 in the League campaign. Other new faces were goalkeeper Edmonds, who played for the latter half of the season when Moger was out, Arthur Donnelly, who filled in both fullback positions, and Hoften, a right-back.

The season reached an exciting climax on the last Saturday, 29 April 1911, when Aston Villa, leading the table by one point, were away to Liverpool, and United were at home to Sunderland.

So fickle is the football supporter that, with the Champion-ship a possibility, only 10,000 made the journey to Old Trafford for what turned out to be a decisive game. A week earlier United had lost 4-2 at Villa Park and that, it seemed, was that. But on that last day of the season Liverpool, lying in the lower half of the table beat Villa 3-1, while United thrashed Sunderland 5-1, two goals from Harold Halse and one each from Turnbull and West, plus an own goal, giving them the title.

It would be 41 years before the League Championship would return to the club, and United's victory once again in the FA Charity Shield of 1911, when they beat Southern League Swindon Town 8-4, marked the end of a great era for the club.

Mangnall joins City

In August 1912, after a season in which United had finished 13th in the First Division, and lost to Blackburn in the fourth round of the FA Cup, they also lost Ernest Mangnall. The manager who had been at their helm throughout their successful years left to join Manchester City.

The *Manchester Evening Chronicle* of 21 August 1912 reported that the United maestro had moved to Hyde Road, home of the Old Trafford club's biggest rivals:

The City directors did not come to a decision without long and anxious consideration, and among the names before them were those of Mr J J Bentley and Mr H C Broomfield. At the last moment there seemed a possibility of the negotiations breaking down, but late last night the directors interviewed Mr Mangnall after a three hours' discussion, and an hour later the announcement was made that he had been appointed. Mr W H Wilkinson (chairman) welcomed the new manager and wished him every success. Mr Mangnall, in reply, said he hoped to see the Hyde Road club soon take the position which Manchester City ought to take. Nothing that he could do to attain that end should be left undone.

Ernest Mangnall's place as secretary-manager was taken by J J Bentley, and under his guidance United reached fourth place in the League in the 1912-13 season. But the great names were drifting out of the game, and those who had been part of those championship-winning sides were now reaching the end of their playing days. Had Ernest Mangnall seen what the future held for the club when he decided to leave?

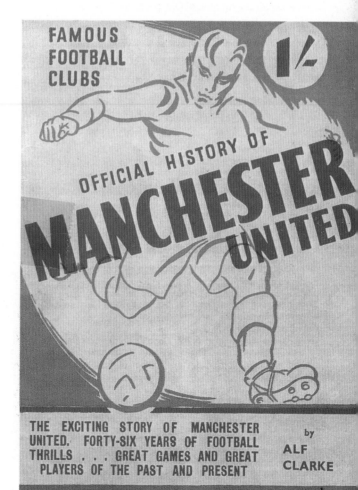

FAMOUS FOOTBALL CLUBS

1/-

OFFICIAL HISTORY OF MANCHESTER UNITED

THE EXCITING STORY OF MANCHESTER UNITED. FORTY-SIX YEARS OF FOOTBALL THRILLS . . . GREAT GAMES AND GREAT PLAYERS OF THE PAST AND PRESENT

by ALF CLARKE

The pocket version of the club's history written by Alf Clarke of the Manchester Evening Chronicle and published in 1948. The booklet told some of the stories included in their history and was printed to coincide with the club's FA Cup achievements of that year. Alf Clarke was one of the journalists who died at Munich.

By the end of the 1913-14 season only Stacey, Duckworth, Meredith, Turnbull, West and Wall were left, and by the end of the following season crowds had dropped to below an average of 15,000, and United escaped relegation by just one point.

To make matters worse Mangnall's Manchester City ended the last season before the First World War, 1914-15, in fifth place, their highest since his departure from Old Trafford. The United side which began the season was almost unrecognisable:

Beale, Hodge, Stacey, Hunter, O'Connell, Knowles, Meredith, Anderson, Travers, West, Wall

Although Ernest Mangnall had often been referred to in newspaper reports as United's 'manager', his actual title was secretary, and it wasn't until 1914 that the first official football manager of the club was appointed. John Robson, who arrived from Brighton and Hove Albion in December 1914, worked under secretary Bentley and took charge of playing arrangements. He stayed in the post until 1921.

The First World War brought football to a standstill and had a crippling effect on United, who were faced with massive overheads for the running of Old Trafford.

The club also lost a lot of its charisma with the departure of Mangnall, who was a great publicist and who took his gift to City.

The war also robbed United of one of its stars. Sandy Turnbull was killed in France, and when life returned to normal in 1919 and football resumed there was a very different line-up for the first game against Derby County:

Mew, Moore, Silcock, Montgomery, Hilditch, Whalley, Hodge, Woodcock, Spence, Potts, Hopkin

Attendances rose following the turmoil of war, and by the end of the 1919-20 season crowds of over 40,000 were commonplace, but the League position of 12th place did little to inspire. A season later John Chapman replaced John Robson as manager, and also filled the secretarial role, but once more Ernest Mangnall stole the Manchester spotlight when his club opened its new ground at Maine Road. Mangnall was clearly leaving his mark on Manchester football.

Relegation and promotion

Then, in 1922, United were relegated, after winning just eight of their 42 games (the First Division had been increased to 22 clubs after the war, when plans were also being made for the

introduction of a Third Division). Billy Meredith had left United in 1921 to re-sign for Ernest Mangnall, and by the time United played their first game in the Second Division for 16 years, none of the great stars of the successful pre-war years remained. They finished fourth in the table, having had hopes of winning promotion until defeats at Blackpool in late March and at home to Leicester in April had seen them slip out of contention.

A season later, 1923-24, they were 14th in the Second Division, but then came a breath of fresh air in the 1924-25 season. It began with a showpiece game at Maine Road, where a combined City and United side played Everton and Liverpool as a testimonial for Ernest Mangnall, now ready to retire from football management and take up a career in journalism. It ended with United winning promotion, finishing second to Leicester City, and a season later in 1925-26 the improvement was maintained with a respectable ninth place in the top flight.

Fate this year twisted the tail of Manchester City. The two Manchester clubs met in the semi-final of the FA Cup with City winning 3-0 at Bramall Lane, but then the Sky-blues not only lost the final 1-0 to Bolton Wanderers, but were relegated to the Second Division.

New stars had begun to emerge for United: Joe Spence, an outside-right who played a record 510 League and Cup games in his 14 years' service; Frank Barson, a towering centre-half who had been a blacksmith before turning to football; and Clarrie Hilditch, a wing-half who became player-manager in 1926-27 as the club looked for a new man to succeed John Chapman.

In 1927 John Henry Davies died. The man who had saved the club from slipping out of existence in 1902, and who had played a crucial role in the creation of Manchester United, could no longer be turned to at difficult times. He was replaced by G H Lawton, who bridged the gap between two major benefactors.

A new manager was appointed. Herbert Bamlett's pedigree for football management was strange and somewhat unorthodox. Bamlett was a former referee – in fact he had gone down in the record books as the youngest to take charge of an FA Cup final when he officiated in 1914 when only 32. He had then moved into management and had been in charge at Oldham Athletic, the now defunct Wigan Borough and Middlesbrough.

Under Bamlett, whose assistant was Louis Rocca, the man who had been general 'dogs-body' at Newton Heath, and who had acted as a scout for the club during its successful years, United slipped slowly down the First Division: 15th in 1926-27; 18th in 1927-28; 12th in 1928-29; 17th in 1929-30; and then, in 1931, relegation as bottom club.

What a terrible season that was. As Tommy Docherty might have described it: 'They started off badly, then deteriorated.'

They lost their first game of the season, at home to Aston, and followed this with eleven more successive defeats, so that by October 1930 their record read:

1892-1949

P	W	D	L	F	A	Pts
12	0	0	12	14	49	0

Something had to be done, but what? United had massive debts and could not afford new players, but even so they plunged recklessly into the transfer market, only adding to their own downfall. By the end of that season they had scored 53 goals in their 42 games, and conceded a massive 115, winning only six times at Old Trafford. No wonder they went down.

Another financial rescue

So began the 1931-32 season, which was to have a lasting effect on the club, or at least, events which occurred during the period were. In the Second Division United again found themselves fighting for their lives. They lost their first two games, to Bradford City in Yorkshire and to Southampton at Old Trafford, before low attendances. Only 3,507 loyal souls turned up to watch the opening game of the season. The United supporters were voting with their feet, and the board of directors got the message.

Herbert Bamlett had lost his job in April 1931, and the manager's role was filled temporarily by Walter Crickmer, the club's secretary since 1926. His assistant was Louis Rocca, still dedicated to the club he had followed since the Newton Heath days. But times were getting harder. By December 1931 Manchester United was on the rocks. Deeply in debt, unable to pay off instalments on the loan made to the club to build Old Trafford, with no chance of paying for players they had obtained from other clubs, they faced bankruptcy. Another saviour was needed, but could Manchester produce another John Henry Davies?

Crisis came in Christmas week when the players went to pick up their wages and were told there was no money available. Stacey Lintott, a sportswriter, picked up the story, but before he wrote it he went to see a contact of his, James W Gibson, whose company was a major garment producer, specialising in army uniforms.

Gibson had a love of sport, and was persuaded to help the club. He met United's directors, laid down his terms and agreed to help out on the understanding that he would become chairman and be able to elect his own colleagues on the board. The directors had no choice – they either went to the wall with their club, or agreed to Gibson's proposals. So the club was once again saved from extinction.

James Gibson invested over £30,000 of his own money in the club – half the original cost of Old Trafford – paid the players' wages, settled outstanding accounts and began to put the ship back on an even keel again.

A new manager was found: Scott Duncan, who had risen to fame as a footballer with Glasgow Rangers and Newcastle United. This time United had an ex-player at the helm, an idea that had worked with other clubs, a former professional knowing how to approach the game in a professional manner. Scott Duncan spent money on new players as he tried to build a strong side, but whether he spent wisely is debatable.

On the brink of obscurity

In the season in which they had almost faded to obscurity United finished 12th in the Second Division, a year later they were sixth, and then in 1933-34 not even Gibson's money could prevent them from sliding to the lowest ebb in the club's history, just one point away from the Third Division.

In fact the future of the club in the Second Division hung by a slender thread as late as the final day of the season. The date, 5 May 1934 is significant in the club's history for on that day, and for the previous week since drawing with Swansea, the club was last but one in the table. Never since the days those railway workers started their team had the club been in such a lowly position.

Lincoln were bottom, and nothing could stop them from being relegated. United were above them, seven points better off, and one point behind Millwall, who filled the 20th position. On 5 May United were away to Millwall, and knew that they had their own fate in their hands.

New signing Hacking was in goal, playing his tenth game since his transfer from Oldham, and in front of him were full-backs Griffiths and Jones. The half-back line of Robertson, Vose and McKay supported a forward line which read: Cape, McLenahan, Ball, Hine and Manley. The last-named normally played wing-half but was brought in to play outside-left so that he would add his defensive qualities if things got tough.

United played their hearts out. Manley scored first, Cape added a second and United won 2-0 . . . but what might have happened to this great club had that result been reversed and Manchester United had begun 1934-35 as a Third Division side? Incidentally, the week that United spent in that lowest point in their history, began the day that Manchester City, with Matt Busby in the side, won the FA Cup.

The new season began with Scott Duncan's new players in the line-up and ended with United fifth from the top, a much improved performance and one which brought the crowds back to Old Trafford, especially those who had been embarrassed by the failure of the Red Devils while Manchester City had lifted the Cup. A season later and United had something to celebrate. Not since Ernest Mangnall's team had won the Championship and the FA Charity Shield in 1911, had Old Trafford's trophy room been blessed with a major piece of silverware. The club had got used to playing second fiddle to Manchester City, but times at last were beginning to change. In 1935-36 they won the Second Division title, not perhaps the most coveted award the game has to offer, but certainly better than facing relegation, and a big improvement on their achievements over the previous quarter of a century.

Scott Duncan's team had achieved this with a tremendous run-in to the end of the season, stringing together 19 games without defeat and clinching promotion with a 3-2 win over Bury at Gigg Lane, where two goals from Tom Manley and another from George Mutch brought the 31,562 fans spilling onto the pitch. It is interesting to note that in 1987, when United were drawn against Bury in the Littlewoods Cup, the game was switched from Gigg Lane to Old Trafford because the ground safety limit at Bury is now restricted to 8,000.

United's only defeat after the beginning of the year, apart from a 2-0 exit from the FA Cup at Stoke, had been to lose by the only goal of the game at Bradford City on 4 January, and even though Charlton Athletic tried to close the gap United won promotion by a single point after both clubs had each won 22 of their 42 games.

Duncan's departure

They had started the 1935-36 season with Hall pushing Breedon out of the goalkeeper's spot after just one game and they had the good fortune to have several players who were virtually ever-presents throughout the season. Tom Curry was responsible for the fitness of the players, and he must have been proud of their response. Of the full-backs, Griffiths and Porter, only John Griffiths missed a single game of the 42, right-half Jim Brown missed just two, one of them a defeat at Blackpool, and centre-half George Vose was absent only for the 4-0 win at home to Burnley. Of the others, George Mutch was an ever-present, playing either at inside-right or centre-forward and scoring 21 goals in the League, and Henry Rowley scored just two fewer despite missing five matches.

Constantly being able to field a virtually unchanged side, Scott Duncan knew that he had a chance of success, and the players he had brought into the club from a variety of backgrounds took United back into the First Division for the first time since the start of the decade. Their stay, however was short. If ever the expression 'after the Lord Mayor's Show comes the dustcart' could be applied to football, here surely was the perfect example as 1936-37 followed the celebrations of 1935-36.

There were changes in the line-up at the start of the season: John, Redwood, Porter, Brown, Vose, McKay, Bryant, Mutch, Bamford, Rowley and Manley starting the campaign. A young man named Walter Winterbottom made his League debut for the club at Elland Road, Leeds, as they slipped to their ninth defeat in 16 games, with only three victories to their name. Winterbottom was never renowned as a player, but became manager of England from 1946 to 1963.

By the end of the season United had won only ten games, eight of them at Old Trafford, and a season after celebrating their return from the Second Division, they were back there.

Scott Duncan resigned and went to manage non-league Ipswich Town, and top-scorer George Mutch took the road to Preston and a place in the game's Hall of Fame. Mutch had scored 46 goals in his 112 League games for United and three more in his eight FA Cup appearances, but it was for one goal he scored for the club which bought him from United for £5,000 that he is remembered. It was in the 1938 FA Cup final at Wembley, when Preston met Huddersfield and the scores were level 0-0 in the dying minutes of extra-time. George Mutch ran into the penalty area with the ball and was tripped. A penalty, and the last kick of the game. Mutch took it and hit the ball with a powerful shot, which struck the underside of the square crossbar, bounced down over the line and spun into the back of the net. George Mutch had made footballing history, but it is worth noting that had Mutch not taken the kick himself, the man who would have gone into the record books in his place was Preston's second-string penalty taker, Bill Shankly.

Back for 36 years at the top

United were not too disappointed at the success of their ex-player, for as the FA Cup came back to the north-west, United also had something to celebrate. Their big-dipper ride through football was back at the top, after plunging to the depths a season earlier. They ended the 1937-38 season as runners-up in the Second division to Aston Villa.

United won promotion by the skin of their teeth. Hot on their heels were Sheffield United, who in their 42 games scored 73 goals against 56, giving them a goal average of 1.738. United, with exactly the same record, 22 wins and nine draws, netted 82 goals against 50, an average of 1.952 – they went up, Sheffield stayed down. Coventry were only a point behind.

The season had seen new players once again take their places in the line-up. Walter Crickmer had been given the reins for another spell as temporary manager, and with Tom Curry and Louis Rocca remaining in the backroom, United tried out a blend of youth and experience.

Rocca, on one of his visits to Ireland, had spotted a young forward, Johnny Carey, and after bringing him to Manchester was delighted with his progress into the first team. Carey made his debut on 25 September 1937, against Southampton, and played just one more game before a ten-match break. He

1892-1949

returned in Christmas week to score in the 3-2 win over Nottingham Forest, the club he would later manage after a career with United which saw him recognised as one of the best full-backs the game had produced.

A month before Duncan had resigned he had bought Jack Rowley from Bournemouth. Rowley was a prolific goal-scorer, making his debut as an outside-left in a home win over Sheffield Wednesday on 23 October 1937. He arrived on the scene at the right time. United had started the season badly, and as it followed their year of relegation, crowds fell off. To make matters worse Manchester City had won the League Championship in 1936-37 and had been the major crowd pullers in the city as the Red fans stayed silent and at home.

Another new player to win his way into the side was Stan Pearson, a Salford-born lad who made his debut in a game which was the turning point of the season. From August until 6 November, three days before Scott Duncan resigned, United had won only five out of 14. The side which started the season was:

Breen, Griffiths, Roughton, Gladwin, Vose, McKay, Bryant, Murray, Bamford, Baird and Manley

On 13 November, after Duncan had gone, the line-up looked different to say the least. Jack Breedon was in goal, Bert Redwood at right-back, Roughton at left. Right-half was Jim Brown, Vose remained at centre-half, and Bert Whalley played left-half. Bill Bryant stayed at outside-right with Baird inside him and Tommy Bamford centre-forward. Young Stan Pearson played inside-left, with Tom Manley outside him, a team of experience blending with young enthusiasm, and Chesterfield, the opposition, never knew what hit them.

Bamford scored four times, and Baird, Bryant and Manley scored to make it a 7-1 win. United lost just five more matches in the remainder of the season and were promoted. If some seasons have been of more importance to the history of Manchester United than others, that 1937-38 season must rank highly, even though the club failed to win any major trophies. Promotion to the First Division at such a time, with war impending, can only be looked upon as an act of good fortune. In that same season Manchester City were relegated along with West Bromwich Albion, and both failed to return a season later. United ended the 1938-39 campaign in 14th place in the First Division, but it was events outside football which would have a long-lasting effect on the club.

At the outbreak of the Second World War football was suspended. From 1939 until 1946-47 there was no League competition, and while United played no serious football during this period, when the game began again after years of

Souvenir Programme. - Price 2d.

COMPLIMENTARY

Testimonial Inter-City Match

TO

Mr. J. E. MANGNALL,

Late Secretary-Manager, Manchester City Football Club.

EVERTON AND LIVERPOOL *v.* MANCHESTER CITY AND MANCHESTER UNITED

Maine Road, Moss Side, Wednesday, September 10th.
KICK OFF 6-20 P.M.

In 1924 Manchester showed its appreciation of Ernest Mangnall's contribution to football with a testimonial game at Maine Road. Under Mangnall's leadership United won the championship in 1908 and 1911 and the Cup in 1909. He was not only influential in the building of Old Trafford, but of Maine Road too after moving to City as their secretary-manager

friendlies, they would start again in the First Division.

A major historical event had once again played an important role in the Manchester United story. Because of the Second World War the club found itself bracketed with the elite and was to remain in the upper section for 36 years. In that time United would achieve successes never dreamt of by Harry Stafford, reach peaks beyond the far-seeing imagination of Ernest Mangnall, and develop its stadium beyond the riches of men like John Henry Davies and James Gibson. It would also find itself a manager to reign longer than any who had gone before him, and that man would step into the breach after the war. His name . . . Matt Busby.

SEASON 1889-1890
FOOTBALL ALLIANCE

21 Sep	Sunderland A	H	W	4-1
23 Sep	Bootle	A	L	1-4
28 Sep	Crewe Alex	A	D	2-2
19 Oct	Walsall T Swifts	A	L	1-4
26 Oct	Birmingham St G	A	L	1-5
9 Nov	Long Eaton R	H	W	3-0
30 Nov	Sheffield Wed	A	L	1-4
7 Dec	Bootle	H	W	3-0
28 Dec	Darwen	A	L	1-4
25 Jan	Sunderland	A	L	0-2
8 Feb	Grimsby T	A	L	1-4
15 Feb	Nottingham F	A	W	3-1
1 Mar	Crewe Alex	H	L	1-2
15 Mar	Small Heath	A	D	1-1
22 Mar	Long Eaton A	A	W	3-1
29 Mar	Darwen	H	W	2-1
5 Apr	Nottingham F	H	L	0-1
7 Apr	Small Heath	H	W	9-1
14 Apr	Grimsby T	H	L	0-1
19 Apr	Birmingham St G	H	W	2-1
21 Apr	Walsall T Swifts	H	W	2-1
26 Apr	Sheffield Wed	H	L	1-2

FA Cup

18 Jan	Preston NE (1)	A	L	1-6

Football Alliance

	P	W	D	L	F:A	Pts	
Newton Heath	22	9	2	11	40:45	20	8th

SEASON 1890-1891
FOOTBALL ALLIANCE

6 Sep	Darwen	H	W	4-2
13 Sep	Grimsby T	A	L	1-3
20 Sep	Nottingham F	H	D	1-1
27 Sep	Stoke C	A	L	1-2
11 Oct	Bootle	A	L	0-5
18 Oct	Grimsby T	H	W	3-1
1 Nov	Crewe Alex	H	W	6-3
8 Nov	Walsall T Swifts	A	L	1-2
22 Nov	Nottingham F	A	L	2-8
29 Nov	Sunderland	H	L	1-5
13 Dec	Small Heath	H	W	3-1
27 Dec	Bootle	H	W	2-1
5 Jan	Stoke C	H	L	0-1
10 Jan	Birmingham St G	A	L	1-6
17 Jan	Walsall T Swifts	H	D	3-3
24 Jan	Sheffield Wed	A	W	2-1
14 Feb	Crewe Alex	A	W	1-0
21 Feb	Sheffield Wed	H	D	1-1
7 Mar	Small Heath	A	L	1-2
14 Mar	Birmingham St G	H	L	1-3
28 Mar	Darwen	A	L	1-2
11 Apr	Sunderland	A	L	1-2

FA Cup

4 Oct	Higher Walton (Q1)	H	W	2-0
	(tie switched to Manchester)			
25 Oct	Bootle Res (Q2)	A	L	0-1

Football Alliance

	P	W	D	L	F:A	Pts	
Newton Heath	22	7	3	12	37:55	12	9th

SEASON 1891-1892
FOOTBALL ALLIANCE

12 Sep	Burton Swifts	A	L	2-3
19 Sep	Bootle	H	W	4-0
26 Sep	Birmingham St G	A	W	3-1
10 Oct	Ardwick	H	W	3-1
17 Oct	Grimsby T	A	D	2-2
31 Oct	Burton Swifts	H	W	3-1
7 Nov	Crewe Alex	A	W	2-0
21 Nov	Lincoln C	H	W	10-1
28 Nov	Walsall T Swifts	A	W	4-1
12 Dec	Sheffield Wed	A	W	4-2
19 Dec	Ardwick	A	D	2-2
26 Dec	Small Heath	H	D	3-3
1 Jan	Nottingham F	H	D	1-1
9 Jan	Bootle	A	D	1-1
30 Jan	Crewe Alex	H	W	5-3
20 Feb	Sheffield Wed	H	D	1-1
27 Feb	Small Heath	A	L	2-3
5 Mar	Walsall T Swifts	H	W	5-0
19 Mar	Nottingham F	A	L	0-3
26 Mar	Grimsby T	H	D	3-3
2 Apr	Lincoln C	A	W	6-1
9 Apr	Birmingham St G	H	W	3-0

FA Cup

3 Oct	Ardwick (Q1)	H	W	5-1
24 Oct	Heywood (Q2)	H	W	W-0
	(scratched)			
14 Nov	South Shore (Q3)	A	W	2-0
5 Dec	Blackpool (Q4)	H	L	3-4

Football Alliance

	P	W	D	L	F:A	Pts	
Newton Heath	22	12	7	3	69:33	31	2nd

SEASON 1892-1893
FOOTBALL LEAGUE (DIVISION 1)

3 Sep	Blackburn R	A	L	3-4
10 Sep	Burnley	H	D	1-1
17 Sep	Burnley	A	L	1-4
24 Sep	Everton	A	L	0-6
1 Oct	WBA	A	D	0-0
8 Oct	WBA	H	L	2-4
15 Oct	Wolverhampton W	H	W	10-1
19 Oct	Everton	H	L	3-4
22 Oct	Sheffield Wed	A	L	0-1

Abbreviations:

Appearances (goals) refer to League games only

Figures shown as 2 etc. refer to goals scored by individual players

* own-goal

---

29 Oct	Nottingham F	A	D	1-1
5 Nov	Blackburn R	H	D	4-4
12 Nov	Notts Co	H	L	1-3
19 Nov	Aston Villa	H	W	2-0
26 Nov	Accrington S	A	D	2-2
3 Dec	Bolton W	A	L	1-4
10 Dec	Bolton W	H	W	1-0
17 Dec	Wolverhampton W	A	L	0-2
24 Dec	Sheffield Wed	H	L	1-5
26 Dec	Preston NE	A	L	1-2
31 Dec	Derby Co	H	W	7-1
3 Jan	Stoke C	A	L	1-7
14 Jan	Nottingham F	H	L	1-3
26 Jan	Notts Co	A	L	0-4
11 Feb	Derby Co	A	L	1-5
4 Mar	Sunderland	H	L	0-5
6 Mar	Aston Villa	A	L	0-2
31 Mar	Stoke C	H	W	1-0
1 Apr	Preston NE	H	W	2-1
4 Apr	Sunderland	A	L	0-6
8 Apr	Accrington S	H	D	3-3

Test Match

22 Apr	Small Heath	D		1-1
	(At Stoke)			

Replay

27 Apr	Small Heath	W		5-2

Newton Heath kept First Division status

FA Cup

21 Jan	Blackburn R (1)	A	L	0-4

Football League

	P	W	D	L	F:A	Pts	
Newton Heath	30	6	6	18	50:85	18	16th

SEASON 1893-1894
FOOTBALL LEAGUE (DIVISION 1)

2 Sep	Burnley	H	W	3-2
9 Sep	WBA	A	L	1-3
16 Sep	Sheffield Wed	A	W	1-0
23 Sep	Nottingham F	H	D	1-1
30 Sep	Darwen	A	L	0-1
7 Oct	Derby Co	A	L	0-2
14 Oct	WBA	H	W	4-1
21 Oct	Burnley	A	L	1-4
28 Oct	Wolverhampton W	A	L	0-2
4 Nov	Darwen	H	L	0-1
11 Nov	Wolverhampton W	H	W	1-0
25 Nov	Sheffield U	A	L	1-3
2 Dec	Everton	H	L	0-3
9 Dec	Sunderland	A	L	1-4
9 Dec	Bolton W	A	L	0-2
16 Dec	Aston Villa	H	L	1-3
23 Dec	Preston NE	A	L	0-2
6 Jan	Everton	A	L	0-2
13 Jan	Sheffield Wed	H	L	1-2
3 Feb	Aston Villa	A	L	1-5
3 Mar	Sunderland	H	L	2-4
10 Mar	Sheffield U	H	L	0-2
12 Mar	Blackburn R	H	W	5-1
17 Mar	Derby Co	H	L	2-6
23 Mar	Stoke C	H	W	6-2
24 Mar	Bolton W	H	D	2-2
26 Mar	Blackburn R	A	L	0-4
31 Mar	Stoke C	A	L	1-3
7 Apr	Nottingham F	A	L	0-2
14 Apr	Preston NE	H	L	1-3

Test Match

28 Apr	Liverpool	L		0-2
	(At Ewood Park)			

Newton Heath were relegated to Division Two

FA Cup

27 Jan	Middlesbrough (1)	H	W	4-0
10 Feb	Blackburn R (2)*	H	D	0-0
17 Feb	Blackburn R (2R)	A	L	1-5
	*after extra time			

Football League

	P	W	D	L	F:A	Pts	
Newton Heath	30	6	2	22	36:72	14	16th

SEASON 1894-1895
FOOTBALL LEAGUE (DIVISION 2)

8 Sep	Burton W	A	L	0-1
15 Sep	Crewe Alex	H	W	6-1
22 Sep	Leicester Fosse	A	W	3-2
6 Oct	Darwen	A	D	1-1
13 Oct	Arsenal	H	D	3-3
20 Oct	Burton Swifts	A	W	2-1
27 Oct	Leicester Fosse	H	D	2-2
3 Nov	Manchester C	A	W	5-2
10 Nov	Rotherham T	H	W	3-2
17 Nov	Grimsby T	A	L	1-2
24 Nov	Darwen	H	D	1-1
1 Dec	Crewe Alex	A	W	2-0
8 Dec	Burton Swifts	H	W	5-1
15 Dec	Notts Co	A	D	1-1
22 Dec	Lincoln C	H	W	3-0
24 Dec	Port Vale	A	W	5-2
26 Dec	Walsall	A	W	2-1
29 Dec	Lincoln C	A	L	0-3
1 Jan	Port Vale	H	W	3-0
5 Jan	Manchester C	H	W	4-1
12 Jan	Rotherham T	A	L	1-2
2 Mar	Burton W	H	D	1-1
23 Mar	Grimsby T	H	D	1-1
30 Mar	Arsenal	A	L	2-3
3 Apr	Walsall	H	W	9-0
6 Apr	Newcastle U	H	W	5-1
12 Apr	Bury	H	D	2-2
13 Apr	Newcastle U	A	L	0-3
15 Apr	Bury	A	L	1-2
20 Apr	Notts Co	H	D	3-3

Football Alliance

	P	W	D	L	F:A	Pts	
Newton Heath	22	12	7	3	69:33	31	2nd

Test Match

27 Apr	Stoke C	L		0-3
	(at Burslem)			

Newton Heath stayed in Division 2

FA Cup

2 Feb	Stoke C (1)	H	L	2-3

Football League

	P	W	D	L	F:A	Pts	
Newton Heath	30	15	8	7	78:44	38	3rd

SEASON 1895-1896
FOOTBALL LEAGUE (DIVISION 2)

7 Sep	Crewe Alex	H	W	5-0
14 Sep	Loughborough T	A	D	3-3
21 Sep	Burton Swifts	H	W	5-0
28 Sep	Crewe Alex	A	W	2-0
5 Oct	Manchester C	H	D	1-1
12 Oct	Liverpool	A	L	1-7
19 Oct	Newcastle U	H	W	2-1
26 Oct	Newcastle U	A	L	1-2
2 Nov	Liverpool	H	W	5-2
9 Nov	Arsenal	A	L	1-2
16 Nov	Lincoln C	H	D	5-5
23 Nov	Notts Co	A	L	0-3
30 Nov	Arsenal	H	W	5-1
7 Dec	Manchester C	A	L	1-2
14 Dec	Notts Co	H	W	3-0
21 Dec	Darwen	A	L	0-3
1 Jan	Grimsby T	H	W	3-2
4 Jan	Leicester Fosse	A	L	0-3
11 Jan	Rotherham T	H	W	3-0
3 Feb	Leicester Fosse	H	W	2-0
8 Feb	Burton Swifts	A	L	1-4
29 Feb	Burton W	H	L	1-2
7 Mar	Rotherham T	A	W	3-2
14 Mar	Grimsby T	A	L	2-4
18 Mar	Burton T	A	L	1-5
23 Mar	Port Vale	H	L	0-3
3 Apr	Darwen	H	W	4-0
4 Apr	Loughborough T	A	W	2-0
6 Apr	Port Vale	A	W	2-1
11 Apr	Lincoln C	A	W	3-2

FA Cup

1 Feb	Kettering (1)	H	W	2-1
15 Feb	Derby Co (2)	H	D	1-1
19 Feb	Derby Co (2R)	A	L	1-5

Football League

	P	W	D	L	F:A	Pts	
Newton Heath	30	15	3	12	66:57	33	6th

SEASON 1896-1897
FOOTBALL LEAGUE (DIVISION 2)

1 Sep	Gainsborough T	H	W	2-1
5 Sep	Burton Swifts	A	W	5-3
7 Sep	Walsall	H	W	2-0
12 Sep	Lincoln C	H	W	3-1
19 Sep	Grimsby T	A	L	0-2
21 Sep	Walsall	A	W	3-2
26 Sep	Newcastle U	H	W	4-0
3 Oct	Manchester C	A	D	0-0
10 Oct	Small Heath	H	D	1-1
17 Oct	Blackpool	A	L	2-4
21 Oct	Gainsborough T	A	L	0-2
24 Oct	Burton W	H	W	3-0
7 Nov	Grimsby T	H	W	4-2
26 Nov	Small Heath	A	L	0-3
19 Dec	Notts Co	H	W	2-1
25 Dec	Manchester C	H	W	2-1
26 Dec	Blackpool	H	W	2-0
2B Dec	Leicester Fosse	A	L	0-1
1 Jan	Newcastle U	H	D	1-1
9 Jan	Burton Swifts	H	D	1-1
6 Feb	Loughborough T	H	W	6-0
20 Feb	Leicester Fosse	H	W	2-1
2 Mar	Darwen	A	W	3-1
13 Mar	Darwen	A	W	2-0
20 Mar	Burton W	A	W	2-1
22 Mar	Arsenal	H	D	1-1
27 Mar	Notts Co	H	D	1-1
1 Apr	Lincoln C	A	W	3-1
3 Apr	Arsenal	A	W	2-0
10 Apr	Loughborough T	A	L	0-2

Test Match

19 Apr	Burnley	A	L	0-2
21 Apr	Burnley	H	W	2-0
24 Apr	Sunderland	H	D	1-1
26 Apr	Sunderland	A	L	0-2

Newton Heath stayed in Division 2

FA Cup

12 Dec	West Manchester (Q1)	H	W	7-0
2 Jan	Nelson (Q2)	H	W	3-0
16 Jan	Blackpool (Q3)	H	D	2-2
20 Jan	Blackpool (Q3R)	A	W	2-1
30 Jan	Kettering (1)	H	W	5-1
13 Feb	Southampton (2)	A	D	1-1
17 Feb	Southampton (2R)	H	W	3-1
27 Feb	Derby Co (3)	A	L	0-2

Football League

	P	W	D	L	F:A	Pts	
Newton Heath	30	17	5	8	56:34	39	2nd

SEASON 1897-1898
FOOTBALL LEAGUE (DIVISION 2)

4 Sep	Lincoln C	H	W	5-0
11 Sep	Burton Swifts	A	W	4-0
18 Sep	Luton T	A	L	1-2
25 Sep	Blackpool	A	W	1-0
2 Oct	Leicester Fosse	H	W	2-0
9 Oct	Newcastle U	A	L	0-2

---

16 Oct	Manchester C	H	D	1-1
23 Oct	Small Heath	A	L	1-2
30 Oct	Walsall	H	W	6-0
6 Nov	Lincoln C	A	L	0-1
13 Nov	Newcastle U	H	L	0-1
20 Nov	Leicester Fosse	A	D	1-1
27 Nov	Grimsby T	H	W	2-1
11 Dec	Walsall	A	D	1-1
25 Dec	Manchester C	A	W	1-0
27 Dec	Gainsborough T	A	L	1-2
1 Jan	Burton Swifts	H	W	4-0
8 Jan	Arsenal	A	L	1-5
12 Jan	Burnley	A	D	0-0
15 Jan	Blackpool	H	W	4-0
26 Feb	Arsenal	H	W	5-1
7 Mar	Burton W	A	L	3-6
19 Mar	Darwen	A	W	3-2
21 Mar	Gainsborough T	H	W	2-1
29 Mar	Loughborough T	H	W	5-1
2 Apr	Grimsby T	A	W	3-1
8 Apr	Gainsborough T	H	W	1-0
9 Apr	Small Heath	H	W	3-1
16 Apr	Loughborough T	A	D	0-1
23 Apr	Darwen	H	W	3-2

FA Cup

29 Jan	Walsall (1)	H	W	1-0
12 Feb	Liverpool (2)	H	D	0-0
16 Feb	Liverpool (2R)	A	L	1-2

Football League

	P	W	D	L	F:A	Pts	
Newton Heath	30	16	6	8	64:35	38	5th

SEASON 1898-1899
FOOTBALL LEAGUE (DIVISION 2)

3 Sep	Gainsborough T	A	W	2-0
10 Sep	Manchester C	H	W	3-0
17 Sep	Glossop	A	W	2-0
24 Sep	Walsall	H	W	1-0
1 Oct	Burton Swifts	A	L	1-5
6 Oct	Port Vale	H	W	2-1
15 Oct	Small Heath	A	L	1-4
22 Oct	Loughborough T	H	W	6-1
5 Nov	Grimsby T	H	W	3-2
12 Nov	Barnsley	H	D	0-0
19 Nov	New Brighton	A	D	0-0
26 Nov	Lincoln C	H	W	1-0
3 Dec	Arsenal	A	L	1-5
10 Dec	Blackpool	H	W	3-1
17 Dec	Leicester Fosse	A	L	0-0
24 Dec	Darwen	H	W	9-0
26 Dec	Manchester C	A	L	0-4
31 Dec	Gainsborough T	H	W	6-1
2 Jan	Burton Swifts	H	D	2-2
14 Jan	Glossop	H	W	3-0
21 Jan	Walsall	A	L	0-1
4 Feb	Port Vale	A	W	1-0
18 Mar	New Brighton	H	L	1-2
25 Mar	Lincoln C	A	L	0-2
1 Apr	Arsenal	H	D	2-2
3 Apr	Blackpool	A	W	2-0
4 Apr	Barnsley	A	W	2-0
8 Apr	Luton T	A	W	1-0
12 Apr	Luton T	H	W	5-0
15 Apr	Leicester Fosse	H	D	2-2
22 Apr	Darwen	A	D	1-1

FA Cup

28 Jan	Tottenham H (1)	A	D	1-1
1 Feb	Tottenham H (1R)	H	L	3-5

Football League

	P	W	D	L	F:A	Pts	
Newton Heath	34	19	5	10	67:43	43	4th

SEASON 1899-1900
FOOTBALL LEAGUE (DIVISION 2)

2 Sep	Gainsborough T	H	D	2-2
9 Sep	Bolton W	A	L	1-2
16 Sep	Loughborough T	H	W	4-0
23 Sep	Burton Swifts	A	D	0-0
30 Sep	Sheffield Wed	A	L	1-2
7 Oct	Lincoln C	H	W	1-0
14 Oct	Small Heath	A	L	0-1
21 Oct	New Brighton	H	W	2-0
4 Nov	Arsenal	H	W	2-0
11 Nov	Barnsley	A	D	0-0
25 Nov	Luton T	A	W	1-0
2 Dec	Port Vale	H	W	3-0
16 Dec	Middlesbrough	H	W	2-1
23 Dec	Chesterfield	A	L	1-2
26 Dec	Grimsby T	H	W	7-0
30 Dec	Gainsborough T	A	D	0-0
6 Jan	Bolton W	H	L	1-2
13 Jan	Loughborough T	A	W	2-0
20 Jan	Burton Swifts	H	W	4-0
3 Feb	Sheffield Wed	H	W	1-0
10 Feb	Lincoln C	A	L	0-1
17 Feb	Small Heath	H	W	3-2
24 Feb	New Brighton	A	W	4-1
3 Mar	Grimsby T	H	W	1-0
10 Mar	Arsenal	A	L	1-2
17 Mar	Barnsley	H	W	3-0
24 Mar	Leicester Fosse	A	L	0-0
31 Mar	Luton T	H	W	5-0
7 Apr	Port Vale	A	L	0-1
13 Apr	Leicester Fosse	H	W	3-0
14 Apr	Walsall	H	W	5-0
21 Apr	Middlesbrough	A	L	0-2
28 Apr	Chesterfield	H	W	2-1

FA Cup

28 Oct	South Shore (Q1)	A	L	1-3

Football League

	P	W	D	L	F:A	Pts	
Newton Heath	34	20	4	10	63:27	44	4th

SEASON 1900-1901
FOOTBALL LEAGUE (DIVISION 2)

1 Sep	Glossop	A	L	0-1
8 Sep	Middlesbrough	H	W	4-0
15 Sep	Burnley	A	L	0-1
22 Sep	Port Vale	H	W	4-0
29 Sep	Leicester Fosse	A	L	0-1
6 Oct	New Brighton	H	W	1-0
13 Oct	Gainsborough T	A	W	1-0
20 Oct	Walsall	H	D	1-1
27 Oct	Burton Swifts	A	L	1-3
10 Nov	Arsenal	A	L	1-2
24 Nov	Stockport Co	A	L	0-1
1 Dec	Small Heath	A	L	0-1
8 Dec	Grimsby T	A	L	0-2
15 Dec	Lincoln C	H	W	4-1
22 Dec	Chesterfield	A	L	1-2
26 Dec	Blackpool	H	W	4-0
29 Dec	Glossop	H	W	3-0
1 Jan	Middlesbrough	A	D	1-1
12 Jan	Burnley	H	L	0-1
19 Jan	Port Vale	A	L	0-1
16 Feb	Gainsborough T	H	D	0-0
19 Feb	New Brighton	A	L	0-1
25 Feb	Walsall	A	D	1-1
2 Mar	Burton Swifts	H	D	1-1
13 Mar	Barnsley	H	W	1-0
16 Mar	Arsenal	H	W	1-0
20 Mar	Leicester Fosse	H	L	2-3
23 Mar	Blackpool	A	W	2-1
30 Mar	Stockport Co	H	W	3-1
5 Apr	Lincoln C	A	L	0-2
8 Apr	Small Heath	A	L	0-1
9 Apr	Barnsley	A	L	2-6
13 Apr	Grimsby T	H	L	2-3
27 Apr	Chesterfield	H	W	1-0

FA Cup

5 Jan	Portsmouth (S)	H	W	3-0
9 Feb	Burnley (1)	H	D	0-0
13 Feb	Burnley (1R)	A	L	1-7

Football League

	P	W	D	L	F:A	Pts	
Newton Heath	34	14	4	16	42:38	32	10th

SEASON 1901-1902
FOOTBALL LEAGUE (DIVISION 2)

7 Sep	Gainsborough T	H	W	3-0
14 Sep	Middlesbrough	A	L	0-5
21 Sep	Bristol C	H	W	1-0
28 Sep	Blackpool	A	W	4-2
5 Oct	Stockport Co	H	D	3-3
12 Oct	Burton U	A	D	0-0
19 Oct	Glossop	A	D	0-0
26 Oct	Doncaster R	H	W	6-0
9 Nov	WBA	H	L	1-2
16 Nov	Arsenal	A	L	0-2
23 Nov	Barnsley	H	W	1-0
30 Nov	Leicester Fosse	A	L	2-3
7 Dec	Preston NE	A	L	1-5
21 Dec	Port Vale	H	W	1-0
25 Dec	Lincoln C	A	L	0-2
1 Jan	Preston NE	H	L	0-2
4 Jan	Gainsborough T	A	D	1-1
18 Jan	Bristol C	A	L	0-4
25 Jan	Blackpool	A	L	0-1
15 Feb	Stockport Co	A	L	0-1
11 Feb	Burnley	A	W	2-0
15 Feb	Glossop	H	W	1-0
22 Feb	Doncaster R	A	L	0-4
1 Mar	Lincoln C	H	D	0-0
8 Mar	WBA	A	L	0-4
15 Mar	Arsenal	H	L	0-1
17 Mar	Chesterfield	A	L	0-3
22 Mar	Barnsley	A	L	2-3
28 Mar	Burnley	A	L	0-1
29 Mar	Leicester Fosse	H	W	2-0
7 Mar	Middlesbrough	H	L	1-2
19 Apr	Port Vale	A	D	1-1
21 Apr	Burton U	H	W	3-1
23 Apr	Chesterfield	H	W	2-0

FA Cup

14 Dec	Lincoln C (1R)	H	L	1-2

Football League

	P	W	D	L	F:A	Pts	
Newton Heath	34	11	6	17	38:53	28	15th

SEASON 1902-1903
FOOTBALL LEAGUE (DIVISION 2)

6 Sep	Gainsborough T	A	W	1-0
13 Sep	Burton U	H	W	1-0
20 Sep	Bristol C	A	L	1-3
27 Sep	Glossop	H	D	1-1
4 Oct	Chesterfield	H	W	2-1
11 Oct	Stockport Co	A	L	1-2
25 Oct	Arsenal	A	W	1-0
8 Nov	Lincoln C	A	W	3-1
15 Nov	Small Heath	A	D	1-1
22 Nov	Leicester F	A	D	1-1
6 Dec	Burnley	A	W	*2-0
13 Dec	Burnley	A	W	2-0
20 Dec	Port Vale	A	D	1-1
25 Dec	Manchester C	H	D	2-2
26 Dec	Blackpool	H	D	2-2
27 Dec	Barnsley	A	W	3-1
3 Jan	Gainsborough T	H	W	3-1
10 Jan	Burton U	A	L	1-3
17 Jan	Bristol C	H	L	1-2
24 Jan	Glossop	A	W	3-1
31 Jan	Chesterfield	A	L	0-2

14 Feb Blackpool   A L 0-2
28 Feb Doncaster R   A D 2-2
7 Mar Lincoln C   H L 1-2
9 Mar Arsenal   H W 3-0
21 Mar Leicester F   H W 5-1
23 Mar Stockport Co   H D 0-0
30 Mar Preston NE   H L 0-1
4 Apr Burnley   H W 4-0
10 Apr Manchester C   A W 2-0
11 Apr Preston NE   A L 1-3
13 Apr Doncaster R   H W 4-0
18 Apr Port Vale   H W 2-1
20 Apr Small Heath   A L 1-0
25 Apr Barnsley   A D 0-0

FA Cup
1 Nov Accrington S. (3Q)   H W 7-0
13 Nov Oswaldtwistle R (4Q)   H W 3-2
29 Nov Southport Cent. (5Q)   H W 4-1
13 Dec Burton U (Int)   H D 1-1
17 Dec Burton U (R)†   H W 3-1
7 Feb Liverpool (1)   H W 2-1
21 Feb Everton (2)   A L 1-3
†away tie switched to Manchester (Bank St.)

Football League
P W D L F:A Pts
Manchester U 34 15 8 11 53:38 38 5th

SEASON 1903-1904
FOOTBALL LEAGUE (DIVISION 2)
5 Sep Bristol C   H D 2-2
7 Sep Burnley   A L 0-2
12 Sep Port Vale   A L 0-1
19 Sep Glossop   A W 5-0
26 Sep Bradford C   H W 3-1
3 Oct Arsenal   A L 0-4
10 Oct Barnsley   H W 4-0
17 Oct Lincoln C   A D 0-0
24 Oct Stockport Co   H W 3-1
7 Nov Bolton W   H D 0-0
21 Nov Preston NE   H L 0-2
19 Dec Gainsborough T   H W 4-2
25 Dec Chesterfield   H W 3-1
26 Dec Burton U   A D 2-2
2 Jan Bristol C   A D 1-1
9 Jan Port Vale   H W 2-0
16 Jan Glossop   H W 3-1
23 Jan Bradford C   A D 3-3
30 Jan Arsenal   H W 1-0
13 Feb Lincoln C   H W 2-0
9 Mar Blackpool   A L 1-2
12 Mar Burnley   H W 3-1
19 Mar Preston NE   A D 1-1
26 Mar Grimsby T   H W 2-0
28 Mar Stockport Co   A W 3-0
1 Apr Chesterfield   A W 2-0
2 Apr Leicester F   A W 1-0
5 Apr Barnsley   A W 2-0
9 Apr Blackpool   H W 3-1
12 Apr Grimsby T   A L 1-3
16 Apr Gainsborough T   A W 1-0
23 Apr Burton U   H W 2-0
25 Apr Bolton W   A D 0-0
30 Apr Leicester   H W 5-2

FA Cup
12 Dec Small Heath (Int)   H D 1-1
16 Dec Small Heath (IntR)†   A D 1-1
21 Dec Small Heath (IntR)†   N D 1-1
    (at Bramall Lane)
11 Jan Small Heath (IntR)   N W 3-1
    (at Hyde Road, Manchester)
6 Feb Notts Co (1)   A D 3-3
10 Feb Notts Co (1R)   H W 2-1
20 Feb Sheffield Wed (2)   A L 0-6
†after extra time

Football League
P W D L F:A Pts
Manchester U 34 20 8 6 65:33 48 3rd

SEASON 1904-1905
FOOTBALL LEAGUE (DIVISION 2)
5 Sep Port Vale   A D 2-2
10 Sep Bristol C   H W 4-1
17 Sep Bolton W   H L 1-2
24 Sep Glossop   A W 2-1
8 Oct Bradford C   A D 1-1
15 Oct Lincoln C   H W 2-0
22 Oct Leicester F   H W 3-0
29 Oct Barnsley   H W 4-0
5 Nov WBA   A W 2-0
12 Nov Burnley   H W 1-0
19 Nov Grimsby T   A W 1-0
3 Dec Doncaster R   A W 1-0
10 Dec Gainsborough T   H W 3-1
17 Dec Burton U   A W 3-2
24 Dec Liverpool   H W 3-1
26 Dec Chesterfield   H W 3-0
31 Dec Port Vale   H W 6-1
2 Jan Bradford C   H W *7-0
3 Jan Bolton W   A W 4-2
7 Jan Bristol C   A D 1-1
21 Jan Glossop   H W 4-1
11 Feb Lincoln C   A L 0-3
18 Feb Leicester F   H W 4-1
25 Feb Barnsley   A D 0-0
4 Mar WBA   H W 2-0
11 Mar Burnley   A L 0-2
18 Mar Grimsby T   H W 2-1
25 Mar Blackpool   A W 1-0
1 Apr Doncaster R   H W 8-0
8 Apr Gainsborough T   A D 0-0
15 Apr Burton U   H W 5-0
21 Apr Chesterfield   A L 0-2
22 Apr Liverpool   A L 0-4
24 Apr Blackpool   H W 3-1

FA Cup
14 Jan Fulham (Int)   H D 2-2
18 Jan Fulham (IntR)†   A D 0-0
23 Jan Fulham (IntR)   N L 0-1
    (at Villa Park)
†after extra time

Football League
P W D L F:A Pts
Manchester U 34 24 5 5 81:30 53 3rd

SEASON 1905-1906
FOOTBALL LEAGUE (DIVISION 2)
2 Sep Bristol C   H W 5-1
4 Sep Blackpool   H W 2-1
9 Sep Grimsby T   A W 1-0
18 Sep Glossop   A W 2-1
23 Sep Stockport C   H W 3-1
30 Sep Blackpool   A W 1-0
7 Oct Bradford C   H D 0-0
14 Oct WBA   A L 0-1
21 Oct Leicester   H W 3-2
25 Oct Gainsborough T   A D 2-2
28 Oct Hull C   A W 1-0
4 Nov Lincoln C   H W 2-1
11 Nov Chesterfield   A L 0-1
18 Nov Port Vale   H W *3-0
25 Nov Barnsley   A W *3-0
2 Dec Clapton O   H W 4-0
9 Dec Burnley   A W 3-1
23 Dec Burton U*   A W 2-0
25 Dec Chelsea   H D 0-0
30 Dec Bristol C   A D 1-1
6 Jan Grimsby T   H W 5-0
15 Jan Leed C   H L 0-3
20 Jan Glossop   H W 5-2
27 Jan Stockport C   A W 1-0
10 Feb Bradford C   A W 5-1
17 Feb WBA   H D 0-0
3 Mar Hull C   H W 5-1
17 Mar Chesterfield   H W 4-1
24 Mar Port Vale   A L 0-1
29 Mar Leicester C   A W 5-2
31 Mar Barnsley   H W 5-1
7 Apr Clapton O   A W 1-0
13 Apr Chelsea   A D 1-1
14 Apr Burnley   H W 1-0
16 Apr Gainsborough T   H W 2-0
21 Apr Leeds C   A W 3-1
25 Apr Lincoln C   A W 3-2
28 Apr Burton U   H W 6-0

FA Cup
13 Jan Staple Hill (1)   H W 7-2
3 Feb Norwich (2)   H W 3-0
24 Feb Aston Villa (3)   H W 5-1
10 Mar Arsenal (4)   H L 2-3

Football League
P W D L F:A Pts
Manchester U 38 28 6 4 90:28 82 2nd

SEASON 1906-1907
FOOTBALL LEAGUE (DIVISION 1)
1 Sep Bristol C   A W 2-1
3 Sep Derby Co   A D 2-2
8 Sep Notts Co   H D 0-0
15 Sep Sheffield U   A W 2-0
22 Sep Bolton W   H L 1-2
29 Sep Derby Co   H D 1-1
6 Oct Stoke C   A W 2-1
13 Oct Blackburn R   H D 1-1
20 Oct Sunderland   A L 1-4
27 Oct Birmingham   H W 2-1
3 Nov Everton   A L 0-3
10 Nov Arsenal   H W 1-0
17 Nov Sheffield Wed   A L 2-6
24 Nov Bury   H L 2-4
1 Dec Manchester C   A L 0-3
8 Dec Middlesbrough   H W 3-1
16 Dec Preston NE   H L 0-2
22 Dec Newcastle U   H L 1-3
25 Dec Liverpool   H D 0-0
26 Dec Aston Villa   A L 0-2
29 Dec Bristol C   H D 0-0
1 Jan Aston Villa   H W 1-0
5 Jan Notts Co   A L 0-3
19 Jan Sheffield U   H W 2-0
26 Jan Bolton W   A W 1-0
2 Feb Newcastle U   A L 0-5
9 Feb Stoke C   H W 4-1
16 Feb Blackburn R   A W 4-2
23 Feb Preston NE   H W 3-0
2 Mar Birmingham   A D 1-1
16 Mar Arsenal   A L 0-4
25 Mar Sunderland   A W 2-0
30 Mar Bury   A W 2-1
1 Apr Liverpool   A W 1-0
6 Apr Manchester C   H D 1-1
10 Apr Sheffield Wed   H W 5-0
13 Apr Middlesbrough   A L 0-2
22 Apr Everton   H W 3-0

FA Cup
12 Jan Portsmouth (1)   A D 2-2
16 Jan Portsmouth (1R)   H L 1-2

Football League
P W D L F:A Pts
Manchester U 38 17 6 13 53:56 42 8th

SEASON 1907-1908
FOOTBALL LEAGUE (DIVISION 1)
2 Sep Aston Villa   A W 4-1
7 Sep Liverpool   H W 4-0
9 Sep Middlesbrough   H W 2-1

Billy Meredith with his footballing achievements collected over 30 years.

14 Sep Middlesbrough   A L 1-2
21 Sep Sheffield U   H W 2-1
26 Sep Chelsea   A W 4-1
5 Oct Nottingham F   H W 4-0
12 Oct Newcastle U   A W 6-1
19 Oct Blackburn R   H W 5-1
26 Oct Bolton W   A W 4-3
2 Nov Birmingham   A W 4-3
9 Nov Everton   H W 4-3
16 Nov Sunderland   A W 2-1
23 Nov Arsenal   H W 4-2
30 Nov Sheffield Wed   A L 0-2
7 Dec Bristol C   H W 2-1
14 Dec Notts Co   A D 1-1
21 Dec Manchester C   H W 3-1
25 Dec Bury   A D 0-0
28 Dec Preston NE   A D 0-0
1 Jan Bury   H W 1-0
16 Jan Sheffield U   A L 0-2
25 Jan Chelsea   H W 1-0
6 Feb Newcastle U   H D 1-1
15 Feb Blackburn R   H L 1-2
29 Feb Birmingham   A D 1-1
14 Mar Sunderland   H W 3-0
21 Mar Arsenal   A L 0-1
25 Mar Liverpool   A L 4-7
28 Mar Sheffield Wed   H W 4-1
4 Apr Bristol C   A D 1-1
8 Apr Everton   A W 3-1
11 Apr Notts Co   H L 0-1
17 Apr Nottingham F   A L 0-2
16 Apr Manchester C   H D 0-0
20 Apr Aston Villa   H L 1-1
22 Apr Bolton W   A W 2-0
25 Apr Preston NE   H W 2-1

FA Cup
*11 Jan Blackpool (1)   H W 3-1
1 Feb Chelsea (2)   H W 1-0
22 Feb Aston Villa (3)   A W 2-0
7 Mar Fulham (4)   A L 1-2

Football League
P W D L F:A Pts
Manchester U 38 23 6 9 61:46 52 1st

SEASON 1908-1909
FOOTBALL LEAGUE (DIVISION 1)
5 Sep Preston NE   A W 3-0
7 Sep Bury   H W 2-0
12 Sep Middlesbrough   H W 6-3
19 Sep Manchester C   A W 2-1
26 Sep Liverpool   H W 3-2
3 Oct Bury   A D 2-2
10 Oct Sheffield U   H W 2-1
17 Oct Aston Villa   A L 1-3
24 Oct Nottingham F   H D 2-2
31 Oct Sunderland   A L 1-6
7 Nov Chelsea   A L 0-1
14 Nov Blackburn R   A W 3-1
21 Nov Bradford   H W 2-0
28 Nov Sheffield Wed   H W 3-1
5 Dec Everton   A L 2-3
12 Dec Leicester F   H W 4-2
19 Dec Arsenal   A W 1-0
25 Dec Newcastle U   A L 1-2
26 Dec Newcastle U   H L 0-1
1 Jan Notts Co   H W 4-3
2 Jan Preston NE   H L 0-2
9 Jan Middlesbrough   A L 0-5
23 Jan Manchester C   H W 3-1
30 Jan Liverpool   A L 1-3
13 Feb Sheffield U   A D 0-0
27 Feb Nottingham F   A D 0-0
13 Mar Chelsea   A D 1-1
15 Mar Sunderland   H D 2-2
20 Mar Blackburn R   H L 0-3

31 Mar Aston Villa   H L 0-2
3 Apr Sheffield Wed   A L 0-2
9 Apr Bristol C   H L 0-1
10 Apr Everton   H D 2-2
12 Apr Bristol C   A D 0-0
13 Apr Notts C   A W 1-0
17 Apr Leicester F   A L 2-3
27 Apr Arsenal   H L 1-4
29 Apr Bradford C   A L 0-1

FA Cup
16 Jan Brighton (1)   H W 1-0
6 Feb Everton (2)   H W 1-0
20 Feb Blackburn R (3)   H W 6-1
5 Mar Burnley (4)   A *
10 Mar Burnley (4)   H W 3-2
27 Mar Newcastle U (SF)   N W 1-0
    (at Bramall Lane)
24 Apr Bristol C (F)   N W 1-0
    (at Crystal Palace)
*match abandoned after 72 minutes because of snow. Score Burnley 1 United 0

Football League
P W D L F:A Pts
Manchester U 38 15 7 16 58:68 37 13th

SEASON 1909-1910
FOOTBALL LEAGUE (DIVISION 1)
1 Sep Bradford C   H W 1-0
4 Sep Bury   H W 2-0
6 Sep Notts Co   H W 2-1
11 Sep Tottenham H   A D 2-2
18 Sep Preston NE   H D 1-1
25 Sep Notts Co   A L 2-3
2 Oct Newcastle U   H D 1-1
9 Oct Liverpool   A L 2-3
16 Oct Aston Villa   H W 2-0
23 Oct Sheffield U   A W 1-0
30 Oct Arsenal   H W 1-0
6 Nov Bolton W   A W 3-2
13 Nov Chelsea   H W 2-0
20 Nov Blackburn R   A L 2-3
27 Nov Nottingham F   H L 2-6
4 Dec Sunderland   A L 0-1
18 Dec Middlesbrough   A W 2-1
25 Dec Sheffield Wed   H L 0-1
27 Dec Sheffield Wed   A L 1-4
1 Jan Bradford C   A W 2-0
8 Jan Bury   A D 1-1
22 Jan Tottenham H   H W 5-0
5 Feb Preston NE   A L 0-1
12 Feb Newcastle U   A W 4-3
19 Feb Liverpool   H L 3-4
26 Feb Aston Villa   A L 1-7
5 Mar Sheffield U   H W 1-0
12 Mar Arsenal   H D 0-0
19 Mar Bolton W   H W 5-0
25 Mar Bristol C   H W 2-0
26 Mar Chelsea   A D 1-1
28 Mar Bristol C   A L 1-2
2 Apr Blackburn R   H W 2-0
6 Apr Everton   H W 3-2
9 Apr Nottingham F   A L 0-2
16 Apr Sunderland   H W 2-0
23 Apr Everton   A D 3-3
30 Apr Middlesbrough   H W 4-1

FA Cup
15 Jan Burnley (1)   A L 0-2

Football League
P W D L F:A Pts
Manchester U 38 9 7 12 69:61 45 5th

SEASON 1910-1911
FOOTBALL LEAGUE (DIVISION 1)
1 Sep Arsenal   A W 2-1
3 Sep Blackburn R   H W 3-2
10 Sep Nottingham F   A L 1-2
17 Sep Manchester C   H W 2-1
24 Sep Everton   A W 1-0
1 Oct Sheffield Wed   H W 3-2
8 Oct Bristol C   A W 1-0
15 Oct Newcastle U   H W 2-0
22 Oct Tottenham H   A D 2-2
29 Oct Middlesbrough   H L 1-2
5 Nov Preston NE   A W 2-0
12 Nov Notts Co   H D 0-0
19 Nov Oldham   A W 3-1
28 Nov Liverpool   A L 2-3
3 Dec Bury   H W 3-2
10 Dec Sheffield U   A L 0-2
17 Dec Aston Villa   H W 2-0
24 Dec Sunderland   A W 2-1
26 Dec Arsenal   H W 5-0
27 Dec Bradford C   A L 0-1
31 Dec Blackburn R   A L 0-1
2 Jan Bradford C   H W *1-0
7 Jan Nottingham F   H W 4-2
21 Jan Manchester C   A D 1-1
28 Jan Everton   H D 2-2
11 Feb Bristol C   H W 3-1
18 Feb Newcastle U   H W 2-0
4 Mar Middlesbrough   A D 2-2
11 Mar Preston NE   H W 5-0
15 Mar Tottenham H   H W 3-2
18 Mar Notts Co   A L 0-1
25 Mar Oldham   H D 0-0
1 Apr Liverpool   H W 2-0
8 Apr Bury   A W 3-0
15 Apr Sheffield U   H D 1-1
17 Apr Sheffield Wed   A D 0-0
22 Apr Aston Villa   A L 2-4
29 Apr Sunderland   H W *5-1

FA Cup
14 Jan Blackpool (1)   A W 2-1
4 Feb Aston Villa (2)   H W 2-1
25 Feb West Ham (3)   A L 1-2

Football League
P W D L F:A Pts
Manchester U 38 22 8 8 72:40 52 1st

SEASON 1911-1912
FOOTBALL LEAGUE (DIVISION 1)
2 Sep Manchester C   A D 0-0
9 Sep Everton   H W 2-1
16 Sep WBA   A L 0-1
23 Sep Sunderland   H D 2-2
30 Sep Blackburn R   A D 2-2
7 Oct Sheffield Wed   H W 3-1
14 Oct Bury   A W 1-0
21 Oct Middlesbrough   H L 3-4
28 Oct Notts C   A L 1-2
4 Nov Tottenham H   A L 1-2
11 Nov Preston NE   H D 0-0
18 Nov Liverpool   A L 2-3
25 Nov Aston Villa   H W 3-1
2 Dec Newcastle U   A W 3-2
9 Dec Sheffield U   H W 1-0
16 Dec Oldham   A D 2-2
23 Dec Bolton W   H W 1-0
25 Dec Bradford C   H L 0-1
26 Dec Bradford C   A L 0-1
30 Dec Manchester C   H L 0-1
1 Jan Arsenal   A L 1-2
6 Jan Everton   A L 0-4
20 Jan WBA   H L 1-2

27 Jan Sunderland A L 0-5
10 Feb Sheffield Wed A L 0-3
1 Feb Bury H D 0-0
2 Mar Notts C H W 2-0
16 Mar Preston NE A D 0-0
23 Mar Liverpool H D 1-1
30 Mar Aston Villa A L 0-6
5 Apr Arsenal A L 1-2
6 Apr Newcastle H L 0-2
9 Apr Tottenham H A D 1-1
13 Apr Sheffield U A L 1-6
17 Apr Middlesbrough A L 0-3
20 Apr Oldham H W 3-1
27 Apr Bolton W A D 1-1
29 Apr Blackburn R H W 3-1

FA Cup
13 Jan Huddersfield T(1) H W 3-1
3 Feb Coventry C (2) A W 5-1
24 Feb Reading (3) A D 1-1
29 Feb Reading (3R) H W 3-0
9 Mar Blackburn R (4) H D *1-1
14 Mar Blackburn R (4R)† A L 2-4
†after extra time

Football League
P W D L F:A Pts
Manchester U 38 13 11 14 45:60 37 13th

SEASON 1912-1913
FOOTBALL LEAGUE (DIVISION 1)
2 Sep Arsenal A D 0-0
7 Sep Manchester C H L 0-1
14 Sep WBA A W 2-1
21 Sep Everton H W 2-0
28 Sep Sheffield Wed A D 3-3
5 Oct Blackburn R H D 1-1
12 Oct Derby C A L 1-2
19 Oct Tottenham H H W 2-0
26 Oct Middlesbrough A L 2-3
2 Nov Notts C H W 2-1
9 Nov Sunderland A L 1-3
16 Nov Aston Villa A L 24
23 Nov Liverpool H W 3-1
30 Nov Bolton W A L 1-2
7 Dec Sheffield U H W 4-0
14 Dec Newcastle U A W 3-1
21 Dec Oldham H D 0-0
25 Dec Chelsea A W 4-1
26 Dec Chelsea H W 4-2
28 Dec Manchester C A W 2-0
1 Jan Bradford C H W 2-0
4 Jan WBA H D 1-1
18 Jan Everton A L 1-4
25 Jan Sheffield Wed H W 2-0
8 Feb Blackburn R A D 0-0
15 Feb Derby C H W 4-0
1 Mar Middlesbrough H L 2-3
8 Mar Notts Co A W 2-1
15 Mar Sunderland H L 1-3
21 Mar Arsenal H W 2-0
22 Mar Aston Villa H W 4-0
25 Mar Bradford C A L 0-1
29 Mar Liverpool A W 2-0
31 Mar Tottenham H A D 1-1
5 Apr Bolton W H W 2-1
12 Apr Sheffield U A L 1-2
19 Apr Newcastle U H W 3-0
26 Apr Oldham A D 0-0

FA Cup
11 Jan Coventry (1) H D 1-1
16 Jan Coventry (1R) A W 2-1
1 Feb Plymouth A (2) A W 2-0
22 Feb Oldham (3) A D 0-0
26 Feb Oldham (3R) H L 1-2

Football League
P W D L F:A Pts
Manchester U 38 19 8 11 69:43 46 4th

SEASON 1913-1914
FOOTBALL LEAGUE (DIVISION 1)
6 Sep Sheffield Wed A W 3-1
8 Sep Sunderland H W 3-1
13 Sep Bolton W H L 0-1
20 Sep Chelsea A W 2-0
27 Sep Oldham H W 4-1
4 Oct Tottenham H A W 2-1
11 Oct Burnley A W 2-1
18 Oct Preston NE H W 2-0
25 Oct Newcastle U A W 1-0
1 Nov Liverpool H W 3-0
8 Nov Aston Villa A L 1-3
15 Nov Middlesbrough H L 0-1
22 Nov Sheffield U A L 0-2
29 Nov Derby Co H D 3-3
6 Dec Manchester C A W 2-0
13 Dec Bradford C H D 1-1
20 Dec Blackburn R A W 1-0
25 Dec Everton H L 0-1
26 Dec Everton A L 0-5
27 Dec Sheffield Wed H W 2-1
1 Jan WBA H W 1-0
3 Jan Bolton W A L 1-6
17 Jan Chelsea H L 0-1
24 Jen Oldham A D 2-2
7 Feb Tottenham H A L 1-2
14 Feb Burnley H L 0-1
21 Feb Middlesbrough A L 1-3
28 Feb Newcastle U H D 2-2
5 Mar Preston NE A L 2-4
14 Mar Aston Villa H L 0-6
4 Apr Derby Co A L 0-2
10 Apr Sunderland A L 0-2
11 Apr Manchester C H L 0-1
13 Apr WBA A L 1-2
15 Apr Liverpool A W 2-1
18 Apr Bradford C A D 1-1

22 Apr Sheffield U H W 2-1
25 Apr Blackburn R H D 0-0

FA Cup
10 Jan Swindon T (1) A L 0-1

Football League
P W D L F:A Pts
Manchester U 38 15 6 17 52:62 36 14th

SEASON 1914-1915
FOOTBALL LEAGUE (DIVISION 1)
2 Sep Oldham H L 1-3
5 Sep Manchester C H D 0-0
12 Sep Bolton W A L 0-3
19 Sep Blackburn R H W 2-0
26 Sep Notts Co A L 2-4
3 Oct Sunderland H W 3-0
10 Oct Sheffield Wed A L 0-1
17 Oct WBA H D 0-0
24 Oct Everton A L 2-4
31 Oct Chelsea H D 2-2
7 Nov Bradford C A L 2-4
14 Nov Burnley H L 0-2
21 Nov Tottenham H A L 0-2
28 Nov Newcastle U H L 0-1
5 Dec Middlesbrough A D 1-1
12 Dec Sheffield U H L 1-2
19 Dec Aston Villa A D 3-3
26 Dec Liverpool A D 1-1
1 Jan Bradford H L 1-2
2 Jan Manchester C A D 1-1
16 Jan Bolton W H W 4-1
23 Jan Blackburn R A D 3-3
30 Jan Notts Co H D 2-2
6 Feb Sunderland A L 0-1
13 Feb Sheffield Wed H W 2-0
20 Feb WBA A D 0-0
27 Feb Everton H L 1-2
13 Mar Bradford C A L 1-0
20 Mar Burnley A L 0-3
27 Mar Tottenham H H D 1-1
2 Apr Liverpool H W 2-0
3 Apr Newcastle A L 0-2
5 Apr Bradford A L 0-5
6 Apr Oldham A L 0-1
10 Apr Middlesbrough H D 2-2
17 Apr Sheffield U A L 1-3
19 Apr Chelsea A W 3-1
26 Apr Aston Villa H W 1-0

FA Cup
9 Jan Sheffield Wed (1) A L 0-1

Football League
P W D L F:A Pts
Manchester U 38 9 12 17 46:62 30 18th

SEASON 1915-1916
Lancs Principal Tournament
4 Sep Oldham A A L 2-3
11 Sep Everton H L 2-4
18 Sep Bolton W A W 5-3
25 Sep Manchester C H D 1-1
2 Oct Stoke C A D 0-0
9 Oct Burnley H L 3-7
16 Oct Preston NE A D 0-0
23 Oct Stockport Co H W 3-0
30 Oct Liverpool A W 2-0
6 Nov Bury H D 1-1
13 Nov Rochdale H W 2-0
20 Nov Blackpool A L 1-5
27 Nov Southport H D 0-0
4 Dec Oldham H W 2-0
11 Dec Everton A L 1-2
18 Dec Bolton W H W 1-0
25 Dec Manchester C A L 1-2
1 Jan Stoke C H L 1-2
8 Jan Burnley A L 4-7
15 Jan Preston NE H W 4-9
22 Jan Stockport Co A L 1-3
29 Jan Liverpool H D 1-1
5 Feb Bury A L 1-2
12 Feb Rochdale A D 2-2
19 Feb Blackpool H D 1-1
26 Feb Southport A L 0-5

P W D L F:A Pts
Manchester U 26 7 8 13 41:51 22 11th

Lancs Subsidiary Tournament
4 Mar Everton H L 0-2
11 Mar Oldham A L 0-1
18 Mar Liverpool H D 0-0
25 Mar Manchester C H L 0-2
1 Apr Stockport Co A L 3-5
8 Apr Everton A L 1-3
15 Apr Oldham H W 3-0
21 Apr Stockport Co H W 3-2
22 Apr Liverpool A L 1-7
29 Apr Manchester C A L 1-2

P W D L F:A Pts
Manchester U 10 2 1 7 12:24 5 6th

SEASON 1916-1917
Lancs Principal Tournament
2 Sep Port Vale H D 2-2
9 Sep Oldham A W 2-0
16 Sep Preston NE H W 2-1
23 Sep Burnley A L 1-7
30 Sep Blackpool A D 2-2
7 Oct Liverpool H D 0-0
14 Oct Stockport Co A L 0-1
21 Oct Bury H W 3-1
28 Oct Stoke C A L 0-3
4 Nov Southport H W 1-1

11 Nov Blackburn H A W 2-1
18 Nov Manchester C H W 2-1
25 Nov Everton A L 2-3
2 Dec Rochdale H D 1-1
9 Dec Bolton W A W 1-0
23 Dec Oldham H W 3-2
30 Dec Preston NE A W 3-1
6 Jan Burnley H W 3-1
13 Jan Blackpool A D 3-3
20 Jan Liverpool A D 3-3
27 Jan Stockport Co H L 0-1
3 Feb Bury A D 1-1
10 Feb Stoke C H W 4-2
17 Feb Southport A W 1-0
24 Feb Blackburn R H W 1-0
3 Mar Manchester C A L 0-1
10 Mar Everton H L 0-2
17 Mar Rochdale A L 0-1
24 Mar Bolton W H W 6-3
6 Apr Port Vale A L 0-3

P W D L F:A Pts
Manchester U 30 13 8 11 48:54 33 7th

Lancs Subsidiary Tournament
31 Mar Stoke C A L 1-2
7 Apr Manchester C H W 5-1
9 Apr Port Vale H W 5-1
14 Apr Stoke C H W 1-0
21 Apr Manchester C A L 0-1
28 Apr Port Vale A L 2-5

P W D L F:A Pts
Manchester U 6 4 0 2 15:9 8 4th

SEASON 1917-1918
Lancs Principal Tournament
1 Sep Blackburn R A W 5-0
8 Sep Blackburn R H W 6-1
15 Sep Rochdale A L 0-3
22 Sep Rochdale H W 3-1
29 Sep Manchester C A L 1-3
6 Oct Manchester C H D 1-1
13 Oct Everton A L 0-3
20 Oct Everton H D 0-0
27 Oct Port Vale H D 3-3
3 Nov Port Vale A W 1-0
10 Nov Bolton W H L 1-3
17 Nov Bolton W A L 2-4
24 Nov Preston NE H W 2-1
1 Dec Preston NE A L 0-3
8 Dec Blackpool H W 1-0
15 Dec Blackpool A W 3-2
22 Dec Burnley A W 5-0
29 Dec Burnley H W 1-0
5 Jan Southport A L 0-3
12 Jan Southport H D 0-0
19 Jan Liverpool A L 1-5
26 Jan Liverpool H L 0-2
2 Feb Stoke C A L 1-5
9 Feb Stoke C H W 2-1
16 Feb Bury H D 0-0
23 Feb Bury A W 2-1
2 Mar Oldham H W 2-1
9 Mar Oldham A L 0-2
16 Mar Stockport Co H W 1-0
23 Mar Stockport Co A L 1-2

P W D L F:A Pts
Manchester U 30 1 8 1 45:49 30 8th

Lancs Subsidiary Tournament
29 Mar Manchester C A L 0-3
30 Mar Stoke C H W 2-1
1 Apr Manchester C H W 2-0
6 Apr Stoke C A D 0-0
13 Apr Port Vale H W 2-1
20 Apr Port Vale A L 0-3

P W D L F:A Pts
Manchester U 6 3 1 2 6:7 7 8th

SEASON 1918-1919
Lancs Principal Tournament
7 Sep Oldham H L 1-4
14 Sep Oldham A W 2-0
21 Sep Blackburn R H W 1-0
28 Sep Blackburn R A D 1-1
5 Oct Manchester C H L 0-2
12 Oct Manchester C A D 0-0
19 Oct Everton H D 1-1
26 Oct Everton A L 2-6
2 Nov Rochdale H W 3-1
9 Nov Rochdale A L 0-1
16 Nov Preston NE A L 2-4
23 Nov Preston NE H L 1-2
30 Nov Bolton W A L 1-3
7 Dec Bolton W H W 2-0
14 Dec Port Vale A L 1-3
21 Dec Port Vale H W 5-1
28 Dec Blackpool A D 2-2
11 Jan Stockport Co H L 1-2
18 Jan Stockport Co A L 0-2
25 Jan Liverpool A D 1-1
1 Feb Liverpool H L 0-1
8 Feb Southport V A L 1-2
15 Feb Southport V H L 1-3
22 Feb Burnley H W 4-0
1 Mar Burnley A W 4-0
8 Mar Stoke C A W 2-1
15 Mar Stoke C H W 3-1
22 Mar Bury A W 2-0
29 Mar Bury H W 5-1

P W D L F:A Pts
Manchester U 30 11 5 14 51:50 27 9th

Lancs Subsidiary Tournament (Sec 'C')
5 Apr Port Vale A W 3-1
12 Apr Port Vale H W 2-1
18 Apr Manchester C A L 0-3
19 Apr Stoke C H L 0-1

21 Apr Manchester C H L 2-4
26 Apr Stoke C A L 2-4
30 Apr Blackpool H W 5-1

P W D L F:A Pts
Manchester U 6 2 0 4 9:14 4 3rd

SEASON 1919-1920
FOOTBALL LEAGUE (DIVISION I)
30 Aug Derby Co A D 1-1
1 Sep Sheffield Wed H D 0-0
6 Sep Derby Co H L 0-2
8 Sep Sheffield Wed A W 3-1
13 Sep Preston NE A W 3-2
20 Sep Preston NE H W 5-1
27 Sep Middlesbrough A D 1-1
4 Oct Middlesbrough H D 1-1
11 Oct Manchester C A D 3-3
18 Oct Manchester C H W 1-0
25 Oct Sheffield U A D 2-2
1 Nov Sheffield U H W 3-0
8 Nov Burnley A L 1-2
15 Nov Burnley H L 0-1
22 Nov Oldham A W 3-0
6 Dec Aston Villa A L 0-2
13 Dec Aston Villa H L 1-2
20 Dec Newcastle U H W 2-1
27 Dec Newcastle U A L 1-2
1 Jan Liverpool A D 0-0
3 Jan Chelsea A L 0-1
17 Jan Chelsea H L 0-1
24 Jan WBA A L 1-2
7 Feb Sunderland A L 0-3
11 Feb Oldham H D 1-1
14 Feb Sunderland H W 2-0
21 Feb Arsenal A W 3-0
25 Feb Arsenal H L 1-2
28 Feb Arsenal H W 1-0
13 Mar Everton A D 0-6
20 Mar Bradford H D 0-6
27 Mar Bradford PA A L 0-1
2 Apr Bradford PA H L 0-1
3 Apr Bolton W A W 4-1
6 Apr Bradford PA A W 5-3
10 Apr Bolton W A W 5-3
17 Apr Blackburn R H D 1-1
24 Apr Blackburn R A L 0-1
26 Apr Notts Co H D 0-0
1 May Notts Co A W 2-0

FA Cup
10 Jan Port Vale (1) A W 1-0
31 Jan Aston Villa (2) H L 1-2

Football League
P W D L F:A Pts
Manchester U 42 13 14 15 54:50 40 12th

SEASON 1920-1921
FOOTBALL LEAGUE (DIVISION I)
26 Aug Bolton W H L 2-3
30 Aug Arsenal A L 0-2
4 Sep Bolton W A D 1-1
6 Sep Arsenal H D 1-1
11 Sep Chelsea H W 3-1
18 Sep Chelsea A W 2-1
25 Sep Tottenham H H L 0-1
2 Oct Tottenham H A L 1-4
9 Oct Oldham H W 4-1
16 Oct Oldham A D *2-2
23 Oct Preston NE A L 1-6
30 Oct Preston NE A D 0-0
6 Nov Sheffield U H W 2-1
13 Nov Sheffield U A D 0-0
20 Nov Manchester C H D 1-1
2 Nov Manchester C A L 1-3
4 Dec Bradford H W 5-1
11 Dec Bradford A W 4-2
18 Dec Newcastle A W 3-0
25 Dec Aston Villa H W 4-3
27 Dec Aston Villa A W 3-0
1 Jan Newcastle U A L 3-6
15 Jan WBA H L 1-4
22 Jan WBA A W 2-0
5 Feb Liverpool H D 1-1
9 Feb Liverpool A L 0-1
12 Feb Everton H L 1-2
20 Feb Sunderland A W 3-0
5 Mar Sunderland A W 3-2
9 Mar Everton A L 0-2
12 Mar Bradford C H D 1-1
19 Mar Bradford C A D 1-1
25 Mar Burnley A L 0-1
26 Mar Huddersfield T A L 2-5
29 Mar Burnley H L 0-1
2 Apr Huddersfield T H W 2-0
9 Apr Middlesbrough A W 4-2
16 Apr Middlesbrough H L 0-1
23 Apr Blackburn R A L 0-2
30 Apr Blackburn R H W 1-0
2 May Derby Co A D 1-1
7 May Derby Co H W 3-0

FA Cup
8 Jan Liverpool (1) A D 1-1
12 Jan Liverpool (1R) H L 1-2

Football League
P W D L F:A Pts
Manchester U 42 15 10 17 64:68 40 13th

SEASON 1921-1922
FOOTBALL LEAGUE (DIVISION I)
27 Aug Everton A L 0-5
29 Aug WBA H W 2-3
3 Sep Everton H W 2-1
7 Sep WBA A D 0-0
10 Sep Chelsea H L 0-0

17 Sep Chelsea H D 0-0
24 Sep Preston NE A L 2-3
1 Oct Preston NE H D 2-2
8 Oct Tottenham H A D 2-2
15 Oct Tottenham H H L 1-4
22 Oct Manchester C A L 1-4
29 Oct Manchester C H L 3-5
5 Nov Middlesbrough A L 3-5
12 Nov Middlesbrough H W 1-0
19 Nov Aston Villa A L 1-3
26 Nov Aston Villa H W 1-0
3 Dec Bradford C A L 2-4
10 Dec Bradford C H L 0-3
17 Dec Liverpool A L 0-0
24 Dec Liverpool H D 0-0
26 Dec Burnley A L 0-1
27 Dec Burnley H L 2-4
31 Dec Newcastle U A L 0-3
2 Jan Sheffield U A L 0-3
14 Jan Newcastle U H L 0-3
21 Jan Sunderland A L 1-2
28 Jan Sunderland H D 1-1
11 Feb Huddersfield T H D 1-1
18 Feb Birmingham A D 1-1
25 Feb Birmingham H D 1-1
27 Feb Huddersfield T A L 1-0
11 Mar Arsenal H W 1-0
18 Mar Blackburn H A L 0-3
25 Mar Blackburn H A L 0-3
1 Apr Bolton W H L 0-1
5 Apr Arsenal A L 1-3
8 Apr Bolton W A L 0-1
15 Apr Oldham H L 0-3
17 Apr Sheffield U H W 3-2
22 Apr Oldham A D 1-1
29 Apr Cardiff C H D 1-1
6 May Cardiff C A L 1-3

FA Cup
7 Jan Cardiff C (1) H L 1-4

Football League
P W D L F:A Pts
Manchester U 42 8 12 22 41:73 28 22nd

SEASON 1922-1923
FOOTBALL LEAGUE (DIVISION 2)
26 Aug Crystal Palace H W 2-1
28 Aug Sheffield Wed A L 0-1
2 Sep Crystal Palace A W 3-2
4 Sep Sheffield Wed H W 1-0
9 Sep Wolverhampton W A W 1-0
16 Sep Wolverhampton W H W 1-0
23 Sep Coventry C A L 0-2
30 Sep Coventry C H W 2-0
7 Oct Port Vale H L 1-2
14 Oct Port Vale A L 0-1
21 Oct Fulham H D 1-1
28 Oct Fulham A D 0-0
4 Nov Clapton O H D 1-1
11 Nov Clapton O A D 1-1
18 Nov Bury A D 2-2
25 Nov Bury H L 0-1
2 Dec Rotherham U H W 3-0
9 Dec Rotherham U A D 1-1
16 Dec Stockport Co H W 1-0
23 Dec Stockport Co A L 0-1
25 Dec West Ham U H L 1-2
26 Dec West Ham U A W 2-0
30 Dec Hull C A L 1-2
1 Jan Barnsley H W 1-0
6 Jan Hull C H W *3-2
20 Jan Leeds U H D 0-0
27 Jan Leeds U A W 1-0
10 Feb Notts Co A W 6-1
17 Feb Derby Co H D 0-0
21 Feb Notts Co H D 1-1
3 Mar Southampton H L 1-2
14 Mar Derby Co A D 1-1
17 Mar Bradford C H W 3-0
21 Mar Bradford C H D 1-1
30 Mar South Shields H W 3-0
31 Mar Blackpool A L 0-1
7 Apr Blackpool H W 3-0
11 Apr Southampton A D 0-0
14 Apr Leicester C H W 1-0
21 Apr Leicester C H L 0-2
28 Apr Barnsley A D 2-2

FA Cup
13 Jan Bradford C (1) A D 1-1
17 Jan Bradford C (1R) H W 2-0
3 Feb Tottenham H (2) A L 0-4

Football League
P W D L F:A Pts
Manchester U 42 17 14 11 51:36 48 4th

SEASON 1923-1924
FOOTBALL LEAGUE (DIVISION 2)
25 Aug Bristol C A W 2-1
27 Aug Southampton H W 1-0
1 Sep Bristol C H W 2-0
3 Sep Southampton A D 0-0
8 Sep Bury A L 0-2
15 Sep Bury H L 0-1
22 Sep South Shields A L 0-1
29 Sep South Shields H D 1-1
6 Oct Oldham A L *2-3
13 Oct Oldham H W 2-0
20 Oct Stockport Co H W 3-0
27 Oct Stockport Co A L 2-3
3 Nov Leicester C A D 2-2
10 Nov Leicester C H W 2-0
17 Nov Coventry C A D *1-1
1 Dec Leeds U H D 0-0
8 Dec Leeds U H W 3-1
15 Dec Port Vale A W 3-0
22 Dec Port Vale H W 5-0
25 Dec Barnsley H L 1-2

Date	Opponent		Res	Score
26 Dec	Barnsley	A	L	0-1
29 Dec	Bradford C	A	D	0-0
2 Jan	Coventry C	H	L	1-2
5 Jan	Bradford C	H	W	3-0
19 Jan	Fulham	A	L	1-3
26 Jan	Fulham	H	D	0-0
6 Feb	Blackpool	A	L	0-1
9 Feb	Blackpool	H	D	0-0
16 Feb	Derby Co	A	L	0-3
23Feb	Derby Co	H	D	0-0
1 Mar	Nelson	A	W	2-0
8 Mar	Nelson	H	L	0-1
15 Mar	Hull C	H	D	1-1
22 Mar	Hull C	A	D	1-1
29 Mar	Stoke C	H	D	2-2
5 Apr	Stoke C	A	L	0-3
12 Apr	Crystal Palace	H	W	5-1
18 Apr	Clapton O	A	L	0-1
19 Apr	Crystal Palace	A	D	1-1
21 Apr	Clapton O	H	D	2-2
26 Apr	Sheffield Wed	H	W	2-0
3 May	Sheffield Wed	A	L	0-2

FA Cup

12 Jan	Plymouth A (1)	H	W	1-0
2 Feb	Huddersfield (2)	H	L	0-3

Football League

	P	W	D	L	F:A	Pts	
Manchester U	42	13	14	15	52:44	40	14th

SEASON 1924-1925
FOOTBALL LEAGUE (DIVISION 2)

30 Aug	Leicester C	H	W	1-0
1 Sep	Stockport Co	A	L	1-2
6 Sep	Stoke C	A	D	0-0
8 Sep	Barnsley	H	W	1-0
13 Sep	Coventry C	H	W	5-1
20 Sep	Oldham	A	W	3-0
27 Sep	Sheffield Wed	H	W	2-0
4 Oct	Clapton O	A	W	1-0
11 Oct	Crystal Palace	H	W	1-0
18 Oct	Southampton	A	W	2-0
25 Oct	Wolverhampton W	H	D	0-0
1 Nov	Fulham	H	W	2-0
8 Nov	Portsmouth	A	D	1-1
15 Nov	Hull C	H	W	2-0
22 Nov	Blackpool	A	D	1-1
29 Nov	Derby Co	H	D	1-1
6 Dec	South Shields	A	W	2-1
13 Dec	Bradford C	H	W	3-0
20Dec	Port Vale	A	L	1-2
25 Dec	Middlesbrough	A	D	1-1
26 Dec	Middlesbrough	H	W	2-0
27 Dec	Leicester C	A	L	0-3
17 Jan	Chelsea	H	W	1-0
3 Jan	Stoke C	H	W	2-0
1 Jan	Coventry C	A	L	0-1
24 Jan	Oldham	H	L	0-1
7 Feb	Clapton O	H	W	4-2
14 Feb	Crystal Palace	A	L	1-2
23 Feb	Sheffield Wed	A	D	1-1
28 Feb	Wolverhampton W	H	W	3-0
7 Mar	Fulham	A	L	0-1
14 Mar	Portsmouth	H	W	2-0
21 Mar	Hull C	A	W	1-0
28 Mar	Blackpool	H	D	0-0
4 Apr	Derby Co	A	L	0-1
10 Apr	Stockport Co	H	W	2-0
11 Apr	South Shields	H	W	1-0
13 Apr	Chelsea	A	D	0-0
18 Apr	Bradford C	A	W	1-0
22 Apr	Southampton	H	D	1-1
25 Apr	Port Vale	H	W	4-0
2 May	Barnsley	A	D	0-0

FA Cup

10 Jan	Sheffield Wed (1)	A	L	0-2

Football League

	P	W	D	L	F:A	Pts	
Manchester U	42	23	11	8	57:23	57	2nd

SEASON 1925-1926
FOOTBALL LEAGUE (DIVISION 1)

29 Aug	West Ham U	A	L	0-1
2 Sep	Aston Villa	H	W	3-0
5 Sep	Arsenal	H	L	0-1
9 Sep	Aston Villa	A	D	2-2
12 Sep	Manchester C	A	D	1-1
16 Sep	Leicester C	H	W	3-2
19 Sep	Liverpool	A	L	0-5
26 Sep	Burnley	H	W	6-1
3 Oct	Leeds U	A	L	0-2
10 Oct	Newcastle U	H	W	2-1
17 Oct	Tottenham H	H	D	0-0
24 Oct	Cardiff C	A	W	2-0
31 Oct	Huddersfield T	H	D	1-1
7 Nov	Everton	A	W	3-1
14 Nov	Birmingham	H	W	3-1
21 Nov	Bury	A	W	3-1
28 Nov	Blackburn R	H	W	2-0
5 Dec	Sunderland	A	L	1-2
12 Dec	Sheffield U	H	L	1-2
19 Dec	WBA	A	L	1-5
25 Dec	Bolton W	H	W	2-1
28 Dec	Leicester C	A	W	3-1
2 Jan	West Ham U	H	W	2-1
16 Jan	Arsenal	A	L	2-3
23 Jan	Manchester C	H	L	1-6
6 Feb	Burnley	A	W	1-0
13 Feb	Leeds U	H	W	2-1
27 Feb	Tottenham H	A	W	1-0
10 Mar	Liverpool	H	D	3-3
13 Mar	Huddersfield T	A	L	0-5
17 Mar	Bolton W	H	L	1-3
20 Mar	Everton	H	D	0-0
2 Apr	Notts Co	A	W	3-0
3 Apr	Bury	H	L	0-1
5 Apr	Notts Co	H	L	0-1
10 Apr	Blackburn R	A	L	0-7
14 Apr	Newcastle U	A	L	1-4
19 Apr	Birmingham	A	L	1-2
21 Apr	Sunderland	H	W	5-1
24 Apr	Sheffield U	A	L	0-2
26 Apr	Cardiff C	H	W	1-0
1 May	WBA	H	W	3-2

FA Cup

9 Jan	Port Vale (3)	A	W	3-2
30 Jan	Tottenham (4)	A	D	2-2
3 Feb	Tottenham (4R)	H	W	2-0
20 Feb	Sunderland (5)	A	D	3-3
24 Feb	Sunderland (SR)	H	W	2-1
6 Mar	Fulham (6)	H	W	2-1
21 Mar	Manchester C (SF)	N	L	0-3
	(at Bramall Lane)			

Football League

	P	W	D	L	F:A	Pts	
Manchester U	42	19	6	17	66:73	44	9th

SEASON 1926-1927
FOOTBALL LEAGUE (DIVISION 1)

26 Aug	Liverpool	A	L	2-4
30 Aug	Sheffield	A	D	2-2
4 Sep	Leeds U	H	D	2-2
11 Sep	Newcastle U	A	L	2-4
15 Sep	Arsenal	H	D	2-2
18 Sep	Burnley	H	W	2-1
25 Sep	Cardiff C	H	W	2-0
2 Oct	Aston Villa	H	W	2-1
9 Oct	Bolton W	A	L	0-4
16 Oct	Bury	A	W	3-0
23 Oct	Birmingham	H	L	0-1
30 Oct	West Ham U	A	L	0-4
6 Nov	Sheffield Wed	H	D	0-0
13 Nov	Leicester C	A	W	3-2
20 Nov	Everton	H	W	2-1
27 Nov	Blackburn R	A	L	1-2
4 Doc	Huddersfield T	H	D	0-0
11 Dec	Sunderland	A	L	0-8
18 Dec	WBA	H	W	2-0
25 Dec	Tottenham H	H	D	1-1
27 Dec	Tottenham H	H	W	2-1
28 Dec	Arsenal	A	L	0-1
1 Jan	Sheffield U	H	W	5-0
15 Jan	Liverpool	H	L	0-1
22 Jan	Leeds U	A	W	3-2
5 Feb	Burnley	A	L	0-1
9 Feb	Newcastle U	H	W	3-1
12 Feb	Cardiff C	H	D	1-1
19 Feb	Aston Villa	A	L	0-2
26 Feb	Bolton W	H	D	0-0
5 Mar	Bury	H	L	1-2
12 Mar	Birmingham	A	W	1-0
19 Mar	West Ham U	H	L	0-3
26 Mar	Sheffield Wed	A	L	0-2
2 Apr	Leicester C	H	W	1-0
9 Apr	Everton	A	D	0-0
15 Apr	Derby Co	H	D	2-2
15 Apr	Blackburn R	H	W	2-0
18 Apr	Derby Co	A	D	2-2
23 Apr	Huddersfield T	H	D	0-0
30 Apr	Sunderland	H	D	0-0
7 May	WBA	A	D	2-2

FA Cup

8 Jan	Reading (3)	A	D	1-1
12 Jan	Reading (3R)†	H	D	2-2
17 Jan	Reading (3R)	N	L	1-2
	(at Villa Park)			
	†after extra time			

Football League

	P	W	D	L	F:A	Pts	
Manchester U	42	13	14	15	52:64	40	15th

SEASON 1927-1928
FOOTBALL LEAGUE (DIVISION 1)

27 Aug	Middlesbrough	H	W	3-0
29 Aug	Sheffield Wed	A	W	2-0
3 Sep	Birmingham	A	D	0-0
7 Sep	Sheffield Wed	H	D	1-1
10 Sep	Newcastle U	H	L	1-7
17 Sep	Huddersfield T	A	L	2-4
19 Sep	Blackburn R	A	L	0-3
24 Sep	Tottenham H	H	W	3-0
1 Oct	Leicester C	A	L	0-1
8 Oct	Everton	A	L	2-5
15 Oct	Cardiff C	H	D	2-2
22 Oct	Derby Co	H	W	5-0
29 Oct	West Ham U	A	W	2-1
5 Nov	Portsmouth	H	W	2-0
12 Nov	Sunderland	A	L	1-4
19 Nov	Aston Villa	H	W	5-1
26 Nov	Burnley	A	L	0-4
3 Dec	Bury	H	L	1-2
10 Dec	Sheffield U	A	L	1-2
17 Dec	Arsenal	H	W	4-1
24 Dec	Liverpool	A	L	0-2
26 Dec	Blackburn R	H	D	1-1
31 Dec	Middlesbrough	A	D	1-1
7 Jan	Birmingham	A	D	1-1
21 Jun	Newcastle U	A	L	1-4
4 Feb	Tottenham H	H	W	1-1
11 Feb	Leicester C	H	W	5-2
25 Feb	Cardiff C	A	L	0-2
7 Mar	Huddersfield T	H	D	0-0
10 Mar	West Ham U	H	L	1-1
14 Mar	Everton	H	W	1-0
17 Mar	Portsmouth	A	L	1-1
28 Mar	Derby Co	A	L	0-5
31 Mar	Aston Villa	A	L	1-3
6 Apr	Bolton W	A	L	2-3
7 Apr	Burnley	H	W	4-3
9 Apr	Bolton W	H	W	2-1
14 Apr	Bury	A	L	3-4
21 Apr	Sheffield U	H	L	2-3
25 Apr	Sunderland	H	W	2-1
28 Apr	Arsenal	A	W	1-0
5 May	Liverpool	H	W	6-1

FA Cup

14 Jan	Brentford (3)	H	W	7-1
28 Jan	Bury (4)	A	D	1-1
1 Feb	Bury (4R)	A	D	1-1
18 Feb	Birmingham (5)	H	W	1-0
3 Mar	Blackburn (6)	A	L	0-2

Football League

	P	W	D	L	F:A	Pts	
Manchester U	42	16	7	19	72:80	39	18th

SEASON 1928-1929
FOOTBALL LEAGUE (DIVISION 1)

25 Aug	Leicester C	H	D	1-1
27 Aug	Aston Villa	A	D	0-0
1 Sep	Manchester C	A	D	2-2
8 Sep	Leeds U	A	L	2-3
15 Sep	Liverpool	H	D	2-2
22 Sep	West Ham U	A	L	1-3
29 Sep	Newcastle U	H	W	5-0
6 Oct	Burnley	A	W	4-3
13 Oct	Cardiff C	H	D	1-1
20 Oct	Birmingham	H	W	1-0
27 Oct	Huddersfield T	A	W	2-1
3 Nov	Bolton W	H	D	1-1
10 Nov	Sheffield Wed	A	L	1-0
17 Nov	Derby Co	H	L	0-1
24 Nov	Sunderland	A	L	1-5
1 Dec	Blackburn R	A	L	1-3
8 Dec	Arsenal	A	L	1-3
15 Dec	Everton	H	D	1-1
22 Dec	Portsmouth	A	L	0-3
25 Dec	Sheffield U	H	D	1-1
26 Dec	Sheffield U	A	L	1-6
29 Dec	Leicester C	A	L	1-2
1 Jan	Aston Villa	H	D	2-2
5 Jan	Manchester C	H	L	1-2
19 Jan	Leeds U	H	L	1-2
2 Feb	West Ham U	H	L	2-3
9 Feb	Newcastle U	A	L	0-5
13 Feb	Liverpool	A	W	3-2
16 Feb	Burnley	H	W	1-0
23 Feb	Cardiff C	A	D	2-2
2 Mar	Birmingham	A	D	1-1
9 Mar	Huddersfield T	H	W	1-0
16 Mar	Bolton W	A	D	1-1
23 Mar	Sheffield Wed	H	W	3-1
29 Mar	Bury	A	W	3-1
30 Mar	Derby Co	A	L	1-8
1 Apr	Bury	H	W	1-0
6 Apr	Sunderland	H	W	3-0
13 Apr	Blackburn R	A	W	3-0
20 Apr	Arsenal	H	W	4-1
27 Apr	Everton	A	W	4-2
4 May	Portsmouth	H	D	0-0

FA Cup

12 Jan	Port Vale (3)	A	W	3-0
26 Jan	Bury (4)	H	L	0-1

Football League

	P	W	D	L	F:A	Pts	
Manchester U	42	14	13	15	68:76	41	12th

SEASON 1929-1930
FOOTBALL LEAGUE (DIVISION 1)

31 Aug	Newcastle U	A	L	1-4
2 Sep	Leicester C	A	L	1-4
7 Sep	Blackburn R	H	W	1-0
11 Sep	Leicester C	H	W	2-1
14 Sep	Middlesbrough	A	W	3-2
21 Sep	Liverpool	H	L	1-2
28 Sep	West Ham U	H	L	1-2
5 Oct	Manchester C	H	L	1-3
7 Oct	Sheffield U	A	L	0-3
12 Oct	Grimsby T	H	L	2-5
19 Oct	Portsmouth	A	L	0-3
28 Oct	Arsenal	H	W	1-0
2 Nov	Anton Villa	A	L	0-1
9 Nov	Derby Co	H	W	3-2
16 Nov	Sheffield Wed	A	L	2-7
23 Nov	Burnley	A	W	4-2
30 Nov	Sunderland	A	W	4-2
7 Dec	Bolton W	H	D	1-1
14 Dec	Everton	A	D	0-0
21 Dec	Leeds U	H	W	3-1
25 Dec	Birmingham	H	D	0-0
26 Dec	Newcastle U	H	W	5-0
4 Jan	Blackburn R	A	L	4-5
18 Jan	Middlesbrough	H	L	0-3
25 Jan	Liverpool	A	L	0-1
1 Feb	West Ham U	H	W	4-2
8 Feb	Manchester C	A	W	1-0
15 Feb	Grimsby T	A	D	2-2
22 Feb	Portsmouth	H	W	3-0
1 Mar	Bolton W	A	L	1-4
8 Mar	Aston Villa	H	L	2-3
12 Mar	Arsenal	A	D	1-1
15 Mar	Derby Co	A	D	0-4
29 Mar	Burnley	H	L	0-4
5 Apr	Sunderland	A	W	2-1
14 Apr	Sheffield Wed	H	D	2-2
18 Apr	Huddersfield T	H	W	1-0
19 Apr	Everton	H	D	3-3
22 Apr	Huddersfield T	A	D	2-2
26 Apr	Leeds U	A	L	1-3
3 May	Sheffield U	H	L	1-5

FA Cup

11 Jan	Swindon (3)	H	L	0-2

Football League

	P	W	D	L	F:A	Pts	
Manchester U	42	15	8	19	67:88	38	17th

SEASON 1930-1931
FOOTBALL LEAGUE (DIVISION 1)

30 Aug	Aston Villa	H	L	3-4
3 Sep	Middlesbrough	A	L	1-3
6 Sep	Chelsea	A	L	2-6
10 Sep	Huddersfield T	H	L	0-6
13 Sep	Newcastle U	H	L	4-7
15 Sep	Huddersfield T	A	L	0-3
20 Sep	Sheffield Wed	H	L	0-3
27 Sep	Grimsby T	H	L	0-2
4 Oct	Manchester C	A	L	1-4
11 Oct	West Ham U	A	L	1-5
18 Oct	Arsenal	H	L	1-2
25 Oct	Portsmouth	A	L	1-4
1 Nov	Birmingham	H	W	2-0
8 Nov	Leicester C	A	L	4-5
15 Nov	Blackpool	H	D	0-0
22 Nov	Sheffield U	A	L	1-3
29 Nov	Sunderland	H	D	1-1
6 Dec	Blackburn R	A	L	1-4
13 Dec	Derby Co	H	W	2-1
20 Dec	Leeds U	A	L	0-5
26 Dec	Bolton W	A	L	1-3
26 Dec	Bolton W	H	D	1-1
27 Dec	Aston Villa	A	L	0-7
1 Jan	Leeds U	H	W	1-0
3 Jan	Chelsea	H	W	1-0
17 Jan	Newcastle U	A	L	3-4
28 Jan	Sheffield Wed	H	W	4-1
31 Jan	Grimsby T	H	L	1-2
7 Feb	Manchester C	H	L	1-3
14 Feb	West Ham U	H	W	1-0
21 Feb	Arsenal	A	L	1-4
7 Mar	Birmingham	A	D	0-0
16 Mar	Portsmouth	H	L	0-1
21 Mar	Blackpool	A	L	1-5
25 Mar	Leicester C	H	D	0-0
28 Mar	Sheffield U	H	L	1-2
3 Apr	Liverpool	A	D	1-1
4 Apr	Sunderland	A	W	2-1
6 Apr	Liverpool	H	W	4-1
11 Apr	Blackburn B	H	L	0-1
18 Apr	Derby Co	A	L	1-6
2 May	Middlesbrough	H	D	4-4

FA Cup

10 Jan	Stoke C (3)	A	D	3-3
14 Jan	Stoke C (3R)†	H	D	0-0
19 Jan	Stoke C (3R)	N	W	4-2
	(at Anfield)			
24 Jan	Grimsby (4)	A	L	0-1
	†after extra time			

Football League

	P	W	D	L	F:A	Pts	
Manchester U	42	7	8	27	53:115	22	22nd

SEASON 1931-1932
FOOTBALL LEAGUE (DIVISION 2)

29 Aug	Bradford	A	L	1-3
2 Sep	Southampton	H	L	2-3
5 Sep	Swansea	H	W	2-1
7 Sep	Stoke C	A	L	0-3
12 Sep	Tottenham H	H	D	1-1
16 Sep	Stoke C	H	D	1-1
19 Sep	Nottingham F	A	L	1-2
26 Sep	Chesterfield	H	W	3-1
3 Oct	Burnley	A	L	0-2
10 Oct	Preston NE	H	W	3-2
17 Oct	Barnsley	A	D	0-0
24 Oct	Notts Co	H	D	3-3
31 Oct	Plymouth A	A	L	1-3
7 Nov	Leeds U	H	L	1-5
14 Nov	Oldham	A	W	5-1
21 Nov	Bury	A	W	2-1
28 Nov	Port Vale	H	W	2-0
5 Dec	Millwall	H	W	2-0
12 Dec	Bradford C	A	L	3-4
19 Dec	Bristol C	H	L	0-1
25 Dec	Wolverhampton W	H	W	3-2
26 Dec	Wolverhampton W	A	L	0-7
2 Jan	Bradford	H	L	0-2
16 Jan	Swansea	A	L	1-3
23 Jan	Tottenham H	A	L	1-4
30 Jan	Nottingham F	H	W	3-2
6 Feb	Chesterfield	A	W	3-1
17 Feb	Burnley	H	W	5-1
20 Feb	Preston NE	A	D	0-0
27 Feb	Barnsley	H	W	3-0
5 Mar	Notts Co	A	W	2-1
12 Mar	Plymouth A	H	W	2-1
19 Mar	Leeds U	A	W	4-1
25 Mar	Charlton A	H	L	0-2
26 Mar	Oldham	H	W	5-1
28 Mar	Charlton A	A	L	0-1
2 Apr	Bury	A	D	0-0
9 Apr	Port Vale	H	W	2-0
16 Apr	Millwall	A	D	1-1
23 Apr	Bradford C	H	W	1-0
30 Apr	Bristol C	A	L	1-2
7 May	Southampton	A	D	1-1

FA Cup

9 Jan	Plymouth A (3)	A	L	1-4

Football League

	P	W	D	L	F:A	Pts	
Manchester U	42	17	8	17	71:72	42	12th

SEASON 1932-1933
FOOTBALL LEAGUE (DIVISION 2)

27 Aug	Stoke C	H	L	0-2
29 Aug	Charlton A	A	W	1-0
3 Sep	Southampton	A	L	*2-4
7 Sep	Charlton A	H	D	1-1
10 Sep	Tottenham H	A	L	1-6
17 Sep	Grimsby T	H	D	1-1
24 Sep	Oldham	A	D	1-1
1 Oct	Preston NE	A	W	3-2
6 Oct	Burnley	A	W	3-2
15 Oct	Bradford	H	W	2-1
22 Oct	Millwall	H	W	7-1
29 Oct	Port Vale	H	D	3-3
5 Nov	Notts Co	H	W	2-0
12 Nov	Bury	A	D	2-2
19 Nov	Fulham	H	W	4-3
26 Nov	Chesterfield	A	D	1-1
3 Dec	Bradford C	A	L	1-3
10 Dec	West Ham U	A	L	1-3
17 Dec	Lincoln C	H	W	*4-1
24 Dec	Swansea	A	D	0-0
26 Dec	Plymouth A	A	D	3-2
31 Dec	Stoke C	A	D	0-0
2 Jan	Plymouth A	H	W	4-0
7 Jan	Southampton	H	L	1-2
21 Jan	Tottenham H	H	W	2-1

Ernest Mangnall was United's first manager.

1889-1949

Matt Busby began his reign at Old Trafford in 1945.

31 Jan	Grimsby T	A	D	1-1
4 Feb	Oldham	H	W	2-0
11 Feb	Preston NE	A	D	3-3
22 Feb	Burnley	H	W	2-1
4 Mar	Millwall	A	L	0-2
11 Mar	Port Vale	H	D	1-1
18 Mar	Notts Co	A	L	0-1
25 Mar	Bury	H	L	1-3
1 Apr	Fulham	A	L	1-3
5 Apr	Bradford	H	W	2-1
8 Apr	Chesterfield	H	W	2-1
14 Apr	Nottingham F	A	L	2-3
15 Apr	Bradford C	A	W	2-1
17 Apr	Nottingham F	H	W	2-1
22 Apr	West Ham U	H	L	1-2
29 Apr	Lincoln C	A	L	2-3
6 May	Swansea	H	D	1-1

FA Cup

14 Jan	Middlesbrough (3)	H	L	1-4

Football League

	P	W	D	L	F:A	Pts	
Manchester U	42	15	13	14	71:88	43	6th

SEASON 1933-1934
FOOTBALL LEAGUE (DIVISION 2)

Date	Opponent	Venue	Result	Score
26 Aug	Plymouth A	A	L	0-4
30 Aug	Nottingham F	H	L	0-1
2 Sep	Lincoln C	H	D	1-1
6 Sep	Nottingham F	A	D	1-1
9 Sep	Bolton W	H	L	1-5
16 Sep	Bradford	A	W	4-3
23 Sep	Burnley	H	W	5-2
30 Sep	Oldham	A	L	0-2
7 Oct	Preston NE	H	W	1-0
14 Oct	Bradford	A	L	1-6
21 Oct	Bury	A	L	1-2
28 Oct	Hull C	H	W	4-1
4 Nov	Fulham	A	W	2-0
11 Nov	Southampton	H	W	*1-0
18 Nov	Blackpool	A	L	1-3
25 Nov	Bradford C	H	W	2-1
2 Dec	Port Vale	A	W	*3-2
9 Dec	Notts Co	H	L	1-2
16 Dec	Swansea	A	L	1-2
23 Dec	Millwall	H	D	1-1
25 Dec	Grimsby T	H	L	1-3
26 Dec	Grimsby T	A	L	3-7
30 Dec	Plymouth A	H	L	0-3
6 Jan	Lincoln C	A	L	1-5
20 Jan	Bolton W	A	L	1-3
27 Jan	Brentford	H	L	1-3
3 Feb	Burnley	A	W	4-1
10 Feb	Oldham	H	L	2-3
21 Feb	Preston NE	H	L	2-3
24 Feb	Bradford	H	L	0-4
3 Mar	Bury	H	W	2-1
10 Mar	Hull C	A	L	1-4
17 Mar	Fulham	H	W	1-0
24 Mar	Southampton	A	L	0-1
30 Mar	West Ham U	H	L	0-1
31 Mar	Blackpool	H	W	2-0
2 Apr	West Ham U	A	L	1-2
7 Apr	Bradford C	A	D	1-1
14 Apr	Port Vale	H	W	2-0
21 Apr	Notts Co	A	D	0-0
28 Apr	Swansea	H	D	1-1
5 May	Millwall	A	W	2-0

FA Cup

13 Jan	Portsmouth (3)	H	D	1-1
17 Jan	Portsmouth (3R)	A	L	1-4

Football League

	P	W	D	L	F:A	Pts	
Manchester U	42	14	6	22	59:85	34	20th

SEASON 1934-1935
FOOTBALL LEAGUE (DIVISION 2)

Date	Opponent	Venue	Result	Score
2 Aug	Bradford C	H	W	2-0
1 Sep	Sheffield U	A	L	2-3
3 Sep	Bolton W	A	L	*1-3
8 Sep	Barnsley	H	W	4-1
12 Sep	Bolton W	H	L	0-3
15 Sep	Port Vale	A	L	2-3
22 Sep	Norwich C	H	W	5-0
29 Sep	Swansea	H	W	3-1
6 Oct	Burnley	A	W	2-1
13 Oct	Oldham	H	W	4-0
20 Oct	Newcastle U	H	W	1-0
27 Oct	West Ham U	H	W	3-1
3 Nov	Blackpool	A	W	2-1
10 Nov	Bury	H	W	1-0
17 Nov	Hull C	A	L	2-3
24 Nov	Nottingham F	H	W	3-2
1 Dec	Brentford	A	L	1-3
8 Dec	Fulham	H	W	1-0
15 Dec	Bradford	A	W	2-1
22 Dec	Plymouth A	H	W	3-1
25 Dec	Notts Co	H	W	2-1
26 Dec	Notts Co	A	L	0-1
29 Dec	Bradford C	A	L	0-2
1 Jan	Southampton	H	W	3-0
5 Jan	Sheffield U	H	D	3-3
19 Jan	Barnsley	A	W	2-0
2 Feb	Norwich C	A	L	2-3
8 Feb	Port Vale	H	W	2-1
9 Feb	Swansea	A	L	0-1
23 Feb	Oldham	A	W	1-3
2 Mar	Newcastle U	H	L	0-1
9 Mar	West Ham U	A	D	0-0
16 Mar	Blackpool	H	W	3-2
23 Mar	Bury	A	W	1-0
27 Mar	Burnley	H	L	3-4
30 Mar	Hull C	H	W	3-0
6 Apr	Nottingham F	A	D	2-2
13 Apr	Brentford	H	D	0-0
20 Apr	Fulham	A	L	1-3
22 Apr	Southampton	A	L	0-1
27 Apr	Bradford	H	W	2-0
4 May	Plymouth A	A	W	2-0

FA Cup

12 Jan	Bristol R (3)	A	W	3-1
26 Jan	Nottingham F (4)	A	D	0-0
30 Jan	Nottingham F (4R)	H	L	0-3

Football League

	P	W	D	L	F:A	Pts	
Manchester U	42	23	4	15	76:55	50	5th

SEASON 1935-1936
FOOTBALL LEAGUE (DIVISION 2)

Date	Opponent	Venue	Result	Score
31 Aug	Plymouth A	A	L	1-3
4 Sep	Charlton A	H	W	3-0
9 Sep	Bradford C	H	W	3-1
11 Sep	Charlton A	A	D	0-0
14 Sep	Newcastle U	H	W	2-0
18 Sep	Hull C	H	W	2-0
21 Sep	Tottenham H	H	D	0-0
28 Sep	Southampton	A	L	1-2
5 Oct	Port Vale	A	W	3-0
12 Oct	Fulham	H	W	1-0
19 Oct	Sheffield U	H	W	3-1
28 Oct	Bradford	A	L	0-1
2 Nov	Leicester C	H	L	0-1
9 Nov	Swansea	A	L	1-2
16 Nov	West Ham U	A	L	2-3
23 Nov	Norwich C	A	W	5-3
30 Nov	Doncaster R	H	D	0-0
7 Dec	Blackpool	A	L	1-4
14 Dec	Nottingham F	H	W	5-0
26 Dec	Barnsley	H	D	1-1
28 Dec	Plymouth A	H	W	3-2
1 Jan	Barnsley	A	W	3-0
4 Jan	Bradford C	A	L	0-1
18 Jan	Newcastle U	H	W	3-1
1 Feb	Southampton	H	W	*4-0
8 Feb	Tottenham H	A	D	0-0
8 Feb	Port Vale	H	W	7-2
22 Feb	Sheffield U	A	D	1-1
29 Feb	Blackpool	H	W	3-2
7 Mar	West Ham U	A	W	2-1
14 Mar	Swansea	H	W	3-0
21 Mar	Leicester C	A	D	1-1
28 Mar	Norwich C	H	W	2-1
1 Apr	Fulham	A	D	2-2
4 Apr	Doncaster R	A	D	0-0
10 Apr	Burnley	A	D	2-2
11 Apr	Bradford	H	W	4-0
13 Apr	Burnley	H	W	4-0
18 Apr	Nottingham F	A	D	1-1
2 Apr	Bury	H	W	2-1
29 Apr	Bury	A	W	3-2
2 May	Hull C	A	D	1-1

FA Cup

11 Jan	Reading (3)	A	W	3-1
25 Jan	Stoke C (4)	A	D	0-0
29 Jan	Stoke C (4R)	H	L	0-2

Football League

	P	W	D	L	F:A	Pts	
Manchester U	42	22	12	8	85:43	56	1st

SEASON 1936-1937
FOOTBALL LEAGUE (DIVISION 1)

Date	Opponent	Venue	Result	Score
29 Aug	Wolverhampton W	H	D	1-1
2 Sep	Huddersfield T	A	L	1-3
5 Sep	Derby Co	A	L	4-5
9 Sep	Huddersfield T	H	W	3-1
12 Sep	Manchester C	H	W	3-2
19 Sep	Sheffield Wed	H	D	1-1
26 Sep	Preston NE	A	L	1-3
3 Oct	Arsenal	H	W	2-0
10 Oct	Brentford	A	L	0-4
17 Oct	Portsmouth	A	L	1-3
24 Oct	Chelsea	H	D	0-0
31 Oct	Stoke C	A	L	0-3
7 Nov	Charlton A	H	D	0-0
14 Nov	Grimsby T	A	L	2-6
21 Nov	Liverpool	H	L	2-5
28 Nov	Leeds U	A	L	1-2
5 Dec	Birmingham	H	L	1-2
12 Dec	Middlesbrough	A	L	2-3
19 Dec	West Brom A	H	D	2-2
25 Dec	Bolton W	H	W	1-0
26 Dec	Wolverhampton W	A	L	1-3
28 Dec	Bolton W	A	W	4-0
1 Jan	Sunderland	H	W	2-1
2 Jan	Derby Co	H	D	2-2
9 Jan	Manchester C	A	L	0-1
23 Jan	Sheffield Wed	A	L	0-1
3 Feb	Preston NE	H	D	1-1
6 Feb	Arsenal	A	D	1-1
13 Feb	Brentford	H	L	1-3
20 Feb	Portsmouth	H	L	0-1
27 Feb	Chelsea	A	L	2-4
6 Mar	Stoke C	H	W	2-1
13 Mar	Charlton A	A	L	0-3
20 Mar	Grimsby T	H	D	1-1
26 Mar	Everton	H	W	2-1
27 Mar	Liverpool	A	L	0-2
29 Mar	Everton	A	L	3-2
3 Apr	Leeds U	H	W	2-1
10 Apr	Birmingham	A	D	2-2
17 Apr	Middlesbrough	H	D	1-1
21 Apr	Sunderland	A	D	1-1
24 Apr	WBA	A	L	0-1

FA Cup

16 Jan	Reading (3)	H	W	1-0
30 Jan	Arsenal (4)	A	L	0-5

Football League

	P	W	D	L	F:A	Pts	
Manchester U	42	10	12	20	55:78	32	21st

SEASON 1937-1938
FOOTBALL LEAGUE (DIVISION 2)

Date	Opponent	Venue	Result	Score
28 Aug	Newcastle U	H	W	3-0
30 Aug	Coventry C	A	L	0-1
4 Sep	Luton T	A	L	0-1
8 Sep	Coventry C	H	D	2-2
11 Sep	Barnsley	H	W	4-1
13 Sep	Bury	A	W	2-1
18 Sep	Stockport Co	A	L	0-1
25 Sep	Southampton	H	L	1-2
2 Oct	Sheffield U	A	L	0-1
9 Oct	Tottenham H	A	W	1-0
16 Oct	Blackburn R	A	D	1-1
23 Oct	Sheffield Wed	H	W	1-0
30 Oct	Fulham	A	L	0-1
6 Nov	Plymouth A	H	D	0-0
13 Nov	Chesterfield	A	W	7-1
20 Nov	Aston Villa	H	W	3-1
27 Nov	Norwich C	A	W	3-2
4 Dec	Swansea	H	W	5-1
11 Dec	Bradford	A	L	0-4
27 Dec	Nottingham F	H	W	4-3
28 Dec	Nottingham F	A	W	3-2
1 Jan	Newcastle U	A	D	2-2
15 Jan	Luton T	H	W	4-2
29 Jan	Stockport Co	H	W	3-1
2 Feb	Barnsley	A	D	2-2
5 Feb	Southampton	A	D	3-3
17 Feb	Sheffield U	A	W	2-1
19 Feb	Tottenham H	H	L	0-1
23 Feb	West Ham U	H	W	4-0
26 Feb	Blackburn R	A	W	2-1
5 Mar	Sheffield Wed	A	W	3-1
12 Mar	Fulham	H	W	1-0
19 Mar	Plymouth A	A	D	1-1
26 Mar	Chesterfield	H	W	2-0
2 Apr	Aston Villa	A	L	0-3
9 Apr	Norwich C	H	D	0-0
15 Apr	Burnley	A	L	0-1
16 Apr	Swansea	A	D	2-2
18 Apr	Burnley	H	W	4-0
23 Apr	Bradford	H	L	0-1
30 Apr	West Ham U	A	L	0-1
7 May	Bury	H	W	2-0

FA Cup

8 Jan	Yeovil (3)	H	W	3-0
22 Jan	Barnsley (4)	A	D	2-2
26 Jan	Barnsley (4R)	H	W	1-0
12 Feb	Brentford (5)	A	L	0-2

Football League

	P	W	D	L	F:A	Pts	
Manchester U	42	22	9	11	82:50	53	2nd

SEASON 1938-1939
FOOTBALL LEAGUE (DIVISION 1)

27 Aug	Middlesbrough	A	L	1-3
31 Aug	Bolton W	H	D	*2-2
3 Sep	Birmingham	H	W	4-1
7 Sep	Liverpool	A	L	0-1
10 Sep	Grimsby T	A	L	0-1
17 Sep	Stoke C	A	D	1-1
24 Sep	Chelsea	H	W	5-1
1 Oct	Preston NE	A	D	1-1
8 Oct	Charlton A	H	L	0-2
15 Oct	Blackpool	H	D	0-0
22 Oct	Derby Co	A	L	1-5
29 Oct	Sunderland	H	L	0-1
5 Nov	Aston Villa	A	W	2-0
12 Nov	Wolverhampton W	H	L	1-3
19 Nov	Everton	A	L	0-3
26 Nov	Huddersfield T	H	D	1-1
3 Dec	Portsmouth	A	D	0-0
10 Dec	Arsenal	H	W	1-0
17 Dec	Brentford	A	W	5-2
24 Dec	Middlesbrough	H	D	1-1
26 Dec	Leicester C	H	W	3-0
27 Dec	Leicester C	A	D	1-1
31 Dec	Birmingham	A	D	3-3
14 Jan	Stoke C	H	W	3-1
21 Jan	Stoke C	H	L	0-1
28 Jan	Chelsea	A	W	1-0
4 Feb	Preston NE	H	D	1-1
11 Feb	Charlton A	A	L	1-7
18 Feb	Blackpool	H	W	5-3
25 Feb	Derby Co	H	D	1-1
4 Mar	Sunderland	A	L	2-5
11 Mar	Aston Villa	H	D	1-1
18 Mar	Wolverhampton W	A	L	0-3
29 Mar	Everton	H	L	0-1
1 Apr	Huddersfield T	A	D	1-1
7 Apr	Leeds U	A	L	1-3
10 Apr	Leeds U	H	L	0-1
15 Apr	Arsenal	A	L	1-2
22 Apr	Brentford	H	W	3-0
29 Apr	Bolton W	A	D	1-1
6 May	Liverpool	H	W	2-0

FA Cup

7 Jan	WBA (3)	A	D	0-0
11 Jan	WBA (3R)	H	L	1-5

Football League

	P	W	D	L	F:A	Pts	
Manchester U	42	11	16	15	57:65	38	14th

SEASON 1939-1940
ALL MATCHES
Western Division Wartime Regional League

Date	Opponent	Venue	Result	Score
21 Oct	Manchester C	H	L	0-4
28 Oct	Chester	A	W	4-0
11 Nov	Crewe Alex	H	W	5-1
18 Nov	Liverpool	A	L	0-1
25 Nov	Port Vale	H	W	8-1
2 Dec	Tranmere R	A	W	4-2
9 Dec	Stockport Co	H	W	7-4
23 Dec	Wrexham	H	W	5-1
6 Jan	Everton	A	L	2-3
20 Jan	Stoke C	H	W	4-3
10 Feb	Manchester C	A	L	0-1
24 Feb	Chester	H	W	5-1
9 Mar	Crewe Alex	A	W	4-1
16 Mar	Liverpool	H	W	1-0
23 Mar	Port Vale	A	W	3-1
30 Mar	Tranmere R	H	W	6-1
6 Apr	Stockport Co	H	W	1-0
6 May	New Brighton	H	W	6-0
13 May	Wrexham	A	L	2-3
18 May	New Brighton	A	L	0-6
25 May	Stoke C	A	L	2-3
1 Jun	Everton	H	L	0-3

	P	W	D	L	F:A	Pts	
Manchester U	22	14	0	8	74:41	28	14th

Football League War Cup

20 Apr	Manchester C (1st leg)	H	L	0-1
27 Apr	Manchester C (2nd leg)	A	W	2-1
4 May	Blackburn R (1st leg)	A	W	2-1
11 May	Blackburn R (2nd leg)	A	L	1-3

SEASON 1940-1941
North Regional League

31 Aug	Rochdale	A	W	3-1
7 Sep	Bury	H	D	0-0
14 Sep	Oldham	A	L	1-2
21 Sep	Oldham	H	L	2-3
28 Sep	Manchester C	A	L	1-4
5 Oct	Manchester C	H	L	0-2
12 Oct	Burnley	A	W	1-0
19 Oct	Preston NE	H	W	4-1
26 Oct	Preston NE	A	L	1-3
2 Nov	Burnley	H	W	4-1
9 Nov	Everton	A	L	2-5
16 Nov	Everton	H	D	0-0
23 Nov	Liverpool	A	D	2-2
30 Nov	Liverpool	H	W	2-0
7 Dec	Blackburn R	A	D	5-5
14 Dec	Rochdale	H	W	2-0
21 Dec	Bury	A	L	1-4
26 Dec	Stockport Co	A	W	3-1
28 Dec	Blackburn R	H	W	9-0
4 Jan	Blackburn R	A	D	2-2
11 Jan	Blackburn R	H	D	0-0
18 Jan	Bolton W	A	L	2-3
25 Jan	Bolton W	H	W	4-1
1 Mar	Chesterfield	A	D	1-1
8 Mar	Bury	H	W	7-3
22 Mar	Oldham	A	W	1-0
29 Mar	Blackpool	A	L	0-2
5 Apr	Blackpool	H	L	2-3
12 Apr	Everton	A	W	2-1
14 Apr	Manchester C	A	W	7-1
19 Apr	Chester	A	W	8-4
26 Apr	Liverpool	A	L	1-2
3 May	Liverpool	H	D	1-1
10 May	Bury	A	L	1-5
17 May	Burnley	H	W	1-0

	P	W	D	L	F:A	Pts	
Manchester U	35	15	7	13	82:85	37	7th*

*Positions according to goal average not points

Football League War Cup

15 Feb	Everton (1st leg)	H	D	2-2
22 Feb	Everton (2nd leg)	A	L	1-2

SEASON 1941-1942
ALL MATCHES

Date	Opponent	Venue	Result	Score
30 Aug	New Brighton	H	W	13-1
6 Sep	New Brighton	A	D	3-3
13 Sep	Stockport Co	A	W	5-1
20 Sep	Stockport Co	H	W	7-1
27 Sep	Everton	H	L	2-3
4 Oct	Everton	A	W	3-1
11 Oct	Chester	A	W	7-1
18 Oct	Chester	H	W	8-1
25 Oct	Stoke C	A	D	1-1
1 Nov	Stoke C	H	W	3-0
8 Nov	Tranmere P	H	W	6-1
15 Nov	Tranmere P	A	D	1-1
22 Nov	Liverpool	A	D	1-1
29 Nov	Liverpool	H	D	2-2
6 Dec	Wrexham	H	W	10-3
13 Dec	Wrexham	A	W	4-3
20 Dec	Manchester C	A	L	1-2
25 Dec	Manchester C	H	D	2-2

Football League North Region: First Championship

	P	W	D	L	F:A	Pts	
Manchester U	18	10	6	2	79:27	26	4th

27 Dec	Bolton W (Cup Q)	H	W	3-1
3 Jan	Bolton W (Cup Q)	A	D	2-2
10 Jan	Oldham (Cup Q)	H	D	1-1
17 Jan	Oldham (Cup Q)	A	W	3-1
31 Jan	Southport (Cup Q)	A	D	1-1
14 Feb	Sheffield U (Cup Q)	A	W	2-0
21 Feb	Preston NE (Cup Q)	H	L	1-2
28 Feb	Preston NE (Cup Q)	A	W	3-1
21 Mar	Sheffield U (Cup Q)	H	D	2-2
28 Mar	Southport (Cup Q)	H	W	4-2

```
4 Apr   Blackburn R (Cup KO)        A  W  2-1
6 Apr   Blackburn R (Cup KO)        H  W  3-1
11 Apr  Wolverhampton W
        (Cup KO)                    H  W  5-4
18 Apr  Wolverhampton W
        (Cup KO)†                   A  L  0-2
25 Apr  Oldham A (Lancs Cup)        H  W  5-1
2 May   Oldham A (Lancs Cup)        A  W  2-1
9 May   Blackburn R (Lancs Cup)     A  D  1-1
16 May  Blackburn R (Lancs Cup)     H  L  0-1
23 May  Manchester C                A  W  3-1
        †after extra time
```

League & Cup games were played as part of the
North Region Second Championship
(Results counted for each competition)

**Football League North Region:
Second Championship**

	P	W	D	L	F:A	Pts	
Manchester U	19	12	4	3	44:25	28	1st

SEASON 1942-1943
ALL MATCHES

```
29 Aug  Everton         A  D  2-2
5 Sep   Everton         H  W  2-1
12 Sep  Chester         H  L  0-2
19 Sep  Chester         A  D  2-2
26 Sep  Blackburn R     A  L  2-4
3 Oct   Blackburn R     H  W  5-2
10 Oct  Liverpool       H  L  3-4
17 Oct  Liverpool       A  L  1-2
24 Oct  Stockport Co    A  W  4-1
31 Oct  Stockport Co    H  W  3-1
11 Nov  Manchester C    H  W  2-1
14 Nov  Manchester C    A  W  5-0
21 Nov  Tranmere R      A  W  5-0
28 Nov  Tranmere R      H  W  5-1
5 Dec   Wrexham         H  W  6-1
12 Dec  Wrexham         A  W  5-2
19 Dec  Bolton W        A  W  2-0
25 Dec  Bolton W        H  W  4-0
```

**Football League North Region:
First Championship**

	P	W	D	L	F:A	Pts	
Manchester U	18	12	2	4	58:26	26	4th

```
26 Dec  Chester (Cup Q)         H  W  3-0
2 Jan   Chester (Cup Q)         A  L  1-4
9 Jan   Blackpool (Cup Q)       A  D  1-1
16 Jan  Blackpool (Cup Q)       H  W  5-3
23 Jan  Everton (Cup Q)         H  L  1-4
30 Jan  Everton (Cup Q)         A  W  3-0
6 Feb   Manchester C (Cup Q)    A  D  0-0
13 Feb  Manchester C (Cup Q)    H  D  1-1
20 Feb  Crewe A (Cup Q)         H  W  7-0
27 Feb  Crewe A (Cup Q)         A  W  3-2
8 Mar   Manchester C (Cup KO)   H  L  0-1
13 Mar  Manchester C (Cup KO)   A  L  0-1
20 Mar  Bury (Lancs Cup)        H  W  4-1
27 Mar  Bury (Lancs Cup)        A  W  5-3
3 Apr   Crewe A (Lancs Cup)     A  W  4-1
10 Apr  Crewe A (Lancs Cup)     A  W  6-0
17 Apr  Oldham (Lancs Cup)      A  W  3-0
24 Apr  Oldham (Lancs Cup)      H  D  1-3
1 May   Sheffield U             H  W  2-0
8 May   Liverpool (Lancs Cup F) A  W  3-1
15 May  Liverpool (Lancs Cup F) H  D  3-3
```

Games played between 26 Dec and 1 May (inc)
formed the **North Region Second Championship**

**Football League North Region:
Second Championship**

	P	W	D	L	F:A	Pts	
Manchester U	19	11	3	5	52:26	25	6th

SEASON 1943-1944
ALL MATCHES

```
28 Aug  Stockport Co    H  W  6-0
4 Sep   Stockport Co    A  D  3-3
11 Sep  Everton         H  W  4-1
18 Sep  Everton         A  L  1-6
25 Sep  Blackburn R     H  W  2-1
2 Oct   Blackburn R     A  L  1-2
9 Oct   Chester         H  W  3-1
16 Oct  Chester         A  L  4-5
23 Oct  Liverpool       A  W  4-3
30 Oct  Liverpool       H  W  1-0
6 Nov   Manchester C    A  D  2-2
13 Nov  Manchester C    H  W  3-0
20 Nov  Tranmere R      H  W  6-3
27 Nov  Tranmere R      A  W  1-0
4 Dec   Wrexham         A  W  4-1
11 Dec  Wrexham         H  W  5-0
18 Dec  Bolton W        H  W  3-1
25 Dec  Bolton W        A  W  3-1
```

**Football League North Region:
First Championship**

	P	W	D	L	F:A	Pts	
Manchester U	18	13	2	3	56:30	28	2nd

```
27 Dec  Halifax T (Cup Q)        H  W  6-2
1 Jan   Halifax T (Cup Q)        A  D  1-1
8 Jan   Stockport Co (Cup Q)     H  W  3-0
15 Jan  Stockport Co (Cup Q)     H  W  4-2
22 Jan  Manchester C (Cup Q)     H  L  1-3
29 Jan  Manchester C (Cup Q)     A  W  3-0
8 Feb   Bury (Cup Q)             A  W  3-0
12 Feb  Bury (Cup Q)             H  D  3-3
19 Feb  Oldham (Cup Q)           H  W  3-2
26 Feb  Oldham (Cup Q)           H  W  4-0
4 Mar   Wrexham (Cup KO)         A  W  4-1
11 Mar  Wrexham (Cup KO)         H  W  2-0
18 Mar  Birmingham (Cup KO)      A  L  1-3
```

```
25 Mar  Birmingham (Cup KO)      H  D  1-1
1 Apr   Bolton W                 H  L  0-3
8 Apr   Bolton W                 H  W  3-2
10 Apr  Manchester C             A  L  1-4
15 Apr  Burnley                  H  W  9-0
22 Apr  Burnley                  A  D  3-3
29 Apr  Oldham                   H  D  0-0
6 May   Oldham                   A  W  3-1
```

**Football League North Region:
Second Championship**

	P	W	D	L	F:A	Pts	
Manchester U	21	10	7	4	55:38	27	9th

SEASON 1944-1945
ALL MATCHES

```
26 Aug  Everton         A  W  2-1
2 Sep   Everton         H  L  1-3
9 Sep   Stockport Co    H  L  3-4
16 Sep  Stockport Co    A  D  4-4
23 Sep  Bury            H  D  2-2
30 Sep  Bury            A  L  2-4
7 Oct   Chester         A  L  0-2
14 Oct  Chester         H  W  1-0
21 Oct  Tranmere R      H  W  6-1
28 Oct  Tranmere R      H  W  4-2
4 Nov   Liverpool       A  L  2-3
11 Nov  Liverpool       H  L  2-5
18 Nov  Manchester C    H  W  3-2
25 Nov  Manchester C    A  L  0-4
2 Dec   Crewe A         A  W  4-1
9 Dec   Crewe A         H  W  2-0
16 Dec  Wrexham         H  W  1-0
23 Dec  Wrexham         A  L  1-2
```

**Football League North Region:
First Championship**

	P	W	D	L	F:A	Pts	
Manchester U	18	8	2	8	40:40	18	30th

```
26 Dec  Sheffield U              A  W  4-3
30 Dec  Oldham (Cup Q)           A  W  4-3
6 Jan   Huddersfield T (Cup Q)   H  W  1-0
13 Jan  Huddersfield T (Cup Q)   A  D  2-2
3 Feb   Manchester C (Cup Q)     H  L  1-3
10 Feb  Manchester C (Cup Q)     A  L  0-2
17 Feb  Bury (Cup Q)             H  W  2-0
24 Feb  Bury (Cup Q)             A  L  1-3
3 Mar   Oldham (Cup Q)           H  W  3-2
10 Mar  Halifax T (Cup Q)        A  L  0-1
17 Mar  Halifax T (Cup Q)        H  W  2-0
24 Mar  Burnley (Cup Q)          A  W  3-2
31 Mar  Burnley (Cup KO)         A  W  4-0
2 Apr   Blackpool                A  L  1-4
7 Apr   Stoke C (Cup KO)         H  W  6-1
14 Apr  Stoke C (Cup KO)         A  W  4-1
21 Apr  Doncaster R (Cup KO)     A  W  2-1
28 Apr  Doncaster R (Cup KO)     H  W  2-0
5 May   Chesterfield (Cup SF)    H  D  1-1
12 May  Chesterfield (Cup SF)    A  L  0-2
19 May  Bolton W (Cup F)         A  L  0-1
26 May  Bolton W (Cup F)         H  D  2-2
```

**Football League North Region:
Second Championship**

	P	W	D	L	F:A	Pts	
Manchester U	22	13	3	6	47:33	29	9th

SEASON 1945-1946
ALL MATCHES

```
25 Aug  Huddersfield T   A  L  2-3
1 Sep   Huddersfield T   H  L  2-3
8 Sep   Chesterfield     H  D  2-2
12 Sep  Middlesbrough    A  L  1-2
15 Sep  Chesterfield     A  W  2-1
20 Sep  Stoke C          A  W  2-1
22 Sep  Barnsley         A  D  2-2
29 Sep  Barnsley         H  D  1-1
6 Oct   Everton          H  D  0-0
13 Oct  Everton          A  L  0-3
20 Oct  Bolton W         A  D  1-1
27 Oct  Bolton W         H  W  2-1
3 Nov   Preston NE       H  W  6-1
10 Nov  Preston NE       A  D  2-2
17 Nov  Leeds U          A  D  3-3
24 Nov  Leeds U          H  W  6-1
1 Dec   Burnley          H  D  3-3
8 Dec   Burnley          A  D  2-2
15 Dec  Sunderland       H  W  2-1
22 Dec  Sunderland       A  L  2-4
25 Dec  Sheffield U      A  L  0-1
29 Dec  Sheffield U      H  L  2-3
29 Dec  Middlesbrough    H  W  4-1
12 Jan  Grimsby T        H  W  5-0
19 Jan  Grimsby T        A  L  0-1
2 Feb   Blackpool        H  W  4-2
9 Feb   Liverpool        H  W  2-1
16 Feb  Liverpool        A  W  5-0
23 Feb  Bury             A  D  1-1
2 Mar   Bury             H  D  1-1
9 Mar   Blackburn R      H  W  6-2
16 Mar  Blackburn R      A  W  3-1
23 Mar  Bradford         A  L  1-2
27 Mar  Blackpool        A  W  5-1
30 Mar  Bradford         H  W  4-0
6 Apr   Manchester C     H  L  1-4
13 Apr  Manchester C     A  W  3-1
17 Apr  Newcastle U      A  W  1-0
20 Apr  Sheffield Wed    H  W  4-0
22 Apr  Newcastle U      H  W  4-1
27 Apr  Sheffield Wed    A  W  3-0
4 May   Stoke C          H  W  2-1
```

Football League North

	P	W	D	L	F:A	Pts	
Manchester U	42	19	11	12	98:62	49	4th

SEASON 1946-1947
FOOTBALL LEAGUE (Division 1)

```
31 Aug  Grimsby T        H  W  2-1
4 Sep   Chelsea          A  W  3-0
7 Sep   Charlton A       A  W  *3-1
11 Sep  Liverpool        H  W  5-0
14 Sep  Middlesbrough    H  W  1-0
18 Sep  Chelsea          H  D  1-1
21 Sep  Stoke C          A  L  2-3
28 Sep  Arsenal          H  W  5-2
5 Oct   Preston NE       H  D  1-1
12 Oct  Sheffield U      A  D  2-2
19 Oct  Blackpool        H  D  0-0
26 Oct  Sunderland       H  L  0-3
2 Nov   Aston Villa      A  W  1-0
9 Nov   Derby Co         H  W  4-1
16 Nov  Everton          A  D  2-2
23 Nov  Huddersfield T   H  W  5-2
30 Nov  Wolverhampton W  A  L  2-3
7 Dec   Brentford        H  W  4-1
14 Dec  Blackburn R      A  L  1-2
25 Dec  Bolton W         A  D  2-2
26 Dec  Bolton W         H  W  1-0
28 Dec  Grimsby T        A  D  0-0
4 Jan   Charlton A       H  W  4-1
18 Jan  Middlesbrough    A  W  4-2
1 Feb   Arsenal          A  L  2-6
5 Feb   Stoke C          H  D  1-1
22 Feb  Blackpool        H  W  3-0
1 Mar   Sunderland       A  D  1-1
8 Mar   Aston Villa      H  W  2-1
15 Mar  Derby Co         A  L  3-4
22 Mar  Everton          H  W  3-0
29 Mar  Huddersfield T   A  D  2-2
5 Apr   Wolverhampton W  H  W  3-1
7 Apr   Leeds U          H  W  3-1
8 Apr   Leeds U          A  W  2-0
12 Apr  Brentford        A  D  0-0
19 Apr  Blackburn R      H  W  *4-0
26 Apr  Portsmouth       A  W  1-0
3 May   Liverpool        A  L  0-1
10 May  Preston NE       A  D  1-1
17 May  Portsmouth       H  W  3-0
26 May  Sheffield U      H  W  8-2
```

FA Cup

```
11 Jan  Bradford (3)     A  W  3-0
25 Jan  Nottingham F (4) H  L  0-2
```

Football League

	P	W	D	L	F:A	Pts	
Manchester U	42	22	12	8	95:54	58	2nd

SEASON 1947-1948
FOOTBALL LEAGUE (Division 1)

```
23 Aug  Middlesbrough    A  D  2-2
27 Aug  Liverpool        H  W  2-0
30 Aug  Charlton A       H  W  6-2
3 Sep   Liverpool        A  W  3-0
6 Sep   Arsenal          A  L  1-2
8 Sep   Burnley          A  D  0-0
13 Sep  Sheffield U      H  L  0-1
20 Sep  Manchester C     H  D  0-0
27 Sep  Preston NE       A  L  1-2
4 Oct   Stoke C          H  D  1-1
11 Oct  Grimsby T        H  L  3-4
18 Oct  Sunderland       A  L  0-1
25 Oct  Aston Villa      H  W  2-0
1 Nov   Wolverhampton W  A  W  6-2
8 Nov   Huddersfield T   H  D  4-4
15 Nov  Derby Co         H  D  1-1
22 Nov  Everton          H  D  2-2
29 Nov  Chelsea          A  W  4-0
6 Dec   Blackpool        H  D  1-1
13 Dec  Blackburn R      A  D  1-1
20 Dec  Middlesbrough    H  W  2-1
```

```
25 Dec  Portsmouth       H  W  3-2
27 Dec  Portsmouth       A  W  3-1
1 Jan   Burnley          H  W  5-0
3 Jan   Charlton A       A  W  2-1
17 Jan  Arsenal          H  D  1-1
31 Jan  Sheffield U      A  L  1-2
14 Feb  Preston NE       H  W  2-0
21 Feb  Stoke C          A  W  2-0
6 Mar   Sunderland       H  W  3-1
17 Mar  Grimsby T        A  D  1-1
20 Mar  Wolverhampton W  H  W  3-2
22 Mar  Aston Villa      A  W  1-0
26 Mar  Bolton W         H  L  0-2
27 Mar  Huddersfield T   A  W  1-0
29 Mar  Bolton W         A  W  1-0
3 Apr   Derby Co         A  W  1-0
7 Apr   Manchester C     H  D  1-1
10 Apr  Everton          A  L  0-2
17 Apr  Chelsea          H  W  5-0
24 Apr  Blackpool        A  L  0-1
1 May   Blackburn        H  W  4-1
```

FA Cup

```
10 Jan  Aston Villa (3)  A  W  6-4
24 Jan  Liverpool (4)    H  W  3-0
        (at Goodison Park)
7 Feb   Charlton A (5)   H  W  2-0
        (at Huddersfield)
28 Feb  Preston NE (6)   H  W  4-1
        (at Maine Road)
13 Mar  Derby Co (SF)    N  W  3-1
        (at Hillsborough)
24 Apr  Blackpool (F)    N  W  4-2
        (at Wembley)
```

Football League

	P	W	D	L	F:A	Pts	
Manchester U	42	19	14	9	81:48	52	2nd

SEASON 1948-1949
FOOTBALL LEAGUE (Division 1)

```
21 Aug  Derby Co         H  L  1-2
23 Aug  Blackpool        A  W  1-0
28 Aug  Arsenal          A  W  1-0
1 Sep   Blackpool        H  L  3-4
4 Sep   Huddersfield T   H  W  4-1
8 Sep   Wolverhampton W  A  L  2-3
11 Sep  Manchester C     A  D  0-0
15 Sep  Wolverhampton W  H  W  2-0
18 Sep  Sheffield U      A  D  2-2
25 Sep  Aston Villa      H  W  3-1
2 Oct   Sunderland       A  L  1-2
9 Oct   Charlton A       H  D  1-1
16 Oct  Stoke C          A  L  1-2
23 Oct  Burnley          H  D  1-1
30 Oct  Preston NE       A  W  6-1
6 Nov   Everton          H  W  2-0
13 Nov  Chelsea          A  D  1-1
20 Nov  Birmingham C     H  W  3-0
27 Nov  Middlesbrough    A  W  4-1
4 Dec   Newcastle U      H  D  1-1
11 Dec  Portsmouth       A  D  2-2
18 Dec  Derby Co         A  W  3-1
25 Dec  Liverpool        A  W  2-0
26 Dec  Liverpool        H  W  2-0
1 Jan   Arsenal          H  W  2-0
22 Jan  Manchester C     H  D  0-0
19 Feb  Aston Villa      A  L  1-2
5 Mar   Charlton A       A  W  3-2
12 Mar  Stoke C          H  W  3-0
19 Mar  Birmingham C     A  L  0-1
6 Apr   Huddersfield T   A  L  1-2
9 Apr   Chelsea          H  D  1-1
15 Apr  Bolton W         A  W  1-0
16 Apr  Burnley          H  W  2-0
18 Apr  Bolton W         H  W  3-0
21 Apr  Sunderland       H  L  1-2
23 Apr  Preston NE       H  D  2-2
```

```
27 Apr  Everton          A  L  0-2
30 Apr  Newcastle U      A  W  1-0
2 May   Middlesbrough    H  W  1-0
4 May   Sheffield U      H  W  3-2
7 May   Portsmouth       H  W  3-2
```

FA Cup

```
8 Jan   Bournemouth (3)   H  W  6-0
29 Jan  Bradford (4)      H  D  1-1
5 Feb   Bradford (4R)     A  D  1-1
7 Feb   Bradford (4R)     H  W  5-0
12 Feb  Yeovil (5)        H  W  8-0
26 Feb  Hull C (6)        A  L  0-1
26 Mar  Wolverhampton W (SF)   N  D  1-1
        (at Hillsborough)
2 Apr   Wolverhampton W (SFR)  N  L  0-1
        (at Goodison)
```

Football League

	P	W	D	L	F:A	Pts	
Manchester U	42	21	11	10	77:44	53	2nd

SEASON 1949-1950
FOOTBALL LEAGUE (Division 1)

```
20 Aug  Derby Co         A  W  1-0
24 Aug  Bolton W         H  W  3-0
27 Aug  WBA              H  D  1-2
31 Aug  Bolton W         A  W  2-1
3 Sep   Manchester C     H  W  2-1
7 Sep   Liverpool        A  D  1-1
10 Sep  Chelsea          A  D  1-1
17 Sep  Stoke C          H  D  2-2
24 Sep  Burnley          A  L  0-1
1 Oct   Sunderland       H  L  1-3
8 Oct   Charlton A       H  W  3-2
15 Oct  Aston Villa      A  W  4-0
22 Oct  Wolverhampton W  A  W  3-0
29 Oct  Portsmouth       H  W  3-0
5 Nov   Huddersfield T   H  W  6-0
12 Nov  Everton          A  D  0-0
19 Nov  Middlesbrough    H  W  2-0
26 Nov  Blackpool        A  D  3-3
3 Dec   Newcastle U      H  D  1-1
10 Dec  Fulham           A  L  0-1
17 Dec  Derby Co         H  L  0-1
24 Dec  WBA              A  W  2-1
26 Dec  Arsenal          H  W  2-0
27 Dec  Arsenal          A  D  0-0
31 Dec  Manchester C     A  W  2-1
14 Jan  Chelsea          H  W  1-0
21 Jan  Stoke C          A  L  1-3
4 Feb   Burnley          H  W  3-2
18 Feb  Sunderland       A  D  2-2
25 Feb  Charlton A       A  W  2-1
8 Mar   Aston Villa      H  W  7-0
11 Mar  Middlesbrough    A  W  3-2
15 Mar  Liverpool        H  D  0-0
18 Mar  Blackpool        H  L  1-2
25 Mar  Huddersfield T   A  L  1-3
1 Apr   Everton          H  D  1-1
7 Apr   Birmingham C     H  L  0-2
8 Apr   Wolverhampton W  A  D  1-1
10 Apr  Birmingham C     A  D  0-0
15 Apr  Portsmouth       H  L  0-2
22 Apr  Newcastle U      A  L  1-2
29 Apr  Fulham           H  W  3-0
```

FA Cup

```
7 Jan   Weymouth (3)      H  W  4-0
28 Jan  Watford (4)       H  W  1-0
11 Feb  Portsmouth (5)    H  D  3-3
15 Feb  Portsmouth (5R)   A  W  3-1
4 Mar   Chelsea (6)       A  L  0-2
```

Football League

	P	W	D	L	F:A	Pts	
Manchester U	42	18	14	10	69:44	50	4th

1889-1949

Johnny Carey, who joined United in 1936, enjoyed a 17-year career with the club.

Manchester United believe that their theatre of dreams is the finest club stadium in the country with its towering triple-deck North Stand taking the capacity to an all-seated 56,000 spectators serviced by unrivalled facilities.

But United are still not content and a £30 million scheme is in the pipeline to extend the stands behind each goal to take the capacity to 67,400 for the start of the 2000-01 season and make Old Trafford a regular venue for big European cup finals and international matches.

The deal will also see the club fund a £1 million package for local environmental improvements.

Old Trafford has come a long way since their ground, built in 1910 by Chairman John H Davies, was bombed twice during the war and closed down.

After reopening in 1949, the club has consistently set the pace in stadium development, building a cantilever stand for the World Cup of 1966, and steadily replacing the old fabric with new stands.

The result is a completely cantilevered stadium with private boxes ringing the entire ground and hosting a variety of corporate suites. Every match day 4,000 meals are served.

Their handsome three-deck North Stand was opened in 1997 at a cost of £28 million to add a hugely significant feature to the Manchester skyline.

All day and nearly every day, visitors tour the ground to get closer to the magical feel of Manchester United. The club museum is just as popular with thousands of visitors a year flocking to the much bigger and more ambitious centre opened on three floors of the North Stand in April, 1998.

Above, left: the Stretford End c. 1966. Old Trafford underwent a major re-building programme (above) before the World Cup.

Top: the modern 'Theatre of Dreams' with the triple-teired North Stand (facing). Plans for the rest of the Stadium would take the capacity up to 67,400

Carrington

Old Trafford is more than a simple football stadium. It plays host these days to a wide range of conferences, exhibitions and entertainment as people come from far and wide to share the stage of Manchester United's theatre of dreams.

But United are also keeping pace on the playing side with work now completed on a new training complex at Carrington, a £14.3 million project which is designed to provide the latest in integrated training, remedial and rehabilitation facilities on a 100-acre site. The centre will be at the cutting edge of football science and will show other clubs the way forward.

"We believe it is a centre which will be a world leader in sport," says Chairman Martin Edwards, as his club plan to make Carrington the hub of their training organisation catering for not just their first-team squad but their Academy for the junior players.

"Our training ground at The Cliff in Salford and the pitches at neighbouring Littleton Road were fine in their day, but we needed to update our facilities in keeping with new technologies and have everything together in one centre." he explained.

"The development represents a significant investment in the local economy and presents Trafford with a unique opportunity for wider environmental and regeneration initiatives in the area of Carrington Moss," he added.

The future of football

The outdoor area contains nine full size grass pitches, four junior grass pitches, training areas, a shale area for small-sided games, shuttle runs, head-tennis, a goalkeeping grass training area and an area with shooting boards.

Inside is a physiotherapy room, massage room, doctor's office, rooms for dietitian and podiatrist, a remedial and hydrotherapy pool, sauna and steam rooms along with changing rooms, canteen and television studio!

Manager Alex Ferguson says: "The pace of football change has accelerated in recent years, both on and off the pitch.

"Players are fitter and faster and it is necessary to give them an integrated medical and training back-up in keeping with our high-tech age. It represents our future and with senior players valued at millions of pounds it would be foolish not to offer the best that sports science can provide.

"I have always felt that the development of youth is at the core of a successful club and I think our present first team reflects that policy. Carrington is going to enable us to continue our work at this very important level... Our staff have visited the big clubs in Europe to study the latest developments in the field of integrated training and remedial work. I have always had this vision of a training centre of real excellence and this is what we have achieved at Carrington Moss,"

Sir Matt Busby lent his name to the most romantic and tragic experiences of football. The 'Busby Babes' of Manchester United fired the imagination of the public as they came bounding onto the scene a few years after the Second World War. They were the creation of a remarkable manager, a man of genius and vision who was to change the face of English football.

Tragically, the Busby Babes were destroyed in the Munich air disaster of 1958 before reaching their prime, and their manager came close to perishing with them. But he survived and Manchester United rose again from the ashes of their despair. Busby started all over again and produced more splendid teams so, as Bobby Charlton said, Old Trafford became a theatre of dreams.

United blazed a trail for English football in Europe. Winning the European Cup in 1968 just ten years after the tragedy at Munich was an incredible achievement and, of course, a testament to the life and work of Matthew Busby, born in 1909 in a two-roomed pitman's cottage in Orbiston, a small Lanarkshire mining village some miles from Glasgow.

The young Busby was no stranger to loss. His father and all his uncles were killed in the First World War. The result was that the remainder of the family, one by one, emigrated to America, looking for a better life than coal mining. Matt's mother was due to join her sister, and Matt himself was only waiting for a visa quota number. Then, just before he was 17, came the invitation to join Manchester City after he had played a few games for Denny Hibs, a local side.

Life at Maine Road was not easy, he was homesick and he struggled to get into the first team. A switch of position to take the place of an injured player at wing half in the reserves finally launched him on a distinguished career with City and won him Scottish international honours.

He won a Cup-winners' medal in 1934 and by 1936 he was captain of City, but he decided he wanted a change and he signed for Liverpool. Like most of the Liverpool team he joined the army when the Second World War started and served in the 9th Battalion of the King's Liverpool Regiment, and eventually in the Army Physical Training Corps. After the war Liverpool wanted him back as a player and as assistant to manager George Kay. But, as Matt says: 'I got this opportunity to go as manager of Manchester United. I had a soft spot for Manchester after my City days and it attracted me.'

So began a 25-year reign in which he produced three great teams, all different in character but reflecting his desire to create and entertain. In his time with United they won five League Championships, the FA Cup twice (from four finals), the FA Youth Cup six times, five of them on the trot as he fashioned the Busby Babes, and achieved crowning glory in 1968 with the winning of the European Cup.

Matt Busby as a player at Manchester City. Busby scrapped plans to go to the United States to play at Maine Road and after a difficult start he had a distinguished career

Left: Matt Busby leads out Manchester United for the final of the 1957 FA Cup at Wembley against Aston Villa. Roger Byrne follows him as captain of the team labelled the Busby Babes in tribute to their youth and precocious talent which had already earned them the championship. It was a team which had already taken Europe by storm, reaching the semi-finals of the European Cup in the first season in the competition

He was awarded the CBE in 1958, he was given the Freedom of Manchester in 1967 and he was knighted the following year. Pope Paul conferred one of the highest civil awards in the Roman Catholic Church on him in 1972 by making him a Knight Commander of St Gregory the Great. When he retired as manager of Manchester United in 1970 he was made a director and then the club's first president. He was appointed manager in 1945. He must have been felt daunted as he looked at a bombed ground and examined the books. United were £15,000 overdrawn at the bank, and it was impossible to play at Old Trafford. The dressing rooms were derelict and there were no facilities for training. Matches had to be played at Maine Road. Of the players on the books, some were still away in the services.

The first great team

The new manager wasted little time, and right from the start showed the character and judgement that eventually became legendary. To start with, he insisted on a five-year contract when the chairman, James Gibson, offered him one of three years.

Players on the books included Carey, Henry Cockburn, Jack Rowley, Johnny Morris, Stan Pearson, Allenby Chilton, Joe Walton, Charlie Mitten, John Aston and goalkeeper Jack Crompton. Some say Busby was lucky to start with such a promising nucleus of established players, but many a manager has taken over as good a squad and made nothing of it. He also soon showed the shrewdness in the transfer market. He paid £4,000 to Glasgow Celtic in February 1946 for Jimmy 'Brittle Bones' Delaney, a fast right-winger.

Behind the scenes he had also made a good signing. Jimmy Murphy, a player in his day with West Bromwich and Wales, was brought to Old Trafford as assistant manager after a friendship formed during the war abroad, and he became Busby's able lieutenant, the hard man to complement his own more fatherly role in an outstanding football partnership. Busby also showed an early appreciation of tactics, making international full-backs from modest inside-forwards John Aston and Johnny Carey.

When he began the job in October 1945 United were 16th, but by the end of the season they were fourth with a team which read:

Crompton, Hamlett, Chilton, Aston, Whalley, Cockburn, Delaney, Pearson, Rowley, Buckle, Wrigglesworth.

United were on their way, and the following season, 1946-47, as football returned to a national league instead of being divided into northern and southern leagues, they finished second, one with their equaliser in the 28th minute, despite their pressure. For it was a misunderstanding between Blackpool goalkeeper Joe Robinson and centre-half Eric Hayward that let Rowley step in to walk the ball over the line. It was an evenly contested match with Blackpool taking the lead again in the 35th minute with a goal hammered home by Mortensen.

Blackpool led 2-1 until the 69th minute, soaking up a whole stream of punishing United raids. Then their defence cracked under the pressure with Rowley heading a free-kick from Morris into the roof of the net. The game was now 2-2 with both teams redoubling their attacking efforts. Crompton saved brilliantly from Mortensen and then within seconds the ball was in the other net to put United in front. Crompton's clearance was switched by Anderson to Pearson who scored off the post from 25 yards.

It was the 'killer' goal and three minutes later United clinched victory. Anderson shot from a long way out and with the help of a deflection Robinson was wrong-footed to give United a memorable 4-2 win. The team was:

Crompton, Carey, Ason, Anderson, Chilton, Cockburn, Delaney, Morris, Rowley, Pearson, Mitten

point behind Liverpool, in the Championship. Busby's talented collection of experienced players, many of them seasoned by life in the services, were runners-up for two more years.

That was impressive consistency, even if they did miss out on the Championship itself. They were not to be denied a deserved honour, though, giving Busby his first trophy by winning the FA Cup in 1947-48. The 4-2 victory over Blackpool at Wembley was regarded as a classic final. United dominated the competition right from the start and reached Wembley by scoring 18 goals in five ties, indicating their great attacking strength.

They had a magnificent forward line. Jimmy Delaney played on the right wing with Charlie Mitten, one of the sweetest strikers of the ball in the game, operating on the left wing to give the Reds a two-winged attack. The dashing Jack Rowley was a traditional centre-forward with a fierce shot. He was flanked by the delightfully skilful Stan Pearson at inside-left and the clever Johnny Morris at inside-right. The most commanding figure of all featured further back in the team at right-back – the captain, Johnny Carey, an influential man both on and off the field.

They arrived at Wembley for the final against Blackpool full of confidence but respecting an opposition that included players like Stanley Matthews, Stan Mortensen and Harry Johnston.

Blackpool gave early notice of their intentions. After only 12 minutes Mortensen broke clean through and was heading for goal when he was brought down by centre-half Allenby Chilton. He fell into the penalty area and Eddie Shimwell beat Jack Crompton with his spot kick. United were a shade lucky

Top: Matt Busby with wife and son at Buckingham Palace after receiving C.B.E. in July 1958

Above: Matt Busby's first postwar peak was the 1948 Cup final against Blackpool

The old sweats still had another shot in their locker, and after finishing runners-up in the League three years on the trot, then fourth followed by another second, the 'nearly men' finally cracked it. They won the Championship in 1951-52, four points ahead of Spurs. They were mean at the back and prolific up front, with 30 goals from Jack Rowley and 22 from Stan Pearson. The team which clinched the title read:

Allen, McNulty, Aston, Carey, Chilton, Cockburn, Berry, Downie, Rowley, Pearson, Byrne

Rowley opened the Championship season in spanking form, scoring hat-tricks in the first two games for a 3-3 draw at West Bromwich and a 4-2 win at home against Middlesbrough.

Portsmouth were the early pace-setters, but they fell away to leave United, Spurs and Arsenal looking the strongest teams.

The destiny of the title was decided on the last game of the season, with a grand finale between two of the top three teams. Arsenal came to Old Trafford on 26 April as outsiders because, thanks to the scoring prowess of Rowley and Pearson, they had an inferior goal average. In fact they needed to win 7-0 to become champions. In the event United established themselves as worthy champions by running rampant for a 6-1 victory.

So United finished on 57 points, with Spurs and Arsenal level on points, four behind. Tottenham took second place on goal average. The big difference was in the scoring. United had notched a magnificent 95 as opposed to 76 from Spurs and 80 by Arsenal. It was a worthy climax for what was still largely the first post-war team.

Jack Rowley

Busby's team was packed with men not just of ability but also of character . . . people like Jack Rowley who was not nicknamed 'The Gunner' for nothing. For this man gunned his shots on the football field with the kind of ferocity and accuracy he had used as an anti-tank gunner with the South Staffordshire infantry.

Until Dennis Viollet came along a few years later Rowley held the United League scoring record for a season with his 30 goals in 1951-52. Overall, he scored 175 goals in 359 League appearances, which is a remarkable record when you consider that the war deprived him of six of his peak years as a player.

Rowley won six caps, playing in four different positions for England, with his highspot the scoring of four goals against Northern Ireland in 1949. His shot was reckoned to be the hardest of his day, a finish in keeping with the strong, aggressive style of the traditional centre-forward of the time.

Born in Wolverhampton, he was a junior at his local club under the legendary Major Frank Buckley, but made his League debut playing for Bournemouth. United signed him for £3,000 in 1937. He was soon among the goals, scoring four out of five against Swansea to help United win promotion to the First Division on the eve of the war.

Jack played for ten years after the war and then joined Plymouth as player-manager for a couple of seasons. His management career saw him twice at Oldham and with Ajax in Amsterdam, Wrexham and Bradford. During his second spell with Oldham he took a local post office and newsagency which became his job when he left the soccer scene until his retirement in the 1980s.

Stan Pearson

Stan Pearson, the other half of the high-scoring partnership, was the perfect foil for Rowley. They often say strikers are born in pairs, and these two players certainly complemented each other.

Pearson was the more subtle, and created a great many of Rowley's goals, while at the same time he himself profited from the big man's more forceful style. He was a lethal finisher as well as the traditional inside-forward of that period, good on the ball and skilful, with a deceptive body swerve. He made 345

League and FA Cup appearances, scoring 149 goals, a tremendous scoring rate. As with Rowley, the war took six years out of his United career.

Pearson was a Salford schoolboy who joined the club at the age of 15 in 1936. He made his debut at the age of 17 in a 7-1 win at Chesterfield, and he scored in each of the next two games. But he had only two seasons before the war interrupted normal football. He served in the Second/Fourth South Lancashires, ending up in India.

Stan signed for Bury in 1954 after a 17-year association with United. He later played for Chester and managed them. Finally, he settled at Prestbury in Cheshire, running the local post office and newsagent's shop.

Johnny Carey

United were a star-studded team in that era, but they had one truly influential player, the captain, Johnny Carey. Carey took Busby's philosophy of attacking football out to the pitch. He had

The 'goal machine' Jack Rowley heads the ball goalwards during the 1948 Cup Final. His two goals twice pulled United level and set up an historic 4-2 win

joined United in 1936 from the Dublin club, St James' Gate, for the modest sum of £250 after being spotted by Louis Rocca, a scout who was one of the founders of the latter-day United.

Rocca had gone to Dublin to watch an entirely different player. It is said that Carey was playing only his third real game of soccer, but his natural ability shone through and Rocca quickly made arrangements for him to come to Old Trafford.

Carey was 17 at the time and made his League debut the following year. He started as an inside-left, became an outstanding right-back, played centre-half, and finished his career as a polished wing-half. In fact he played in every position except wing for United, including a game in goal when Jack Crompton was taken ill on the day of a match. In all he played 344 League and FA Cup games spanning 17 years with the club. He would have made many more appearances for the club but for army service in Italy during the war. A fine international, he had the distinction of playing for both Northern Ireland and the Republic. Perhaps his greatest honour was captaining the Rest of Europe against Great Britain in 1947. Two years later he was voted Footballer of the Year by the Football Writers' Association.

Carey retired from playing in 1953 and started in management as coach at Blackburn. He was promoted to manager there before managing Everton, Leyton Orient, Nottingham Forest and Blackburn again. A genial, pipe-smoking man, he was known as 'Gentleman John' and as a manager the gist of his team talks would be to urge his players to 'fizz it around'.

He ended his managerial days by returning to Old Trafford as a part-time scout while working in the borough treasurer's office at Sale, Cheshire.

Jack Crompton

Another of the stalwarts in the post-war period was Jack Crompton, who joined the club in 1944 from the local works side, Goslings, having played for Oldham as an amateur.

Jack was born in 1921 and United was his only club as a professional. He made about 200 League appearances before joining Luton Town as their trainer in 1956. Just over a year later he returned to Old Trafford as trainer to help Jimmy Murphy in the crisis of Munich.

He served Matt Busby well as both player and staff man, and admits that in the early days he did not appreciate the impact Busby was going to make on the soccer world.

'He was such a quiet, unassuming and modest man that at first you didn't know the strength,' said Jack. 'The first thing I remember he did was to change the them and us of management and players to we, and he kept it that way. Naturally, when he first took charge he had to fight to make his presence felt and he had still to win the great respect he enjoyed later.

'He was accurate in his assessment of players and always thoughtful. I remember our first flight to the Continent after the Munich disaster. After we had landed at Amsterdam, Bill Foulkes telephoned his wife to let her know we had arrived safely. Teresa Foulkes already knew. Busby had been on the phone to tell her.

'As a manager he had a tremendous memory for players'

Stan Pearson was one of the most gifted inside forwards to play for United in post 1945 football. He struck a particularly effective partnership with Jack Rowley, and together they formed one of the highest scoring strike forces in football. Salford born, Stan joined the club before the war and returned with a number of his colleagues to provide Busby with his first successful team

strengths and failings. He never lost the common touch, the knack of understanding, and being in touch with players. He never forgot a player, past or present, and his memory for people's names was uncanny. There are many facets to the character of Matt Busby.'

Jack Crompton later tried management himself at Barrow and Preston. A keen YMCA member in his youth, he was always fitness minded, and in the mid-1980s he was still coaching youngsters at Manchester's splendid Platt Lane sports complex used by Manchester City.

The 1951-52 Championship side

Jack played only a handful of games in the Championship year after losing his place to Reg Allen, the first goalkeeper to attract a five-figure transfer fee. Busby paid Queen's Park Rangers £11,000 for him and he held the first-team job down for two seasons, including the Championship year, before he was overtaken by illness which finished his career.

John Anderson had gone from wing-half to prompt the masterly switch of Carey to form the dominating half-back line of Carey on the right, Allenby Chilton at centre-half and Henry Cockburn on the left. Tom McNulty took Carey's place at right-back with John Aston still on the left, though starting to concede that place to Roger Byrne.

It was the balance and blend of the half-back line which was

1949-59

the key to the way the team took charge in so many games and managed to supply their marvellous front runners and wingers with quality service.

Henry Cockburn, recruited like Crompton from the local works team Goslings, which had become something of a United nursery, was the typical little guy who made up for lack of inches with fire and determination. He also had class and timing, which meant he often outjumped taller men for the ball.

He made his first-team debut in war-time football and he was there for the first League game after the war in a 2-1 win against Grimsby at Maine Road. He was still working in an Oldham mill and had played only a handful of League games when he was selected for the first of his 13 England caps. For United he played in the 1948 Cup-winning team and in the 1951-52 Championship side. In all he spent ten years at Old Trafford before moving in 1954 to Bury. Later he worked as a coach for Ian Greaves, the former United full-back, at Huddersfield.

The pillar of the team and the kind of player Matt Busby always preferred at centre-half was the remarkable Allenby Chilton, a man who played before the war yet lasted to see the Busby Babes settling in around him. After being signed from Seaham Colliery in the north-east, he made his League debut against Charlton in September 1939. War was declared the following day and sliced out seven years of his United career.

Chilton fought in France and was wounded at Normandy, and he was nearly 28 before he was able to resume his life with United. But he played in the first team for another ten seasons,

Johnny Carey is hoisted shoulder high by his team-mates after leading United to victory in the FA Cup competition of 1948. The genial Irishman enjoyed many successes, including the captaincy of the Rest of the World when they played against Great Britain in 1947. He was voted Footballer of the Year in 1949, the season he skippered the Republic of Ireland to a notable 2-0 win against England at Goodison Park

with Busby always claiming that he played his best football in his later years. In all, he played nearly 400 League and Cup games and he was the only player ever-present in the Championship side, not that that was anything special to Chilton, who was as durable as he was big and strong. Towards the end he took over the captaincy from Johnny Carey, and when he lost his place to Mark Jones in 1955 he had achieved a club record of 166 consecutive League appearances. He played twice for England. After Old Trafford, he led Grimsby to the Third Division North Championship as player-manager and then had spells in management with Wigan and Hartlepool.

Johnny Carey has been discussed already. His switch to right-half with Tommy McNulty coming in at right-back was a masterly move in the second half of the Championship season.

Up front, Rowley and Pearson were still the scoring stars but Busby had brought in new wingers and changed one of the inside-forwards.

After sacrificing Johnny Morris from the 1948 team on a point of principle, selling him for a British record fee of £24,500 to Derby County, Busby bought Johnny Downie for a club record £18,000 from Bradford Park Avenue in 1949. Downie had established himself in the team the season before the Championship, and he is perhaps not so well remembered as some of the other players of that era. He simply wasn't there as long as most of the others, but he certainly played his part in bringing the title to Old Trafford and he scored 35 goals in the 110 League appearances he made in his five seasons with the Reds. Later he played for Luton, Hull City, Mansfield and Darlington, yet another Scotsman with a good career in English football.

Delaney and Mitten depart

The 1948 wingers had also gone by 1951-52. Jimmy Delaney had been given something of an Indian summer when Matt Busby made him his first signing in 1946, and he played a total of 164 League games plus 19 in the FA Cup spread over five seasons. But there was still a lot more football left in him, despite his spate of injuries before coming down from Scotland. At the end of 1950 he went back home to Scotland to join Aberdeen. Later he played for Derry City to win an Irish FA Cup medal and complete a unique hat-trick of winners' medals. In 1937, when he was with Glasgow Celtic, he had been in their Scottish Cup-winning team, and while with United he collected a medal with the 1948 team.

Delaney finally hung up his boots back home in Scotland with Highland League club Elgin City after 23 years as a player.

The transfer of Delaney came soon after the departure of his fellow winger, Charlie Mitten, though he left for a quite different reason. Charlie, one of the great characters of all time at the club, joined straight from school locally in 1936 and was just about ready for his League debut when war broke out. His debut proper came in the first League fixture after hostilities and he was one of the 'famous five' forwards who helped win the 1948 Cup. Always a speedy winger, he gave superb service from the left and he scored a lot of goals himself as well.

Then, in the summer of 1950, he became one of the 'rebels' of English football who rocked the boat to try for fame and fortune, especially fortune, in Colombia. United were on an end-of-season tour in South America when Charlie was approached by a representative of the Bogota club, Sante Fe, to play in Colombia. There was talk of a £5,000 signing-on fee, a lot of money in those days, plus wages of £60 a week, four times as much as the maximum pay at home. Neil Franklin, the England and Stoke centre-half, threw in his lot with the South American adventure, perhaps influencing men like Mitten.

Busby counselled caution, pointing out that playing outside FIFA jurisdiction would mean suspension at home. Charlie gave it a year, and with a lot of the promises unfulfilled returned to England. He was duly banned and had to be transfer-listed by United. After completing his suspension, he joined Fulham for five years, subsequently becoming player-manager of Mansfield.

The whole affair was a sad blow for United fans, who saw Charlie in their colours for only four seasons. His tally of 50 goals in 142 League appearances reflected his ability as a high-scoring winger. In all, he played nearly 400 League games. After Mansfield he became manager of Newcastle United where it seems he indulged his passion for dog racing.

The new wingers

So with both Delaney and Mitten gone, Busby had need of new wingers. He bought Harry McShane, a player who later became the club announcer and then a scout, from Bolton, and he also played Ernie Bond. But four games into the Championship season he was still casting around, when he recalled a match the previous season against Birmingham City. He remembered the performance of a little winger who had scored an outstanding goal against them at Old Trafford.

Busby swooped for Johnny Berry at a cost of £25,000 and was delighted with his capture. Berry's debut against Bolton ended in defeat, but he soon settled down to solve the right-wing position with his tricky, ball-playing ability, which also saw him net half-a-dozen goals. Berry made the position his own for the next seven seasons, making nearly 300 League and Cup appearances for 43 goals until he was severely injured in the Munich crash. He was critically ill with head injuries for some weeks and made only a slow recovery. There was never any chance of him playing again.

By the end of the Championship season the new outside-

Jimmy Delaney was Matt Busby's first signing after becoming manager at the end of the Second World War. He was tagged Brittle Bones because of a number of broken limbs and he was generally regarded as being past his best, but he proved a brilliant buy at £5,000 from Glasgow Celtic. He was a speedy winger who played a key role in helping to win the FA Cup in 1948

left was Roger Byrne. He had made his League debut midway through the campaign at left-back but was switched to the left-wing with devastating effect, playing in the last six games and scoring seven times. Roger, later to become a distinguished captain, was the first of the home-grown kids to come pushing through the ranks as the Busby Babes concept gathered force behind the scenes and at junior level.

The season after the Championship Roger Byrne returned after a few games to left-back, where he played with great distinction using his instinct as a winger to attack down his flank. His flair took him into the England team at left-back in 1954 and he won 33 successive caps until he was a victim of the Munich disaster. He was only 28 when he died. His wife, Joy, gave birth to their son, Roger, eight months after his death.

In all Byrne made nearly 300 League and Cup appearances involving three Championships. Few who were there at the time will forget, though, his dramatic impact on the wing to help clinch that first vital title in 1952.

Busby finally captures title

Manchester United's achievement, perhaps because of its then rarity, was considered worthy of a tribute from the Manchester Guardian in their esteemed leader column, usually reserved for weightier matters. The leader writer eulogised:

'After an interval of forty-one years, Manchester United have regained the Championship of the Football League. The title has never been better earned.

'Not only has the team, in the five seasons before this one, finished second four times and fourth once in the League and won the FA Cup; it has been captained, managed and directed in a way that is a lesson to many others. J. Carey, the captain in this period, has been a model footballer – technically efficient, thanks to hard work; a fighter to the last, without ever forgetting that he is a sportsman; a steadier of the younger and inexperienced, an inspirer of the older and tiring, and at all times the most modest of men, though he has won every football honour open to him.

'M. Busby, the manager, has shown himself as great a coach as he was a player, with an uncannily brilliant eye for young local players' possibilities, whether in their usual or in other positions; a believer in the certainty of good football's eventual reward, and a kindly, yet, when necessary, firm father of his family of players.

'Between them they have built up a club spirit which is too rare in these days, a spirit which enables men to bear cheerfully personal and team disappointments and to ignore personal opportunities to shine for the good of the whole.'

1949-59

The emergence of the Babes

After winning the Championship in 1951-52, Busby naturally kicked off the following season with his winning team, but it was soon obvious that the first great post-war side had passed its peak. Six of the first 11 matches were lost, and Busby realised he had to start drafting in new players, and making changes. The situation did not take him altogether by surprise because he had already laid the foundations for the future.

Always in his mind had been the creation of a team based

Roger Byrne clutching the cherished championship trophy after leading the Reds to success. He won three championship medals in his seven seasons at United. He went on to become an integral part of the Busby Babes as their captain

on youngsters he had taken from school and brought up in his ways. Right from the start he had paid a lot of attention to this aspect of the club and he had taken great care to appoint the right kind of men to make a success of his plan. The result was that in addition to having Jimmy Murphy as his right-hand man, he had Joe Armstrong busy signing the best schoolboy players he could find, with Northern Ireland and the Republic of Ireland proving rich recruiting areas. Then Busby had Bert Whalley as a dedicated, gifted coach and Tom Curry as the

kindly trainer. Helped by enthusiastic part-timers like Jack
Pauline, they put great emphasis on grooming the youngsters.
They had good material to work with, and they made sure the
finished product had excellence. United dominated the game in
this area, as can be seen in their FA Youth Cup record. They
won the competition for five successive seasons, starting from
its inception in the 1952-53 season, the year the first team
started to come apart.

The result was that towards the end of that rather troubled
season players such as David Pegg, Jeff Whitefoot, John
Doherty, Jackie Blanchflower, Bill Foulkes, Dennis Viollet and
Duncan Edwards started to get the occasional game.

Busby also went into the transfer market to pay £29,999 to
Barnsley for Tommy Taylor. The team finished a modest
eighth, but Busby knew he had talent in the making. He made
his decisive move in October the following season. Busby
explained:

*'We played a friendly at Kilmarnock and I played half-a-dozen
of the youngsters. They did well and we won 3-0. Then, as I
walked the golf course in the next few days, I pondered
whether this was the moment to play them all in the League
team. One or two had already come into the side, and I decided
that I would go the whole way with the youngsters.'*

This meant that Edwards, Viollet and Blanchflower
squeezed out three more of the veterans to give the team a
more youthful look. Most things in football have to be worked

Manchester at the start of the
1952-53 season complete with
the League trophy and FA
Charity Shield which they won
by beating Newcastle United
4-2. Jack Rowley scored twice
with the other goals from
Johnny Downie and a young
Roger Byrne. Back row: Tom
Curry (trainer), Walter
Crickmer (secretary), Alan
Gibson (director), Dr W McLean
(director), George Whittaker
(director), Bill Petherbridge
(director), Matt Busby
(manager). Middle: Johnny
Downie, Jack Rowley, John
Aston, Reg Allen, Allenby
Chilton, Roger Byrne, Stan
Pearson. Front: Johnny Berry,
Johnny Carey, Henry Cockburn,
Tommy McNulty. They were
champions for the first time
under Matt Busby in 1951-52

for, and the Busby Babes didn't find overnight success. They
finished only fourth in that 1953-54 season, and then, with more
youngsters like Albert Scanlon, Mark Jones and Billy Whelan
occasionally drafted in, the best they could do in 1954-55 was
fifth place.

Babes storm to title

But then everything began to click and the Busby Babes hit the
headlines. They took the First Division by storm in 1955-56,
winning the Championship by a devastating 11 points from
Blackpool and with an average age of barely 22. By this time
precociously talented youngsters were rolling out of the Busby
academy. Eddie Colman, whose shimmy of the hips was said to
send even the crowd the wrong way, had forced his way into
the team while top-class reserves like Ian Greaves and Geoff
Bent were ready in case there were any injuries.

The team which played most for the 1955-56 title lined up:

**Wood, Foulkes, Byrne, Whitefoot then Colman,
Jones, Edwards, Berry, Blanchflower or Doherty or
Whelan, Taylor, Viollet, Pegg**

Ian Greaves, Albert Scanlon and Colin Webster also played.

Only right-winger Johnny Berry and left-back Roger Byrne
bridged the four-year transition from the 1951-52
Championship side to the 1955-56 Championship.

Ray Wood had taken over in goal from Allen by this time.
United had signed him as a teenager from Darlington in 1949
and he gradually worked his way through to the first team after
providing cover for Allen and Crompton. He played in all but
one of the 1955-56 Championship games. He collected a second Championship medal the following season and was the
central figure in the controversy with Peter McParland in the
1957 FA Cup final.

Just before the air crash Ray lost his place to new signing
Harry Gregg. He recovered from the relatively minor injuries he
suffered to play again, but he was forced to move on, playing
for Huddersfield Town, Bradford City and Barnsley. Later he
turned to coaching with great success in Cyprus, the Middle
East and Africa. He won three caps for England.

Roger Byrne was at left-back, but with a new partner. Bill
Foulkes had dug in at right-back with the kind of dour tenacity
associated with his coalmining background. His father was a
miner at St Helens, and Bill was also working at the pit when
he was picked up by United as an amateur with Whiston Boys

1949-59

Club. He became a full-time professional and won a regular place in 1953, going on to become one of the club's greatest ever servants.

Foulkes lasted a long course, playing First Division football for 18 years, involving some 600 games for the club. He won just about everything in the course of his career: four Championship medals, an FA Cup winner's medal and he went on to win a 1968 European Cup medal. As a survivor of Munich he played an important part in bridging the gap between the Babes and later teams, at one point captaining the club. He was never regarded as one of the more skilful stars, but he had them all licked for staying power, as Allenby Chilton had before him, and like Chilton he played at centre-half later in his career.

After retiring as a player in 1970 Bill became a youth coach at Old Trafford. Then he played and managed in the United States and more recently in Norway. Such is the esteem of his old team-mates that they elected him the first chairman of the association of former Manchester United players.

Jeff Whitefoot started the season at right-half, and indeed won a Championship medal, but such was the competition for places that he was forced to concede to Eddie Colman. Whitefoot was a schoolboy international and he was only 16 when he was given his League debut in 1950. He was a brilliant, cultured wing-half, yet he played only 95 League and Cup games for United before being squeezed out by the stream of starlets coming through. He underlined his great ability by going on to play nearly 300 games for Nottingham Forest, and win an FA Cup medal with them.

There was no holding back Colman, though. 'Snake Hips' played the second half of the season at right-half, striking up an uncanny understanding with Duncan Edwards at left-half. They both loved to attack, which is probably why Busby went for the rocklike steadiness of Mark Jones between them at centre-half.

Mark was a traditional 'stopper', arriving as a schoolboy from Barnsley and fitting perfectly into the mould established by Allenby Chilton. Together Colman, Jones and Edwards formed one of the finest half-back lines ever assembled. All three were to die tragically young at Munich.

Edwards and Taylor

Duncan Edwards is probably the player mentioned most often as the best-ever footballer to wear a Manchester United shirt. Certainly Jimmy Murphy, assistant to Sir Matt Busby until the day they both retired, had not the slightest doubt in his mind.

'When I used to hear Muhammad Ali proclaim to the world that he was the greatest, I used to smile. You see, the greatest of them all was an English footballer named Duncan Edwards. 'If I shut my eyes I can see him now. Those pants hitched up,

Duncan Edwards emerged as the exciting icon of the Busby Babes. Jimmy Murphy first saw him at the age of 14: 'he looked like and played with the assurance of a man, with legs like tree trunks, a deep and powerful chest and an unforgettable zest for the game... He was quite simply a soccer Colossus.'

the wild leaps of boyish enthusiasm as he came running out of the tunnel, the tremendous power of his tackle – always fair but fearsome – the immense power on the ball. In fact the number of times he was robbed of the ball once he had it at his feet could be counted on one hand. He was a players' player. The greatest . . . there was only one and that was Duncan Edwards.'

Jimmy told the story of when he was manager of Wales and preparing a team to play against Duncan Edwards and England. He carefully went through all the England players, detailing their strengths and weaknesses. Then, at the end of his team talk, Reg Davies, the Newcastle and Welsh inside-forward, said to Jimmy that he hadn't mentioned Edwards, the player probably marking him. Replied Murphy: 'There is nothing to say that would help us. Just keep out of his way, son.'

Duncan Edwards played his first League game for United at the age of 15 and 285 days, against Cardiff City at Old Trafford on Easter Monday 1953. During the next five years he became the youngest England international, making his debut at the age of 17 and 8 months in a 7-2 victory against Scotland at Wembley. He won two Championship medals and played 19 times for England. He would have been a natural successor as captain to Billy Wright.

By 1955-56 the attack had also taken on a new look, and not every player had come from the youth ranks. The gap at centre-forward caused by the absence of Jack Rowley was filled by a man they found at Barnsley, Tommy Taylor.

United were not his only admirers. Jimmy Murphy said that the last time he saw him play at Barnsley there were so many managers and club chairmen there that he thought it was an extraordinary general meeting of the Football League. Altogether 20 clubs were chasing the 21-year-old forward, and Murphy said that the biggest problem was trying to persuade him he was good enough to play for Manchester United in the First Division.

'He had this mop of black hair and a perpetual smile on his face which prompted one sportswriter of the time, George Follows, to christen him "the smiling executioner". 'He didn't really want to leave Barnsley where everyone knew him. Eventually Matt Busby's charm won him over, and convinced him that if he came to Old Trafford to link up with the young-sters we had produced ourselves, the sky was the limit to his future in football.'

Taylor was signed for the odd-sounding fee of £29,999 so as not to burden him with a £30,000 tag, and he was an immediate success with his penetrating stride, fierce shot and powerful heading. He crossed the Pennines in 1953 and two months after signing he won the first of 19 England caps. He played 163 League games for United, scoring 112 goals. He scored 25 of them from 33 appearances to help win the 1956 Championship.

The inside-right berth was causing something of a problem, with first Jackie Blanchflower, then John Doherty and finally another exciting youngster, Billy Whelan, all sharing in the Championship race. Inside-left was more settled with Dennis Viollet now a regular, but more of him later as a Munich sur-vivor who hit the scoring headlines in 1960.

Johnny Berry was still at outside-right, while the youthful David Pegg occupied the left wing for most of the title season. David was another of the successful youth team, a Busby Babe recruited at Doncaster. He was able to make only 127 League appearances in his five seasons before losing his life at Munich. He played just once for the full England team, joining team-mates Roger Byrne, Tommy Taylor and Duncan Edwards against the Republic of Ireland. Munich was England's loss as well as Manchester United's.

Free-scoring Reds retain title

United were at the forefront of the 1955-56 Championship race right from the start, though it wasn't until around Christmas that the rest of the First Division felt their real power. They went to the top of the table in early December when they beat Sunderland 2-1 at Old Trafford. They lost only twice in the sec-ond half of the season. They clinched the title with two games to spare by beating their closest rivals, Blackpool, 2-1.

Tommy Taylor's 25 goals were backed by 20 from Viollet and nine from Pegg. United's 11-point margin from Blackpool at the top of the table equalled the record shared in the previ-ous century by Preston, Sunderland and Aston Villa.

All but three of the team had been nurtured as home-produced players. As Jimmy Murphy would say: 'As ye sow . . . so shall ye reap.'

Busby summed up: 'From the very start I had envisaged making my own players, having a kind of nursery so that they could be trained in the kind of pattern I was trying to create for Manchester United.'

The League champions were now in peak form and they won the title again the following season, this time romping home eight points in front of Spurs. The team had settled down to read:

Wood, Foulkes, Byrne, Colman, Jones, Edwards, Berry, Whelan, Taylor, Viollet, Pegg

There was one other notable player who began to crop up in this season, playing whenever Taylor or Viollet was injured, another home-produced starlet, Bobby Charlton. Making his debut at Charlton Athletic in October, he scored twice in a 4-2 win. Altogether that season he made 14 League appearances, scoring ten goals. Clearly he was a youngster with a great future, as events subsequently bore out.

It was a high-scoring season, with United's goals topping the ton thanks to Charlton's youthful contribution, plus 16 from Dennis Viollet, 22 from Tommy Taylor and an outstanding 26 from Billy Whelan.

Billy, or back home in Dublin, Liam, was a ball-playing inside-forward, very gifted and a surprisingly good marksman for one whose main job was to create for others. But then most of this talented team were good all-rounders and Whelan was at the peak of his powers. He had joined the club as a young-ster from Home Farm, the Irish team which served United well over the years. In four seasons at Old Trafford before the crash he played 96 League and Cup games for a total of 52 goals. He won four Republic of Ireland caps, and was a player with immaculate control.

United were named as League champions by Easter. Busby rang the changes for the following match because of Cup com-mitments and he played seven reserves. The Football League could hardly complain because United won 2-0 with a goal from Alex Dawson on his debut and another from Colin Webster. To illustrate the club's great strength in depth, the 'reserve' side made up mostly of youth team players won 3-1 at Burnley on the same day.

United's final points total of 64 was the highest for 26 years.

1949-59

United just miss double

The 1956-57 season was notable not only for winning the Championship for the second successive season. The Busby Babes were also flying high in the FA Cup as well as storming along in the European Cup. In the FA Cup they went to Wembley and came within an ace of achieving the elusive League and FA Cup double. Matt Busby said that when he came downstairs on the morning of the final against Aston Villa he had never been more sure of victory before in his football life. The Championship was already in the bag, and the form book pointed only one way for the winner at Wembley. But just six minutes into the match goalkeeper Ray Wood was carried off the field suffering from a smashed cheekbone. Peter McParland had headed the ball into Wood's arms and it seemed a routine matter for the goalkeeper to kick it clear. But McParland, perhaps fired up for the final, kept on coming to crash into the United man. Even allowing for the fact that in those days goalkeepers did not enjoy the kind of protection they get now from referees, it was an outrageous charge, and in 1957 there were no substitutes.

Jackie Blanchflower took over in goal and, with the rest of the defence, performed heroically to keep the game goalless at

Above and top: Manchester United's goalkeeper Ray Wood lies clutching his broken face watched by anxious teammates. Jackie Blanchflower took over in goal, but though United fought bravely they couldn't prevent Aston Villa emerging 2-1 winners with the villain of the piece Peter McParland, scoring Villa's two goals

the interval. Ray Wood bravely returned to the field for spells at outside-right, but could not do much. The team's pattern had been destroyed and Villa scored twice, even though Tommy Taylor managed to pull one back with a fine header.

McParland the villain then became Villa's hero by scoring two second-half goals for a 2-1 victory. Towards the end Busby sent the dazed Wood back into goal in a desperate gamble to pull the game out of the fire. The players responded by giving a tantalising glimpse of what might have been but for the injury to their goalkeeper, but Wood was really in no condition to play. It was rough, tough luck for United, and the incident helped bring in the substitute rule, but that was little consolation at the time as the dream of the double collapsed.

There was no denying that Manchester United in 1957 were the outstanding team in the country, playing some majestic football and so young that they were only on the threshold of their full potential. At home and in Europe they had covered themselves in glory and there was a tremendous expectation and excitement as they readied themselves for another treble bid in season 1957-58. But all these hopes were to come crashing to the ground in the February snow and ice in what was to be one of the saddest seasons in English football history.

CHAPTER **3**
MUNICH:END OF A DREAM

The team Matt Busby had built from the club's successful youth policy seemed destined to dominate football for many years. Such was the power of the Babes that they seemed invincible. The average age of the side which won the Championship in 1955-56 was just 22, the youngest ever to achieve such a feat. A year later, when they were Champions again, nothing, it seemed, would prevent the young braves of Manchester United from reigning supreme for the next decade.

United had taken their first steps into European football in defiance of the football authorities and it was on foreign soil that the final chapter in the story of the Babes was to be written. The aircraft carrying the United party back from a victorious visit to Yugoslavia crashed in the snow of Munich airport and the Babes were no more.

The young Champions flew out of Manchester to face Red Star Belgrade remembering the cheers of 63,000 intoxicated football fans. Five days before Munich, United had played Arsenal at Highbury and thrilled all those who witnessed that game with a display of the attacking football that they had made their trademark. Nine goals were scored . . . four by Arsenal, five by United.

That game, on Saturday, 1 February 1958, had typified the Busby Babes. They played with such flair and enthusiasm that they thought nothing of conceding four goals in their efforts to score five. United were trying to win the League Championship for the third successive season and by then had already reached the fifth round of the FA Cup.

1957-58 Season

To set the scene for the tragedy which was to shock football, let us consider how the 1957-58 season led up to a symbolic game with Arsenal and the fateful journey to Yugoslavia. For United, the season had started well, victories over Leicester at Filbert Street, then Everton and Manchester City at Old Trafford being the perfect launch towards the title. Their scoring record was remarkable with 22 goals coming in the opening six games. Yet when they lost for the first time it was not by just an odd goal, but by 4-0 at Burnden Park, where Bolton Wanderers ran rampant in front of a crowd of 48,003.

As 1957 drew to an end the Babes lost 1-0 to Chelsea at Old Trafford, then picked themselves up to beat luckless Leicester 4-0. On Christmas Day goals from Charlton, Edwards and Taylor secured two points against Luton in Manchester. On Boxing Day they met Luton again at Kenilworth Road and drew

Left: the snow falls on the wreckage of the Elizabethan that crashed on the runway of Munich airport on Thursday, 6 February 1958, claiming the lives of 23 people

Below: players, officials and journalists prepare to board the BEA Elizabethan which was to crash at Munich. The aircraft stopped at the snowbound German airport to refuel as the party made its way back to England from Yugoslavia

2-2 and two days later the 'derby' game with Manchester City ended in the same scoreline at Maine Road. A crowd of 70,483 watched that game as the old rivals battled for pride as well as points.

As the European Cup-tie with Red Star approached, the side also made progress in the FA Cup with a 3-1 win at Workington and a 2-0 victory over Ipswich at Old Trafford to see them through to the fifth round, where they were to meet Sheffield Wednesday.

Before Munich

But the third target for Matt Busby, success in Europe, was perhaps the greatest. In 1956 United had become the first English club to compete in the European Champions' Cup, falling at the semi-final to the might of Real Madrid, winners of the trophy in the competition's first five years.

That year, the European seed had been sown. Manchester had witnessed the skills of di Stefano, Kopa and Gento, had seen United score ten times against Belgian club Anderlecht, then hang on against Borussia Dortmund before a remarkable quarter-final against Atletico Bilbao. In this match the Babes defied the odds by turning a 5-3 deficit from the first leg into a 6-5 victory, with goals from Taylor, Viollet and Johnny Berry, to win the right to challenge Real Madrid in the penultimate round.

That was where the run ended, but when United qualified to enter the European competition again in the 1957-58 season it was clear where the club's priorities lay. Matt Busby wanted a side which was good enough to win everything. The FA Cup had been snatched out of his grasp because of an injury to goalkeeper Ray Wood in the 1957 final, but his Babes were capable of reaching Wembley once again, and having secured the League Championship in 1956 and 1957 they could certainly emulate the great sides of pre-war Huddersfield Town and Arsenal and win it for a third successive time.

United's second European campaign saw them stride over Shamrock Rovers before beating Dukla Prague 3-1 on aggregate to reach the quarter-final against Red Star.

The Yugoslavs came to Manchester on 14 January 1958, and played a United side which was smarting from a 1-1 draw at Elland Road against Leeds United, who had been beaten 5-0 at Old Trafford earlier in the season.

Bobby Charlton and Eddie Colman scored the goals which gave United the edge in a 2-1 first-leg victory over Red Star, but it would be close in Belgrade. The run-up to the second leg was encouraging. A 7-2 win over Bolton, with goals from Bobby Charlton (3), Dennis Viollet (2), Duncan Edwards and Albert Scanlon, was just the result United needed before visiting Highbury, then leaving on the tiring journey behind the Iron Curtain.

The great match at Highbury

The United side which faced Arsenal was the eleven which was to line up against Red Star four days later. With Irish international Harry Gregg, a new signing, in goal, United were without some of their regulars. Jackie Blanchflower, the centre-half who had replaced Ray Wood in goal in the FA Cup final, was missing from the side along with wingers David Pegg and Johnny Berry and the creative inside-forward Liam Whelan, all of whom were being rested by Busby.

The two full-backs were Bill Foulkes and captain Roger Byrne, with the half-back line of Eddie Colman, Mark Jones and Duncan Edwards supporting the forward line of Ken Morgans, Bobby Charlton, Tommy Taylor, Dennis Viollet and Albert Scanlon.

Jack Kelsey was in goal for the Gunners and he was first to feel the power of United. Only ten minutes had gone when Dennis Viollet laid off a pass to an advancing Duncan Edwards who struck the ball with such ferocity that it was past Kelsey and in the net despite the efforts of the Welsh international.

Arsenal fought back, urged on by the huge crowd, and it took a superb save by Gregg to prevent them from equalising. He somehow kept out a certain scoring chance by grabbing the ball just under the crossbar and his clearance led to United's second. The ball was pushed out to Albert Scanlon on the left wing and he ran virtually the full length of the field before crossing. Two Arsenal defenders had been drawn into the

1949-59

corner by the United winger and his centre found Bobby Charlton running into the penalty area from the right. Charlton's shot was unstoppable and all Kelsey could do was throw up both arms in a token gesture as he dived to his right, but the shot was past him and the young Charlton was turning to celebrate the Babes' 2-0 lead.

By half-time it was 3-0, and again Scanlon's speed had played its part. The winger broke down the left, rounded Arsenal right-back Stan Charlton and crossed to the far side of the pitch where right-winger Kenny Morgans met the cross and chipped the ball back into the penalty area. England centre-forward Tommy Taylor scored his 111th goal in the First Division after five seasons with United.

For 15 minutes of the second half there was no further score, then Arsenal took heart when David Herd, who was to become a United player, broke through and hit a fierce shot at Gregg's goal. The big Irishman tried to keep the ball out but Herd's power and accuracy beat him. It was 3-1 with half an hour remaining.

Within two minutes the scores were level as Arsenal staged a sensational fight back. Wing-half Dave Bowen was the man driving Arsenal forward. It was from his cross that Herd had got the first of the home side's goals and he was involved in the move which led to the second Arsenal strike. Vic Groves jumped above the United defence to head down a cross from Gordon Nutt which fell to Jimmy Bloomfield, who scored. It was Nutt again who made the pass to Bloomfield some 60 seconds later for the London-born striker to dive full length and head home a magnificent goal which turned Highbury into a deafening stage for the final drama.

No scriptwriter could have dreamt up the plot for the last chapter of the Babes' challenge for Football League supremacy.

Would United collapse under the Arsenal onslaught? Lesser teams would have been forgiven if they had defended in depth to hold out for a draw, having seen a three-goal lead disintegrate, but Manchester United went all out in search of more goals, and got them.

The speed of Scanlon and the skill of young Charlton combined to give Dennis Viollet a goal. The Manchester supporters screamed their delight, and were in raptures a few minutes later when Kelsey had to retrieve the ball from his goal for a fifth time, after Eddie Colman had found Morgans with a precise pass and Tommy Taylor had scored his last goal.

Yet even then this magnificent game had not ended. Derek Tapscott ran through the centre of United's near exhausted defence to put Arsenal within one goal of United again. But it was the final goal of the afternoon. The referee blew for time and the players collapsed into one another's arms.

Fate had decided that for fans at home this game would be the epitaph to those young heroes of Manchester.

The stained glass window at St Francis in the Priory Church in Dudley, Worcestershire in memory of Duncan Edwards. Although only 21 when he died, Duncan played a total of 175 games for United and scored 21 times. He played for his country 18 times

Left: Keeper Ray Wood was a regular in Matt Busby's team during the 1953-54 season, winning League Championship medals in 1956 and 1957. Busby said of him: 'You didn't get miracles from Ray, he was just there when it mattered.' Having survived the 1958 Munich air crash, he was later sold to Huddersfield Town. Ironically, Busby tried to buy him back some years later.

The fatal European Cup trip

After that symbolic game, all thoughts were now on Europe. Could United hold on to that slender lead from the first leg? For the supporters left behind it seemed a narrow margin, but they had faith in those young players – after all had they not proved themselves time and again in similar circumstances?

For the players the damp, grey smog of Manchester's winter was replaced by the fresh crispness of mid-Europe. They had seen snow on their journey to the Yugoslav capital yet they had been welcomed with warmth by the people of Belgrade who understood the greatness of Manchester United in the common language of football.

It was time for the game and as the two sides lined up in the stadium the roar of thousands of Yugoslav voices rang in the ears of the Babes. Cameras clicked as last-minute photographs were taken, and above the players in the press area British journalists filed stories which were to be read in England the following morning.

Among them was Frank Swift, a giant of a man who had kept goal for Manchester City and England, and who had a reputation of being the gentle giant. Big 'Swifty' had retired from the game and taken a job as a sportswriter with the *News of the World,* and his role in Belgrade was to write a column for the following Sunday edition.

Also looking out from that crowded press box were journalists who had travelled to Europe for each of United's previous games: Tom Jackson of the *Manchester Evening News* and his close friend and rival Alf Clarke of the now defunct *Manchester Evening Chronicle*. Both men loved Manchester United and lived to see their every game. Alf Clarke had been on United's books as an amateur, and was with the club before Matt Busby arrived to rebuild it after the war.

Because Manchester was a printing centre for the northern editions of the national newspapers, and also because of the tremendous popularity of the United side, most other daily newspapers were represented.

From the *Daily Mirror* was Archie Ledbrooke, who had only just made the trip having been on the point of being replaced by Frank McGhee because he (Ledbrooke) had still to complete an outstanding feature only hours before the flight had left England. Others included Eric Thompson from the Daily Mail, George Follows of the *Daily Herald* – the daily newspaper which was succeeded by *The Sun* following its closure – Don Davies of the *Manchester Guardian,* Henry Rose of the *Daily Express* and Frank Taylor from the *News Chronicle,* another publication which has since gone out of existence.

Don Davies wrote under the pen-name of 'Old International' and had been in the England amateur side which played Wales in 1914, having been a member of the famous Northern Nomads side. On 5 February 1958 this is the story Davies filed back to the *Manchester Guardian* office:

*Who would be a weather prophet? At Belgrade today in warm
sunshine and on a grass pitch where the last remnants of
melting snow produced the effect of an English lawn flecked
with daisies, Red Star and Manchester United began a battle of
wits and courage and rugged tackling in the second leg of their
quarter-final of the European Cup competition. It ended in a
draw 3-3, but as United had already won the first leg at Old
Trafford by 2-1 they thus gained the right to pass into the
semi-final round of the competition for the second year in succession on a 5-4 aggregate.*

*Much to the relief of the English party and to the consternation
of the 52,000 home spectators, Viollet had the ball in the net
past a dumbfounded Beara in ninety seconds. It was a beautifully taken goal – a characteristic effort by that player – but
rather lucky in the way a rebound had run out in United's
favour. But, as Jones remarked, 'You need luck at this game';
and he might have added, 'a suit of chain mail also would not
have come amiss'. A second goal almost came fourteen minutes later, delightfully taken by Charlton after a corner kick by
Scanlon had been headed by Viollet, but this was disallowed,
because of offside, by the Austrian referee whose performance
on the whistle so far had assumed the proportions of a flute
obligato. That was due to the frequency which fouls were
being committed by both sides after Sekularac had set the
fashion in shabbiness by stabbing Morgans on the knee.*

*. . . Further success for United was impending. Charlton this
time was the chosen instrument. Dispossessing Kostic about
forty yards from goal, this gifted boy leaned brilliantly into his
stride, made ground rapidly for about ten yards, and then beat
the finest goalkeeper on the Continent with a shot of tremendous power and superb placing. There, one thought, surely
goes England's Bloomer of the future. Further evidence of
Charlton's claim to that distinction was to emerge two minutes later. A smartly taken free kick got the Red Star defence
into a real tangle. Edwards fastened on the ball and did his
best to oblige his colleagues and supporters by bursting it (a
feat, by the way, which he was to achieve later), but he
muffed his kick this time and the ball rolled to Charlton,
apparently lost in a thicket of Red Star defenders. Stalemate
surely. But not with Charlton about. His quick eye detected
the one sure route through the circle of legs; his trusty foot
drove the ball unerringly along it. 3-0 on the day: 5-1 on the
aggregate. Nice going.*

*As was natural, the Red Star players completely lost their poise
for a while. Their forwards flung themselves heatedly against a
defence as firm and steady as a rock; even Sekularac, after a
bright beginning in which he showed his undoubted skill, lost
heart visibly and stumbled repeatedly. Nevertheless there was
an upsurge of the old fighting spirit when Kostic scored a fine*

*goal for Red Star two minutes after half time. It ought to have
been followed by another one only three minutes later when
Sekularac placed the ball perfectly for Cotic. Cotic's terrific
shot cleared the bar by a foot – no more. Next, a curious mix-
up by Foulkes and Tasic, Red Star's centre-forward, ended in
Foulkes falling flat on top of Tasic and blotting him completely
out of view. According to Foulkes, Tasic lost his footing, fell
over, and pulled Foulkes over with him. But it looked bad and
the whistle blew at once with attendant gestures indicating a
penalty. Tasic had the satisfaction of converting that one,
although his shot only just evaded Gregg's finger tips.*

Top: Over 60,000 copies of this
programme were sold as Red
Star of Belgrade came to Old
Trafford for the first leg of the
European Cup quarter-final in
1958. United won the game 2-1
thanks to goals from Bobby
Charlton and Eddie Colman

Above: The final team talk.
Matt Busby chats to his players
following their pre-match meal
in Belgrade, shortly before the
Red Star game. Listening to his
words Bert Whalley rests an
arm on the shoulder of Tommy
Taylor as next to him stand
Jackie Blanchflower and
Duncan Edwards. Seated right
is Dennis Viollet and in the
foreground Bobby Charlton
(right) and Ken Morgans

*The score was now 3-2 and the crowd broke into an uncon-
trolled frenzy of jubilation and excitement . . . A quarter of an
hour from the end Red Star, with their confidence and self-
respect restored, were wheeling and curvetting, passing and
shooting in their best style, and the United's defenders had to
fight their way out of a regular nightmare of desperate situa-
tions. It was significant hereabouts that United's inside
forwards were not coming back to chase the ball as they had
done so effectively in the first half and this, of course, threw
added pressure on the rearguard. As soon as this fault was rec-
tified the Red Star attacks, though frequent enough, lost
something of their sting. In fact, United began to pile on the
pressure at the other end and once Morgans struck a post with
a glorious shot.*

*The furious pace never slackened, and as England's champi-
ons tried to find their flowing, attacking play of the first half,
they were pelted by a storm of snowballs. Two minutés from
time Harry Gregg came racing out of his goal, and hurled himself full length at Zebec's feet. He grasped it safely, but the
impetus of his rush took him outside the penalty area with the*

1949-59

ball, and Red Star had a free kick some twenty yards out. Kostic watched Gregg position himself by the far post, protected by a wall of United players. There was just a narrow ray of light, a gap, by the near post, and precision player Kostic threaded the ball through as Gregg catapulted himself across his goal. Too late. The ball eluded his grasping fingers, and hit the back of the net. The score was 3-3.

It had always been Davies's ambition to be a football writer. For most of his life he had worked as an education officer with a Manchester engineering firm, but after it was suggested that he should try his hand at journalism he had been taken onto the Guardian staff when the editor saw a report of a fictitious match. It was the key he needed to open the door to a career of full-time writing. His style was that of the essayist, ideally suited to the *Manchester Guardian*, and contrasting totally with that of Henry Rose, the most popular daily writer of that time – certainly with the Old Trafford supporters.

Rose saw the game from the same vantage point as Davies, yet his description was totally different:

The last line-up in Belgrade, 5 February, 1958 and the Busby Babes are ready for their final game. Left to right: Duncan Edwards, Eddie Colman, Mark Jones, Ken Morgans, Bobby Charlton, Dennis Viollet, Tommy Taylor, Bill Foulkes, Harry Gregg, Albert Scanlon, and captain Roger Byrne who leans forward to shout encouragement to his colleagues before the European cup tie

Red Star 3 Manchester United 3
Star Rating ***

Manchester United survived the Battle of Belgrade here this afternoon and added another shining page to their glittering history by drawing 3-3 with Red Star and winning the two-leg tie 5-4.

They had to fight not only eleven desperate footballers and a fiercely partisan 52,000 crowd, but some decisions of Austrian referee Karl Kainer that were double-Dutch to me. I have never witnessed such a one-sided exhibition by any official at home or abroad.

The climax of Herr Kainer's interpretations, which helped inflame the crowd against United, came in the 55th minute when he gave a penalty against Foulkes, United's star defender. Nothing is wrong with my eyesight – and Foulkes confirmed what I saw . . . that a Red Star player slipped and pulled the United man back down with him. A joke of a ruling it would have been had not Tasic scored from the spot.

Later in his report, Rose wrote:

*Gregg was hurt, Morgans and Edwards were limping; Byrne
was warned for wasting time. United players were penalised
for harmless-looking tackles.*

*I thought Herr Kainer would have given a free-kick against
United when one of the ballboys fell on his backside!*

He described the United side as:

*Heroes all. None greater than Billy Foulkes. None greater than
Bobby Charlton, who has now scored twelve goals in the
eleven games he has played since he went into the side at
inside-right on 21 December. But all eleven played a noble part
in this memorable battle.*

After the game

The game over and the work completed, it was time to relax,
and the party of journalists joined the United officials, players
and their opposite numbers from the Red Star club at a banquet in the Majestic Hotel in Belgrade. It was a friendly affair,
despite the disappointment felt by the host club at losing such
an important game. There was a great friendship between the
clubs in those early years of the European competition.

In a moving scene the meal ended when waiters entered the
dining room carrying trays of sweetmeats lit by candles set in
ice. The United party stood to applaud the skill of the Yugoslav
chef, and Roger Byrne led his colleagues in song:

'We'll meet again,
Don't know where, don't know when,
But we know we'll meet again
some sunny day . . .'

That scene was remembered clearly by Yugoslav writer Miro
Radojcic in an article for his newspaper *Politika*, which he
translated into English 20 years later for Geoffrey Green, and
which was published in *There's Only One United* (Hodder and
Stoughton, 1978). Part of it read:

*Then followed the simple warm-hearted words of Matt Busby
and Walter Crickmer as they said: 'Come and visit us, the
doors of Old Trafford will always be open to you' . . . and after
that lovely, crazy night as I parted from 'Old International' –
Don Davies from the Manchester Guardian – he said to me:
'Why didn't you score just one more goal then we could have
met for a third time?'*

Radojcic sat up throughout most of the night musing over a
feature article he planned to write for his newspaper. *Politika*
was not a sporting publication – in fact he was a political writer
– but he had a great love for football and the flair of Manchester
United's young side attracted him.

After chatting and drinking with Tommy Taylor and Duncan
Edwards in a bar named Skadarija, Radojcic was left alone with
his thoughts. He decided that he would arrange to fly back to

Manchester with the team, and write his story from the
Manchester angle, a look at England's top team seen through
the eyes of one of Yugoslavia's most celebrated journalists.

The players had gone off to bed when Radojcic came to his
decision so he went back to his flat, packed a bag and made his
way to the airport only to discover that he had left his passport
at home. He asked the airport authorities to hold the aircraft for
as long as possible while he took a return taxi trip back to his
hime. By the time he got back with his passport the twin-
engined Elizabethan had taken off, bound for England via
Munich where it was to stop to re-fuel.

The tragedy at Munich airport

Those on board were in a relaxed mood when the plane landed
on German soil. They had played cards, chatted over the latest
news, read books and magazines which were around and passed
the time away as best they could. There was the usual air of ner-
vous apprehension about the flight, but card schools and con-
versation hid any fears of flying and some even managed to catch
up on lost sleep rather than gaze out on the snowscape below.

By around 2 pm G-ALZU AS 57 was ready once more for
take-off with Captain Kenneth Rayment, the second in command, at the controls. The man in charge, Captain James
Thain, had flown the plane out to Belgrade, and his close friend
and colleague was now taking the 'Lord Burleigh' home again.

At 2.31 pm the control tower was told that '609 Zulu Uniform
is rolling'. Captain Thain later described what happened:

*Ken opened the throttles which were between us and when they
were fully open I tapped his hand and held the throttles in the
fully open position. Ken moved his hand and I called for 'full
power'. The engines sounded an uneven note as the aircraft
accelerated and the needle on the port pressure gauge started to*

After the second unsuccessful
take-off the players and
journalists decided that it
would be impossible to leave
Munich until the next day.
Duncan Edwards sent this
telegram to his landlady back in
Manchester telling her of the
delay. . . but a third attempt at
take-off was made. The
telegram was delivered after
the crash

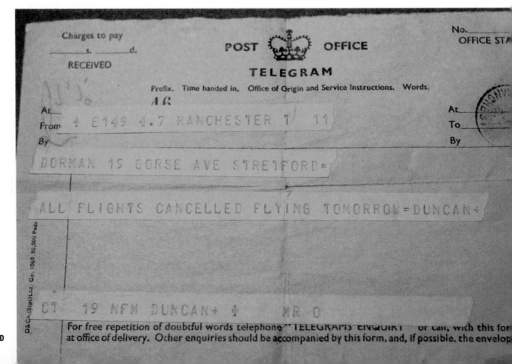

fluctuate. I felt a pain in my hand as Ken pulled the throttles back and said: 'Abandon take-off'. I held the control column fully forward while Ken put on the brakes. Within 40 seconds of the start of its run the aircraft was almost at a halt again.

The cause of the problem had been boost surging – a very rich mixture of fuel causing the engines to over-accelerate – a fault which was quite common in the Elizabethan. As the two men talked over the problem Captain Rayment decided that he would attempt a second take-off, this time opening the throttles gradually before releasing the brakes, and then moving to full power.

At 2.34 pm permission for a second take-off attempt was given by air traffic control and for a second time the plane came to a halt. During their wait while the aircraft was being refuelled, the passengers had gone into a lounge for coffee. Now, after the two aborted attempts to take off, the party was in the lounge once more. It had begun to snow quite heavily. Full-back Bill Foulkes remembers:

We'd been playing cards for most of the flight from Belgrade to Munich, and I remember when we left the aircraft thinking how cold it was. We had one attempt at taking off, but didn't leave the ground, so I suppose a few of those on board would start to worry a little bit, and when the second take-off failed we were pretty quiet when we went back into the lounge.

Some of the players must have felt that they would not be flying home that afternoon. Duncan Edwards sent a telegram to his landlady back in Manchester: 'All flights cancelled returning home tomorrow'. The telegram was delivered at around 5 pm.

Bill Foulkes recalls how after a quarter of an hour delay the passengers were asked to board again but it was another five minutes before everyone was back in the aircraft.

Alf Clarke from the Evening Chronicle had put a call through to his office and we had to wait for him to catch up with us. We got back into our seats, but we didn't play cards this time. . . . I slipped the pack into my jacket pocket and sat back waiting for take-off.

I was sitting about half-way down the aircraft next to a window, on the right-hand side of the gangway. Our card school was Ken Morgans, who was on my right, and facing us David Pegg and Albert Scanlon. Matt Busby and Bert Whalley were sitting together on the seat behind us and I remember how Mark Jones, Tommy Taylor, Duncan Edwards and Eddie Colman were all at the back.

David Pegg got up and moved to the back: 'I don't like it here, it's not safe,' he said and went off to sit with the other players. I saw big Frank Swift back there too, he also felt that the rear was the safest place to be.

There was another card school across the gangway from us, Ray Wood and Jackie Blanchflower were sitting on two of the seats, Roger Byrne, Billy Whelan and Dennis Viollet let on the others with one empty seat amongst them.

A last photograph of football writer Henry Rose (right), and Tommy Taylor as they share a moment together on the Elizabethan aircraft which crashed at Munich. Eight journalists died in the disaster, among them former England goalkeeper Frank Swift who was working as a correspondent for the *News of the World*

Back on the flight deck Captain Thain and Captain Rayment had discussed the problem they were having with the station engineer William Black, who had told them that the surging they were having was quite common at airports like Munich because of its altitude. At 3.03 pm 609 Zulu Uniform was rolling again. Captain Thain describes the next attempt at take-off:

I told Ken that if we got boost surging again, I would control the throttles. Ken opened them to 28 inches with the brakes on. The engines were both steady so he released the brakes and we moved forward again.

He continued to open the throttles and again I followed with my left hand until the levers were fully open. I tapped his hand and he moved it. He called 'Full power' and I checked the dials and said: 'Full power'.

Captain Thain again noticed that there was a sign of boost surging and called this out to Captain Rayment. The surging was controlled and the throttle pushed back until it was fully open:

I glanced at the air speed indicator and saw it registered 105 knots and was flickering. When it reached 117 knots I called out 'V1' [Velocity One, the point on the runway after which it isn't safe to abandon take-off]. Suddenly the needle dropped to about 112 and then 105. Ken shouted, 'Christ, we can't make it' and I looked up from the instruments to see a lot of snow and a house and a tree right in the path of the aircraft.

Inside the passengers' compartment Bill Foulkes had sensed that something was wrong:

There was a lot of slush flying past the windows and there was a terrible noise, like when a car leaves a smooth road and starts to run over rough ground.

The Elizabethan left the runway, went through a fence and crossed a road before the port wing struck a house. The wing and part of the tail were torn off and the house caught fire. The cockpit struck a tree and part of the fuselage hit a wooden hut containing a truck loaded with fuel and tyres. This exploded.

Matt Busby lies in an oxygen tent as he fights for his life in the Rechts der Isar Hospital. The United manager told Jimmy Murphy to keep the flag flying when his assistant visited him the day after the disaster

The End of the Babes

Bill Foulkes remembered afterwards a terrific bang, then after being unconscious for a few moments, seeing a gaping hole in front of him. Foulkes was unscathed, but he recalled the horror of what he saw later in the hospital:

We went in and saw Matt in an oxygen tent, and Duncan Edwards, who seemed to be badly hurt. Bobby Charlton had a bandaged head, Jackie Blanchflower was nursing a badly gashed arm which had been strapped up by Harry Gregg in the snow of the night before. Albert Scanlon lay with his eyes closed, he had a fractured skull, and Dennis Viollet had a gashed head and facial injuries. Ray Wood's face was cut and he had concussion and Ken Morgans and Johnny Berry lay quite still in their beds. I spoke to a nurse and she told me that she thought Duncan had a better chance of making a full recovery than Johnny did. . .

We came across Frank Taylor in another bed; he was the only journalist around and he asked if we'd like to have a beer with him. Like us, he didn't know the full implications of what had happened the afternoon before.

We were about to leave the hospital when I asked a nurse where we should go to see the other lads. She seemed puzzled so I asked her again: 'Where are the other survivors?' . . . 'Others?

There are no others, they are all here.' It was only then that we knew the horror of Munich.

The Busby Babes were no more.

Roger Byrne, Geoff Bent, Mark Jones, David Pegg, Liam Whelan, Eddie Colman and Tommy Taylor had been killed instantly. Club secretary Walter Crickmer had also died, along with the first team trainer, Tom Curry, and coach Bert Whalley.

Duncan Edwards and Johnny Berry were critically injured and fighting for their lives, Matt Busby had suffered extensive injuries and was the only club official to survive the crash.

Eight of the nine sportswriters on board the aircraft had also perished: Alf Clarke, Don Davies, George Follows, Tom Jackson, Archie Ledbrooke, Henry Rose, Eric Thompson and the gentle giant, Frank Swift.

One of the aircrew had been killed, together with two other passengers: the travel agent who had arranged the flight details, and a supporter who had flown out to watch the game. Nine players had survived, but two of them, Johnny Berry and Jackie Blanchflower – brother of Tottenham Hotspur's Danny – never played again.

Two photographers, the travel agent's wife, and two Yugoslav passengers, one with a young baby, had survived, together with Frank Taylor. On the afternoon of the crash 21 people had died, 18 had survived, of whom four were close to death.

Of those four, Duncan Edwards, Matt Busby, Johnny Berry and Captain Kenneth Rayment, two would survive. Three weeks after the aircrash which had become known simply as 'Munich', Duncan Edwards and Kenneth Rayment had lost their battle to live.

The news reaches Manchester

On the afternoon of the crash Alf Clarke had telephoned the Evening Chronicle sports desk to say that he thought the flight would be held up by the weather and made arrangements to return the following day. By three in the afternoon the paper had more or less 'gone to bed', and the final editions were leaving Withy Grove.

Then on the teleprinter came an unbelievable message: 'Manchester United aircraft crashed on take off. . . heavy loss of life feared.' The BBC interrupted its afternoon programming to broadcast a news flash. The football world listened to the words but few understood their meaning.

Jimmy Murphy, was manager of the Welsh national side, and a World Cup qualifying game had coincided with the Red Star fixture. Murphy told Matt Busby that he would go to Yugoslavia rather than the game at Ninian Park, Cardiff, but his manager told him that his place was with the Welsh side.

'I always sat next to Matt on our European trips, but I did what he said and let him go off to Red Star without me. Mind you,

1949-59

I've got to be honest – my mind was more on our game in Yugoslavia than the match I was watching. When I heard that we were through to the semi-final it was a great load off my mind; I didn't like not being there.'

He had just returned to Old Trafford from Wales when the news reached him. Alma George, Matt Busby's secretary, told him that the charter flight had crashed. Murphy failed to react.

'She told me again. It still didn't sink in, then she started to cry. She said many people had been killed, she didn't know how many, but the players had died, some of the players. I couldn't believe it. The words seemed to ring in my head. Alma left me and I went into my office. My head was in a state of confusion and I started to cry.'

At the Hospital

The following day Jimmy Murphy flew out to Munich and was stunned by what he saw: 'Matt was in an oxygen tent and he told me to "keep the flag flying". Duncan recognised me and spoke. It was a terrible, terrible time.'

Murphy was given the job of rebuilding. Life would go on despite the tragedy, and Manchester United would play again: 'I had no players, but I had a job to do.'

After the agency newsflash had reached the Manchester evening newspapers, extra editions were published. At first details were printed in the Stop Press. By 6 pm a special edition of the *Manchester Evening Chronicle* was on sale:

About 28 people, including members of the Manchester United football team, club officials, and journalists are feared to have been killed when a BEA Elizabethan airliner crashed soon after take-off in a snowstorm at Munich airport this afternoon. It is understood there may be about 16 survivors. Four of them are crew members.

The newspaper, which was carrying Alf Clarke's match report and comments from the previous night's game, said on its front page: 'Alf Clarke was talking to the Evening Chronicle reporters in Manchester just after 2.30 pm when he said it was unlikely that the plane would be able to take off today.' Even though only three hours had elapsed since the crash the newspaper had a detailed report of how the disaster occurred.

Twenty-four hours later, as the whole of Europe reacted to the news, the *Evening Chronicle* listed the 21 dead on its front page under a headline: 'Matt fights for life: a 50-50 chance now'. There was a picture of Harry Gregg and Bill Foulkes at the bedside of Ken Morgans, and details of how the other injured were responding to treatment. The clouds of confusion had lifted – Munich had claimed 21 lives, 15 were injured and, of these, four players and Matt Busby were in a serious condition.

In the days following, Manchester mourned as the bodies of

A youthful Bobby Charlton sits at the bedside of goalkeeper Ray Wood in the Rechts der Isar Hospital in Munich a few days after the crash.
Charlton was able to return home in time to play in the sixth round of the FA Cup on 1 March 1958, but Wood played just one more League game for United following Munich. Six weeks before the disaster he had lost his place to Harry Gregg and although Wood returned to Old Trafford in the weeks following the crash he was unable to win back his position and was transferred to Huddersfield Town

its famous footballing heroes were flown home to lie overnight in the gymnasium under the main grandstand before being passed on to relatives for the funerals.

Thousands of supporters turned out to pay their last respects. Where families requested that funerals should be private, the United followers stayed away from gravesides but lined the route to look on in tearful silence as corteges passed.

Desmond Hackett wrote a moving epitaph to Henry Rose, whose funeral was the biggest of all. A thousand taxi drivers offered their services free to anyone who was going to the funeral and there was a six-mile queue to Manchester's Southern Cemetery. The cortege halted for a moment outside the *Daily Express* offices in Great Ancoats Street where Hackett wrote in the style of Henry: 'Even the skies wept for Henry Rose today. . .'

Football returns to Old Trafford

Rival clubs offered helping hands to United. Liverpool and Nottingham Forest were first to respond by asking if they could do anything to assist. Football had suffered a terrible blow. To give United a chance of surviving in football the FA waived its rule which 'cup-ties' a player once he has played in an FA Cup round in any particular season. The rule prevents him from playing for another club in the same competition, so that if he is transferred he is sidelined until the following season. United's need for players was desperate and the change of rules allowed Jimmy Murphy to begin his rebuilding by signing Ernie Taylor from Blackpool. Manchester United took a deep breath. Football would return to Old Trafford.

Thirteen nights after news of Munich had reached Jimmy Murphy the days of torture ended when United played again. Their postponed FA Cup-tie against Sheffield Wednesday

Colin Webster at outside-right had joined United in 1952 and made his League debut in the 1953-54 season. He had won a League Championship medal in 1956 after 15 appearances, but had since been edged out of the side by Johnny Berry. Ernie Taylor was inside-right, and at centre-forward was Alex Dawson, a brawny Scot who had made his debut as a 16-year-old in April 1957, scoring against Burnley. Inside-left was Mark Pearson, who earned the nickname 'Pancho' because of the Mexican appearance his sideburns gave him. The new United outside-left was Shay Brennan, who was a reserve defender. Such was United's plight that the 20-year-old was to begin his League career not as a right-back but as a left-winger.

Sheffield Wednesday had no chance. Murphy's Manchester United were playing for the memory of their friends who had died less than a fortnight earlier, the final score was United 3 Wednesday 0.

Playing in the Sheffield side was Albert Quixall, later to join United in a record transfer deal, who recalls: 'I don't think anyone who played in the game or who watched it will ever forget that night. United ran their hearts out, and no matter how well we had played they would have beaten us. They were playing like men inspired. We were playing more than just eleven players, we were playing 60,000 fans as well.'

United scored in the 27th minute after two errors by Brian Ryalls in the Wednesday goal. Bill Foulkes had taken a free-kick outside the penalty area and his shot was going wide when Ryalls palmed it away for a corner. There had seemed no danger from the shot, but Brennan's corner kick brought his first senior goal. Ryalls tried to collect the cross under the bar and could only turn the ball into his own net. Brennan got a second later in the game when a Mark Pearson shot rebounded off the 'keeper and straight into the Irishman's path. He made no mistake and United led 2-0. Five minutes from the end Alex Dawson scored the third. United had reached the quarter-finals of the FA Cup.

The crowd turned for home, their heads full of memories of a remarkable game, their hearts full of sadness as they realised the full extent of Munich. The new team had carried on where the Babes had left off... but they would never see their heroes again.

Two days after that cup-tie Duncan Edwards lost his fight to survive, and the sadness of Munich was rekindled.

The flowers of Manchester

Manchester United had to continue and chairman Harold Hardman had made this clear in his message on the front cover of the Sheffield Wednesday programme:

United will go on . . . the club has a duty to the public and a duty to football. We shall carry on even if it means that we are heavily defeated.

drew a crowd of 60,000 on a cold February evening of immense emotion. Spectators wept openly, many wore red-and-white scarves draped in black – red, white and black were eventually to become United's recognised colours – and the match programme added a poignant final stroke to a tragic canvas. Under the heading 'Manchester United' there was a blank teamsheet.

Spectators were told to write in the names of the players. Few did, they simply listened in silence as the loudspeaker announcer read out the United team. Harry Gregg in goal and Bill Foulkes at right-back had returned after the traumas of Munich, other names were not so familiar.

At left full-back was Ian Greaves who had played his football with United's junior sides and found himself replacing Roger Byrne: 'I can remember the dressing room was very quiet. I couldn't get Roger out of my mind, I was getting changed where he would have sat. I was wearing his shirt...'

At right-half was Freddie Goodwin, who had come through from the reserve side after joining United as a 20-year-old. Another reserve regular was centre-half Ronnie Cope, who had come from United's juniors after joining the club in 1951. At left-half was Stan Crowther, whose transfer to United was remarkable. He played for Aston Villa, and was not very keen to leave the Midlands club. Jimmy Murphy recalled: 'Eric Houghton was Villa manager at the time and he had told Stan that we were interested in him. He didn't want to leave Villa, but Eric got him to come to Old Trafford to watch the Sheffield Wednesday game. On the way up he told him he thought that he should help us out, but Stan told him he hadn't brought any kit with him. "Don't worry, I've got your boots in my bag," Eric said. We met at about half-past five and an hour before the kick-off he'd signed!'

Bare headed workmen pay their respects as a cortege leaves Old Trafford. Immediately after the disaster the bodies of those who died were brought back to Old Trafford where they lay in the club gymnasium until arrangements for the funerals were completed. Supporters kept vigil at the stadium as the football world mourned the passing of the Babes

Here is a tragedy which will sadden us for years to come, but in this we are not alone. An unprecedented blow to British football has touched the hearts of millions. Wherever football is played United is mourned.

The weeks following the tragedy revealed moving stories about the players who lost their lives.

Roger Byrne would have learned when he returned to Manchester that his wife Joy was expecting a child. Thirty-eight weeks after his death Roger had a son.

Geoff Bent treasured a picture of himself taking the ball off Tom Finney in one of the 12 First Division games he played, and the newspaper cutting was kept by his young wife Marion. His daughter Karen was a babe in arms when he died.

Eddie Colman, the 'cheekie chappie' from Salford, was just three months past his 21st birthday when he was killed.

Duncan Edwards, the youngest player to appear for England, was planning to get married to his fiancée, Molly. He had been a senior footballer for only four years, and was 22. Today, a stained glass window in St Francis's Church in his home town of Dudley remains as a tribute to a great player.

Mark Jones left a young wife, June, and a baby son, Gary. The ex-bricklayer was just 24 years of age. He doted on his black Labrador retriever, Rick. The dog pined away to its death shortly after the disaster.

David Pegg was only 22 and had edged himself into the England side at a time when Tom Finney and Stan Matthews were ending their international careers. His ambition was to be successful with United, and he had achieved that aim.

Tommy Taylor was also planning to marry and had told his fiancée, Carol, that he was looking forward to getting home from Belgrade for a pint of Guinness and to listen to his records with her.

Liam Whelan was a deeply religious boy, and Harry Gregg remembers clearly his last words as the aircraft accelerated down the runway: 'If the worst happens I am ready for death . . . I hope we all are.'

Eleven years later an official inquiry cleared Captain James Thain of any responsibility for the accident. The official cause was recorded as a build-up of melting snow on the runway which prevented the Elizabethan from reaching take-off speed.

Through the Munich Air Disaster a bond between Manchester United and its supporters was welded. Since that day, the club has been one of the best supported in Britain, and even though it never achieved the domination threatened by the potential of the Babes, since 1972-73 Old Trafford's attendances have been the highest in the Football League. Anyone who was a supporter at the time of Munich has remained loyal to the club. Those who came afterwards perhaps failed to understand the magnitude of the club's loss but have absorbed the meaning of Munich. It was the day a team died, but still plays on.

THE FLOWERS OF MANCHESTER

One cold and bitter Thursday in Munich Germany,
Eight great football stalwarts conceded victory,
Eight men will never play again who met destruction there,
The Flowers of British football, the Flowers of Manchester.

Matt Busby's boys were flying, returning from Belgrade,
This great United family, all masters of their trade,
The pilot of the aircraft, the skipper Captain Thain,
Three times they tried to take off and twice turned back again.

The third time down the runway disaster followed close,
There was slush upon that runway and the aircraft never rose,
It ploughed into the marshy ground, it broke, it overturned
And eight of the team were killed when the blazing wreckage burned.

Roger Byrne and Tommy Taylor who were capped for England's side
And Ireland's Billy Whelan and England's Geoff Bent died,
Mark Jones and Eddie Colman, and David Pegg also,
They lost their lives as it ploughed on through the snow.

Big Duncan he went too, with an injury to his frame,
And Ireland's brave Jack Blanchflower will never play again,
The great Matt Busby lay there, the father of his team,
Three long months passed by before he saw his team again.

The trainer, coach and secretary, and a member of the crew,
Also eight sporting journalists who with United flew,
And one of them Big Swifty, who we will ne'er forget,
The finest English 'keeper that ever graced the net.

Oh, England's finest football team its record truly great,
Its proud successes mocked by a cruel turn of fate.
Eight men will never play again, who met destruction there,
The Flowers of English football, the Flowers of Manchester.

'The Flowers of Manchester', words anon. Recorded by The Spinners on their album 'Black and White', Phillips International 6382 047.

SEASON 1950-1951
FOOTBALL LEAGUE (Division 1)

19 Aug	Fulham	H W	1-0
23 Aug	Liverpool	A L	1-2
26 Aug	Bolton W	A L	0-1
30 Aug	Liverpool	H W	1-0
2 Sep	Blackpool	H W	1-0
4 Sep	Aston Villa	A W	3-1
9 Sep	Tottenham H	A L	0-1
13 Sep	Aston Villa	H D	0-0
16 Sep	Charlton A	H W	3-0
23 Sep	Middlesbrough	A W	2-1
30 Sep	Wolverhampton W	A D	0-0
7 Oct	Sheffield Wed	H W	3-1
14 Oct	Arsenal	A L	0-3
21 Oct	Portsmouth	H D	0-0
28 Oct	Everton	A W	4-1
4 Nov	Burnley	H D	1-1
11 Nov	Chelsea	A L	0-1
18 Nov	Stoke C	H D	0-0
25 Nov	W B A	A W	1-0
2 Dec	Newcastle U	H L	1-2
9 Dec	Huddersfield T	A W	3-2
16 Dec	Fulham	A D	2-2
23 Dec	Bolton W	H L	2-3
25 Dec	Sunderland	A L	1-2
26 Dec	Sunderland	H L	3-5
13 Jan	Tottenham H	H W	2-1
20 Jan	Charlton A	A W	2-1
3 Feb	Middlesbrough	H W	1-0
17 Feb	Wolverhampton W	H W	2-1
26 Feb	Sheffield Wed	A W	4-0
3 Mar	Arsenal	H W	3-1
10 Mar	Portsmouth	A D	0-0
17 Mar	Everton	H W	3-0
23 Mar	Derby Co	A D	2-2
24 Mar	Burnley	A W	2-1
26 Mar	Derby Co	A W	2-1
31 Mar	Chelsea	H W	4-1
7 Apr	Stoke C	A L	0-2
14 Apr	W B A	H W	3-0
21 Apr	Newcastle U	A W	2-0
28 Apr	Huddersfield T	H W	6-0
5 May	Blackpool	A D	1-1

FA Cup

6 Jan	Oldham (3)	H W	*4-1
27 Jan	Leeds U (4)	H W	4-0
10 Feb	Arsenal (5)	H W	1-0
24 Feb	Birmingham C (6)	A L	0-1

Football League

	P	W	D	L	F:A	Pts	
Tottenham H	42	25	10	7	82:44	60	1st
Manchester U	42	24	8	10	74:40	56	2nd

SEASON 1951-1952 FOOTBALL LEAGUE (DIVISION 1)

18 Aug	W B A	H D	3-3	Allen	Carey	Redman	Cockburn	Chilton	McGlen	Mcshane	Pearson	Rowley3	Downie	Bond
22 Aug	Middlesbrough	H W	4-2	..	..	..	Gibson	..	Cockburn	..	..1	..3	..	..
25 Aug	Newcastle U	H W	2-1	..	..	..	..	..	..	..	..1	..1	..1	..
29 Aug	Middlesbrough	A W	4-1	..	..	..	..	..	..	..	..	..	..	..
1 Sep	Bolton W	A L	0-1	..	..	..	..	..	..	Berry	..	..	..	..
5 Sep	Charlton A	H W	3-2	..	..	..	..	..	..	..	..	..2	..	..
8 Sep	Stoke C	H W	4-0	..	..	..	..	..	..	..1	..	..3	..	McShane
12 Sep	Charlton A	A D	2-2	..	..	..	..	..	..	..	..	..	..2	..
15 Sep	Manchester C	A W	2-1	..	..	..	..	..	..	..1	Cassidy	..	..	..1
22 Sep	Tottenham H	A L	0-2	..	..	..	..	..	..	..	Rowley	..	..	..
29 Sep	Preston NE	H L	1-2	..	..	..	..	..	..	Walton	Aston1	Pearson	Rowley	
8 Oct	Derby Co	H W	2-1	..	..	..	..	..	..	..1	Rowley	..	..	McShane
13 Oct	Aston Villa	A W	5-2	..	McNulty	..	..	..	..	Pearson2	..2	Downie	Bond1	
20 Oct	Sunderland	A L	0-1	..	Carey	..	..	..	McGlen	Downie	..	Pearson	McShane	
27 Oct	Wolverhampton W	A W	2-0	..	..	..	..	Cockburn	McShane	Pearson1	..1	Birch	Bond	
3 Nov	Huddersfield T	H D	1-1	..	..	..	..	..	..	..1	..	..	..	
10 Nov	Chelsea	A L	2-4	..	..	..	..	..	Berry	..1	Aston	Downie	Rowley1	
17 Nov	Portsmouth	H L	1-3	..	..	..	..	..	..	..1	..	..	..	
24 Nov	Liverpool	A D	0-0	Crompton	..	Byrne	Blanchflower	..	..	..	Rowley	..	Bond	
1 Dec	Blackpool	H W	3-1	..	McNulty	..	Carey	..	..	..	..1	..2	..	
8 Dec	Arsenal	A W	*3-1	Allen	..	..	..	..	..	..1	..1	..	..	
15 Dec	W B A	H W	5-1	Allen	..	..	..	..	..	..1	..2	..2	..	
22 Dec	Newcastle U	A D	2-2	..	..	..	Chilton	JonesM	..1	..	..	..	..1	
25 Dec	Fulham	H W	3-2	..	..	..	Chilton	..	..1	..	..1	..1	..1	
26 Dec	Fulham	A D	3-3	..	..	..	..	..	..	..	..1	..1	..1	
29 Dec	Bolton W	H W	1-0	..	..	..	..	..	..	..	..1	..	..	
5 Jan	Stoke C	A D	0-0	..	..	..	Carey	Chilton	..	..	..	..	..	
19 Jan	Manchester C	H D	1-1	..	..	..	..1	..	..	..	Aston	..	Rowley	
28 Jan	Tottenham H	H W	*2-0	..	..	..	..	..	..	Clempson	..	Pearson1	..	
9 Feb	Preston NE	A W	2-1	..	..	..	..	..	..1	..	..1	..	..1	
16 Feb	Derby Co	A W	3-0	Crompton	..	..	..	..	..	..	..1	..1	..1	
1 Mar	Aston Villa	H D	1-1	..	..	..	..	..	..1	..	..	..	..	
8 Mar	Sunderland	A W	2-1	..	..	..	..	..	..1	..	..1	..	..1	
15 Mar	Wolverhampton W	A W	2-0	..	..	..	..	..	..	..	..1	..1	..	
22 Mar	Huddersfield T	A L	2-3	..	..	..	..	..	..	..1	..	..1	..	
5 Apr	Portsmouth	A L	0-1	..	..	..	..	Whitefoot	..	..	..	Downie	Bond	
11 Apr	Burnley	A D	1-1	Allen	..	Aston	..	..	Cockburn	..	Downie	Pearson	Byrne1	
12 Apr	Liverpool	H W	4-0	..	..	..	..	..	Whitefoot	..	Rowley	Pearson	..2	
14 Apr	Burnley	H W	6-1	..	..	..	..1	..	..	..	..1	..1	..1	
19 Apr	Blackpool	A D	2-2	..	..	..	..	Cockburn	..	..	..1	..1	..1	
21 Apr	Chelsea	A W	*3-0	..	..	..	..	..	..	..	..1	..1	..	
26 Apr	Arsenal	H W	6-1	..	..	..	..	..	..	..	..3	..2	..1	

FA Cup

12 Jan	Hull City (3)	H L	0-2	Allen	McNulty	Byrne	Carey	Chilton	Cockburn	Berry	Pearson	Rowley	Downie	Bond

Appearances (goals)

Allen	33	
Aston	16	4
Berry	36	6
Birch	2	
Blanchflower	1	
Bond	19	4
Byrne	24	7
Carey	36	3
Cassidy	1	
Chilton	42	
Clempson	6	2
Cockburn	36	2
Crompton	9	
Downie	31	11
Gibson	17	
Jones M	3	
McGlen	2	
McNulty	24	
McShane	12	1
Pearson	41	22
Redman	16	
Rowley	40	30
Walton	2	
Whitefoot	3	
Own goals	3	
Total 24 players		95

Football League

	P	W	D	L	F:A	Pts	
Manchester U	42	23	11	6	95:52	57	1st

SEASON 1952-1953 FOOTBALL LEAGUE (DIVISION 1)

23 Aug	Chelsea	H W	2-0	Wood	McNulty	Aston	Carey	Chilton	Gibson	Berry1	Downie1	Rowley	Pearson	Byrne
27 Aug	Arsenal	A L	1-2	Crompton	..	..	..	..	Cockburn	..	..1	..	..	..
30 Aug	Manchester C	A L	1-2	..	..	..	..	..	..	..	..1	..	..	..
3 Sep	Arsenal	H D	0-0	..	Carey	Byrne	Gibson	..	..	..	Clempson	Aston	..	Bond
6 Sep	Portsmouth	A L	0-2	..	McNulty	..	..	..	..	..	..	..	..	Rowley
10 Sep	Derby Co	A W	3-2	..	..	Aston	Carey	..	Gibson	..	Downie	Rowley	..3	Byrne
13 Sep	Bolton W	H W	1-0	Allen	..	..	..	..	..	..1	..	..	..	..
20 Sep	Aston Villa	A D	3-3	Wood	..	..	..	..	..	..	..2	..	..	..
27 Sep	Sunderland	H D	0-1	..	..	..	Jones M	..	..	..	Clempson	..	..	..
4 Oct	Wolverhampton W	A L	2-6	Allen	..	..	Carey	..	..	..	Rowley2	..	..	Scoff
11 Oct	Stoke C	H L	0-2	Wood	..	..	..	..	..	Clempson	..	Downie	..	..
18 Oct	Preston NE	A W	5-0	Crompton	Carey	Byrne	Whitefoot	..	..	Downie	Aston2	Pearson2	Rowley1	
25 Oct	Burnley	H L	1-3	..	..	..	..	..	..	..	..1	..	..	
1 Nov	Tottenham H	A W	2-1	..	McNulty	..	..	..	..2	..	..	..	McShane	
8 Nov	Sheffield Wed	H D	1-1	..	..	..	..	..	..	..	..	..1	..	
15 Nov	Cardiff C	A W	2-1	..	..	..	Cockburn	..	..	..	..1	..1	..	
22 Nov	Newcastle U	H D	2-2	..	..	..	..	..	..	..	..1	..1	..	
29 Nov	W B A	A L	1-3	..	..	..	..	..	..	Lewis1	..	..	..	
8 Dec	Middlesbrough	H W	3-2	..	..	..	Carey	..	Cockburn	Doherty	Aston1	..2	Pegg	
13 Dec	Liverpool	A W	2-1	..	Foulkes	..	..	..	..	..1	..2	..1	..	
20 Dec	Chelsea	A W	3-2	..	..	..	..	..	..	..	..2	..1	..	
25 Dec	Blackpool	A D	0-0	Wood	McNulty	..	..	..	..	..	..	..	..	
26 Dec	Blackpool	H W	2-1	..	..	..	..1	..	..	..	..	..1	..	
1 Jan	Derby Co	H W	1-0	..	Redman	..	..	..	..	Lewis1	Aston	..	..	
3 Jan	Manchester C	H D	1-1	..	Aston	..	..	Whitefoot	..	Doherty	Lewis1	..	..	
17 Jan	Portsmouth	H W	1-0	..	..	..	..	Cockburn	..	Rowley	..	..1	..	
24 Jan	Bolton W	A L	1-2	..	..	..	..	..	..	..	..	..	..	
7 Feb	Aston Villa	H W	3-1	..	..	..	..	..	..	Lewis1	Rowley2	..	..	
18 Feb	Sunderland	A D	2-2	Carey	..	..	Gibson	..	..	..	..	..	..1	
21 Feb	Wolverhampton W	H L	0-3	Wood	..	..	Carey	..	..	..	..	..	..	
28 Feb	Stoke C	A L	1-3	Crompton	McNulty	..	Chilton	Jones M	Gibson	..1	Aston	..	Downie	
7 Mar	Preston NE	H W	5-2	..	Aston	..	Carey	Chilton	Cockburn	..	Rowley1	Taylor T2	Pearson	..2
14 Mar	Burnley	A L	1-2	..	..	..1	..	..	..	..	..	..	..	
25 Mar	Tottenham H	H W	3-2	..	..	..	Gibson	..	..	..	..	..2	..	..1
28 Mar	Sheffield Wed	A D	0-0	..	..	..	Carey	..	..	..	..	..	..	
3 Apr	Charlton A	A D	2-2	..	..	..	..	..	Blanchflower	..2	..	..1	..	
4 Apr	Cardiff C	H L	1-4	..	..	..	Gibson	..	Edwards	..	..	..	..	
6 Apr	Charlton A	H W	3-2	..	McNulty	..	Carey	..	Whitefoot	Lewis	..2	..	Rowley1	
11 Apr	Newcastle U	A W	2-1	Olive	..	..	..	..	..	Viollet	Pearson	Aston	Taylor T2	
18 Apr	WBA	H D	2-2	..	..	..	..	..	..	..1	..1	..	..	
20 Apr	Liverpool	A W	3-1	..	Crompton	Aston	..	..	..	Berry1	Downie	Taylor T	Pearson 1	..1
25 Apr	Middlesbrough	A L	0-5	..	..	McNulty	..	..	..	Viollet	Aston	Taylor T	..	

Appearances (goals)

Allen	2	
Aston	40	8
Berry	40	7
Blanchflower	1	
Bond	1	
Byrne	40	2
Carey	32	1
Chilton	42	
Clempson	4	
Cockburn	22	
Crompton	25	
Doherty	5	2
Downie	20	3
Edwards	1	
Foulkes	2	
Gibson	20	
Jones M	2	
Lewis	10	7
McNulty	23	
McShane	5	
Olive	2	
Pearson	39	16
Pegg	19	4
Redman	1	
Rowley	26	11
Scott	2	
Taylor T	11	7
Viollet	3	1
Whitefoot	10	
Wood	12	
Total 30 players		69

Football League

	P	W	D	L	F:A	Pts	
Arsenal	42	21	12	9	97:64	54	1st
Manchester U	42	16	10	14	69:72	46	8th

SEASON 1953-1954 FOOTBALL LEAGUE (DIVISION 1)

19 Aug	Chelsea	H D	1-1	Crompton	Aston	Byrne	Gibson	Chilton	Cockburn	Berry	Rowley	Taylor T	Pearson1	Pegg
22 Aug	Liverpool	H D	4-4	..	..	..	..1	..	..	..	..1	..1	Lewis1	
26 Aug	W B A	H L	1-3	..	..	..	..	..	..	..	..	..	..1	
29 Aug	Newcastle U	H D	1-1	Wood	McNulty	Aston	Whitefoot	..1	..	..	Byrne	..	..	Rowley
2 Sep	W B A	A L	0-2	..	..	Aston	Byrne	..	..	..	Lewis	..	Viollet	
5 Sep	Manchester C	A L	0-2	..	..	..	..	..	..	..	Viollet	..	Pearson	
9 Sep	Middlesbrough	H D	2-2	..	McNulty	..	..	..	..	..	Lewis	Rowley2	..	McShane
12 Sep	Bolton W	A D	0-0	..	..	..	..	..	..	..	Taylor T	..	..	
16 Sep	Middlesbrough	A W	4-1	..	..	..	..1	..	..	..	..	..	..	
19 Sep	Preston NE	H W	1-0	..	..	..	Foulkes	..1	..	..	..2	..	..	
26 Sep	Tottenham H	A D	1-1	..	..	..	..	..	..	..	..	..	..	
3 Oct	Burnley	H L	1-2	..	..	..	..	..	..	..	..	..	..1	
10 Oct	Sunderland	H W	1-0	..	..	Aston	..	..	..	..	..	..	..	

Abbreviations:

Appearances (goals) refer to League games only

Figures shown as 2 etc. refer to goals scored by individual players

* own-goal

(Season 1953-1954 — continued)

Date	Opponent	Venue	Res	Score	Notes
17 Oct	Wolverhampton W	A	L	1-3	Foulkes; Pearson, Taylor T1, Rowley
24 Oct	Aston Villa	H	W	1-0	
31 Oct	Huddersfield	A	D	0-0	Edwards; Blanchflower, Viollet, Rowley
7 Nov	Arsenal	H	D	2-2	
14 Nov	Cardiff C	A	W	6-1	
21 Nov	Blackpool	H	W	4-1	
28 Nov	Portsmouth	A	L	1-1	Webster, Berry
5 Dec	Sheffield U	H	D	2-2	
12 Dec	Chelsea	A	L	1-3	
19 Dec	Liverpool	H	W	5-1	
25 Dec	Sheffield Wed	H	W	5-2	
26 Dec	Sheffield Wed	A	W	1-0	
2 Jan	Newcastle U	A	W	2-1	Pegg
16 Jan	Manchester C	H	D	1-1	
23 Jan	Bolton W	H	L	1-5	Rowley1
6 Feb	Preston NE	A	W	3-1	Crompton
13 Feb	Tottenham H	H	W	2-0	McFarlane, Berry; Pegg
20 Feb	Burnley	A	L	0-2	Rowley
27 Feb	Sunderland	A	W	2-0	Wood
6 Mar	Wolverhampton W	H	W	1-0	
13 Mar	Aston Villa	A	D	2-2	Crompton; Cockburn
20 Mar	Huddersfield T	H	W	3-1	Edwards
27 Mar	Arsenal	A	L	1-3	
3 Apr	Cardiff C	H	L	2-3	Redman, Byrne; Gibson, Whitefoot; Lewis, Aston
10 Apr	Blackpool	A	L	0-2	
16 Apr	Charlton A	H	W	2-0	Gibson; Pegg
17 Apr	Portsmouth	H	W	2-0	
19 Apr	Charlton A	A	L	0-1	Cockburn
24 Apr	Sheffield U	A	W	3-1	Berry; Rowley

FA Cup

Date	Opponent	Venue	Res	Score	Lineup
9 Jan	Burnley (3)	A	L	3-5	Wood, Foulkes, Bryne, Whitefoot, Chilton, Edwards, Berry, Blanchflower1, Taylor T1, Viollet1, Rowley

Appearances (goals)

Player	Apps	Goals
McFarlane	1	
McNulty	4	
McShane	9	
Pearson	11	2
Pegg	9	
Redman	1	
Rowley	36	12
Taylor T	35	22
Viollet	29	11
Webster	1	
Whitefoot	38	
Wood	27	
Total 23 players		**73**

Football League

	P	W	D	L	F:A	Pts	
Wolves	42	25	7	10	96:56	57	1st
Manchester U	42	16	12	12	73:56	46	4th

SEASON 1954-1955 FOOTBALL LEAGUE (DIVISION 1)

Regular lineup: Wood, Foulkes, Byrne, Whitefoot, Chilton, Edwards, Berry, Blanchflower, Webster, Viollet, Rowley

Date	Opponent	Venue	Res	Score	Notes
21 Aug	Portsmouth	H	L	1-3	
23 Aug	Sheffield Wed	A	W	4-2	
28 Aug	Blackpool	A	W	4-2	
1 Sep	Sheffield Wed	H	W	2-0	
4 Sep	Charlton A	H	W	3-1	Taylor1
8 Sep	Tottenham H	A	W	2-0	Webster1
11 Sep	Bolton W	A	D	1-1	
15 Sep	Tottenham H	H	W	2-1	Taylor
18 Sep	Huddersfield T	H	D	1-1	
25 Sep	Manchester C	A	L	2-3	Gibson
2 Oct	Wolverhampton W	A	L	2-4	Crompton, Greaves, Kennedy; Cockburn; Edwards
9 Oct	Cardiff C	H	W	5-2	Wood, Foulkes, Byrne; Edwards; Blanchflower
16 Oct	Chelsea	A	W	6-5	
23 Oct	Newcastle U	H	D	*2-2	
30 Oct	Everton	A	L	2-4	
6 Nov	Preston NE	H	W	2-1	
13 Nov	Sheffield U	A	L	0-3	
20 Nov	Arsenal	H	W	2-1	Goodwin, Edwards; Scanlon
27 Nov	WBA	A	L	0-2	Whitefoot
4 Dec	Leicester C	H	W	3-1	Webster1; Rowley1
11 Dec	Burnley	A	W	4-2	Bent
18 Dec	Portsmouth	A	D	0-0	Byrne; Edwards
27 Dec	Aston Villa	H	L	0-1	
28 Dec	Aston Villa	A	L	1-2	Webster, Taylor1; Pegg; Blanchflower2
1 Jan	Blackpool	H	W	4-1	
22 Jan	Bolton W	H	D	1-1	Rowley
5 Feb	Huddersfield T	A	W	3-1	Whitefoot; Webster, Edwards1; Pegg1
12 Feb	Manchester C	H	L	0-5	
23 Feb	Wolverhampton W	H	L	2-4	Webster, Viollet, Taylor1
26 Feb	Cardiff C	A	L	0-3	Jones; Berry, Taylor, Webster; Scanlon
5 Mar	Burnley	H	W	1-0	
19 Mar	Everton	H	L	1-2	Whelan, Taylor
26 Mar	Preston NE	A	W	2-0	Taylor2
2 Apr	Sheffield U	H	W	5-0	Bent; Viollet1, Edwards2
8 Apr	Sunderland	A	L	3-4	Byrne
9 Apr	Leicester C	A	L	0-1	Crompton
11 Apr	Sunderland	H	D	2-2	
16 Apr	WBA	H	W	3-0	Goodwin, Gibson; Viollet1
18 Apr	Newcastle U	A	L	0-2	
23 Apr	Arsenal	A	W	*3-2	Wood; Goodwin; Blanchflower2
26 Apr	Charlton A	A	D	1-1	
30 Apr	Chelsea	H	W	2-1	

FA Cup

Date	Opponent	Venue	Res	Score	Lineup
8 Jan	Reading (3)	A	D	1-1	Wood, Foulkes, Byrne, Gibson, Chilton, Edwards, Berry, Blanchflower, Webster1, Viollet, Rowley
12 Jan	Reading (3R)	H	W	4-1	
29 Feb	Manchester C (4)	A	L	0-2	Taylor

Appearances (goals)

Player	Apps	Goals
Bent	2	
Berry	40	3
Blanchflower	29	10
Byrne	39	2
Chilton	29	
Cockburn	1	
Crompton	7	
Edwards	33	6
Foulkes	41	
Gibson	32	
Goodwin	5	
Greaves	1	
Jones	13	
Kennedy	1	
Pegg	6	1
Rowley	22	7
Scanlon	14	4
Taylor	30	20
Viollet	34	20
Webster	17	8
Whelan	7	1
Whitefoot	24	
Wood	37	
Own goals		2
Total 23 players		**84**

Football League

	P	W	D	L	F:A	Pts	
Chelsea	42	20	12	10	61:57	52	1st
Manchester U	42	20	7	15	54:74	47	5th

SEASON 1955-1956 FOOTBALL LEAGUE (DIVISION 1)

Regular lineup: Wood, Foulkes, Byrne, Whitefoot, Jones, Edwards, Webster/Berry, Blanchflower, Taylor, Viollet, Scanlon

Date	Opponent	Venue	Res	Score	Notes
20 Aug	Birmingham C	A	D	2-2	Wood, Foulkes, Byrne, Whitefoot, Jones, Edwards, Webster, Blanchflower, Taylor, Viollet2, Scanlon; Berry1, Webster1
24 Aug	Tottenham H	H	D	2-2	Webster; Lewis1
27 Aug	WBA	H	W	3-1	
31 Aug	Tottenham H	A	W	2-1	..2; Edwards
3 Sep	Manchester C	A	L	0-1	Goodwin
7 Sep	Everton	H	W	2-1	
10 Sep	Sheffield U	A	L	0-1	Berry; Whelan; Blanchflower, Doherty, Berry
14 Sep	Everton	A	L	2-4	Whitehurst, Whitefoot; Webster1; Blanchflower, Taylor1, Viollet1, Pegg1
17 Sep	Preston NE	H	W	3-2	
24 Sep	Burnley	A	D	0-0	Berry
1 Oct	Luton T	H	W	3-1	Bent; Webster1
8 Oct	Wolverhampton W	H	W	4-3	Byrne, Foulkes; Byrne; Doherty1; Blanchflower
15 Oct	Aston Villa	A	D	4-4	McGuinness; Blanchflower1
22 Oct	Huddersfield T	H	W	3-0	Crompton; Bent; Edwards; Viollet
29 Oct	Cardiff C	A	W	1-0	Wood; Byrne
5 Nov	Arsenal	H	D	1-1	
12 Nov	Bolton W	A	L	1-3	Colman; Webster
19 Nov	Chelsea	H	W	3-0	Doherty; Viollet
26 Nov	Blackpool	A	D	0-0	Greaves, Foulkes
3 Dec	Sunderland	H	W	2-1	
10 Dec	Portsmouth	A	L	2-3	
17 Dec	Birmingham C	H	W	2-1	
24 Dec	WBA	A	W	4-1	
26 Dec	Charlton A	H	W	5-1	
27 Dec	Charlton A	A	L	0-3	
31 Dec	Manchester C	H	W	2-1	
14 Jan	Sheffield U	H	W	3-1	Scott; Whelan; Webster
21 Jan	Preston NE	A	L	1-3	Berry; Taylor1
4 Feb	Burnley	H	W	2-0	Greaves
11 Feb	Luton T	A	W	2-0	Goodwin; Blanchflower, Edwards
18 Feb	Wolverhampton W	H	W	2-0	Colman
25 Feb	Aston Villa	H	W	1-0	
3 Mar	Chelsea	A	W	4-2	
10 Mar	Cardiff C	H	D	1-1	
17 Mar	Arsenal	A	D	1-1	
24 Mar	Bolton W	H	W	1-0	
30 Mar	Newcastle U	H	W	5-2	Doherty1
31 Mar	Huddersfield T	A	W	2-0	

Appearances (goals)

Player	Apps	Goals
Bent	4	
Berry	34	4
Blanchflower	18	3
Byrne	39	3
Colman	25	
Crompton	1	
Doherty	16	4
Edwards	33	3
Foulkes	26	
Goodwin	8	
Greaves	15	
Jones	42	1
Lewis	4	1
McGuinness	4	
Pegg	35	9
Scanlon	8	1
Scott	1	
Taylor	33	25
Viollet	34	20
Webster	15	4
Whelan	13	4
Whitetoot	15	
Whitehurst	1	
Wood	41	
Total 24 players		**83**

Football League

	P	W	D	L	F:A	Pts	
Manchester U	42	25	10	7	83:51	80	1st

Date	Opponent	V	R	Score	1	2	3	4	5	6	7	8	9	10	11
2 Apr	Newcastle U	A	D	0-0	..	..									
7 Apr	Blackpool	H	W	2-1	..	..					..1				
14 Apr	Sunderland	A	D	2-2	..	..	Bent	..	..	McGuinness1	..	Whelan1	Blanchflower	..	..
21 Apr	Portsmouth	H	W	1-0	..	..	Byrne	..	..	Doherty	..	Doherty	Taylor	..1	..

FA Cup

Date	Opponent	V	R	Score	1	2	3	4	5	6	7	8	9	10	11
7 Jan	Bristol R (3)	A	L	0-4	Wood	Foulkes	Byrne	Colman	Jones	Whitefoot	Berry	Doherty	Taylor	Viollet	Pegg

SEASON 1956-1957 FOOTBALL LEAGUE (DIVISION 1)

Date	Opponent	V	R	Score	1	2	3	4	5	6	7	8	9	10	11
18 Aug	Birmingham C	H	D	2-2	Wood	Foulkes	Byrne	Colman	Jones M	Edwards	Berry	Whelan	Taylor T	Viollet2	Pegg
20 Aug	Preston NE	A	W	3-1	..	..	..	..	..	..	..	..1	..2	..	..
25 Aug	W B A	A	W	3-2	..	..	..	..	..	..	..	..1	..1	..1	..
29 Aug	Preston NE	H	W	3-2	..	..	..	..	..	..	..	..	..	..3	..
1 Sep	Portsmouth	H	W	3-0	..	..	..	..	..	..	..1	..	..	..1	..1
5 Sep	Chelsea	A	W	2-1	..	..	..	..	..	..	..	..1	..	..	..
8 Sep	Newcastle U	A	D	1-1	..	..	..	..	..	..	..	..1	..	..	..
15 Sep	Sheffield Wed	H	W	4-1	..	..	..	..	..	..	..1	..1	..1	..	..
22 Sep	Manchester C	H	W	2-0	..	..	..	..	..	..	..	..1	..1	..	..
29 Sep	Arsenal	A	W	2-1	..	..	..	..	Cope	..	..1	..1	..	..1	..
8 Oct	Charlton A	H	W	4-2	..	..	Bent	..	Jones M	McGuinness	..1	..1	Charlton2	..	..
13 Oct	Sunderland	A	W	*3-1	..	..	Byrne	..	..	Edwards	..	..1	Taylor T	..1	..
20 Oct	Everton	H	L	2-5	..	..	..	..	..	..	..	..1	..	Charlton1	..
27 Oct	Blackpool	A	D	2-2	Hawksworth Wood	..	..	..	..	..	..	..	..2	Viollet	..
3 Nov	Wolverhampton W	H	W	3-0	..	..	..	..	..	..	..	..1	..1	Charlton	..
10 Nov	Bolton W	A	L	0-2	..	..	..	..	..	..	..	..	..	..	..1
17 Nov	Leeds U	H	W	3-2	..	..	..	..	..	McGuinness	..	..2	..	..1	..
24 Nov	Tottenham H	A	D	2-2	..	..	..	..1	Blanchflower	..	..1	..	..	Edwards	..
1 Dec	Luton T	H	W	3-1	..	..	..	..	Jones M	..	..	..1	..1	..	..
8 Dec	Aston Villa	A	W	3-1	..	..	Bent	..	..	Edwards	..	..	..2	Viollet1	..1
15 Dec	Birmingham C	A	L	1-3	..	..	..	..	..	..	..	..1	..	..	..
26 Dec	Cardiff C	H	W	3-1	..	..	Byrne	..	..	..	..1	..1	..1	..1	..
29 Dec	Portsmouth	H	W	3-1	..	..	..	..	..	McGuinness	..	..	Edwards1	..1	..
1 Jan	Chelsea	H	W	3-0	..	..	..	..	..	Edwards	..	..1	Taylor T2	..	..1
12 Jan	Newcastle U	H	W	6-1	..	..	..	..	..	..	..	..2	..	..1	..
19 Jan	Sheffield Wed	A	L	1-2	..	..	..	..	..	..	..	..	..1	..	..2
2 Feb	Manchester C	A	W	4-2	..	..	..	..	..	..1	..	..1	..1	..1	..
9 Feb	Arsenal	H	W	6-2	..	..	..	..	..	..1	..2	..2	..1	..	..
18 Feb	Charlton A	A	W	5-1	..	Byrne	Bent	..	..	McGuinness	..	..	..2	Charlton3	..
23 Feb	Blackpool	H	L	0-2	..	Foulkes	Byrne	..	..	Edwards	..	..	..	..	..
6 Mar	Everton	A	W	2-1	..	Byrne	Bent	Goodwin	Blanchflower	McGuinness	..	..	Webster2	Doherty	..
9 Mar	Aston Villa	H	D	1-1	..	Foulkes	Byrne	..	..	Edwards	..	..	Edwards	Charlton1	..
16 Mar	Wolverhampton W	A	D	1-1	Clayton Wood	..	..	Colman	..	Edwards	..	..	Webster	..	..
25 Mar	Bolton W	H	L	0-2	Wood	..	..	..	..	McGuinness	..	..	Edwards	..	..
30 Mar	Leeds U	A	W	2-1	..	..	..	..	..	Edwards	..1	..	Webster	..	..
6 Apr	Tottenham H	H	D	0-0	..	..	Bent	..	..	McGuinness	..	..	Taylor T	Viollet	Scanlon
13 Apr	Luton T	A	W	2-0	..	..	Byrne	Goodwin	..	Edwards	..	Viollet	..2	Charlton	..
19 Apr	Burnley	A	W	3-1	..	..	..	..	..	..	..	Whelan3	..	..	Pegg
20 Apr	Sunderland	H	W	4-0	..	..	..	Colman	..	..	..	..2	..	..	..
22 Apr	Burnley	H	W	2-0	..	..	Greaves	Goodwin	Cope	McGuinness	Webster1	Doherty	Dawson1	Viollet	Scanlon
27 Apr	Cardiff C	A	W	3-2	..	..	..	Colman	Blanchflower	..	..	Whelan	..1	..	..2
29 Apr	W B A	H	D	1-1	Clayton	Greaves	Byrne	Goodwin	Jones M	..	Berry	Doherty	..1	..	..

FA Cup

Date	Opponent	V	R	Score	1	2	3	4	5	6	7	8	9	10	11
5 Jan	Hartlepool U (3)	A	W	4-3	Wood	Foulkes	Byrne	Colman	Jones M	Edwards	Berry1	Whelan2	Viollet	Pegg	..
26 Jan	Wrexham (4)	A	W	5-0	..	..	..1	..	..	..	..	Webster	..2	..	..
16 Feb	Everton (5)	H	W	1-0	..	..	..	..	..	..1	..	..	..	..	..
2 Mar	Bournemouth (6)	A	W	2-1	..	..	..	..	..	McGuinness	..2	Edwards	..	..	..
23 Mar	Birmingham C (SF)	N	W	2-0	..	..	..	..	Blanchflower	Edwards	..1	Charlton1	..	..	..
(at Hillsborough)															
4 May	Aston Villa (F)	N	L	1-2	..	..	..	..	..	..	..	Taylor T1	Charlton	..	..
(at Wembley)															

European Cup

Date	Opponent	V	R	Score	1	2	3	4	5	6	7	8	9	10	11
12 Sep	RSC Anderlecht (P)	A	W	2-1	Wood	Foulkes	Byrne	Colman	Jones M	Blanchflower	Berry	Whelan	Taylor T1	Viollet1	Pegg
26 Sep	RSC Anderlecht (P)	†H	W	10-0	..	..	..	..	..	Edwards	..2	..3	..4	..	..1
17 Oct	Borussia D'mund (1)	†H	W	3-2	..	..	..	..	..	..	..	..	..2	Edwards	..1
21 Nov	Borussia D'mund (1)	A	D	0-0	..	..	..	..	..	McGuinness	..	..	Edwards	..	..
16 Jan	Athletico Bilbao (2)	A	L	3-5	..	..	..	..	..	Edwards	..	..1	..1	Viollet1	..
6 Feb	Athletico Bilbao (2)	†H	W	3-0	..	..	..	..	..	..	..1	..1	..1	..	..
11 Apr	Real Madrid (SF)	A	L	1-3	..	..	..	..	Blanchflower	..	..	..	..1	..	..
25 Apr	Real Madrid (SF)	†H	D	2-2	..	..	..	..	..	..	..	..1	Charlton 1	..	..
†at Maine Road															

Appearances (goals)

Player	Apps	Goals
Bent	8	
Berry	40	8
Blanchflower	11	
Byrne	36	
Charlton	14	10
Clayton	2	
Colman	36	1
Cope	2	
Dawson	3	3
Doherty	3	
Edwards	34	5
Foulkes	39	
Goodwin	8	
Greaves	3	
Hawksworth	1	
Jones M	29	
McGuinness	13	
Pegg	37	6
Scanlon	5	2
Taylor T	32	22
Viollet	27	16
Webster	5	3
Whelan	39	26
Wood	39	
Own goals		1
Total 24 players		**103**

Football League

	P	W	D	L	F:A		Etc
Manchester U	42	28	8	8	103:54	64	1st

SEASON 1957-1958 FOOTBALL LEAGUE (DIVISION 1)

Date	Opponent	V	R	Score	1	2	3	4	5	6	7	8	9	10	11
24 Aug	Leicester C	A	W	3-0	Wood	Foulkes	Byrne	Colman	Blanchflower	Edwards	Berry	Whelan3	Taylor T	Viollet	Pegg
28 Aug	Everton	H	W	*3-0	..	..	..	..	..	..	..	..1	..1	..	..
31 Aug	Manchester C	H	W	4-1	..	..	..	..	..	..1	..	..1	..1	..1	..
4 Sep	Everton	A	D	3-3	..	..	..	..	..	..1	..1	..1	..	..1	..
7 Sep	Leeds U	H	W	5-0	..	..	..	..	..	..2	..	..	..2	..1	..
9 Sep	Blackpool	A	W	4-1	..	..	..	..	..	..	..2	..	..	..2	..
14 Sep	Bolton W	A	L	0-4	..	..	..	..	..	..	..	..	..	..	..
18 Sep	Blackpool	H	L	1-2	..	..	..	..	..	..1	..	..	..	..	..
21 Sep	Arsenal	H	W	4-2	..	..	..	..	..	..	..	..2	..1	..	..1
28 Sep	Wolverhampton W	A	L	1-3	..	..	McGuinness	Goodwin	Jones M	McGuinness	..	Doherty1	..	Charlton	..
5 Oct	Aston Villa	H	W	*4-1	..	..	Byrne	Colman	Blanchflower	Edwards	..	Whelan	..1	Viollet1	..
12 Oct	Nottingham F	A	W	2-1	..	..	..	..	Blanchflower	Edwards	..	..1	Dawson	Viollet1	..
19 Oct	Portsmouth	H	L	0-3	..	..	Jones MP	..	..	McGuinness	..	..	Dawson	..	..
26 Oct	W B A	A	L	3-4	..	..	Byrne	Goodwin	..	Edwards	..	..1	Taylor T2	Charlton	Webster
2 Nov	Burnley	H	W	1-0	..	..	..	..	..	..	..	..	..	..	..1
9 Nov	Preston NE	A	D	1-1	..	..	..	..	..	..	..	..1	..	..	..
16 Nov	Sheffield Wed	H	W	2-1	..	..	..	Colman	..	..	..	..	..	..2	..
23 Nov	Newcastle U	A	W	2-1	..	..	..	..	..	..1	Scanlon	..1	..	..	..
30 Nov	Tottenham H	H	L	3-4	Gaskell	..	..	..	..	..	..	..	Webster	Charlton	..2
7 Dec	Birmingham C	A	D	3-3	Wood	..	..	..	Jones M	..	Berry	..	Taylor T1	Viollet2	..
14 Dec	Chelsea	H	L	0-1	..	..	..	..	..	..	..	..	..	..	..
21 Dec	Leicester C	H	W	4-0	Gregg	..	..	..	..	..	Morgans	Charlton1	..	..	Scanlon1
25 Dec	Luton T	H	W	3-0	..	..	..	..	..	..1	..	..	..1	..	..
26 Dec	Luton T	A	D	2-2	..	..	..	..	..	..	Berry	..	..1	..	..
28 Dec	Manchester C	A	D	2-2	..	..	..	..	..	..	Morgans	..	Dawson	..1	..1
11 Jan	Leeds U	A	D	1-1	..	..	..	..	..	..	..	..	Taylor T	..1	..
18 Jan	Bolton W	H	W	7-2	..	..	..	..	..	..1	..	..3	..1	..2	..1
1 Feb	Arsenal	A	W	5-4	..	..	..	..	..	..	..	..2	..1	..	..
22 Feb	Nottingham F	H	D	1-1	..	..	Greaves	Goodwin	Cope	Crowther	Webster	Taylor E	Dawson	Pearson	Brennan
8 Mar	W B A	H	L	0-4	..	..	..	..	..	Harrop	..	..	..	Charlton	..
15 Mar	Burnley	A	L	0-3	..	..	..	Cope	..	Crowther	..	Harrop	..	..	..
29 Mar	Sheffield Wed	A	L	0-1	..	..	..	..	Greaves	..	..	Taylor E	..	Charlton	Brennan
31 Mar	Aston Villa	A	L	2-3	..	..	..	..	..	..	..1	Pearson	..1	..	..
4 Apr	Sunderland	H	D	2-2	..	..	..	Greaves	Cope	..	..	Taylor E	..	..	..
5 Apr	Preston NE	H	D	0-0	..	..	..	..	..	Morgans	..	..	Webster	..	Heron
7 Apr	Sunderland	A	W	2-1	..	..	..	..	Harrop	McGuinness	..	..2	..	..	Pearson
12 Apr	Tottenham H	A	L	0-1	..	..	..	Cope	Crowther	..	..	..	..	..	..
16 Apr	Portsmouth	A	D	3-3	..	..	..	Crowther	..	McGuinness	Dawson1	..1	..	Pearson	Morgans
19 Apr	Birmingham C	H	L	0-2	..	..	..	Goodwin	Crowther	..	..	..	..	..	..
21 Apr	Wolverhampton W	H	L	0-4	..	..	..	..	Crowther	McGuinness	..	Brennan	Viollet	..	..
23 Apr	Newcastle U	H	D	1-1	..	..	..	Crowther	..	..	Taylor E	..	Charlton	..	..
26 Apr	Chelsea	A	L	1-2	..	..	..	Goodwin	..	Crowther	..	..1	Charlton	Viollet	Webster

FA Cup

Date	Opponent	V	R	Score	1	2	3	4	5	6	7	8	9	10	11
4 Jan	Workington T (3)	A	W	3-1	Gregg	Foulkes	Byrne	Colman	Jones M	Edwards	Morgans	Charlton	Taylor T	Viollet3	Scanlon
25 Jan	Ipswich T (4)	H	W	2-0	..	..	..	..	..	..	..	..2	..	..	..

Appearances (goals)

Player	Apps	Goals
Berry	20	4
Blanchflower	18	
Brennan	5	
Byrne	25	
Charlton	21	8
Colman	24	
Cope	13	
Crowther	11	
Dawson	12	5
Doherty	1	1
Edwards	26	6
Foulkes	42	
Gaskell	3	
Goodwin	16	
Greaves	12	
Gregg	19	
Harrop	5	
Heron	1	
Jones M	10	
Jones P	1	
McGuinness	7	
Morgans	13	
Pearson	8	
Pegg	21	4
Scanlon	9	3
Taylor E	11	2
Taylor T	25	16
Viollet	22	16
Webster	20	6
Whelan	20	12
Wood R	20	
Own goals		2
Total 31 players		**85**

Football League

	P	W	D	L	F:A	Pts	
Wolverhampton W	42	28	8	6	103:47	64	1st
Manchester U	42	16	11	15	85:75	43	9th

Abbreviations:

Appearances (goals) refer to League games only

Figures shown as 2 etc. refer to goals scored by individual players

* own-goal

Date	Opponent	V	R	Score											
19 Feb	Sheffield Wed (5)	H	W	3-0	..	..	Greaves	Goodwin	Cope	Crowther	Webster	Taylor E	Dawson1	Pearson	Brennan2 / Charlton
1 Mar	W B A (6)	A	D	2-2	..	..	..	..	..	..	..1	..1	..1	..	
5 Mar	W B A (6R)	H	W	1-0	..	..	..	..	..	Harrop	..	..	..	Charlton2	Pearson
22 Mar	Fulham (SF) (at Villa Park)	N	D	2-2	..	..	..	..	..	Crowther	..	..	..	Charlton2	Pearson
26 Mar	Fulham (SFR) (at Highbury)	N	W	5-3	..	..	..	..	..	..	..	..	..3	..1	Brennan1
3 May	Bolton W (F) (at Wembley)	N	L	0-2	..	..	..	..	..	..	Dawson	..	Charlton	Viollet	Webster

European Cup

Date	Opponent	V	R	Score											
25 Sep	Shamrock R (P)	A	W	6-0	Wood	Foulkes	Byrne	Goodwin	Blanchflower	Edwards	Berry1	Whelan2	Taylor T2	Viollet	Pegg1
2 Oct	Shamrock R (P)	H	W	3-2	..	..	..	Colman	..	..	..	Webster	..	..	..1
21 Nov	Dukla Prague (1)	H	W	3-0	..	..	..	..	Blanchflower	Edwards	..	Whelan	..1	Webster1	..1
4 Dec	Dukla Prague (1)	A	L	0-1	..	..	..	..	Jones M	..	Scanlon	..	..	..	..
14 Jan	Red Star Belgrade (2)	H	W	2-1	Gregg	..	..	..1	..	..	Morgans	Charlton1	..	Viollet	Scanlon
5 Feb	Red Star Belgrade (2)	A	D	3-3	..	..	..	..	..	..	..2	..1	..	..1	..1
8 May	A C Milan (SF)	H	W	2-1	..	..	Greaves	Goodwin	Cope	Crowther	..	Taylor E1	Webster	..1	Pearson
14 May	A C Milan (SF)	A	L	0-4	..	..	..	..	..	..	..	..	..	..	..

SEASON 1958-1959 FOOTBALL LEAGUE (DIVISION 1)

Date	Opponent	V	R	Score											
23 Aug	Chelsea	H	W	5-2	Gregg	Foulkes	Greaves	Goodwin	Cope	McGuinness	Dawson	Taylor E	Viollet	Charlton3	Scanlon
27 Aug	Nottingham F	A	W	3-0	..	..	..	..	..	..	..	..	..	..2	..1
30 Aug	Blackpool	A	L	1-2	..	..	..	..	..	..	..	..	..1	..	
3 Sep	Nottingham F	H	D	1-1	..	..	..	..	..	..	Webster1	..	..2	..1	..
6 Sep	Blackburn R	H	W	6-1	..	..	..	..	..	..	..1	..	..	..2	..1
8 Sep	West Ham U	A	L	2-3	..	..	..	..	..	Crowther	..	..	..	..1	..
13 Sep	Newcastle U	A	D	1-1	..	..	..	..	..	McGuinness	..1	..	Dawson	..	..3
17 Sep	West Ham U	H	W	4-1	..	..	..	..	..	..	..2	Quixall	..	..	
20 Sep	Tottenham H	H	D	2-2	..	..	..	..	..	..	Viollet	..	Webster	..1	
27 Sep	Manchester C	A	D	1-1	..	..	..	..	..	..	..	..	Pearson	..	
4 Oct	Wolverhampton W	A	L	0-4	Wood	..	..	..	..	Harrop	Crowther	..	Dawson	Charlton	
8 Oct	Preston NE	H	L	0-2	Gregg	..	..	..	Cope	McGuinness	..	Taylor E	Quixall	Charlton	Taylor E
11 Oct	Arsenal	H	D	1-1	..	..	..	..	..	..	..1	..	Charlton	
18 Oct	Everton	A	L	2-3	..	..	..	..	..2	..	..	Dawson	Charlton	
25 Oct	W B A	H	L	1-2	..	..	..	..	..1	Harrop	..	..	..	
1 Nov	Leeds U	A	W	2-1	..	..	..	..	..1	..	Morgans	..	..	..1
8 Nov	Burnley	H	L	1-3	..	..	..	..	..	..	..1	..	
15 Nov	Bolton W	A	L	3-6	..	..	..	..	Cope	..	Bradley	Viollet1	..2	
22 Nov	Luton T	H	W	2-1	..	..	Carolan	..	..	..	..1	..	..2	
29 Nov	Birmingham C	A	W	4-0	..	..	..	..	..	..	..1	..1	..1	
6 Dec	Leicester C	H	W	4-1	..	..	..	..	..	..	..1	..1	..1	
13 Dec	Preston NE	A	W	4-3	..	..	..	..	..	..	..1	Pearson	..1	
20 Dec	Chelsea	A	W	*3-2	..	..	..1	..	..	..	..1	..1	
26 Dec	Aston Villa	H	W	2-1	..	..	..	Greaves	..	..	Hunter	..	..1	Charlton2
27 Dec	Aston Villa	A	W	2-0	..	..	..	Carolan	..	..	Bradley	..	..1	
3 Jan	Blackpool	H	W	3-1	..	..	..	..	..	..	..	..1	..2	..1
31 Jan	Newcastle U	H	D	4-4	..	..	..	Harrop	Goodwin	..	..	..1	..1
7 Feb	Tottenham H	A	W	3-1	..	Greaves	..	Goodwin	Cope	..	..1	..1	..1
16 Feb	Manchester C	H	W	4-1	..	..	..	..1	..	..2	..1	..1
21 Feb	Wolverhampton W	H	W	2-1	..	..	..	..	..1	..	..1
28 Feb	Arsenal	A	L	2-3	..	..	..	..	..1	..	..2	..1
2 Mar	Blackburn R	A	W	3-1	..	..	..	..	..1	..1
7 Mar	Everton	H	W	2-1	..	..	..	..1	..	..1
14 Mar	W B A	A	W	3-1	..	..	..	..1	..3	..1
21 Mar	Leeds U	H	W	4-0	..	..	..	..2	..1
27 Mar	Portsmouth	H	W	*6-1	..	..	..	..1	..1	..2
28 Mar	Burnley	A	L	2-4	..	..	..1	..	..1	..1
30 Mar	Portsmouth	A	W	3-1	..	..	..	Foulkes	..	..1	..2	..1
4 Apr	Bolton W	H	W	3-1	..	..	..	..	..1
11 Apr	Luton T	A	D	0-0	..	..	..	Pearson	
18 Apr	Birmingham C	H	W	1-0	..	..	..	..1	Charlton
25 Apr	Leicester C	A	L	1-2	..	..	..	Brennan	..1

FA Cup

Date	Opponent	V	R	Score											
10 Jan	Norwich C (3)	A	L	0-3	Gregg	Foulkes	Carolan	Goodwin	Cope	McGuinness	Bradley	Quixall	Viollet	Charlton	Scanlon

Appearances (goals)

Player	Apps	Goals
Bradley	24	12
Brennan	1	
Carolan	23	
Charlton	38	29
Cope	32	2
Crowther	2	
Dawson	11	4
Foulkes	32	
Goodwin	42	6
Greaves	34	
Gregg	41	
Harrop	5	
Hunter	1	
McGuinness	39	1
Morgans	2	
Pearson	4	1
Quixall	33	4
Scanlon	42	16
Taylor E	11	
Viollet	37	21
Webster	7	5
Wood	1	
Own goals		2
Total 22 players		**103**

Football League

	P	W	D	L	F:A	Pts	
Wolves	42	28	5	9	110:49	61	1st
Manchester U	42	24	7	11	103:66	55	2nd

SEASON 1959-1960 FOOTBALL LEAGUE (DIVISION 1)

Date	Opponent	V	R	Score											
22 Aug	W B A	A	L	2-3	Gregg	Greaves	Carolan	Goodwin	Foulkes	McGuinness	Bradley	Quixall	Viollet2 / Dawson	Charlton / Viollet	Scanlon / Charlton
26 Aug	Chelsea	H	L	0-1	..	Cope	..	..	..	..	..	..2	Viollet2	Charlton1	Scanlon
29 Aug	Newcastle U	H	W	3-2	..	..	..	Brennan	..	..	..2	..1	..2	..1	..1
2 Sep	Chelsea	A	W	6-3	..	..	..	..	..	..	..	..2	..	..	..1
5 Sep	Birmingham C	A	D	1-1	..	..	..	..	..	..	..2	..	..1	..2	..1
9 Sep	Leeds U	H	W	6-0	..	..	..	..	..	..	..	Giles	..1	..	
12 Sep	Tottenham H	H	L	1-5	..	..	..	Goodwin	..	..	..	Quixall	..	..1	
16 Sep	Leeds U	A	D	*2-2	..	..	Foulkes	Brennan	Cope	..	..	..	..1	
19 Sep	Manchester C	A	L	0-3	..	..	..	Viollet	..	..	Dawson	..	
26 Sep	Preston NE	A	L	0-4	..	..	..	Goodwin	..	..	Viollet2	..1	
3 Oct	Leicester C	H	W	4-1	Gaskell	..	..	..	..	..1	..1	
10 Oct	Arsenal	H	W	*4-2	Gregg	..	..	..	..	Giles	..1	Pearson	
17 Oct	Wolverhampton W	A	L	*2-3	..	..	..	..	Quixall	..2	Charlton	
24 Oct	Sheffield Wed	H	W	3-1	..	..	..	..	..1	
31 Oct	Blackburn R	A	D	1-1	..	..	..	..	..1	..1	
7 Nov	Fulham	H	D	3-3	..	..	..	..	..1	..1	Dawson1
14 Nov	Bolton W	A	D	1-1	..	..	..	..	..2	Scanlon
21 Nov	Luton T	H	W	4-1	..	..	..1	..	..1	
28 Nov	Everton	A	L	1-2	..	..	..	..	..1	
5 Dec	Blackpool	H	W	3-1	Gaskell	..	..	Brennan	Dawson	..2	Pearson
12 Dec	Nottingham F	A	W	5-1	..	..	..	..1	..3	
19 Dec	W B A	H	L	2-3	..	..	..	..	..1	Charlton
28 Dec	Burnley	H	L	1-2	..	..	..	..	..2	
26 Dec	Burnley	A	W	4-1	..	..	..	..2	..2
2 Jan	Newcastle U	A	L	3-7	..	..	..	..1	
16 Jan	Birmingham C	H	W	2-1	Gregg	..	Setters	Bradley	..1	
23 Jan	Tottenham H	A	L	1-2	..	..	..	..1	
6 Feb	Manchester C	H	D	0-0	..	..	..	
13 Feb	Preston NE	H	D	1-1	..	..	..	..	..1	
24 Feb	Leicester C	A	L	1-3	..	..	Viollet	..	Dawson	..3	..1
27 Feb	Blackpool	A	W	6-0	..	..	..	..1	
5 Mar	Wolverhampton W	H	L	0-2	..	..	Giles	Viollet	..1	Pearson	Charlton2
19 Mar	Nottingham F	H	W	3-1	..	..	..1	..2	..1	..1	
26 Mar	Fulham	A	W	5-0	Gaskell	..	Heron	..	..1	
30 Mar	Sheffield Wed	A	L	2-4	..	..	Carolan	Bradley	Giles	..2
7 Apr	Bolton W	H	W	2-0	..	..	..	..1	
9 Apr	Luton T	A	W	3-2	Gregg	..	..	..2	Lawton	Scanlon
15 Apr	West Ham U	A	L	1-2	..	..	..	..1	Charlton
16 Apr	Blackburn R	H	W	1-0	..	..	..	..1	
18 Apr	West Ham U	H	W	5-3	..	..	Giles	Quixall	..2	Viollet	..2
23 Apr	Arsenal	A	L	2-5	..	..	..	Pearson1	
30 Apr	Everton	H	W	5-0	..	..	..	Bradley1	..1	..3	

FA Cup

Date	Opponent	V	R	Score											
9 Jan	Derby Co (3)	A	W	*4-2	Gregg	Foulkes	Carolan	Goodwin1 / Setters	Cope	Brennan	Damson / Bradley1	Quixall	Viollet	Charlton1	Scanlon1
30 Jan	Liverpool (4)	H	W	3-1	..	..	..	..	..	..	Bradley1	..	..2	..	
20 Feb	Sheffield Wed (5)	A	L	0-1	..	..	..	..	..	..	..	..	..	..	

Appearances (goals)

Player	Apps	Goals
Bradley	29	8
Brennan	29	
Carolan	41	
Charlton	37	18
Cope	40	
Dawson	22	15
Foulkes	42	
Gaskell	9	
Giles	10	2
Goodwin	18	1
Greaves	2	
Gregg	33	
Heron	1	
Lawton	3	
McGuinness	19	
Pearson	10	3
Quixall	33	13
Scanlon	31	7
Setters	17	
Viollet	36	32
Own goals		3
Total 20 players		**102**

Football League

	P	W	D	L	F:A	Pts	
Burnley	42	24	7	11	85:61	55	1st
Manchester U	42	19	7	16	102:80	45	7th

1950-1959

CHAPTER 4
THE 1960s: GREATNESS AND GLORY

The great side of the 1960s

Some men are born great, some achieve greatness and some have greatness thrust upon them. Jimmy Murphy came to appreciate what Shakespeare had in mind when Busby whispered to him: 'Keep the flag flying', and suddenly the responsibility for the survival of Manchester United was laid on his shoulders.

A ticket stub for the 1958 Cup Final clash with Bolton. Post-Munich Manchester United proved that they were still a footballing force with a Cup run that saw them beat Sheffield Wednesday, West Bromwich Albion and Fulham

How do you continue playing a game against a background of death and destruction with so much suffering and grief? As Jimmy wrote in his book:

At first I felt as if I was going out of my mind, not knowing where to start. Previously Old Trafford had worked like a machine with Matt at the top presiding over all our efforts, sound in judgement and experience, with that incredible flair for public relations, always courteous, urbane and seemingly never forgetting anyone's face, so that he was always able to put people at their ease and talk to them.

But now I had to try and keep the club in business, without Matt's guidance and strength to fall back on, without dear Bert Whalley's unflagging energy and zeal for the club, without Tom Curry, the quiet-spoken yet highly professional team trainer, who also had a lifetime of football experience to draw on. On the administrative side we had lost the club secretary, Walter Crickmer, a man with a shrewd brain which worked with a computer-like efficiency.

Murphy's problem was to get a side out for the next match, but he also had to attend to the survivors, help the bereaved and go to the funerals. He did all these things. Cometh the hour, cometh the man, and though he started in management as an assistant and retired in a similar capacity, during his time in command he brought order out of chaos and was a born leader.

Jimmy Murphy assembled the boys and his new signings to beat Sheffield Wednesday in the rearranged fifth round of the FA Cup. He took away his youngsters to prepare them for men's work in the comparative calm of the Norbreck Hydro Hotel at Blackpool. For the rest the season he kept taking his squad to the Norbreck, so that many of the accompanying football writers will forever associate the smell of the chlorine from the indoor baths with those emotional weeks in the aftermath of Munich.

Three days after United beat Wednesday in that emotional post-Munich Cup-tie they were plunged back into League football with 66,000 packed into Old Trafford to see a 1-1 draw with Nottingham Forest. The patched-up team won only one of the remaining 14 League fixtures after Munich, but they never lost heart. They picked up five draws which with the win at Sunderland saw them hang on for an extremely commendable ninth place.

Left: 18 April 1958 and Matt Busby is home again. Seventy-one days after the air crash the United manager arrives at his home in Kings Road, Chorlton, to be welcomed by a group of supporters. For the schoolboys of the fifties the effect of the Munich disaster was lasting: those who followed the club at that time would always remain loyal. They had lost their heroes and would find new ones under the leadership of Busby

United march to Wembley

United's really sterling efforts came in the FA Cup, of course. After beating Sheffield Wednesday they had to travel to West Bromwich for the sixth round. They ran themselves ragged to lead 2-1 with four minutes to go, but then Harry Gregg was ruled to have carried a cross over his goal line. It didn't matter, as inspired by the Old Trafford crowd and Bobby Charlton's return they won the replay 1-0. Colin Webster provided the winner after a last-minute run down the wing by Charlton.

Then it was back to the Midlands for a 2-2 draw in the semi-final at Villa Park with Fulham. The replay at Highbury, with Fulham enjoying almost a home tie, was a momentous match, won by United 5-3 with the help of a hat-trick from Alex Dawson, nicknamed the Black Prince. So United were through to Wembley for a final against Bolton. A telephone call from Munich saying that Matt Busby was no longer on the danger list seemed to set the seal on a truly remarkable achievement.

Nat Lofthouse, the legendary 'Lion of Vienna' after his exploits for England in Austria, and the Bolton captain, recalls the final vividly:

Some of the fellows who died at Munich were among my pals. Barely a fortnight before the disaster I was having a drink with them at Old Trafford after they had thrashed us 7-2 in the League.

The thousands of neutrals at Wembley wanted United to beat us. Their incredible fight-back from Munich had captured the imagination of the world. We walked out of that tunnel into an incredibly emotional atmosphere. But I would not be honest if I did not say that I was only interested in beating them. I was a professional who played for Bolton Wanderers. All that mattered was for Bolton to win the FA Cup.

The teams for the final were:

BOLTON: Hopkinson, Hartle, Banks, Hennin, Higgins, Edwards, Birch, Stevens, Lofthouse, Parry, Holden

MANCHESTER UNITED: Gregg, Foulkes, Greaves, Goodwin, Cope, Crowther, Dawson, Taylor, Charlton, Viollet, Webster

Had United scored first, it is likely that the wave which carried them to Wembley would have engulfed Bolton. But Lofthouse saw to it that whatever the Reds wanted they would have to fight for. Inside five minutes the old warhorse struck the first decisive blow. A corner from Holden was only half cleared and fell to the feet of Bryan Edwards. His centre towards the far post was met by Lofthouse, whose low drive gave Gregg no chance. It was as if

Above: Jimmy Murphy leads out the team at Wembley for the 1958 FA Cup final. Matt Busby was there as a spectator on sticks, barely recovered from the Munich accident. United had battled on after the crash, carried on a tide of emotion through ties against Sheffield Wednesday, West Bromwich Albion and Fulham. Though the second goal by Nat Lofthouse when he knocked goalkeeper Harry Gregg into the back of the net was controversial, Bolton were worthy winners

Left: Harry Gregg receives treatment after Nat Lofthouse's infamous goal in the '58 Cup final. Gregg had caught the ball after initially parrying a shot from Bolton's Dennis Stevens. Lofthouse ran in and clearly barged Gregg over the line. The goal was given by Sheffield referee J. Sherlock

in that moment the Red bubble had burst – as if the tragic events of the recent past had suddenly caught up with them.

Deflated, they fell apart. A terrific drive from Charlton did crash against the Bolton upright, and had that gone in the magic may have stirred them again. But within minutes Bolton scored again at the other end . . . although it was a goal which to this day the United lads claim should never have been allowed. Dennis Stevens hit a fierce shot from out on the left. Gregg, perhaps deceived by the pace of the shot, could only palm the ball into the air. As he jumped to catch it, the onrushing Lofthouse barged the ball and Gregg into the back of the net. Even Lofthouse could hardly believe his luck when referee Sherlock awarded a goal:

I am quite convinced that I did foul Gregg, but you could hardly expect me to argue when the referee gave a goal!

The heroes of the post-Munich season

The following season might have been expected to come as an anti-climax. Certainly another Wembley trip was soon out of the picture with a third round exit at Norwich, but in the League the Reds finished the 1958-59 season as runners-up behind Wolves.

That was an incredible achievement and it was done without any dramatic rush into the transfer market. Dennis Viollet and

1960-69

Albert Scanlon returned to action after recovering from injuries.

Warren Bradley, an England amateur international winger from Bishop Auckland was signed midway through the season and Matt Busby had recovered sufficiently by the end of September to pay a then record £45,000 for Albert Quixall from Sheffield Wednesday. The rest of the team was made up of reserves and, of course, the youngsters. The success of the team spoke volumes for the quality of the juniors who had been working in the shadow of the Busby Babes.

The team took a few weeks to settle, but a run of 11 wins out of 12 games between November and February put them in the frame with the Wolverhampton team of Stan Cullis. United was a team built for attack and they netted more than a 100 League goals with 29 from Charlton, the best scoring season of his career, 21 from Viollet, 16 from Scanlon and 12 from 24 appearances by Bradley.

The team had emerged by the end of the season to line up:

Gregg, Greaves, Carolan, Goodwin, Foulkes (Cope), McGuinness, Bradley, Quixall, Viollet, Charlton, Scanlon

Both inside-forward Ernie Taylor and wing-half Stan Crowther, the emergency signings after Munich, had departed, their brief but vital holding missions accomplished. They had helped give United a breathing space, Crowther bringing vigour to the team while Taylor used his experience to put his foot on the ball and direct operations. He had played only 30 League and

Bobby Charlton rides a challenge from Tommy Banks during the 1958 FA Cup Final

Cup games for United, but the little general had been priceless. He was 33, with his great years of winning FA Cup medals with Newcastle and Blackpool well behind him. He was only 5ft 4in (1.63m), with tiny feet, but his reading of the game and his passing more than made up for the lack of inches. United let him move on to his home team of Sunderland and he still managed another 70 games before going into non-League football with Altrincham. He died in 1985. His short career at Old Trafford had been long enough to see others pick up the baton.

Bobby Charlton

Bobby Charlton went into Munich a boy and came out of that season a man. He had of course already given ample notice of his prodigious talent in the youth team and as a young player beginning to nudge the original Busby Babes. His 14 appearances and 10 goals had brought him a championship medal in 1957 and he had won a first-team place again just before the crash. He says about those early days leading up to his League debut in a 4-2 win at Charlton Athletic in October 1956:

I thought I was never going to get into the team. I was scoring a lot of goals in the reserves and I kept thinking surely Matt Busby would play me now. Everyone kept telling me I would get a game soon, but it never seemed to happen. Ironically three weeks before my debut I sprained my ankle in a collision with Keith Marsden of Manchester City when playing for the reserves. Then just before the Charlton match, Sir Matt asked me if I was OK. Actually I wasn't, but I wasn't going to let my long awaited chance go by, so I crossed my fingers and said yes.

The Boss said good and that I would be playing the next day. I carried the leg a little, but it went well for me and I managed to score two goals, one from close in and one from outside the box. I was still dropped for the next game, which just shows you how severe the competition was that season. I had played in place of Tommy Taylor who had been injured and he was fit again so had to come back.

I got back into the team for the following match in place of the injured Dennis Viollet, and that's how it went for the rest of the season, in and out whenever Tommy, Dennis or Billy Whelan was injured. I didn't become a regular until the following season, about two months before the Munich accident. Then I was in off my own bat. In those days they didn't put you in until you were really ready. For ages they just seemed to move the more experienced players around.

Bobby Charlton was such an outstanding figure at Old Trafford and played for such a long time that it is difficult to know at what point of the club's history a tribute should be made. He had many fine moments in his career for both Manchester United and England, spanning 17 seasons of First Division football.

In terms of facts and figures, Charlton made 604 League appearances, scoring 198 goals, a club record on both counts which looks capable of standing for all time. In the FA Cup he played in 78 ties to score 20 goals. In European competition he made 45 appearances for a tally of 22 goals. He collected three championship medals, an FA Cup winner's medal in 1963 and of course the European Cup winner's medal in 1968, as well as helping to win the World Cup for England in 1966 in an international career of 106 appearances, during which he set a scoring record of 49 goals, another achievement likely to stand the test of time.

He was awarded the OBE in 1969, and the CBE in 1974. In 1966 he was voted Footballer of the Year in both England and Europe. But even the stream of honours and medals don't really do justice to his career, because there was both a warmth and a dignity about him which endeared him not just to Manchester United fans, but to followers of football all over the world.

It was certainly a fitting move by the board of Manchester United when they asked him to become a director in 1986, an invitation which keeps alive great traditions of the past while introducing an able man who will contribute to the future. But this is running on far ahead of our story. Bobby Charlton in 1959 was a fledgling. He had joined United as a schoolboy from Ashington in Northumberland. He came from good footballing stock, his mother, Cissie, being from the well-known Milburn soccer family. Two uncles, Jim and George, played for Leeds. Uncle Stan played for Leicester. His cousin Jackie Milburn was Newcastle United's great centre-forward of the 1950s.

Bobby did not have an easy apprenticeship. Murphy reckons they had to work hard on him to improve his short-passing game and curb his tendency to hit speculative long balls all the time. Charlton well remembers the lessons. 'Jimmy used to play with us in practice matches and he used to come up behind me and kick me on the back of the legs. I think he was trying to toughen me up, and also perhaps to encourage me to pass the ball a bit quicker,' he says now.

Certainly Bobby proved a quick learner as he emerged after Munich as one of the key players round whom Manchester United could build. He missed two games immediately after the crash and then resumed playing with a heightened responsibility. By the start of the 1958-59 season he was in full flow.

Really United had no right to finish runners-up after the grievous blow suffered at Munich just the previous season. Such a position was really beyond their wildest dreams and even Busby admitted that it had been far better than he had expected.

What was so startling of course was that the club had been able to find so many players from within. Warren Bradley enjoyed great success after joining as an amateur. He was quickly launched into the England team and won three caps to add to 11 amateur appearances. Born in Hyde, Cheshire, he was a school teacher and soon made himself at home among the elite.

Bobby Charlton scoring against Burnley in 1966/67. Charlton proved himself to be a match winner. His career saw him win everything the game had to offer and Bobby received a knighthood in 1994

Albert Quixall

The only real concession United had made to the transfer market following the emergency signings of Taylor and Crowther was in recruiting inside-forward Albert Quixall from Hillsborough. The blond-haired Yorkshireman was bought in keeping with Busby's policy of putting players on to the Old Trafford stage who had personality and entertainment value as well as being able to do a job of work. Albert was the golden boy of his day. In his native Sheffield he had swept everything before him . . . captain of his school, his city, his county, his country and then playing for the full England team by the age of 18.

1960-69

Quixall helped to maintain the Busby tradition for creative, skilful football in a difficult period. He had charisma, though he didn't make a fortune from football. Looking back he says: 'I suppose I was born 20 years too early. I remember an article on me at the time saying that my record transfer fee made me worth my weight in gold. Perhaps that was true, but it didn't do much for me personally. I don't harp on that though because you can't translate everything into money. I achieved a lot in my teens and had some great times in football. I'm not bitter by any means.'

You could hardly blame him if he was. Working after football for years in a scrap metal yard near Manchester where he settled, he was young enough to see near-contemporaries prosper out of all proportion with a fraction of his talent . . . yet he was too old to have caught the gravy train himself.

Dennis Viollet

Dennis Viollet was another supremely gifted player who hit the heights just a little too soon to catch the explosion in football wages and finances. Dennis, a local youngster who grew up playing ball around Maine Road, was in fact a Manchester City fan like the rest of his family. Joe Armstrong and Jimmy Murphy persuaded him to come to Old Trafford and his career straddled the Munich disaster. He was one of the Busby Babes who survived the crash to play a vital role in the rebuilding period.

Viollet's best season came as United embarked on the 1959-60 season, hoping to build on their runners-up position of the previous season. That they finished only seventh was hardly the fault of Viollet, who broke Jack Rowley's club scoring record by notching 32 League goals.

He was a master craftsman, a sleek ghost of a player who scored goals with stealth, skill and speed. He was not a robust centre-forward, but his rather frail-looking appearance belied his strength. He was resilient, and overall he scored 159 goals in 259 League appearances over ten seasons of first-team soccer.

He eventually left Old Trafford in 1962 to play for Stoke, and helped them win the Second Division Championship for Tony Waddington. He played in the States for a spell, then after winning an Irish FA Cup winners' medal with Linfield he settled in America, becoming involved in their football. His next visits to England were to accompany his talented tennis daughter on trips to play at Junior Wimbledon.

Viollet's record scoring season should have brought him more than two caps for England. There was, in fact, a case to be made out around 1960 for playing the entire United forward line at international level. United again topped 100 League goals in that 1959-60 season, with Dennis's 32 being followed by 18 from Charlton, 13 from Quixall, and eight and seven from wingers Bradley and Scanlon.

United were too erratic to win the title. One week they would score four, the next they would concede four. Things came to a head in January when the team lost 7-3 at Newcastle. Busby suddenly swooped on the transfer market and paid £30,000 for wing-half Maurice Setters from West Bromwich Albion. He wanted the bandy-legged, tough-tackling Setters to stiffen the midfield. What a contrast he made with Quixall. Their styles were completely different and there was no love lost between them.

It was a period of consolidation for United, with Busby taking the rebuilding in steady fashion. At the end of 1960 he bought again, paying £29,000 for the West Ham and Republic of Ireland left-back Noel Cantwell.

The intelligent and articulate Irishman became a sound influence and a splendid captain. But there was no instant success with United unable to improve on seventh in the League in the 1960-61 season, and making a fourth-round exit in the FA Cup.

The 1961-62 season did bring a run in the Cup, United reaching the semi-finals only to lose 3-1 against Spurs at Hillsborough. The League, however, saw them slip to 15th. Busby knew it was time for action. There were not enough tal-

Even as a young man Bobby Charlton was the Pied Piper of football. Back home in Beatrice Street, Ashington, Northumberland, he shows the local youngsters how it's done at Old Trafford

ented youngsters coming through fast enough. Just before the start of the 1961-62 season he had bought centre-forward David Herd, son of his former team-mate Alex, from Arsenal for £32,000. Herd had obliged by scoring 14 goals, but the goal touch had deserted the others and Herd's tally was the best effort.

The arrival of Law and Crerand

So in the summer of 1962 Busby spent again and pulled off his best-ever transfer coup. He brought Denis Law home from Italy's Torino for a record £115,000.

United now had a twin strike force of Law and Herd, backed by Charlton and Quixall and a new youngster, Johnny Giles, with another home product, Nobby Stiles, occasionally forcing his way into the team at half-back.

Still it wasn't quite right. The attack looked full of goals, but they only clicked spasmodically. Busby decided that the service to the men up front wasn't good enough. So he went out to buy a player who could supply the right kind of ammunition for Law and Herd to fire. The result was the arrival, in February 1963 for £43,000 from Glasgow Celtic, of right-half Pat Crerand. Busby now had the right balance in the half-back line, Setters the ball-winner on the left and Crerand the distributor on the right.

It was too late to pull things round in the League and the Reds ended the 1962-63 season in 19th place, their lowest position under Busby's management. But the potential was there, and it showed in the FA Cup as the Reds sailed through every round without a replay, to beat Southampton 1-0 in the semi-final at Villa Park and face Leicester City at Wembley.

For a change, because of their League position, the Reds were the underdogs. Leicester had finished fourth in the First Division and had the reputation of being a side with an iron defence. So the stage was set for a clash between the irre-sistible force and the immovable object when the following teams took the field at Wembley on 25 May 1963:

MANCHESTER UNITED: Gaskell, Dunne, Cantwell, Crerand, Foulkes, Setters, Giles, Quixall, Herd, Law, Charlton

LEICESTER: Banks, Sjoberg, Norman, McLintock, King, Appleton, Riley, Cross, Keyworth, Gibson, Stringfellow

From the first whistle it was obvious that the Reds had torn up the form book. Law, in particular, was in one of those moods when it would have taken a Centurion tank to stop him. The famous Leicester 'iron curtain' looked more like a torn cur-tain, as Law danced through at will.

Crerand, who had taken time to settle into the side, was also having a field day on Wembley's wide-open spaces, and it was one of those inch-perfect passes which enabled Law to swivel and drive home the first goal after 29 minutes. The longer the game went on, the more composed and confident United looked. In the 58th minute, they underlined their superiority when Herd rounded off a sweet move, involving Giles and Charlton, by sweeping the ball past Gordon Banks. The game was as good as won. In a late flurry Keyworth scored for Leicester, but Herd grabbed his second to make the final scoreline 3-1 to United.

Gordon Banks clears from Denis Law at Wembley in 1963, but the Leicester City and England goalkeeper couldn't stop United winning 3-1 to take the FA Cup. It was sweet relief for United who struggled all season in the League, looking relegation candidates at one stage, and finishing in 19th place, the low water mark in Matt Busby's management career

The victory more than made up for the Reds' disappointing League form, and finally buried the memory of their two Wembley defeats in 1957 and 1958. More than that, it indicated that from the ashes of Munich, Busby was on the way towards building another side capable of taking English soccer by storm.

United had flexed their muscles and had given notice that they were back in business as a top team again. They looked forward to season 1963-64 in more confident mood, and used their Cup victory as a launching pad to go with more conviction for the big prizes. They didn't do too well in the European Cup Winners' Cup, squandering a first leg win of 4-1 against Sporting Lisbon by losing 5-0 in Portugal. It was United's most embarrassing defeat in their history and the story is told more fully in the chapter on Europe.

However, they reached the semi-finals of the FA Cup to play West Ham and finished runners-up in the League. Denis Law, the matador of Old Trafford, enjoyed his best scoring season in a year which was also significant for the debut in League football of a young, black-haired Irishman with flashing eyes.

Matt Busby gave George Best his first game on 14 September 1963, playing him at outside-right against West Bromwich Albion at Old Trafford. David Sadler, the young bank clerk from Maidstone, Kent, with whom he shared digs at Mrs Fullaway's in Davyhulme, scored in a 1-0 win.

Ian Moir replaced Best for the next League match, but Busby had noted his performance and called up the youngster to play against Burnley at Old Trafford in December. Busby was ringing the changes because two days previously, on Boxing Day, his team had gone down 6-1 at Turf Moor. Best came in for the return and scored in a sweet 5-1 revenge win.

The famous football litany of Charlton, Law and Best had now come together, though at this stage Best was very much the junior partner. The man at the height of his powers was Law, scoring a fantastic total of 46 goals in League and Cup. Thirty of them came from 30 League appearances, helping the Reds finish second to Liverpool, four points adrift. He scored ten in six FA Cup-ties and notched another eight in ten games in the European Cup Winners' Cup. There was the usual 20 from David Herd, while Bobby Charlton weighed in with nine, but Busby was still tinkering with the team.

He changed goalkeepers at one point, replacing Harry Gregg for a spell with David Gaskell. Halfway through he switched Tony Dunne to left-back in place of Noel Cantwell and brought in Shay Brennan at right-back. Inside-right was causing him problems with one of his youngsters, Phil Chisnall, dropped in favour of Graham Moore, the Welsh international. David Sadler was in and out, still searching for his best position, defender, midfield or striker. Nobby Stiles was brought in at left-half to take over from Maurice Setters, and give nothing away in terms of matching fire with fire. Ian Moir played half a season on the wing. There had probably been just a few too many changes to get the better of Liverpool, who proved their right to be champions by winning 1-0 at Old Trafford in November and then beating United 3-0 at Anfield on the run-in for the title. Those four points separated the two teams at the end of the season.

The kids won the FA Youth Cup after a seven-year gap, heralding the arrival of more promising youngsters.

George Best, Willie Anderson and David Sadler had already played in the first team. Other players from the successful youth team who went on to play in the League side were Jimmy Rimmer, the goalkeeper, full-back Bobby Noble, winger John Aston and wing-half John Fitzpatrick.

United were blooming again at all levels accompanied by imaginative development off the field. Plans were announced for the building of a new cantilever stand in readiness for Old Trafford as a venue for the 1966 World Cup. The bulk of the finance was to be raised by a football pool run by a Development Association on a scale not previously seen in soccer.

There was a buzz about the place again, though Busby knew he needed a more settled side than the one which had just chased Liverpool home, and despite his many changes he felt he needed a top-class winger. So during the summer of 1964 he bought the experienced John Connelly from Burnley

for £60,000. The winger, equally at home on either flank, had already won a League Cup medal and an FA Cup runners-up medal at Turf Moor and it proved to be an inspired signing.

Champions again

Connelly was the final piece in the jigsaw which turned a team of runners-up into champions. The whole thing fell into place as the Reds swept to success in season 1964-65, pipping Leeds United for the title. In the days when goal average, rather than difference, settled issues, United won by the narrow margin of 0.686 of a goal.

Celebration time for Pat Crerand, Albert Quixall and David Herd after winning the FA Cup in 1963. The Sheffield-born Quixall, crowned with the Cup, was the golden boy of his era, playing international football at every level and costing a then record fee of £45,000 from Sheffield Wednesday

United still had a game in hand when they knew they had won the Championship, so the final game at Villa Park didn't matter all that much and it was duly lost. The significant aspect was that they were champions for the first time since Munich. Bobby Charlton and Bill Foulkes were the only crash survivors remaining in the team.

Connelly more than played his part, scoring 15 goals from outside-right while Best dazzled on the left to score ten. Charlton, now operating in a midfield role, scored ten as well, while Law led the scoring with 28, supported again by 20 from

Herd. But while the forwards attracted the headlines, they owed a great deal to the defence. Bill Foulkes, the centre-half, and the two full-backs, Shay Brennan and Tony Dunne, were ever-presents. They conceded only 39 goals to help provide their personable new goalkeeper, Pat Dunne, with a championship medal. A modest £10,000 signing from Shamrock Rovers, Pat spent less than three seasons at United. He seemed to come from nowhere and disappear as quickly, but he played his part.

The team's championship qualities had not been immediately apparent when only one win had come in the opening six games, but they picked up thereafter, dropping only one point in their next 14 games. The highlight was a 7-0 thrashing of Aston Villa at Old Trafford with four of the goals down to Law.

They dropped a few points in mid-season, but put in another searing run of ten wins in 11 games to take the title.

United had an all-round strength now that also saw them do well in the other competitions. They were, in fact, chasing a treble for most of the season. They reached the semi-finals of the European Fairs Cup (later to become the UEFA Cup), and at the same time stormed through to the semi-finals of the FA Cup. It had been a mighty year with many memorable games on the three fronts, and they had made their mark with the Championship trophy back at Old Trafford to show for their efforts. The team, a well-balanced, strong side, showed few changes and the medals went to:

Pat Dunne, Brennan, Tony Dunne, Crerand, Foulkes, Stiles, Connelly, Charlton, Herd, Law, Best

Denis Law

Law was at his peak in that Championship season as the attacking star, yet when he had started his career in England with Huddersfield Town in 1955, Bill Shankly had said of him: 'He looked like a skinned rabbit.' But once Shankly had seen him play he knew that here was something special. After only 80 games, and with Huddersfield having slid into the Second Division, he was sold for £56,000 to First Division Manchester City.

City kept Law for a season and then made a handsome profit, selling him to Torino for £110,000, giving him what he describes as the worst 12 months of his life.

'It was like a prison' said Law. 'I am not one for the high life. All I wanted was to be treated like a human being. It wasn't long before I realised I had made a ghastly mistake. It all finally blew up when Torino refused me permission to play for Scotland. That was the end as far as I was concerned. I stormed out so quickly that I left all my clothes behind. I never saw them again.'

Torino threatened Law with all sorts of legal sanctions to try to get him back to Italy, but in the end they gave in. So on 12 July 1962, Denis Law signed for Manchester United for a record fee of £115,000. And what a marvellous deal it turned out to be. For a decade, the 'king' ruled over his Old Trafford empire. The United fans respected the skills of Bobby Charlton, they revelled at the sight of the genius which was George Best, but they worshipped Denis Law, the hero of the Stretford End.

'What I walked into from Italy was the finest football club in the world with the finest manager,' said Law. 'Matt Busby always stuck by me through thick and thin. Your problems at home, your illnesses, any little worries – they were all his business. That's what made him so different. That is why you gave everything for him on the field.'

Not that Law was always the apple of Busby's eye. Three times between 1963 and 1967, his fiery temperament landed him in trouble with referees. Twice he was suspended for 28 days. And that is not the type of record that endeared you to Matt Busby.

The Demon King was electric near goal. When he jumped he seemed to have a personal sky hook, so long did he hang in the air above defenders.

His razor reflexes and courage brought him 171 goals from 305 League appearances in his ten years at Old Trafford. In the FA Cup he had an incredible return of 34 goals in 44 appearances, while European competition brought him the even more impressive scoring rate of 28 goals in 33 matches. The Stretford End took him to their heart: they perhaps loved not just his goals but the streak of villainy that also ran through his game.

Denis Law signing for United in 1962 after a record fee of £115,000 brought him from Torino. It proved to be a bargain and he was instrumental in United's Championship seasons of '65 and '67

In July 1973, after battling against a knee injury for two years, United allowed him to join Manchester City on a free transfer in recognition of his services. The best way to illustrate the bond between Law and Old Trafford is to recall an incident in April 1974, when Law's back-heeled goal for City condemned United to another defeat as they headed for the Second Division. This time there was no punching of the air in celebration. Law, head down, walked slowly back to the centre circle with the look of a man who had just stabbed his best friend in the back.

Law scored 30 goals in 55 international appearances for Scotland. His career brought him 217 League goals in 452 games. After retiring in 1974, at the end of his second spell with Manchester City, he virtually hung up his boots. His bravery had left him with a legacy of injuries which wouldn't permit him to play any more. That was the price he paid for his storming career.

The other Championship winners

Like Law, there was something of the lost waif about George Best when he arrived at Old Trafford. He was a skinny 15-year-old from Belfast, desperately homesick at being away from home for the first time in his life. Indeed, after 24 hours, he and his young Irish companion from Belfast, Eric McMordie, fled back to Ireland. But Busby was quickly on the phone, and with the help of his father, George was persuaded to give it another go.

Best had been recommended by United's legendary Northern Ireland scout Bob Bishop, who sent this simple note to Busby: 'I think I have found a genius.' It wasn't long before Harry Gregg and his United team-mates found out that Bishop was not exaggerating. Gregg recalls:

I think the first time I ever saw George in action was when I volunteered to go to our training ground, The Cliff, one afternoon to help with the kids. There was a bit of a practice game planned and I went in goal on one side with George on the other. After a while he got the ball and raced clear of our defence. I had always prided myself on the fact that I could make forwards do what I wanted in these circumstances. But this slip of a boy shook his hips and had me diving at fresh air while the ball went in the other corner of the net.
I thought, right, you won't get away with that again. But blow me, a few minutes later he brought the ball up to me again . . . and did exactly the same thing. I knew in that moment that the club had a very rare talent on their hands.

Best brought his young genius to bear on the left wing, often roaming far for the ball, while the more orthodox Connelly supplied penetration on the right flank. Law and Herd fired in most of the ammunition, scoring nearly 50 goals between them.

Charlton and Crerand generated ideas and movement while the whole pattern was based on solid defence. Centre-half Bill

Foulkes was rightly proud of his department's contribution and was the first to point up the increasingly effective role of the fast emerging Nobby Stiles. He had worn glasses from a young age and naturally took them off for football. It left him short on visual judgement. As Bobby Charlton once said: 'Nobby doesn't so much tackle people as bump into them.' It's said that his sight was so poor that he once left a football banquet, returned, sat down and then realised he was at someone else's dinner.

Certainly there was a marked improvement in Stiles' timing when he started to wear contact lenses, and he went on to become one of England's heroes when they won the World Cup at Wembley in the summer of 1966. Who can forget the merry jig he did round Wembley without his front teeth but with a grin that seemed to spread across his entire face? Stiles and Bobby Charlton reflected great credit on Manchester United with the way they performed for England on the World Cup stage.

Disciplinary problems

What did not reflect so well on United around this period was the number of times United players were in trouble with referees.

The black streak contrasted so vividly with the man at the helm, a manager who throughout his career represented all that was fair and best in the game of football. There is no simple explanation except to say that United were playing more games than most, matches of high tension, in this period, and that many of their offences were in retaliation. Crerand for one couldn't abide cheats, and if he felt an opponent was taking a liberty with him he was more inclined to take an immediate swing at him than wait in the time-honoured way to get his own back with a hard tackle when the chance arose.

Law was a highly strung character who reacted fiercely to provocation and Stiles was another impatient character who couldn't suffer fools, poor referees and poor linesmen gladly.

Busby never went in for the tactics of Don Revie at Leeds, but possibly, after the experience of Munich, he was prepared to turn a blind eye to some of the excesses of his players in his ambition to make Manchester United a power in the game again. As the years went by he was not getting any younger and he was a man in a hurry. In any case how did you control the emotions of a player like Denis Law, so explosive and so often kicked black and blue by opponents seeking to contain him?

The 1965-66 Season

United launched into the 1965-66 season as champions determined to make an impression on three fronts and that is exactly what they did, even though they failed to land a trophy.

They were playing in their beloved European Cup again and produced some splendid football until stopped by Partizan Belgrade in the semi-finals. The Reds reached the semi-finals of the FA Cup as well after one or two scares. For instance in the fifth round at Wolves they were two goals down after only nine minutes, both from penalties, but recovered for Law (two), Best and Herd to give them a 4-2 win. They beat Preston in the sixth round after a replay at Old Trafford to reach the semi-finals for the fifth successive season. But a hectic season seemed to catch up with them when they played Everton at Burnden Park just three days after meeting Partizan Belgrade in the second leg of the European semi-final. Best was missing with a knee injury and his colleagues looked jaded in contrast to Everton, who had fielded virtually a reserve team the previous Saturday in order to rest their senior players. They were later fined £2,000, but that was little consolation for United, who fought stubbornly but without any spark on their way to a 1-0 defeat.

It seemed as if the two Cup runs had dissipated United's strength in the League, too. David Herd scored 24 League goals, Charlton got 16 and Law 15, but the Reds never strung more than three wins together on the trot. They were always among the leading group of clubs and put in a great finish, beating Blackburn 4-1 away and whipping Aston Villa 6-1 at Old Trafford, but they had to be content with fourth place while Liverpool took the title six points ahead of Leeds and Burnley and ten ahead of United.

Bobby Charlton and Nobby Stiles went off to play for England in the World Cup triumph and everybody reported back for the start of season 1966-67 determined to learn from the near-misses.

A second title in 1966-67

They didn't make a particularly good start, but Busby made a few changes. He had Bobby Noble and Johnny Aston ready after coming through with the team which had won the FA Youth Cup in 1964. Noble took over at left-back and Aston at outside-left, with Best switched to the right to replace the departed Connelly. David Sadler also won a regular place as an attacking midfield player.

Busby bought a new goalkeeper, paying Tommy Docherty at Chelsea £50,000 for Alex Stepney. At the end of the season the manager described the arrival of Stepney as the biggest single factor behind the winning of the 1966-67 Championship four points in front of Nottingham Forest. United were particularly strong in the second half of the season, perhaps helped by the fact that they were not in Europe and that they were knocked out of both the FA Cup and the League Cup in early rounds.

The Reds certainly clinched the title with a flourish, beating West Ham 6-1 in London to take the honours with a match to

spare. It was the biggest away win of the season in the First Division. The team went through the season unbeaten at home, where they were watched by a League average crowd of 53,800. They were in relentless mood, even to the end. As Nobby Stiles said afterwards: 'Just after we had scored our sixth goal at West Ham I trotted over to Bill Foulkes and said: "Congratulations, Bill, on your fourth championship medal", but all he did was give me a rollicking and tell me to concentrate on the game.'

It was determination by Stiles that had started the scoring, though. The England wing-half thrust for goal and pressured the West Ham defence into trouble. The ball spun loose across the area for Bobby Charlton to streak through a gap between two players and hammer home a goal after only two minutes. Pat Crerand, Bill Foulkes and George Best added goals to put the Reds four up in the first 25 minutes. Denis Law scored twice in the second half, one from the penalty spot, for a swashbuckling finale.

It was a crashing climax to a season in which the Reds paced the title with a perfect sense of timing and produced a remorseless last lap that was too good for their opponents. For this was a Championship won on the classical formula of winning at home and drawing away. This was the pattern from Christmas as they turned for home into the second half of the season. The sequence started with a 1-0 win at Old Trafford against Spurs on 14 January. The following week at Maine Road the Reds drew 1-1 with Manchester City. And they never looked back as they marched on to a run of eight away draws backed by eight home victories. This was the solid base, consistent and relentless, from which they sprang to tear West Ham to pieces and take the title.

At the turn of the year United had been locked in a three-horse race, jockeying for top place with Liverpool, while

Nobby Stiles was a terrier defender for United and a versatile midfielder for England. As a sweeper and as a wing-half he was busy, uncompromising and displayed more natural talent than people gave him credit for, but in a team with Law, Best and Charlton many were overshadowed. In both positions he was always vociferous

Nottingham Forest were the dark horses rising swiftly after a long and powerful winning run. By mid-March United were still level pegging with Liverpool, though ahead on goal average, and Forest had dropped back a little. On 25 March came one of those decisive games, for on that day United, the challengers, took on Liverpool, the reigning champions, in the lion's den at Anfield.

The Reds had feared Liverpool all season, particularly after only drawing with them at Old Trafford in December. In fact Denis Law was having nightmares. He dreamed that he was playing at Anfield, took the ball up to Ron Yeats, beat him, scored a goal . . . and then fell into The Kop! As it turned out, no-one scored, but the point was a great result for United and a bad one for Bill Shankly's men, who slowly slid out of the picture after failing to close the gap that the match had offered.

Forest now turned out to be the greater danger. The Forest fire was spreading and they were breathing down United's neck. They got within a point at one stage, and the game that proved decisive for them was on 11 February when they came to play at Old Trafford.

There was a 62,727 attendance, with the gates locked. It took the Reds until five minutes from the end to crack Forest, but the scoring maestro, Law, then banged in the winner. That was the beginning of the end for the team, managed by old United maestro Johnny Carey, though no-one at Old Trafford will forget the first encounter of the season between the two clubs at Nottingham in October. The Reds crashed to their heaviest defeat of the season, beaten 4-1, and they slipped to eighth in the table, the low water mark of the campaign.

The 'Busby boobies' had been one football writer's description of that performance. Hardly that perhaps, but it was a critical game, and a significant one for Bobby Noble, who along with Noel Cantwell was drafted into the team after the defeat. The choice of Noble meant that Matt Busby had once again turned to his fruitful youth in an hour of need. The youngster took his chance brilliantly until a car accident following his return from Sunderland robbed him of the last few games and his career.

Shay Brennan slipped quietly but effectively back into his place to keep the victory push going. A much more difficult problem was posed when David Herd broke his leg against Leicester City at Old Trafford on 18 March in the act of scoring his 16th League goal. It could easily have been Herd's best scoring season with United and it was with some anxiety that the manager waited to see whether the team could get by without any more goals from him.

No doubt he recalled the injury to George Best at a similar stage of the previous season. For when Best had injured his knee, leading to a cartilage operation, the whole team faded and they lost the FA Cup semi-final and the European Cup semi-final. But this time they stayed steady, and others came forward to help shoulder the scoring burden.

The talented trinity of Denis Law, George Best and Bobby Charlton celebrate a goal for Manchester United against Wolves in March 1966. It was because of the entertainment value of players like this famous trio, coupled with success, that attendances at Old Trafford started to boom. An average League crowd of 53,984 watched the team in 1966-67. The following season a record was established with a League average at Old Trafford of 57,759, a figure only likely to be beaten in the 2000-01 season.

The stars of '67

Law, of course, remained the leading spirit in United's sparkling attack. Charlton came back to his best in the second half of the season, and after Herd's injury stepped up his scoring rate, notably with a fine pair against Sheffield Wednesday at Hillsborough. The United manager also helped cover Herd's absence by switching Stiles into the attack to add more fire and bringing David Sadler, a most versatile performer, back from the forward line to form a fine double centre-half pairing with Foulkes.

Stiles, now wearing his dental plate for matches because he considered that his fierce toothless appearance as seen on television during the World Cup frightened referees and got him into trouble, finished the season in fine form. Although the attack dazzled in many games with George Best another brilliant ace in the pack, United's defence paved the way by holding on through some lean scoring spells and hard away games. Foulkes started the season with many people wondering whether the club should have bought a new centre-half; he gave the answer himself with some uncompromising displays.

Every player played his part, including Tony Dunne, brilliant at full-back and Irish Footballer of the Year; Pat Crerand, the architect of so much of United's midfield play; the young left-winger John Aston, who came through a critical spell superbly, and players who came in for brief but vital periods like Noel Cantwell, wing-half John Fitzpatrick and forward Jimmy Ryan.

And what wonderful support urged them to the Championship. The Old Trafford crowd – over a million watched United's home League games – and the fans who travelled to bring record gates at many away matches, also helped bring European football back to Old Trafford. Matt Busby gave notice he would be there to lead the next campaign. 'I'm too young to retire,' said the longest serving club manager in the game.

It wasn't just winning the Championship that brought the crowds flocking to watch United home and away in such numbers: it was the quality of their football and the personalities packed into their team.

George Best

George Best had become a cult figure by this time. He took your breath away with his finesse on the field and he was worshipped off it, especially by the girls. He was a new breed of footballer, with a following more like that of a pop star.

It was the age of the Beatles and the swinging sixties and George, with his cute eyes and Beatle haircut was ready to swing with the best of them. Girls sobbed as they stared at him through the windows of the team coach. Writers flocked to his door to examine the magic not just of his play but of his appeal for beauty queens and actresses.

Busby had already declared: 'George has the lot. He's a world-class footballer.' Alf Ramsey was sighing: 'I wish he had been born in England.' Of course it all went wrong at the end, but in 1967 he was simply a brilliant player. His life style off the field was still regarded as a bit of a lark, certainly by the media.

After all, he was different. By early 1966 he had opened a men's boutique with a partner, Malcolm Mooney, in Cheshire. Later he moved his shop into the centre of Manchester. Later still he had a night club. But at the beginning he simply swept everything before him, a prince of players who also planned to become the first British footballer millionaire.

It was already difficult to appreciate that this was the young boy who had come over from Belfast to join United aged 15 and almost immediately gone back to Ireland because he was homesick and didn't like it. Now he was so cool that he was always the last man into the dressing room to get changed for the match.

Defining what made him such a great player is difficult. Most simply, he could do virtually everything just a little better than almost everybody else. His balance was exquisite, helped by a

natural grace of movement. He had a perfectly proportioned physique, and was much stronger than he appeared. He had the ability not only to take the ball past opponents but to get himself past as well, skipping neatly over flying boots and avoiding all the other physical attempts to stop him which his skill provoked.

Few succeeded in nailing him, and he was rarely injured, although often going into areas where players get hurt. He was just so nimble, a quality which also made him a very good ball-winner. He seemed able to go in for the ball and come out with it without even making contact with the man in possession.

He could run with the ball seemingly tied to his proverbial bootlaces. He could play one-twos off an opponent's legs; it would look like a lucky break the first time, and then you realised he was doing it deliberately. On reflection he didn't seem to score many headers, but it didn't matter because he could do so much with his feet; he was a true footballer.

The players all had their own ideas about how the team came

Even the likes of Ron Harris could not contain the delicate talents of George Best. From a shy, homesick youngster blossomed a confident and dazzling footballer. At times he liked to taunt opponents, at least those who tried to kick him

1960-69

to win the 1966-67 Championship. Bobby Charlton said: 'We won it because we believed right from the start that we could do it.'

Pat Crerand said: 'Being knocked out of the FA Cup so early was a blessing in disguise. Also the fact that we weren't competing in Europe. There were no Wednesday matches to worry about, no race against time to get players fit. By Saturday everybody was bursting to play. There was no pressure. In fact it was our easiest season.

George Best reflected: 'If the Championship were decided on home games we would win it every season. This time our away games made the difference. We got into the right frame of mind.'

Tony Dunne added: 'We realised that teams without as much ability as us were giving more effort. Our great players in particular realised this and came through at just the right time.'

Noel Cantwell, no longer a regular, summed up: 'It's simply that Matt Busby has built another great team.'

So United celebrated the success which had given them

Below: The arrival of Best coincided with the swinging sixties and he was both glorified by, and caught up in, the mood of the times. The trappings of stardom are all evident ... cars, girls and fashion. George could cause both admiration and envy in all male football fans

another tilt at the European Cup after the disappointment of failing to do justice to themselves in foreign competition against Partizan Belgrade two years previously.

David Herd

Busby, now in his 21st year as manager at Old Trafford, had only one cloud on his horizon. He needed another forward to take over from David Herd, who had broken his leg the previous season.

Herd knew all about scoring long before Busby had persuaded Arsenal to part with him in the summer of 1961 for £40,000. The previous season he had finished second to Jimmy Greaves as the First Division's top marksman. The United manager had played with his father, Alex Herd, at Manchester City and watched father and son achieve the rare distinction of playing in the same League team together at Stockport County.

The Manchester clubs had let Herd slip through their fingers as a youngster. His father still lived near the Edgeley Park ground when David travelled north to join an exciting era at Old Trafford. Because of players like Charlton, Law and Best, Herd often seemed to get second billing, but his contribution should never be underestimated.

In his first season at Old Trafford, while still settling in, he scored 14 League goals, but then he reeled off a string of 19, 20, 20 and 24 before breaking his leg in March of the 1966-67 Championship season with his tally at 16. He was actually in the process of scoring against Leicester in a 5-2 win when the fracture occurred. It was a bad one and you could see his foot hanging at a broken angle.

'I was watching my shot on its way into goal when Graham Cross came sliding in and that was it,' he recalls now. 'I was getting a bit long in the tooth, and there were a few in the team in a similar position, so the following season I was transferred to Stoke. I had two good seasons there, but the broken leg was the end of the good times for me with Manchester United.'

After Stoke, and two years in management at Lincoln, he retired from football to concentrate on his motor car and garage business in Davyhulme, near Manchester, and play cricket locally at Timperley and Brooklands. He has been a United season ticket holder for years and has seen a procession of strikers struggle to achieve what seemed to come so naturally to him and reach the target of 20 League goals in a season.

He says: 'I don't like harking back, but in my day 20 goals was quite commonplace, not just by me but by Denis Law, George Best and Bobby Charlton. When we won the Championship the first time in 1964-65 five of us were in double figures. The second time in 1966-67 there were four of us with at least ten apiece. United have had a lot of good players since those days, but because of the way the game is played now by so many teams it is more difficult to score. Actually I feel sorry for the strikers of today.'

Brian Kidd arrives

United certainly found the right man to follow in David Herd's footsteps in 1967. Brian Kidd, born downtown in Collyhurst,

The FA Charity Shield against Spurs saw the debut of Brian Kidd who was quickly made part of the Old Trafford set up. A dream start in first-team football culminated in him scoring in the European Cup final on his 19th birthday

went to St. Patrick's School, a place of soccer learning which had already produced Nobby Stiles and many more. His father was a bus driver on the route which went past Old Trafford; perhaps being held up in traffic jams on match days accounted for dad being a Manchester City fan, though he raised no objections to his son joining United when he left school. Busby took young Brian on tour to Australia in 1967, and deemed him ready.

Kidd was always solidly built and strong on the ball and Busby put him in the FA Charity Shield match against Spurs at the beginning of 1967-68, a match entertainingly drawn 3-3. He made his League debut in the opening match of the season, lost 3-1 at Everton. Still only 18, he stayed in the side for the rest of the season to score 15 goals in 38 appearances. After three months of senior football he was picked for the first of his England Under-23 caps, playing on the wing against Wales with team-mate David Sadler at centre-half.

United lose out to City

The season saw yet another youngster from the juniors reach the first team. Francis Burns, who had captained the Scottish schoolboys, had also been on the tour of Australia, and after recovering from a close-season cartilage operation was brought in at left-back, with Tony Dunne switching sides to squeeze Shay Brennan out for lengthy spells. The shaggy haired John Fitzpatrick, a Scottish terrier of a wing-half also from the youth team, played quite a few games, but it was still basically the team of the previous season.

Despite losing the opening game, United went the next 11 without defeat and just after the turn of the year, the reigning champions held a five-point lead at the top of the table. They seemed on course to keep their title, and there were many who saw their FA Cup third-round exit in a replay against Spurs as confirmation that they would see success in the League again.

A poor spell which started in mid-February saw them lose their advantage. Five defeats in a run of eight games let Manchester City into the race. Losing to the Blues 3-1 at Old Trafford at this point didn't exactly help their cause.

The two Manchester clubs were level on points when they went into their final matches. With the second leg of their European Cup semi-final against Real Madrid in Spain only four days distant, United wavered and lost 2-1 at home to lowly Sunderland. Manchester City on the other hand finished with a flourish to beat Newcastle United 4-3 at St James's Park and so take the title by two points.

Blame certainly could not be laid at the feet of George Best, who played 41 League games and scored 28 goals, his best season as a marksman, which coupled with his feats in European competition saw him voted Footballer of the Year. In any case finishing second was not exactly failure, particularly when set against their achievement this season of winning the European Cup. The pursuit of the elusive trophy which had cost them so dearly in 1958 had become something of an obsession by this time, and as the quarter-finals approached in late February, their concentration was focusing more and more on Europe.

Law was missing in the last couple of championship games with a further recurrence of knee trouble which finally put him into hospital for an operation while his team were playing Benfica in the final of the European Cup. The Scot had been troubled for a long time by his knee, and at one point he was told that there was nothing physically wrong with it and that the problem was his imagination. Subsequently after an operation had removed some foreign bodies from the joint, he had them bottled in preservative and labelled: 'They said they were in my mind.'

No-one could really begrudge City their Championship. The partnership of Joe Mercer and Malcolm Allison had produced a fine team featuring players like Francis Lee, Colin Bell, Mike

Matt Busby leads his players round Old Trafford on a lap of honour after United won the championship again in 1966-67. Bill Foulkes holds the trophy aloft followed by, from left, Charlton, Brennan, Aston, Best, Stiles (barely visible), Stepney, Crerand, Law, Dunne, and Ryan. The manager named Stepney as the biggest single factor behind the title success after buying him from Chelsea for £50,000 early in the campaign. United went through the season unbeaten at home and clinched the title with a flourish, winning 6-1 at West Ham, the best away win of the season in the First Division

Summerbee, Tony Book, Mike Doyle and Alan Oakes.

The United fans had also seen some splendid matches and had responded to the achievements of the team, their colourful personalities and their entertaining brand of football in unbelievable numbers. The average League attendance at Old Trafford was 57,696, an all-time British record surpassing Newcastle United's crowds of the immediate post-war boom years. United's figures will probably only be beaten in the 2000-01 season following the extensive redevelopment work which has increased the stand sizes behind the goals.

The supporters had no time really to feel disappointment at seeing the Championship move across the city. As soon as the Sunderland match was over, the club were packing for Spain and a date with their old friends, the matadors of Madrid. Anticipation was at fever pitch, and after all, it was really a season which belonged to Europe. One only felt sorry for Manchester City, whose Championship achievement after so many long lean years was to be so soon overshadowed by their neighbours' triumph in the European Cup!

Eric Cantona strides like a giant across the pages of Manchester United's history, confirmed now from two sources as the club's greatest player of all time.

A galaxy of stars has appeared on the Old Trafford stage over the years but the overwhelming choice as the best of them points to the Frenchman who led United out of the Championship wilderness and inspired Alex Ferguson's team of the Nineties.

Despite plunging United into controversy with his infamous kung-fu kick and record suspension, fans from two quite distinct areas of support have voted Cantona their top man.

United's official museum came face to face with the problem of naming a list of all-time greats when they were deciding which players should be included in their display of legends.

Knowing the complexities they decided to ballot among the committee which designed and created the £4 million development in their new North Stand.

The results of their voting are now on show along each side of a wide corridor with cases containing photographs and memorabilia of the 15 players chosen for their hall of fame.

Above: the undisputed King of Manchester United: Eric Cantona. It was his leadership that set up Ferguson's team of the Nineties

Left: Duncan Edwards (here taking the field against Red Star in 1958) has reached legendary status since his premature death and deserves his place among Old Trafford's greatest

The leading lights in the museum are:

ERIC CANTONA
GEORGE BEST
BOBBY CHARLTON
DUNCAN EDWARDS
DENIS LAW
BRYAN ROBSON
PETER SCHMEICHEL
JOHNNY CAREY
BILLY MEREDITH
ROGER BYRNE
MARTIN BUCHAN
MARK HUGHES
CHARLIE ROBERTS
STEVE BRUCE
NOBBY STILES

So there is no great conflict over the greatest ever with Eric Cantona the most popular in the magazine vote after figuring as a major player in the museum list.

In fact three out of the top four stars named by the museum committee form the first three in the magazine readers' choice.

Ryan Giggs is the odd man out, voted the third best by the magazine, but failing to make the 15 in the museum's list of legends. We suspect Giggs had not been around long enough to tempt the committee into voting for him.

Understandably in their desire to take a broad look at the history of the club the museum committee were concerned to delve further back to find some of their great footballers with the result that Billy Meredith, Charlie Roberts and Johnny Carey, great names from a rather more dim and distant past, are included.

The readers of the biggest selling football magazine in the country no doubt have a lot of young readers so that in addition to Giggs, they go for David Beckham and Andy Cole from the present team, as well as showing great respect for the Busby Babes killed in the Munich air crash by including Tommy Taylor as well as Roger Byrne and Duncan Edwards who both figure in the museum display.

In all, there are 10 players who find favour in the top 15 lists of both the magazine and museum. It's clear that in addition to Cantona, Best and Charlton, there is no quibble about recognising players like Denis Law, Bryan Robson, Mark Hughes and Steve Bruce as all-time legends.

Peter Schmeichel is the most modern player to appear in both lists, though the museum have said that they expect several of the current team to join their hall of fame once they have passed the test of time. Skipper Roy Keane has reserved his place and if the deadly duo, Dwight Yorke and Andy Cole, continue to knock in goals well into the new millennium, stand by for two more legends!

Cantona in fact was only joint top in the Museum vote, polling exactly the same as three other players, George Best, Sir Bobby Charlton and Duncan Edwards.

There the matter might have rested, with supporters left to argue over which of the leading four was in fact the all-time best, but the Manchester United Magazine have brought the issue out into the open again by asking their readers to vote for their top 50.

Their voting produced a leading 15 of:	
ERIC CANTONA	DAVID BECKHAM
GEORGE BEST	MARK HUGHES
RYAN GIGGS	DENIS LAW
SIR BOBBY CHARLTON	NORMAN WHITESIDE
BRYAN ROBSON	STEVE BRUCE
DUNCAN EDWARDS	ROGER BYRNE
PETER SCHMEICHEL	TOMMY TAYLOR
	ANDY COLE

Top: The idol of late-sixties United and a footballing icon, George Best dazzled defenders and thrilled fans

Left: It would be unusual for a 'keeper to figure in a club's all time greatest, but Peter Schmeichel is no ordinary 'keeper. He was instrumental in United's Nineties triumphs and ended his United career with the treble in 1999

CHAPTER 5
EUROPE! EUROPE! EUROPE!

Manchester United travelled through a vale of tears to become the champions of Europe. It had been a long, hard journey, setting out in recriminations with the Football League and enduring the misery and woe of Munich before arriving at that golden triumph. So many Busby Babes had perished on the way.

Certainly there was sadness as well as joy when Busby and Bobby Charlton fell into each other's arms out on the pitch at Wembley. It was much more than the glow of victory as one of the surviving players of the Munich tragedy turned to the manager who had himself come back from the brink of death. It was the journey's end, the climax to a great adventure, which like life itself had contained sorrows and successes.

As Bill Foulkes, the other crash survivor who also shared a winning hug with Busby, reflects:

'I had come the whole way with the Boss trying to make Manchester United the champions of Europe. I thought the destruction of our team at Munich would have been the end of it, but he patiently put together another side. I'm proud to have been a part of it, and for those of us who lost our friends coming home from a European Cup-tie in 1958, our victory seemed the right tribute to their memory.'

Even the youngest, Brian Kidd, who celebrated his 19th birthday on the day of the final, was gripped by the significance of the game.

'I want us to win for the Boss', he kept saying.

The team that played Benfica reflected the patience, planning and philosophy of Busby. It was basically a team fashioned from boys recruited when they left school and groomed at Old Trafford. With Denis Law watching the final from a hospital bed after a knee operation, only Alex Stepney and Pat Crerand had cost fees among the 12 men named for the big day.

By now George Best had arrived in world class. He was at his peak. With Benfica obsessed with the necessity for marking Best – no doubt they had vivid memories of their massacre at his hands two years previously – other players were left with more freedom. David Sadler, for instance, missed more than one opportunity of opening the scoring. Bobby Charlton saved his embarrassment when he leapt into the air to head a centre from Sadler high into the far corner of the net. A Charlton header was a rarity, and this one was beautifully timed.

Perhaps sensing victory, John Aston began the first of many brilliant runs on the left wing and Best contributed a dazzling piece of football to help Sadler to another near-miss. Ten minutes from the end Benfica pulled themselves together and Jaime Graca hit an equaliser after Torres, who up to this point had been well held by Bill Foulkes, had headed the ball down to him.

Top: David Sadler Misses a chance to open the scoring during the 1968 European Cup Final at Wembley

Middle: Sadler (on the ball) is aided in attack by Brian Kidd who was to score during the match. A perfect way to celebrate your 19th Birthday

Bottom: Best finally evades the Benfica defence to slot home United's second in extra time.

Now it was United's turn to wilt as the Portuguese surged forward and Eusebio, for once escaping the close attentions of Nobby Stiles, had victory at his feet. He burst through and hammered a tremendous shot but Stepney pulled off a seemingly impossible reaction save. Perhaps if Eusebio had been content to try and score in a more modest style, he would have made it easily; but the Portuguese star hit the ball hard and his shot was too close to Stepney, whose reflexes were tested as he parried the ball away. It was the save of the match and Eusebio stayed behind to pat his opponent on the back and contribute his applause.

Aston led the offensive, but in the first minute of extra time it was Stepney who kicked a long clearance which Kidd headed forward for Best. Watch-dog Cruz was tiring now and he failed to hold his opponent as Best tore away. Henrique came out of his goal to narrow the angle, but Best swerved to his left on a curve round the Benfica goalkeeper before clipping the ball into the net.

Benfica were on their knees as United came in for the kill.

Kidd headed Charlton's corner kick at Henrique. The goalkeeper somehow beat out the ball but Kidd was there again to head in off the bar for a real birthday celebration. Charlton supplied the final touch as he flicked Kidd's right-wing centre high into the Benfica goal to hammer home a 4-1 win.

United's long quest was over, the European Championship was at Old Trafford at last. Best was voted Footballer of the Year by the English soccer writers, and a little later he was elected European Player of the Year, the youngest ever. Soon afterwards Matt Busby was knighted for his services to sport.

The teams for the final of the European Cup at Wembley on 29 May 1968 were:

MANCHESTER UNITED: Stepney, Brennan, A. Dunne, Crerand, Foulkes, Stiles, Best, Kidd, Charlton, Sadler, Aston. Sub: Rimmer.
BENFICA: Henrique, Adolfo, Humberto, Jacinto, Cruz, Jaime Graca, Coluna, Jose Augusto, Torres, Eusebio, Simoes. Sub: Nascimento.
REFEREE: Concetto Lo Bello of Italy.
ATTENDANCE: 100,000

Above: Charlton lifts the European Cup at Wembley Stadium in 1968, and United become the first English team to win the trophy

Below: As the heroes parade atop an open top bus, the whole of Manchester celebrate

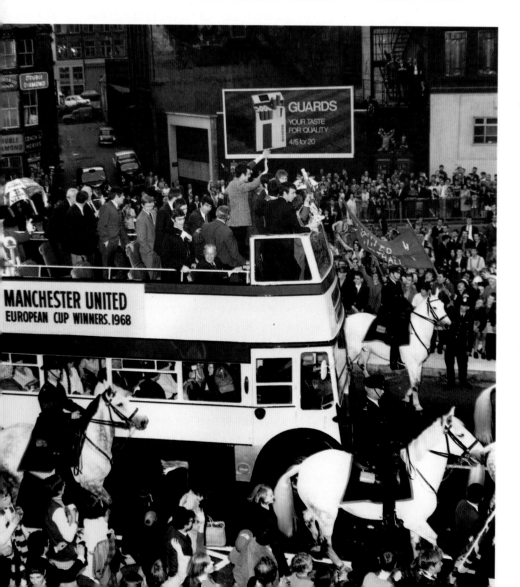

MANCHESTER UNITED
EUROPEAN CUP WINNERS. 1968

United enter Europe

Of course the story of Manchester United in Europe began a lot earlier than Wembley 1968, 12 years earlier to be precise.

In 1956 United entered the European Cup after Chelsea had been refused permission by the Football League the previous season. In 1956 they were drawn in the preliminary round against Anderlecht, the champions of Belgium. It was a step into the unknown for the Reds, who were disappointed that for their first competitive match on foreign soil they were going to be without the powerful Duncan Edwards.

In the event Jackie Blanchflower, who took his place, turned in a star performance. Eddie Colman created a goal for Dennis Viollet and Tommy Taylor scored to give the Manchester men a 2-0 win.

The return leg was played a fortnight later at Maine Road – the Old Trafford floodlights weren't yet ready – and United were in a purposeful mood.

They would have beaten any club side in the world that night. Ten times in 90 minutes the Anderlecht keeper picked the ball out of his net. It would have made news if an English First Division side had beaten a Fourth Division side by that margin. But this was Anderlecht, one of the top sides in Europe. The poor keeper must have felt he was having a nightmare as the goals poured past him from Viollet (4), Tommy Taylor (3), Billy Whelan (2) and Johnny Berry. Busby, who before that night must have thought he had seen it all, could scarcely believe his eyes.

However, the cocky Busby boys were nearly shot out of the Cup in the next round when they took on West German champions Borrussia Dortmund. Thousands packed into Maine Road expecting another goal glut. It looked possible for 35 minutes as Viollet (2) and David Pegg put United in a commanding position. But the Red Devils took things too easily. Silly mistakes gave the Germans a second, to cut United's lead to 3-2.

Now United had a real battle on their hands when they travelled to the Ruhr for the return. They were cheered on by 7,000 British servicemen and held the Germans to a goalless draw with an uncharacteristic backs-to-the-wall performance.

Six weeks later England's new soccer ambassadors took on Spanish champions Bilbao in the first leg of the quarter-finals. It looked as if the Babes were to learn their first bitter European lesson when they trooped off at half-time trailing 3-0. Amazingly, within eight minutes of the restart, they had pulled back to 3-2 with goals from Taylor and Viollet. But United slumped and Bilbao were coasting home again at 5-2. With five minutes to go the Reds were as good as out of the European Cup. Then Billy Whelan, picked up the ball in his own half beating man after man in a wriggling 40-yard run before drawing keeper Carmelo and thumping the ball into the top left-hand corner.

The return at Maine Road was not a masterly display of football. Busby, on the touch-line, lost his usual composure. As half-time approached he waved big Duncan Edwards upfield to try to break the deadlock. A minute later Edwards struck – a drive which was speeding towards the net until a defender stuck out a foot. The ball flew to the unmarked Viollet and the Reds needed only two goals.

The game restarted even more feverishly. Now it was Tommy Taylor's big moment. He took the game by the scruff of the neck and shook it until victory was won. In the 70th minute he danced around Garay and cracked a left-foot drive against the post. Two minutes later he sailed around Garay again. This time there was no woodwork to help Bilbao.

Five minutes to go and still Bilbao hung on. Then Taylor again made a breathtaking dash along the right touchline. Little Johnny Berry, anticipating the move, had raced into the centre-forward position. Gently Taylor rolled the ball back. Berry's right foot did the rest.

Real Madrid, United's opponents in the semi-final, were the greatest football team in the world. The first game at Real's magnificent Bernabeu Stadium was watched by a crowd of 120,000, and from the whistle it was obvious what was Busby's trump card. The man he set to mark maestro di Stefano was not the powerful Duncan Edwards but the little man from Salford, Eddie Colman.

Nevertheless Real's artistic, colourful football opened up a two-goal lead. The Reds pulled one back through Tommy Taylor, but the Spanish champions scored a third through Mateos late in the second half.

The game at Old Trafford, with floodlights now installed, illustrated once again the gap between top-class Continental soccer and the best in Britain. Real Madrid did not fall into the same defensive trap as Bilbao. For 20 minutes they absorbed everything that the Reds could throw at them and then struck with lightning speed. Gento opened up the United defence for Kopa to put Real ahead. Another burst from the flying left-winger created a goal for di Stefano. The 60,000 crowd were shocked into silence.

Sheer guts brought the Reds back into the game with a goal from Taylor and another from young Bobby Charlton. For once the Real defenders were glad to kick for safety but like true `European champions they withstood the assault, and won the tie on a 5-3 aggregate.

The tragic '57-58 campaign

There is no knowing what Manchester United might have achieved in season 1957-58 and thereafter but for the calamity at Munich. They were in the European Cup again as champions, of

course, and they opened their campaign in convincing manner with a 6–0 win over Shamrock Rovers in Dublin. United took the return leg at Old Trafford in casual mood, much to the delight of the Irishmen, who scored twice before going down 3-2 as Dennis Viollet struck a couple of times and Pegg scored again.

Dukla Prague presented stiffer opposition in the first round proper. But they could not prevent the Reds from establishing a 3-0 lead from the first leg at Old Trafford.

United were more accustomed now to the niceties of two-legged ties and they adopted a careful approach in Prague. With the help of some sterling play from Eddie Colman at wing-half they restricted Dukla to a 1-0 win to sail through with an aggregate 3-1 victory.

United had a fright on the way back home, though. Their plane back to London couldn't take off from Prague because the airport in England was closed through fog. Busby knew that the

Top: Johnny Berry was a key player in Matt Busby's first championship team of 1952. He was a tricky winger who won four England caps before the Munich accident ended his career

Above: Dennis Viollet had an enormous amount of skill and vision. His greatest attributes were his pace and shooting ability. He still holds United's all-time scoring record, hitting 32 League goals in one season (1959-60)

League would come down on them like a ton of bricks if they were late for a domestic fixture. Hastily they made other arrangements. They caught a flight to Amsterdam and completed the journey by taking a boat from the Hook of Holland to Harwich and then travelling by train and coach to Manchester.

They arrived home weary on the Friday, a day later than planned. It was the experience in Prague that made the club take the first ill-fated decision to charter a plane for their next foreign trip . . . to play Red Star in Belgrade.

In the first leg at Old Trafford United got the goals they deserved through Eddie Colman and Bobby Charlton for a 2-1 win.

The next European adventure

The FA Cup success in 1963 put the Reds into the European Cup Winners' Cup the following season.

They opened convincingly enough, drawing 1-1 against Willem II in Holland and then going to town on the Dutchmen in the second leg at Old Trafford. Denis Law grabbed a hat-trick while Bobby Charlton, Phil Chisnall and Maurice Setters also scored to complete a rousing 6-1 win to go through 7-2 on aggregate.

The next round brought the kind of opposition disliked in European football, a tie against fellow countrymen. On this occasion Spurs, as holders, were their opponents. The first leg was at White Hart Lane where Spurs registered a 2-0 win with goals from Dave Mackay and winger Terry Dyson. Tottenham were confident they could turn their advantage into an aggregate win. But the second leg went sour for the Londoners. Mackay broke his leg in an accidental collision and they went down to a 4-1 defeat. David Herd and Bobby Charlton shared United's four goals.

In the next round they ran up a handsome 4-1 lead against Sporting Lisbon in the first leg at Old Trafford.

But no-one expected the collapse that occurred in the second leg of the Cup Winners' Cup against Sporting Lisbon in Portugal. The Reds squandered their three-goal advantage to lose by an incredible 5-0.

As runners-up in the League, United qualified for the Fairs Cup in 1964-65. Although they only drew 1-1 in the first leg of their opening round against Djurgaarden in Sweden, they went to town in the return to the tune of 6-1. Law got a hat-trick.

Borussia Dortmund in the next round didn't know what had hit them. Charlton scored a hat-trick in another 6-1 win in Dortmund, and narrowly missed repeating his three-goal salvo in the second leg 4-0 victory in Manchester.

The scoring slowed in the third round when United drew English opponents. Everton did well to hold them to a 1-1 draw in the first leg at Old Trafford, Connelly providing the lifeline for the Reds. Everton were favourites at Goodison Park for the return, but United, with goals from Connelly and Herd, won 2-1.

The Reds were quickly back in form in the next round, banging in five against Racing Club in Strasbourg.

United had been the new League Champions for a month by the time the first leg of the semi-final against Ferencvaros came round on 31 May 1965.

After a 3-2 win at Old Trafford it was with some misgiving that the Reds set off for the second leg, and their mood was not helped by the difficulties of the journey, with a strike delay at London Airport and a hold-up in Brussels. Misfortune spilled over into the match. Just before half-time Albert set Varga off running for goal. He was still some way out when he tried a speculative shot which Pat Dunne looked to have well

The second round of the 1963/64 Cup Winners' Cup saw the unlikely tie against Spurs. United lost the first leg 2-0 but bounced back at Old Trafford to win 4-3 with two each from Herd and Charlton

They hadn't had such a slender lead to take abroad before and everyone wondered whether it would be enough.

We have dealt in detail with that fateful final match in Belgrade before the disaster. The club were jubilant at the end of the game, of course, because their 3-3 result for an aggregate 5-4 win had put them into the semi-finals of the European Cup for the second season running.

Just as Manchester United had had to carry on in the FA Cup and the League, so they had to face up to their commitments in Europe. By the time the semi-finals came round it was May. Five days after losing to Bolton at Wembley they were facing up to AC Milan at Old Trafford.

It seemed that sentiment for United had run out in high places. England picked Bobby Charlton for a friendly against Portugal at Wembley, so that the Reds were unnecessarily deprived of one of their quality players, the kind needed for a match against a team like AC Milan. United also lost him to England for the second leg as he was chosen to play against Yugoslavia – in Belgrade of all places. Little wonder he had a poor game.

So the patched-up Reds fought bravely in the first leg to win 2-1 with a penalty from Taylor and a goal from Viollet. But it was a slim lead to take to the San Siro Stadium for the second leg six days later. There an 80,000 crowd bombarded the English players with cabbages and carrots, a quite new experience for most of the United team who slowly but surely slid to a 4-0 defeat.

covered. The ball struck Stiles on the shoulder and he cleared. The referee amazingly awarded a penalty for handball.

Novak scored with the penalty and United lost their cool. Pat Crerand was sent off along with Orosz when they finally turned on each other after a running battle. But it still wasn't their lucky day, and Matt Busby returned grimly to the dressing room having lost the toss for choice of venue for the replay. Back to Budapest went United, now a month into the close season and lost.

The Championship put the Reds back into the top competition, the European Cup, in 1965-66 and they produced another brave campaign on three fronts.

The European season will be remembered for an incredible performance at the quarter-final stage against Benfica in Lisbon which was inspired by George Best, who returned as El Beatle.

When that season opened Best was just making the English soccer fans sit up and take notice. However, glimpses of his future lifestyle were beginning to emerge. A string of late nights took the edge off his form and brought the first of many dressing-downs from Busby. Then, after a miserable performance against Newcastle, he was dropped for three games, including the opening round of the European Cup against HJK Helsinki.

United won 3-2 in Finland, but he was restored for the second leg after turning in a brilliant performance for Northern Ireland against Scotland. The shock of losing his place had done the trick and George was back to his impudent best, running the Finns ragged in a 6-0 victory in which he scored twice.

The East Berlin army team Vorwaerts were beaten 2-0 away and 3-1 at home to give United a quarter-final tie against Benfica.

Best can still vividly recall the first leg at Old Trafford on 2 February 1966: 'It was one of those nights when you could almost feel the crackle of the atmosphere. I recall best of all the fantastic pace at which the game was played and then thinking during the second half that our lead of 3-1 was ideal. Then Eusebio worked one of his tricks to get his side a valuable goal. He sent our defence the wrong way with a quick shuffle of his feet and curled in a centre for a goal which Torres scored with his knee.'

A fantastic victory in Lisbon

So the Reds were going to Lisbon with the slenderest of leads, and with bitter memories of their last visit two years.

Busby wanted United to hold Benfica for the first 20 minutes. But Best refused to be held in check. He took the game by the scruff of the neck and didn't let go until victory was assured. He scored the first goal after only six minutes when he soared to head a free-kick from Tony Dunne past Costa Pereira. Then six minutes later he scored one of the finest ever seen when he weaved around three Benfica defenders before stroking the ball into the corner.

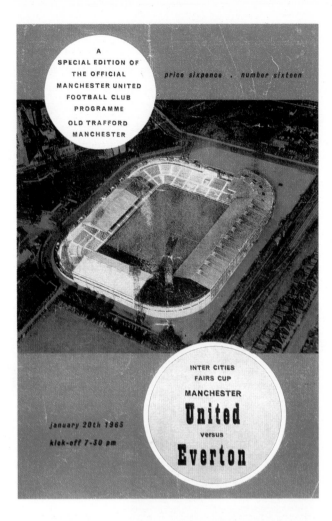

Above, left: The second round of the 1964-65 Inter-Cities Fairs Cup saw United hit 10 goals past Borussia Dortmund. The Germans would wait 32 years for revenge as they beat United in the semi-finals of their successful 1997 Champion's League campaign

Above, right: A tight tie against Everton in the 1964-65 Fairs Cup saw United win by one goal on aggregate thanks to a 2-1 victory at Goodison Park. United eventually were put out by Ferencvaros in the semi-final

Another tremendous burst brought a third goal for John Connelly. As Benfica reeled, Shay Brennan put through his own net to bring Benfica back in the game, but the Reds struck again in the last quarter, Law laying on a goal for Crerand and Charlton waltzing through at the end for a 5-1 win (an incredible 8-3 on aggregate).

A fortnight later in the sixth round of the FA Cup Best was brought down from behind, fell awkwardly and twisted his right knee. It was a classic case of a torn cartilage, the occupational hazard of footballers, and behind the scenes they worked round the clock trying to get him fit for the first leg of the European semi-final against Partizan Belgrade in Yugoslavia.

Partizan were an ordinary side without much flair, but they were as hard and unrelenting as the Partizans of the war whom their club was named after.

The Reds started as if capable of carrying on where they had left off in Lisbon. After only five minutes Best had wriggled through only to miss with a fair chance. Then he put Denis Law clear with a centre, but the Scot could only bounce the ball against the bar off his body as he tried to run it into the net. After that United faded. Hasanagic scored for Partizan and soon after Best began to feel the nagging pain in his knee return. Becejac made it a 2-0 win for the home team.

The Belgrade game was the last of the season for Best, who on the return home went straight into hospital for a cartilage operation. Willie Anderson took Best's place for the second leg a week later but again United were below par. United attacked all night but Partizan held out, losing 1-0 on the night, but going through on a 2–1 aggregate.

The Championship challenge had also fizzled out with the result that they finished fourth in the League, not good enough for a place in Europe the following season. Liverpool had taken the honours, but could not get past Ajax of Holland in the first round proper.

United emerged Champions of 1966–67 to go forward for their big date with destiny in the European Cup.

The Semi-Final in Madrid witnessed an amazing finale with an unlikely goal-scoring hero. Experienced European Cup campaigner Bill Foulkes left his station to side foot the winning goal. United won 4–3 on aggregate after being 3–2 down at half-time during the second leg

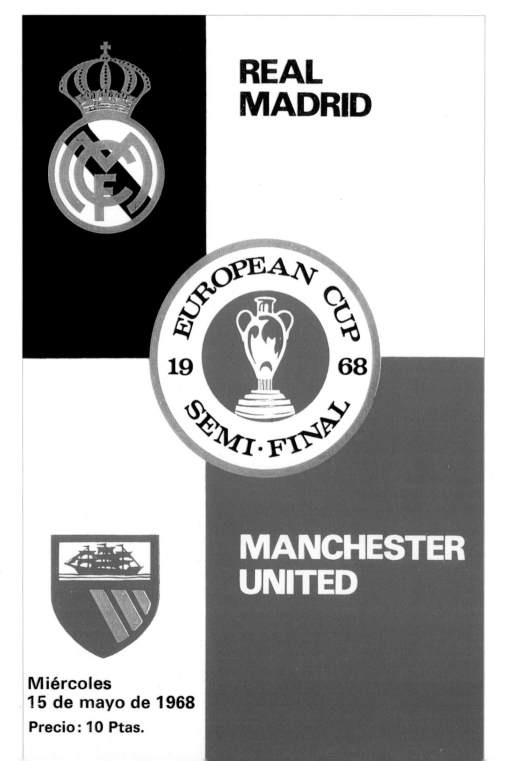

REAL MADRID

EUROPEAN CUP 19 68 SEMI·FINAL

MANCHESTER UNITED

Miércoles
15 de mayo de 1968
Precio: 10 Ptas.

The 1967-68 campaign

The 1967-68 campaign opened with an easy tie against the Hibernian part-timers of Malta and Denis Law and David Sadler scored two goals each for a 4-0 win.

The next round brought a much tougher draw. United's opponents were Sarajevo, kinsmen of the Partizan team which had dashed their hopes two years previously. Matt Busby, stifling memories of Munich, ordered a charter plane for the first time since to ease a long, difficult journey. The Reds at least kept their heads and came home with a goalless draw, a good result in the circumstances. Sarajevo were just as hard at Old Trafford, so United were delighted when Best avoided the flying boots to reach Kidd's centre with a header which the goalkeeper could only palm out. John Aston whipped the ball back in for an 11th minute lead.

Best rammed a second home, scoring in the 65th minute. Outside-right Salih Delalic headed a goal for Sarajevo, but too late to influence the game three minutes from the end. So the Reds moved on with a 2-1 win to meet Gornik Zabrze in the quarter-finals.

The first leg in Manchester came as a refresher after the previous round and was a splendidly sporting affair. A 2-0 win was fair especially with Law missing again, this time with the start of his knee problem. Jimmy Ryan had played well in his place, but was replaced by the more defensive John Fitzpatrick for the second leg to help protect the two-goal advantage.

It was bitterly cold and snowing in Gornik where United, wilier now in the art of European football, played a mature game. Gornik scored 20 minutes from the end through their danger man, Lubanski but it was an aggregate defeat.

So Manchester United were in the semi-finals of the European Cup for the fourth time, and were drawn against their old friends and rivals, Real Madrid. The stage was set for what many fans would have preferred to see as the final. After a first leg at Old Trafford United were thankful to take a one-goal lead to Madrid – scored by George Best – but that was a frighteningly slender advantage against a team like Real in front of their own fanatical supporters.

Foulkes the hero of Madrid

Twenty-one days after the Old Trafford tie the two teams met again in Madrid. For the most important game in the history of the club Busby decided not to risk Law, but recalled the ageing defender Bill Foulkes for his 29th European Cup tie. David Sadler kept his place as an extra attacker and Shay Brennan came in at full-back in place of Francis Burns.

Real were the exact opposite of the team which had played at Old Trafford. The ball was whisked from man to man as if on an invisible string and with United defenders chasing shadows it came as no surprise when Pirri headed a free-kick past Stepney after half an hour.

An uncharacteristic error by Shay Brennan allowed Gento to make it 2-0 and although Zoco sliced Dunne's centre past his own keeper, Amancio quickly scored again after fooling two defenders to give Real a 3-1 interval lead. United, it seemed, were down and almost out.

Busby's half-time pep-talk helped to change the players' outlook.

In the second period the Reds ran their opponents ragged. But the vital goal wouldn't come. Then Crerand lobbed the ball forward. A header by Foulkes fell between the Real goalkeeper and his defenders, and before anyone could move, Sadler had stolen in to glance the ball home. Now the scores were level with just under 15 minutes to go and the stage was set for one of the most memorable, emotional moments in United's various European games.

Bill Foulkes, the most unlikely goal-scoring hero of all time, a survivor of the other semi-final between the two clubs 11 years earlier, booked a place in the final with his only European Cup goal. Foulkes insists:

Leading up to the goal, I had called for the ball when Paddy Crerand took a throw-in. He threw it to George Best instead who shot off down the field. Perhaps it was with moving slightly forward to call for the throw-in which prompted me to keep running. Anyway I reached the corner of the box and found myself calling for the ball again. I thought George was going to shoot, but instead he cut back a beautiful pass to me. It was perfect and I just had to side-foot it in at the far side.

In the dressing-room after the match Bobby Charlton and Matt Busby were both unashamedly crying. 'I can't help it, I can't help it,' said Busby. As already described, United went on to win the Cup in that never-to-be-forgotten final at Wembley, making them the first English winners.

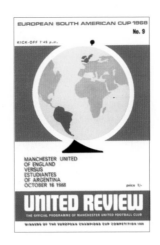

The World Championship match with Estudiantes opened United's horizons considerably. Although the fixture between the champions of Europe and South America had an unhappy history of violence, it hadn't really prepared United for the naked aggression and general hostility they met in Buenos Aires. As Matt Busby summed up: 'Holding the ball out there put you in danger of your life.' United lost the first leg 1-0 and then drew 1-1 at Old Trafford in the return, with Willie Morgan their goal scorer.

next round because of a two-match suspension, but Law was still in form near goal and scored twice in a 3-0 home win. There was nearly a hiccup in the away leg. United lost 3-1 in Belgium, but survived thanks to the goal scored by newcomer Carlo Sartori, another young lad from Collyhurst.

The Reds were back to their best for the quarter-final against Rapid Vienna, who arrived at Old Trafford for the first leg with the boost of having just knocked Real Madrid out of the tournament. They received short shrift from United in the second half, though, and were sent back home to Austria as 3–0 losers. Best made up for his absence in the previous round with a sparkling performance. He scored the first and third goals, with Willie Morgan, United's £100,000 summer signing from Burnley marking his European debut by notching the other.

United conformed more now to European tactics and played carefully in Vienna for a 0-0 result.

With Best in the side the team's performance just could not be predicted; to a large extent it was the secret of their European success, though they more than met their match when they came up against AC Milan in the semi-finals.

They certainly found Milan a tough nut to crack. A goal from Angelo Sormani in the 33rd minute and one from Kurt Hamrin just after the interval gave AC Milan a 2-0 win in the San Siro.

United were not without hope for the second leg. The Reds flung themselves forward but didn't break through until the 70th minute. It was a fine goal, created when Best at last eluded Anquilletti, and was scored fittingly enough by Bobby Charlton. It was United's 100th in European football. But it wasn't enough on the night. The fans thought their team had equalised 13 minutes from the end when Crerand chipped a ball in. The players swore that the ball had crossed the line, but it wasn't given.

It was in fact eight years before United qualified for a European return, a completely different era with a new generation of players and staff.

The European Cup defence

Winning the European Cup meant United qualified for the World Club Championship against Estudiantes. The Reds drew the second game 1-1 with Willie Morgan scoring on a violent night at Old Trafford but the Inter-continental Cup went to Buenos Aires on the strength of their 1-0 home victory.

United hoped for better things as they began to defend their precious European Cup. They went willingly to work on Waterford in the opening round, winning 3-1 in Ireland with a hat-trick from Denis Law and piling on the agony with a 7-1 win at Old Trafford. This time Law went one better and scored four.

George Best missed both legs against Anderlecht in the

The return to Europe under Docherty

Tommy Docherty was the manager who led the Reds back to the Continent, and he did not disguise either his excitement or the way he was going to try to uphold the tradition established by Sir Matt Busby.

The Doc led the charge with a place in the 1976-77 UEFA Cup on the strength of third place in the League the previous season, and true to his promise they opened like the cavalry against Ajax in Holland's Olympic Stadium. Yet the Dutchmen survived to emerge 1-0 winners when Rudi Krol, their World Cup star and a survivor from the days when Ajax ruled the European roost, left his sweeper's post to jink through to slip the ball past Alex Stepney just before the interval.

United were disappointed to lose, but as Docherty chortled at the end to the Ajax president: 'Sorry, my friend, one goal won't be enough for you in Manchester.'

That's how it worked out. Brian Greenhoff stepped up the tempo after Lou Macari had scored two minutes before the interval to make it 1-1 on aggregate. He powered down the right and with the help of Steve Coppell crossed for Sammy McIlroy to touch home the winner.

Round two brought United up against Juventus, who had just knocked neighbouring Manchester City out of the competition. United won the first leg at Old Trafford 1-0 with a beautifully struck goal in the 31st minute from Gordon Hill but if they had any doubts about the class of the opposition, they were soon dispelled in Turin. Roberto Boninsegna struck a brilliant goal after half an hour and another just after the hour. Romeo rubbed in the defeat with a goal five minutes from the end for 3-0 on the night.

At least the club didn't have to wait long for another crack at Europe. For though dispatched very efficiently by Juventus in their European adventure, they had picked themselves up in splendid style in the FA Cup to beat Liverpool at Wembley and so qualify for the European Cup Winners' Cup in season 1977-78.

Trouble with the fans

By then they were under new management of course with Dave Sexton having replaced the sacked Tommy Docherty, and Sexton could hardly have had a more traumatic baptism when he took his team to France to play at St Etienne. For this was a tie fought on two fronts, on and off the field. Out on the pitch United performed well in a 1-1 draw. Gordon Hill smashed home a right-wing centre from Stuart Pearson in the 76th minute, with Christian Synaeghel scrambling in an equaliser just three minutes later.

But the real drama was happening on the terraces where the French club had ignored all United's appeals for segregation of the fans. Fighting broke out and the riot police swept in to charge at the English fans and lay about them indiscriminately.

The reaction of UEFA's disciplinary committee was simply to toss United out of the competition and award the tie to St Etienne. But United appealed and won the day in front of a tribunal in Zurich. The appeal commission ruled that the original sanction had been too severe and allowed United to stay in the competition, but ordered them to pay a £7,500 fine and play the second leg at a neutral stadium at least 200 kilometres from Manchester.

The club kept cool heads and after deciding to play at Plymouth won 2-0.

United reached the semi-finals in defence of their European crown in 1969, but found AC Milan too strong for them. The Italians won the tie with a powerful performance in the first leg on their own ground. Milan won 2-0 and then defended with all the expertise the Italians can muster to escape with a 1-0 defeat at Old Trafford. Bobby Charlton scored United's 100th in European football but otherwise it was an unhappy night with missile throwing from the Stretford End

Unfortunately for the second year running United came to grief in the next round. FC Porto proved far too good for them. The power, pace and precision of the Portuguese men o' war sank the Reds 4-0 in Portugal. It was like the Juventus away leg all over again, only this time United responded much better at home. In fact they came close to turning the tie upside down with a dazzling 5-2 victory at Old Trafford.

United missed a couple of seasons of European competition, but finishing runners-up in the Championship to Liverpool in 1979-80 saw them return to Europe for season 1980-81 in the UEFA Cup again.

This proved to be their shortest ever European run, as they failed at the first fence against Widzew Lodz.

Ron Atkinson took over; it was another blank season on the European front but Bryan Robson, Remi Moses, Frank Stapleton and Norman Whiteside were all introduced to help the club finish third in the League. This meant another run in the UEFA Cup 1982-83, though once again it was a short-lived campaign.

After losing to Valencia, United went on to beat Brighton in the final of the FA Cup to earn a return to the European Cup Winners' Cup in season 1983-84. The first-round draw against Dukla Prague also sent the minds of older fans racing down memory lane, but United went through on the away goals rule.

Spartak Varna were gobbled up without too much trouble.

Then came a mighty tussle with Barcelona in the quarter-final. The first leg in the magnificent Nou Camp Stadium was lost 2-0.

The great match with Barcelona

Robson seemed to take the second leg as a personal challenge and he led a fight back which belongs in the top drawer of United's European achievements. There was a tremendous rapport from the 58,000 fans as United took the game to their opponents, at the same time keeping a wary eye on Diego Maradona.

They pulled back the first goal after 25 minutes, Hogg touching on a Wilkins corner for Robson to score with a diving header, bravely ignoring the flying boots. Robson smashed in number two after the Spanish goalkeeper had failed to hold a drive from Wilkins. Whiteside headed a ball down for Stapleton to score the winner. It was a nail-biting finish with Mark Hughes lucky to escape being penalised in the area for a foul on Alonso.

Unhappily United were without the injured Robson and Arnold Muhren for the first leg of the semi-final against Juventus at Old Trafford, and to make matters worse Wilkins was serving a suspension. The Reds tried willingly enough but couldn't stop Paolo Rossi scoring with the help of a deflection off Hogg after 15 minutes. Substitute Alan Davies made it 1-1, but most fans feared the worst in Turin.

The Reds were still without Robson, and Whiteside was only fit enough to make the substitutes' bench. He came on late in the game to demonstrate his liking for the big occasion by scoring an equaliser after Boniek had given Juventus an early lead. It seemed likely to be enough to take the match into extra time, but with only a minute remaining, Rossi sped away to score a beautiful winner.

United finished fourth in the League that season to give them their final run in Europe before the ban on English clubs which followed the tragedy at the European Cup final at the Heysel Stadium, Brussels, in 1985. They opened season 1984-85 in the UEFA Cup with a home first leg against Raba Gyor of Hungary and won comfortably 3-0 with goals from Robson, Hughes and Muhren. The Hungarians made more of a show in their own country but goals from Alan Brazil and Muhren, a penalty, provided the Reds with a 2-2 draw and safe passage through to meet PSV Eindhoven.

The Dutchmen provided two tight games, goalless in Holland and then 1-0 in United's favour at Old Trafford, the

The quarter-final against Barcelona in the European Cup Winners' Cup in 1984 produced an epic, with a fight-back by Manchester United. United lost the first leg in Spain 2-0. The second leg at Old Trafford was a personal triumph for the captain who was mobbed and carried off shoulder high by fans at the end of United's inspiring 3-0 victory. The confrontation with Barcelona brought United up against world star Diego Maradona. In this European collision, Maradona was eclipsed by Robson who scored two of the goals

goal coming from a penalty by Gordon Strachan. Dundee United saw the Reds at their best. The Scots came to Old Trafford first and played well for a 2-2 draw. Robson scored and Strachan got another penalty, though he also let his countrymen off the hook by missing one as well. United played a storming game in Dundee with goals from Hughes and Muhren along with an own-goal seeing them safe with a 3-2 win.

Videoton, another Hungarian club, whom United played in the quarter-finals provided a huge anti-climax. United outplayed them over the two legs but couldn't finish them off. In the first leg in Manchester Frank Stapleton had two goals disallowed for offside before netting one that counted for a 1-0 win. It wasn't much of a lead but everyone was confident it would be enough because there had been nothing special about the Hungarians. But the goals wouldn't come in Hungary either, and Videoton sneaked a 1-0 win. For the first time in Europe United went into a penalty shoot-out . . . and lost 4-5. Stapleton and Hughes missed their penalties, while luckless Bailey dived the wrong way for every one of Videoton's kicks!

It was 1990 when UEFA decided to lift the ban on English clubs and United were invited to play in the Cup Winners' Cup competition of the 1990-91 season.

FINAL

MANCHESTER UNITED
FC BARCELONA
MAY 15 - 1991
STADION FEIJENOORD ROTTERDAM

Football was returning to normal and for a second time Manchester United became England's ambassadors in Europe having been first to show the way in the Fifties.

This was Alex Ferguson's first European campaign as United manager and having succeeded in the Cup Winners' Cup when in charge at Aberdeen, he was determined to repeat the feat.

The first round saw an easy 3-0 aggregate victory over Hungarian side Pecsi Munkas with goals from Clayton Blackmore and Neil Webb at Old Trafford, and Brian McClair in picturesque Pecs.

In Round Two United were paired with Wrexham, home town of Mark Hughes and beat them 5-0 over the two legs.

Montpellier proved tougher opposition for the next stage when, despite a great start with McClair scoring in the first attack of the match, the French sprang a surprise and a Lee Martin own goal gave them a 1-1 draw at Old Trafford.

United performed much better in the second leg. Blackmore scored with a long range free-kick, and Steve Bruce from the penalty spot to put them in the semi-final.

There they face Polish club Legia Warsaw but a 3-1 away win, and a 1-1 second leg at Old Trafford took United to the final against Barcelona in Rotterdam.

Two of United's heroes in Rotterdam, Mark Hughes and Steve Bruce. The final was particularly meaningful to Hughes because it had been Barcelona that prised him away from Old Trafford in 1986. Hughes' spell with the Catalan giants wasn't a success, but his two goals in the final demonstrated that the magic that had commanded the original £1.8 million fee was still working. Bruce's contribution to the Cup run, too, was impressive. In defence, United concede only three goals, and at the other end the big defender hit four, making him the Reds' joint top scorer with Brian McClair

United's Second European Final

United knew they would be up against it and with goalkeeper Les Sealey protecting a badly gashed knee sustained in the League Cup Final less than a month earlier the odds against an English victory were stacked high.

The first shock of the final was Ferguson's decision to drop Neil Webb to make way for Michael Phelan as United lined up:

		Sealey		
Irwin	Bruce		Pallister	Blackmore
Phelan	Ince		Robson	Sharpe
	McClair		Hughes	

The second shock was the way United outplayed Barcelona.

After 67 minutes it looked as if Steve Bruce had given United the lead with a powerful header but Hughes ripped in to claim the goal as he pushed the ball over the line, and tied up victory eight minutes later with a splendidly taken goal . . . an angled shot from the edge of the penalty area as the team's 100th of the season brought the European Cup Winners' Cup to Old Trafford for the first time.

1960-69

Barcelona punished the struggling Sealey to make it 2-1 from a Ronald Koeman free kick but it was too late.

Rotterdam belonged to Manchester United as Alex Ferguson was hailed as the most successful manager since Sir Matt Busby.

United began the defence of their trophy with a visit to Greece and after 180 goal-less minutes against Athinaikos, Hughes and McClair saved the blushes with two extra-time goals in the second leg at Old Trafford.

The campaign was short lived.

Handicapped by UEFA's 'foreigner' ruling which restricted the use of Scottish, Welsh and Irish players as well as those from overseas, United fell to Atletico Madrid, losing the Spanish leg 3-0 before drawing 1-1 at Old Trafford.

There was some success that season however as the European Super Cup was won thanks to a 1-0 victory over Red Star Belgrade.

European disappointments

As Premiership champions in 1993, United were back in the European Cup, but it was a new style competition following the introduction of the Champions' League.

They failed to reach the Group stage, falling to Turkish side Galatasaray who drew 3-3 at Old Trafford and held out for a 0-0 stalemate in Istanbul.

The following year they were back but, still handicapped by the 'foreigner' rule, they performed poorly in their group.

They beat Gothenburg and Galatasaray at home but defeat by Barcelona and in the return game against the Swedes – for whom Jesper Blomqvist starred – saw them fail to reach the quarter finals.

In 1995, the UEFA Cup brought a swift exit and the sensation of a Peter Schmeichel headed goal rescuing the long standing home record. It was little consolation as Rotor Volgograd knocked them out thanks to a 1-1 away result.

Europe was United's priority for the 1996-97 season. Qualifying for the knock-out stage in second place, behind Juventus, United emphatically beat FC Porto 4-0 in the quarter-final. The semi-final against Borussia Dortmund proved to be a frustrating experience, the German champions winning 1-0 in Germany after United had dominated the game. The return at Old Trafford followed a similar pattern, Dortmund scored in the eighth minute while United spurned numerous scoring chances; it was a bitter blow.

UEFA were forced by European law to lift their restrictions on non-national players but it was a similar story the following season when, after reaching the quarter finals by winning their group, they fell to Monaco.

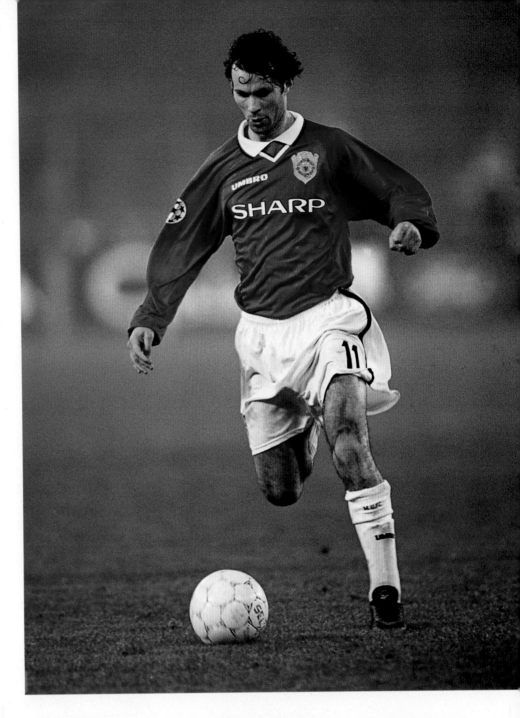

Against Juventus, in October 1997, Ryan Giggs was outstanding in the 3-2 victory over the Italian giants at Old Trafford, and his late goal will be long remembered by all who saw it. Giggs himself claimed it to be the best of his career, and there are few who would argue. Sadly while United topped their group it was second placed Juventus who eventually reached the final as United lost out to Monaco in the quarter finals

United had promised so much. In the qualifying stages, Juventus were beaten 3-2 at Old Trafford on a sensational night of exciting football, Ryan Giggs sealing victory with a classic third goal.

Kosice and Feyenoord provided little opposition as United won all their Group games except their final fixture in Turin. They easily qualified for the quarter finals but injury to Schmeichel and Giggs, ruled them out of the decider with Monaco.

After a 0-0 tussle in the Principality, a surprise 1-1 draw at Old Trafford brought proceedings to an end and saw the French League side through.

For the 1998-99 campaign see page 194, and for the 1999-2000 season turn to page 198.

CHAPTER 6

BEYOND BUSBY:
SEARCH FOR A SUCCESSOR

and it was unanimously agreed that Sir Matt be appointed general manager of the club which he is very happy to accept. The chairman added:

Of course we knew that it had to come but this does not mean that Sir Matt will be any less involved with Manchester United. In fact the post of general manager carries even wider responsibilities and my board are well content to think that in future they can call upon Sir Matt's unique football experience in both home and international fields.

The press had a field day searching out likely candidates. The names of Don Revie, Johnny Carey, Ron Greenwood, Jimmy Adamson and Brian Clough were freely mentioned, but few questioned whether such experienced managers would be willing to work under Sir Matt Busby.

The Busby Babes were the personification of a renaissance period for the whole of football as folk flocked back to the game after the grim days of the Second World War. Under Busby's guidance, United emerged a giant, surviving the most terrible of blows to conquer Europe. But even Sir Matt Busby couldn't go on for ever, nor could his great team of 1968. The great man needed a new commander to take his beloved club into the 1970s.

Even as they were winning the European Cup in 1968 and finishing runners-up for the Championship it was clear that some of the players were no longer in their prime and that changes would have to be made. Some of the decisions were going to be difficult, both in terms of judgement and feeling, and Busby thought long and hard about whether he wanted to be the manager to close one book and open yet another.

Busby tried to bolster the team by buying winger Willie Morgan, a Scottish international, for £110,000 from Burnley, but in September, October and November they managed just three wins. Disappointingly, the most frequent result was only a draw.

Denis Law and George Best manfully shouldered the burden, but by the end of the season their goal figures were down on previous seasons. Law scored 19 and Best 14, and Bobby Charlton was reduced to five. Morgan managed six, and the slump was eventually reflected in a League placing of 11th. Three defeats in succession around Christmas gave Sir Matt food for thought and by January he had reached a decision . . . he would 'go upstairs' to become general manager and leave a new man to run the team. The club issued a statement which read:

Sir Matt has informed the board that he wishes to relinquish the position of team manager at the end of the present season. The chairman and directors have tried to persuade him to carry on and it was only with great reluctance that his request has been accepted. The board fully appreciates the reason for his decision

Above: Manchester United at the start of the 1968-69 season proudly displaying the European Cup they had won the previous May. From right to left, back row: Bill Foulkes, John Aston, Jimmy Rimmer, Alex Stepney, Alan Gowling, David Herd, Middle: David Sadler, Tony Dunne, Shay Brennan, Pat Crerand, George Best, Francis Burns, Jack Crompton (trainer). Front: Jimmy Ryan, Nobby Stiles, Denis Law, Matt Busby (manager), Bobby Charlton, Brian Kidd, John Fitzpatrick. But despite the European triumph, the team had peaked. It was a side growing old gracefully and lacking the edge to keep them competing for fresh honours. Matt Busby was preparing to retire and a few of his stars were of like mind. They finished 11th that season and they never finished higher than eighth before relegation arrived six years after winning the European Cup

Left: As the '70s loomed, Busby was contemplating his future. Many of his match-winners – Charlton (left), Law and Best – were out of sorts and that meant United were not the force they once were. Despite protests from the board, Busby became general manager and, in so doing, made himself the hardest of acts to follow

Wilf McGuinness

The club solved the problem by looking within and deciding to promote one of their junior staff to take charge of the players with a title of chief coach. Wilf McGuinness, the 31-year-old trainer with the reserves, was the man chosen to follow in the great man's footsteps.

Wilf McGuinness was Busby's recommendation and the appointment had the advantage of keeping the management within the family of Old Trafford; it did however beg the question of total control, and was in marked contrast to the conditions insisted upon by Busby when he was brought to the club as a young man.

McGuinness had the additional problem of being asked to take charge of players who were his contemporaries, but these thoughts were only clouds on a distant horizon when the enthusiastic Wilf assembled his players for pre-season training in the summer of 1969. Wilf was certainly steeped in the tradition of the club and had always possessed qualities of leadership. As a schoolboy he captained not only Manchester Boys, but Lancashire and England as well. In fact he quite enjoys pointing out that a certain Bobby Charlton played under his command at schoolboy level!

As a junior, McGuinness was one of the Busby Babes and played in three of the FA Youth Cup winning teams in the 1950s.

His problem was that he was a left-half, and the great Duncan Edwards played in that position. His best season didn't come until after Munich. In 1958-59 he made 39 League appearances. Sadly, in the middle of the following season, he broke his leg playing for the reserves against Stoke. It was a bad break, and though he attempted a come-back he was forced to retire at the age of 22. But at least he had his qualities of leadership and United had no hesitation recruiting him as assistant trainer to Jack Crompton in charge of the reserve team.

Before long the Football Association made him the England youth team coach and in 1968 he was appointed their manager after helping Sir Alf Ramsey as a training assistant during preparations for the 1966 World Cup.

So the youthful McGuinness was not without management experience when he was handed command of the Busby empire. Yet, looking back, was there a veiled doubt in the minds of the board from the start?

On the pitch at least the difficulties soon manifested themselves. The opening game of the 1969-70 season, away to Crystal Palace, was drawn 2-2, a fair start in the circumstances, but then came three successive defeats, including losing 2-0 to Everton at Old Trafford and then going down at home again 4-1 to Southampton. This was followed by a 3-0 defeat at Everton and the fans were starting to worry.

United bought a new centre-half to replace the veteran Bill Foulkes, who had been given quite a chasing by centre-forward Ron Davies in the Southampton game. They bought Ian Ure from Arsenal for £80,000. It later transpired that Ure was not McGuinness's choice but Busby's, underlining at a very early stage the difficulties of dividing responsibility for running a team.

The team continued to hold their own, but in terms of winning the Championship it was becoming clear that new blood was required. The goal scoring was shared mainly by George Best again with 15, a welcome increase to 12 by Bobby Charlton and a useful 12 from Brian Kidd. Willie Morgan scored seven. There were lapses like a 4-0 beating at Manchester City and a 5-1 crash at Newcastle, immediately avenged by a 7-0 win against West Bromwich at Old Trafford in the next match.

For the third season in succession, more than a million spectators had packed Old Trafford, but behind the scenes there were rumblings. No-one knew better than McGuinness that, despite two semi-finals, changes were needed, and at the end of the season came reorganisation and a clear-out of players.

Bill Foulkes retired after a glorious career spanning 18 seasons of First Division football. Denis Law was put up for sale at £60,000, Don Givens was listed at £15,000 and nine other players were given free transfers, including Shay Brennan, who had joined the club with Wilf McGuinness 16 years previously. The two of them were great pals. Each was best man at the other's wedding and it must have been difficult when Wilf had to break the news to his friend.

The club were looking ahead, promoting McGuinness from chief coach to team manager. But there was still the feeling that the youthful McGuinness was heading for a crisis on the pitch as season 1970-71 began. Another slow start posed questions.

One of the problems was that while individually the older players still had a lot to offer, collectively they were aged. On their day they were still capable winning performances, as they showed by reaching the semi-final of the League Cup.

Wilf McGuinness had the unenviable task of taking over from Sir Matt Busby as manager of Manchester United. United wanted to make the appointment from within the club, so McGuinness was called up from the reserve team to be first-team coach. Later he was promoted to team manager, but though he did well enough by ordinary standards, it wasn't quite good enough for Old Trafford. He was in charge for 20 months, starting in April 1969, before being offered his old job back in December 1970

But they struggled in the first leg against Aston Villa at Old Trafford. Perhaps demoralised by a 4-1 home defeat against Manchester City four days earlier, they found they just could not master their opponents.

The flaws of the first half of the season were mirrored as they slid to a 2-1 defeat in the second leg and exit from the competition. To lose yet again just one step short of Wembley, and this time to a Third Division team, was a bitter blow to the fans who thought they had a good Cup team, even if it was a side with problems sustaining an effort in the League. The defeat was the death warrant for Wilf McGuinness, and after a 4-4 draw at Derby County three days later on Boxing Day, he was relieved of his first-team duties. Sir Matt announced in a statement:

The directors had a special meeting last night to discuss the performances of the team and decided to release Wilf

1969-72

McGuinness from his duties as team manager. As he did not wish to leave the club, and as the club felt he still had a part to play, he was offered his former position as trainer of the Central League side, which he has accepted. The board have asked me to take over team matters for the time being and until a new appointment is made in the close season.

Sir Matt, grim-faced and upset, explained:

I did not want to take charge of the team again, but my directors asked me to. At my age, I feel I have had enough of managerial worries at team level. It means becoming involved with players again. I shall be at their training sessions again. It's something I think I am capable of doing for a while, though I would have preferred we were not in this situation. It is unfortunate that things have not worked out. I feel very sorry for Wilf, who was appointed on my recommendation. He might have been a wee bit raw.

Later Sir Matt told his protegé where he thought he had gone wrong. 'You failed to get the players with you,' he said.

This was an apt summing up – whether the fault lay in McGuinness or the players is a moot point. Certainly at least two of the senior men had been to see Sir Matt behind the manager's back, perhaps in a genuine concern for the club's plight, though hardly a move calculated to help the manager's authority.

One player was reported anonymously in the *Sunday Times* as saying:

The problem for Wilf McGuinness was he had no personality. He did not understand that the team he was controlling needed handling in a special way. I am not saying we were special, but after all, we had won the European Cup and we were being told what to do by a man who had never been anywhere. People go on about us buying our way out of trouble, but I believe we would have been screwed even if Wilf had had a million quid to spend.

Denis Law was the king as far as United fans were concerned. They liked the streak of villainy which ran through his play as well as his excellence as a goal scorer. Not a big man by any means, but as quick as lightning in front of goal, he spent 11 seasons at Old Trafford, scoring a remarkable 236 goals in 393 appearances in League, domestic cup and European competition. Born in Aberdeen, he came into English football with Huddersfield Town, moved to Manchester City and then went abroad to play for Torino in Italy. Matt Busby brought him back to England, paying a then record £115,000. He rejoined City and scored his final League goal with a back-flick which confirmed United's descent into the Second Division

Busby returns

Sir Matt himself could still control them. The team clawed their way back to finish eighth again, while McGuinness went back to running the reserves. Not for long though. After two months he decided to quit the club he loved, saying:

I thought I had time. I was on a contract which still had 18 months to run, but the simple truth is that the results went badly for me. We have been in three Cup semi-finals, something that cannot be claimed by any other club, and yet each time we fell short of reaching the final. If we had made it in any one of those competitions, things might have been so different.

The extent of the turmoil within McGuinness can be judged by the fact that soon afterwards, as he attempted to rebuild his career in Greece, his hair fell out almost overnight and what little grew again was white.

With hindsight it seems the board were more concerned with persuading Matt Busby to stay on as manager than in properly preparing a successor. Perhaps Wilf McGuinness should been brought on to the first-team scene a year earlier as a senior trainer instead of being thrust right into the deep end.

The experience certainly did nothing for the image of Manchester United who were right back to square one with few, if any, of their problems solved. It had been the worst playing record since the Second World War, for although the club had finished lower in the League on occasions there had invariably been a good FA Cup run.

So there were still enormous difficulties waiting to be resolved. The fans were demanding new blood. United hadn't bought anyone for two years, with Ian Ure their last signing. In fact they had bought only three players in six years – Ure, Willie Morgan and Alex Stepney.

The behaviour of George Best did not help much either. Although he was top scorer with 18 League goals, he was becoming increasingly difficult to manage. Apart from periodic petulance on the field, usually involving referees, the first sign that all was not well came on Christmas Day. He simply failed to turn up for training, the only player to shirk an obviously unpopular chore. McGuinness was considerably annoyed because the player had no real excuse, beyond perhaps a sore head after Christmas Eve celebrations. It was agreed that he should be sent home when he reported the next day for the match at Derby County. Then came second thoughts. They fined him £50 instead and played him. Of course he scored to help achieve a 4-4 draw. But should expediency have come before discipline?

United received a poor reward for their leniency. Less than a fortnight later the player was due to meet Busby at Piccadilly Station to catch a train to London for an appearance in front of the FA disciplinary committee to answer for three bookings. He failed to turn up, and Sir Matt had to travel down on his own and then use all his eloquence to placate the commission whose members were in no mood to indulge a young man who could not even arrive on time for his disciplinary hearing. The hearing was put back until later in the day so that Best, who had pleaded feeling unwell when his housekeeper had arrived at his home in Bramhall first thing in the morning, could catch a later train. When he eventually arrived at Euston Station he was mobbed by photographers, reporters, television cameras and girls. George Best was a show on his own. It took him 10 minutes to fight his way through in his smart blue suit, pink shirt and white tie.

He was given a suspended six-week suspension, but just five days later he failed to report for morning training before the team set off for London in readiness for a match at Chelsea the following day. Sir Matt expected him at the station, but he was still missing. John Aston was sent for as a replacement and Busby announced that Best need not bother coming at all. The player travelled to London anyway and went to ground hiding in the flat of his latest girlfriend. Busby expected him to report to the ground on Monday, but he was still in London besieged by the media. He was suspended by the club for a fortnight and it took the combined efforts of his agent, Ken Stanley, and business partner, Malcolm Mooney, to bring him back to face the music.

It emerged later that it wasn't just his playboy streak that turned him into the runaway soccer star. He had also grown somewhat disillusioned with the decline of the team, and he felt, probably rightly too, that too much was being expected of him. He once remarked: 'Everyone makes mistakes – mine just seem to get more publicity than other people's.'

That was certainly true, just as it was true that he had presented Wilf McGuinness with a stack of problems which even the experienced Busby found difficult enough. For a young man in his first big job it must have seemed like a nightmare. What should he have done for instance when he caught a girl in the player's room a hours before a semi-final? Drop his best player in the interests of discipline, or play him and risk the rest of the team grumbling about a rule for one and another for the others?

It all added up to a most difficult period of change which had proved too much for the youthful Wilf McGuinness, and though Sir Matt had galloped to the rescue, the problems were still there as the board looked for a man to follow the legendary manager.

Frank O'Farrell takes over

The club were looking for an experienced manager this time and they finally settled on Frank O'Farrell, who had a good, solid record of achievement. He was to bring with him from Leicester City his partner at Filbert Street, Malcolm Musgrove, a coach who like his boss had grown up as a player in the think-tank era of West Ham with the likes of Malcolm Allison, Dave Sexton, Noel Cantwell, John Bond and Ken Brown.

The parallels with Sir Matt were strong, even down to strong convictions as Roman Catholics. They had both started from modest family backgrounds. Frank's first ambition was to follow in his father's footsteps and drive the express trains from Cork to Dublin. He did indeed start his working life shovelling coal on the Irish Railways.

O'Farrell started on the ground floor as player-coach with Weymouth and made club history by taking the Southern League team to the fourth round of the FA Cup. This brought him an invitation to manage Torquay and in his first season he brought them up from the Fourth Division to the Third. He followed Matt Gillies as manager of Leicester in December 1968, and failed to save them from dropping into the Second Division, but he did enjoy a run to Wembley in the FA Cup, losing to Manchester City. After two seasons he brought Leicester back to the First Division as Champions and it was his steady managerial progress through all levels which attracted United.

O'Farrell looked an eminently sound choice and he accepted the invitation to come to Old Trafford proffered in the chairman's car parked on a lonely side road at Mackworth just outside Derby, and he said about his contract: 'It's long enough to achieve what I hope to achieve.'

Stung by criticism that his presence as general manager had not given McGuinness a fair chance, Sir Matt voluntarily gave up his paid post and joined the board as a director. He said:

The idea seemed to build up that if I stayed as general manager I would want to interfere. It was a wrong impression, but it was splashed about and I admit the talk influenced me. Frank O'Farrell did not make an issue of it, in fact he said he hoped his coming was not the reason and he didn't mind whether I stayed on as general manager or director.

So O'Farrell had a clear field and he voiced firm ideas for the future, in keeping with the Busby traditions:

I have no preconceived ideas. I don't prejudge any situation or individual. I just want to see for myself and make up my own mind. The entertaining image must be maintained, but at the same time if modifications in style are necessary to make the team a more efficient unit, then they must be made. In principle a team needs a sound defence. That is the basis, but it doesn't mean that I have to be defensive minded.

Malcolm Musgrove, who followed Jimmy Hill as chairman of the Professional Footballers' Association, believed United had made the right appointment. He said:

Frank O'Farrell is one of the few people who could have come to Old Trafford. The job is so big it's hardly true. Yet Frank will measure up. He is the ideal choice. His greatest quality is his honesty, yet you don't pull the wool over his eyes. I think we make a good partnership and I hope it will show for Manchester United.

That partnership was going to be sorely tried and tested in

1969-72

the next 18 months, both on and off the pitch, but there were no such fears as the new management team got off to a brilliant start. Although they drew 2-2 at Derby on the opening day, they won the next three and only lost one of their first 14 games. By early October they were top of the First Division, and as Christmas approached they had a five-point lead.

The inspiration of a new manager and the fresh coaching techniques of Malcolm Musgrove had fired some of the old skill and enthusiasm in the first half of the season, but it all vanished in the seven-match burn-out. O'Farrell knew it was time to turn to the transfer market, and he made two excellent signings in the space of a fortnight. First he moved to Aberdeen with £125,000 for Martin Buchan and then paid £200,000 for Ian Storey-Moore from Nottingham Forest.

Martin Buchan

Buchan at 23 was a super signing, who went on to play 455 League and Cup games for United, becoming their captain and a remarkable character. Already a Scottish international, he was the exception from Scotland who proved the rule, adjusting immediately to the pace of English football. His debut was marked by a 2-0 defeat at Spurs, but his influence on those around him was very evident and he quickly slowed the rate of descent down the League table. United lost only four of their last 12 games with Buchan playing.

Signing Buchan in February 1972 was O'Farrell's best day's work and a handsome legacy to leave. O'Farrell's second signing, a week later, was also a good buy, but Ian Moore eventually ran into bad luck with numerous injuries.

The question marks against Best were mounting. During the summer the player went missing again, this time failing to report for duty with Northern Ireland, and the episode ended with him threatening to retire from football. He had been a source of worry for the new manager right from the start of the season. In only the second League game he was sent off against Chelsea at Stamford Bridge by Norman Burtenshaw for abusive language. An FA disciplinary commission cleared him after accepting his plea that his swearing had been directed at team-mate Willie Morgan and not at the referee.

Morgan backed up the player, who was well represented by Cliff Lloyd, the secretary of the Professional Footballers' Association who outshone Perry Mason on the day. United were worried because if Best had been found guilty a six-week suspended ban would have come in to operation as well as any other further punishment. Many people thought Best lucky to escape, and O'Farrell privately indicated which version he believed.

At least Best behaved for a while and in fact enjoyed fabulous form again, but in January he failed to turn up for training, and

Martin Buchan was the most valuable legacy of Frank O'Farrell's management. The United manager signed the Scot from Aberdeen for £125,000 in March 1972, and he played at Old Trafford for 12 seasons. He was a remarkable defender, a man who knew his own mind and an obvious captain. In 1977 he captained United to victory in the FA Cup against Liverpool to become the first player to skipper both English and Scottish Cup-winning teams. He subsequently played for Oldham and was briefly a manager at Burnley before returning to his native Aberdeen

just when the team needed him. O'Farrell immediately dropped him, fined him two weeks' pay, ordered him to train in the afternoons as well as the mornings and cancelled his days off for five weeks to make up for the week's training he had skipped.

Then at the end of the season, after signing off with a goal in a 3-0 win against Stoke, the team which had knocked United out of the FA Cup in the sixth round, Best disappeared on the eve of the British Championships. The day after he should have joined the Northern Ireland squad he turned up at a luxury hotel in Marbella on the Spanish coast. Against a background of jet-set living and champagne by the side of a sun-soaked swimming pool, he announced that he had had his fill of football, Manchester United and the Irish international team. The day after announcing his retirement he celebrated his 26th birthday. Frank O'Farrell said:

I know he has been drinking a lot and has been going out with a lot of girl friends and keeping late hours. These things and pressures from outside the game have wrecked him.

Best was expected to link up with his club in Tel Aviv for the final game of their summer tour, but he didn't make that either and was posted absent without leave. A few days later he crept back into Manchester and at a secret meeting with O'Farrell said it was all a big mistake and that he wanted to play again after all.

On the brighter side another boy from Belfast made a significant entrance on to the Old Trafford stage. Sammy McIlroy, sent over from Ireland by Bob Bishop, the scout who had nurtured Best as a boy, was given his League debut at the age of 17 against Manchester City at Maine Road. He scored an exciting goal in a 3-3 draw to win a bottle of champagne from Best, and in fact scored in each of his first four League games. He made such an impact that he played for Northern Ireland within three months of his League debut, still only 17.

There was a lot still to accomplish, as Frank O'Farrell readily admitted, but few could have anticipated the disasters lying in wait as season 1972-73 got under way.

The team opened with a terrible string of results. They lost the first three games, drew the next four and then lost two more. Those first nine games saw them score only three goals. The alarm bells were ringing for Frank and he turned urgently to the transfer market.

He bought Wyn Davies from Manchester City for £60,000, and the Welshman scored on his debut against Derby at Old Trafford to help notch the first win of the season. But by now the Reds had gone to the bottom like a lead weight. A week later Frank swooped again to land Ted MacDougall from Third Division Bournemouth for £200,000. MacDougall scored on his second appearance for a 1-0 win against Birmingham, but pressure was building up. Losing 4-1 at home to Spurs didn't help; nor did a morale-sapping derby defeat at Maine Road.

The departures of O'Farrell and Best

Ironically United won their next two games, but the board were already making plans for a new manager. The *Manchester Evening News* carried a story with the headline 'Be Fair to Frank', urging the club to give the manager time, but that only succeeded in getting the joint author of this history, David Meek, banned from travelling on the team coach.

The final blow for O'Farrell came on 16 December at Crystal Palace where his team crashed 5-0. Significantly, Tommy Docherty, then manager of Scotland, was watching from the stands. After the game Sir Matt Busby seized the opportunity to ask him if he was interested in coming to Old Trafford. The Doc indicated that he was; he could do little else since it had been his burning ambition to manage Manchester United for 25 years!

First had to come the night of the long knives, an evening of wining, dining and dancing to celebrate the finale of Bobby Charlton's testimonial. Frank O'Farrell, Malcolm Musgrove and

Above: Sir Matt with George Best speaks at a press conference in 1971 after Best had returned from going AWOL

Right: Bobby Charlton made his debut for Manchester United in October 1956, scoring twice in a 4-2 win against Charlton Athletic at Old Trafford. Here he is pictured stepping out for last time on 28 April 1973 after 604 League appearances

John Aston were all at the banquet and ball which went on into the early hours. There could have been little sleep for the directors before they met at the offices of chairman Louis Edwards and the decision was taken to sack the management team. The statement issued on Tuesday, 19 December 1972, read:

In view of the poor position in the League, it was unanimously decided that Mr O'Farrell, Malcolm Musgrove and John Aston be relieved of their duties forthwith.

Side by side with the sacking of the manager almost inevitably ran another chapter in the saga of George Best. Once again the Irishman was in crisis and gave notice that he was quitting in a letter to the board. He wrote:

. . . therefore I have decided not to play football again, and this time no-one will change my mind. I would like to wish the club the best of luck for the remainder of the season and for the future. Because even though I personally have tarnished the club's name in recent times, to me and thousands of others, Manchester United still means something special.

The club were at some pains at the end to make it clear that they had in fact 'sacked' George Best as well as the manager before the player's letter of resignation had reached them. The statement announcing the sacking of Frank O'Farrell also said:

Furthermore, George Best will remain on the transfer list and will not be selected again for Manchester United as it is felt it is in the best interest of the club and the player that he leaves Old Trafford.

So it turned out the board had beaten the player to the punch by a few hours, though it is difficult to see how it mattered, except perhaps to Frank O'Farrell, who might well have wished for that kind of backing from the directors a little earlier in the whole protracted drama with the player. Frank left the club with great bitterness, a feeling which persisted for many years, and perhaps will for the rest of his life. His departure certainly ended his career in football as a top manager, though he did return in an advisory capacity with Torquay for a while.

The senior players saw Frank O'Farrell as someone distant

1969-72

and remote. Denis Law, for instance, once quipped: 'Frank O'Farrell – who's he?' He later summed up: 'Mr O'Farrell came as a stranger and went as a stranger.'

From where Frank stood, other teams had left United behind in terms of effort and team-work. He considered that players who had enjoyed success under the old regime resented his new methods. He likened Old Trafford to Sleepy Valley. The old stars were going out. Even that most dedicated and conscientious of players, Bobby Charlton, was on the brink of retirement. And all the time there had been the divisive problem of the wandering Best. Willie Morgan didn't pull any punches when he said:

George thought he was the James Bond of soccer. He had everything he wanted and he pleased himself. He had money, girls and tremendous publicity. He lived from day to day. Until right at the end, he got away with it when he missed training or ran away. So he didn't care. People always made excuses for him; he didn't even have to bother to make them himself.

The Irishman's letter of resignation was not quite the end of his links with United. He continued to flirt with the game, but his night club, Slack Alice, claimed most of his attention.

Certainly there was need for a dynamic personality and bold leadership when the United directors looked round for Frank O'Farrell's successor, and of course in Tommy Docherty they found just the man.

But though things were bad on the field, there was still a lot going for the club. The ground itself, for instance, was looking better than ever, and the club was very healthy from the financial point of view. The enthusiasm for the club was boundless, as was shown on the night Glasgow Celtic came to Old Trafford to play a testimonial in honour of Bobby Charlton.

Tribute to Charlton

The date was 18 September 1972. The team had yet to win a League game that season, but the fans put that behind them to pay tribute to one of their favourites who had graced the game for 20 years. There were 60,538 people packed into Old Trafford probably feeling a little like Sir Matt Busby when he wrote in the testimonial programme:

He has broken all records and won everything possible that there is to win. Yet he has remained completely unspoiled, still prepared to do more than his fair share for the cause of Manchester United. The shy boy has blossomed now into a man with a great sense of assurance, confidence and responsibility.

It was a night of nostalgia, which to a certain extent had been the problem for Frank O'Farrell. United had become a club living on its past. The giant was slumbering again . . . but not for long as Manchester braced itself for the arrival of Tommy Docherty, who reckoned he had the right prescription for an ailing club.

SEASON 1960-1961 FOOTBALL LEAGUE (DIVISION 1)

Date	Opp		Res											
20 Aug	Blackburn R	H	L	1-3	Gregg	Cope	Carolan	Setters	Haydock	Brennan	Giles	Quixall	Viollet	Charlton1	Scanlon
24 Aug	Everton	H	D	0-4		Brennan				Nicholson					
31 Aug	Everton	H	W	4-0		Foulkes	Brennan			..1		Giles	Dawson2	Viollet	Charlton1
3 Sep	Tottenham H	A	L	1-4									..1		
5 Sep	West Ham U	A	L	1-2				Cope			..1				
10 Sep	Leicester C	H	D	1-1								..1			
14 Sep	West Ham U	H	W	6-1							..1		Viollet2	Charlton2	Scanlon1
17 Sep	Aston Villa	A	L	1-3							Giles	Quixall	..1		
24 Sep	Wolverhampton W	H	L	1-3									..1		
1 Oct	Bolton W	A	D	1-1		Setters		Stiles	Foulkes		Moir	Giles1	Dawson		
15 Oct	Burnley	A	L	3-5			Dunne A	Brennan			Quixall		Viollet3	Pearson	Charlton
22 Oct	Newcastle U	H	W	3-2		..1					Dawson1			Charlton	Scanlon
24 Oct	Nottingham F	H	W	2-1		Dunne A							..2	Pearson	
29 Oct	Arsenal	A	L	1-2		Brennan	Heron						Quixall1	Charlton	
5 Nov	Sheffield Wed	A	D	0-0		Setters	Brennan								
12 Nov	Birmingham C	A	L	1-3									Pearson	..1	
19 Nov	W B A	H	W	3-0							Bradley	Quixall1	Dawson1		
26 Nov	Cardiff C	A	L	0-3		Brennan	Cantwell	Setters					Viollet1		
3 Dec	Preston NE	H	W	1-0									..1	Pearson	
10 Dec	Fulham	A	D	4-4								..2		..1	..1
17 Dec	Blackburn R	A	W	2-1							Quixall	Stiles		..2	..1
24 Dec	Chelsea	A	W	2-1									..1		
26 Dec	Chelsea	H	W	6-0							..2		..3		..1
31 Dec	Manchester C	H	W	5-1									..3		..1
14 Jan	Tottenham H	H	W	2-0								..1			..2
21 Jan	Leicester C	A	L	0-6	Briggs										
4 Feb	Aston Villa	H	D	1-1	Pinner									..1	
11 Feb	Wolverhampton W	A	L	1-2						..1					
18 Feb	Bolton W	H	W	3-1				Stiles		Setters	Morgans	Quixall1	..2		
25 Feb	Nottingham F	A	L	2-3	Gregg			Setters		Nicholson		..1		..1	..1
4 Mar	Manchester C	A	W	3-1						Stiles	Moir		..1		..1
11 Mar	Newcastle U	A	D	1-1	Pinner								Lawton		
16 Mar	Arsenal	H	W	1-1	Gaskell					..1				Dawson	
25 Mar	Sheffield Wed	A	L	1-5											..1
31 Mar	Blackpool	A	L	0-2											
1 Apr	Fulham	H	W	3-1						Nicholson	Giles				
3 Apr	Blackpool	H	W	*2-0						..1					
8 Apr	W B A	A	D	1-1										..1	Moir
12 Apr	Burnley	H	W	6-0						Stiles		..3	..3	..1	
15 Apr	Birmingham C	H	W	4-1								..1	..1	..2	
22 Apr	Preston NE	A	W	4-2		Dunne A	Brennan	..2							Charlton2
29 Apr	Cardiff C	H	D	3-3		Brennan	Cantwell	..1							..2

FA Cup

7 Jan	Middlesbrough (3)	H	W	3-0	Gregg	Brennan	Cantwell1	Setters	Foulkes	Nicholson	Quixall	Stiles	Dawson2	Pearson	Charlton
26 Jan	Sheffield Wed (4)	A	D	1-1	Briggs		..1				Viollet				
1 Feb	Sheffield Wed (4R)	H	L	2-7							Quixall		..1	..1	

Football League Cup

19 Oct	Exeter C (1)	A	D	1-1	Gregg	Setters	Brennan	Stiles	Foulkes	Nicholson	Dawson1	Lawton	Viollet	Pearson	Scanlon
26 Oct	Exeter C (1R)	H	W	4-1	Gaskell	Dunne A	Carolan			Cope		Giles1	Quixall2	..1	
2 Nov	Bradford C (2)	A	L	1-2	Gregg	Setters	Brennan	Bratt	Foulkes				Viollet1		

Appearances (goals)

Bradley	4	
Brennan	41	
Briggs	1	
Cantwell	24	
Carolan	2	
Charlton	39	21
Cope	6	
Dawson	28	16
Dunne A	3	
Foulkes	40	
Gaskell	10	
Giles	23	2
Gregg	27	
Haydock	4	
Heron	1	
Lawton	1	
Moir	8	1
Morgans	2	
Nicholson	31	5
Pearson	27	7
Pinner	4	
Quixall	38	13
Scanlon	8	1
Setters	40	4
Stiles	26	2
Viollet	24	15
Own goals		1
Total 26 players		**88**

Football League

	P	W	D	L	F:A	Pts	
Tottenham H	42	31	4	7	115:55	66	1st
Manchester U	42	18	9	15	88:76	45	7th

SEASON 1961-1962 FOOTBALL LEAGUE (DIVISION 1)

Date	Opp		Res											
19 Aug	West Ham U	A	D	1-1	Gregg	Brennan	Cantwell	Stiles1	Foulkes	Setters	Quixall	Viollet	Herd	Pearson	Charlton
23 Aug	Chelsea	H	W	3-2									..1		
26 Aug	Blackburn R	H	W	6-1							..1		..2		..1
30 Aug	Chelsea	A	L	0-2											
2 Sep	Blackpool	A	W	3-2							Bradley	..2			..1
9 Sep	Tottenham H	H	W	1-0							Quixall1				
16 Sep	Cardiff C	A	D	1-1	Gaskell		Dunne A	..1			..1		Dawson1		
18 Sep	Aston Villa	H	W	2-1	Gregg			..1					Herd		
23 Sep	Manchester C	H	W	*3-2	Gregg							..1	Dawson		
30 Sep	Wolverhampton W	H	L	0-2			Cantwell	..1		Lawton		Giles	Dawson		
7 Oct	W B A	A	D	1-1	Gaskell						Moir	Quixall	1	Giles	
14 Oct	Birmingham C	H	L	0-2	Gregg				Haydock		Bradley	Giles	Herd	Moir	
21 Oct	Arsenal	A	L	1-5				Nicholson	Foulkes		Moir		Herd	Viollet1	Charlton
28 Oct	Bolton W	A	L	0-3			Dunne A	Cantwell		Setters		Quixall	Herd		
4 Nov	Sheffield Wed	H	W	1-1				Stiles			Bradley	Giles	Viollet1	Charlton	McMillan
11 Nov	Leicester C	H	D	2-2	Gaskell								Herd		
18 Nov	Ipswich T	A	L	1-4			Dunne A						Herd		
25 Nov	Burnley	H	L	1-4										Quixall	Charlton
2 Dec	Everton	A	L	1-5				Nicholson				Chisnall		Lawton	
9 Dec	Fulham	H	W	3-0										..1	
16 Dec	West Ham U	H	L	1-2										..1	
26 Dec	Nottingham F	H	W	6-3			..1						..1	..3	..1
13 Jan	Blackpool	H	L	0-1											
15 Jan	Aston Villa	H	W	2-0									Quixall1		..1
20 Jan	Tottenham H	A	D	2-2								Stiles1	Lawton	Giles	..1
3 Feb	Cardiff C	H	W	3-0								..1	..1	1	..1
10 Feb	Manchester C	A	W	2-0				Stiles	Setters	Nicholson	..1	Giles	Herd	Lawton	
24 Feb	W B A	H	W	4-1	Briggs				Foulkes	Setters1	Quixall1				
28 Feb	Wolverhampton W	A	D	2-2				Setters		Nicholson		Stiles	..1		
3 Mar	Birmingham C	A	D	1-1				Stiles		Setters		Giles	..1		
17 Mar	Bolton W	A	L	0-1				Nicholson							
20 Mar	Nottingham F	A	L	0-1									Lawton	Stiles	
24 Mar	Sheffield Wed	H	D	1-1	Gaskell			Stiles			Moir		Viollet	Herd	Charlton1
4 Apr	Leicester C	A	L	3-4			Setters			Nicholson		Quixall1	Herd		McMillan2
7 Apr	Ipswich T	H	W	5-0	Briggs	Brennan		..1		Setters1		Giles	Quixall3	McMillan	Charlton
10 Apr	Blackburn R	A	L	0-3	Gaskell								Cantwell	Pearson	Charlton
14 Apr	Burnley	A	W	3-1	Briggs						Giles	Pearson	Herd1		McMillan
16 Apr	Arsenal	H	L	2-3			Cantwell1						Herd	Viollet1	..1
21 Apr	Everton	H	D	1-1	Gaskell		Dunne A					Cantwell	Herd1	McMillan	Charlton
23 Apr	Sheffield U	H	L	0-1									Herd	McMillan	
24 Apr	Sheffield U	A	W	3-2				Nicholson1					McMillan2	Stiles1	
28 Apr	Fulham	A	L	0-2				Setters		Nicholson					

FA Cup

6 Jan	Bolton W (3)	H	W	2-1	Gaskell	Brennan	Dunne A	Nicholson1	Foulkes	Setters	Chisnall	Giles	Herd1	Lawton	Charlton
31 Jan	Arsenal (4)	H	W	1-0							..1		Stiles		
17 Feb	Sheffield Wed (5)	H	D	0-0				Setters		Nicholson			Herd		
21 Feb	Sheffield Wed (5R)	A	W	2-0				Stiles		Setters	Quixall		..1		..1
10 Mar	Preston NE (6)	A	D	0-0				Nicholson			Chisnall		Cantwell		
14 Mar	Preston NE (6R)	H	W	2-1				Stiles			Quixall		Herd1		..1
31 Mar	Tottenham H (SF)	N	L	1-3			Dunne A	Cantwell					..1		
	(at Hillsborough)														

Appearances (goals)

Bradley	6	
Brennan	41	2
Briggs	8	
Cantwell	17	2
Charlton	37	8
Chisnall	9	1
Dawson	4	2
Dunne A	28	
Foulkes	40	
Gaskell	21	
Giles	30	2
Gregg	13	
Haydock	1	
Herd	27	14
Lawton	20	6
McMillan	11	6
Moir	9	
Nicholson	17	
Pearson	17	1
Quixall	21	10
Setters	38	3
Stiles	34	7
Viollet	13	7
Own goals		1
Total 23 players		**72**

Football League

	P	W	D	L	F:A	Pts	
Ipswich	42	24	8	10	93:67	56	1st
Manchester U	42	15	9	18	72:75	39	15th

SEASON 1962-1963 FOOTBALL LEAGUE (DIVISION 1)

Date	Opp		Res											
18 Aug	W B A	H	D	2-2	Gaskell	Brennan	Dunne A	Stiles	Foulkes	Setters	Giles	Quixall	Herd1	Law1	Moir
22 Aug	Everton	A	L	1-3									Pearson		1
25 Aug	Arsenal	A	W	3-1				Nicholson		Lawton		Chisnall1	..2		
29 Aug	Everton	H	W	0-1											
1 Sep	Birmingham C	H	W	2-0								..1		..1	
5 Sep	Bolton W	A	L	0-3							Quixall				
8 Sep	Leyton O	A	L	0-1						Moir	Setters				McMillan
12 Sep	Bolton W	H	W	3-0				Stiles		Giles	Lawton		..2		Cantwell1
15 Sep	Manchester C	H	L	2-3						Nicholson			..1	..1	
22 Sep	Burnley	H	L	2-5						Lawton		Law 2		..2	Moir
29 Sep	Sheffield Wed	A	L	0-1	Gregg							Quixall	Herd	Chisnall	McMillan
6 Oct	Blackpool	A	D	2-2						Nicholson			Herd2	Lawton	
13 Oct	Blackburn R	H	L	0-3											Charlton
20 Oct	Tottenham H	A	L	2-6			Cantwell			Setters		Quixall1		Law	Charlton
27 Oct	West Ham U	A	W	3-1								..1	4	..1	
3 Nov	Ipswich T	A	W	5-3									..1	..4	..1
10 Nov	Liverpool	H	D	3-3										4	..2
17 Nov	Wolverhampton W	H	W	3-2							..1			..2	..2
24 Nov	Aston Villa	H	D	2-2									..2		
1 Dec	Sheffield Wed	A	D	1-1									Lawton		
8 Dec	Nottingham F	H	W	5-1				Nicholson			Lawton	..1		..2	Law1
15 Dec	W B A	A	L	0-3				Stiles			Nicholson			Moir	..1
26 Dec	Fulham	A	W	1-0							Setters			Charlton1	
23 Feb	Blackpool	H	D	1-1									Chisnall		
2 Mar	Blackburn R	A	D	2-2							Crerand		Chisnall	Law1	
9 Mar	Tottenham H	H	L	0-2											..1
18 Mar	West Ham U	H	L	1-3						Stiles			Stiles		
23 Mar	Ipswich T	H	L	0-1						Setters			Quixall		
1 Apr	Fulham	H	L	0-2			Dunne A						Chisnall	Quixall	
9 Apr	Aston Villa	A	W	2-1			Cantwell						Stiles1	Herd	Quixall
13 Apr	Liverpool	A	L	0-1			Dunne A							Quixall	Law
15 Apr	Leicester C	A	L	3-4							Quixall				..1
18 Apr	Leicester C	H	L	2-3									Herd1		..1
20 Apr	Sheffield U	H	D	1-1										..3	..1
22 Apr	Wolverhampton W	H	W	2-2	Gaskell									..1	..1
1 May	Sheffield Wed	H	L	1-3			Cantwell						Quixall		..1
4 May	Burnley	A	L	1-0			Dunne A				Giles		Quixall		..1
6 May	Arsenal	H	L	2-3										..1	..1
10 May	Birmingham C	A	L	1-2								Stiles	Quixall	Giles	Herd
15 May	Manchester C	A	D	1-1										..1	
18 May	Leyton O	H	W	*3-1								Setters	Giles		
20 May	Nottingham F	A	L	2-3					Haydock			Brennan	Stiles	Giles	Walker

FA Cup

4 Mar	Huddersfield T (3)	H	W	5-0	Gregg	Brennan	Cantwell	Stiles	Foulkes	Setters	Giles1	Quixall1	Herd	Law3	Charlton
11 Mar	Aston Villa (4)	H	W	1-0								..1			
16 Mar	Chelsea (5)	H	W	2-1								..1			
30 Mar	Coventry C (6)	A	W	3-1			Dunne A	Crerand			..1		..1		..2
27 Apr	Southampton (SF)	N	W	1-0	Gaskell	Dunne A	Cantwell				Stiles		..1		
	(at Villa Park)														
25 May	Leicester C (F)	N	W	3-1								Quixall	..2		..1
	(at Wembley)														

Appearances (goals)

Brennan	37	
Cantwell	25	1
Charlton	28	7
Chisnall	6	1
Crerand	19	
Dunne A	25	
Foulkes	41	
Gaskell	18	
Giles	36	4
Gregg	24	
Haydock	1	
Herd	37	19
Law	38	23
Lawton	12	
McMillan	4	
Moir	9	1
Nicholson	10	
Pearson	2	
Quixall	31	7
Setters	27	1
Stiles	31	2
Walker	1	
Own goals		1
Total 22 players		**67**

Football League

	P	W	D	L	F:A	Pts	
Everton	42	25	11	6	84:42	61	1st
Manchester U	42	12	10	20	67:81	34	19th

Date	Opponent				Gregg	Dunne A	Cantwell	Crerand	Foulkes	Setters	Moir1	Chisnall	Sadler	Law	Charlton2
24 Aug	Sheffield Wed	A	D	3-3										..2	
28 Aug	Ipswich T	H	W	2-0						Stiles		..2	..1	..2	
31 Aug	Everton	H	W	5-1						Setters1		..1	..1	..2	
3 Sep	Ipswich T	A	W	7-2								..1		..1	
7 Sep	Birmingham C	A	D	1-1									..1		..2
11 Sep	Blackpool	H	W	3-0						Best	Stiles	..1		Chisnall	
14 Sep	W B A	H	W	1-0						Moir					
16 Sep	Blackpool	A	L	0-1						Herd1	Chisnall		Law		
21 Sep	Arsenal	A	L	1-2						Moir			Herd2		
28 Sep	Leicester C	H	W	3-1					..1						
2 Oct	Chelsea	A	D	1-1					..1						
5 Oct	Bolton W	A	W	1-0						Herd1			Stiles		
19 Oct	Nottingham F	H	W	2-1						Quixall1		Herd			
26 Oct	West Ham U	H	L	0-1						Moir					
28 Oct	Blackburn R	H	D	2-2						Stiles		Quixall2			
2 Nov	Wolverhampton W	A	L	0-2						Setters					
9 Nov	Tottenham H	H	W	4-1						Quixall	Moore	Herd1	..3		
16 Nov	Aston Villa	A	L	0-4											
23 Nov	Liverpool	H	L	0-1									..2		
30 Nov	Sheffield U	A	W	2-1	Gaskell								..4		
7 Dec	Stoke C	H	W	5-2							Chisnall	Sadler	Herd3		
14 Dec	Sheffield Wed	H	W	3-1		Brennan	Dunne A				Moir				
21 Dec	Everton	A	L	0-4		Dunne A	Cantwell				Quixall	Charlton	..1		Brennan
26 Dec	Burnley	A	L	1-6							Anderson		..2		Best1
28 Dec	Burnley	H	W	5-1							Herd	..2			
11 Jan	Birmingham C	H	L	1-2								Sadler1	Law		
18 Jan	W B A	A	W	4-1								Charlton1	..2		
1 Feb	Arsenal	H	W	3-1		Brennan	Dunne A	Stiles		..1			..1		..1
8 Feb	Leicester C	A	L	2-3				Crerand		..1					
19 Feb	Bolton W	H	W	5-0						..2	Stiles		..2		..1
22 Feb	Blackburn R	A	W	3-1							Chisnall1				
7 Mar	West Ham U	A	W	2-0					Tranter	Stiles	Anderson	Sadler1	Herd1		Moir1
21 Mar	Tottenham H	A	W	3-2					Foulkes		Best	Moore1	Law1		Charlton1
23 Mar	Chelsea	H	D	1-1									Herd		
27 Mar	Fulham	A	D	2-2								Chisnall	..1	Setters	..1
28 Mar	Wolverhampton W	H	D	2-2	Gregg		Cantwell				Moir	Moore	..1	Law	
30 Mar	Fulham	H	W	3-0			Duane A	..1	..1		Best	Stiles			
4 Apr	Liverpool	A	L	0-3						Setters		Charlton	..1		Moir1
6 Apr	Aston Villa	H	W	1-0						Stiles					..1
13 Apr	Sheffield U	H	W	2-1			Cantwell					..1	Sadler	Herd	Charlton
18 Apr	Stoke C	A	L	1-3			Dunne A							Law2	
25 Apr	Nottingham F	H	W	3-1	Gaskell					Setters		Moore1	Herd		

FA Cup

Date	Opponent				Gaskell	Dunne A	Cantwell	Crerand1	Foulkes	Setters	Herd1	Moore1	Charlton	Herd1	Best
4 Jan	Southampton (3)	A	W	3-2	Gaskell	Dunne A	Cantwell	Crerand1	Foulkes	Setters	Herd1	Moore1	Charlton	Herd1	Best
25 Jan	Bristol R (4)	H	W	4-1							..1	Chisnall		Law3	..1
15 Feb	Barnsley (5)	A	W	4-0		Brennan	Dunne A					Stiles	..2		..1
29 Feb	Sunderland (6)	H	D	3-3									..1		..1
4 Mar	Sunderland (6R)	A	D	2-2								Chisnall	..1		..1
9 Mar	Sunderland (6R) (at Huddersfield)	N	W	5-1						..1		Chisnall1	..1	..3	
14 Mar	West Ham U (SF) (at Hillsborough)	N	L	1-3									..1		

European Cup Winners' Cup

Date	Opponent				Gregg	Dunne A	Cantwell	Crerand	Foulkes	Setters	Herd1	Chisnall	Sadler	Law	Charlton
25 Sep	Willem II (1)	A	D	1-1	Gregg	Dunne A	Cantwell	Crerand	Foulkes	Setters	Herd1	Chisnall	Sadler	Law	Charlton
15 Oct	Willem II (1R)	H	W	6-1						..1	Quixall	..1	Herd	..3	..1
3 Dec	Tottenham H (2)	A	L	0-2	Gaskell							Stiles			
10 Dec	Tottenham H (2)	H	W	4-1								Chisnall	Sadler	Herd2	..2
26 Feb	Sporting Lisbon (3)	H	W	4-1		Brennan	Dunne A				Herd	Stiles	Charlton1	Law3	Best
18 Mar	Sporting Lisbon (3)	A	L	0-5								Chisnall			

Appearances (goals)

Player	Apps	Goals
Anderson	2	
Best	17	4
Brennan	17	
Cantwell	28	
Charlton	40	9
Chisnall	20	6
Crerand	41	1
Dunne A	40	
Foulkes	41	1
Gaskell	17	
Gregg	25	
Herd	30	20
Law	30	30
Moir	18	3
Moore	18	4
Quixall	9	3
Sadler	19	5
Setters	32	4
Stiles	17	
Tranter	1	
Total 20 players	**90**	

Football League

	P	W	D	L	F:A	Pts	
Liverpool	42	26	5	11	92:45	57	1st
Manchester U	42	23	7	12	90:62	53	2nd

Date	Opponent				Gaskell	Brennan	Dunne A	Setters	Foulkes	Stiles	Connelly	Charlton1	Herd	Law1	Best
22 Aug	W B A	H	D	2-2	Gaskell	Brennan	Dunne A	Setters	Foulkes	Stiles	Connelly	Charlton1	Herd	Law1	Best
24 Aug	West Ham U	A	L	1-3									Sadler1	..1	..1
29 Aug	Leicester C	A	D	2-2				Crerand						..1	
2 Sep	West Ham U	H	W	3-1							..1			..1	
5 Sep	Fulham	A	L	1-2							..1		Herd1		
8 Sep	Everton	A	D	3-3	Dunne P						..1		..2	Stiles	
12 Sep	Nottingham F	H	W	3-0						Setters	..1			Law	
16 Sep	Everton	H	W	2-1						Stiles				Stiles	
19 Sep	Stoke C	A	W	2-1						Setters	..1		..1	Stiles	
26 Sep	Tottenham H	H	W	4-1				..2		Stiles				Law2	
30 Sep	Chelsea	A	W	2-0										..1	..1
6 Oct	Burnley	A	D	0-0											
10 Oct	Sunderland	H	W	1-0									..1		
17 Oct	Wolverhampton W	A	W	*4-2									..2	..4	
24 Oct	Aston Villa	H	W	7-0				..1		Setters	..1	Stiles	..2		
31 Oct	Liverpool	A	W	2-0						Stiles		Charlton	..1		
7 Nov	Sheffield Wed	H	W	1-0									..1		
14 Nov	Blackpool	A	W	2-1							..1		..1		Moir
21 Nov	Blackburn R	H	W	3-0							..1		..1		Best1
28 Nov	Arsenal	A	W	3-2							..1			..2	
5 Dec	Leeds U	H	L	0-1											
12 Dec	W B A	A	D	1-1										..1	
16 Dec	Birmingham C	H	D	1-1									Sadler	Herd	
26 Dec	Sheffield U	A	W	1-0							..1			..1	
28 Dec	Sheffield U	H	D	1-1									Herd	Law2	
16 Jan	Nottingham F	A	D	2-2										..1	
23 Jan	Stoke C	H	D	1-1									..1		
6 Feb	Tottenham H	A	L	0-1											
13 Feb	Burnley	H	W	3-2							..1		..1		..1
24 Feb	Sunderland	A	L	0-1						Fitzpatrick					
27 Feb	Wolverhampton W	H	W	3-0						Stiles	..1	..2	..2	..1	
13 Mar	Chelsea	H	W	4-0							..2		..2		
15 Mar	Fulham	H	W	4-1										..1	
20 Mar	Sheffield Wed	A	L	0-1											
22 Mar	Blackpool	H	W	2-0											
3 Apr	Blackburn R	A	W	5-0							..1	..3	..1	Best	Aston
12 Apr	Leicester C	H	W	1-0							..1			Law	Beat
17 Apr	Leeds U	A	W	1-0							..1			Cantwell1	..2
19 Apr	Birmingham C	A	W	4-2							..1	..1		..2	
24 Apr	Liverpool	H	W	3-0									Herd	..2	
26 Apr	Arsenal	H	W	3-1							..1			..2	
28 Apr	Aston Villa	A	L	1-2				Fitzpatrick						..1	

FA Cup

Date	Opponent				Dunne P	Brennan	Dunne A	Crerand	Foulkes	Stiles	Connelly	Charlton	Herd	Kinsey1	Best1
9 Jan	Chester (3)	H	W	2-1	Dunne P	Brennan	Dunne A	Crerand	Foulkes	Stiles	Connelly	Charlton	Herd	Kinsey1	Best1
30 Jan	Stoke C (4)	A	D	0-0										Law	
3 Feb	Stoke C (4R)	H	W	1-0									..1		
20 Feb	Burnley (5)	H	W	2-1							..1		..1		
10 Mar	Wolverhampton W (6)	A	W	5-3							..1		..1		
27 Mar	Leeds U (SF) (at Hillsborough)	N	D	0-0											
31 Mar	Leeds U (SFR) (at City Ground)	N	L	0-1											

Inter-Cities Fairs Cup

Date	Opponent				Dunne P	Brennan	Dunne A	Crerand	Foulkes	Stiles	Connelly	Charlton	Hurd1	Setters	Best
23 Sep	Djurgaardan	A	D	1-1	Dunne P	Brennan	Dunne A	Crerand	Foulkes	Stiles	Connelly	Charlton	Hurd1	Setters	Best
27 Oct	Djurgaarden (1)	H	W	6-1								..2		Law3	..1
11 Nov	Borussia Dortmund (2)	A	W	6-1								..3	..1		..1
2 Dec	Borussia Dortmund (2)	H	W	4-1								..2			
20 Jan	Everton	H	D	1-1							..1				
9 Feb	Everton	A	W	2-1							..1		..1		
12 Mar	Racing Strasbourg (4)	A	W	5-0							..1	..1	..1		..2
19 May	Racing Strasbourg (4)	H	D	0-0											
31 May	Ferencvaros (5)	H	W	3-2										..2	..1
6 Jun	Ferencvaros (5)	A	L	0-1											
18 Jun	Ferencvaros (5)	A	L	1-2							..1				

Appearances (goals)

Player	Apps	Goals
Aston	1	
Best	41	10
Brennan	42	
Cantwell	2	1
Charlton	41	10
Connelly	42	15
Crerand	39	3
Dunne A	42	
Danne P	37	
Fitzpatrick	2	
Foulkes	42	
Gaskell	5	
Herd	37	20
Law	36	28
Moir	1	
Sadler	6	1
Setters	5	
Stiles	41	
Own goals		1
Total 18 players	**89**	

Football League

	P	W	D	L	F:A	Pts	
Manchester U	42	28	9	7	89:39	61	1st

Date	Opponent				Dunne P	Brennan	Dunne A	Crerand	Foulkes	Stiles	Anderson	Charlton	Herd1	Best	Aston
21 Aug	Sheffield Wed	H	W	1-0	Dunne P	Brennan	Dunne A	Crerand	Foulkes	Stiles	Connelly	Charlton	Herd1	Best	Aston
24 Aug	Nottingham F	A	L	2-4									..1		Best
28 Aug	Northampton T	A	D	1-1	Gaskell	Dunne A	Cantwell							Law	
1 Sep	Nottingham F	H	D	0-0		Brennan	Dunne A								
4 Sep	Stoke C	H	D	1-1							..1				
8 Sep	Newcastle U	A	W	2-1									..1		
11 Sep	Burnley	A	L	0-3											
15 Sep	Newcastle U	H	D	1-1						..1					
18 Sep	Chelsea	H	W	4-1								..1	..3		Aston
25 Sep	Arsenal	A	L	2-4	Dunne P							Charlton	..1		..1
9 Oct	Liverpool	H	W	2-0							Beast1	Charlton			
16 Oct	Tottenham H	A	L	1-5									Herd3		
23 Oct	Fulham	H	W	4-1									..2		
30 Oct	Blackpool	A	W	2-1	Gregg										
6 Nov	Blackburn R	H	D	2-2							Best	Law1	..1		Connelly1
13 Nov	Leicester C	H	W	5-3		Dunne A	Cantwell				..1	..1	..1		
20 Nov	Sheffield U	H	W	3-1					Sadler		..1	..1	..2		
4 Dec	West Ham U	A	W	2-0	Dunne P				Foulkes		..2		..1		
11 Dec	Sunderland	A	W	3-2									..1		
15 Dec	Everton	H	W	3-0	Gregg							..2	..1		
18 Dec	Tottenham H	H	W	*5-1								..2	..2		
27 Dec	W B A	H	D	1-1								..1			
1 Jan	Liverpool	A	L	1-2									..1		Aston
8 Jan	Sunderland	H	D	1-1											

Fitzpatrick for Law

Connelly for Aston

Date	Opponent		Result											Notes
12 Jan	Leeds U	A	D	1-1								.1	.1	
15 Jan	Fulham	A	W	1-0										
29 Jan	Sheffield Wed	A	D	0-0										
5 Feb	Northampton T	H	W	6-2						.2	.3		Connelly1	
19 Feb	Stoke C	A	D	2-2	Brennan	Dunne A			Connelly1	Best	Law	.1	Aston	
26 Feb	Burnley	H	W	4-2					Best	Law	.1	.3	Connelly	
12 Mar	Chelsea	A	L	0-2										
19 Mar	Arsenal	H	W	2-1				Fitzpatrick	.1					
6 Apr	Aston Villa	A	D	1-1	Gaskell			Connelly	.1	Anderson	Cantwell1			
9 Apr	Leicester C	H	L	1-2	Gregg	Noble		Sadler	Stiles	Best	Anderson	Herd	.1	
16 Apr	Sheffield U	A	L	1-3		Cantwell	Fitzpatrick	Foulkes	Connelly	Sadler1				
25 Apr	Everton	A	D	0-0		Dunne A	Crerand	Cantwell	Anderson	Law		Aston		
27 Apr	Blackpool	H	W	2-1					Connelly	.1		Charlton		
30 Apr	West Ham U	A	L	2-3				.1				.1		
4 May	W B A	A	D	3-3		..1			Ryan		Charlton1	Herd1	.1	
7 May	Blackburn R	A	W	4-1					Stiles		.2	Herd1		
9 May	Aston Villa	A	W	6-1					.1		Charlton			
19 May	Leeds U	H	D	1-1		Noble			Dunne A		Law			Herd for Dunne A / Anderson for Fitzpatrick

FA Cup

22 Jan	Derby Co	A	W	5-2	Gregg	Dunne A	Cantwell	Crerand	Foulkes	Stiles	Best2	Law2	Charlton	Herd1	Aston
12 Feb	Rotherham U (4)	H	D	0-0											Connelly
15 Feb	Rotherham U (4R)	A	W	1-0		Brennan	Dunne A								..1
5 Mar	Wolverhampton W (5)	A	W	4-2							..1	.2			..1
26 Mar	Preston NE (6)	A	D	1-1								..1			
30 Mar	Preston NE (6R)	H	W	3-1							Connelly1	.2			Aston
23 Apr	Everton (SF)	N	L	0-1							Anderson				Connelly
	(at Burnden Park)														

European Cup

22 Sep	HJK Helsinki (P)	A	W	3-2	Gaskell	Brennan	Dunne A	Fitzpatrick	Foulkes	Stiles	Connelly1	Charlton	Herd1	Law1	Aston
6 Oct	HJK Helsinki (P)	H	W	6-0	Dunne P			Crerand			.3	Best2	Charlton1		
17 Nov	ASK Vorwaerts (1)	A	W	2-0	Gregg	Dunne A	Cantwell				Best	Law		Herd	Connelly
1 Dec	ASK Vorwaerts (1)	H	W	3-1	Dunne P									.3	
2 Feb	Benfica (2)	H	W	3-2	Gregg				..1			.1		.1	
9 Mar	Benfica (2)	A	W	5-1		Brennan	Dunne A	.1				.1		.1	
13 Apr	FK Partizan	A	L	0-2						Anderson					
	Belgrade (SF)														
20 Apr	FK Partizan	H	W	1-0					.1						
	Belgrade (SF)														

Appearances (goals)

Anderson 23 (4) – Aston 22 (4) – Best 31 (9) – Brennan 28 – Cantwell 23 (2) – Charlton 38 (16) – Connelly 31 (5) – Crerand 41 – Dunne A 40 (1) – Dunne P (8) – Fitzpatrick 3 – Foulkes 33 – Gaskell 8 – Gregg 26 – Herd 36 (24) – Law 33 (15) – Noble 2 – Ryan 4 (1) – Sadler 10 (4) – Stiles 39 (2) – Own goals 1 – **Total 20 players 84**

Football League

	P	W	D	L	F:A	Pts	
Liverpool	42	26	9	7	79:34	61	1st
Manchester U	42	16	15	9	84:59	51	4th

SEASON 1966-1967 FOOTBALL LEAGUE (DIVISION 1)

20 Aug	W B A	H	W	5-3	Gaskell	Brennan	Dunne A	Fitzpatrick	Foulkes	Stiles1	Best1	Law2	Charlton	Herd1	Connelly
23 Aug	Everton	A	W	2-1								.2			
27 Aug	Leeds U	A	L	1-3							..1				
31 Aug	Everton	H	W	3-0				Crerand			Connelly1	..1			Best
3 Sep	Newcastle U	H	W	3-2	Gregg			..1			..1			..1	
7 Sep	Stoke C	A	L	0-3											
10 Sep	Tottenham H	A	L	1-2	Gaskell						Best	..1	Sadler		Charlton
17 Sep	Manchester C	H	W	1-0	Stepney						Herd1	..1		Charlton	Aston	Aston for Sadler
24 Sep	Burnley	H	W	4-1				..1			..1	..1	..1		Bent
1 Oct	Nottingham F	A	L	1-4							Best	Charlton1		Hard	Aston	Aston for Law
8 Oct	Blackpool	A	W	2-1		Dunne A	Noble		Cantwell		Herd	Law2		Charlton	Aston
15 Oct	Chelsea	H	D	1-1										Charlton	Best
29 Oct	Arsenal	H	W	1-0									..1		
5 Nov	Chelsea	A	W	3-1		Brennan			Foulkes			Aston2			..1
12 Nov	Sheffield Wed	H	W	2-0		Dunne A					..1	Law		..1		Aston for Foulkes
19 Nov	Southampton	A	W	2-1					Cantwell				.2			Aston for Cantwell
26 Nov	Sunderland	H	W	5-0					Sadler		Best	..1	Charlton	Herd4	Aston
30 Nov	Leicester C	A	W	2-1							..1	..1			
3 Dec	Aston Villa	A	L	1-2								..1		..1	
10 Dec	Liverpool	H	D	2-2		Brennan				Dunne A	.2	Ryan		..1	
17 Dec	W B A	A	W	4-3						Stiles		Law1		.3		Anderson for Dunne A
26 Dec	Sheffield U	A	L	1-2			Donna A		Foulkes	Sadler				..1	
27 Dec	Sheffield U	H	W	2-0				..1						..1	
31 Dec	Leeds U	H	D	0-0										..1	
14 Jan	Tottenham H	H	W	1-0							Ryan			..1	
21 Jan	Manchester C	A	D	1-1					..1	Stiles	Charlton	Sadler		Best	
4 Feb	Burnley	A	D	1-1							Best	Law			Charlton
11 Feb	Nottingham F	H	W	1-0								..1			Ryan for Foulkes
25 Feb	Blackpool	H	W	*4-0									Charlton2	Aston	
3 Mar	Arsenal	A	D	1-1								..1		..1	
11 Mar	Newcastle U	A	D	0-0											
18 Mar	Leicester C	H	W	5-2								..1	Charlton1	Herd1	..1	Sadler1 for Herd
25 Mar	Liverpool	A	D	0-0									Sadler	Charlton	
27 Mar	Fulham	A	D	2-2						.1	.1				
28 Mar	Fulham	H	W	2-1					..1		..1				
1 Apr	West Ham U	H	W	3-0							..1	..1		..1	
10 Apr	Sheffield Wed	A	D	2-2							..1	..1		.3	
18 Apr	Southampton	H	W	3-0								..1		.2	..P
22 Apr	Sunderland	A	D	0-0								..1		..1	
29 Apr	Aston Villa	H	W	3-1		Brennan	Dunne A				..1	..1			..1
6 May	West Ham U	A	W	6-1				.1	..1		..1	.2		..1	
13 May	Stoke C	H	D	0-0								Ryan			

FA Cup

| 28 Jan | Stoke C (3) | H | W | 2-0 | Stepney | Dunne A | Noble | Crerand | Foulkes | Stiles | Best | Law1 | Sadler | Herd1 | Charlton |
| 18 Feb | Norwich C (4) | H | L | 1-2 | | | | | Sadler | | Ryan | ..1 | Charlton | | Best |

Football League Cup

| 14 Sep | Blackpool (2) | A | L | 1-5 | Dunne P | Brennan | Dunne A | Crerand | Foulkes | Stiles | Connelly | Best | Sadler | Herd1 | Aston |

Appearances (goals)

Aston 26 (5) – Best 42 (10) – Brennan 16 – Cantwell 4 – Charlton 42 (12) – Connelly 6 (2) – Crerand 59 (3) – Dunne A 40 – Fitzpatrick 3 – Foulkes 33 (4) – Gaskell 5 – Gregg 2 – Herd 28 (16) – Law 36 (23) – Noble 29 – Ryan 4 – Sadler 35 (3) – Stepney 35 – Stiles 37 (3) – Own goals 1 – **Total 19 players 84**

Football League

	P	W	C	L	F:A	Pts	
Manchester U	42	24	12	6	84:45	60	1st

SEASON 1967-1968 FOOTBALL LEAGUE (DIVISION 1)

19 Aug	Everton	A	L	1-3	Stepney	Brennan	Dunne A	Crerand	Foulkes	Stiles	Best	Law	Charlton1	Kidd	Aston	Sadler for Crerand
23 Aug	Leeds U	H	W	1-0							Ryan		..1		
26 Aug	Leicester C	H	D	1-1				Sadler		..1	Best				
2 Sep	West Ham U	A	W	3-1		Dunne A	Burns	Crerand			Ryan1	Sadler1		..1	Best
6 Sep	Sunderland	A	D	1-1										..1	
9 Sep	Burnley	H	D	2-2										..1	Fitzpatrick for Stiles / Kopel for Fitzpatrick
16 Sep	Sheffield Wed	A	D	1-1			..1	..1		Fitzpatrick			Law	Kidd	
23 Sep	Tottenham H	H	W	3-1						Stiles	Best1		..1		
30 Sep	Manchester C	A	W	2-1							.2		..2		Aston for Foulkes
7 Oct	Arsenal	H	W	1-0						Sadler		Kidd		Aston1	Aston for Law
14 Oct	Sheffield U	A	W	3-0								..1		..1	Fitzpatrick for Stiles
25 Oct	Coventry C	H	W	4-0						Fitzpatrick			..1		..2
28 Oct	Nottingham F	A	L	1-3		Kopel					..1		..1		
4 Nov	Stoke C	H	W	1-0		Dunne A			Foulkes	Sadler	Ryan			Best	
8 Nov	Leeds U	A	L	0-1									..1		Fitzpatrick for Ryan
11 Nov	Liverpool	A	W	2-1							Fitzpatrick			.2	
18 Nov	Southampton	H	W	3-2								..1		..1	
25 Nov	Chelsea	A	D	1-1		Brennan	Dunne A				Burns	..1			..1
2 Dec	W B A	H	W	2-1								..1		.2	
9 Dec	Newcastle U	A	D	2-2			..1					..1			
16 Dec	Everton	H	W	3-1		Dunne A	Burns			..1	Best			Law1	..1
23 Dec	Leicester C	A	D	2-2										..1	
26 Dec	Wolverhampton W	H	W	4-0							.2		..1		..1
30 Dec	Wolverhampton W	A	W	3-2									..1		..1
6 Jan	West Ham U	H	W	3-1					Sadler	Fitzpatrick	..1		..1		..1
20 Jan	Sheffield Wed	H	W	4-2							.2		..1		
3 Feb	Tottenham H	H	L	1-2							..1		..1		
17 Feb	Burnley	A	L	1-2						Stiles	..1			Herd	
24 Feb	Arsenal	H	W	*2-0							..1			Law	
2 Mar	Chelsea	H	L	1-3								..1		Ryan	
16 Mar	Coventry C	A	L	0-2		Brennan							Fitzpatrick	Fitzpatrick	Herd	Aston for Kidd
23 Mar	Nottingham F	H	W	3-0		..1		..1			Fitzpatrick	Herd1	Charlton	Best	Aston
27 Mar	Manchester C	H	L	1-3								Law		..1	Herd	Aston for Herd
30 Mar	Stoke C	A	W	4-2						Fitzpatrick	Best1	Gowling1		Herd	Aston1	Ryan1 for Gowling
5 Apr	Liverpool	H	L	1-2		Dunne A								Herd	
12 Apr	Fulham	A	W	4-0						Stiles	.2	Kidd1		Law1	
13 Apr	Southampton	A	D	2-2					Foulkes	Sadler	..1		..1	Gowling	
15 Apr	Fulham	H	W	3-0	Rimmer						..1		..1	Law	
20 Apr	Sheffield U	H	W	1-0	Stepney	Brennan	Dunne A		Sadler	Stiles				Law	..1
27 Apr	W B A	A	L	3-6			Burns						..2		
4 May	Newcastle U	H	W	6-0		Brennan	Dunne A		Foulkes	Sadler1	.3			Gowling	
11 May	Sunderland	H	L	1-2						Stiles				Sadler		Gowling for Foulkes

FA Cup

| 27 Jan | Tottenham H (3) | H | D | 2-2 | Stepney | Dunne A | Burns | Crerand | Sadler | Fitzpatrick | Best1 | Kidd | Charlton1 | Law | Aston |
| 31 Jan | Tottenham H (3R) | A | L | 0-1 | | | | | | | | | | Herd | |

European Cup

20 Sep	Hibernians (Malta) (1)	H	W	4-0	Stepney	Dunne A	Burns	Crerand	Foulkes	Stiles	Best	Sadler2	Charlton	Law2	Kidd
27 Sep	Hibernians (1)	A	D	0-0											
15 Nov	FK Sarajevo (2)	H	D	0-0						Sadler	Fitzpatrick	Kidd		Best	Aston
29 Nov	FK Sarajevo (2)	A	W	2-1		Brennan	Dunne A			Burns				..1	
28 Feb	Gornik Zabrze (3)	H	W	*2-0			Burns		Sadler	Stiles	Best			Ryan	
13 Mar	Gornik Zabrze (3)	A	L	0-1							Fitzpatrick	Charlton	Herd	Kidd	Best
24 Apr	Real Madrid (SF)	H	W	1-0							Best1	Kidd	Charlton	Law	Aston

Date	Opponent			Score	Stepney	Brennan	Dunne A	Crerand	Foulkes	Stiles	Best	Kidd	Charlton	Law	Aston	Notes
15 May	Real Madrid (SF)	A	D	*3-3		Brennan	Dunne A		Foulkes1			..1	..1	..2	Sadler1	
29 May	Benfica (F) (at Wembley)	N	W	4-1												

Appearances (goals)

Aston 34 (10) – Best 41 (28) – Brennan 13 (1) – Burns 36 (2) – Charlton 41 (15) – Crerand 41 (1) – Dunne A 37 (1) – Fitzpatrick 14 – Foulkes 24 (1) – Gowling 4 (1) – Herd 6 (1) – Kidd 34 (15) – Kopel 1 – Law 23 (7) – Rimmer 1 – Ryan 7 (2) – Sadler 40 (3) – Stepney 41 – Stiles 20 – Own goals 1 – **Total 19 players 89**

Football League

	P	W	D	L	F:A	Pts	
Manchester C	42	26	8	10	86:43	58	1st
Manchester U	42	24	8	10	89:55	55	2nd

SEASON 1968-1969 FOOTBALL LEAGUE (DIVISION 1)

Date	Opponent			Score	Stepney	Brennan	Dunne A	Crerand	Foulkes	Stiles	Best	Kidd	Charlton	Law	Aston	Notes
10 Aug	Everton	H	W	2-1	Stepney	Brennan	Dunne A	Crerand	Foulkes	Stiles	Best1	Kidd	Charlton1	Law	Aston	
14 Aug	W B A	A	L	1-3									..1			Sadler for Foulkes
17 Aug	Manchester C	A	D	0-0		Kopel		Fitzpatrick	Sadler			Gowling		Kidd		Burns for Aston
21 Aug	Coventry C	H	W	1-0							Ryan1	Kidd		Burns	Best	
24 Aug	Chelsea	H	L	0-4				Crerand			Morgan			Law		
28 Aug	Tottenham H	H	W	3-1		Brennan		Fitzpatrick2					..1	..2	..1	Burns for Dunne A
31 Aug	Sheffield Wed	A	L	4-5					Foulkes			Sadler				
7 Sep	West Ham U	H	D	1-1		Dunne A	Burns							..1	..2	Kidd for Crerand
14 Sep	Burnley	A	L	0-1												
21 Sep	Newcastle U	H	W	3-1				Crerand	Sadler			Fitzpatrick		..1		Sartori for Burns
5 Oct	Arsenal	H	D	0-0					Foulkes					..1		
9 Oct	Tottenham H	A	D	2-2				..1						Gowling	Sartori	Fitzpatrick for Foulkes
12 Oct	Liverpool	A	L	0-2		Brennan	Kopel		James		Ryan			Sartori	Best1	
19 Oct	Southampton	H	L	1-2		Kopel	Dunne A		Foulkes		Morgan	Sadler		Sartori	..2	
26 Oct	QPR	A	W	3-2		Brennan			Sadler			Kidd		Law1		
2 Nov	Leeds U	H	D	0-0											Sartori	
9 Nov	Sunderland	A	D	1-1										..1		Kopel for Kidd
16 Nov	Ipswich T	H	D	0-0					James			Best		Fitzpatrick	Sartori	
23 Nov	Stoke C	A	D	0-0		Kopel			Sadler			Sartori		Law1	Best1	Fitzpatrick for Stiles
30 Nov	Wolverhampton W	H	W	2-0										..1	..1	
7 Dec	Leicester C	A	L	1-2		Dunne A	Burns				Best	Sadler		..1		
14 Dec	Liverpool	H	W	1-0					James			Sadler		..1	Sartori	
21 Dec	Southampton	A	L	0-2										Kidd		Sartori for Crerand
26 Dec	Arsenal	A	L	0-3										Sartori		
11 Jan	Leeds U	A	L	1-2					Fitzpatrick		Morgan	Fitzpatrick	..1	..3	Best1	
18 Jan	Sunderland	H	W	4-1	Rimmer			Crerand				Sartori				
15 Feb	Ipswich T	A	L	0-1	Stepney	Fitzpatrick	Dunne A			Sadler		Kidd	..1	Sartori	..1	Foulkes for Sartori
8 Mar	Manchester C	H	L	0-1		Brennan	Fitzpatrick		Foulkes	Stiles				Sadler		
10 Mar	Everton	A	D	0-0			Dunne A		James		Best		Fitzpatrick	Aston		Foulkes for Brennan
15 Mar	Chelsea	A	L	2-3		Fitzpatrick			..1		Morgan		Sadler	Law1	Best	
19 Mar	QPR	H	W	8-i						..1	..3		..1	Aston1	..2	
22 Mar	Sheffield Wed	H	W	1-0									Best1		Aston	
24 Mar	Stoke C	H	D	1-1										Best		Sadler for Morgan
29 Mar	West Ham U	A	D	0-0							Ryan			..1		Sadler for Dunne A
31 Mar	Nottingham F	A	W	1-0			Stiles			Sadler				Kidd	..2	Foulkes for Ryan
2 Apr	W B A	H	W	2-1							Morgan	Ryan		Law	Charlton	
5 Apr	Nottingham F	H	W	3-1							..2	Kidd		Charlton	..1	
8 Apr	Coventry C	A	L	1-2	Rimmer		..1						Charlton	Law		
12 Apr	Newcastle U	A	L	0-2		Brennan	Fitzpatrick		Foulkes	Stiles			Aston	..1		
19 Apr	Burnley	H	W	*2-0			Burns				..1		Charlton	..1		
17 May	Leicester C	H	W	3-2												

FA Cup

Date	Opponent			Score												Notes
4 Jan	Exeter C (3)	A	W	*3-1	Stepney	Dunne A	Burns	Fitzpatrick1	James	Stiles	Best	Kidd1	Charlton	Law	Sartori	Sadler for Best
25 Jan	Watford (4)	H	D	1-1	Rimmer	Kopel	Dunne A				Morgan	Best		..1		
3 Feb	Watford (4R)	A	W	2-0	Stepney	Fitzpatrick		Crerand				Kidd		..2	Best	
8 Feb	Birmingham C (5)	A	D	2-2										..1	..1	
24 Feb	Birmingham C (5R)	H	W	6-2			..1				..1		..3			
1 Mar	Everton (6)	H	L	0-1												

European Cup

Date	Opponent			Score												Notes
18 Sep	Waterford (1)	A	W	3-1	Stepney	Dunne A	Burns	Crerand	Foulkes	Stiles	Best	Law3	Charlton	Sadler	Kidd	Rimmer for Stepney
2 Oct	Waterford (1)	H	W	7-1						..1		..4	..1			
13 Nov	RSC Anderlecht (2)	H	W	3-0		Brennan	Dunne A		Sadler		Ryan	Kidd1		Law 2	Sartori	
27 Nov	RSC Anderlecht (2)	A	L	1-3		Kopel			Foulkes		Fitzpatrick	Law		Sadler	..1	
26 Feb	Rapid Vienna (3)	H	W	3-0		Fitzpatrick			James		Morgan1	Kidd		Law	Best2	
5 Mar	Rapid Vienna (3)	A	D	0-0										Sadler		
23 Nov	AC Milan (SF)	A	L	0-2	Rimmer	Brennan	Fitzpatrick		Foulkes					Law		Burns for Stiles
15 May	AC Milan (SF)	H	W	1-0			Burns						..1			

World Club Championship

Date	Opponent			Score												Notes
25 Sep	Estudiantes	A	L	0-1	Stepney	Dunne A	Burns	Crerand	Foulkes	Stiles	Morgan	Sadler	Charlton	Law	Best	Sartori for Law
16 Oct	Estudiantes	H	D	1-1		Brennan	Dunne A			Sadler	..1	Kidd				

Appearances (goals)

Aston 13 (2) – Best 41 (19) – Brennan 13 – Burns 14 – Charlton 32 (5) – Crerand 35 (1) – Dunne A 33 – Fitzpatrick 28 (3) – Foulkes 10 – Gowling 2 – James 21 (1) – Kidd 26 (1) – Kopel 7 – Law 30 (14) – Morgan 29 (8) – Rimmer 4 – Ryan 8 (1) – Sadler 26 – Sartori 11 – Stepney 36 – Stiles 41 (1) – Own goals 3 – **Total 21 players 57**

Football League

	P	W	U	L	F:A	Pts	
Leeds U	42	27	13		66:26	67	1st
Manchester U	42	15	12	15	57:53	42	11th

SEASON 1969-1970 FOOTBALL LEAGUE (DIVISION 1)

Date	Opponent			Score	Rimmer	Dunne A	Burns	Crerand	Foulkes	Sadler	Morgan	Kidd	Charlton	Law	Best	Notes
9 Aug	Crystal Palace	A	D	2-2	Rimmer	Dunne A	Burns	Crerand	Foulkes	Sadler	Morgan1	Kidd	Charlton1	Law	Best	Givens for Dunne A
13 Aug	Everton	H	L	0-2		Brennan										Givens for Foulkes
16 Aug	Southampton	H	L	1-4							..1					
19 Aug	Everton	A	L	0-3	Stepney	Fitzpatrick			Edwards				Givens	Best	Aston	
23 Aug	Wolverhampton W	A	D	0-0					Ure				Charlton	Law	Best	Givens for Law
27 Aug	Newcastle U	H	D	0-0			Dunne A							Givens	..1	
30 Aug	Sunderland	H	W	3-1			Burns					Givens		Gowling	..2	
6 Sep	Leeds U	A	D	2-2								Kidd				
13 Sep	Liverpool	H	W	1-0								..1			..2	Aston for Gowling
17 Sep	Sheffield Wed	A	W	3-1								..1			..1	
20 Sep	Arsenal	A	D	2-2					..1	..1			Aston		..1	
27 Sep	West Ham U	H	W	5-2					..1			..1			..2	
4 Oct	Derby Co	A	L	0-2				..1								Sartori for Aston
8 Oct	Southampton	A	W	3-0								..1			..1	Brennan for Best
11 Oct	Ipswich T	H	W	2-1											..1	
18 Oct	Nottingham F	H	D	1-1								..1				
25 Oct	W B A	A	L	1-2		Brennan							..1			Givens for Kidd
1 Nov	Stoke C	H	D	1-1							Sartori Law	Best		Law1	Aston1	
8 Nov	Coventry C	A	W	2-1												Kidd for Sartori
15 Nov	Manchester C	A	L	0-4								Kidd	..2	Best		Edwards for Fitzpatrick
22 Nov	Tottenham H	H	W	3-1		Fitzpatrick			..1					Stiles		
29 Nov	Burnley	A	D	1-1		Edwards					Best1					Ryan for Kidd
6 Dec	Chelsea	H	L	0-2												Sartori for Aston
13 Dec	Liverpool	A	W	*4-1		Brennan			..1		Morgan1		Crerand	..1		
26 Dec	Wolverhampton W	H	D	0-0		Edwards						Crerand	Kidd	Best		
27 Dec	Sunderland	A	D	1-1			Brennan							..1	Aston	
10 Jan	Arsenal	H	W	2-1			Dunne A				..1	Sartori				Sartori1 for Dunne A
17 Jan	West Ham U	A	D	0-0	Rimmer	Burns	Crerand						..1			
26 Jan	Leeds U	H	D	2-2	Stepney				..1				..1			
31 Jan	Derby Co	H	W	1-0									..1		Best	
10 Feb	Ipswich T	A	W	1-0			Dunne A						..1			
14 Feb	Crystal Palace	H	D	1-1									..1			
28 Feb	Stoke C	A	D	2-2							..1				..1	Burns for Sadler
17 Mar	Burnley	H	D	3-3	Rimmer				..1					Law1		
21 Mar	Chelsea	A	L	1-2	Stepney		Burns				..1	Stiles			..1	Law for Sartori
28 Mar	Manchester C	H	L	1-2			Dunne A			Sadler	Burns			Kidd1		Burns for Kidd
30 Mar	Coventry C	H	D	1-1					Fitzpatrick	Ure	Sadler		Best	Law	Aston	
31 Mar	Nottingham F	A	W	2-1		Stiles		Crerand	James			Fitzpatrick	Charlton1	Gowling	Best	Sartori for Aston
4 Apr	Newcastle U	A	L	1-5		Fitzpatrick						Gowling	..1	Stiles	Aston	
8 Apr	W B A	H	W	7-0		Stiles			Ure			Fitzpatrick2	..2	Gowling2	Best1	
13 Apr	Tottenham H	A	L	1-2		Edwards						..1		Kidd		Gowling for Morgan
15 Apr	Sheffield Wed	H	D	2-2						Sadler						

FA Cup

Date	Opponent			Score												Notes
3 Jan	Ipswich T (3)	A	W	*1-0	Stepney	Edwards	Brennan	Burns	Ure	Sadler	Morgan	Crerand	Charlton	Kidd	Best	Aston for Morgan
24 Jan	Manchester C (4)	H	W	3-0		Burns	Crerand					..1	Sartori		..2	Aston
7 Feb	Northampton T (5)	A	W	8-2			Dunne A							..2	Best6	Burns for Charlton
21 Feb	Middlesbrough (6)	A	D	1-1								..1				
25 Feb	Middlesbrough (6R)	H	W	2-1		Dunne A	Burns				..1		..1			
14 Mar	Leeds U (SF) (at Hillsborough)	N	D	0-0		Edwards	Dunne A									
23 Mar	Leeds U (SFR) (at Villa Park)	N	D	0-0						Sadler	Stiles					Law for Sartori
26 Mar	Leeds U (SFR) (at Burnden Park)	N	L	0-1												Law for Sartori
10 Apr	Watford (playoff) (at Highbury)	N	W	2-0			Stiles		Ure	Sadler		Fitzpatrick		..2		

League Cup

Date	Opponent			Score												Notes
3 Sep	Middlesbrough (2)	H	W	1-0	Stepney	Fitzpatrick	Dunne A	Crerand	James	Sadler1	Morgan	Kidd	Charlton	Givens	Best	Gowling for Kidd
23 Sep	Wrexham (3)	H	W	2-0			Burns		Ure						Aston	
14 Oct	Burnley (4)	A	D	0-0												
20 Oct	Burnley (4R)	H	W	1-0												Sartori for Fitzpatrick
12 Nov	Derby Co (5)	A	U	0-0		Brennan					Sartori	Best		Law	Aston	
19 Nov	Derby Co (5R)	H	W	1-0		Fitzpatrick					Best	Kidd1				Sartori for Law
3 Dec	Manchester C (SF)	A	L	1-2		Edwards				Stiles			..1	Stiles		
17 Dec	Manchester C (SF)	H	D	2-2			..1					Morgan	Crerand	Law1	Best	

Appearances (goals)

Aston 21 (1) – Best 37 (15) – Brennan 8 – Burns 30 (3) – Charlton 40 (12) – Crerand 25 (1) – Dunne A 33 – Edwards 18 – Fitzpatrick 20 (3) – Foulkes 3 – Givens 4 (1) – Gowling 6 (3) – James 2 – Kidd 33 (12) – Law 10 (2) – Morgan 35 (7) – Rimmer 5 – Sadler 40 (2) – Sartori 13 (2) – Stepney 37 – Stiles 8 – Ure 34 (1) – Own goals 1 – **Total 22 players 66**

Football League

	P	W	D	L	F:A	Pts	
Everton	42	29	8	5	72:34	66	1st
Manchester U	42	14	17	11	66:61	45	8th

CHAPTER 7

THE 1970s:
DOCHERTY AND SEXTON

Docherty's 'wind of change' was a hurricane. It swept through Old Trafford, whipping up clouds of dust which for years had hidden the harsh truth from not only those in charge, but from the thousands who followed the team. Docherty could look at the situation from the position of the outsider, he had no axe to grind, neither had he any reason to feel that his actions would offend. It was no time to be sentimental, his target was success, and if it meant that his decisions might upset the normal pattern, he would make them anyway.

The re-building had to start quickly, and having been in charge of the Scottish side it was obvious where the new manager would turn. George Graham, from Arsenal's recent double-winning side, was bought for £120,000, a considerable increase on the £6,000 Docherty had paid for him when he signed him from Aston Villa in 1964 while manager of Chelsea. The story had hardly made the sports pages when another Scot was bought. Alex Forsyth, a sturdy full-back from Partick Thistle, signed for £100,000. Two days later Docherty added to his backroom staff by bringing Tommy Cavanagh from Hull City, where he left Terry Neill's coaching team.

Docherty's threat that he would not allow players to 'perform on their reputations' became apparent early in his reign as manager. 'There are players here who are not up to Manchester United standard,' he had said.

On 30 December United were due to play Everton at Old Trafford but the game was called off because of bad weather. It gave Tommy Docherty a little more breathing space. He needed time to get new players and to assess those already in his squad. As he said:

I had other players in mind, but it was getting hold of them. I had already drawn up a list of who I would like to get and the chairman was fantastic, he just let me get on with it, he didn't want to see United in trouble and neither did I.

The first game under Docherty's direct influence was against Arsenal and the side was a mixture of the remnants of the Busby side of the 1960s, players brought in by O'Farrell and the Doc's new boys:

Stepney, Young, Forsyth, Graham, Sadler, Buchan, Morgan, Kidd, Charlton, Law, Storey-Moore

The changes did little to stop United slipping into further trouble and they lost 3-1. United had gone in the direction Docherty feared – instead of moving up the table they were now bottom.

The Scottish take-over

The rebuilding had to continue and the sports pages that weekend gave a clue as to who might be next on the Docherty shopping list. From Scotland came the news that Lou Macari had asked Glasgow Celtic for a transfer.

With United knocked out of the FA Cup 1-0 by Wolves, it was time to buy again, and Jim Holton a big, solid centre-half, was bought from Shrewsbury to increase the Docherty clan of Scots. Five days after the Cup defeat the club paid £200,000 for Macari, a record to a Scottish club at the time, and snatched him away from the grasp of Bill Shankly at Anfield.

Mick Martin, a Republic of Ireland midfield player, was bought from the Irish League club Bohemians, and was waiting in the wings as United played West Ham at Old Trafford, and the Stretford End became the tartan army.

There were 50,878 in Old Trafford to see goals from Bobby Charlton and Lou Macari, but still United could not take maximum points, and had to settle for a draw.

The crowd hoped for success for United and were perhaps disappointed that they had not seen a victory, but they certainly were not totally disheartened, because four days later just under 59,000 turned up for the re-arranged game with Everton, hoping that United could avenge the 2-0 defeat they had suffered at Goodison in the third game (and the third defeat) of the season. Everton were in mid-table, United bottom, and even though the game ended goalless it gave the United fans hope that the revival had started.

Since the sacking of Frank O'Farrell and the appointment of Tommy Docherty, United had hardly been out of the headlines and the Everton game produced another as Ted MacDougall stormed away from Old Trafford before the game ended, after being brought off and replaced by Brian Kidd.

Docherty's first win was on 10 February 1973, when once again a crowd of over 50,000 packed the stadium for the visit of Wolverhampton Wanderers.

Joy was short-lived. A week later at Ipswich they lost 4-1 to Bobby Robson's side, and again the threat of relegation loomed large.

The game at Ipswich turned out to be Ted MacDougall's last for the club. A week later he was sold to West Ham United for £150,000.

Charlton retires and Law is transferred

Against all odds, United now had their best run of the season, and wins over Newcastle and Southampton sandwiching a draw at Tottenham kept three clubs below them in the table – West Brom, Norwich and Crystal Palace. They played Norwich next, and won 1-0 thanks to a Mick Martin goal. Four days later they beat Crystal Palace, and then they drew 2-2 at Stoke to ease themselves up into 16th place. Surely they were safe now.

Bobby Charlton took the opportunity to tell Tommy Docherty that he was retiring. The player who had been Britain's best ambassador for football had decided that he would go out at the top: 'I have had a wonderful life in the greatest game in the world, and I always said that only I would know when I would want to retire. That time has come, and I'll leave the game with some marvellous memories.'

Eighteenth place was the reward for United's run, and Crystal Palace and West Bromwich Albion were relegated. But although the campaign was over United were still in the news. Denis Law and Tony Dunne were given free transfers as Tommy Docherty prepared his squad for the following season, and the move was not seen as a compliment by Law.

Docherty promised the supporters that the future was bright: 'We have some good young players coming through. Boys like Sammy McIlroy, Brian Greenhoff and Gerry Daly are all going to make it to the top. All they need is time.'

But did Docherty have time? His critics were swift to point out that Denis Law, who had signed for Manchester City during the close season, still had his golden touch, and had scored twice on his debut against Birmingham City. Could Law still have offered United something had he been allowed to stay?

The sixth of September 1973 and George Best is back at Old Trafford. The bearded wanderer agreed to play again after retiring from football but his stay with United was both turbulent and short and after 12 appearances and two goals Best had gone again. 'It is one of the tragedies of life that we never saw the full potential of George,' said Tommy Docherty

Ironically, no sooner had Law and Charlton left Old Trafford than the third member of the trinity which had achieved greatness, George Best, decided to return. George left behind the sunshine of Spain and told his club that he would like to play again. The prodigal son was allowed the opportunity.

Then nobody realised the extent of Best's drink problem, and it was only later that it became apparent that it was one of the reasons for George's waywardness. He reappeared on 20 October 1973, not fully match fit, yet still capable of demonstrating that his skills had not deserted him in a 1-0 win over Birmingham City. Mick Martin replaced him when his tiredness showed.

The only goal of that game was scored not by Best, but by Alex Stepney, the goalkeeper. It was his second goal of the season, the first being against Leicester at Old Trafford, when United were awarded a penalty. He had filled the role in pre-season friendlies, and Docherty had handed him the task when the new campaign began.

With Alex Forsyth still out of the side, Tommy Docherty was forced to sign another full-back, this time a recognised left-sided player, Stewart Houston, from Frank Blunstone's former club, Brentford. Docherty had come across the player briefly during his last months as manager of Chelsea, and the tall, strong Scot held his place in the side for the remainder of the season.

1972-80

Fracas at Maine Road

By early March, when United travelled to Bramall Lane to face Sheffield United, only one side had a worse record than them in the First Division and that was Norwich City, who added a twist to the story by signing none other than Ted MacDougall from West Ham in an effort to stay in the top flight. United won at Sheffield thanks to a Lou Macari goal. Then, eleven days later came a remarkable game, the clash with Manchester City.

The tension was higher than that of a normal derby and it reached boiling point when suddenly the diminutive Macari and City's rugged defender Mike Doyle began throwing punches at one another, close to the touchline in front of the main grandstand. The boxing mismatch was quickly over as players from both sides intervened, but referee Clive Thomas had his hands full to prevent a battle as the staff from both benches ran on to the field. The linesmen raced to help, and the Welsh referee ordered Macari and Doyle off.

They refused to go.

With the crowd howling, and fighting breaking out amongst pockets of supporters, Thomas marched both sets of players off the field, and it seemed at first as if he had abandoned the game, only for both teams to return minutes later without the two offenders.

Another Scot was bought, Jim McCalliog from Wolves, and another member of the European Cup-winning side played his final game for the club: Brian Kidd's last game was the 3-1 win at Chelsea which once more gave hope that Docherty could again play Houdini.

United were living from day to day, hanging on to the First Division by the tips of their fingers. Then they won three suc-cessive games – at Norwich then at home to Newcastle and Everton – with McCalliog scoring three times.

City and Law send United down

United had two games remaining and their rivals in relegation were ending the season that afternoon. Norwich City were bottom with 29 points, United above them with 32. Occupying the new relegation position of 20th place were Southampton on 34 points, one behind the club above them, Birmingham City. United's lifeline was thin but it was still there. If Birmingham were to lose and United could win their two remaining fixtures, the Midlands club would be relegated and United would survive. Southampton were away to Everton, and United at home to City!

The 57,000 crowd was hushed at half-time when the electronic scoreboard at Old Trafford printed out the scores from the other games . . . Everton 0 Southampton 2, Birmingham 2 Norwich 1. The derby game was goalless, but still there was hope. If United could win, and Norwich fight back.

Then, with eight minutes remaining, the death blow was struck. Through a ruck of players the ball bobbled and rebounded. The scrambling Alex Stepney was helpless as it passed out of his reach. A City player had his back to the goal, only feet away from the line. He back-heeled the ball over the line, and turned slowly upfield as his supporters and teammates leapt in celebration. Denis Law had sealed United's fate, but he felt only a bitter sadness.

As it happened, Birmingham won their game, so no matter what the outcome of the derby United could not have stayed in the top Division that they had occupied since before the Second World War. Docherty wept in the dressing room, but bravely faced the media only minutes after the game was called off. He said: 'Words can't describe how sick I feel at the moment. I can't believe that this has happened, but I know it has. All I can say is that we have gone down with the makings of a good side, and that hopefully that side will bring us back again as quickly as possible.'

Manchester United were in the Second Division: after the glory years of the 1960s, the brilliance of the 1950s and the building of the 1940s, the unbelievable had become a reality.

Tommy Docherty's team had been improving but he knew that there were certain areas which needed to be strengthened, and he was quick to move. In cloak and dagger style Stuart Pearson was signed from Tommy Cavanagh's former club Hull City. The transfer – £200,000 cash plus the lanky Peter Fletcher – went through on the eve of the Liverpool-Newcastle FA Cup final, and was lost in the publicity previewing the Wembley clash.

Brian Kidd against Derby in 1973. A 1-0 defeat at Old Trafford put the writing on the wall for United. By Boxing day they had lost 11 of their 21 matches and by the end of April Law's backheeled goal confirmed the Reds' relegation scored the first. It was a victory in the style the long-serving supporters had come to associate with United.

A week later, however, there was major upset in another thrilling game. Jim Holton, by now well established as a Scottish international, broke his leg in a 4-4 draw at Sheffield Wednesday's Hillsborough. It turned out to be Holton's last senior game for the club.

The cricketing Arnie Sidebottom and Steve James filled the gap left by the big man and took United into the New Year still ahead of the pack, but Docherty was not yet satisfied. He sold McCalliog to Southampton and used the £40,000 he received to buy university graduate Steve Coppell from Tranmere Rovers. Coppell had played for the Wirral club while completing his studies at Liverpool University, and came on as substitute for United in the 4-0 victory over Cardiff City at Old Trafford, as a replacement for Willie Morgan.

Coppell's arrival signalled the end for Morgan, who played just four more games before leaving to join his former club Burnley during the summer of 1975. Morgan's departure was not amicable. He left after a series of much publicised incidents, and then a television condemnation of Tommy Docherty led to him being sued by his former manager for libel. The case was heard in 1978 and this in turn led to Docherty being charged with perjury after withdrawing from the first battle. Docherty appeared at the Old Bailey in 1981 and was found not guilty.

With Coppell firmly established in the side, nothing could stop United from winning promotion, and a Macari goal at the Dell put United back in the First Division on 5 April 1975. A fortnight later they were confirmed as Second Division Champions after drawing 2-2 with Notts County.

United's start to the 1975-76 season was remarkable. They won five of their first six games, three of them away from home. By mid-September they had been top of the First Division for five weeks. Tommy Jackson, an experienced midfield player with Everton and Nottingham Forest, had been added to the side, and by November, after a loss of form had seen the side slump to fifth place, Docherty paid out £70,000 for another bright young player, Millwall winger Gordon Hill.

United bounce straight back

United stepped into the unknown the following season, 1974-75, at London's Brisbane Road, Orient's ground having the claim to stage the first Manchester United Second Division game since 7 May 1938. United won 2-0 with goals from Stewart Houston and Willie Morgan.

Attendances at all games had risen, and at Old Trafford huge audiences witnessed the revival. When Sunderland, lying second, came to Manchester the biggest Second Division crowd in United's history turned out to watch the game: 60,585. The home supporters were stunned when Sunderland took a 2-1 lead through two goals from Billy Hughes, but such was the confidence of United that they fought back and goals from Morgan and McIlroy pushed them to a 3-2 win. Pearson had

George Graham was the first player bought by Docherty as he added experience to the squad he had inherited from Frank O'Farrell. When his playing days had ended Graham himself moved into management. After four successful years at Millwall he returned to Arsenal, the club which sold him to United and quickly brought the championship trophy to Highbury

Cup Final disappointment

While League form had slipped, United had a great run in the FA Cup, reaching the final. Home wins over Oxford and Peterborough, and a 2-1 away victory at Leicester, had seen them tipped to do well in the competition. Having reached the quarter-finals it looked as if their hopes had been dashed when they could only manage a draw with Wolves at Old Trafford on 6 March. But three days later they pulled off a remarkable victory at Molineux, taking the game 3-2 in extra time.

1972-80

Their opponents in the semi-final were Derby County, one of the challengers for the League Championship, but neither side, each at one time chasing the 'double', were to win any honours. Gordon Hill's two goals took United to Wembley where they were to lose to Southampton.

By the time the 1976-77 season started only Alex Stepney and Martin Buchan were left of the players brought to the club by managers before Tommy Docherty. The Doc had built his team, and young hopefuls were emerging from Blunstone's efforts with the youth teams. Jimmy Nicholl was able to force the right full-back's role away from Alex Forsyth, Arthur Albiston proved himself to be a player of promise, and David McCreery was on the edge of the team being used regularly as substitute.

Yet another link with the European Cup side of 1968 had left the club. Pat Crerand, who had been appointed Docherty's assistant, left to move into full management.

United reached that second final after a slump in League form of alarming proportions. At one stage they led the First Division, then went eight games without a victory and slumped to 17th. Out came the Docherty cheque book again and Jimmy Greenhoff, older brother of Brian, was bought from Stoke City. Luck had taken United through to round five and the draw for that part of the competition made the headlines: 'United to meet Saints – play it again Reds'.

Southampton versus Manchester United, a repeat of the 1976 final, and at the Dell. Had United's luck run out? No home advantage, and facing a side that had already beaten them, they had to be second favourites.

It ended in a 2-2 draw.

Two Jimmy Greenhoff goals saw United into the sixth round with a 2-1 win, David Peach again scoring for Southampton to nurse the unhappy memory of having netted three times and ending on the losing side.

The quarter-final draw gave United home advantage against Aston Villa, and Houston and Macari scored in a 2-1 win in front of the fourth successive crowd of over 57,000 in games at Old Trafford. The biggest of those attendances had been for the League game with Leeds United, when 60,612 filled the ground . . . and it was Leeds who provided the semi-final opposition.

In the other semi-final Mersey rivals Liverpool and Everton met at Maine Road, while United travelled into Yorkshire to face Leeds at Hillsborough.

Wembley again

Within a quarter of an hour United had booked their ticket to Wembley. They played with confidence as Leeds seemed to be overcome by the occasion. First Jimmy Greenhoff scored, then Steve Coppell, and United's lively forward line continued to

Steve Coppell's graduation into the Second Division was swift. During his university days he played with Tranmere Rovers, but even though he was on the doorsteps of Liverpool and Everton he slipped through the Merseyside net and was bought for a bargain £40,000 in April 1975. He made his debut as substitute against Cardiff City and was a regular in the side until injury forced his retirement eight years and three managers later

cause problems for the Leeds defence all through the match.

All hopes of the Championship vanished in the days after the semi-final, as the team picked up only one point in four games. Then 18 days before the Wembley final, United lost to Liverpool at Anfield and Tommy Docherty amazed everyone by saying: 'We have learned something tonight. We can beat Lverpool at Wembley.'

Had they discovered the Achilles heel of Paisley's side? There were many who watched the 1-0 defeat who felt that United had been the better team, but had given away an unlucky goal to the side which was aiming for an incredible treble of League, FA Cup and European Cup. Kevin Keegan had scored in what, amazingly, was to be Liverpool's last win of the League campaign. They drew three out of their last four fixtures and lost the last, yet still won the Championship.

As for United's run-in to Wembley, they were hit by a devastating blow in a rough-house of a game at Bristol City when Stewart Houston was stretchered off with a broken ankle. Wembley was just a fortnight away when Arthur Albiston, a 19-year-old Scot, was called into the side. He played three full games before the final.

United and Docherty win the Cup

Liverpool were clear favourites to win. As League Champions and European Cup finalists their pedigree far outweighed Docherty's Dynamos, but it was United who rose to the occasion. The final was played at a hectic pace, with Liverpool pressurising young Albiston, who showed that he had a bright future ahead of him as he handled the foraging of McDermott, and the speed of Heighway who kept switching wings to cause confusion.

United held out till half-time, and realised as the second half started that they were not playing an invincible side. With five minutes gone Jimmy Greenhoff broke downfield and found Pearson with a precision header. The striker ran forward, brushing aside a challenge and fired a low shot towards the right-hand post. Clemence in the Liverpool goal seemed late to move to cover it and the ball passed his outstretched left arm before he could fully dive. United were ahead!

Back came Liverpool and a Joey Jones cross from the left was hit firmly by Case into the roof of Alex Stepney's net – two goals within three minutes and the cheers of the United fans choked by the sudden upsurge from Liverpool.

Another three minutes and United were ahead again thanks to a remarkable goal, and a strike which had a certain amount

of luck attached to it. Tommy Smith and Jimmy Greenhoff tangled, Smith blocking a scoring chance from the United forward. The ball ran off to Macari who fired at goal, but the shot was completely off target, and Clemence moved to his left to cover. The shot hit Greenhoff who was still between Macari and Smith, and deflected from his chest, over his right shoulder and into the net well beyond Clemence, for the winning goal.

The celebrations went on into the night. An official banquet at the Royal Lancaster Hotel was followed by a private party for the players and officials, their wives and friends at the Royal Garden Hotel where they were staying.

Martin Buchan ordered a trolley full of champagne and the joy of winning the cup was apparent . . . but Tommy Docherty had left the group to walk in Hyde Park, alone with his thoughts. He spent most of the night strolling in the silence of the park, making what for him was an important personal decision. Docherty was deciding how to break the news, before the media discovered it and splashed it, that he was leaving his wife to set up permanent home with another woman. That the woman was Mary Brown, wife of the club physiotherapist Laurie, made the situation more difficult than if she had no connections with United.

1972-80

Docherty forced to go

News of the love affair became public. Accusing fingers were pointed at the club, and at the couple who had been forced to make the heartbreaking decision of ending two marriages in order that they could share their lives together. 'The Mary Brown Affair' was headline news for weeks and eventually, even though he claimed that he was given an assurance that his private life would not affect his position as manager, Tommy Docherty was called before the board.

The meeting was held in Louis Edwards' home in Alderley Edge. The directors met the man who had taken their club to Wembley 44 days earlier and asked for his resignation. He refused, and was dismissed.

Ten years after their private lives had become public, Tommy Docherty and Mary Brown were free to marry and did so.

Dave Sexton arrives

Just ten days after Docherty's dismissal, Dave Sexton was appointed manager, following in the Scot's footsteps for the third time in his career. Sexton succeeded Docherty at Chelsea, and Docherty had briefly been manager of Queen's Park Rangers before Sexton.

Having left Loftus Road Sexton realised the size of the task which lay ahead of him at Old Trafford. He was following the

Left: Docherty and co. celebrate victory in the 1977 FA Cup. Goals from Stuart Pearson and Jimmy Greenhoff beat Liverpool, but every silver lining has a cloud and Docherty left the club during the summer

Below: No manager, but Manchester United display their silverware in 1977. Tommy Docherty took United back to Wembley to win the FA Cup for the first time since 1963, but had lost his job by the time the official photograph was taken. The players pose with the cup and the Charity Shield as chairman Louis Edwards fills the place normally reserved for the manager. His fellow directors stand behind him and (left to right) are today's chairman Martin Edwards, Bill Young, Alan Gibson, Sir Matt Busby and Denzil Haroun

most successful manager the club had seen since Busby, and a man who was extremely popular with the supporters. The extrovert Docherty was a complete contrast to the introvert Sexton and Sexton would find him a hard act to follow.

The 1977-78 season could have had no better start for Sexton, Lou Macari scoring a hat-trick in a 4-1 home victory over Birmingham City – but this was the team Docherty had built and the supporters were quick to remind the new manager of this fact, chanting the Doc's name regularly.

It was these same supporters who involved the club in one of the most embarrassing moments in its history when the first season under Sexton was just a month old. Crowd trouble in St Etienne resulted in United at first being banned from the Cup Winners' Cup, then reinstated and ordered to play the second leg of their tie with the French club at around 300 kilometres from Manchester. They chose Home Park, Plymouth.

Sexton made his first major move in the transfer market on 6 January 1978 when he signed Joe Jordan from Leeds United for £350,000, but the big striker did not play for almost a month because he was 'Cup-tied' and under suspension. During his enforced absence United were knocked out of the FA Cup by West Brom after scraping through the third round with a replay victory over Carlisle.

On 9 February, Sexton bought again, bringing centre-half Gordon McQueen from Leeds for £495,000 to join his best friend Joe Jordan. Jordan had made his debut on 8 February, and McQueen made his first appearance at Anfield 17 days later. Even so, it was 8 April before United won a game with both their signings in the side.

A series of draws during March kept United in mid-table, and then in April the supporters were stunned when Gordon Hill, one of the most popular players in the side, was sold for £250,000. The buyer? Tommy Docherty, now managing Derby County.

The following season, 1978-79, saw the visit of Real Madrid for the club's centenary game with Dave Sexton proud to be in charge:

> No club has captured the imagination like Manchester United, and it is a great thrill for me to be here. But rather than looking back over what has happened before, I'd like to look ahead. I feel that in the next ten years there will be changes. Football is a family game and I would like to see stadiums providing areas for family seating.
>
> Sponsorship is another aspect of the game which can be developed and I wouldn't be surprised to see players wearing shirts bearing a sponsor's name before long.
>
> We must also get ready to accept foreign players into our game, as well as some of our players going abroad. The only snag in this area, as far as I can see it, is our taxation system does not make a move to this country as attractive as one abroad.

United had opened the new season with Roche in goal and, despite winning only five games by November, were in the top six. They had been knocked out of the League Cup in a surprising game, Third Division Watford scoring twice through Luther Blissett, a self-confessed United supporter.

On 11 October 1978 United were away to Birmingham City and lost 5-1. Immediately Sexton moved for the chequebook and agreed to buy Coventry City goalkeeper Jim Blyth. He said that Roche's confidence had been shattered, not just by the Birmingham scoreline, but by the lack of support he was getting from the fans, who felt that Stepney was being wasted in the Central League side. Blyth arrived at Old Trafford to face the bright lights of television crews who had been told of the signing. The media gathered for interviews and photographs, but then the extraordinary news came through that the deal was off. Blyth had not passed the insurance medical, and was not eligible to play.

Sexton was in a difficult position. Stepney had not played any first team games, Roche had already been told by the move to sign Blyth that he was no longer being considered as first choice goalkeeper, and United were 48 hours away from their next game. So on 18 November the name of Gary Bailey was written on the team sheet for the first time, and the tall young blond prepared to face Ipswich Town, the side from his Suffolk birthplace.

Bailey had arrived at Old Trafford after playing university football in South Africa, where he had lived since his family emigrated there when he was four years old. Goalkeeping was in Bailey's blood, as his father Roy had kept goal for Ipswich Town from 1955 to 1964, and had been a member of the 1962 League Championship-winning side.

Young Gary Bailey had a steady debut in a 2-0 victory, and his form kept him in the side for the rest of the season.

The possibility of a Wembley return ended all rumblings about poor League form, but luck was again against the team when the sixth-round draw paired them with Tottenham at White Hart Lane. When a solid, professional performance earned them a replay at Old Trafford, the scent of Wembley was really in their nostrils. In the second game goals from McIlroy and Jordan powered United through to their third FA Cup semi-final in four years, but once more it was Lverpool who stood in their way.

The semi-final was at Maine Road and it was Liverpool who struck the first blow, Kenny Dalglish putting them ahead, but Jordan restored the balance. There was a moment of panic when Liverpool were awarded a hotly disputed penalty, but when McDermott missed United rallied, and Brian Greenhoff followed his brother's example by scoring a vital Cup goal to put them ahead. Six minutes from the end Hansen equalised, forcing United into their eighth game of the Cup campaign.

Four nights later, at Goodison Park, the elder Greenhoff

scored yet another crucial goal, and although Liverpool at times laid siege in the United half of the field, they were beaten. United were back at Wembley, and Dave Sexton had the chance of emulating Docherty and finally erasing all the disadvantageous comparisons.

The 'five-minute' final

For the massive United contingent amongst the supporters the final was a dull affair. The eleven who had beaten Liverpool ould start the final against Arsenal:

Bailey, Nicholl, Albiston, McIlroy, McQueen, Buchan, Coppell, Jimmy Greenhoff, Jordan, Macari, Thomas

The yellow and blue banners of Arsenal were held high as first Talbot, and then Frank Stapleton scored before half-time. Sexton's side seemed to offer little resistance and all United had won was the toss of the coin to decide who would wear their normal red on the big day.

Then, with five minutes remaining United found hope. Gordon McQueen, lunging forward, scored. The United chants at last were louder than those of the Londoners. Suddenly supporters who had been preparing to make an unhappy exit from the stadium stopped gathering their belongings to turn their attention to the game again. Journalists who had already written the story of United's defeat began to scribble new words on their notepads, and when Sammy McIlroy danced through the tiring Arsenal defence and slid the ball into the net for a second goal, the game took on a whole new life.

The 'five-minute final' and United celebrate after Sammy McIlroy's incredible equaliser. United trailed 2-0 with five minutes to go, then Gordon McQueen put them back in the game before McIlroy's goal. Joy was short-lived as straight from the kick-off Arsenal scored another to win the 1979 FA Cup

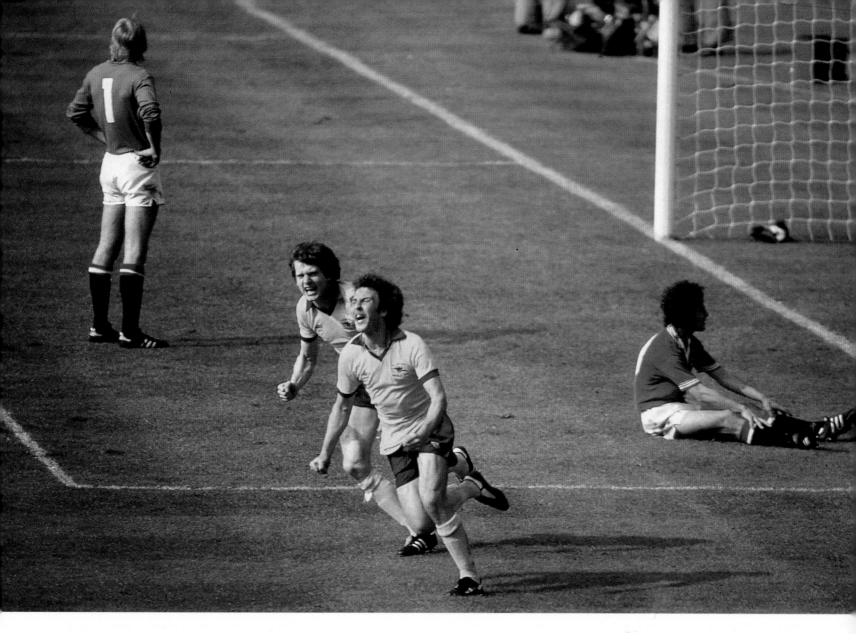

The scores were level with seconds rather than minutes left. United had earned extra time and, looking the fresher team, were looking forward to the whistle and the extra half-hour.

Instead, Liam Brady ran forward for Arsenal, crossing into the United half unchallenged. Macari went after him, but Brady's pass out to the left found Graham Rix. He ran forward again evading his opponents and sent over a high cross. Bailey appeared to hesitate, expecting his defence to cover, and Alan Sunderland forced the ball home. Arsenal had won what became known as 'the five-minute final', 3-2.

Seven days later Dave Sexton continued the building of a side which he could call his own, and bought Ray Wilkins from Chelsea for a massive £777,777, as two more of Docherty's players were sold. The first of these was David McCreery, bought by the new Queen's Park Rangers manager Tommy Docherty. He had joined the relegated London club on the eve of United's Cup final. The next player sold was Brian Greenhoff, reversing his brother's move by joining Leeds for

Alan Sunderland breaks United hearts as he scores the winner in the 89th minute of the 1979 Cup Final

£350,000. The side which began the 1979-80 season contained five players introduced by Sexton.

Criticism of fans and chairman

However, it was events away from the field which made the headlines. First, two Middlesbrough fans were killed when a wall collapsed on spectators as they left Ayrsome Park, and accusing fingers were pointed at United's rowdy supporters. Then a television programme accused the club of operating outside the rules.

Granada Television's 'World in Action' produced by Geoffrey Seed, a United supporter, accused chairman Louis Edwards of instigating payments to young players as a method of persuading them to join the club. It claimed that United operated a secret cash fund to use for matters such as this, and also accused the chairman of irregular share dealings. Louis Edwards strongly denied the accusations, which became the subject of a joint inquiry by the Football League and the Football Association, and said: 'I have never done anything at Manchester United that I am ashamed of I have always been proud to be chairman of this great club, and anything I have done has been in its best interests.'

A month after the allegations Louis Edwards died of a heart attack, to be succeeded by his son Martin as chairman of the club.

The battle for the Championship continued between Liverpool and United but an amazing scoreline on 1 March caused concern: Ipswich Town 6 United 0. And that match included two penalties saved by Bailey!

Since his arrival, Ray Wilkins had missed only two games. The first was the home defeat by Wolves, the second the trouncing at Ipswich in a game which Sir Matt Busby, the club's president-elect, described thus:

It was not the sort of result to make you feel confident of winning the Championship, but I remember that one player was outstanding. Arnold Muhren, the Dutch midfielder was brilliant – his part in the victory for his side was one of great importance, and he linked up well with his fellow countryman Frans Thijssen.

Was Sexton's premonition about the influx of foreign players coming true? Perhaps it was, because United's substitute that afternoon was Nikola Jovanovic, the Yugoslav defender, signed from Red Star Belgrade.

From the Ipswich disgrace to the end of the season only three more games were lost, the final result deciding the destiny of the title. The first of these upsets came at Nottingham's City Ground, where in an ill-tempered game Sammy McIlroy was ordered off by Clive Thomas after disputing a penalty from which John Robertson put the home side in front. Forest won 2-0, with Garry Birtles scoring the second.

Three days later United and Liverpool began their run-in to the end of the season when they met at Old Trafford, and a 2-1 win for United narrowed the gap to four points with six games remaining. The game also saw Jimmy Greenhoff playing his first full match of the season – and scoring the winner.

During what turned out to be the club's most successful season since 1968, as far as League position was concerned, United were accused by the media of lacking warmth. Under a headline of 'Cold Trafford', Dave Sexton's weakness in handling day-to-day press inquiries was exposed. The article alleged that Sexton was so unlike his predecessor that journalists who specialised in reporting the club's affairs were having difficulty in going about their work.

His approach was directly opposite to that of Docherty, who was never out of the news, eager to talk about anything whether it involved his club or not. Yet, as the Championship battle reached its end, Sexton was willing to give his views: 'We are in with a definite chance. If we can do well in the last six fixtures then we can win the title, but we are also hoping for mistakes from Liverpool.'

Five successive wins following the Liverpool game was the players' response to the challenge, but it was to no avail. On the last afternoon of the season United lost 2-0 at Leeds, Liverpool won 4-1 at Anfield against Aston Villa, and the race was lost by two points.

Injuries sink Sexton

Injuries became a millstone around Dave Sexton's neck. Slowly they pulled him down, causing him to use 16 players in the first three fixtures of 1980-81.

Nothing went right for United. In the first game Jordan limped off with a knee injury. Gary Bailey was able to disguise the fact that he had dislocated a finger making a save towards the end of the game, but he too was ruled out for the next two matches.

In the second game Grimes was hurt, and in the third Moran's bravery cost him dearly. He lunged at Birmingham's Keith Bertschin, and badly twisted his ankle, to be replaced by League debutant Mike Duxbury.

Moran, who had joined United from Pegasus, was missing for the next five League games and the two-legged League Cup clash with Coventry City. These League Cup-ties saw United out of the competition by early September, losing 1-0 at Old Trafford, and by the same scoreline at Highfield Road, with spurned goalkeeper Jim Blyth adding irony to the event by playing in both games for Coventry without conceding a goal.

Scoring goals was proving a problem and the club went six games with only one successful strike and that came from central defender Jovanovic in a 1-1 draw with Sunderland. By 13 September 1980 United had won just one game in the League, and drawn three of their four other First Division games. Sexton had tried Andy Ritchie at striker, alongside the rejuvenated Jimmy Greenhoff, who was fighting through the pain of a pelvic injury, and elsewhere gambled with young players. He was even forced to recall Chris McGrath from the reserve pool for his first game in three years. McGrath played one game, away to Birmingham, and that was his last appearance for the club.

Ritchie also played his last game for United early that season in the 0-0 draw at Tottenham, which came four days after the League Cup exit. Injuries and the continuing poor results were increasing the pressure on Sexton to pull the club out of its misery.

By mid-October the murmurings of discontent were growing louder, as the injury list grew longer. Buchan had been added to the ever-growing numbers unfit to play, and McQueen aggravated his injury again when he tried a return in the derby game at Old Trafford which ended in another predictable draw. After 12 League games there had been one defeat, but only three wins and the eight drawn games were the subject of most contention.

The unhappy Ritchie was sold to Brighton, and the £500,000 paid for the teenager was used to balance the books when Sexton plunged for Garry Birtles of Nottingham Forest, a prolific scorer who had netted 32 times in his 87 League games under Brian Clough. This, it was felt, was a better pedigree than young Ritchie's 13 goals in 26 full appearances. Ritchie was, however, still a month away from his 20th birthday, and revealed after the move that he felt he had been the target of too much criticism from assistant manager Tommy Cavanagh, and this contributed to his eagerness to leave.

Birtles cost United a massive £1,250,000, the largest amount up to that time (October 1980) that the club had paid for any player. His inclusion in the side brought two successive victories, although Birtles himself failed to score.

After defeats at Arsenal and to West Brom, United stepped into 1981 with three games against Ritchie's club Brighton. Such is the irony of football that the clubs were paired against each other in the third round of the FA Cup a week before their League meeting at Old Trafford.

United won 2-0 and Garry Birtles scored his first goal since his expensive move. Wilkins played in both matches although it was obvious that he was below full fitness.

Would the selling of Ritchie, a player who had cost the club nothing, prove to be an expensive mistake by Sexton? Certainly Birtles had not shown anything like the goalscoring he had produced for Clough, and the result was a slump from the end of January until mid-March, when the club went without a win.

The solidarity given to the defence by the presence of McQueen had been a vital factor missing from the side. He had been out for all but four League games of that season by the time that a revival began.

United were in mid-table and had lost four out of five games, one of these at home to Leeds United, when a lacklustre performance had the crowd shouting for Sexton's head. Was this the type of result to get a manager the sack? Sexton's response was a cold stare, and a reluctant reply:

'That's not the sort of question I can answer. We have had terrible injury problems this season, and everyone knows it.'

His players' response after the fourth of those defeats was to stage a late rally of nine games without losing, and after McQueen's return, seven successive victories, which was the best run by the team since the days of Busby in 1964. But it was too late and on 30 April 1980, five days after the closing victory over Norwich was watched by an Old Trafford crowd of 12,000 fewer than that of the previous season, Dave Sexton lost his job.

He was stunned by the news, but refused to criticise the club. He had taken United higher than anyone since Busby yet had failed, but he remained the gentleman to the end, saying only in private: 'There can be few managers who have lost their job after seven consecutive victories . . .'

Ray Wilkins was a fine ambassador for United both on and off the field. Injury led to him losing the captaincy of club and country to his friend Bryan Robson but it never affected his dedication to the game. Wilkins was bought by Dave Sexton in 1979 having been signed by the United manager when he was a 15-year-old starting his career with Chelsea. Ron Atkinson transferred him to AC Milan who paid a then record £1.5 million for the midfield player

SEASON 1970-1971 FOOTBALL LEAGUE (DIVISION 1)

Positions: 1 Stepney · 2 Edwards · 3 Dunne A · 4 Crerand · 5 Ure · 6 Sadler · 7 Fitzpatrick · 8 Stiles · 9 Charlton · 10 Kidd · 11 Best

Date	Opp	V	R	Score	1	2	3	4	5	6	7	8	9	10	11	Substitute
15 Aug	Leeds U	H	L	0-1	Stepney	Edwards	Dunne A	Crerand	Ure	Sadler	Fitzpatrick	Stiles	Charlton	Kidd	Best	Gowling for Stiles
19 Aug	Chelsea	H	D	0-0	..	..	..	..	..	..	Morgan	Fitzpatrick	..	Stiles	..	
22 Aug	Arsenal	A	L	0-4	..	Stiles	..	Fitzpatrick	..	..	..		..	Law	..	Edwards for Stepney
25 Aug	Burnley	A	W	2-0	Rimmer	Edwards	..	Fitzpatrick	..	..	..	Law2	..	Stiles	..	
29 Aug	West Ham U	H	D	1-1	..	..	..	.1	..	..	..	Stiles	..	..	..	Gowling for Stiles
2 Sep	Everton	H	W	2-0	..	..	..	..	..	..	Stiles	..	..1	Kidd	.1	
5 Sep	Liverpool	A	D	1-1	..	..	..	..	..	..	..	..	..	..1		
12 Sep	Coventry C	H	W	2-0	..	..	..	..	..	..	..	..	..1	..	..1	
19 Sep	Ipswich T	A	L	0-4	..	..	..	..	..	..	..	..	Gowling	..		Young for Dunne A
26 Sep	Blackpool	H	D	1-1	..	Watson	Burns	..	James	..	Morgan	Gowling	Kidd	..1		Sartori for James
3 Oct	Wolverhampton W	A	L	2-3	..	..	..	..	..	..	.1	..	..1			Sartori for James
10 Oct	Crystal Palace	H	L	0-1	..	Edwards	Dunne A	..	Ure	Stiles	..	Best	..	Aston		Sartori for Stiles
17 Oct	Leeds U	A	D	2-2	..	..	..	.1	..	..	Burns	..	..1	..		
24 Oct	W B A	H	W	2-1	..	..	..	..	..	..	Burns	Law1	..	..1	..	
31 Oct	Newcastle U	A	L	0-1	..	..	..	..	James	Sadler	Burns	..	..	..		
7 Nov	Stoke C	H	D	2-2	..	..	Burns	..	..	..	..1	Law1	..			
14 Nov	Nottingham F	A	W	2-1	..	Watson	Dunne A	..	..	..	..	..	Gowling1	Sartori1		
21 Nov	Southampton	A	L	0-1	..	..	..	..	..	..	.1	..	Kidd	Aston		Sartori for Fitzpatrick
28 Nov	Huddersfield T	H	D	1-1	..	..	..	..	..	..	.1	..	..	..		
5 Dec	Tottenham H	A	D	2-2	..	..	..	..	..	Stiles	..1	..1	..	..		Sartori for Law
12 Dec	Manchester C	H	L	1-4	..	..	..	Crerand	..	Fitzpatrick	Morgan	..	..1	Sartori1		Sartori for Law
19 Dec	Arsenal	H	L	1-3	..	Fitzpatrick	..	..	Ure	Sadler	..	..1	..1	Law2		
26 Dec	Derby Co	A	D	4-4	..	Fitzpatrick	..	..	Ure	Sadler	..1	..1	..1	Law2		
9 Jan	Chelsea	A	W	2-1	Stepney	..	..	..	Edwards	Stiles	..1	Law	Gowling1	Aston		
16 Jan	Burnley	H	D	1-1	..	..	..	..	..	..	..	..	..	Best		
30 Jan	Huddersfield	A	W	2-1	..	..	Burns	..	..	Sadler	..	..1	..	Best		Aston1 for Law
6 Feb	Tottenham H	H	W	2-1	..	..	..	..	..	..	.1	Kidd	..	.1		
20 Feb	Southampton	H	W	5-1	..	..	..	..	..	..	.1	Best	..	.4	Aston	
23 Feb	Everton	A	L	0-1	..	..	Dunne A	..	..	..	..	..	..	..		Burns for Gowling
27 Feb	Newcastle U	H	W	1-0	..	..	..	..	..	..	..	..	Kidd	..		
6 Mar	W B A	A	L	3-4	..	..	..	..	..	..	.1	..	.1	..1		
13 Mar	Nottingham F	H	W	2-0	..	..	..	..	..	..	.1	..	..	Law1		Burns for Aston
20 Mar	Stoke C	A	W	2-1	..	..	..	..	..	..	.2	..	..	..		
3 Apr	West Ham U	A	L	1-2	..	..	..	..	..	..	.1	..	..	..		Burns for Sadler
10 Apr	Derby Co	H	L	1-2	..	Dunne A	Burns	..	Stiles	..	..	..	..1	..		Gowling for Aston
12 Apr	Wolverhampton W	H	W	1-0	..	..	..	..	..	Best	Gowling1	..	..	Morgan		Kidd for Law
13 Apr	Coventry C	A	L	1-2	..	..	..	..	..	.1	..	..	Kidd	..		
17 Apr	Crystal Palace	A	W	5-3	..	Fitzpatrick	Dunne A	..	Sadler	.2	..	..	Law3	..		Burns for Crerand
19 Apr	Liverpool	H	L	0-2	..	..	Dunne A	Burns	..	..	..	..	..	..		
24 Apr	Ipswich T	H	W	3-2	..	..	..	James	..	Law	..	..	..1	Kidd1	Best1	Sartori for Sadler
1 May	Blackpool	A	D	1-1	..	..	..	..	..	..	..	..	..	..		
5 May	Manchester C	A	W	4-3	..	O'Neil	..	..	..	..	..1	..	..1	..	..2	

FA Cup
Date	Opp	V	R	Score	1	2	3	4	5	6	7	8	9	10	11	Substitute
2 Jan	Middlesbrough (3)	H	D	0-0	Rimmer	Fitzpatrick	Dunne A	Crerand	Ure	Sadler	Morgan	Best	Charlton	Kidd	Law	
5 Jan	Middlesbrough (SR)	A	L	1-2	..	..	..	..	Edwards	..	..	..1	..	..	..	Gowling for Kidd

League Cup
Date	Opp	V	R	Score	1	2	3	4	5	6	7	8	9	10	11	Substitute
9 Sep	Aldershot (2)	A	W	3-1	Rimmer	Edwards	Dunne A	Fitzpatrick	Ure	Sadler	Stiles	Law1	Charlton	Kidd1	Best1	James for Dunne A
7 Oct	Portsmouth (3)	H	W	1-0	..	Donald	Burns	..	..	..	Morgan	Gowling	..1	..	..	Aston for Sadler
28 Oct	Chelsea (4)	H	W	2-1	..	..	Edwards	Dunne A	..	James	..	Law	Best1	..1	Aston	Burns for Law
18 Nov	Crystal Palace (5)	H	W	4-2	..	Watson	..	..1	..	..	..	..	..	..2		
16 Dec	Aston Villa (SF)	H	D	1-1	..	..	..	..	..	Stiles	Sartori	..	..	..1		
23 Dec	Aston Villa (SF)	A	L	1-2	..	Fitzpatrick	..	Crerand	Ure	Sadler	Morgan	..	..	..1	Law	

Appearances (goals)

Aston 19 (3) — Best 40 (18) — Burns 16 — Charlton 42 (5) — Crerand 24 — Dunne A 35 — Edwards 29 — Fitzpatrick 35 (2) — Gowling 17 (8) — James 13 — Kidd 24 (8) — Law 29 (15) — Morgan 25 (3) — O'Neil 1 — Rimmer 20 — Sadler 32 (1) — Sartori 2 (2) — Stepney 22 — Stiles 17 — Ure 13 — Watson 8 — **Total 21 players 65**

Football League
	P	W	D	L	F:A	Pts	
Arsenal	42	29	7	6	71:29	65	1st
Manchester U	42	16	11	15	65:66	43	8th

SEASON 1971-1972 FOOTBALL LEAGUE (DIVISION 1)

Positions: 1 Stepney · 2 O'Neil · 3 Dunne A · 4 Gowling · 5 James · 6 Sadler · 7 Morgan · 8 Kidd · 9 Charlton · 10 Law · 11 Best

Date	Opp	V	R	Score	1	2	3	4	5	6	7	8	9	10	11	Substitute
14 Aug	Derby Co	A	D	2-2	Stepney	O'Neil	Dunne A	Gowling1	James	Sadler	Morgan	Kidd	Charlton	Law1	Best	
18 Aug	Chelsea	A	W	3-2	..	Fitzpatrick	..	..	..	..	..	..1	..1	..1	..	
20 Aug	Arsenal (Anfield)	H	W	3-1	..	O'Neil	..	.1	..	..	..	..1	..1	..	..	Aston for Best
23 Aug	W B A (Stoke)	H	W	3-1	..	..	..	.1	..	..	..	..	..	Best2	Aston	Burns for Charlton
28 Aug	Wolverhampton W	A	D	1-1	..	..	..	..	..	..	..	..	..	Law	Best	
31 Aug	Everton	A	L	0-1	..	..	..	..	..	..	..	..	..	..	..	
4 Sep	Ipswich T	H	W	1-0	..	..	..	..	..	..	..	..	..	..	..1	Aston for Law
11 Sep	Crystal Palace	A	W	3-1	..	..	..	..	..	..	..	..1	..	..2	..1	Aston for Gowling
18 Sep	West Ham U	H	W	4-2	..	..	..	..	..	..	..	..	..1	..	..3	
25 Sep	Liverpool	A	D	2-2	..	..	Burns	..	..	..	..	..	..1	..1	..	
2 Oct	Sheffield U	H	W	2-0	..	..	Dunne A	..1	..	..	..	..	..	Best1	Aston	Burns for Dunne A
9 Oct	Huddersfield T	A	W	3-0	..	..	..	..	..	..	..	..	..1	Law1	Best1	
16 Oct	Derby Co	A	W	1-0	..	..	..	..	..	..	..	..	..	..	..1	
23 Oct	Newcastle U	A	W	1-0	..	..	..	..	..	..	..	..	..	..	..1	Aston for Gowling
30 Oct	Leeds U	A	L	0-1	..	..	..	..	..	..	..	..	..	..	..	Sartori for Kidd
6 Nov	Manchester C	A	D	3-3	..	..	..	..1	..	..	..	..1	..	McIlroy1	..	Aston for Dunne A
13 Nov	Tottenham H	H	W	3-1	..	..	Burns	..	..	..	..	..	..	Law2	..	
20 Nov	Leicester C	A	W	3-2	..	..	..	..	..	Edward	..	McIlroy1	..	..2	..	McIlroy for Law
27 Nov	Southampton	A	W	5-2	..	..	..	..	..	Sadler	..	Kidd1	..	McIlroy1	..3	Aston for Best
4 Dec	Nottingham F	H	W	3-2	..	..	..	..	..	..	..	..	..	Law1	..	McIlroy for Kidd
11 Dec	Stoke C	A	D	1-1	..	..	..	..	..	..	..	..1	..	..1	..	
18 Dec	Ipswich T	A	D	0-0	..	..	Dunne A	..	..	..	..	..	..	..	..	
27 Dec	Coventry C	H	D	2-2	..	..	..	..	.1	..	..	..	..	..1	..	
1 Jan	West Ham U	A	L	0-3	..	..	..	..	Edwards	..	..	..	..	..	..	
8 Jan	Wolverhampton W	H	L	1-3	..	..	..	..	..	..	..	..	..	..	McIlroy1	Sartori for Gowling
22 Jan	Chelsea	H	L	0-1	..	O'Neil	..	..	..	..	..	McIlroy	..	..	Best	Aston for McIlroy
29 Jan	W B A	A	L	1-2	..	..	Dunne A	Burns	James	..	..	Kidd1	..	..	..	
12 Feb	Newcastle U	H	L	0-2	..	..	Burns	Gowling	..	..	..	..	..	..	..	
19 Feb	Leeds U	A	L	1-5	..	..	Dunne A	Burns1	..	..	..	..	..	Gowling	..	McIlroy for Kidd
4 Mar	Tottenham H	A	L	0-2	..	..	..	Buchan	..	..	..	Gowling	..	Law	..	McIlroy for Gowling
8 Mar	Everton	H	D	0-0	..	..	..	..	..	..	Burns	..	..	Best1	..	
11 Mar	Huddersfield T	H	W	2-0	..	..	..	..	..	..	Morgan	Kidd	Kidd	Best1	Storey-Moore1	McIlroy for Kidd
25 Mar	Crystal Palace	H	W	4-0	..	..	..	..	..	Gowling1	Bent	..	Charlton1	Law1	..	McIlroy for Kidd
1 Apr	Coventry C	A	W	3-2	..	..	..	..	..	..	Morgan	Best1	..1	..	..1	
3 Apr	Liverpool	H	L	0-3	..	..	..	..	..	..	..	..	..	..	..	Young for Law
4 Apr	Sheffield U	A	D	1-1	Connaughton	..	..	..	..	Sadler1	Best	McIlroy	..	Young	..	
8 Apr	Leicester C	A	L	0-2	..	..	..	..	Sadler	Morgan	..	..	..	..	..	Gowling for McIlroy
12 Apr	Manchester C	H	L	1-3	..	..	..	..	.1	James	Sadler	Gowling	..	Kidd	..	Law for Gowling
15 Apr	Southampton	H	W	3-2	Stepney	..	..	..	..	..	.1	Young	..	Law	..1	
22 Apr	Nottingham F	A	D	0-0	..	..	..	..	..	..	Morgan	Kidd	Kidd1	..	..	Young for James
25 Apr	Arsenal	A	L	0-3	..	..	..	..	..	Sadler	Gowling	Best	Young	Charlton	Kidd	McIlroy for Young
29 Apr	Stoke C	H	W	3-0	..	..	..	..	James	Young	..1	McIlroy	..1	Law	..1	Gowling for Charlton

FA Cup
Date	Opp	V	R	Score	1	2	3	4	5	6	7	8	9	10	11	Substitute
15 Jan	Southampton (S)	A	D	1-1	Stepney	O'Neil	Burns	Gowling	Edwards	Sadler	Morgan	Kidd	Charlton1	Law	Best	McIlroy for Kidd
19 Jan	Southampton (SR)	H	W	4-1	..	..	..	..	..	..1	..	McIlroy	..	..	..2	Aston1 for McIlroy
5 Feb	Preston NE (4)	A	W	2-0	..	..	Dunne A	..	James	..	..	Kidd	..	..	..	
26 Feb	Middlesbrough (5)	H	D	0-0	..	..	O'Neil	Dunne A	Burns	..	..	Gowling	..	..	..	
29 Feb	Middlesbrough (5R)	A	W	3-0	..	..	..	..	..	..	..	..1	..	.1	..	
18 Mar	Stoke C (6)	H	D	1-1	..	..	..	..	Buchan	..	..	Kidd	..	..	..1	Gowling for Sadler
22 Mar	Stoke C (6R)	A	L	1-2	..	..	..	Gowling	..	Buchan	..	..	..	..	..1	McIlroy for Morgan

Abbreviations:

Appearances (goals) refer to League games only

Figures shown as 2 etc. refer to goals scored by individual players

* own-goal

Players' names in final column, are substitutes

League Cup

				Stepney	O'Neil	Dunne A	Gowling	James	Sadler	Morgan	Kidd	Charlton	Best	Aston	
7 Sep	Ipswich T (2)	A	W 3-1	Stepney	O'Neil	Dunne A	Gowling	James	Sadler	Morgan1	Kidd	Charlton	Best	Aston	
6 Oct	Burnley (3)	H	D 1-1	..	..	..	..	..	..	..	..	..1	..	..	
18 Oct	Burnley (SR)	A	W 1-0	..	..	..	..	..	..	..	..	..1	Law	Best	
27 Oct	Stoke C (4)	H	D 1-1	..	..	Burns	..1	..	..	..	..	..	..	..	Aston for Kidd
8 Nov	Stoke C (4R)	A	D 0-0	...	...	...	...	...	...	...	..	McIlroy	Best	..	Aston for Kidd
15 Nov	Stoke C (4R)	A	L 1-2	..	..	..	..	..	..	..	McIlroy	Sartori	..1		

Appearances (goals)

Aston 2 – Best 40 (18) – Buchan 13 (1) – Burns 15 (1) – Charlton 40 (8) – Connaughton 3 – Dunne A 34 – Edwards 4 – Fitzpatrick 1 – Gowling 35 (6) – James 37 (1) – Kidd 34 (10) – Law 32 (13) – McIlroy 8 (4) – Morgan 35 (1) – O'Neil 37 – Sadler 37 (1) – Stepney 39 – Storey-Moore 11 (5) – Young 5 – **Total 20 players 69**

Football League

	P	W	D	L	F:A	Pts	
Derby Co	42	24	10	8	69:33	58	1st
Manchester U	42	19	10	13	69:61	48	8th

SEASON 1972-1973 FOOTBALL LEAGUE (DIVISION 1)

Date	Opp		Res	Stepney	O'Neil	Dunne A	Morgan	James	Buchan	Best	Kidd	Charlton	Law	Storey-Moore	Substitute
12 Aug	Ipswich T	H	L 1-2	Stepney	O'Neil	Dunne A	Morgan	James	Buchan	Best	Kidd	Charlton	Law1	Storey-Moore	McIlroy for Charlton
15 Aug	Liverpool	A	L 0-2	..	..	..	Young	..	..	Morgan	..	..	Best	..	McIlroy for Kidd
19 Aug	Everton	A	L 0-2	..	..	..	Buchan	..	Sadler	..	Fitzpatrick	Kidd	..	..	McIlroy for James
23 Aug	Leicester C	H	D 1-1	..	..	..	..	..	..	..	..	McIlroy	..1	..	Kidd for McIlroy
26 Aug	Arsenal	H	D 0-0	..	..	..	..	..	..	..	Young	..	..	..	
30 Aug	Chelsea	H	D 0-0	..	..	..	..	..	..	..	Fitzpatrick	Law	..	..	Charlton for Storey-Moore
2 Sep	West Ham U	A	D 2-2	..	..	..	..	..	..	..	Law	Charlton	..1	..1	McIlroy for Law
9 Sep	Coventry C	H	L 0-1	..	..	Buchan	Fitzpatrick	..	..	McIlroy	..	..	..	..	Young for Charlton
16 Sep	Wolverhampton W	A	L 0-2	..	Buchan	Dunne A	..	..	..	Young	McIlroy	..	..	..	Kidd for Sadler
23 Sep	Derby Co	H	W 3-0	..	Donald	..	Young	..	Buchan	Morgan1	Davies1	..	..	..1	McIlroy for Storey-Moore
30 Sep	Sheffield U	A	L 0-1	..	..	..	..	..	..	..	Macdougall1	Davies	..1	..	
7 Oct	W B A	A	D 2-2	..	Watson	..	..	.Sadler	..	..	..1	..	..	..1	Charlton for Storey-Moore
14 Oct	Birmingham C	H	W 1-0	..	..	..	..	..	..	..	..	..	Charlton1	Storey-Moore	
21 Oct	Newcastle U	A	L 1-2	..	Donald	..	Law	..	..	Best1	..1	Charlton	Davies1		McIlroy for Dunne A
26 Oct	Tottenham H	H	L 1-4	..	O'Neil	..	Morgan	..	..	..	..1	Charlton	Davies1	..	Kidd for Morgan
4 Nov	Leicester C	A	D 2-2	..	..	..	..	..	Edwards	..	..1	..	..1	..	
11 Nov	Liverpool	H	W 2-0	..	..	..	..	..	Sadler	Young	..1	..	..	..1	
18 Nov	Manchester C	A	L 0-3	..	..	..	..	..	Young	Morgan	..	..	..	..	Law for Young
25 Nov	Southampton	H	W 2-1	..	..	..	..	..	..	..	..	Kidd	..	..	Law for Dunne A
2 Dec	Norwich C	A	W 2-0	..	..	..	Law	..	..	..	..1	Charlton	..	..1	Kidd for Law
9 Dec	Stoke C	H	L 0-2	..	..	..	Kidd	..	..	..	..	..	..	..	Young for Dunne A
16 Dec	Crystal Palace	A	L 0-5	..	Young	Forsyth	Graham	..	..	Kidd1	..	Low	..	Davies for Law
23 Dec	Leeds U	H	D 1-1	..	..	..	Law	Holton	..	Macdougall	..1	Macari1	Graham	Kidd for Macdougall
26 Dec	Derby Co	A	L 1-3	..	..	..	Martin	..	..	..	..	..	Martin		
6 Jan	Arsenal	A	L 1-3	..	..	..	Graham	..1	..	..	..	..2	..		
20 Jan	West Ham U	H	D 2-2	..	Forsyth	Dunne A	..	..	Martin	..	..	..1	Kidd		
24 Jan	Everton	H	D 0-0	..	Young	Forsyth	..	James	..	Morgan	Kidd1	..	..1	Storey-Moore	Martin for Storey-Moore
27 Jan	Coventry C	A	D 1-1	Rimmer	..	..	..	..	..	..	..1	..	..1		Martin for Storey-Moore
10 Feb	Wolverhampton W	H	W 2-1	..	..	James	..	Holton1	..	..	..	..	Martin1		
17 Feb	Ipswich T	A	L 1-4	..	..	..	..1	..	..	..	..1	..	..		Anderson for Kidd
3 Mar	W B A	H	W 2-1	..	..	..	..1	..	..	..	..	Law	..1		Anderson for Kidd
10 Mar	Birmingham C	A	L 1-3	Stepney	..	..	..	..	..	..	..1	..	Macari	Anderson for Kidd
17 Mar	Newcastle U	H	W 2-1	..	..	..	..	..	..	..	Anderson	..	..1	Fletcher for Anderson
24 Mar	Tottenham H	A	D 1-1	..	..	..	..	..	..	..	..1	..	..	Fletcher for Anderson
31 Mar	Southampton	A	W 2-0	..	..	Sidebottom	..	..	..	..	Kidd	..	..	Anderson for James
7 Apr	Norwich C	H	W 1-0	..	..	..	..	..	..	..	..1	..	..	Anderson for Kidd

FA Cup

				Stepney	Young	Forsyth	Law	Sadler	Buchan	Morgan	Davies	Charlton	Kidd	Graham	
13 Jan	Wolverhampton W (3)	A	L 0-1	Stepney	Young	Forsyth	Law	Sadler	Buchan	Morgan	Davies	Charlton	Kidd	Graham	Dunne A for Kidd

League Cup

				Stepney	O'Neil	Dunne A	Buchan	James	Sadler	Morgan	Charlton	Law	Best	Storey-Moore	
6 Sep	Oxford U (2)	A	D 2-2	Stepney	O'Neil	Dunne A	Buchan	James	Sadler	Morgan	Charlton1	Law1	Best	Storey-Moore	McIlroy for Dunne A
12 Sep	Oxford U (2R)	H	W 3-1	..	Fitzpatrick	Buchan	Young	..	..	..	Law	Charlton	..2	..1	McIlroy for Law
3 Oct	Bristol R (3)	A	D 1-1	..	Donald	Dunne A	..	..	Buchan	..	Kidd	..	..	..	
11 Oct	Bristol R (3R)	H	L 1-2	..	..	Watson	Dunne A	..	..	..1	..	..	..	..	McIlroy1 for Kidd

Appearances (goals)

Anderson 2 (1) – Best 19 (4) – Buchan 42 – Charlton 34 (6) – Davies 15 (4) – Donald 4 – Dunne A 24 – Edwards 1 – Fitzpatrick 5 – Forsyth 8 – Graham 18 (1) – Holton 15 (3) – James 22 – Kidd 17 (4) – Law 9 (1) – Macari L 16 (5) – Macdougall 18 (5) – McIlroy 4 – Martin 14 (2) – Morgan 39 (2) – O'Neil 18 – Rimmer 4 – Sadler 19 – Sidebottom 2 – Stepney 38 – Storey-Moore 26 (5) – Watson 3 – Young 28 – Own goals 1 – **Total 28 players 44**

Football League

	P	W	D	L	F:A	Pts	
Liverpool	42	25	10	7	72:42	60	1st
Manchester U	42	12	13	17	44:60	37	18th

Bobby
Charlton

SOUVENIR TESTIMONIAL PROGRAMME

Bobby Charlton's Testimonial was against Celtic on 18th September 1972.

1970-1971

SEASON 1973-1974 FOOTBALL LEAGUE (DIVISION 1)

Date	Opponent			Score	1	2	3	4	5	6	7	8	9	10	11	Substitutes
25 Aug	Arsenal	A	L	0-3	Stepney	Young	Buchan M	Daly	Holton	James	Morgan	Anderson	Macari	Graham	Martin	McIlroy for Daly
29 Aug	Stoke C	H	W	1-0	..	..	..	Martin	..	..1	..	..	..	..	McIlroy	Fletcher for James
1 Sep	Q P R	H	W	2-1	..	..	..	..	..	Sidebottom	..	..	..	..	..1	Fletcher for Martin
5 Sep	Leicester C	A	L	0-1	..	..	..	Daly	..	Sadler	..	Kidd	..	..	..	Martin for Daly
8 Sep	Ipswich T	A	L	1-2	..	..	..	..	Sadler	Greenhoff	..	..1	Macari	..	Storey-Moore	Macari for Kidd
12 Sep	Leicester C	H	L	1-2	..1	Buchan M	Young	Martin	Holton	James	..	Kidd1	Anderson	..		Buchan G for Holton
15 Sep	West Ham U	H	W	3-1	..	..	..	..	..	..	..	Anderson	Macari	Kidd	Graham	Buchan G for Macari
22 Sep	Leeds U	A	D	0-0	..	..	..	Greenhoff	..	..	..	..	..	..	..	Buchan G for Graham
29 Sep	Liverpool	H	D	0-0	..	..	..	..	..	..	..	..	..	..	..	McIlroy1 for Anderson
8 Oct	Wolverhampton W	A	L	1-2	..	..	..	..	..	..	..	Young	Kidd	Anderson	..	
13 Oct	Derby Co	H	L	0-1	..	..	..	Forsyth	..	..	..	Kidd	Macari	Graham	Best	Martin for Best
20 Oct	Birmingham C	H	W	1-0	..1	..	..	Young	..	..	..	..	..	..	..	Sadler for Kidd
27 Oct	Burnley	A	D	0-0	..	..	..	..	..	James	Griffiths	..	..	..	..	
3 Nov	Chelsea	H	D	2-2	..	..	..	A	..1	..	..	Macari	Kidd	..1	..	
10 Nov	Tottenham H	A	L	1-2	..	..	..	..	Holton	James	..	..	..	..	..1	
17 Nov	Newcastle U	A	L	2-3	..	..	..	..	..	..	..	..1	..	..1	..	Fletcher for Morgan
24 Nov	Norwich C	H	D	0-0	..	..	..	..	..	..	..	..	..	..	..	Anderson for Kidd
8 Dec	Southampton	H	D	0-0	..	..	..	Forsyth	James	Griffiths	..	Young	..	McIlroy	..	Martin for James
15 Dec	Coventry C	H	L	2-3	..	..	..	..	..	..	..1	Macari	McIlroy	Young	..1	McIlroy for Kidd
22 Dec	Liverpool	A	L	0-2	..	..	Young	..	Sidebottom	..	..	Kidd	Graham	..		
26 Dec	Sheffield U	H	L	1-2	..	Young	Griffiths	..	Holton	Buchan M	..	..1	McIlroy	..	..	
29 Dec	Ipswich T	H	W	2-0	..	..	..	..	..	..	..	..1	..1	..	..	
1 Jan	Q P R	A	L	0-3	..	..	Houston	..	..	..	..	..	..	..	..	
12 Jan	West Ham U	A	L	1-2	..	Forsyth	..	..	..	..	..	Kidd	Young	Graham	McIlroy for Kidd
19 Jan	Arsenal	H	D	1-1	..	Buchan M	..	..	..	James1	..	McIlroy	..	..	Martin	
2 Feb	Coventry C	A	L	0-1	..	..	..	..	..	..	..	..	Kidd	Young	Forsyth for McIlroy
9 Feb	Leeds U	H	L	0-2	..	..	..	..	..	..	..	..	Young	Forsyth	McIlroy for Forsyth
16 Feb	Derby Co	A	D	2-2	..	Forsyth	..1	..1	..	Buchan M	..	Fletcher	..	Macari	McIlroy	Daly for Morgan
23 Feb	Wolverhampton W	H	D	0-0	..	..	..	..	..	..	..	Macari1	McIlroy	Daly	Martin	Daly for McIlroy
2 Mar	Sheffield U	A	W	1-0	..	..	..	..	..	..	..	..	Greenhoff	..	Bielby	Graham for Martin
13 Mar	Manchester C	A	D	0-0	..	..	..	Martin	..	..	McCalliog	..	..	Graham	..	
16 Mar	Birmingham C	A	L	0-1	..	..	..	..	..	..	Morgan	McIlroy	Kidd	McCalliog	Daly	Bielby for Kidd
23 Mar	Tottenham H	H	L	0-1	..	..	..	Greenhoff	James	..	..1	Greenhoff	..	Martin	Bielby for James
30 Mar	Chelsea	A	W	3-1	..	..	..	Daly	..	..	..1	..	..	..	..	
3 Apr	Burnley	H	D	3-3	..	..1	..	..	Holton1	..	..1	Macari1	McIlroy	..	Daly	
6 Apr	Norwich C	A	W	2-0	..	..	..	Greenhoff1	..	..	..	Daly	McCalliog1	Macari	..	McIlroy
13 Apr	Newcastle U	H	W	1-0	..	..	..	..	..	..	..	Macari	McIlroy	McCalliog2	Daly	Martin for McIlroy
15 Apr	Everton	H	W	3-0	..	Young	..1	..	..	..	..	..	..	..1	..	
20 Apr	Southampton	A	D	1-1	..	..	..	..	..	..	..	..	..	..	..	
23 Apr	Everton	A	L	0-1	..	Forsyth	..	..	..	..	..	..	..	..	..	
27 Apr	Manchester C	H	L	0-1	..	..	..	..	..	..	..	..	..	..	Martin	
29 Apr	Stoke C	A	L	0-1	..	..	..	..	..	..	..	..	..	..	..	

FA Cup

Date	Opponent			Score												Substitutes
5 Jan	Plymouth A (3)	H	W	1-0	Stepney	Young	Forsyth	Greenhoff	Holton	Buchan M	Morgan	Macari1	Kidd	Graham	Martin	McIlroy for Martin
26 Jan	Ipswich T (4)	H	L	0-1	..	Buchan M	..	..	..	James	..	..	McIlroy	Young	..	Kidd for Macari

League Cup

Date	Opponent			Score												Substitutes
8 Oct	Middlesbrough (2)	H	L	0-1	Stepney	Buchan M	Young	Greenhoff	Holton	James	Morgan	Daly	Macari	Kidd	Graham	Buchan G for Macari

Appearances (goals)

Anderson 11 (1) – Best 12 (2) – Bielby 2 – Buchan M 42 – Daly 14 (1) – Fletcher 2 – Forsyth 18 (1) – Graham 23 (1) – Greenhoff 36 (3) – Griffiths C 7 – Holton 34 (2) – Houston 20 (2) – James 21 (2) – Kidd B 21 (2) – Macari 34 (5) – McCalliog 11 (4) – McIlroy 24 (6) – Martin 12 – Morgan 41 (2) – Sadler 2 – Sidebottom 2 – Stepney 42 (2) – Storey-Moore 2 (1) – Young 29 (1) – **Total 24 players 58**

Football League

	P	W	D	L	F:A	Pts	
Leeds	42	24	14	4	66:31	62	1st
Manchester U	42	10	12	20	38:48	32	21st

SEASON 1974-1975 FOOTBALL LEAGUE (DIVISION 2)

Date	Opponent			Score	1	2	3	4	5	6	7	8	9	10	11	Substitutes
17 Aug	Orient	A	W	2-0	Stepney	Forsyth	Houston1	Greenhoff B	Holton	Buchan M	Morgan1	Macari	Pearson	McCalliog	Daly	McIlroy for Macari
24 Aug	Millwall	H	W	4-0	..	..	..	..	..	..	..	McIlroy	..1	Martin	..3	
28 Aug	Portsmouth	H	W	2-1	..	..	..	..	..	..	..	..1	..	..	..1	
31 Aug	Cardiff C	A	W	1-0	..	..	..	..	..	..	..	..	..	Martin	McCalliog	Young for Pearson
7 Sep	Nottingham F	H	D	2-2	..	..	..	..	..	..	..	..	Pearson1	..	..1	Macari for Greenhoff B
14 Sep	W B A	A	D	1-1	..	..	..	Martin	..	..	..	..	..	..	..	Greenhoff B for Martin
16 Sep	Millwall	A	W	1-0	..	..	..	Greenhoff B	Sidebottom	..	..	Macari	..	..	..1	Young for Daly
21 Sep	Bristol R	H	W	2-0	..	..	..1	..1	Holton	..	..	..	..	..	..	Young for McCalliog
25 Sep	Bolton W	H	W	*3-0	..	..	..	..	Sidebottom	..	..1	..	..	..		
26 Sep	Norwich C	A	L	0-2	..	..	..	..	Holton	..	..	..	..	..	..	Young for Morgan
5 Oct	Fulham	A	W	2-1	..	..	..	..	..	..	..	..	Pearson2	..	..	Macari for Daly
12 Oct	Notts Co	H	W	1-0	..	..	..	..	..	..	..	..1	Macari	..	..	Young for McCalliog
15 Oct	Portsmouth	A	D	0-0	..	..	Albiston	..	..	..	..	..	..	..	..	McCreery for Morgan
19 Oct	Blackpool	A	W	3-0	..	..	..1	Houston	..	..	..	..	..1	..1	..	McCreery for Daly
28 Oct	Southampton	H	W	1-0	..	..	..	..	..	..	..	..	..	..	..	Pearson1 for Morgan
2 Nov	Oxford U	H	W	4-0	..	..	..	..	Sidebottom	..	Macari1	..	Pearson3	..	..	Morgan for Greenhoff B
9 Nov	Bristol C	A	L	0-1	..	..	..	..	..	..	..	..	..	..	..	Graham for Daly
16 Nov	Aston Villa	H	W	2-1	..	..	..	Macari	..	..	Morgan	..	..	..	..2	Greenhoff B for Pearson
23 Nov	Hull C	A	L	0-2	..	..	..	Greenhoff B	..	..	..	Greenhoff B	..	Macari	..	Davies for Greenhoff B
30 Nov	Sunderland	H	W	3-2	..	..	..	Greenhoff B	Holton	..	..1	..1	Pearson1	Macari	..	Davies for Holton
7 Dec	Sheffield Wed	A	D	4-4	..	..	..1	..	..	..	..	..1	..2	..	McCalliog	Davies for Greenhoff B
14 Dec	Orient	H	D	0-0	..	..	..	..	Sidebottom	..	..	..	..	..	Daly	Davies for Sidebottom
21 Dec	York C	A	W	1-0	..	Young	..	..	..	..	..	..1	..1	..	..	
26 Dec	W B A	H	W	2-1	..	..	..	..	..	..	..	..1	..1	..	..1	
28 Dec	Oldham	A	L	0-1	..	..	Albiston	..	..	..	..	..	..	..	..	Davies for Greenhoff B
11 Jan	Sheffield Wed	H	W	2-0	..	Forsyth	Houston	..	James	..	..	..	..	..	McCalliog2	Daly for Morgan
18 Jan	Sunderland	A	D	0-0	..	..	..	..	..	..	..	Baldwin	..	..		Young for Daly
1 Feb	Bristol C	H	L	0-1	..	..	..	Daly	..	..	..	..	Pearson	..	Young	Davies for Morgan
8 Feb	Oxford U	A	L	0-1	Roche	..	..	Greenhoff B	..	..	..	..	..1	..	Martin	Davies for James
15 Feb	Hull C	H	W	2-0	..	..	..1	..	..	..	Young	..	..	..	..	Davies for Martin
22 Feb	Aston Villa	A	L	0-2	Stepney	..	..	..	Sidebottom	..	..	..	..	..	Daly	Coppell for Morgan
1 Mar	Cardiff C	H	W	4-0	..	..	..1	..	James	..	Morgan	..1	..1	..1	..	Young for Houston
8 Mar	Bolton W	A	W	1-0	..	..	..	..	..	..	Coppell	..	..1	..	..	Young for Coppell
15 Mar	Norwich C	H	D	1-1	..	..	..	..	..	..	..	..	..1	..	..	
22 Mar	Nottingham F	A	W	1-0	..	..	..	..	..	..	..	..	..	..	..1	
28 Mar	Bristol R	A	D	1-1	..	..	..	..	..	..	..	..	..1	..	..	Morgan for James
29 Mar	York C	H	W	2-1	..	..	..	Morgan	Greenhoff B	..	..1	..	..1	..	..	
31 Mar	Oldham	H	W	3-2	..	..	..	..	..	..	..1	..1	..	..1	..	Martin for Daly
5 Apr	Southampton	A	W	1-0	..	..	..	Young	..	..	Morgan	..	..	..	..	Nicholl for Buchan M
12 Apr	Fulham	H	W	1-0	..	..	..	Greenhoff B	James	Morgan	Coppell	..	..	..	..1	
19 Apr	Notts Co	A	D	2-2	..	..	..1	..1	..	..	..	..	..2	..1	..	
26 Apr	Blackpool	H	W	4-0	..	..	..	..1	..	..	..	..	..	..	..	

FA Cup

Date	Opponent			Score												Substitutes
4 Jan	Walsall (3)	H	D	0-0	Stepney	Young	Houston	Greenhoff B	Sidebottom	Buchan M	Morgan	McIlroy	Pearson	Macari	Daly	Davies for Morgan
7 Jan	Walsall (3R)	A	L	2-3	..	..	..	..	..	..	McCalliog	..1	..	..	..1	Davies for Daly

League Cup

Date	Opponent			Score												Substitutes
11 Sep	Charlton A (2)	H	W	*5-1	Stepney	Forsyth	Houston1	Martin	Holton	Buchan M	Morgan	McIlroy1	Macari2	McCalliog	Daly	Young for Forsyth
9 Oct	Manchester C (3)	H	W	1-0	..	..	Albiston	Greenhoff B	..	..	..	..	Pearson	..	..1	Macari for Pearson
13 Nov	Burnley (4)	H	W	3-2	..	..	Houston	..	Sidebottom	..	Macari2	..	..	Macari	..	Morgan1 for Greenhoff B
4 Dec	Middlesbrough (5)	A	D	0-0	..	..	..	..	Holton	..	Morgan	..	..	..	..	Young for Morgan
18 Dec	Middlesbrough (5R)	H	W	3-0	..	Young	..	..	Sidebottom	..	..	..1	..	..1	..	McCalliog for Greenhoff B
15 Jan	Norwich C (SF)	H	D	2-2	..	Forsyth	..	..	James	..	..	..	Daly	..	McCalliog	Young for Daly
22 Jan	Norwich C (SF)	A	L	0-1	..	..	..	..	..	..	..	..	..	..	..	Young for James

Appearances (goals)

Albiston 2 – Baldwin 2 – Buchan M 41 – Connell 9 (1) – Daly 36 (11) – Forsyth 39 (1) – Greenhoff B 39 (4) – Holton 14 – Houston 40 (6) – James 13 – Macari 36 (11) – McCalliog -20 (3) – McIlroy 41(7) – Martin 7 – Morgan 32 (3) – Pearson 30 (17) – Roche 2 – Sidebottom 12 – Stepney 40 – Young 7 – Own goals 2 – **Total 20 players 66**

Football League

	P	W	D	L	F:A	Pts	
Manchester U	42	26	9	7	66:30	61	1st

Date	Opponent	V	R	Score	Stepney	Forsyth	Houston	Jackson	Greenhoff B	Buchan M	Coppell	McIlroy	Pearson	Macari	Daly	Substitutes
16 Aug	Wolverhampton W	A	W	2-0	Stepney	Forsyth	Houston	Jackson	Greenhoff B	Buchan M	Coppell1	McIlroy	Pearson	Macari2	Daly	Nicholl for Pearson
19 Aug	Birmingham C	A	W	2-0	..	..	..	..	..	..	..	..2	..	McCreery	..	Nicholl for Stepney
23 Aug	Sheffield U	H	W	5-1	..	..	..	..	..	..	..	..1	Pearson2	..1	..1	Nicholl for Forsyth
27 Aug	Coventry C	H	D	1-1	..	..	..	..	..	..	..	..	..1	..	..	
30 Aug	Stoke C	A	W	*1-0	..	..	..	..	..	..	..	..	..	..	..	
6 Sep	Tottenham H	H	W	*3-2	..	Nicholl	..	..	..	..	..	..	..	..	..2	
13 Sep	Q P R	A	L	0-1	..	..	..	Albiston	..	Houston	..	..	..	..	..	Young for Jackson
20 Sep	Ipswich T	H	W	1-0	..	..	..	Houston1	McCreery	Greenhoff B	..	..	..	..	..1	
24 Sep	Derby Co	A	L	1-2	..	..	..	..	..	..	..	..	..	..	..1	
27 Sep	Manchester C	A	D	2-2	..	..	..	..1	..	..	..	..	..	..1	..	
4 Oct	Leicester C	H	D	0-0	..	..	..	Jackson	..	..	..	..	..	..	..	
11 Oct	Leeds U	A	W	2-1	..	..	..	..	..	..	..	..2	..	..	..	Grimshaw for Houston
18 Oct	Arsenal	H	W	3-1	..	..	..	..	..	..	..2	..	..1	..	..	
25 Oct	West Ham U	A	L	1-2	..	..	..	..	..	..	..	..	..	..1	..	McCreery for Daly
1 Nov	Norwich C	H	W	1-0	Roche	..	..	..	..	..	..	..	..	..1	..	McCreery for Jackson
8 Nov	Liverpool	A	L	1-3	..	..	..	..	..	..1	..	..	..	..1	..	McCreery for Jackson
15 Nov	Aston Villa	H	W	2-0	..	..	..	..	Daly	..	..1	..1	..	..1	..Hill	
22 Nov	Arsenal	A	L	1-3	..	..	..	..	..	..1	..1	..	..	..1	..	McCreery for McIlroy
29 Nov	Newcastle U	H	W	1-0	Stepney	..	..	..	..1	..	..	..	..	..	..	McCreery for Pearson
6 Dec	Middlesbrough	A	D	0-0	..	Forsyth	..	..	..	..	..	..	..	..	..	Nicholl for Forsyth
13 Dec	Sheffield U	A	W	4-1	..	..	..	..	..	..	..	..	..2	..1	..1	McCreery for McIlroy
20 Dec	Wolverhampton W	H	W	1-0	..	..	..	..	..	..	..	..	..	..1	..1	Kelly for Greenhoff B
23 Dec	Everton	A	D	1-1	..	..	..	..	..	..	..	..	..	..1	..	
27 Dec	Burnley	H	W	2-1	..	..	..	..	..	..	..	..1	..	..1	..	McCreery for Pearson
10 Jan	Q P R	H	W	2-1	..	..	..	..	..	..	..	..1	..	..	..1	
17 Jan	Tottenham H	A	D	1-1	..	..	..	..	..	..	..	..	..	..	..1	McCreery for McIlroy
31 Jan	Birmingham C	H	W	3-1	..	..1	..	..	..	..	..	..	..	..1	..	McCreery for Pearson
7 Feb	Coventry C	A	D	1-1	..	..	..	..	..	..	..	..	..	..1	..	McCreery for Pearson
18 Feb	Liverpool	H	D	0-0	..	..	..	..	..	..	..	..	..	..	..	McCreery for McIlroy
21 Feb	Aston Villa	A	L	1-2	..	..	..	..	..	..	..	..	..	..1	..	Coyne for Macari
25 Feb	Derby Co	H	D	1-1	..	..	..	..	..	..	..	..	..1	..	..	McCreery for Hill
28 Feb	West Ham U	H	W	4-0	..	..1	..	..	..	..	..	..	..1	..1	..	McCreery for McIlroy
13 Mar	Leeds U	H	W	3-2	..	..	..	..1	..	..1	..	..	..1	McCreery	..	
16 Mar	Norwich C	A	D	1-1	..	..	..	..	..	..	..	..	..	..	..1	
20 Mar	Newcastle U	A	W	*4-3	..	..	..	..	..	..	..	..	..	..2	..	
27 Mar	Middlesbrough	H	W	3-0	..	..	..	..	..1	..	..	..	..	..1	..1	
10 Apr	Ipswich T	A	L	0-3	..	..	..	..	..	..	..	..	..	..	..	
17 Apr	Everton	H	W	*2-1	..	..	..	..	..	..	..	..	..	Macari	..	McCreery1 for Coppell
19 Apr	Burnley	A	W	1-0	..	..	..	..	..	..	McCreery	..	..	..1	..	Jackson for Pearson
21 Apr	Stoke C	H	L	0-1	..	..	..	..	..	..	Jackson	..	McCreery	..	..	Nicholl for Jackson
24 Apr	Leicester C	A	L	1-2	..	..	..	..	Nicholl	..	..	McCreery	Coyne1	..	..	Albiston for Houston
4 May	Manchester C	H	W	2-0	..	..	..	..	Daly	Albiston	..	Coppell	McIlroy1	Pearson	Jackson	..1 — McCreery for Pearson

FA Cup

Date	Round	V	R	Score	Stepney	Forsyth	Houston	Daly	Greenhoff B	Buchan M	Coppell	McIlroy	Pearson	Macari	Hill	Substitutes
3 Jan	Oxford U (3)	H	W	2-1	Stepney	Forsyth	Houston	Daly2	Greenhoff B	Buchan M	Coppell	McIlroy	Pearson	Macari	Hill	Nicholl for Forsyth
24 Jan	Peterborough (4	H	W	3-1	..	..1	..	..	..	..	..	..1	..	..	..1	
14 Feb	Leicester C (5)	A	W	2-1	..	..	..	..1	..	..	..	..	..	..1	..	McCreery for Hill
6 Mar	Wolverhampton W (6)	H	D	1-1	..	..	..	..	..1	..	..	..	..	..	..	
9 Mar	Wolverhampton W (6R)	A	W	3-2	..	..	..	..	..	..1	..	..	..1	..	..	Nicholl for Macari
3 Apr	Derby Co (SF) (at Hillsborough)	N	W	2-0	..	..	..	..	..	..	..	..	..	McCreery	..2	
1 May	Southampton (F) (at Wembley)	N	L	0-1	..	..	..	..	..	..	..	..	..	Macari	..	McCreery for Hill

League Cup

Date	Round	V	R	Score	Stepney	Nicholl	Houston	Jackson	Greenhoff B	Buchan M	Coppell	McIlroy	Pearson	Macari	Daly	Substitutes
10 Sep	Brentford (2)	H	W	2-1	Stepney	Nicholl	Houston	Jackson	Greenhoff B	Buchan M	Coppell	McIlroy1	Pearson	Macari1	Daly	Grimshaw for Jackson
8 Oct	Aston Villa (3)	A	W	2-1	..	..	..	..	..	..	..1	..	..	..1	..	
12 Nov	Manchester C (4)	A	L	0-4	Roche	..	..	..	..	..	..	..	..	..	..	

Appearances (goals)

Albiston 2 – Buchan M 42 – Coppell 39 (4) – Coyne 1 (1) – Daly 41 (7) – Forsyth 28 (2) – Greenhoff B 40 – Hill 26 (7) – Houston 42 2 – Jackson 18 – Macari 36 (13) – McCreery 12 (4) – McIlroy 41 (10) – Nicholl 15 – Pearson 39 (13) – Roche 4 – Stepney 38 – Own goals 8 – **Total 17 players (88)**

Football League

	P	W	D	L	F:A	Pts	
Liverpool	42	23	14	5	66:31	60	1st
Manchester U	42	23	10	9	68:42	56	3rd

Date	Opponent	V	R	Score	Stepney	Nicholl	Houston	Daly	Greenhoff B	Buchan M	Coppell	McIlroy	Pearson	Macari	Hill	Substitutes
21 Aug	Birmingham C	H	D	2-2	Stepney	Nicholl	Houston	Daly	Greenhoff B	Buchan M	Coppell1	McIlroy	Pearson1	Macari	Hill	Foggon for Daly
24 Aug	Coventry C	A	W	2-0	..	..	..	..	..	..	..	..	..	..1	..1	
28 Aug	Derby Co	A	D	0-0	..	..	..	..	..	..	..	..	..	..	..	
4 Sep	Tottenham H	H	L	2-3	..	..	..	..	..	..	..1	..	..1	..	..	McCreery for McIlroy
11 Sep	Newcastle U	A	D	2-2	..	..	..	..	..1	..	..1	..	..	..	..	Foggon for Hill
18 Sep	Middlesbrough	H	W	*2-0	..	..	..	..	..	..	..1	..	..1	..	..	Foggon for Daly
25 Sep	Manchester C	A	W	3-1	..	..	..	..1	..	..	..1	..	..	..	..	McCreery1 for Pearson
2 Oct	Leeds U	A	W	2-0	..	..	..	..1	..	..	..1	..	..	..	..	McCreery for Pearson
16 Oct	W B A	A	L	0-4	..	..	..	..	..	Waldron	..	..	..	..	..	McCreery for Macari
23 Oct	Norwich C	H	D	2-2	..	..	..	..1	..	..	..	..	..	..	..1	McGrath for McIlroy
30 Oct	Ipswich T	H	L	0-1	..	..	Albiston	..	..	Houston	..	..	..	..	..	McCreery for Macari
6 Nov	Aston Villa	A	L	2-3	..	..	..	..	..	..	McGrath	..	..1	..	Coppell1	McCreery for Macari
10 Nov	Sunderland	H	D	3-3	Roche	Albiston	Houston	..	Paterson	Waldron	Coppell	Greenhoff B1	..1	Macari	..1	Clark for Waldron
20 Nov	Leicester C	A	D	1-1	Stepney	Nicholl	Albiston	..1	Greenhoff B	Paterson	..	McIlroy	..	Greenhoff J	..	
27 Nov	West Ham U	H	L	0-2	..	..	Forsyth	Houston	..	Buchan M	..	..	..	..	..	
18 Dec	Arsenal	A	L	1-3	..	..	Houston	McIlroy1	..	Buchan M	..	..	Macari	..	..	McGrath for Greenhoff B
27 Dec	Everton	H	W	4-0	..	Nicholl	..	..	..	..	Coppell	..1	Greenhoff J	..1	..2	McCreery for Coppell
1 Jan	Aston Villa	H	W	2-0	..	..	..	..	..	..	McCreery	..	..	..1	..	McCreery for Pearson
3 Jan	Ipswich T	A	L	1-2	..	..	Albiston	..	..	..	Coppell1	..	..	..1	..	McGrath for Pearson
15 Jan	Coventry C	H	W	2-0	..	..	Houston	..	..	..	Coppell1	..	..	..1	..	McCreery for Hill
19 Jan	Bristol C	H	W	2-1	..	..	..	..	..	..1	..	..	..1	..1	..	
22 Jan	Birmingham C	A	W	3-2	..	..	..	..1	..	..	..	..1	..1	..1	Daly	
5 Feb	Derby Co	H	W	3-1	..	..	..	..1	..	..	..	..	..	..1	Hill1	
12 Feb	Tottenham H	A	W	3-1	..	..	..	..	..1	..	..1	..	..	..1	..	
16 Feb	Liverpool	H	D	0-0	..	..	..	..	..	..	..	..	..	..	..	
19 Feb	Newcastle U	H	W	3-1	..	..	..	..	..	..	..3	..	..	..	..	Albiston for Hill
5 Mar	Manchester C	H	W	3-1	..	..	..	..	..	..	..	..1	..	..	..1	McCreery for Hill
12 Mar	Leeds U	H	W	1-0	..	..	..	..	..	..	..1	..	..	..	..	McCreery for Hill
23 Mar	W B A	H	D	2-2	..	..	Albiston	..	Houston	..	..	..	..	McCreery	..	McCreery for McIlroy
2 Apr	Norwich C	A	L	1-2	..	..	Houston	..	Greenhoff B	..	..	Pearson	McCreery	..2	..	McGrath for Hill
5 Apr	Everton	A	W	2-1	..	..	Albiston	..	..	..	..	McCreery	Macari1	..1	..	McGrath for Hill
9 Apr	Stoke C	H	W	3-0	..	..	Houston1	..	..	..	..	..	..	..1	..	McCreery for Greenhoff J
11 Apr	Sunderland	A	L	1-2	..	..	..	..	..	..	McCreery	Greenhoff J1	..	..	..	Albiston for Macari
16 Apr	Leicester C	H	D	1-1	..	..	Albiston	..	..	..	..	..	..	..	McCreery	Hill for McCreery
19 Apr	Q P R	A	L	0-4	..	..	..	..	..	Houston	..	..	..	..	Hill	Forsyth for Greenhoff B
26 Apr	Middlesbrough	A	L	0-3	..	..	Houston	..	..	Buchan M	..	..	..	..	Hill	
30 Apr	Q P R	H	W	1-0	..	..	..	..	..	..	..	..	..1	..	..	McCreery for Hill
3 May	Liverpool	A	L	0-1	..	..	..	..	Forsyth	Albiston	..	..	..	..	Albiston	McCreery for Greenhoff J
7 May	Bristol C	A	D	1-1	..	..	..	Jackson	Greenhoff B	Buchan M	..	..1	McCreery	..	Hill2	McIlroy for Houston
11 May	Stoke C	A	D	3-3	..	..	Albiston	..	..	..	McCreery	McGrath	..	..	..1	McCreery for Pearson
14 May	Arsenal	H	W	3-2	..	..	..	McIlroy	..	..	Greenhoff J1	Pearson	..	..1	..1	McCreery for Greenhoff J
16 May	West Ham U	A	L	2-4	Roche	..	..	..	..	..	..	..	..1	..	..1	McCreery for Greenhoff J

FA Cup

Date	Round	V	R	Score	Stepney	Nicholl	Houston	McIlroy	Greenhoff B	Buchan M	Coppell	Greenhoff J	Pearson	Macari	Hill	Substitutes
8 Jan	Walsall (3)	H	W	1-0	Stepney	Nicholl	Houston	McIlroy	Greenhoff B	Buchan M	Coppell	Greenhoff J	Pearson	Macari	Hill	McCreery for Hill
29 Jan	Q P R (4)	H	W	1-0	..	..	..	..	..	..	..	..	..	..1	..1	
26 Feb	Southampton (5)	A	D	2-2	..	..	..	..	..	..	..	..	..	..1	..1	McCreery for Greenhoff J
8 Mar	Southampton (5R)	H	W	2-1	..	..	..	..	..	..	..	..	..	..1	..1	
19 Mar	Aston Villa (6)	H	W	2-1	..	..	..	..1	..	..	..	..	..	..1	..	McCreery for Greenhoff B
23 Apr	Leeds U (SF) (at Hillsborough)	N	W	2-1	..	..	..	..	..	..	..1	..1	..	..	..	
21 May	Liverpool (F) (at Wembley)	N	W	2-1	..	..	..	Albiston	..	..	..	..	..1	..1	..	McCreery for Hill

League Cup

Date	Opp		Result	1	2	3	4	5	6	7	8	9	10	11	Subs
1 Sep	Tranmere R (2)	H W	5-0	Stepney	Nicholl	Houston	Daly2	Greenhoff B	Buchan M	Coppell	McIlroy	Pearson1	Macari1	Hull1	McCreery for McIlroy
22 Sep	Sunderland (3)	H D	*2-2	..	..	..	..	..	..	McCreery	..	..1	..	..	
4 Oct	Sunderland (3R)	A D	2-2	..	..	..	..1	Waldron	..	Coppell	..	McCreery	Greenhoff B1	..	Albiston for Greenhoff B
6 Oct	Sunderland (3R)	H W	1-0	..	..	..	..	Greenhoff S1	..	..	..	Macari	..	..	Albiston for Hill
27 Oct	Newcastle U (4)	H W	7-2	..	..	..1	Albiston	..	..	Houston1	..1	..	Pearson1	..3	McGrath for Pearson
1 Dec	Everton (5)	H L	0-3	..	Forsyth	..	..	Paterson	Greenhoff B	..	..	..	Jackson	..	McCreery for Daly

UEFA Cup

Date	Opp		Result	1	2	3	4	5	6	7	8	9	10	11	Subs
15 Sep	Ajax (1)	A L	0-1	Stepney	Nicholl	Houston	Daly	Greenhoff B	Buchan M	Coppell	McIlroy	Pearson	Macari	Hill	McCreery for Daly
29 Sep	Ajax (1)	H W	2-0	..	..	..	..	..	..	..	..	McCreery	..1	..	Albiston for Daly, Paterson for Hill
20 Oct	Juventus (2)	H W	1-0	..	..	Albiston	..	..	Houston	..	..	Pearson	..	..1	McCreery for Daly
3 Nov	Juventus (2)	A L	0-3	..	..	..	..	..	..	..	..	..	..	..	McCreery for McIlroy, Paterson for Macari

Appearances (goals)

Albiston 14 – Buchan M 33 – Coppell 40 (7) – Daly 16 (4) – Forsyth 3 – Greenhoff B 40 (3) – Greenhoff J 27 (8) – Hill 38 (15) – Houston 37 (3) – Jackson 2 – Macari 3 (89) – McCreery 9 (2) – McGrath 2 – McIlroy 39 (2) – Nicholl 39 – Paterson 1 – Pearson 39 (15) – Roche 2 – Stepney 40 – Waldron 3 – Own goals 3 – **Total 20 players (71)**

Football League

	P	W	D	L	F:A	Pts	
Liverpool	42	23	11	8	62:33	57	1st
Manchester U	42	18	11	13	71:62	47	6th

SEASON 1977-1978 FOOTBALL LEAGUE (DIVISION 1)

Date	Opp		Result	1	2	3	4	5	6	7	8	9	10	11	Subs
20 Aug	Birmingham C	A W	4-1	Stepney	Nicholl	Albiston	McIlroy	Greenhoff B	Buchan M	Coppell	McCreery	Pearson	Macari2	Hill	Grimes for Pearson
24 Aug	Coventry C	H W	2-1	..	..	..	..	..	..	..	..1	..	..	..1	
27 Aug	Ipswich T	H D	0-0	..	..	..	..	..	..	McGrath	..	Coppell	..	..	Grimes for McIlroy
3 Sep	Derby Co	A W	1-0	..	Forsyth	..	..	Nicholl	..	Coppell	..	Pearson	..1	..	
10 Sep	Manchester C	A L	1-3	..	..	..	..	..1	..	..	..	..	..	..	McGrath for Macari
17 Sep	Chelsea	H L	0-1	..	Nicholl	..	..	Greenhoff B	..	..	..	..	..	..	McGrath for Buchan M
24 Sep	Leeds U	A D	1-1	..	..	..	..1	..	Houston	McGrath	Coppell	..	..	..1	
1 Oct	Liverpool	H W	2-0	..	..	..	..1	..	Buchan M	..	..	Greenhoff J	..1	..	
8 Oct	Middlesbrough	A L	1-2	..	..	..	McCreery	..	..	..	Greenhoff	J Coppell1	..	..	
15 Oct	Newcastle U	H W	3-2	..	..	..	McIlroy	Houston	..	..	..1	..1	..1	..	
22 Oct	W B A	A L	0-4	..	Forsyth	Rogers	..	Nicholl	..	Coppell	McCreery	Pearson	..	..	MoGrath for McCreery
29 Oct	Aston Villa	A L	1-2	..	Nicholl1	Albiston	..	Houston	..	McGrath	Coppell	..	McCreery	..	Grimes for Hill
5 Nov	Arsenal	H L	1-2	..	..	..	..	..	..	..	..	..	..	..1	Grimes for McGrath
12 Nov	Nottingham F	A L	1-2	Roche	..	Houston	..	Greenhoff B	..	..	..	..	..	..	
19 Nov	Norwich C	H W	1-0	..	..	..	..	..	..	Coppell	Greenhoff J	..1	Macari	..	McCreery for McIlroy
26 Nov	Q P R	A D	2-2	..	..	..	Grimes	..	..	..	..	..	..	..2	McGrath for Macari
3 Dec	Wolverhampton W	H W	3-1	..	..	Albiston	McIlroy1	..	Houston	..	..1	..	Grimes	..	McGrath for Grimes
10 Dec	West Ham U	A L	1-2	..	..	..	Coppell	..	..	McGrath1	..	..	..	..	
17 Dec	Nottingham F	H L	0-4	..	..	Houston	McIlroy	..	Buchan M	Coppell	..	..	Macari	..	Grimes for Pearson
26 Dec	Everton	A W	6-2	..	..	..	..1	..	..	..1	..1	Ritchie	..2	..1	
27 Dec	Leicester C	H W	3-1	..	..	Albiston	..	Houston	..	..1	..1	..	..	..1	
31 Dec	Coventry C	A L	0-3	..	..	Houston	..	Greenhoff B	..	..	..	..	..	..	McGrath for Buchan M
2 Jan	Birmingham C	H L	1-2	..	..	..	..	..	..	..	..	..	..	..	
14 Jan	Ipswich T	A W	2-1	..	..	Albiston	..1	Houston	..	..	..	Pearson1	..	..	
21 Jan	Derby Co	H W	4-0	..	..	..	..	..	..	..	..1	..	..	..2	
8 Feb	Bristol C	H D	1-1	..	..	..	..	..	..	Jordan	..	..	..	..1	Greenhoff for Buchan M
11 Feb	Chelsea	A D	2-2	..	..	..	..1	..	Greenhoff B	..	..	..	..	..	
25 Feb	Liverpool	A L	1-3	..	..	..	..1	McQueen	Houston	..	..	..	..	..	
1 Mar	Leeds U	H L	0-1	..	..	..	..	Greenhoff B	..	..	Greenhoff J	Jordan	..	..	McGrath for Hill
4 Mar	Middlesbrough	H D	0-0	..	..	Houston	..	McQueen	Greenhoff B	..	..	..	..	..	
11 Mar	Newcastle U	A D	2-2	..	..	..	..	..	..	..	..	..1	..	..1	
15 Mar	Manchester C	H D	2-2	Stepney	..	..	..	..	..	..	..	..	..	..2	Albiston for Jordan
18 Mar	W B A	H D	1-1	..	..	..	..	..	..1	..	..	Pearson	..	..1	
25 Mar	Leicester C	A W	3-2	..	..	..	..	..	..	..	..1	..1	..	..1	
27 Mar	Everton	H L	1-2	..	..	Albiston	..	..	..	..	..	..1	..	..1	
29 Mar	Aston Villa	H D	1-1	..	Greenhoff B	Houston	..1	..	Buchan M	..	..	..	..1	Jordan	
1 Apr	Arsenal	A L	1-3	..	..	..	..	..	..	Jordan1	..	..	..	Hill	
8 Apr	Q P R	H W	3-1	..	..	..	..	..	..1	..	..2	..	Grimes1	McCreery	
15 Apr	Norwich C	A W	3-1	..	Albiston	..	..1	..	..	..	..1	..	Greenhoff B	..	
22 Apr	West Ham U	H W	3-0	..	..	..	Greenhoff B	..	..	..	..1	Grimes1	McIlroy1	..	
25 Apr	Bristol City	A W	1-0	Roche	..	..	McIlroy	..	Nicholl	..	..1	..	..	Greenhoff B	McCreery for Greenhoff B
29 Apr	Wolverhampton W	A L	1-2	Stepney	..	..	..	..	..	..	..	..	Greenhoff B1	Grimes	

FA Cup

Date	Opp		Result	1	2	3	4	5	6	7	8	9	10	11	Subs
7 Jan	Carlisle U (3)	A D	1-1	Roche	Nicholl	Albiston	McIlroy	Greenhoff B	Buchan M	Coppell	Greenhoff J	Pearson	Macari1	Grimes	McCreery for Grimes
10 Jan	Carlisle U (3R)	H W	4-2	..	..	..	..	Houston	..	..	..2	..	..2	Hill	
28 Jan	W B A (4)	H D	1-1	..	..	..	..	..	..	..1	Jordan	..	..	..	
1 Feb	W B A (4R)	A L	2-3	..	..	..	..	..	..	..	..	..1	..	..1	Greenhoff for Albiston

League Cup

Date	Opp		Result	1	2	3	4	5	6	7	8	9	10	11	Subs
30 Aug	Arsenal (2)	A L	2-3	Stepney	Nicholl	Albiston	Grimes	Greenhoff B	Buchan M	Coppell	McCreery1	Pearson1	Macari	Hill	McGrath for Greenhoff B

European Cup-Winners' Cup

Date	Opp		Result	1	2	3	4	5	6	7	8	9	10	11	Subs
14 Sep	St Etienne (1)	A D	1-1	Stepney	Nicholl	Albiston	McIlroy	Greenhoff B	Buchan M	McGrath	McCreery	Pearson	Coppell	Hill1	McGrath for Pearson
5 Oct	St Etienne (1) (at Plymouth)	N W	2-0	..	..	..	..	..	..	Coppell1	Greenhoff J	..1	Macari	..	
19 Oct	F C Porto (2)	A L	0-4	..	..	..	..	Houston	..	McGrath	McCreery	Coppell	..	..	Forsyth for Houston, Grimes for Coppell
2 Nov	F C Porto (2)	H W	*5-2	..	..	..1	..	..	..	Coppell2	Pearson	McCreery	..	..	

Appearances (goals)

Albiston 27 – Buchan M 28 (1) – Coppell 42 (5) – Greenhoff B 31 (1) – Greenhoff J 22 (6) – Grimes 7 (2) – Hill 37 (17) – Houston 30 – Jordan 14 (3) – Macari 32 (8) – McCreery 13 (1) – McGrath 9 (1) – McIlroy 39 (9) – McQueen 14 (1) – Nicholl 37 (2) – Pearson 30 (10) – Ritchie 4 – Roche 19 – Rogers 1 – Stepney 23 – **Total 20 players (67)**

Football League

	P	W	D	L	F:A	Pts	
Nottingham F	42	25	14	3	69:24	64	1st
Manchester U	42	16	10	16	67:63	42	10th

SEASON 1978-1979 FOOTBALL LEAGUE (DIVISION 1)

Date	Opp		Result	1	2	3	4	5	6	7	8	9	10	11	Subs
19 Aug	Birmingham C	H W	1-0	Roche	Greenhoff B	Albiston	McIlroy	McQueen	Buchan M	Coppell	Greenhoff J	Jordan1	Macari	McCreery	
23 Aug	Leeds United	A W	3-2	..	..	..	..1	..1	..	..	..	..	..1	..	McGrath for McCreery
26 Aug	Ipswich T	A L	0-3	..	..	..	..	..	..	..	..	..	..	..	Grimes for McCreery
2 Sep	Everton	H D	1-1	..	Nicholl	..	..	Greenhoff B	..1	..	..	..	..	..	
9 Sep	Q P R	A D	1-1	..	Greenhoff B	..	..	McQueen	..	..	..1	..	..	..	
16 Sep	Nottingham F	H D	1-1	..	..	..	..	..	..	..	..1	..	..	..	Grimes for McCreery
23 Sep	Arsenal	A D	1-1	..	..	Albiston	Houston	Greenhoff B	..	..	..	..	..	McIlroy	
30 Sep	Manchester C	H W	1-0	..	..	..	..	..	..	..	..1	..	..	..	
7 Oct	Middlesbrough	H W	3-2	..	..	..	McCreery	..	..	..	..1	..	..2	..	Grimes for Greenhoff J
14 Oct	Aston Villa	A D	2-2	..	..	..	McIlroy1	..	..	..	..	..	..1	Grimes	
21 Oct	Bristol C	H L	1-3	..	..	..	..	..	..	..	..1	..	..	..	Greenhoff B for McIlroy
28 Oct	Wolverhampton W	A W	4-2	..	Nicholl	..	Greenhoff B1	..	..	..	..2	..1	..	McIlroy	Grimes for McQueen
4 Nov	Southampton	H U	1-1	..	..	..	McIlroy	Greenhoff B	..	..	..1	..	..	Grimes	
11 Nov	Birmingham C	A L	1-5	..	..	..	McCreery	..	..	..	..	..	..	McIlroy	Albiston for Nicholl
18 Nov	Ipswich T	H W	2-0	Bailey	Albiston	..	Greenhoff B	McQueen	..	..1	..1	..	Sloan	..	McGrath for Sloan
21 Nov	Everton	A L	0-3	..	..	..	..	..	..	..	..	..	..	..	Macari for Sloan
25 Nov	Chelsea	A W	1-0	..	Greenhoff B	..	McIlroy	..	..	..	..1	..	Macari	Thomas	
9 Dec	Derby Co	A W	3-1	..	..	..	..1	..	..	..	..1	Ritchie1	..	..	Paterson for Houston
16 Dec	Tottenham H	H W	2-0	..	..	..	..	..	..	..	..	..	..	..	Nicholl for Greenhoff J
22 Dec	Bolton W	A L	0-3	..	..	Connell	..	..	..	..	..	..	..	..	
28 Dec	Liverpool	H L	0-3	..	..	..	..	..	..	..	..	..	..	..	
30 Dec	W B A	H L	3-5	..	..1	Houston	..	..1	..	..	..	..	McCreery	..	Sloan for Greenhoff J
3 Feb	Arsenal	H L	0-2	..	..	..	Nicholl	..	..	..	Macari	McIlroy	..	Ritchie for Greenhoff J
10 Feb	Manchester C	A W	3-0	..	..	Albiston	McIlroy	..	..2	..	Ritchie1	Macari	..	
24 Feb	Aston Villa	H D	1-1	..	..	..	..	..	..1	..	..	..	..	Nicholl for Macari
28 Feb	Q P R	H W	2-0	..	..	..	..	..	..1	..	Nicholl	..	..	
3 Mar	Bristol C	A W	2-1	..	Nicholl	..	..1	..	..	..	..1	Grimes	..	
20 Mar	Coventry C	A L	3-4	..	..	..	..	..	..2	..	Greenhoff B	..	Jordan	Paterson for Greenhoff J
24 Mar	Leeds U	H W	4-1	..	..	..	..	..	..	..	Ritchie3	..	..1	
27 Mar	Middlesbrough	A D	2-2	..	..	..	..1	..	..1	..	Jordan	..	..	
7 Apr	Norwich C	A D	2-2	..	Albiston	Houston	..1	..	..	..	..	Macari1	..	
11 Apr	Bolton W	H L	1-2	..	Nicholl	Albiston	..	..	..1	..	Ritchie	..	..	

Sammy McIlroy scored on his debut for United at the tender age of 17. A decade at Old Trafford saw him collect an FA Cup medal in 1977 and score a dazzling equaliser against Arsenal in the 1979 Cup final.

Season 1978-79 (continued)

Date	Opponent	V	R	Score	1	2	3	4	5	6	7	8	9	10	11	Substitutes
14 Apr	Liverpool	A	L	0-2	..	..	..	..	Greenhoff B	..	..	..	Greenhoff B	..		Houston for Ritchie
16 Apr	Coventry C	H	D	0-0	..	..	..	..	McQueen	..	..	..1	Greenhoff B	..		McCreery for Ritchie
18 Apr	Nottingham F	A	D	1-1	..	..	..	..	..	..	McCreery	..1		Macari	..	Grimes for Buchan M
21 Apr	Tottenham H	A	D	1-1	..	..	..	..	..1	Greenhoff B	..			..1		Grimes for Thomas
25 Apr	Norwich C	H	W	1-0	..	..	..	..	..	Buchan M	..					Grimes for Buchan M
28 Apr	Derby Co	H	D	0-0	McCreery	Houston			Houston	Nicholl		Ritchie		Nicholl	Grimes	Grimes for Ritchie
30 Apr	Southampton	A	D	1-1	Albiston	Houston	Sloan	McQueen	Moran		Paterson	Ritchie1			Grimes	Grimes for Thomas
5 May	W B A	A	L	0-1			McIlroy		Greenhoff B		Greenhoff J	Jordan			Thomas	
7 May	Wolverhampton W	A	W	3-2		Nicholl	Albiston	Greenhoff B	Houston	Buchan M	..1	Ritchie1	..1			Grimes for Greenhoff B
16 May	Chelsea	H	D	1-1		Albiston	Houston	McIlroy	McQueen	Nicholl	..1	Greenhoff J		McCreery	..	Grimes for Greenhoff J

FA Cup

Date	Opponent	V	R	Score	1	2	3	4	5	6	7	8	9	10	11	Substitutes
15 Jan	Chelsea (3)	H	W	3-0	Bailey	Greenhoff B	Houston	McIlroy	McQueen	Buchan M	Coppell1	Greenhoff J1	Pearson	Nicholl	Grimes1	
31 Jan	Fulham (4)	A	D	1-1	..	..	..	..	..	..	..	..	..	Macari	Thomas	Nicholl for Pearson
12 Feb	Fulham (4R)	H	W	1-0	..	..	Albiston	..	..	..	..1	Ritchie	..	..		
20 Feb	Colchester (5)	A	W	1-0	..	..	..	..	..	..	..1	..	..	..	..	Nicholl for Greenhoff B
10 Mar	Tottenham H (6)	A	D	1-1	..	Nicholl	..	..	..	..	..	..	Grimes	..1		Jordan for Ritchie
14 Mar	Tottenham H (6R)	H	W	2-0	..	..	..	..	..	..	..	Jordan1	..1			
31 Mar	Liverpool (SF) (at Maine Road)	N	D	2-2	..	..	..	..	..	..	..1		Greenhoff B1			
4 Apr	Liverpool (SFR) (at Goodison Park)	N	W	1-0	..	..	..	..	..	..	..1		Macari			Ritchie for Macari
12 May	Arsenal (F) (at Wembley)	N	L	2-3	..	..	..1	..1	..	..	..		..			

League Cup

Date	Opponent	V	R	Score	1	2	3	4	5	6	7	8	9	10	11	Substitutes
30 Aug	Stockport Co (2)	H	W	3-2	Roche	Greenhoff B	Albiston	McIlroy1	McQueen	Buchan M	Coppell	Greenhoff J1	Jordan1	Macari	Grimes	
4 Oct	Watford (3)	H	L	1-2	..	Albiston	Houston	Greenhoff B	..	..	..	..1	McIlroy	..		McCreery for Greenhoff B

Appearances (goals)

Albiston 32 – Bailey 28 – Buchan M 37 (2) – Connell 2 – Coppell 42 (11) – Greenhoff B 32 (2) – Greenhoff J 33 (11) – Grimes 5 – Houston 21 – Jordan 30 (6) – Macari 31 (8) – McCreery 14 – McIlroy 40 (8) – McQueen 38 (6) – Moran 1 – Nicholl 19 – Paterson 1 – Ritchie 18 (9) – Roche 14 – Sloan 3 – Thomas 25 (1) – **Total 21 players (60)**

Football League

	P	W	D	L	F:A	Pts	
Liverpool	42	30	8	4	85:18	68	1st
Manchester U	42	15	15	12	60:63	45	9th

SEASON 1979-1980 FOOTBALL LEAGUE (DIVISION 1)

Date	Opponent	V	R	Score	1	2	3	4	5	6	7	8	9	10	11	Substitutes
18 Aug	Southampton	A	D	1-1	Bailey	Nicholl	Albiston	McIlroy	McQueen1	Buchan M	Coppell	Wilkins	Jordan	Macari	Thomas	Ritchie for McIlroy
22 Aug	W B A	H	W	2-0	..	..	..	..	..1	..	..1	..	..	..	..	
25 Aug	Arsenal	A	D	0-0	..	..	..	..	..	..	..	..	..	..	..	Paterson for Coppell
1 Sep	Middlesbrough	H	W	2-1	..	..	..	..	..	..	..	..	..	..2	..	
8 Sep	Aston Villa	A	W	3-0	..	..	..	..	..	..	..1	..	Ritchie	..1	Grimes	Grimes1 for Jordan
15 Sep	Derby Co	H	W	*1-0	..	..	..	..	..	..	Grimes	..	Coppell	..1	Thomas	
22 Sep	Wolverhampton W	A	L	1-3	..	..	..	..	..	..	..1	..	..	..	..	
29 Sep	Stoke C	H	W	4-0	..	..	..	..1	..2	..	..	..	..1	..	..	Sloan for Macari
6 Oct	Brighton	H	W	2-0	..	..	..	..	..	..	..	..	..1	..1	..	
10 Oct	W B A	A	L	0-2	..	..	..	..	..	..	..	..	..	..	..	
13 Oct	Bristol C	A	D	1-1	..	..	..	..	..	..	..	..	..	..1	..	
20 Oct	Ipswich T	H	W	1-0	..	..	..	..	..	..	..1	..	..	..	..	
27 Oct	Everton	A	D	0-0	..	..	..	..	..	..	..	..	..	..	..	Sloan for Albiston
3 Nov	Southampton	H	W	1-0	..	..	Houston	..	Moran	..	..	..	..	..1	..	
10 Nov	Manchester C	A	L	0-2	..	..	..	..	..	..	..	..	..	..	..	
17 Nov	Crystal Palace	H	D	1-1	..	..	..	..	..	..	Coppell	..	Jordan1	..	..	Grimes for Thomas
24 Nov	Norwich C	H	W	5-0	..	..	Grimes	..	..1	..	..1	..	..2	..1	..	
1 Dec	Tottenham H	A	W	2-1	..	..	..	..	..1	..	..	..	..	..1	..	
8 Dec	Leeds U	H	D	1-1	..	..	..	..	..	..	..	..	..	..	..1	
15 Dec	Coventry C	A	W	2-1	..	..	Houston	..	McQueen1	..	..	..	..	..1	..	
22 Dec	Nottingham F	H	W	3-0	..	..	..	..	..1	..	..	..	..2	..	..	
26 Dec	Liverpool	A	L	0-2	..	..	..	..	..	..	..	..	..	..	..	Grimes for Thomas
29 Dec	Arsenal	H	W	3-0	..	..	..	..1	..1	..	..	..	..1	..	..1	
12 Jan	Middlesbrough	A	D	1-1	..	..	..	..	..	..	..	..	..	..	..1	McGrath for Thomas
2 Feb	Derby Co	A	W	*3-1	..	..	..	..	..1	..	..	Jovanovic	..	..	..1	Grimes for Jovanovic
9 Feb	Wolverhampton W	H	L	0-1	..	..	..	..	..	..	..	Wilkins	..	..	..	Grimes for Wilkins
16 Feb	Stoke C	A	D	1-1	..	..	..	..	..	..	..1	..	..	..	Grimes	Ritchie for Macari
23 Feb	Bristol C	H	W	*4-0	..	..	..	..1	..	..	..	..	..2	..	..	Ritchie for McQueen
27 Feb	Bolton W	H	W	2-0	..	..	..	..	..1	..	..	..	..1	..	..	Sloan for Wilkins
1 Mar	Ipswich T	A	L	0-6	..	..	..	..	..	..	..	Sloan	..	..	..	Jovanovic for Nicholl
12 Mar	Everton	H	D	0-0	..	..	Albiston	..	..	..	..	Wilkins	..	..	..	Greenhoff for Macari
15 Mar	Brighton	A	D	0-0	..	..	..	..	..	..	..	..	..	..	..	
22 Mar	Manchester C	H	W	1-0	..	..	..	..	..	..	..	..	..	..1	Thomas1	Grimes for Thomas
29 Mar	Crystal Palace	A	W	2-0	..	..	..	..	..	..	..	..	..	..	..1	
2 Apr	Nottingham F	A	L	0-2	..	..	..	..	..	..	..	..	..	..	..1	
5 Apr	Liverpool	H	W	2-1	..	..	..	Greenhoff1	..	..	..	..	..	..	..1	
7 Apr	Bolton W	A	W	3-1	..	..	..	McIlroy	..1	..	..	..	..	Grimes	..1	Ritchie for Wilkins
12 Apr	Tottenham H	H	W	4-1	..	..	..	..	..1	..	..	..1	..	Ritchie2	..	Ritchie for Wilkins
19 Apr	Norwich C	A	W	2-0	..	..	..	..	Moran	..	..	..	..2	..	..	
23 Apr	Aston Villa	H	W	2-1	..	..	..	..	..	..	Greenhoff	..	..2	Macari	..	
26 Apr	Coventry C	H	W	2-1	..	..	..	..2	..	..	..	..	..	..	..	Sloan for Greenhoff
3 May	Leeds U	A	L	0-2	..	..	..	..	McQueen	..	..	..	..	..	..	Ritchie for Buchan M

FA Cup

Date	Opponent	V	R	Score	1	2	3	4	5	6	7	8	9	10	11	Substitutes
5 Jan	Tottenham H (3)	A	D	1-1	Bailey	Nicholl	Houston	McIlroy1	McQueen	Buchan M	Coppell	Wilkins	Jordan	Macari	Thomas	
9 Jan	Tottenham H (3R)	H	L	0-1	..	..	..	..	..	..	..	..	..	..	..	

League Cup

Date	Opponent	V	R	Score	1	2	3	4	5	6	7	8	9	10	11	Substitutes
29 Aug	Tottenham H (2)	A	L	1-2	Bailey	Nicholl	Albiston	Paterson	McQueen	Buchan M	Ritchie	Wilkins	Jordan	Macari	Thomas1	Ritchie for Houston
5 Sep	Tottenham H (2)	H	W	*3-1	..	..	..	McIlroy	Houston	..	Coppell1	..	..	..	..1	Ritchie for McIlroy
28 Sep	Norwich C (3)	A	L	1-4	..	..	..	..	..1	McQueen	..	Grimes	Coppell	..	..	

Appearances (goals)

Albiston 25 – Bailey 42 – Buchan M 42 – Coppell 42 (8) – Greenhoff J 41 – Grimes 20 (2) – Houston 14 – Jordan 32 (13) – Jovanovic 1 – Macari 39 (9) – McIlroy 41 (8) – McQueen 33 (9) – Moran 9 – Nicholl 42 – Ritchie 33 – Sloan 1 – Thomas 35 (8) – Wilkins 37 (2) – Own goals 3 – **Total 18 players 65**

Football League

	P	W	D	L	F:A	Pts	
Liverpool	42	25	10	7	81:30	60	1st
Manchester U	42	24	10	8	65:35	58	2nd

1970-1979

MANAGERS

During the past century, only three of the 14 men to take charge of Manchester United, have led the club to the League Championship. Others have tried, and some have come close to taking the club to football's pinnacle, but just three managers earn the right of a place in the Manchester United Hall of Fame and that is why Ernest Mangnall, Sir Matt Busby and Alex Ferguson, stand out from the rest.

Today's manager, Alex Ferguson is close to becoming the club's most successful manager. Perhaps before he stands down, the Scot will surpass the achievements of the legendary Sir Matt who led the club for a quarter of a century.

That question will be answered in the new Millennium but before both Busby and Ferguson, came a man whose contribution to the success of United is unquestioned.

The first great manager

Ernest Mangnall took charge in 1903. The club had by then changed its name from Newton Heath to Manchester United and after five years under his guidance, became a true force in football.

In 1908, the League Championship was won by Mangnall's men for the first time then, a year later, the feat was repeated in the FA Cup.

To illustrate their strength, a second league title was won in 1911, but Mangnall was to leave a more lasting memorial when he eventually departed from the club to take charge of Manchester City. It was during his reign in charge that Old Trafford Football Ground was built, and he had much to do with its planning and development from waste land to the showpiece stadium of its era.

The Busby reign

That was in 1910. Thirty-six years later Old Trafford was bomb-damaged when Matt Busby took charge at the end of the Second World War. Despite the set back the club rose from the wreckage to become the institution it is today.

Busby created three great sides, one in each decade of his leadership.

In 1948 a gap of 39 years was bridged as the FA Cup was won again, then in 1952, came the club's third championship.

Busby's visionary policy of youth development created a team of homespun and carefully bought players, which was to take football by storm.

"The Busby Babes" won successive championships in 1956 and 1957, then set their sights beyond home shores, when for the first time, United entered the European Cup. In 1957 they reached the semi-final.

A year later the dream ended in the Munich Air Disaster. Matt Busby survived, his great team was destroyed.

He rebuilt and his third great side won the championship twice more in 1965 and 1967, before achieving the ultimate success when United became the first English side to win the European Champions' Cup. Sir Matt went on to become United's first president, holding the position until his death on January 20, 1994.

Above: Sir Matt Busby celebrates the 1968 European Cup Victory, the pinnacle of an illustrious managerial career

Left: Tommy Docherty brought the good times back to Old Trafford during the mid-1970s

Above, right: It seemed impossible that any manager could match Busby's achievements but Alex Ferguson's Treble of 1999 equals the great man's triumphs

THE MANAGERS

Until 1914 the 'Secretary' was responsible for team affairs.

1892 – 1900	A.H. ALBUT
1900 – 1903	JAMES WEST
1903 – 1912	ERNEST MANGNALL
9/9/12 – 28/10/12	T.J. WALLWORTH (Acting Secretary)
28/10/12 – 16/9/16	J.J. BENTLEY
28/12/14 – 31/10/21	JOHN ROBSON
31/10/21 – 8/10/26	JOHN CHAPMAN
8/10/26 – 13/4/27	CLARENCE HILDITCH (Player/Manager)
13/4/27 – 9/11/31	HERBERT BAMLETT
9/11/31 – 1/8/32	WALTER CRICKMER (Acting Manager)
1/8/32 – 9/11/37	SCOTT DUNCAN
1938 – 1944	JIMMY PORTER
1944 – 15/2/45	WALTER CRICKMER (Acting Manager)
15/2/45 – 11/8/70	MATT BUSBY
11/8/70 – 29/12/70	WILF MCGUINNESS
29/12/70 – 8/6/71	SIR MATT BUSBY
8/6/71 – 19/12/72	FRANK O'FARRELL
22/12/72 – 4/7/77	TOMMY DOCHERTY
14/7/77 – 30/4/81	DAVE SEXTON
9/6/81 – 4/11/86	RON ATKINSON
6/11/86	ALEX FERGUSON

Ferguson's new era

Four months after Busby's death Alex Ferguson's side went further than any of its predecessors by winning the club's first-ever league and FA Cup double.

Ferguson was a highly successful manager before taking charge at Old Trafford in 1986. Under him Aberdeen won the Scottish championship three times and the European Cup Winners' Cup. They collected the Scottish Cup four times, completing a League and Cup double in 1984, and won the Scottish League Cup in 1986.

His first success at Old Trafford came in 1990, when United won the FA Cup for a seventh time. So began the most successful period in the club's history.

In 1991 Ferguson repeated his Scottish success in the Cup Winners' Cup, then two years later, as one of the founders of the FA Premier League, United were its first winners.

The Premiership and FA Cup double in 1994 was repeated in 1996, and a fifth title won in 1997 and the treble of 1999.

As the club steps into a new century no-one knows what will be achieved when football develops beyond the dreams of its creators, but Ernest Mangnall, Matt Busby and Alex Ferguson, will always have their place in the story of Manchester United.

CHAPTER 8

THE 1980s: ATKINSON AND FERGUSON

Success, it would seem, is not the sole criteria by which the manager of Manchester United is judged. He can achieve success on the field yet still fail in the eyes of his employers, or the majority of supporters, or both. It is not the success but how it is achieved which matters most, and the narrowness of the line between pleasing board and fans or leaving them cold illustrates the fragility of the manager's position.

The man walking the tightrope may well be able to cross from end to end without a fall, but if he does so with no excitement for his audience, no hint that he might slip, then what is the point of him being up there in the first place?

Docherty walked the tightrope with a touch of flair and showmanship, yet still stumbled. Sexton was sure-footed but lost his balance when the audience failed to respond to his obvious talents. Whoever was to follow these two would need to be a combination of them both.

United search for successor

Such is the enormity of the managerial task it could be beyond the grasp of a man who simply knows how to select a winning side. He needs to be able to project the right image, mingle with both grass-root supporter and distinguished guest and not seem out of place with either, and have the gift of man management as well as a steady hand when dealing with large cash transactions. All this in one man?

Immediately after the decision to terminate the contracts of both Sexton and his assistant Tommy Cavanagh, United began the search for a replacement. As in the past, the name of Brian Clough was associated with United and reasons were given by the newspaper speculators as to why, and why not, the Nottingham Forest manager could be approached.

Lawrie McMenemy, who had taken Southampton from obscurity to success, was said to be the name at the top of the club's short list. McMenemy had the right public image to prove popular with the fans, had the obvious ability to manage, and if he could achieve such heights at a club as small as Southampton, then what would he do with a giant like United? McMenemy had been the man who had brought England's biggest star since George Best back to the Football League after he had earned his fortune in West Germany, and if he could persuade Kevin Keegan to play for him, could he get other world stars to respond in the same way?

McMenemy had his own views on management which seemed so close to the unwritten guidelines of the club: 'You don't have to win trophies to be successful. The biggest thing

Above: The Dutch master, Arnold Muhren whose move to Old Trafford came when his contract at Ipswich Town ended. Muhren later returned to the Netherlands to continue his career with Ajax and in 1988 was in the Dutch side which won the European Championships in West Germany

Left: Republic of Ireland striker Frank Stapleton eludes Mark Lawrenson of Liverpool, one of his international colleagues. Only a decision to move to Anfield rather than Old Trafford prevented the two playing together at club level. Stapleton was bought by Atkinson in the summer of 1981 in a move which caused ill-feeling between United and the directors of Arsenal the club which reluctantly sold him

is getting the best out of what you have got, and giving the public what it wants.'

But, when given the chance, McMenemy turned down the opportunity to give Manchester United's public what it wanted.

Ron Atkinson gets the job

Bobby Robson's name was also linked with the vacancy, before eventually, in June 1981, the new man was chosen. He was a Liverpudlian, whose managerial rise had been swift. From the parochial surroundings of Kettering Town to the awe-inspiring heights of Old Trafford was the route for Ronald Frederick Atkinson.

Ron Atkinson had shown at West Bromwich Albion that he was capable of producing a first-class team with limited resources, and the step he took from the Hawthorns to United was perhaps for him not such a giant stride as had been his moving to West Bromwich from his first League club after Kettering, Cambridge United. His credentials were based on his previous successful managership. Ron Atkinson had been a hero of Oxford United in his playing days, taking part in their drive from Southern League to Second Division, but it was not his playing background which had seen him recognised as the right material to lead Manchester United back to greatness.

A larger-than-life character, his arrival at Old Trafford brought swift changes. In came Atkinson, and out went coaches Harry Gregg and Jack Crompton, youth coach Syd Owen, and physiotherapist Laurie Brown. The new broom was indeed making a clean sweep as Atkinson brought in his own backroom staff to replace those with links to the past. Crompton and Gregg had ties with the great sides of the three decades after the Second World War, but Ron Atkinson wanted his own men in the backroom.

Mick Brown, his right-hand man at West Brom, was appointed assistant manager. Brian Whitehouse, another from the Hawthorns, became chief coach, and Eric Harrison took charge of the youth team after leaving Everton's staff. The man who replaced Laurie Brown was Jim Headridge, physiotherapist at Bolton Wanderers, but tragedy struck before the new season was under way when, during a training session, he collapsed and died at the Cliff Training Ground. The man described by Atkinson as 'the best physio in the business' was eventually replaced by Jim McGregor, a popular choice, who had been at Goodison Park with Harrison, and before that at Oldham Athletic.

The first gap Atkinson had to fill on the field was that left by Joe Jordan who, as soon as his contract allowed him, had signed for Italian giants AC Milan, adding more weight to the predictions of Sexton in 1978. The new manager bought Frank

Stapleton from Arsenal, who unlike Brady, his fellow country-man, decided to seek his fortune in Manchester rather than follow him abroad when his contract also ended.

Atkinson signs Bryan Robson

In a deal worth more than £2 million West Brom agreed to sell Bryan Robson and Remi Moses to United. This fee, together with the £70,000 compensation for the loss of their manager certainly made the Midlands club richer financially, if poorer in the playing area. While the haggling over the total cost of both players went on, Moses was allowed to move north to his home town. He had been raised in Manchester's Moss Side, and he made his debut by coming on as substitute in the side's first win of the new season against Swansea City at Old Trafford.

That game also marked another milestone. Garry Birtles scored his first League goal, after 29 previous games without

success. Was this to be the turning point Atkinson hoped for?

Robson was eventually signed too late to make his debut against Wolves on 3 October 1981, but he was paraded before a crowd of close on 47,000 and his presence, after the spectacle of an on-the-pitch signing, seemed to rub off on his new col-leagues. The carnival atmosphere created by the event probably contributed to United running in their biggest win of the season, overwhelming struggling Wolves 5-0. Sammy

McIlroy, sensing that his days in midfield might now be num-bered, hit a hat-trick, and Birtles and Stapleton scored the other goals. Robson's fee had finally been settled at £1.5 mil-lion, making him the costliest player in Britain at that time, and he eventually made his league debut in the perfect setting of the derby game at Maine Road, in front of 52,037 supporters, who saw him give a solid performance in a 0-0 draw.

The extrovert Atkinson was also keen to encourage young players, giving Norman Whiteside, a strongly built boy who had joined straight from school in Belfast, his full League debut just a week after his 17th birthday. He took the team into third place in his first season and then the following year in 1982-83 had the Reds in the finals of both the Milk Cup and the FA Cup. The first trip to Wembley brought a 2-1 defeat against Liverpool but it was a different story in the FA Cup.

The other finalist, Brighton arrived at the stadium by heli-copter, but it was a story of a different kind which made the headlines. After just two League games United had called up an unknown youngster, Alan Davies, a Manchester-born player who claimed a loyalty to Wales because his grandparents came from there.

There were fears in the United camp that the game might go the same way as the 1976 final, when underdogs Southampton had beaten the favourites, and when Brighton scored first and still led at the interval Ron Atkinson had to lift his players. Ten minutes into the second period Mike Duxbury broke down the right, overlapping with Davies, and crossed the ball towards the edge of the penalty area. Whiteside flicked on across the face of the Brighton goal, and Frank Stapleton was there at the far post to force the ball home. Brighton's goalkeeper, Graham Moseley (a Manchester-born player) had no chance, and even less with United's second. Ray Wilkins had scored few goals during his time at Old Trafford, but in the 74th minute he set Wembley alight with a bending long-range shot which curled around Moseley and into the net.

Sixteen minutes remained and United led 2–1. It seemed as if the Cup was destined for Old Trafford until three minutes before the end of the game. Brighton's Gary Stevens then fired home a shot which beat Gary Bailey. The goal came from a corner taken by Jimmy Case, scorer of Liverpool's equaliser against United in 1977. Was this to be his revenge for that previous defeat?

The game went into extra time and in one last desperate surge Brighton almost stole the Cup. Michael Robinson, whose career had seen him at one time playing in Manchester with City, pulled a cross over to the feet of Gordon Smith, scorer of the afternoon's first goal. Smith ran into the six-yard box, but Bailey, possibly remembering the last moments of his previous FA Cup final, threw himself bravely at the Brighton player, blocking the shot completely.

The game ended in deadlock, with a replay five days later.

Cup winners again

Brighton had the suspended Foster back, but Moses' two-match suspension meant that he also missed the replay. However, he was there to celebrate as United ran Brighton into the ground.

Davies was magnificent and his performance caught the eye of the Welsh FA, who called him up for their summer internationals. It was Davies who combined with Arthur Albiston to lay on the first of two first-half goals which destroyed the Brighton challenge. Robson scored from the final pass and then two minutes later Davies tipped on a corner from Arnie Muhren and Norman Whiteside scored to add another line to his pedigree. In a year when he had played his first full season, and with a World Cup behind him, he had scored in both Wembley finals of 1983.

Brighton hit back and Case came close to scoring, but Bailey made a good save as the ball seemed to be passing over his

Left: £1.5 million seemed a costly gamble, but Bryan Robson was a dead cert for greatness. The England midfielder arrived at Old Trafford from West Bromwich Albion in October 1981

Left, bottom: Gordon McQueen clashes with Danny Wallace of Southampton at the Dell in 1983. United lost the game 3-0 but managed to finish 4th in the League. During the early and mid '80s Merseyside teams were dominant, but United did record five consecutive top four finishes

head. Then, almost on half time, Robson scored his second, running on to a Stapleton header. Three goals in front at the break, United were out of Brighton's reach. There was only one additional goal in the second half, scored from the penalty spot by Arnie Muhren after Robson had been pulled back by Gary Stevens, and the Cup was on its way back to Old Trafford.

Mark Hughes

United began the 1983-84 season with a 3-1 win over Queen's Park Rangers, but after leading 1-0 at half-time, lost to Nottingham Forest in the second successive home fixture.

The side began by playing attractive football, and eight wins and just two defeats in the eleven games to the end of October saw them sitting on top of the First Division, and there were signs that the future might be even brighter as a young striker emerged from the youth team.

Above: For Brighton's goalkeeper Graham Moseley the 1983 FA Cup final is a bad memory. He became the first 'keeper in post-war finals to concede a total of six goals, two in the original match and four in the replay. Here a Ray Wilkins' challenge leads to Whiteside grabbing United's second

Mark Hughes was beginning to cause a minor sensation in the lower teams. In a pre-season friendly against Port Vale he scored five times in a 10-0 win, and when United were paired with the Potteries club in the Milk Cup, Hughes came on as substitute in a 3-0 aggregate win.

Hughes eventually made his full debut at Oxford's Manor Ground in the fourth round of the Milk Cup, and scored in a 1-1 draw, but the tie proved to be the end of United in the competition that season. The replay at Old Trafford ended 1-1 after extra time and in the third game United were beaten 2-1 by an extra-time goal on a night when Gary Bailey was missing through injury, and Bryan Robson limped off before the final whistle.

The defence of the FA Cup was no luckier and Ron Atkinson's fury after his players were beaten 2-0 by Third Division Bournemouth was only matched by that of the supporters, who chanted 'Atkinson out!' And this to a manager whose team had won the FA Cup and Charity Shield the previous season and which was currently lying second in the table to Liverpool.

If Atkinson's turn on the Old Trafford tightrope was not providing the supporters with thrills, then they were hard to please, and by March, when Hughes was brought back into the side and played at Barcelona in the third round of the Cup-winners' Cup, the excitement reached fever pitch. This was the brilliant tie in which, after losing 2-0 at Nou Camp Stadium, United won 3-0 before 58,547 at Old Trafford, beating Barcelona and Maradona 3-2 on aggregate.

Once toppled from the top of the League table, United were constantly in the shadow of Liverpool, yet beat them at Old Trafford and drew at Anfield after leading for most of the game. Liverpool finished Champions, United fourth. During the season Graeme Hogg was introduced to the side, replacing McQueen, who was again injured at the start of 1984.

Top: The dreams of Brighton are shattered as Arnold Muhren scores United's fourth goal in the 1983 FA Cup final replay

Above: Distant horizons for Ray Wilkins brought an end to his days at Old Trafford. The player who lost both the England and United captaincy to his close friend Bryan Robson, reluctantly moved on to play in Italy with AC Milan.

Wilkins goes to Italy

However, it was the transfer of a player away from the club which made the biggest impact. Ray Wilkins was sold to AC Milan for £1.4 million. Wilkins was a popular player, especially with the younger supporters, and had been a great ambassador for the club, always willing to talk to fans, in a patient, well-mannered and understanding way. Wilkins left sadly, despite the financial attractions of his new life abroad. He said later: 'I never wanted to leave, but it was obvious that there was no place for me in future plans, so when the deal was drawn up between Milan and United that was that.'

There was also a question mark over the future of Norman Whiteside. Although the young striker had proved himself at every level, he lost his place to Hughes at the close of the 1983-84 campaign, and during the summer Atkinson's efforts in the transfer market finalised the purchases of Strachan from Aberdeen, Jesper Olsen, the Danish winger who was playing for Dutch club Ajax, and Alan Brazil from Tottenham, a player Atkinson had pursued for over a year.

Mark Hughes makes his mark

United's chances of winning the League and Cup double in season 1984-85 were realistic, even though Everton were well ahead in the title race, and after beating Aston Villa 4-0 at Old

1980-89

Right: Mark Hughes was the second influential player to emerge from the youth team of the 1980s, the first being Norman Whiteside. Hughes made his debut in a Milk Cup tie at Oxford and scored, an action he was to repeat when he played his first senior League game and his first international for Wales

Below: The jubilant players celebrate victory in the replay of the 1983 FA Cup final

Trafford, Atkinson was being tipped as the man to emulate Busby as a creator of champions. Hughes scored a hat-trick in this match and his performances in his first full season earned him the 'Young Footballer of the Year' award, given to him through the votes of his fellow professionals in the PFA.

It was the FA Cup which became the main target and supporters began to look forward to the possibility of a sixth Wembley final within a decade. United met Liverpool at Goodison Park, while Everton faced Luton Town in the other semi-final at Villa Park. The prospect of an all-Merseyside final had caught the imagination of the sporting press and the build-up to the games helped to create an amazing atmosphere, especially at the Everton ground.

The first goal came after a first half in which Hogg had been booked for a foul on Rush, Whiteside had been floored by Whelan and had clashed with Sammy Lee, and Gidman had created a scoring chance from a free-kick.

It was in the 69th minute when Hughes struck, ramming the ball home after a Robson shot had been blocked. The game seemed over until Ronnie Whelan tried a shot from outside the box four minutes from time and levelled the scores. Once more a Liverpool-United game went into extra time, and eight minutes into the first period Frank Stapleton's shot was deflected to make it 2-1 to United.

Surely this time United were through? But no, back came Liverpool, and in the final minute referee George Courtney ignored a linesman's flag and allowed a Paul Walsh goal to stand. It was a bitter blow for Atkinson: 'We had the game won, we did everything that we had to do this afternoon and still we haven't got to Wembley.'

The game was replayed at Maine Road four nights later and the own-goal jinx once again struck United. In the 39th minute Paul McGrath tried to head a cross over his own bar, and instead beat Bailey to put Liverpool in front. United were stunned, but having had the better of the play up to that time, were in confident mood and came back immediately the second half had started. Bryan Robson ran at the Liverpool defence and unleashed a powerful shot which Grobbelaar could not reach and it was 1-1. Twelve minutes later the dynamic Hughes forced himself through the Liverpool back four as he chased a Strachan pass and hit the winner.

Everton, the League leaders, provided the opposition for the Wembley final on 18 May. Before that United saw their Championship hopes disappear completely as they drew with Southampton and Sunderland at Old Trafford, and even though they had victories at Luton and Norwich on each side of those games the four points lost were vital. A 3-1 win at QPR was followed by a debacle at Vicarage Road, Watford, where the Hornets beat United 5-1 in the last League game, but the players' minds by then were on the Cup final which was five days away.

and swaying as if about to faint.

Moran had to sit on the United bench as the game went into extra time. He said afterwards:

It was the worst moment of my life. I couldn't believe what had happened to me, I honestly didn't think that I'd fouled Peter, but even if I did I didn't think it warranted a sending off. I went crazy, I didn't know what was happening, except that here was a man sending me off for something I thought I hadn't done. I asked for mercy and got none.

No goals had come in the first 90 minutes, but in extra time the ten men from Manchester found the inspiration to create just one vital opportunity, and it fell to Norman Whiteside.

Hughes, in his own half, pushed the ball forward beyond the Everton midfield. Whiteside ran after it, lengthening his stride as he found extra strength. Strachan raced alongside in support, and Van den Hauwe, the Everton left-back, came to challenge. Whiteside turned inwards, the fullback stumbled and Whiteside hit a left-foot shot goalwards as Van den Hauwe fell, obscuring the ball momentarily from the view of Southall in the Everton goal. The ball was level with the goalkeeper when he became aware of the danger, throwing himself outwards in an effort to block its path, but the ball was round

Agony of Moran

Everton, by now champions, were favourites to win the final, but it was a game remembered not so much for its football as for a moment during the second half when Kevin Moran carved an unwanted niche in the history of the game.

It happened when Peter Reid, that dynamo of a midfielder, was running at full speed towards the United penalty area. The Everton player had picked up the ball from a moment of hesitation by McGrath and was clear of the Reds' defence. Moran threw himself feet first at Reid, his right foot pushing the ball away, his left catching the Everton player. Reid's momentum carried him into the air and he dramatically rolled over several times. Referee Peter Willis blew for a foul and called Moran to him.

The United player seemed angry that his challenge should be thought unfair by the referee, but said nothing, turning his back to the official so that Willis could note his number. Moran began to walk away after the caution and was then shocked to learn that he had been sent off. He was unhappily the first player ever to be dismissed in an FA Cup final.

Moran was stunned. He grabbed referee Willis in a vain attempt to plead his innocence. Willis stood firm, pointing to the touchline and growing angry at the player's attitude. Moran was incensed and had to be pulled away from the official by his team-mate at both club and international level, Frank Stapleton.

Bryan Robson pleaded with Willis and was ignored. The Everton players joined in, and Reid walked alongside Moran as he was led from the field by Jim McGregor, holding back tears

Top: Drama in the 1985 FA Cup Final at Wembley as Kevin Moran becomes the first player to be sent off in football's showpiece. Referee Peter Willis points to the touchline, 'I almost hit the referee' Moran said afterwards

him and into the net. United had won the FA Cup again.

The players went to collect their medals. Moran accompanied them and was told by an FA official that his was being withheld. A player sent off at Wembley does not qualify for a medal, winner or loser. However, such was the public outcry, backed by the television evidence, that several weeks later Moran was justly rewarded with his medal.

The sending-off had turned an ordinary final into one of major significance, and the interest created by Moran's misfortune transformed him into a folk hero.

1980-89

United had won another major trophy. They ended their First Division campaign by once again occupying fourth place.

The 1985-86 season began by United losing to Everton in the Charity Shield, Graeme Hogg replacing Moran who was suspended, and the new campaign proved to be one of great importance for Ron Atkinson.

Since his arrival his side had not ended a season outside the top four, had qualified for Europe and won the FA Cup twice, but he had still been unable totally to convince the majority of supporters that he was the right man for the managerial seat at Old Trafford. His record proved he was successful, but the supporters' comments, and their acceptance of Atkinson the man, showed that he was walking the tightrope without winning over his audience.

He was accepted by the media as a man who was easy to work with unless angered. He had dealt with a difficult personal problem in a way which caused not the slightest embarrassment to the club when he had called a 'press conference' to announce that he had left his wife to set up home with another woman, thus preventing any sensational exposures in the tabloid newspapers. He had a circle of close friends with whom he could confide, yet that vital relationship with the grass-roots supporter was missing, the same problem that had eventually spelled the end of the Old Trafford career of Dave Sexton.

from Coventry City, moved to Old Trafford in a player-plus-cash deal which took Alan Brazil to Highfield Road.

After the tremendous start things began to go wrong. After the Sheffield Wednesday defeat United were knocked out of the Milk Cup at Anfield, and got just two points from three further League games.

Injuries still plagued the club. Playing for England, Bryan Robson limped off at Wembley after chasing a ball behind the goal and tearing a hamstring. He returned for the game at Sheffield Wednesday and repeated the injury which kept him out until the New Year. Robson missed the remainder of the Milk Cup games after taking part in the two-legged second round against Crystal Palace – Steve Coppell's club – as goals from Peter Barnes and Norman Whiteside gave United a 1-0 win in each match.

In the third round there was controversy as United beat West Ham 1-0 at Old Trafford. Norman Whiteside scored what turned out to be the only goal of the game, converting an Olsen pass from the goal-line in the 76th minute, but it was a 'goal' that was not a goal which caused a stir. Mark Ward fired a 25-yard free-kick into Gary Bailey's net but as referee Frank Roberts had indicated that it was indirect there was no goal. Ward argued that Bailey had touched the ball in his efforts to make a save, which Bailey denied.

Brilliant start to the 1985-86 season

However, anyone with any doubts about his managerial capabilities had little evidence to use against him as United began their 1985-86 season by setting an impressive new club record for successive victories.

After the Charity Shield they beat Aston Villa, Ipswich, Arsenal, West Ham, Nottingham Forest, Newcastle, Oxford, Manchester City, West Brom and Southampton in the League. Ten games, ten wins, and naturally top of the First Division.

The victories had a price. John Gidman broke his leg in the second game at Ipswich, Jesper Olsen was hurt before the West Ham match, allowing Peter Barnes, signed during that summer, to make an impressive debut, and Gordon Strachan dislocated his shoulder scoring for United at West Brom.

United's run of victories ended with a draw at Luton but it was November before they lost their first League game, going down 1-0 to Sheffield Wednesday at Hillsborough. Injuries had forced Atkinson to use no fewer than 18 players up to that fixture, only one of them, goalkeeper Turner, not having competed in the League.

Colin Gibson was bought from Aston Villa as Ron Atkinson decided that he wanted to strengthen his left full-back options and early in the new year a second Gibson, Terry

Top: Quick talking, quick witted and quick off the mark, Gordon Strachan found himself playing under Alex Ferguson for a second time when United replaced Ron Atkinson in 1986

Above: The slightly built Jesper Olsen was brought to Old Trafford six months before he became a United player. The Dane was out of the game through injury when he agreed to move to English football from Dutch club Ajax

Left: FA Cup final 1985: Everton goalkeeper Neville Southall flings himself across goal in a vain attempt to stop Norman Whiteside's extra-time cup-winning shot from the far edge of the penalty area

Drop in form

By December United were still top of the League, but their form slipped dramatically. Just one win in five games was followed by a 3-1 win at Villa Park. Then, when the first home defeat of the season occurred against Arsenal on 21 December a small section of the supporters demonstrated against the manager. 'What do they think they're talking about?' was Atkinson's retort. 'They seem to forget I've brought them the Cup twice – and would Bryan Robson be playing here if it wasn't for me? They have very short memories.'

Defeat at Goodison Park followed, and only bad weather prevented what might have been a tragic run of defeats as the long trip to Newcastle on 28 December was postponed.

Mark Hughes' form had also taken a significant slide. In his opening 13 games he had scored ten goals, then in the next 13 League fixtures, just two. The period bridged the start of the New Year and the start of the FA Cup campaign.

This opened with a tie against Rochdale, switched to Old Trafford because Spotland could not cater for the numbers who might attend, and United won 2-0. The tie saw the return to football of Mark Higgins, who had been forced to retire from the game after a bad injury. The former Everton captain had turned to Atkinson for a chance to try again and after training with United joined them, repaying the insurance claim he had received when he quit.

Robson returned for the next round of the Cup, against Sunderland at Roker Park. The game ended goalless, but the talking point was a clash between Robson and Barry Venison. Both players fell to the ground, Robson got up first and tried to step over the Sunderland player, catching him on the head with his boot. The linesman closest to the incident saw it as a deliberate kick, and Robson was sent off for the first time ever in his career.

United won the replay 3-0 with Robson in the side, but by the time his two-match suspension started he was injured again. Four days after the second Sunderland game the England captain limped off at Upton Park after twisting his

ankle during a 2-1 League defeat, as United found themselves knocked off the top of the table.

Meanwhile the news had leaked out that Mark Hughes was set to join Barcelona for £1.8m at the end of the season. This angered United's supporters when they read of the speculation in the newspapers.

Atkinson is sacked

On Tuesday, 4 November 1986, United played their final game under Ron Atkinson. It was the replay against Southampton at the Dell, and a game which increased the injury burden which had weighed Atkinson down. Colin Gibson tore his hamstring again after just two partial outings at the start of the season,

Top: Mark Higgins seemed finished in football when he quit Everton with a back injury, but United gave him a second life by repaying his insurance money to take him back into the Football League

Above: Remi Moses beats Adrian Heath to the ball during a 3–1 defeat for United at Goodison in September 1986. Following this, a 1-0 loss to Chelsea and an away draw at Forest heralded the end of Atkinson's reign

and Norman Whiteside limped off with a knee ligament injury before half-time. He was replaced by Nicky Wood, who had ended his studies at Manchester University to concentrate on his playing career. Moran was on instead of Gibson. A minute before half-time Southampton scored, and in the second half took control, winning 4-1.

The United manager was far from happy:

Up to half-time I thought that we were the better team, I honestly believed that we would get into the game in the second half and make something of it, but George Lawrence ran riot. It's seldom that you can find any consolation in defeat, but we had problems with injuries again and I thought that the players battled terribly well considering those. Jimmy Case ran the show though, and there was nothing we could do about it.

Jimmy Case, tormentor of Manchester United, had contributed to the end of Ron Atkinson's spell on the Old Trafford tightrope.

The next day the club's directors met informally to discuss the situation, and 24 hours later at 10.30 am on 6 November, Martin Edwards summoned Ron Atkinson and Mick Brown to his office at Old Trafford.

An hour later a statement was issued which said that the contracts of both men had been terminated. Atkinson was no longer manager.

The men and women of the media gathered outside the normally open gates of the Cliff training ground hoping for an opportunity to see the man who had been forced to stand down from his post, and shortly before noon were allowed into the courtyard where Atkinson held his final audience with the press:

Obviously I'm disappointed. I'd go on record as saying that I have been at the club for five and a half years. Five of them have been very good years which I have enjoyed immensely, but this year things went against us and you have seen the outcome today. I actually had no indication of what was going to happen. I came down here today expecting to have a nice five-a-side and some training, but the chairman sent for me and told me reluctantly – I felt reluctantly – that they had decided to dispense with my services, because of the results over the last few months, and I accept that totally. I don't feel bitter about it, I don't hold any bitterness against the club. I honestly feel that we had just started to turn the corner with our recent run of results but I never expected this to happen. I don't think if you are a positive person you ever look on the black side, you look on the positive side. I came here this morning knowing that we are playing Oxford on Saturday and to get a side capable of winning there. Now someone else has got that responsibility, and whoever it is I sincerely hope they do well. I've no axe to grind at all. I've worked for a chairman who I consider to be as good as any chairman in the game, and I don't think that this job is any harder than being manager of

1980-89

any other club. True this is the biggest club in the country and the manager has his problems, but I don't think the manager of Rochdale would feel that his problems were any smaller than mine have been, or any bigger.

You are always aware that these things might happen but you must never look at it in that light. But I am sure that there are good times ahead for the club, once whoever takes over gets all the key players fit again.

Alex Ferguson is appointed

Atkinson bowed out and drowned his sorrows that night with a party at his Rochdale home, but by then he knew who would succeed him, for Martin Edwards was swift to appoint a new man. Three hours after sacking Ron Atkinson, the United chairman flew to Scotland where he had been given permission to talk to Aberdeen's manager, Alex Ferguson. The man who was to succeed Atkinson remembers the day clearly:

It was a beautiful sunny morning and I drove back to Pittodrie from a training session and I saw the chairman's car there. And I thought to myself 'the old yin's here early today' – it was about a quarter to twelve. I went into my office and he was sitting at my desk, and he had his hand on the telephone. I said hello to him and told him he was in early, and he threw me a piece of paper. 'I've been asked to phone this gentleman,' he said. On the paper was Martin Edwards' name and phone number.

He said 'Do you want me to 'phone him?' and I said that I did, and I went out of the room because I didn't want to be there. I just asked if he would tell me what had happened after the call. I went back after going down to the dressing rooms and he said that he had spoken to Mr Edwards and that he was flying up straight away and would go to my house. He said that his son would collect the United chairman from the airport and take him there. I said it was quick, and he said 'If you want the job there's nothing we can do to stop you.'

There was nothing else I could do, so I went home and told my wife and sons, and right away they were against the idea. I think they were just shocked at the thought of leaving Aberdeen, because it's a lovely city and the boys were settled in at school. We had good players and a good club, but we sat down and my wife said that I was right, I had to take the job.

The following morning Alex Ferguson arrived at the Cliff, met his new players and immediately was impressed:

This is luxury for me, because at Aberdeen we didn't have our own training ground, we used school pitches. But I've got to put these things to good use and get down to picking a winning side. I know the club's had injury problems and my sympathy goes to Ron Atkinson in that sense. You need luck in football and he didn't have any.

During the 1986-87 campaign Paul McGrath was at the peak of his powers. However, after a series of knee operations he was sold to Villa in the summer of '89

The new manager was an optimist:

We aren't in a desperate position, the League can still be won. It's no use me coming here and not thinking that every game we play we can win, that's the only way that we can attack things. That's the attitude I had at Aberdeen – there's a game to be played and we must go out and win it. Tomorrow we have to win, simply that.

His new chairman, Martin Edwards said:

I am sure that we have made a wise choice. We had to move quickly – once we had decided to get rid of Ron we wanted to replace him as quickly as possible.

When we had the meeting to decide that we wanted to make the change we decided that Alex Ferguson was the man that we wanted to replace Ron Atkinson.

It was also evident that the United chairman knew what he expected from his new manager:

We are looking to be the premier club in England and obviously to be that we have to win the First Division Championship. That was our aim throughout Ron Atkinson's reign and will continue to be our main priority. It would be very rash to call Ron Atkinson a failure because he didn't win the title. In the five full seasons he was here he never finished outside the top four, he won us the FA Cup twice and got us to the final of the Milk Cup, plus the semi-final of the European Cup Winners' Cup, so I don't think under any circumstances you could class Ron Atkinson a failure. The only thing is that he didn't achieve the First Division Championship.

Ferguson's first changes

Ferguson brought Archie Knox, his assistant at Aberdeen, to be his right-hand man at Old Trafford, and the Scots injected new spirit into the club. Training became longer and harder and players responded to the new methods. Bryan Robson said after a few weeks:

There's no doubt about it, things have changed, and the players seem to like the way things are being done. I've got to be honest and say that I've never felt stronger in my legs than I do now. I have had a lot of trouble with my hamstring, but the manager has got me doing different routines to strengthen my legs and they seem to be working.

On the pitch the new methods showed. United became a side which used fitness as well as skill to compete, and their willingness to run led to victory over Liverpool at Anfield – their only away win of the whole First Division campaign – as Ferguson tested his squad.

He used no fewer than 23 players during his first season, amongst them Terry Gibson, who had almost joined Watford in the week Atkinson was replaced, but who was eventually transferred to Wimbledon after waiting almost a year for his home debut. Gibson was given a chance by Ferguson, playing 12 First Division games and taking part in both FA Cup ties played during that season.

The first was against Manchester City at Old Trafford, when a crowd of 54,295 witnessed Norman Whiteside scoring the only goal of the afternoon in the 67th minute. But the state of the pitch was poor, and pointed the way to the trouble that was brewing and which would come to a head in the fourth round.

Media criticism and regular comments from supporters had led to the club installing an under-soil heating system, but, as if to back up comments previously made by chairman Edwards, it had proved unsatisfactory. Although costing over £80,000, sections of it had failed and consequently, when there was a hard frost, parts of the ground were frozen while others were perfect for play. Before the City tie, hot air machines were placed around the frozen sections pumping warmth under large blankets borrowed from the nearby cricket ground. The makeshift scheme worked and the pitch was perfect.

It was different for the next round, however, when United were again drawn at home, to Coventry City. Alex Ferguson took the players away to the Lake District to prepare for the game. Five wins and four draws had lifted them away from the relegation zone and the prospect of a good Cup run justified such preparations. On the morning of the game the manager was stunned when he arrived at Old Trafford. The pitch was bone hard, a sudden frost having caught out the groundstaff. The game was turned into a lottery, and United were the losers. Keith Houchen scored for Coventry with a 20th minute shot after the ball bobbled away from Turner on the slippery surface. Coventry went on to win the FA Cup and United replaced their undersoil heating during the summer of 1987.

After their Cup hopes ended, United spent the remainder of the season in mid-table, finishing the campaign in 11th place, their lowest position since the relegation season of 1973-74. But there were signs that the 1987-88 season would have more to offer.

During the months of Ferguson's management Gary Walsh, an 18-year-old goalkeeper, was drafted into the squad, and his presence led to Chris Turner asking for a transfer. Gary Bailey came back from injury and played in five games before announcing that he was being forced into retirement by a knee problem identical to that which had led to the end of Steve Coppell's playing days.

Bailey returned to his parents' home in South Africa to continue the university studies he had abandoned to take up his footballing career, after a hastily arranged testimonial. He said:

> Obviously I am very sad to be giving up the game, when I could have another ten years or more at the top. But I am leaving with some tremendous memories and I feel honoured to have played for a club as great as Manchester United.

During the summer of 1987 Frank Stapleton was transferred to the Dutch team Ajax, where his former club-mate Arnie Muhren was extending his career, and John Sivebaek was sold to St Etienne of France.

Viv Anderson and Brian McClair arrive

In their places came Ferguson's first signings, England full-back Viv Anderson, and Scotland's Brian McClair.

Anderson had been a trialist with United as a boy, but had not been taken on and had eventually become a player with his home town club Nottingham Forest. He was then transferred to

Left: Arthur Albiston made his debut for the club in 1977 and gave an impressive display in the FA Cup final that year as United beat Liverpool to win the cup. The Scottish left full-back won three FA Cup winning medals with United, the first player ever to achieve this feat. In 1988 Albiston was granted a testimonial and given a free transfer. 'In view of his fine record with the club it would not have been right for us to ask for a fee,' said Alex Ferguson

Right: Brian McClair signed for United at a joint signing ceremony with Viv Anderson in the club trophy room in 1987. Alex Ferguson obtained McClair for under £1 million, and in the next seven seasons the hardworking McClair made 330 appearances for the club.

Arsenal after winning major honours with Forest, including the European Cup and the First Division Championship, and was a regular in the England side.

Anderson and McClair signed together on 1 July and both players had their transfer fees finalised by the Football League's independent tribunal. United paid £250,000 for Anderson, but McClair, scorer of 35 goals in his final season with Celtic, cost over three times as much. Celtic valued the player at £2 million, United offered well below that, and eventually a cheque was signed for £850,000.

For Ferguson it was the first step towards greater success and the drive towards a championship win:

> When I first arrived at this club I felt that I had to give myself time to look at the players I had taken over. I knew that I would

eventually make changes, and I have gone on record as saying that I think I need to strengthen as many as five positions. It may be that I have the players for those positions already, it's up to them to show me that, but if not then I will find them elsewhere.

By the time the first full season under his management was about to commence Alex Ferguson had stamped out a clear message of intent to his players. He selected his strongest side from the squad and this shocked some.

Young Walsh was again in goal, although Turner had played in some pre-season matches, Anderson was at right-back, and Mike Duxbury on the left, in preference to the left-footed Albiston. Gibson was one of several players who had been informed that they might be made available for transfer should there be any enquiries, the others being Hogg and goalkeeper Turner. Peter Davenport was linked to other clubs, but began the season as one of the two substitutes allowed in all games after a change in the rules during the summer break.

For the opening game at Southampton McGrath and Moran formed the centre of the defence, Moses, Strachan, Robson and Olsen were in midfield and Whiteside returned to his role of attacker alongside McClair.

Hughes returns to partner McClair

The Scot quickly began to repay his transfer fee, and by Christmas had scored 14 goals, more even than Hughes in his first full term, and Alex Ferguson added fuel to the flames of speculation by hinting that the prospect of McClair and the Welsh striker playing together was not simply wishful thinking.

Hughes was finding that life with Barcelona was not what he had expected. He had flown home early in 1987 after being de-registered by the Spanish giants, which made him unable to play for them under the two-foreign-players rule, and he was immediately linked with his old club.

He played in the Gary Bailey Testimonial and scored four spectacular goals. Afterwards he said:

I am still a Barcelona player and can do nothing unless my club wants me to do it. I have always said that if ever I came back to English football then there is only one club I would want to play for and that's United. I have a lot of friends here and get on well with the supporters.

Unofficially Hughes had hinted that he was ready to return, and this led to Alex Ferguson flying to Barcelona for talks with Hughes and his manager Terry Venables. After his trip he said:

I want to bring Mark back to United, but at present the main problem is with the Inland Revenue. Mark has to stay abroad until after April 1988 otherwise he would be liable for taxation on the money he has earned since he left this country. We can do nothing until then, but I promise that I will do my best to get him playing for United again.

A fee of £750,000 brought Scotland's goalkeeper Jim Leighton to Old Trafford. He played over 94 games for the Reds before being loaned to Reading. He moved back across the border to Dundee in 1991

Ferguson captures Bruce

An injury to Paul McGrath forced Ferguson into the transfer market again in December 1987 and the target this time was Steve Bruce of Norwich City. The club was on the verge of paying £1 million to Glasgow Rangers for their England international centre-back Terry Butcher, but 24 hours before the deal would have become public knowledge, the player broke his leg. United had revealed their hand and when they turned to Norwich City for Bruce, after being rejected by Middlesbrough in a bid for Gary Pallister, they found the club difficult to deal with.

During the summer Alex Ferguson had failed to persuade Norwich to part with striker Kevin Drinkell, whom he saw as a likely partner for McClair, and when negotiations for Bruce opened he was told that the price was £1 million – the fee he had been ready to pay for Butcher. The clubs seemed to have reached agreement on a fee of £800,000 some 48 hours before United were due to play Oxford at Old Trafford on 12 December 1987. Nothing happened; the player had his bags packed ready to move north but was told that he was not being allowed to go. By 5 pm on Friday 11 December Bruce was still a Norwich player, and it took another six days before he was signed.

At first Norwich said they wanted to sign a replacement, then, after John O'Neill from QPR joined them, they said Bruce would not be released until a second player had been bought. Eventually Alex Ferguson called the deal off on 17 December, after Norwich chairman Robert Chase apparently attempted to increase the fee. Finally the Norfolk club had a change of heart and Bruce signed later that day.

Bruce made his debut in a game at Portsmouth which saw the almost rejected Turner playing in goal for his third successive game, all of them victories. Turner had won back his place after Walsh was concussed for the second time that season. The first injury was in the victory over Sheffield Wednesday at Hillsborough, the first time United had taken maximum points since the Yorkshire club's return to the First Division in 1984. The second came during a trip to Bermuda which caused a sensation for another reason, and also revealed Ferguson's strength as a man capable of dealing with a difficult situation.

Trial by media

The trip was arranged to coincide with United's 'blank Saturday', the fate befalling each First Division club during the 1987-88 season, when there were 21 teams competing. United played two games on the island, but it was not their football which made headline news.

Clayton Blackmore was arrested and held by police while investigations were carried out regarding a serious accusation being made against him by a young American woman. The police eventually released him after the Bermudan Attorney General ruled that there was no case to answer, but the woman told newspapers her version of the alleged incident.

News reporters besieged the airport as the team returned, but Blackmore had travelled back a day ahead of his colleagues with club solicitor Maurice Watkins. United found themselves the centre of media attention, but Alex Ferguson remained calm. He allowed sports journalists into the training ground, and as the team were about to leave for the game at QPR called Blackmore into his Friday press conference, where he answered questions from the same newspaper representatives who regularly gathered information from the club. By the week-

Steve Bruce joined United in December 1987 after a fortnight of negotiations with Norwich City. In the end he cost £800,000 and made his debut at Fratton Park, Portsmouth, on 19 December. Bruce's commitment made him a popular player immediately with the supporters and took him to the verge of full international honours in his first season at Old Trafford

end the spotlight had burnt itself out and the matter was closed.

Discipline was mentioned by Alex Ferguson when he faced shareholders at the club's annual meeting, and he told them that he had his own methods of dealing with such matters, but he added that these were not being discussed in such a public place as the packed Europa Suite, part of the club's lavish restaurant complex. As he looked out on the supporters gathered before him Alex Ferguson must have felt that he was amongst friends. He was the new man on the tightrope, but in his short time in charge he had shown that his heart was as much in the club as theirs. He was taking his first steps with caution, but with style. He had won over the staff under him, from the laundry ladies with whom he and Archie Knox share a daily cup of tea at 8.00 am to the chairman and his board of directors.

His natural gift for dealing with people from every walk of life was self-evident and he was filling the role of public relations officer as well as team manager. Small things mattered to Alex Ferguson. Requests for autographs became important and these were organised to coincide with Friday training sessions, when his players were faced with the week's demands for signed books, photographs and footballs, used to raise money for charity.

Pre-match preparation was re-organised. Instead of meeting at the ground and travelling to a city centre hotel for a Saturday morning meal the players were told to report to Old Trafford, where they would eat in the grill room, then relax in their lounge, or mingle with supporters.

Ferguson's influence led to the appointment of a new groundsman, the building of new dressing rooms, and a general awareness amongst his players and the administrative staff that all were responsible for the success of Manchester United.

The future for United

In 1987 the club introduced its own membership scheme to fall in line with government measures to curb football hooliganism. The United scheme was designed to give those who joined something in return for their entry fee. The club gave discount for all home games, and for goods bought at the souvenir shop. Members were sent badges and year books, and given free admission to all reserve games as well as a complimentary ticket for the club museum.

The scheme came in for some criticism in its early stages but by the end of 1987 over 40,000 supporters had joined. The idea had developed from suggestions put to the club by Bobby Charlton, and it was he, speaking at the 1987 annual meeting, who outlined his hopes for the future of Manchester United:

I have been to Barcelona and seen the way that their membership scheme works. It enables them to raise huge amounts of capital domestic cup competitions,' Alex Ferguson said after losing 2-0 at the Manor Ground, 'now we have only the FA Cup to aim for.' He called for a positive response from his players, but unhelpful newspaper speculation that he would stage a wholesale clear-out at the end of the season did nothing to boost morale within the squad.

There was a glimmer of hope as the Oxford game was followed by a 2-1 televised win at Highbury, then victory over Chelsea before the biggest crowd of the season at Old Trafford as 50,700 witnessed a 2-0 win which took United through to the fifth round of the FA Cup and another visit to Arsenal's ground. This was a game which could have devastated the side for the rest of the season. After trailing 2-0 at halftime Brian McClair scored to put United back in the game. Confidence was restored and the pendulum swung United's way. After being totally dominated for the first 45 minutes they took the upper hand and pressurised Arsenal who were lucky to clear several chances away from their besieged goal, then Norman Whiteside was tripped with three minutes remaining and United were awarded a penalty, which McClair failed to convert.

It was an incident which would have left a lasting impression on many players, but McClair faced the media immediately after the game, claiming: 'When you score you are ready to take the bouquets, so you also have got to be prepared to stand up and take the criticism when you miss.' He also stepped forward to take the next penalty when the opportunity arose weeks later at Oxford. However, Alex Ferguson had removed this responsibility from his leading scorer who would have left Highbury with 21 goals to his name that season had his penalty been converted.

at the start of every season, and that is one of the ways that they are able to compete with the best in Europe. It may take several years before this club can stand alongside them from a financial point of view, but we have started to take a step in that direction. Financial security is important, and in order to be successful on the field you have to be successful off it.

As far as I, and my fellow directors are concerned, we have in Alex Ferguson the perfect man to lead us to success. Even in the short time he has been here he has shown us that he is doing things the right way. I can see no reason why Alex should not be here for the next 30 years, and I wish him every success for the future . . . the future of Manchester United.

United entered 1988 with optimism. Victory over champions Everton at Old Trafford had restored them to fourth place in the table, and although slim, the chance of Alex Ferguson taking the club to its first championship win for 21 years remained.

Liverpool stood in their way, leading the First Division and unbeaten in the League by the turn of the year. It seemed that nothing could prevent the First Division title from once more returning to Anfield, and when United drew with lowly Charlton Athletic on New Year's Day it became obvious that the fight was not only uphill, but virtually impossible.

Defeat in the Littlewoods Cup quarter-final at Oxford was soul-destroying: 'We were hoping for success in one of the

Above: Bryan Robson shrugs off a challenge from Chelsea's Graham Roberts. If there were changes afoot under Ferguson, one thing was for sure... the captain was staying

Right: August 1989 heralded the arrival of Gary Pallister from Middlesbrough for the princely sum of £2.3 million. The 6ft 4in centre-half proved to be a majestic presence in defence for almost a decade

Unsettled players

The media used the defeat to emphasise that United's season had ended even though February had not. Crowds began to fall and a League defeat at Norwich had Alex Ferguson demanding that his players 'show me that they want to play for Manchester United'. Many responded but Norman Whiteside and Paul McGrath reacted unexpectedly. Both said that they were unhappy at Old Trafford and asked for transfers in highly publicised moves which stunned United's followers. 'I have had some great years at Old Trafford,' said Whiteside, 'but I feel that the time has come for a change. I want to play abroad, I would not consider playing for another English club except United, but I would like to try my hand on the continent.'

McGrath's demand for a move came a short time after Whiteside's, although there had been newspaper speculation that all was not well between the player and the club following a much publicised motoring accident which led to McGrath being injured and later fined and banned from driving on a drinks charge. 'I feel that I have gone stale,' he said, 'and I would like a new challenge.' The Republic of Ireland defender had been out of action for five months when Alex Ferguson decided that he was fit to play again but the supporters showed whose side they were on when McGrath was booed by the home fans during the game against Luton, and Whiteside was the target of chants of 'You only want the money!' as he sat on the substitute's bench during the same game.

Liverpool were champions elect, and the rivalry between the two clubs reached boiling point on Easter Monday – a week before the Luton game – when United held the Merseysiders to a 3-3 draw at Anfield in an inspired performance. United led as early as the second minute through a Bryan Robson goal, but Liverpool fought back and by the first minute of the second half were 3-1 ahead. To add to their problems United had Colin Gibson sent off for a second bookable offence but the ten men played inspired football, Robson got a second with a deflected shot and Gordon Strachan levelled the scores in the 77th minute.

A month later Liverpool were champions and United had secured second place just nine points behind them, cutting down a 17-point lead to just a three-game difference. Nottingham Forest were third, eight points adrift and Everton, who at one time had been favourites to finish runners-up to Liverpool, ended their season 11 points behind United and 20 points behind their Merseyside neighbours.

United collected 81 points, their biggest tally since the three-points-a-win system was introduced and there was much cause for optimism as the season ended: 'I know that we are not very far away from having a side which can take the championship. During the coming weeks I shall make every effort to strengthen areas of the team which I feel should be improved, and I know that we will challenge the best in our next campaign,' said Alex Ferguson at the end of his first full season as United's manager.

In May 1988 he bought Aberdeen's Scottish international goalkeeper Jim Leighton for a record £750,000 as his plans for rebuilding were put into action, but only one player was told that his services would no longer be required at the club. Arthur Albiston was given a free transfer as a career spanning 11 years of League football with the club came to a close with a testimonial game against Manchester City.

So Alex Ferguson was able to look towards the future with the words of his chairman echoing the thoughts of every United supporter: 'Time alone will tell but I am sure that Alex Ferguson will lead us to greater success than we have enjoyed in recent years. The fruits of his labours in rebuilding a vigorous youth policy, completely overhauling our scouting system and instilling a feeling of pride in everyone who wears a United shirt will I am positive be clear for all to see before very long. . . and I look forward to the future of Manchester United.'

The changes begin

The close season saw the return to Old Trafford of a player the fans had never wished to part with. Mark Hughes had left for Barcelona in 1986 but his stay there had not been a success. His return was greeted with great excitement and with Jim Leighton in goal United began the 1988-89 season confidently.

After seven games the new 'keeper had conceded just one goal – a Jan Molby penalty at Anfield – but Hughes and McClair had scored just one goal each and Ferguson's search for the right formula was constantly thwarted by injuries.

Davenport played alongside Hughes with McClair on the right side of midfield and Olsen the left.

Strachan found the going tough and after being subbed in four out of seven games began to doubt his future at the club.

Lee Martin played in the first game, a scoreless draw against Queens Park Rangers but two days later joined the queue of players in the treatment room and was out for three months.

McGrath and Whiteside were still at the club though openly seeking pastures new and there was newspaper speculation that Ferguson was about to start a clear out.

The first player to leave was Peter Davenport who was bought by Middlesbrough. A month later Jesper Olsen was sold to Bordeaux, then Liam O'Brien began a new career with

During the summer of 1989 United signed Neil Webb from Nottingham Forest and Mike Phelan of Norwich for a combined fee of £2 million. They were intended to fill the gap in midfield left by the departure of Gordon Strachan to Leeds United for £300,000. Less mobile than the diminutive Scot, Webb created many chances for his teammates with his long passing. Unfortunately for Webb – and Alex Ferguson – his first season at Old Trafford was blighted by an injury he picked up while on international duty in Sweden in September 1989

Newcastle United. Viv Anderson had surgery on his back, Mike Duxbury was hospitalised because of a hernia and not surprisingly the manager was forced to buy, with Northern Ireland skipper Mal Donaghy ending a long career at Luton Town.

Ferguson's revamped youth system was paying dividends and talent was coming through.

One such player was just 17 years old when he made his First Division debut in the home game against West Ham. He had been bought by United at the end of the 1987-88 season after some Ferguson cloak and dagger work in Torquay. At the time United were involved in a two day Festival of Football at Wembley, one of the events during the 100th anniversary year of the Football League. The manager went missing from the team hotel and the following day confessed that he and Archie Knox had driven to the south coast to get their man:

I signed a young player last night who is the most expensive teenager I have ever bought but I'm sure he'll be worth every penny. His name is Lee Sharpe.

Sharpe himself recalls:

It was late one night and I was told by my manager, the late Cyril Knowles, that Manchester United wanted to sign me. I don't remember too much about the details only that I agreed to come to Old Trafford.

1980-89

Sharpe began his United career as a left full back as his new manager carefully guided him into top level football, but it was as a left sided attacking player that he made his name before injury slowed down his progress.

By the end of the 1988 season, Ferguson had used 23 players in 24 games.

Fergie's Fledglings

The arrival of Leighton eventually led to the departure of Chris Turner who moved to Wednesday in his native Sheffield, and the media was swift to emphasise signs that the Scottish 'keeper might be finding it difficult to adjust to the English game.

Leighton's confidence was dented in a much publicised incident when he dropped a harmless cross from Southampton's Graham Baker over his shoulder and into his own goal.

Statistics also showed a change of form and Leighton was under the microscope. In his first ten appearances he conceded just five goals, in the final ten matches of 1988 he was beaten on 11 occasions and had just three clean sheets.

But the goalkeeper alone was not to blame for United's slump in form. McClair and Hughes had not exactly struck gold up front.

In their first 25 games together Hughes scored 12 times but McClair had found himself restricted by his midfield role and had just eight goals to his credit. The previous season he had scored 16 in the same period.

United had been knocked out of the Littlewoods (League) Cup during a controversial game at Wimbledon's Plough Lane and many thought that a successful FA Cup run would be the season's only salvation. But the New Year's Day League clash with Liverpool gave some hope.

Martin was back in the side, and in his second League game for the club Russell Beardsmore, just out of his teens, gave a performance which overshadowed his more experienced colleagues. He scored one goal and helped McClair and Hughes to find the net as United won 3-1 to move to 6th in the League.

Within the next ten days more of "Fergie's Fledglings" emerged.

United were drawn at home to Queens Park Rangers in the Third Round of the FA Cup and at the last minute Ferguson found himself forced to make changes. Lee Sharpe had 'flu and Paul McGrath was withdrawn.

Mark Robins, a prolific goalscorer with the junior teams, was plunged into the side and two youngsters, Deiniol Graham and David Wilson found themselves on the substitutes' bench even though both had already played a game earlier on that morning.

The tie ended nil-nil.

For the replay four days later Sharpe had recovered and joined Beardsmore, Martin and Tony Gill in the starting line-up with Graham and Wilson on the bench.

A pulsating game went into extra-time after Gill equalised, then United took the lead when Wilson crossed and Graham stabbed the ball home only for Rangers to force a second replay with a late goal.

Eventually United reached the quarter final stages of the competition but lost at home to Nottingham Forest.

Strachan goes to Leeds

More young players were given an opportunity to make the grade as Alex Ferguson realised that United had little chance of gaining any honours.

Guiliano Maiorana, a Cambridge boy with Italian parents, made his full debut in a televised game against Arsenal, Robins had his League debut against Derby County and Gill delighted the home supporters with an exciting goal against Millwall just seven days after that strike at QPR.

But injuries devastated the "Fledglings".

Deiniol Graham badly broke his arm and eventually left the club, Tony Gill broke a leg in March 1989, an injury which ended his career, and young Maiorana so badly damaged his knee it took two years to recover. Gill's injury came in the week that the player he replaced had left the club.

Gordon Strachan was transferred to Leeds United for £300,000 moving to the Second Division club with the words:

My one wish now is that I can return to Old Trafford in the not too distant future as Leeds celebrate promotion to the First Division and United are the champions.

Who would have thought that within the next three years and with Strachan as captain, Leeds would not only achieve their target of promotion but would beat United to the championship!

The season ended with murmurings of unrest on the terraces. Ferguson's critics used the tabloid press as well as radio and television to snipe at the manager.

Not surprisingly he hit back refusing access to certain journalists and making it clear to former players and managers that they, and their comments were not welcome.

The Michael Knighton affair

Then came a period in the club's history when its activities off the field received as much publicity as those on it.

There was understandable optimism when, during the summer of 1989 Ferguson spent £2 million on Neil Webb from Nottingham Forest and Michael Phelan the Norwich City captain.

Left: Clayton Blackmore emerged to prominence during the 1988/89 season. However, he had a chequered career at Old Trafford and never really got a decent run in the team until the 1991/92 season

juggling act in front of the 47,000 gathered for the game against Arsenal, making it difficult to imagine that this was a man who 24 hours earlier had claimed to be quiet and shy!

The showbiz start rubbed off on the players who slammed new champions Arsenal 4-1 with Neil Webb having a dream debut and scoring ten minutes from time. Mark Hughes and Brian McClair also got onto the scoresheet following a Steve Bruce goal in the second minute.

Ferguson had been criticised for his summer selling of Norman Whiteside to Everton and Paul McGrath to Aston Villa but the victory helped to silence those who spoke out against the manager.

With the season three games old he spent again, a record £2.3 million on Gary Pallister of Middlesbrough.

In mid-September he completed the £2 million purchase of Paul Ince of West Ham after a medical snag and bought Danny Wallace the speedy winger from Southampton for £1.5 million, but only after seeing the injury jinx hit another of his players.

Neil Webb was carried off during a Sweden-England game in Gothenburg after rupturing his Achilles tendon and was ruled out for the next seven months.

By the time Webb played again Michael Knighton no longer made the headlines but our story of United in the 1980s ends by looking at the spectacular series of events which followed the announcement that he was taking control of the club.

But on the eve of the opening game of 1989-1990 news broke that businessman Michael Knighton was to buy the majority shareholding in the club. Chairman Martin Edwards called a press conference at Old Trafford and Knighton was introduced as a man who was ready to invest cash in the club. He eagerly outlined his plans, which included spending £10 million on the Stretford End. Knighton promised great things for the future of his new club:

Clearly this is a very big day in my life, but what I would like to say, and this is very important, Martin Edwards and myself have not just met, and it didn't just happen last night. We have reached a synergy together over the last six weeks, we've grown together as friends. I look forward to working with Alex Ferguson, he's got my 150 per cent support at the moment. I'm very anxious to make public from the outset that we intend completing this marvellous stadium we have at Old Trafford and making it literally one of the finest in the world . . . perhaps even the Mecca. Who knows? We've certainly got the legend to go with that. We will start immediately at the end of this season with the development of the Stretford End and certainly funds are in place to do that.

Knighton stole the headlines the following day when Old Trafford gave him a rapturous welcome as he performed a ball

In mid-September 1989, Ferguson extended his purchasing programme by paying West Ham £2 million for midfielder Paul Ince and Southampton £1.5 million for lightning winger Danny Wallace. Ince's career at Old Trafford began encouragingly enough on 16 September with a 5-1 demolition of Millwall. The following Saturday, however, Ince and United were swept aside by derby rivals Manchester City at Maine Road. The final score – 5-1 to City

Robert Maxwell v Michael Knighton

So began a 55 day guessing game which saw media moguls using all their big guns to shoot down a man they claimed was insignificant.

The trouble started for Michael Knighton when doubts were cast about his wealth. He had two months to come up with the capital to buy the Edwards shareholding and there were many who claimed he would fail.

The biggest campaign against him came from the *Daily Mirror*, the newspaper owned by Robert Maxwell whose efforts to take over United in January 1984 had themselves proved abortive.

A week after Knighton's arrival the *Manchester Evening News* printed a story naming two businessmen claiming to be providing Knighton's financial backing.

A relative of one of these men, Stanley Cohen, had allegedly told a neighbour that it was Cohen who was buying United and not Knighton, and from that tiny acorn . . .

The other alleged partner was Robert Thornton, chairman of Debenhams, who Knighton claimed was both his neighbour and friend.

By Friday 15 September the deal was said to be off because Cohen and Thornton had pulled out, but Knighton stunned his opponents by holding another Old Trafford press conference to announce that despite eveything that had been said, it was definitely on.

Aware of the Takeover Panel's rigid rules, newspaper publisher Eddie Shah claimed Knighton's representatives had approached him with documents which seemed to imply that control of the club was for sale. He had immediately contacted Martin Edwards and returned the dossier to him.

Edwards took out a high court injunction against Knighton to stop him approaching any other would-be buyers.

Within the United boardroom the directors were not happy with the situation and Amer Midani and Bobby Charlton openly said that they felt that the club should be floated on the Stock Market, with supporters investing.

Michael Edelson, Nigel Burrows, Maurice Watkins and Bobby Charlton held late night meetings at Old Trafford as newsmen waited outside. Then late on Tuesday, 10 October they streamed out of one such meeting and drove to the Midland Hotel (The Holiday Inn Crown Plaza) in the city centre.

In the hotel where Rolls met Royce the fate of Manchester United was decided.

On Wednesday, 11 October, 12 hours before the takeover deadline there was another press conference.

Rumour had it that Knighton had pulled out, unable to find the capital but he turned up, and faced the media flanked by Maurice Watkins, and Martin Edwards the man he had hoped to succeed.

The gathering was told that the contract under which M.K. Trafford Holdings (Knighton's company) was to buy the 50.6 per cent share-holding of Martin Edwards had been cancelled by mutual consent.

In return for withdrawing from the agreement Michael Knighton had been given a seat on the United board.

He firmly stood by his claim that he was ready to complete the takeover:

There was no question in anyone's mind and certainly not my mind that the funding was there to move ahead, and that the contract was legally watertight.

Had I been the incredibly selfish and mercenary character that some people claim I might be, then I would not be here today, I would be going along to my bank and placing very large deposits of money.

The Knighton affair had amazed the fans who found it hard to believe. As for the players perhaps the final word on the matter should come from Bryan Robson:

Obviously the players have been concerned about what has been happening during the take-over situation because it does affect us. But when people say to me that Manchester United has been dragged down into the gutter I can't agree. I think it all went on a long time and people made a lot of it because it was United.

SEASON 1980-1981 FOOTBALL LEAGUE (DIVISION 1)

Date	Opponent		Result												Substitutes
16 Aug	Middlesbrough	H	W	3-0	Bailey	Nicholl			...ov	Moran	Buchan M	Coppell	Greenhoff J	Jordan	Macari1	Thomas1	Grimes1 for Jordan
19 Aug	Wolverhampton W	A	L	0-1	Roche							Grimes		Coppell			Ritchie for Grimes
23 Aug	Birmingham C	A	D	0-0								McGrath	Coppell	Ritchie			Duxbury for Grimes
30 Aug	Sunderland	H	D	1-1	Bailey				Jovanovic1			Coppell	Greenhoff J				Duxbury for Moran
6 Sep	Tottenham H	A	L	0-0													
13 Sep	Leicester C	H	W	5-0								Grimes1		Coppell1	..1		Duxbury for Ritchie
20 Sep	Leeds U	A	D	0-0													McGarvey for Macari
27 Sep	Manchester C	H	C	2-2					..en					..1	Duxbury		Duxbury for Macari
4 Oct	Nottingham F	A	W	2-1					...vic	Moran	Duxbury	Coppell1	Jordan	Macari 1			Sloan for Duxbury
8 Oct	Aston Villa	H	C	3-3									..1				Greenhoff J for Macari
11 Oct	Arsenal	H	C	0-0								Grimes		Duxbury			
18 Oct	Ipswich T	A	D	1-1								Coppell	Duxbury	Macari			
22 Oct	Stoke C	A	W	2-1									Birtles	..1	..1		Duxbury for Jovanovic
25 Oct	Everton	H	W	2-0							Duxbury	..1		..1			
1 Nov	Crystal Palace	A	L	0-1					...novic	Moran							
8 Nov	Coventry C	H	D	0-0													Sloan for Jovanovic
12 Nov	Wolverhampton W	H	C	0-0						Moran	Duxbury						
15 Nov	Middlesbrough	A	D	1-1										..1			
22 Nov	Brighton	A	W	4-1				..1		Jovanovic	Moran			..2	Duxbury1		Grimes for Birtles
20 Nov	Southampton	H	C	1-1	Jovanovic					Moran	Duxbury			..1	Macari	Grimes	Whelan for Birtles
6 Dec	Norwich C	A	C	*2-2	Nicholl					Jovanovic	Buchan M	..1	Greenhoff J	..1		Duxbury	
13 Dec	Stoke C	H	C	2-2							Moran		Duxbury	..1		Thomas	
20 Dec	Arsenal	A	L	1-2									Moran	..1			
26 Dec	Liverpool	H	C	0-0													
27 Dec	W B A	A	L	1-3					..1					..1			
10 Jan	Brighton	H	W	2-1				Wilkins	McQueen1	Buchan M		Birtles		..1			Duxbury for Wilkins
28 Jan	Sunderland	A	L	0-2				Duxbury						..1			
31 Jan	Birmingham C	H	W	2-0									..1	..1			McIlroy for Thomas
7 Feb	Leicester C	A	L	0-1						Jovanovic							Wilkins for Jovanovic
17 Feb	Tottenham H	H	C	0-0						Moran			Wilkins	Birtles		McIlroy	
21 Feb	Manchester C	A	L	0-1													McGarvey for Duxbury
28 Feb	Leeds U	H	L	0-1				Wilkins					Birtles	Jordan			
7 Mar	Southampton	A	L	0-1												..1	
14 Mar	Aston Villa	A	C	3-3										..2			
18 Mar	Nottingham F	H	C	*1-1													Duxbury for McIlroy
21 Mar	Ipswich T	A	W	2-1		..1		Moran	McQueen						Duxbury	Thomas1	Macari for Nicholl
28 Mar	Everton	A	W	1-0											..1		Wilkins for Thomas
4 Apr	Crystal Palace	H	W	1-0		Duxbury1									Macari		
11 Apr	Coventry C	A	W	2-0											..2	Wilkins	
14 Apr	Liverpool	A	W	1-0								..1					
18 Apr	W B A	H	W	2-1											..1	..1	
25 Apr	Norwich C	H	W	1-0											..1		

FA Cup
Date	Opponent		Result												Substitutes
3 Jan	Brighton (3)	H	D	2-2	Bailey	Nicholl	Albiston	McIlroy	Jovanovic	Moran	Coppell	Birtles	Jordan	Macari	Thomas1	Duxbury1 for McIlroy
7 Jan	Brighton (3R)	A	W	2-0		..1		Wilkins	McQueen	Buchan M		..1				Duxbury for Wilkins
24 Jan	Nottingham F (4)	A	L	0-1												

League Cup
Date	Opponent		Result												Substitutes
27 Aug	Coventry C (2)	H	L	0-1	Bailey	Nicholl	Albiston	McIlroy	Jovanovic	Buchan M	Coppell	Greenhoff J	Ritchie	Macari	Thomas	Sloan for Greenhoff J
2 Sep	Coventry C (2)	A	L	0-1												

UEFA Cup
Date	Opponent		Result												Substitutes
17 Sep	Widzew Lodz (1)	H	D	1-1	Bailey	Nicholl	Albiston	McIlroy1	Jovanovic	Buchan M	Grimes	Greenhoff J	Coppell	Macari	Thomas	Duxbury for Nicholl
1 Oct	Widzew Lodz (1)	A	D	0-0								Coppell	Jordan	Duxbury		Moran for Buchan M

Appearances (goals)

Albiston 42 (1) – Bailey 40 – Birtles 25 – Buchan M 26 – Copell 42 (6) – Duxbury 27 (2) – Greenhoff J 8 – Grimes 6 (2) – Jordan 33 (15) – Jovanovic 19 (4) – Macari 37 (9) – McGrath 1 – McIlroy 31(5) – McQueen 11(2) – Moran 32 – Nicholl 36 (1) – Ritchie 3 – Roche 2 – Thomas 30 (2) – Wilkins 11 – Own goals 2 – **Total 20 players (51)**

Football League
	P	W	D	L	F:A	Pts	
Aston Villa	42	26	8	8	72:40	60	1st
Manchester U	42	15	18	9	51:36	48	8th

SEASON 1981-1982 FOOTBALL LEAGUE (DIVISION 1)

Date	Opponent		Result												Substitutes
29 Aug	Coventry C	A	L	1-2	Bailey	Gidman	Albiston	Wilkins	McQueen	Buchan M	Coppell	Birtles	Stapleton	Macari1	McIlroy	
31 Aug	Nottingham F	H	D	0-0												
5 Sep	Ipswich T	H	L	1-2										..1		Duxbury for McIlroy
12 Sep	Aston Villa	A	D	1-1										..1		
19 Sep	Swansea	H	W	1-0								..1				Moses for McIlroy
22 Sep	Middlesbrough	A	W	2-0								..1	..1		Moses	Duxbury for Buchan M
26 Sep	Arsenal	A	D	0-0												
30 Sep	Leeds U	H	W	1-0									..1	McIlroy		Duxbury for McQueen
3 Oct	Wolverhampton W	H	W	5-0					Moran			..1	..1	..3		
10 Oct	Manchester C	A	D	0-0						Robson						Coppell for Birtles
17 Oct	Birmingham C	H	D	1-1									Moses	Coppell1		
21 Oct	Middlesbrough	H	W	1-0					Duxbury					..1		
24 Oct	Liverpool	A	W	2-1				..1	Moran1							
31 Oct	Notts Co	H	W	2-1					Duxbury		..1			..1		
7 Nov	Sunderland	A	W	5-1					Moran1		..1	..1	..2			Macari for Robson
21 Nov	Tottenham H	A	L	1-3	Roche	Duxbury					..1	..1			McIlroy	Duxbury for Gidman
28 Nov	Brighton	H	W	2-0		Gidman				McQueen		..1	..1			Nicholl for Buchan M
5 Dec	Southampton	A	D	2-3							..1					
6 Jan	Everton	H	D	1-1	Bailey					Buchan M	McGarvey	..1	McIlroy	Coppell		
23 Jan	Stoke C	A	W	3-0		Duxbury				McQueen		Birtles1	..1	Macari	..1	
27 Jan	West Ham U	H	W	1-0										..1		
30 Jan	Swansea	A	L	0-2												
6 Feb	Aston Villa	H	W	4-1		Gidman			..2	Buchan M	..1			Duxbury	..1	Gidman for McQueen
13 Feb	Wolverhampton W	A	W	1-0								..1				McGarvey for Birtles
20 Feb	Arsenal	H	D	0-0												
27 Feb	Manchester C	H	D	1-1					..1							
6 Mar	Birmingham C	A	W	1-0								..1				
17 Mar	Coventry C	H	L	0-1									Moses			McGarvey for Moran
20 Mar	Notts Co	A	W	3-1										..1	..2	Duxbury for Robson
27 Mar	Sunderland	H	D	0-0					McQueen							McGarvey for Moran
3 Apr	Leeds U	A	D	0-0		Duxbury			Moran		McGarvey					McGarvey for Birtles
7 Apr	Liverpool	H	L	0-1												
10 Apr	Everton	H	D	3-3		Gidman				Duxbury					..2	Grimes for Buchan M
12 Apr	W B A	H	W	1-0						McQueen				Grimes		Grimes 1 for Moses
17 Apr	Tottenham H	H	W	2-0								..1				
20 Apr	Ipswich T	A	L	1-2		..1									Duxbury	
24 Apr	Brighton	H	W	1-0					..1							Birtles for Wilkins
1 May	Southampton	H	W	1-0					Duxbury			..1			Davies	Whiteside for Duxbury
5 May	Nottingham F	A	W	1-0					Moran	Duxbury			..1		Coppell	
8 May	West Ham U	A	D	1-1					..1		Moses	Birtles				McGarvey for Birtles
12 May	W B A	A	W	3-0					McQueen	Robson1	..1				..1	
15 May	Stoke C	H	W	2-0							..1		Whiteside1			McGarvey for Birtles

FA Cup
Date	Opponent		Result												Substitutes
2 Jan	Watford (3)	A	L	0-1	Bailey	Gidman	Albiston	Wilkins	Moran	Buchan M	Robson	Birtles	Stapleton	Moses	McIlroy	Macari for Moses

Milk Cup
Date	Opponent		Result												Substitutes
7 Oct	Tottenham H (2)	A	L	0-1	Bailey	Gidman	Albiston	Wilkins	Moran	Buchan M	Coppell	Birtles	Stapleton	McIlroy	Robson	Duxbury for Birtles
28 Oct	Tottenham H (2)	H	L	0-1							Robson			Moses	Coppell	

Appearances (goals)

Albiston 42 (1) – Bailey 39 – Birtles 32 (11) – Buchan M 27 – Coppell 35 (9) – Davies 1 – Duxbury 19 – Gidman 35 (1) – Grimes 9 (1) – Macari 10 (2) – McGarvey 10 (2) – McIlroy 12 (3) – McQueen 21 – Moran 30 (7) – Moses 20 (2) – Robson 32 (5) – Roche 3 – Stapleton 41 (13) – Whiteside 11 – Wilkins 42 (1) – **Total 20 players 59**

Football League
	P	W	D	L	F:A	Pts	
Liverpool	42	26	9	7	80:32	87	1st
Manchester U	42	22	12	8	59:29	78	3rd

Abbreviations:

Appearances (goals) refer to League games only

Figures shown as 2 etc. refer to goals scored by individual players

***** own-goal

Players' names in final column, are substitutes

SEASON 1982-1983 FOOTBALL LEAGUE (DIVISION 1)

Date	Opponent	V	R	Score	Bailey	Duxbury	Albiston	Wilkins	Moran	McQueen	Robson	Muhren	Stapleton	Whiteside	Coppell	Subs / Notes
28 Aug	Birmingham C	H	W	3-0	Bailey	Duxbury	Albiston	Wilkins	Moran1	McQueen	Robson	Muhren	Stapleton1	Whiteside	Coppell1	
1 Sep	Nottingham F	A	W	3-0	..	..	..	..1	..	..	..1	..	..	..1	..	
4 Sep	W B A	A	L	1-3	..	..	..	..	..	..	..1	..	..	..	..	
8 Sep	Everton	H	W	2-1	..	..	..	..	..	..	..	..	..	..1	..	
11 Sep	Ipswich T	H	W	3-1	..	..	..	..	..	..	..	..	..	..2	..1	
18 Sep	Southampton	A	W	1-0	..	..	..	..	Buchan M	..	..	Grimes	..	..		Macari1 for Coppell
25 Sep	Arsenal	H	U	0-0	..	..	..	..	Moran	..	..	..	..	..	Macari	
2 Oct	Luton T	A	D	1-1	..	..	..	..	..	..	..1	..1	..	..	Moses	
9 Oct	Stoke C	H	W	1-0	..	..	..	..	..	..	..	..	..	..	Coppell	
16 Oct	Liverpool	A	D	0-0	..	..	..	..	..	..	..	..	..	..	..	
23 Oct	Manchester C	H	U	2-2	..	..	..	..	..	..	..	Muhren	..2	..	..	Macari for Muhren
30 Oct	West Ham U	A	L	1-3	..	..	..	Grimes	..1	Buchan M	..	..	..	..	..	Macari for Moran
6 Nov	Brighton	A	L	0-1	..	..	..	Moses	Moran	McQueen	..	..	..	..	..	
13 Nov	Tottenham H	H	W	1-0	..	..	..	..	McGrath	..	..1	..	..	..	..	
20 Nov	Aston Villa	A	L	1-2	..	..	..	..	Moran	..	..	..1	..	..	..	McGarvey for Whiteside
27 Nov	Norwich C	H	W	3-0	..	..	..	..	..	..	..2	..1	..	..	..	
4 Dec	Watford	A	W	1-0	..	..	..	..	Buchan M	..	..1	..	..	..	..	
11 Dec	Notts Co	H	W	4-0	..	..1	..	..	Moran	..	..1	..	..1	..1	..	Grimes for Robson
18 Dec	Swansea	A	D	0-0	..	..	..	..	..	..	..	..	..	..	..	
27 Dec	Sunderland	H	D	0-0	..	..	..	..	..	..	..	..	..	..	..	
28 Dec	Coventry C	A	L	0-3	..	..	..	..	..	..	Wilkins	Muhren	McGarvey	Grimes	..	
1 Jan	Aston Villa	H	W	3-1	..	..	..	..	..	..	..	Muhren	..2	Whiteside	Coppell1	
3 Jan	W B A	H	D	0-0	..	..	..	..	..	..	..	..	..	..	..	
15 Jan	Birmingham C	A	W	2-1	..	..	..	..	..	..	..1	..	..	..	..1	
22 Jan	Nottingham F	H	W	2-0	..	..	..	..	..	..	..	..1	..	..	..1	
5 Feb	Ipswich T	A	D	1-1	..	..	..	..	..	..	..	..	..1	..	..	
26 Feb	Liverpool	H	D	1-1	..	..	..	..	..	..	Wilkins	..1	..	..	..	Macari for Moran
2 Mar	Stoke C	A	L	0-1	..	..	..	..	McGrath	..	..	..	..	..	..	
5 Mar	Manchester	A	W	2-1	..	..	..	..	..	..	..	..	..2	..	..	
19 Mar	Brighton	H	D	1-1	..	Gidman	..1	Grimes	..	Duxbury	..	..	..	..	..	Macari for Wilkins
22 Mar	West Ham U	H	W	2-1	..	..	..	Moses	..	..	..	..	..1	McGarvey1	..	Macari for Stapleton
2 Apr	Coventry C	H	W	*3-0	Wealands	Duxbury	..	..	..	McQueen	..	..	..1	Whiteside	Macari	Macari1 for Whiteside
4 Apr	Sunderland	A	D	0-0	..	..	..	..	..	..	..	..	..	Macari	..	MoGarvey for Macari
9 Apr	Southampton	H	D	1-1	Bailey	..	..	..	..	..	Robson1	..	..	Whiteside	Wilkins	
19 Apr	Everton	A	L	0-2	Wealands	..	..	..	..	..	..	Wilkins	..	..	Grimes1	Cunningham for Whiteside
23 Apr	Watford	H	W	2-0	Wealands	..	..	..	..	..	..	..	..	..	Cunningham	Cunningham1 for Albiston
30 Apr	Norwich C	A	D	1-1	Bailey	..	Grimes	..	Moran	..	McGrath	..	McGarvey	..1	Cunningham	
2 May	Arsenal	A	L	0-3	..	..	..	..	..	..	McGrath	..	McGarvey	..	..	
7 May	Swansea	H	W	2-1	..	..	..	Wilkins	..	..	Robson1	Muhren	Stapleton1	..	..	Davies for Muhren
9 May	Luton T	H	W	3-0	..	..	..	McGrath2	..	..	..	..	..1	..	Davies	McGarvey for Whiteside
11 May	Tottenham H	A	L	0-2	..	..	Albiston	Moses	..	McGrath	..	..	..	Grimes	Davies	
14 May	Notts Co	A	L	2-3	Wealands	Gidman	..	..	McGrath1	Duxbury	Wilkins	..	..1	..	Davies	McGarvey for Robson

FA Cup

Date	Opponent	V	R	Score	Bailey	Duxbury	Albiston	Wilkins	Moran	McQueen	Robson	Muhren	Stapleton	Whiteside	Coppell	Subs / Notes
8 Jan	West Ham U (3)	H	W	2-0	Bailey	Duxbury	Albiston	Moses	Moran	McQueen	Robson	Muhren	Stapleton1	Whiteside	Coppell1	
29 Jan	Luton T (4)	A	W	2-0	..	..	..	..1	..1	..	..	..	..	..	..	
19 Feb	Derby Co (5)	A	W	1-0	..	..	..	..	..	..	..	..	..	..1	..	
12 Mar	Everton (6)	H	W	1-0	..	..	..	..	..	..	Wilkins	..	..1	..	..	Macari for Duxbury
16 Apr	Arsenal (SF) (at Villa Park)	N	W	2-1	..	..	..	..	..	..	Robson1	Wilkins	..1	Grimes	..	McGrath for Moran
21 May	Brighton (F) (at Wembley)	N	D	2-2	..	..	..	Wilkins1	..	..	..	Muhren	..1	Davies	..	
26 May	Brighton (FR) (at Wembley)	N	W	4-0	..	..	..	..	..	..	..2	..1	..	..1	..	

Milk Cup

Date	Opponent	V	R	Score	Bailey	Duxbury	Albiston	Wilkins	Moran	McQueen	Robson	Muhren/Grimes	Stapleton	Whiteside	Coppell/Moses	Subs / Notes
6 Oct	Bournemouth (2)	H	W	*2-0	Bailey	Duxbury	Albiston	Wilkins	Moran	McQueen	Robson	Grimes	Stapleton1	Beardsley	Moses	Whiteside for Beardsley
26 Oct	Bournemouth (2)	A	D	2-2	..	..	..	..	Grimes	Buchan M	..	Muhren1	..	Whiteside	Coppell1	Macari for Wilkins
10 Nov	Bradford C (3)	A	D	0-0	..	..	..	Moses	McGrath	McQueen	..	..	..	..	..	
24 Nov	Bradford C (3R)	H	W	4-1	..	..	..1	..1	Moran1	..	..	..	..	Macari	..1	Whiteside for Coppell
1 Dec	Southampton (4)	H	W	2-0	..	..	..	..	..	..1	..	..	..	Whiteside1	..	
19 Jan	Nottingham F (5)	H	W	4-0	..	..	..	..	..1	..	..2	..	..	..	..1	
15 Feb	Arsenal (SF)	A	W	4-2	..	..	..	..	..	..	..	..	..1	..1	..2	
23 Feb	Arsenal (SF)	H	W	2-1	..	..	..	..	..1	..	..	..	..	..	..1	Wilkins for Robson
26 Mar	Liverpool (F) (at Wembley)	N	L	1-2	..	..	..	..	..	..	Wilkins	..	..	..1	..	

UEFA Cup

Date	Opponent	V	R	Score	Bailey	Duxbury	Albiston	Wilkins	Moran	McQueen	Robson	Grimes	Stapleton	Whiteside	Coppell	Subs / Notes
15 Sep	Valencia (1)	H	D	0-0	Bailey	Duxbury	Albiston	Wilkins	Buchan M	McQueen	Robson	Grimes	Stapleton	Whiteside	Coppell	
29 Oct	Valencia (1)	A	L	1-2	..	..	..	..	Moran	Buchan M	..	..	..1	..	Moses	Coppell for Moses, Macari for Buchan M

Appearances (goals)

Albiston 38 (1) – Bailey 37 – Buchan M 3 – Coppell 29 (4) – Cunningham 3 (1) – Davies 2 – Duxbury 42 (1) – Gidman 3 – Grimes 15 (2) – Macari 2 (2) – McGarvey 3 (1) – McGrath 14 (3) – McQueen 37 – Moran 29 (2) – Moses 29 – Muhren 32 (5) – Robson 33 (10) – Stapleton 41 (14) – Wealands 5 – Whiteside 39 (8) – Wilkins 26 (1) – Own goals 1 – **Total 21 players (56)**

Football League

	P	W	D	L	F:A	Pts	
Liverpool	42	24	10	8	87:37	82	1st
Manchester U	42	19	13	10	56:38	70	3rd

SEASON 1983-1984 FOOTBALL LEAGUE (DIVISION 1)

Date	Opponent	V	R	Score	Bailey	Duxbury	Albiston	Wilkins	Moran	McQueen	Robson	Muhren	Stapleton	Whiteside	Graham	Subs / Notes
27 Aug	Q P R	H	W	3-1	Bailey	Duxbury	Albiston	Wilkins	Moran	McQueen	Robson	Muhren2	Stapleton1	Whiteside	Graham	Macari for Whiteside
29 Aug	Nottingham F	H	L	1-2	..	..	..	..	..1	..1	..	..	..	..	..	Macari for Duxbury
3 Sep	Stoke C	A	W	1-0	..	Gidman	..	..	..	..	..	..	..	..	..	
6 Sep	Arsenal	A	W	3-2	..	..	..	..	..1	..	..1	..	..1	..	..	Moses for Graham
10 Sep	Luton T	H	W	2-0	..	..	..1	..	..	..	..	..1	..	..	..	Moses for Robson
17 Sep	Southampton	A	L	0-3	..	Duxbury	..	..	..	..	Moses	..	..	..	..	
24 Sep	Liverpool	H	W	1-0	..	..	..	..	..	..	Robson	..	..1	..	..	
1 Oct	Norwich C	A	D	3-3	..	..	..	..	..	McGrath	..	..	..1	..2	..	Moses for Muhren
15 Oct	W B A	H	W	3-2	..	..	..1	..	..	McQueen	..	..	..	..1	..1	
22 Oct	Sunderland	A	W	1-0	..	..	..	..1	..	..	..	Moses	..	..	..	Macari for McQueen
29 Oct	Wolverhampton W	A	W	3-0	..	Gidman	..	..	Duxbury	..	..1	Muhren	..2	..	..	Moses for Gidman
5 Nov	Aston Villa	H	L	1-2	..	..	..	..	Moran	..	..1	Moses	..	..	..	Macari for Whiteside
12 Nov	Leicester C	A	D	1-1	..	..	..	..	..	..	..1	..	..	..	..	
19 Nov	Watford	H	W	4-1	..	Moses	..	..	Duxbury	..	..1	Muhren	..	..3	Crooks	
27 Nov	West Ham U	A	D	1-1	..	..	..	..1	..	..	..	..	..	..	..	Whiteside for Muhren
3 Dec	Everton	H	L	0-1	..	Duxbury	..	..	Moran	..	..	Moses	..	..	Whiteside	
10 Dec	Ipswich T	A	W	2-0	..	..	..	..	..	..	..	Moses	..	..1	Graham1	
16 Dec	Tottenham H	H	W	4-2	..	Moses	..	..	..	..	..2	Duxbury	Muhren	Whiteside	..2	Macari for Stapleton
26 Dec	Coventry C	A	D	1-1	..	Duxbury	..	..	..	..	McQueen	Moses	..1	Crooks	..	
27 Dec	Notts Co	H	D	3-3	Wealands	..	..	..	..	..	..	..	..1	..1	..1	Whiteside for Crooks
31 Dec	Stoke City	A	W	1-0	..	..	..	..	..	..	..	..	..	Whiteside	..1	
2 Jan	Liverpool	A	D	1-1	Bailey	..	..	..	..	..	..	..	..	..	..1	Crooks for McQueen
13 Jan	Q P R	A	D	1-1	..	..	..	Moses	..	..	Hogg	Robson1	..	..	..	Hughes for Whiteside
21 Jan	Southampton	H	W	3-2	..	..	..	..	..	..	..1	..1	..1	..	..	Graham for Robson
4 Feb	Norwich C	H	D	0-0	..	Moses	Albiston	..	..	..	Duxbury	..	..	..	..	Graham for Wilkins
7 Feb	Birmingham C	A	D	2-2	..	Duxbury	..	..	..	..	Hogg1	Moses	..	..1	..	Graham for Moran
12 Feb	Luton T	A	W	5-0	..	..	..	..	..	..	..	..2	Muhren	..2	Moses	Graham for Robson
18 Feb	Wolverhampton W	A	D	1-1	..	..	..	..	..	..	..	..	..1	..	..	Graham for Wilkins
25 Feb	Sunderland	H	W	2-1	..	..	..	..	..2	..	..	..	..	..	..	Graham for Moran
3 Mar	Aston Villa	A	W	3-0	..	..	..	..	McGrath	..	..1	..	..	..1	..1	Graham for Whiteside
10 Mar	Leicester C	H	W	2-0	..	..	..	..	Moran	..	..	..	..	Hughes1	..1	Hughes for Whiteside
17 Mar	Arsenal	H	W	4-0	..	..	..	..	..	..	..1	..2	..	Whiteside	..	Hughes for Whiteside
31 Mar	W B A	A	L	0-2	..	..	..	..	..	..	..	Graham	..	..	..	Graham for Robson
7 Apr	Birmingham C	H	W	1-0	..	..	..	..	..	..	..1	..	..	..	..	Hughes for Whiteside
14 Apr	Notts Co	A	L	0-1	..	..	..	..	..	McGrath	Moses	..	..	..	Davies	Hughes for Davies
17 Apr	Watford	A	L	0-1	..	..	..	..	..	Davies	McGrath	..	..	..	Graham	
21 Apr	Coventry C	H	W	4-1	..	..	..	..1	..	..	McGrath1	Moses	..	Hughes2	..	Whiteside for Wilkins
28 Apr	West Ham U	H	D	0-0	..	..	..	..	..	..	..	..	..	..	..	Whiteside for McGrath
5 May	Everton	A	D	1-1	..	..	..	..	..	..	Robson	..	..1	..	Davies	Whiteside for Davies
7 May	Ipswich	H	L	1-2	..	..	..	..	McGrath	..	..	..	..1	..	Graham	Whiteside1 for Stapleton
12 May	Tottenham H	A	D	1-1	..	..	..	..	..	..	..	..	..	..	..	Whiteside for Graham
16 May	Nottingham F	A	L	0-2	..	..	..	..	..	..	..	Blackmore	..	..	..	

FA Cup

Date	Opponent														Substitutes
7 Jan	Bournemouth (3)	A	L	0-2	Bailey	Moses	Albiston	Wilkins	Hogg	Duxbury	Robson	Muhren	Stapleton	Whiteside	Graham	Macari for Albiston

Milk Cup

Date	Opponent															Substitutes
3 Oct	Port Vale (2)	A	W	1-0	Bailey	Duxbury	Albiston	Wilkins	Moran	McGrath	Robson	Muhren	Stapleton1	Whiteside	Graham	Moses for Duxbury
26 Oct	Port Vale (2)	H	W	2-0	..	Gidman	..	..1	Duxbury	McQueen	..	Moses	..	..1	..	Hughes for Whiteside
8 Nov	Colchester U (3)	A	W	2-0	..	Duxbury	..	..	Moran	..1	..	..1	..	..	..	Macari for Whiteside
30 Nov	Oxford U (4)	A	D	1-1	..	..	..	..	..	..	..	..	..	Hughes1		
7 Dec	Oxford U (4R)	H	D	1-1	..	..	..	..	..	..	..	..	..1	Graham		
19 Dec	Oxford U (4R)	A	L	1-2	Wealands	Moses	..	..	..	Duxbury	..	Muhren	..	..1		Macari for Robson

European Cup-Winners' Cup

Date	Opponent															Substitutes
14 Sep	Dukla Prague (1)	H	D	1-1	Bailey	Duxbury	Albiston	Wilkins1	Moran	McQueen	Robson	Muhren	Stapleton	Macari	Graham	Moses for Muhren Gidman for Robson
27 Sep	Dukla Prague (1)	A	D	2-2	..	..	..	..	..	..	..1	..	..1	Whiteside		
19 Oct	Spartak Varna (2)	A	W	2-1	..	..	..	..	..	..	..1	..	..	..	..1	
2 Nov	Spartak Varna (2)	H	W	2-0	..	..	..	Moses	..	..	..	Macari	..2	..		Dempsey for Moran, Hughes for Whiteside
7 Mar	Barcelona (3)	A	L	0-2	..	..	..	Wilkins	..	Hogg	..	Muhren	..	Hughes	Moses	
21 Mar	Barcelona (3)	H	W	3-0	..	..	..	..	..	..	..2	..	..1	Whiteside	..	Hughes for Whiteside
11 Apr	Juventus (SF)	H	D	1-1	..	..	..	McGrath	..	..	Graham	Moses	..	..	Gidman	Davies1 for Gidman
26 Apr	Juventus (SF)	A	L	1-2	..	..	..	Wilkins	..	..	McGrath	..	..	Hughes	Graham	Whiteside1 for Stapleton

Appearances (goals)

Albiston 40 (2) – Bailey 40 – Blackmore 1 – Crooks 6 (2) – Davies 3 – Duxbury 39 – Gidman 4 – Graham 33 (5) – Hogg 16 (1) – Hughes 7 (4) – McGrath 9 (1) – McQueen 20 (1) – Moran 38 (7) – Moses 31(2) – Muhren 26 – Robson 33 (12) – Stapleton 42 (13) – Wealands 2 – Whiteside 30 (10) – Wilkins 42 (3) – **Total 20 players (71)**

Football League

	P	W	D	L	F:A	Pts	
Liverpool	42	22	14	6	73:32	80	1st
Manchester U	42	20	14	8	71:41	74	4th

SEASON 1984-1985 FOOTBALL LEAGUE (DIVISION 1)

Date	Opponent															Substitutes
25 Aug	Watford	H	D	1-1	Bailey	Duxbury	Albiston	Moses	Moran	Hogg	Robson	Strachan1	Hughes	Brazil	Olsen	Whiteside for Brazil
28 Aug	Southampton	A	D	0-0	..	..	..	..	..	..	..	..	..1	..	..	
1 Sep	Ipswich T	A	D	1-1	..	..	..	..	..	..	..	..	..1	..	..	Whiteside for Brazil
5 Sep	Chelsea	H	D	1-1	..	..	..	..	..	..	..	..	..	Whiteside	..1	
8 Sep	Newcastle U	H	W	5-0	..	..	..	..1	..	..	..	..2	..1	..	..1	
15 Sep	Coventry C	A	W	3-0	..	..	..	..	..	..	..1	..	..	..2	..	
22 Sep	Liverpool	H	D	1-1	..	..	..	..	..	..	..	..1	..	..	..	Muhren for Moran
29 Sep	W B A	A	W	2-1	..	..	..(/)	..	..	..	..1	..1	..	Brazil	..	
6 Oct	Aston Villa	A	L	0-3	..	..	..	..	..	..	Strachan	Muhren	..	..	..	
13 Oct	West Ham U	H	W	5-1	..	..	Gidman	..1	McQueen1	..	Robson	Strachan	..1	..1	..	
20 Oct	Tottenham H	H	W	1-0	..	..	..	..	Moran	..	..	..	..1	..	..	
27 Oct	Everton	A	L	0-5	..	Moran	..	..	McQueen	..	..	..	..	..	..	Stapleton for Moran
2 Nov	Arsenal	H	W	4-2	..	Gidman	..	..	Moran	..1	..2	..1	Stapleton	..		
10 Nov	Leicester C	A	W	3-2	..	..	..	..	Garton	..	..1	..1	Brazil1	..		Whiteside for Olsen
17 Nov	Luton T	H	W	2-0	..	..	..	..	McQueen	Duxbury	..	..	Whiteside2	..		Stapleton for Robson
24 Nov	Sunderland	A	L	2-3	..	..	Duxbury	..	Garton	..1	..	..1	..	..		Muhren for Olsen
1 Dec	Norwich C	H	W	2-0	..	..	..	..	..	McGrath	..1	..	..1	..		
8 Dec	Nottingham F	A	L	2-3	..	Duxbury	Blackmore	..	..	..	..2	Stapleton	Brazil	Muhren		
15 Dec	Q P R	H	W	3-0	..	Gidman1	Albiston	..	..	Duxbury1	..	..	..1	Olsen		
22 Dec	Ipswich T	H	W	3-0	..	..1	..	..	..	..	..1	Hughes	Stapleton	..		
26 Dec	Stoke C	A	L	1-2	..	..	..	..1	..	..	..	..	..	Muhren		Brazil for Strachan
29 Dec	Chelsea	A	W	3-1	..	Duxbury	..	..1	McGrath	..	..	Stapleton1	Hughes1	Brazil		Brazil for Robson
1 Jan	Sheffield Wed	H	L	1-2	..	..	..	..	..	..	..	Hughes1	Brazil	..		
12 Jan	Coventry C	H	L	0-1	Pears	..	..	..	..	..	..	Stapleton	Hughes	..		Brazil for Robson
2 Feb	W B A	H	W	2-0	..	Gidman	..	..	Moran	Hogg	McGrath	..2	Hughes	Whiteside	Olsen	Stapleton for Olsen
9 Feb	Newcastle U	A	D	1-1	..	..	..	..	..1	..	..	..	..	Stapleton	..	Whiteside1 for Moran
23 Feb	Arsenal	A	W	1-0	Bailey	..	..	Duxbury	..	..	Strachan	Brazil	..	Stapleton	..	
2 Mar	Everton	H	D	1-1	..	..	..	..	McGrath	..	Strachan	Whiteside	..	..1		
12 Mar	Tottenham H	A	W	2-1	..	..	..	..	..	..	Whiteside1	..1	Stapleton	..		
15 Mar	West Ham U	A	D	2-2	..	..	..	..	..	..	Robson	Strachan	..1	..		Robson1 for Whiteside
23 Mar	Aston Villa	H	W	4-0	..	..	..	Whiteside1	..	..	Robson	Strachan	..3	..		
31 Mar	Liverpool	A	W	1-0	..	..	..	..	..	..	..	..	..1	..		
3 Apr	Leicester C	H	W	2-1	..	..	..	..	..	..	..1	..	..1	..		
6 Apr	Stoke C	H	W	5-0	..	..	..	..1	..	..	..	..2	..	..2		Duxbury for Robson
9 Apr	Sheffield Wed	A	L	0-1	Pears	..	..	Duxbury	..	..	..	..	..	..		Brazil for Duxbury
21 Apr	Luton T	A	L	1-2	Bailey	..	..	Whiteside1	..	..	Muhren	..	..	..		Duxbury for Stapleton
24 Apr	Southampton	H	D	0-0	..	..	..	..	..	..	Strachan	..	..	..		Duxbury for Gidman
27 Apr	Sunderland	H	D	2-2	..	..	..	..	Moran1	..1	..	..	Brazil	..		
4 May	Norwich C	A	W	1-0	..	..	..	..	..	..1	..	..	Stapleton	..		Muhren for Moran
6 May	Nottingham F	H	W	2-0	..	..1	..	..	Moran	Hogg	McGrath	..	Stapleton	Brazil	..	Muhren for Hogg
11 May	Q P R	A	W	3-1	..	..	..	..	McGrath	..	Duxbury	..1	..	..2		Muhren for Whiteside
13 May	Watford	A	L	1-5	..	..	..	..	Moran1	..	..	..	Hughes	Stapleton	Brazil	

FA Cup

Date	Opponent															Substitutes
5 Jan	Bournemouth (3)	H	W	3-0	Bailey	Duxbury	Albiston	Moses	McQueen1	McGrath	Robson	Strachan1	Stapleton1	Hughes	Muhren	
26 Jan	Coventry C (4)	H	W	2-1	Pears	Gidman	..	..	Moran	Hogg	McGrath1	Whiteside	..1	Brazil	Olsen	Brazil for Hughes
15 Feb	Blackburn R (5)	A	W	2-0	Bailey	..	..	..	..	..	..1	..1	Hughes	Whiteside	..	
9 Mar	West Ham U (6)	H	W	4-2	..	..	..	Duxbury	McGrath	..	Strachan	Whiteside3	..1	Stapleton	..	
13 Apr	Liverpool (SF) (at Goodison Park)	N	D	2-2	..	..	..	Whiteside	..	..	Robson	Strachan	..1	..1	..	
17 Apr	Liverpool (SFR) (at Maine Road)	N	W	2-1	..	..	..	..	..	..	..1	..	..1	..	..	
18 May	Everton (F)† (at Wembley) †after extra time	N	W	1-0	..	..	..	..1	Moran	..1	..	..	..	..		Duxbury for Albiston

Milk Cup

Date	Opponent															Substitutes
26 Sep	Burnley (2)	H	W	4-0	Bailey	Duxbury	Albiston	Moses	Garton	Hogg	Robson1	Graham	Hughes3	Whiteside	Muhren	Brazil for Whiteside
9 Oct	Burnley (2)	A	W	3-0	..	..	..	..	Moran	..	Strachan	Blackmore	Stapleton	Brazil2	Olsen1	
30 Oct	Everton (3)	H	L	1-2	..	Gidman	..	..	..	..	Robson	Strachan	Hughes	..1	..	Stapleton for Olsen

UEFA Cup

Date	Opponent															Substitutes
19 Sep	Raba Gyor(1)	H	W	3-0	Bailey	Duxbury	Albiston	Moses	Moran	Hogg	Robson1	Muhren1	Hughes1	Whiteside	Olsen	
3 Oct	Raba Gyor (1)	A	D	2-2	..	..	..	..	..	..	..	..1	..	Brazil1	..	Gidman for Robson
24 Oct	Eindhoven (2)	A	D	0-0	..	Gidman	..	..	..	..	..	Strachan	..	..		Garton for Moran, Whiteside for Stapleton
7 Nov	Eindhoven (2)	H	W	1-0	..	..	..	..	..	..	..	..1	..	Stapleton	..	Stapleton for Whiteside
28 Nov	Dundee U (3)	H	D	2-2	..	..	..	..	McQueen	Duxbury	..1	..1	..	Whiteside	..	
12 Dec	Dundee U (3)	A	W	*3-2	..	..	..	..	..	..	..	..	Stapleton	Hughes1	Muhren1	
6 Mar	Videoton (4)	H	W	1-0	..	..	..	Duxbury	McGrath	Hogg	Strachan	Whiteside	Hughes	Stapleton1	Olsen	
20 Mar	Videoton (4) (4-5 pens after extra time)	A	L	0-1	..	..	..	..	..	..	Robson	Strachan	..	..	Whiteside	Olsen for Robson

Appearances (goals)

Albiston 39 – Bailey 38 – Blackmore 1 – Brazil 17 (5) – Duxbury 27 (1) – Garton 2 – Gidman 27 (3) – Hogg 29 – Hughes 38 (16) – McGrath P 23 – McQueen 12 (1) – Moran 19 (4) – Moses R 26 (3) – Muhren 7 – Olsen 36 (5) – Pears 4 – Robson 32 (9) – Stapleton 21(6) – Strachan 41(15) – Whiteside 23 (9) – **Total 20 players (77)**

Football League

	P	W	D	L	F:A	Pts	
Everton	42	26	6	8	88:43	90	1st
Manchester U	42	22	10	10	77:47	76	4th

SEASON 1985-1986 FOOTBALL LEAGUE (DIVISION 1)

Date	Opp			Score	1	2	3	4	5	6	7	8	9	10	11	Subs
17 Aug	Aston Villa	H	W	4-0	Bailey	Gidman	Albiston	Whiteside1	McGrath	Hogg	Robson	Moses	Hughes2	Stapleton	Olsen1	Duxbury for Moses
20 Aug	Ipswich T	A	W	1-0	..	..	..	..	..	..	..1	Strachan	.1	..	..1	Duxbury for Gidman
24 Aug	Arsenal	A	W	2-1	..	Duxbury	..	..	..1	..	..	..	.1	..	..	
26 Aug	West Ham U	H	W	2-0	..	..	..	..	..	..	..	..1	.1	..	..	
31 Aug	Nottingham F	A	W	3-1	..	..	..	..	..	..	..	..	.1	..1	Barnes1	Brazil for Strachan
4 Sep	Newcastle U	H	W	3-0	..	..	..	..	..	..	..	..	.1	..2	..1	Brazil for Stapleton
7 Sep	Oxford U	H	W	3-0	..	..	..	..1	..	..	..1	..	..	..	..1	Brazil for Stapleton
14 Sep	Manchester C	A	W	3-0	..	..1	..1	..	..	..	..1	..	..	..		Brazil for Stapleton
21 Sep	W B A	A	W	5-1	..	..	..	..	..	..	..1	Brazil2	.1	Blackmore1		Moran for Strachan
28 Sep	Southampton	H	W	1-0	..	..	..	..	Moran	..	Moses	Hughes1	..	Barnes		Brazil for Whiteside
5 Oct	Luton T	A	D	1-1	..	..	..	..	..	..	Olsen1	.1	..			
12 Oct	Q P R	H	W	2-0	..	..	..	..	..	..	Olsen1	.1	..			
19 Oct	Liverpool	H	D	1-1	..	..	..	..	Moran	Hogg	McGrath1	Moses	..	Olsen		Barnes for Moses
26 Oct	Chelsea	A	W	2-1	..	..	..	..	..	..	Olsen1	.1	Barnes			
2 Nov	Coventry C	H	W	2-0	..	Garton	..	..	..	..	..2	..	..			
9 Nov	Sheffield Wed	A	L	0-1	..	Gidman	..	..	McGrath	Moran	Robson	Strachan	..	..		Strachan tor Robson
16 Nov	Tottenham H	H	D	0-0	..	..	..	..	..	Strachan	..	..	..			
23 Nov	Leicester C	A	L	0-3	..	..	..	Moran	Hogg	McGrath	Strachan	..	Olsen			Brazil for Albiston
30 Nov	Watford	H	D	1-1	..	..	Gibson C	..	..	..	..	..				Brazil1 for Moran
7 Dec	Ipswich T	H	W	1-0	..	..	..	McGrath	..	Dempsey	..	..1	..			Brazil for Hughes
14 Dec	Aston Villa	A	W	3-1	Turner	..	..	..	Garton	Blackmore1	.1	.1	..			Brazil for Stapleton
21 Dec	Arsenal	H	L	0-1	Bailey	..	..	..	..	..	..	..				
26 Dec	Everton	A	L	1-3	..	..	..	Hogg	..	..	..1					Wood for Olsen
1 Jan	Birmingham C	H	W	1-0	Turner	..	Albiston	Garton	..	..	Gibson C1					Brazil for McGrath
11 Jan	Oxford U	A	W	3-1	Bailey	..	..1	Moran	..	..	.1	..1				
18 Jan	Nottingham F	H	L	2-3	..	..	..	Olsen2	Olsen	..						
2 Feb	West Ham U	A	L	1-2	..	..	..	McGrath	Moran	Robson1	Olsen	..				Gibson T for Robson
9 Feb	Liverpool	A	D	1-1	Turner	..	..	..	Sivebaek	Gibson T	..	Gibson C1	Olsen			Stapleton for Olsen
22 Feb	W B A	H	W	3-0	..	..	..	Blackmore	..	..	Strachan	Gibson C	..	Stapleton	..3	Gibson T for Gidman
1 Mar	Southampton	A	L	0-1	..	Duxbury ..	..	Gibson C	..	..	Robson	Strachan	..	Gibson C		Gibson T for Olsen
15 Mar	Q P R	A	L	0-1	..	..	..	Blackmore	..	..	Olsen	..	Davenport	Gibson C		Gibson T for Olsen
19 Mar	Luton T	H	W	2-0	..	..	..	Whiteside	..1	..	Gibson C	..	Hughes1	Davenport	Olsen	Stapleton for Moran
22 Mar	Manchester C	H	D	2-2	..	..	..	..	Higgins	.1	..1	..	Barnes			Stapleton for Barnes
29 Mar	Birmingham C	A	D	1-1	..	Gidman	..	..	Robson1	..	..	Gibson C				Stapleton for Gibson C
31 Mar	Everton	H	D	0-0	..	..	..	..	..	..	..					Stapleton for Davenport
5 Apr	Coventry C	A	W	3-1	..	..	..	..	..1	..	..	..1				Stapleton for Gibson C
9 Apr	Chelsea	H	L	1-2	..	..	Duxbury	..	..	..	Olsen1					Stapleton for Strachan
13 Apr	Sheffield Wed	H	L	0-2	..	..	..	..	Sivebaek	..	..					Gibson T for Davenport
16 Apr	Newcastle U	A	W	4-2	..	..	Whiteside1	..	Garton	..1	Gibson T	..2	Stapleton	Blackmore		Sivebaek for Gibson T
19 Apr	Tottenham H	A	D	0-0	..	..	..	..	Duxbury	Davenport	..	..				Olsen for Davenport
26 Apr	Leicester C	H	W	4-0	..	..	..	..	..1	.1	..1	..1				Olsen for Whiteside
3 May	Watford	A	D	1-1	Garton	..	..	Hogg	..	.1						Olsen for Davenport

FA Cup

Date	Opp			Score	1	2	3	4	5	6	7	8	9	10	11	Subs
9 Jan	Rochdale (3)	H	W	2-0	Turner	Duxbury	Albiston	Whiteside	Higgins	Barton	Blackmore	Strachan	Hughes1	Stapleton1	Gibson C	Olsen for Hughes
25 Jan	Sunderland (4)	A	D	0-0	Bailey	Gidman	..	..	McGrath	Moran	Robson	..	Stapleton	Blackmore	Olsen	
29 Jan	Sunderland (4R)	H	W	3-0	..	..	..	..1	..	..	..	Olsen2	Gibson C			Blackmore for Strachan
5 Mar	West Ham U (5)	A	D	1-1	Turner	Duxbury	..	..	..	..	Hughes	Stapleton1	..			Olsen for Robson
9 Mar	West Ham U (5R)	H	L	0-2	..	..	..	..	Higgins	Olsen	..	..				Blackmore for Higgins

Milk Cup

Date	Opp			Score	1	2	3	4	5	6	7	8	9	10	11	Subs
24 Sep	Crystal Palace (2)	H	W	1-0	Bailey	Duxbury	Albiston	Whiteside	McGrath	Moran	Robson	Blackmore	Brazil	Stapleton	Barnes1	Brazil for Hughes
9 Oct	Crystal Palace (2)	H	W	1-0	..	..	..	..1	..	..	..	Olsen	Hughes	..		Brazil for Duxbury
29 Oct	West Ham U (3)	H	W	1-0	..	..	..1	Moran	Hogg	McGrath	..	..				
26 Nov	Liverpool (4)	A	L	1-2	..	Gidman	Blackmore	..	..	..1	Strachan	Stapleton	Brazil	Olsen		

Appearances (goals)

Albiston 37 (1) – Bailey 26 – Barnes 12 (2) – Blackmore 12 (3) – Brazil 1 (3) – Davenport 11 (1) – Dempsey 1 – Duxbury 21 (1) – Garton 10 – Gibson C 18 (5) – Gibson T 2 – Gidman 24 – Higgins 6 – Hughes 40 (17) – Hogg 17 – McGrath 40 (3) – Moran 16 – Moses 4 – Olsen 25 (11) – Robson 21 (7) – Sivebaek 2 – Stapleton 34 (7) – Strachan 27 (5) – Turner 17 – Whiteside 37 (4) –
Total 25 players (70)

Football League

	P	W	D	L	F:A	Pts	
Liverpool	42	26	10	6	89:37	88	1st
Manchester U	42	22	10	10	70:36	76	4th

Not even the skills of Glenn Hoddle can evade Paul McGrath's reading of the game.

SEASON 1986-1987 FOOTBALL LEAGUE (DIVISION 1)

Date	Opponent			Score												Substitutes
23 Aug	Arsenal	A	L	0-1	Turner	Duxbury	Albiston	Whiteside	McGrath	Moran	Strachan	Blackmore	Stapleton	Davenport	Gibson C	Olsen for Gibson C
25 Aug	West Ham U	H	L	2-3	..	..	..	..	..	..	..	..	..1	..1	Olsen for Gibson C
30 Aug	Charlton A	H	L	0-1	..	..	..	..	..	..	..	..			Olsen	Gibson T for Whiteside
6 Sep	Leicester C	A	D	1-1	..	Sivebaek	..	..1	..	Hogg	..	Duxbury		Gibson T		Davenport for Gibson T
13 Sep	Southampton	H	W	5-1	..	..	..	..1	..	Moran	Robson	Strachan	..2	Davenport1	..1	Gibson T for Strachan
16 Sep	Watford	A	L	0-1	..	..	..	Moses	..	..	..	Blackmore	..			
21 Sep	Everton	A	L	1-3	..	..	..	Whiteside	..	..	..	Strachan	..		Moses	Olsen for Whiteside
26 Sep	Chelsea	H	L	0-1	..	..	..	..	..	..	..	..	..		Olsen	Olsen for Whiteside
4 Oct	Nottingham F	A	D	1-1	..	..	..	..	..	..	..1	..	..		Olsen	
11 Oct	Sheffield Wed	H	W	3-1	..	..	..	..1	..	Hogg	..	..		..2	Barnes	
18 Oct	Luton T	H	W	1-0	..	..	..	..	..	..	..	..	..1			Gibson T for Strachan
26 Oct	Manchester C	A	D	1-1	..	..	..	..	..	..	..	Moses	..1			
1 Nov	Coventry C	H	D	1-1	..	..	..	..	..	..	Strachan	..		..1	Olsen	Moses for Robson
8 Nov	Oxford U	A	L	0-2	..	Duxbury	..	Moran	..	..	Blackmore	Moses	..		Barnes	Olsen for McGrath
15 Nov	Norwich C	A	D	0-0	..	Sivebaek	Duxbury	Moses	..	..	Olsen	Blackmore	..			Moran for Sivebaek
22 Nov	Q P R	H	W	1-0	..	..1	..	..	..	..	..	..	..			Strachan for Barnes
29 Nov	Wimbledon	A	L	0-1	..	..	..	..	..	Moran	..	..	..			Robson for Barnes
7 Dec	Tottenham H	H	D	3-3	..	..	..	..	..	..	Robson	Strachan	Whiteside1	..2	Olsen	Stapleton for McGrath
13 Dec	Aston Villa	A	D	3-3	Walsh	..	..	..	Moran	Hogg	..	..	..1	..2		Stapleton for Davenport
20 Dec	Leicester C	H	W	2-0	..	..	Gibson C1	O'Brien	..	..	..	..	Stapleton			Stapleton1 for O'Brien
26 Dec	Liverpool	A	W	1-0	..	..	..	Whiteside1	..	Duxbury	..	..	Stapleton			
27 Dec	Norwich C	H	L	0-1	..	..	..	..	Garton	..	..	..				O'Brien for Robson
1 Jan	Newcastle U	H	W	*4-1	Turner	..	..	O'Brien	..	Moran	Duxbury	..	Whiteside1		..1	Stapleton1 for Whiteside
3 Jan	Southampton	A	D	1-1	..	Duxbury	..	..	..	..	Gill	..	Stapleton	Gibson T	..1	Davenport for Gill
24 Jan	Arsenal	H	W	2-0	..	Sivebaek	Duxbury	Whiteside	..	..	Blackmore	..1	..	..1		McGrath for Duxbury
7 Feb	Charlton A	A	D	0-0	..	..	Gibson C	Duxbury	..	..	Robson	..	..			Davenport for Gibson T
14 Feb	Watford	H	W	3-1	..	Garton	..	..	McGrath1	..	..	..1	Davenport1			Stapleton for Garton
21 Feb	Chelsea	A	U	1-1	Bailey	Duxbury	..	Whiteside	..	..	..	..	..1			Stapleton for Olsen
26 Feb	Everton	H	D	0-0	..	..	..	..	..	..	Hogg	..			Strachan	O'Brien for Davenport
7 Mar	Manchester C	H	W	*2-0	..	Sivebaek	..	Duxbury	..	..	..1	..	Whiteside		O'Brien	Davenport for Strachan
14 Mar	Luton T	A	L	1-2	..	..	..	..	..	..	..1	..	..			Davenport for Gibson C
21 Mar	Sheffield Wed	A	L	0-1	..	Garton	Duxbury	O'Brien	..	..	..	..	Davenport	Gibson C		Gibson T for Garton
28 Mar	Nottingham F	H	W	2-0	Walsh	Sivebaek	Gibson C	..	..1	Duxbury	..1	Moses	Stapleton	Whiteside	Wood	Albiston for Wood
4 Apr	Oxford U	H	W	3-2	..	..	..	..	..	..	..1	Moses		Wood	Davenport2	Albiston for Wood
14 Apr	West Ham U	A	D	0-0	..	Duxbury	..	Moses	..	Moran	Strachan	..	Gibson T			Albiston for Robson
18 Apr	Newcastle U	A	L	1-2	..	..	..	..	..	..	O'Brien	..1	Gibson T	Whiteside		Stapleton for Gibson T
20 Apr	Liverpool	H	W	1-0	..	Sivebaek	Albiston	..	..	..	Duxbury	..1	Whiteside	Davenport1	Gibson C	Stapleton for Albiston
25 Apr	Q P R	A	D	1-1	..	Duxbury	..	..	..	..	Robson	..1	..			Sivebaek for Moses
2 May	Wimbledon	H	L	0-1	..	..	..	..	..	..	..	..	Davenport	Olsen	..	Stapleton for Moses
4 May	Tottenham H	A	L	0-4	..	Sivebaek	Duxbury	Duxbury	..	..	..	..	Gibson T	Whiteside	Olsen	Blackmore for Sivebaek
6 May	Coventry C	A	D	1-1	..	Garton	Albiston	..	..	..	..	..	Whiteside1	Davenport	Gibson C	Blackmore for Strachan
9 May	Aston Villa	H	W	3-1	..	..	..	..	..	..	..	Blackmore	..			Olsen for Whiteside

FA Cup

Date	Opponent			Score												Substitutes
10 Jan	Manchester C (3)	H	W	1-0	Turner	Sivebaek	Gibson C	Whiteside1	Garton	Moran	Duxbury	Strachan	Stapleton	Davenport	Olsen	Gibson T for Davenport
31 Jan	Coventry C (4)	H	L	0-1	..	..	..	Duxbury	..	..	Blackmore	..		Gibson T	..	Davenport for Stapleton, McGrath for Blackmore

Littlewoods Cup

Date	Opponent			Score												Substitutes
24 Sep	Port Vale (2)	H	W	2-0	Turner	Duxbury	Albiston	Whiteside1	McGrath	Moran	Robson	Strachan	Stapleton1	Davenport	Moses	Whiteside for Moran, Gibson T for Stapleton
7 Oct	Port Vale (2)	A	W	5-2	..	Sivebaek	..	Moses2	..	..	..	..	..1	..1	Barnes1	Olsen for Moses, Gibson T for Davenport
29 Oct	Southampton (3)	H	D	0-0	..	Duxbury	..	Whiteside	..	Hogg	..	Moses	..			Moran for Gibson C, Wood for Whiteside
4 Nov	Southampton (SR)	A	L	1-4	..	..	..	..	..	..	Moses	Olsen	..		Gibson C	

Appearances (goals)

Albiston 19 – Bailey 5 – Barnes 7 – Blackmore 10 (1) – Davenport 34 (14) – Duxbury 32 (1) – Garton 9 – Gibson C 24 (1) – Gibson T 12 (1) – Gill 1 – Hogg 11 – McGrath 34 (2) – Moran 32 – Moses 17 – O'Brien 9 – Olsen 22 (3) – Robson 29 (7) – Sivebaek 27 (1) – Stapleton 25 (7) – Strachan 33 (4) – Turner 23 – Walsh 14 – Whiteside 31 (8) – Wood 2 – Own goals 2 – **Total 24 players (52)**

Football League

	P	W	D	L	F:A	Pts	
Everton	42	26	8	8	76:31	86	1st
Manchester U	42	14	14	14	52:45	56	11th

SEASON 1987-1988 FOOTBALL LEAGUE (DIVISION 1)

Date	Opponent			Score												Substitutes
15 Aug	Southampton	A	D	2-2	Walsh	Anderson	Duxbury	Moses	McGrath	Moran	Robson	Strachan	McClair	Whiteside2	Olsen	Albiston for Moses, Davenport for Olsen
19 Aug	Arsenal	H	D	0-0	..	..	..	..	..	..	..	..	..	..	..	Albiston for Olsen, Davenport for Strachan
22 Aug	Watford	H	W	2-0	..	..	..	..	..1	..	..	..	..1	..	Gibson C for Duxbury, Davenport for Olsen
29 Aug	Charlton A	A	W	3-1	..	..	..	..	..1	..	..1	..	..1	..	Gibson C for Albiston
31 Aug	Chelsea	H	W	3-1	..	..	Albiston	..	..	..	Duxbury	..1	..1	..	Gibson C for Albiston, Davenport for Olsen
5 Sep	Coventry C	A	D	0-0	..	..	..	..	..	..	..	..	..	..	Davenport for Olsen
12 Sep	Newcastle U	H	D	2-2	..	..	Duxbury	..	..	..	Robson	..	..	..1	Davenport for Olsen
19 Sep	Everton	A	L	1-2	..	..	..	..	..	Hogg	..	..	..1	..	Garton for Hogg, Davenport for Strachan
26 Sep	Tottenham H	H	W	1-0	..	..	Gibson C	Garton	..	Duxbury	..	..	..	..	Blackmore for Anderson, Davenport for Strachan
3 Oct	Luton T	A	D	1-1	..	Blackmore	..	..	..	..	..	..	..1	..	O'Brien for Blackmore
10 Oct	Sheffield W	A	W	4-2	..	Garton	..	Duxbury	..	Moran	..1	..	..2	..	Blackmore1 for Moran, Davenport for Strachan
17 Oct	Norwich C	H	W	2-1	..	..	..	..	..	Davenport1	..1	Blackmore	..	..	Moran for Gibson C, O'Brien for Blackmore
25 Oct	West Ham U	A	D	1-1	..	..	Anderson	..1	..	Moran	..	Strachan	..	..	Blackmore for Strachan
31 Oct	Nottingham F	H	D	2-2	..	..	..	..	Garton	..	..1	Davenport	..	Whiteside1	Strachan for Whiteside
15 Nov	Liverpool	H	D	1-1	..	..	..	..	Blackmore	..	..	Strachan	..	..1	Davenport for Moran
21 Nov	Wimbledon	A	L	1-2	..	..	..	Duxbury	Moses	..1	..	Graham	..	..	Albiston for Duxbury, O'Brien for Graham
5 Dec	Q P R	A	W	2-0	Turner	Duxbury	Albiston	..	..	Moran	O'Brien	..1	Strachan	..	Davenport1	
12 Dec	Oxford United	H	W	3-1	..	..	..	Gibson C	..	..	Davenport	..	..2	Whiteside	..1	Albiston for Robson
19 Dec	Portsmouth	A	W	2-1	..	..	..	..	Bruce	..	Moses	..	..1	..	Davenport for Olsen
26 Dec	Newcastle U	A	L	0-1	..	Anderson	..	..	..	..	Duxbury	..	..	Davenport	Anderson for Gibson C, Olsen for Moses
28 Dec	Everton	H	W	2-1	..	..	Anderson	..	..	..	Duxbury	..	..2	Olsen	Davenport for Whiteside, Moses for Strachan
1 Jan	Charlton A	H	D	0-0	..	..	..	..	Duxbury	Moses	..	..	Davenport	Blackmore for Olsen, O'Brien for Moses
2 Jan	Watford	A	W	1-0	..	..	Albiston	..	Moran	Duxbury	..	..	..1	Whiteside	Gibson C	Davenport for Albiston, O'Brien for Moran
16 Jan	Southampton	H	L	0-2	..	..	Gibson C	..	..	Moses	..	Duxbury	..	Davenport	Olsen	Strachan for Gibson C, O'Brien for Moran
24 Jan	Arsenal	A	W	2-1	..	..	Duxbury	..	Blackmore	Hogg	..	Strachan1	..	Whiteside	..	O'Brien for Blackmore
6 Feb	Coventry C	H	W	1-0	..	..	..	..	O'Brien1	..	..	..	..	..	Albiston for O'Brien
10 Feb	Derby Co	A	W	2-1	..	..	..	..	..	..	..1	..	..	..1	Albiston for Duxbury, Davenport for Olsen
13 Feb	Chelsea	A	W	2-1	..	..	Albiston	..1	..1	..	Davenport	..	..	Gibson C	Blackmore for Gibson C
23 Feb	Tottenham H	A	D	1-1	..	..	Duxbury	..	..	..	Davenport	Blackmore	..	..	Strachan for Hogg, Olsen for Anderson
5 Mar	Norwich C	A	L	0-1	..	Blackmore	..	..	..	Moran	Robson	Strachan	..	Davenport	..	Olsen for Duxbury
12 Mar	Sheffield W	H	W	4-1	..	..	..1	Gibson C	..	Duxbury	Hogg	..	..	..2	..1	Olsen
19 Mar	Nottingham F	A	D	0-0	..	Anderson	Blackmore	..	..	..	Whiteside	Olsen	..	..	Gibson C	O'Brien for Gibson C, McGrath for Hogg
26 Mar	West Ham U	H	W	3-1	..	..	..1	..	McGrath	Duxbury	Robson1	Strachan1	..	..	Olsen for Strachan
2 Apr	Derby Co	H	W	4-1	..	..	..	Duxbury	..	Hogg	..	..	..3	..	Olsen for Davenport, O'Brien for McGrath
4 Apr	Liverpool	A	D	3-3	..	..	..	Bruce	..	Duxbury	..2	..1	..	..1	Olsen for Blackmore, Whiteside for McGrath
12 Apr	Luton T	H	W	3-0	..	..	..	..	..	..	..	..1	..	..	Olsen for Gibson C
30 Apr	Q P R	H	W	*2-1	..	..	..1	..	..	..	..	..	..	Olsen	O'Brien for Blackmore
2 May	Oxford U	A	W	2-0	..	..	..1	Gibson C	..	..	..	..	..1	..	Blackmore for Anderson
7 May	Portsmouth	H	W	4-1	..	..	..	..	..	..	..1	..	..2	..1	Blackmore for Anderson, Hogg for McGrath
9 May	Wimbledon	H	W	2-1	..	Duxbury	Blackmore	..	..	Moses	..	..	..2	Gibson C	Martin for Moses

FA Cup

Date	Opponent			Score												Substitutes
10 Jan	Ipswich Town (3)	A	W	*2-1	Turner	Anderson1	Duxbury	Bruce	Moran	Moses	Robson	Strachan	McClair	Whiteside	Gibson C	Davenport for Moses, Olsen for Gibson C
30 Jan	Chelsea (4)	H	W	2-0	..	..	..	..	Blackmore	Hogg	..	..	..1	..1	Olsen	O'Brien for Blackmore
20 Feb	Arsenal (5)	A	L	1-2	..	..	Gibson C	..	Duxbury	..	Davenport	..	..1	..	O'Brien for Hogg, Blackmore for Olsen

Littlewoods Cup

Date	Opponent			Score												Substitutes
23 Sep	Hull C (2)	H	W	5-0	Walsh	Anderson	Gibson C	Moses	McGrath1	Duxbury	Robson	Strachan1	McClair	Whiteside1	Davenport1	Garton for Moses
7 Oct	Hull C (2)	A	W	1-0	Turner	Blackmore	..	Garton	..	Moran	..	..	McClair1	..	Olsen	O'Brien for Gibson C, Graham for Duxbury
26 Oct	Crystal Palace (3)	H	W	2-1	..	Anderson	..	Duxbury	Garton	Moran	..	..	..2	..	Davenport	Blackmore for Robson, Davenport for Garton
16 Nov	Bury (4)	H	W	2-1	Walsh	..	..	..	Blackmore	Davenport	..	..	..1	..1	Olsen	O'Brien for Gibson C, Moses for Davenport
20 Jan	Oxford U (5)	A	L	0-2	Turner	..	..	Blackmore	Moran	Duxbury	..	..	..	..	Hogg for Moran, Davenport for Strachan

Appearances (goals)

Albiston 5 – Anderson 30 (2) – Blackmore 15 (3) – Bruce 21 (2) – Davenport 21 (5) – Duxbury 39 – Garton 5 – Gibson C 26 (2) – Graham 1 – Hogg 9 – McClair 40 (24) – McGrath 21 (2) – Moran 20 – Moses 16 – O'Brien 6 (2) – Olsen 31 (2) – Robson 36 (11) – Strachan 33 (6) – Turner 24 – Walsh 16 – Whiteside 25 (7) – Own goals 1 – **Total 21 players (71)**

Football League

	P	W	D	L	F:A	Pts	
Liverpool	40	26	12	2	87:24	90	1st
Manchester U	40	23	12	5	71:36	81	2nd

Peter Davenport clashes with the West Ham defence during a 2-2 draw in 1986.

SEASON 1988-1989 FOOTBALL LEAGUE (DIVISION 1)

Date	Opp			Score												
27 Aug	Q P R	H	D	0-0	Leighton	Blackmore	Martin	Bruce	McGrath	McClair	Robson	Strachan	Davenport	Hughes	Olsen	O'Brien for Davenport
3 Sep	Liverpool	A	L	0-1	..	Anderson	Blackmore	..	McGrath	Duxbury	..	..	McClair	..	..	Garton for McGrath, Davenport for Strachan
10 Sep	Middlesbrough	H	W	1-0	..	Garton	..	..	..	..	..1	Davenport	..	..	..	
17 Sep	Luton	A	W	2-0	..	..	..	..	..	..	..1	..1	..	..	..	
24 Sep	West Ham	H	W	2-0	..	Blackmore	Sharpe	..	Garton	..	..	Strachan	..	..1	Davenport1	Beardsmore for Garton, Olsen for Sharpe
1 Oct	Tottenham	A	D	2-2	..	Garton	..	..	McGrath	..	..	..	..1	..1	..	Anderson for Garton, Olsen for Davenport
22 Oct	Wimbledon	A	D	1-1	..	Blackmore	..	..	Garton	..	..	..	..	..1	..	Beardsmore for Strachan, Robins for Davenport
26 Oct	Norwich	H	L	1-2	..	..	..	..	..	..	..	..	..	..1	..	Olsen for Davenport
30 Oct	Everton	A	D	1-1	..	Garton	Blackmore	..	Duxbury	Donaghy	..	..	..	..1	Olsen	Gibson for Strachan, O'Brien for Duxbury
5 Nov	Aston V	H	D	1-1	..	Blackmore	Gibson	..1	O'Brien	..	..	..	..	..	..	Duxbury for Gibson
12 Nov	Derby C	A	D	2-2	..	Garton	Blackmore	..	Duxbury	..	..	..	..1	..1	Sharpe	Olsen for Duxbury
19 Nov	Southampton	H	D	2-2	..	..	Sharpe	..	Blackmore	..	..1	..	..	..1	Milne	Gill for Sharpe
23 Nov	Sheffield Wed	H	D	1-1	..	..	..	..	..	..	..	..	..	..1	..	Gill for Strachan, Wilson for Blackmore
27 Nov	Newcastle	A	D	0-0	..	..	Blackmore	..	Gill	..	..	Milne	..	..	Sharpe	Martin for Milne, Robins for Sharpe
3 Dec	Charlton	H	W	3-0	..	..	Martin	..	Blackmore	..	..	Strachan	..1	..1	Milne1	
10 Dec	Coventry	A	L	0-1	..	..	..	..	..	..	..	..	..	..	Sharpe	Gill for Garton, Milne for Gill
17 Dec	Arsenal	A	L	1-2	..	Martin	Sharpe	..	..	..	..	..	..	..1	Milne	Gill for Blackmore, Beardsmore for Martin
26 Dec	Nottingham F	H	W	2-0	..	..	..	..	Beardsmore	..	..	..	..	..1	..1	
1 Jan	Liverpool	H	W	3-1	..	..	..	..	..1	..	..	..	..	..1	..1	McGrath for Martin, Robins for Strachan
2 Jan	Middlesbrough	A	L	0-1	..	Gill	..	..	McGrath	..	..	Beardsmore	..	..	..	Robins for McClair, Wilson for Gill
14 Jan	Millwall	H	W	3-0	..	Martin	..	..	Beardsmore	..	Gill	Blackmore1	..	..1	..	Wilson for Beardsmore, Maiorana for Milne
21 Jan	West Ham	A	W	3-1	..	Gill	Martin1	..	Blackmore	..	Robson	Strachan1	..	..1	..	Sharpe for Strachan
5 Feb	Tottenham	H	W	1-0	..	Martin	Sharpe	..	..	..	..	..	..	..1	..	McGrath for Sharpe, Beardsmore for Strachan
11 Feb	Sheffield Wed	A	W	2-0	..	Blackmore	Martin	..	McGrath	..	..	..	..	..2	..	Beardsmore for McClair
25 Feb	Norwich	A	L	1-2	..	..	Sharpe	..	..	..	..	..	..	..	..	Martin for Milne, Beardsmore for Blackmore
12 Mar	Aston Villa	A	D	0-0	..	Beardsmore	Martin	..	..	..	..	..	..	..	Sharpe	Blackmore for Beardsmore, Milne for Martin
25 Mar	Luton	H	W	2-0	..	Martin	Blackmore	..	..	..	..	Beardsmore	..	..	Milne1	Maiorana for Beardsmore
27 Mar	Nottingham F	A	L	0-2	..	Anderson	..	..	..	..	..	..	..	..	..	Martin for McGrath, Gill for Martin
2 Apr	Arsenal	H	D	*1-1	..	..	Donaghy	..	..	Whiteside	..	..	..	..	Maiorana	Blackmore for Beardsmore, Martin for Maiorana
8 Apr	Millwall	A	D	0-0	..	..	..	..	..	..	..	..	..	..	Martin	Maiorana for McGrath
15 Apr	Derby	H	L	0-2	..	..	Martin	..	Donaghy	Robins	..	..	..	..	Maiorana	Duxbury for Robins, Wilson for Anderson
22 Apr	Charlton	A	L	0-1	..	Duxbury	Donaghy	..	Whiteside	Robson	..	..	..	..	Milne	Robins for Milne
29 Apr	Coventry	H	L	0-1	..	..	..	..	..	..	..	..	..	..	Martin	Robins for Martin
2 May	Wimbledon	H	W	1-0	..	..	..	..	..	..	..	..	..1	..	..	Maiorana for Whiteside
6 May	Southampton	A	L	1-2	..	..	..	..	..	..	..	..1	..	..	..	Sharpe for Martin, Milne for Robson
8 May	Q P R	A	L	*2-3	..	..	Sharpe	..1	Blackmore1	Donaghy	Milne	..	..	..1	..	Robins for Blackmore, Brazil for Duxbury
10 May	Everton	H	L	1-2	..	..	..	..	..	..	..	..	..	..	..	
13 May	Newcastle	H	W	2-0	..	..	Martin	..	..	..	Robson1	..	..	..1	Milne	Sharpe for Blackmore, Robins for Milne

FA Cup

Date	Opp			Score												
7 Jan	Q P R (3)	H	D	0-0	Leighton	Gill	Martin	Bruce	Beardsmore	Donaghy	Robson	Robins	McClair	Hughes	Milne	
11 Jan	Q P R (3R)	A	D	2-2	..	Martin	Sharpe	..	..	..	Gill1	Blackmore	..	..	..	Wilson for Sharpe, Graham1 for Blackmore
23 Jan	Q P R (3R2)	H	W	3-0	..	..	..	..	Blackmore	..	Robson1	Strachan	..2	..	..	McGrath for Milne, Beardsmore for Blackmore
28 Jan	Oxford (4)	H	W	*4-0	..	Blackmore	..	..	McGrath	..	..1	..	..	..1	..	Gill for McGrath, Beardsmore for Sharpe
18 Feb	B'mouth (5)	A	D	1-1	..	..	Martin	..	..	..	..	..	..	..1	..	Sharpe for Martin
22 Feb	B'mouth (5R)	H	W	1-0	..	..	Sharpe	..	..	..	..	..	..	..1	..	Gill for Milne
18 Mar	Nott For (6)	H	L	0-1	..	Beardsmore	..	..	..	..	..	..	..	..	..	Martin for Sharpe, Blackmore for Milne

*Includes own goal
†After extra time

Littlewoods Cup

Date	Opp			Score												
28 Sep	Rth'ham (2)	A	W	1-0	Leighton	Blackmore	Sharpe	Bruce	McGrath	Duxbury	Robson	Strachan	McClair	Hughes	Davenport1	Beardsmore for Sharpe, Olsen for Strachan
12 Oct	Rth'ham (2)	H	W	5-0	..	Beardsmore	Blackmore	..1	Garton	..	..1	..	..3	..	..	Davenport for Robson, Robins for Duxbury
2 Nov	Wimbledon (3)	A	L	1-2	..	Blackmore	Gibson	..1	..	..	..1	O'Brien	..	..	Olsen	Anderson for Olsen, Strachan for Duxbury

F.A. Centenary Trophy

Date	Opp			Score												
29 Aug	Everton	H	W	1-0	Leighton	Anderson	Blackmore	Bruce	Garton	Duxbury	Robson	Strachan1	McClair	Hughes	Olsen	Davenport for Olsen
21 Sep	Newcastle	H	W	2-0†	..	Blackmore	Sharpe	..1	..	..	..	Davenport	..1	..	..	Beardsmore for Olsen, O'Brien for Davenport
9 Oct	Arsenal (F)	N	L	1-2	..	..	..1	..	..	..	..	..	..	..	..	Strachen for Olsen, Beardsmore for Davenport

(at Villa Park)

Appearances (goals)

Anderson 8 – Beardsmore 33 (2) – Blackmore 40 (4) – Brazil 1 – Bruce 51 (5) – Davenport 13 (3) – Donaghy 37 – Duxbury 23 – Garton 19 – Gibson 3 – Gill 14 (2) – Graham 11 – Hughes 51 (16) – Leighton 5 – Maiorana 8 – Martin 30 (1) – McClair 51 (17) – McGrath 26 (1) – Milne 29 (3) – O'Brien 7 – Olsen 15 – Robins 12 – Robson 46 (8) – Sharpe 32 – Strachan 31 (2) – Whiteside 8 – Wilson 5 – Own Goals 2 – **Total 27 players (67)**

Football League

	P	W	D	L	F:A	Pts
Arsenal	38	22	10	6	73:36	78	1st
Manchester U	38	13	12	13	45:45	51	11th

Manchester United are the giants of English football, a footballing Colossus and the wealthiest club not only in the country, but in the world. Financial reports place United as the top earner in Europe with clearly the best supported team drawing on fans from far and wide.

It's the worldwide support which has played such a big part in making United rich beyond the dreams of ordinary clubs by pouring money into their merchandising operation via the sale of replica shirts and hundreds of other items ranging from a David Beckham duvet cover for your bed to the latest Ryan Giggs video.

Their corporate hospitality activity also brings in vast amounts and together with sponsorship United earn more from their commercial operations than they do from gate receipts.

Their success is highlighted in a report from the football specialist accountants, Deloitte and Touche of London, indicating that the valuation of United outstrips not only every English club but the top clubs of Italy, Spain and South America as well as saying that the club possesses the most valuable sporting brand in the world.

The analysis is based on financial turnover and the list of the 20 wealthiest clubs worldwide includes five English Premiership teams and six Italian Serie A clubs. But United dwarf them all with an annual turnover which in the financial year 1997-98 reached £87.94 million compared with the next best, Barcelona, who turned over £58.97 million. The third richest club is Real Madrid with a £55.7 million turnover.

Juventus are fourth in the list with £53.22 million, Bayern Munich next (£51.6 million) and AC Milan sixth (£47.48m). The other English clubs which come into the equation are Newcastle who are reckoned to turn over £41.4 million in eighth place, followed by Liverpool (£39.2m), Spurs (£27.9m) and then Arsenal scraping into 20th place with £27.2 million.

United's financial domination was reflected by the bid from Rupert Murdoch's television company, BSkyB, to buy the club for £635 million. The takeover was blocked by the Government's Office of Fair Trading, but it confirmed United's strength in the market place.

The club stand to become even richer if the Office of Fair Trading wins its High Court battle to outlaw the present right of the Premier League to negotiate television agreements on behalf of the League.

If this becomes illegal, clubs will be able to make their own private arrangements and as United are the team with the widest TV appeal, they will be in a position to demand unprecedented deals.

A decision in favour of individual agreements would also open the door for pay-to-view football with United again in the driving seat. Already United have their own cable television company in a link-up with Sky screening reserve and junior matches along with chat shows and lifestyle programmes every day of the week.

The Recipe for Success

United are already a cash giant and are set to become even stronger – but what has made them so wealthy and powerful? The tragedy of the Munich air crash which destroyed the Busby Babes, killing eight players, finishing the careers of two

Chairman, Martin Edwards (left) has presided the club's healthiest financial era with capacity crowds assured of watching stars like Dwight Yorke (top), who cost a record £12.6 million. His financial ventures, such as the Superstore (far right) assure the club has a healthy and wealthy future

players which has given the club such universal appeal.

Right from the early days United established a tradition that encouraged their teams to express themselves.

Billy Meredith, the toothpick chewing Welsh wizard who was a key figure in the re-forming of the players' union, was a major character at the turn of the century, while the half-back line of Duckworth, Roberts and Bell was the foundation of

United's first great era which won two Championships and the FA Cup between 1908 and 1911.

New stars and new fans

Brilliant footballers like Johnny Carey, Stan Pearson, Jack 'Gunner' Rowley, Johnny Morris and Charlie Mitten brought United back to the honours board after the last war and then Matt Busby put the accent on the club developing its own players to create his Babes with outstanding figures like Duncan Edwards, Dennis Viollet, Eddie Colman, David Pegg and many more.

Who knows what they might have gone on to achieve had it not been for the Munich tragedy.

The club were forced more into the transfer market after the air disaster but still always looking for quality with transfer records repeatedly broken over the years to bring players like Albert Quixall, Denis Law, Alex Stepney, Gary Pallister, Roy Keane, Andy Cole, and more recently, Dwight Yorke, Jaap Stam and Jesper Blomqvist, to Old Trafford.

But the emphasis on home-grown talent is also back in favour under the managership of Alex Ferguson whose FA Youth Cup winning team of 1992 is now taking football by storm for both club and country.

Players like Ryan Giggs, David Beckham, Nicky Butt, Paul Scholes, Gary and Philip Neville are just the latest star names to light up the game for Manchester United and perform in front of capacity crowds of over 60,000.

others and taking Sir Matt Busby to death's door, undoubtedly won them wide sympathy and gave them an emotional appeal which has lasted down the years both home and abroad.

But there is also a common thread which has stitched together the history. Right from the beginning they have cultivated personality players and entertainers who have shone as individuals with a brilliance that has made them loved throughout the world.

Old Trafford has always provided a unique and privileged platform for their skills, but in return it was the magic of the

CHAPTER
THE 1990s:
A DECADE OF DOMINANCE
9

Alex Ferguson stepped into the 1990s wondering if he was in fact going to see much of them as manager of Manchester United. He was going backwards in the League and the ever eager media hawks were busy adding up the vast amounts of money he had spent only to find the elusive Championship looking further away than ever.

But the turn of the decade also proved the turning point in the career of Ferguson at Old Trafford and for that he can thank the FA Cup. The road to Wembley had its anxious moments but it was a life-saver as far as his future with United was concerned, especially winning at Nottingham Forest in the third round as the storm clouds were gathering. United went to the City Ground against a background of a run of eight League games without a win, half of them defeats and the tabloid newspapers were seeking a vote of confidence from chairman Martin Edwards about the manager's future, invariably a kiss of death.

There was never any likelihood of the papers getting one because the chairman was well aware of the implications and as far as he was concerned the issue was simply not up for debate. Edwards and his fellow directors were well satisfied with the manager's work. Although naturally disappointed with the lack of progress in the League, they understood the reasons, such as the injuries to Bryan Robson and Neil Webb which had wrecked what Ferguson had hoped would be his midfield engine-room. The board were also impressed with the way their manager had completely restructured the scouting and coaching systems and they felt that given time things would start to come together.

United in the past have been as guilty as the rest of football in this respect, but this time they stuck with their man, and a wise policy it proved to be. Nevertheless there was an unmistakable tension about the place as the Reds prepared for the Cup tie without the services of Robson, Webb, Wallace and Ince. Ferguson was forced to turn to his young ones like Mark Robins and Russell Beardsmore, and they didn't fail him. In fact Robins scored the goal in a 1-0 win which brought a great sigh of relief for those who felt that it was important Ferguson should be allowed to continue with his work at Old Trafford.

Above: Brian McClair and Neil Webb celebrate. McClair's 46 goals in the first two seasons of the decade were instrumental in United's improving form

Left: The prodigious talent of Welsh-born Ryan Giggs was one of the reasons why Manchester United came so close to winning the coveted First Division title in 1991-92. Yet another product of the youth policy instigated by Alex Ferguson in his first years at Old Trafford, Giggs made 51 League and Cup appearances, scored seven goals and thrilled fans up and down the country with his dazzling skills and pinpoint crossing. The quality of young players like Giggs married with the established reputations of some of the more expensive playing assets, make United a real force in the new Premier League

Youth fail to improve League form

The youngster had pumped new life into the club the previous season at a crisis point and Robins went on to show that given a decent run in the team he could produce goals, whatever his other failings might be. That season he finished with a total of 10 goals in League and Cup, yet he started in only 13 games. He was brought on as a substitute in a further 10 matches, but it is

still a remarkable scoring rate and one which has made a lot of people wonder why he wasn't a more regular player in the first team.

The team continued to limp along in the League to finish 13th in the First Division. They could not have expected better when Mark Hughes was their top scorer in the League with 13 goals, Robins was next with seven while Brian McClair limped along with a mere five.

But the team had correctly sniffed Wembley and they somehow pulled themselves together for the FA Cup ties. The fourth round took them to Hereford and a very muddy pitch. It seemed tailor made for a Cup upset given United's erratic form in the League. It rained so hard that spectators who had parked early alongside the ground came out to find their cars marooned in a sea of water. Clayton Blackmore took the honours by scoring the only goal of the match with just four minutes to go.

The next round was at Newcastle where United won an exciting tussle 3-2 with goals from Danny Wallace, Brian McChair and Mark Robins again. United certainly did not get to Wembley the easy way, for the sixth round brought them yet another away tie, a tricky one against a hard-running Sheffield United side calculated to rattle the more sophisticated yet fragile Reds. McClair got them a 1-0 victory to line them up for a Lancashire derby semi-final against Oldham Athletic at Maine Road. At least United went into this match on the back of a couple of League wins, though this hardly prepared them for a tremendous onslaught by their Second Division opponents who played out of their skins for a 3-3 draw after extra time. Robson and Webb scored the United goals with one from Wallace after coming on as a substitute. Robins proved the Cup hero again with the score locked at 1-1 at the end of normal time. He came on as an extra-time sub to score the winner and rescue Ferguson's season with an FA Cup final against Crystal Palace.

Palace force replay

Palace manager Steve Coppell shocked his old club with the physical intensity of his team's approach, quite foreign to his own performances as a winger at Old Trafford in the 1970s. United still seemed to have the game sewn up after goals from Robson and Hughes had given them a 2-1 lead with half an hour to go. But Coppell had an ace up his sleeve and he brought on the dashing Ian Wright to score and send the tie into extra time. Wright, a couple of seasons later the First Division's top scorer with Arsenal, put Palace in front almost from the kick off in the extra period. It took another goal from Hughes to give the Reds a replay following the 3-3 see-saw match.

Jim Leighton had been worrying his manager for a few weeks and he was widely blamed for two of the goals. Ferguson, who had given the Scottish international his debut as a boy at Aberdeen agonised long and hard, and then finally dropped him for the replay. The United manager has since said that if he had his time over again he couldn't make the same decision, not because it was a wrong one for the team but because of the way it wrecked the career of a player who by now was virtually a friend, so long had they known each other. The decision made sense, though his replacement, Les Sealey, still represented a gamble. Sealey had been brought to Old Trafford on loan from Luton as emergency cover and because he had been frozen out at Kenilworth Road he had played only two first-team games in 18 months. Confidence is not lacking in the chirpy Cockney from Bethnal Green though and he took Wembley in his stride to steady the defence and present a more reliable front to Palace.

The Londoners again tried to rough the Reds up but underdogs rarely get a second chance and United won 1-0 with a goal after 60 minutes from a man who nearly didn't play. Lee Martin was within an ace of being left out of the replay because the manager was concerned about his ability to last through extra time without getting cramp. The full-back had been substituted in the three previous rounds after going down with leg muscle problems. But as Ferguson said later: 'It was touch and go whether I kept him in the side, but we decided that if we

Above: Danish goalkeeper Peter Schmeichel (left) and England international Paul Parker (right) were two more astute signings at the commencement of the 1991-92 season

played our best defenders we could win in normal time. That's football for you, the one you nearly dropped wins the FA Cup for you.' It was only Martin's second goal for United in the first team and it crowned a splendid season for the Hyde-born youngster who had joined the club as a YTS boy.

As a result of his part in the victory Sealey earned himself a permanent contract; Leighton retreated into the shadows and made only one more first-team appearance before going back home to Scotland two years later. Ferguson felt for him, but he was fighting for his own skin and winning the FA Cup silenced the doubters and gave him time to develop his team.

They immediately made a strong challenge in all three cup competitions the following season, reaching the sixth round of the FA Cup and the final of the Rumbelows Cup where they underestimated the opposition and lost 1-0 to Sheffield Wednesday. They were not helped by the preparations of a subdued Archie Knox leaving to become coach of Glasgow Rangers, though the promotion of Brian Kidd to fill the Knox role was to become a great success in subsequent seasons.

The board's faith in their manager was certainly rewarded, as the team won the European Cup Winners' Cup by beating Barcelona 2-1 in the final in Rotterdam. Mark Hughes scored both goals to give the club their first European trophy since 1968.

1990-00

Off the field, the club was floated as a public company, raising £7m for the redevelopment of the Stretford End and along the way netting chairman Martin Edwards a similar amount as majority shareholder.

Season 1991-92 saw the team gathering even more momentum to finish brave runners-up to Leeds for the championship with the Rumbelows Cup their consolation after beating Nottingham Forest 1-0 in the final, the single goal coming from Brian McClair.

Then as United entered the newly formed Premiership League for season 1992-93 Alex Ferguson made a move in the transfer market which was to prove the turning point in the club's fortunes.

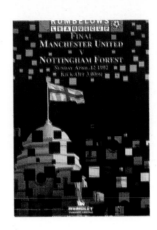

The arrival of Cantona

On Thursday 26 November chairman Edwards received a call from Bill Fotherby, the managing director of Leeds United. It was an inquiry about the possible purchase of Denis Irwin. Ferguson was with the chairman and refused, but asked, somewhat tongue-in-cheek, if Leeds were willing to part with Eric Cantona. Within days he was bought for £1 million.

The French international had arrived in England earlier in the year amid controversy. He was about to sign for Sheffield Wednesday when instead he opted for Leeds. His undeniable

Below: McClair scores the winner in United's 1-0 victory over Nottingham Forest in the 1992 Rumbelows League Cup final. He was also named 'Man of the Match'

contribution to their Championship success had not gone unnoticed at Old Trafford.

That purchase would be seen by many as the moment when United took a major step towards the ending of the 26-year wait since the last Championship win. It led to Ferguson's comments as Cantona signed:

I see Eric as a Manchester United player, the kind we want at this club. He has style, he has class and this club will suit him. His goal scoring was instrumental in the success of Leeds last year. I am happy to bring another striker to the club, one who has a good reputation and one who won't in any way be overawed at playing at Old Trafford.

He was right. Cantona was soon to be hailed 'Le Roi de Old Trafford', a new 'King' to succeed the last to carry that title, Denis Law.

Cantona was registered too late to play against Arsenal at Highbury but he saw his new colleagues win 1-0 thanks to a Mark Hughes goal. The Frenchman came on as substitute during the 2-1 derby win over Manchester City on 6 December, then made his full debut six days later in the victory over leaders Norwich. In that game Hughes scored again, his fourth strike in as many appearances. Cantona was providing the flair as well as the opportunities with a seemingly endless supply of passes to his colleagues. United moved into third place.

The unbeaten run continued into the New Year and included a sensational 3-3 draw at Hillsborough, where at one point United trailed 3-0. It was Cantona who scored the equaliser and in the last six frantic minutes just failed to get what would have been a sensational winner. Next, Coventry were beaten 5-0 at Old Trafford and Tottenham fell in similar style losing 4-1. United won 3-1 at Loftus Road against a Queens Park Rangers side which had been going well and Nottingham Forest were beaten 2-0 in a game which saw the return to Old Trafford of Neil Webb, sold back to his former club for £800,000 shortly before Cantona's arrival.

The season's fifth defeat came at Ipswich, then was followed by another surge, as with 11 games left the wheel turned full circle. United beat Liverpool 2-1 at Anfield to go top and avenge the disappointment of the previous year. They had been knocked out of the FA Cup at Bramall Lane by Sheffield United, the eventual semi-finalists.

Oldham Athletic decided that they would put an abrupt end to any Championship talk. Fighting for survival, they won 1-0 at Boundary Park. The newspapers loved it when it was revealed that Ron Atkinson promised Oldham manager Joe Royle a bottle of champagne if Oldham did Villa a favour. After the game Royle demanded a whole case and the newspaper headlines asked:

Has Fergie got the bottle?

He was unmoved. His players would do the talking, but drawn games against Villa and Arsenal at Old Trafford, then City at Maine Road, saw them slip back to third. Villa led.

Andrei Kanchelskis adapted quickly to the United style and made a major contribution to both Championship campaigns of 1993 and 1994. He scored some important goals, perhaps none more so than against Leeds at Elland Road when United opened up a telling lead during the run-in to the 1994 title

United's title push

So began the most crucial period of the season and the club's most important run of results for 26 years. Norwich regained the leadership with a home win over Villa. Then came United's turn to go to Carrow Road and they would face the leaders without a key player. Mark Hughes was suspended, but manager Ferguson bravely named an attacking side which included Cantona, Kanchelskis, Giggs, Sharpe and McClair.

They hit Norwich with speed and skill and the home side had no answer. By the end of the night United were top of the League once more after a resounding 3-1 victory.

Giggs, Kanchelskis and Cantona each plundered goals in the first 21 minutes as they were inspired by the midfield efforts of Paul Ince. Before facing his former club an optimistic Steve Bruce had said:

'Seven matches left and if we win all of them nobody can stop us!'

Such optimism, but he was right and that is exactly what happened! That defeat at Oldham was the last of the season, and it was Bruce himself who played a crucial role in engineering the first of those seven victories. It was against Sheffield Wednesday, who came to Old Trafford threatening to steal victory in a game that was filled with incident as well as time-wasting tactics.

Wednesday played with a packed midfield. Tension was high and to add to the drama the crowd witnessed the unusual sight of a substitute referee. Michael Peck was replaced after pulling a muscle. Linesmen John Hilditch took over and almost immediately awarded Sheffield Wednesday a penalty from which John Sheridan scored. With six minutes to go Bruce equalised and twelve minutes later headed the winner. The second half ended 53 minutes after it had commenced because of time added on.

A 1-0 win at Coventry was followed by a 3-0 home victory over Chelsea and then the night which in the eye of the United faithful decided the destiny of the Championship.

United were away to Crystal Palace as Aston Villa played Blackburn Rovers at Ewood Park. Before United had kicked off Villa were 2-0 down and went on to lose 3-0. Mark Hughes and Paul Ince scored at Selhurst Park and the United fans taunted their former manager:

Are you watching big fat Ron?

Is it true your bottle's gone?

As for Alex Ferguson, for the first time he spoke as though he felt the Championship could now be won:

We have got ourselves into a fantastic position: two games left and four points clear. We have a far superior goal difference. Now we need to finish the job properly. It would be lovely to win the Championship at Old Trafford in our last home game so that we can pay back a support that has waited so long.

Champions again at last

That game was against Blackburn on Monday, 3 May but United were Champions before that.

The previous day and against all odds Oldham beat Aston Villa 1-0 at Villa Park. There was no talk about champagne this time. The defeat ended Villa's aspirations and the Manchester fans celebrated.

The Blackburn game became a showpiece with United fighting from behind to win 3-1. Ryan Giggs, Paul Ince and Gary Pallister scored as the players were urged on by a fanatical crowd which chanted, sang and danced its way through a carnival 90 minutes.

One game remained, a return to Selhurst Park for a 2-1 victory over Wimbledon. Paul Ince got the opening goal, and fittingly it was Robson who scored his first of the season and the last of the season's campaign.

During the summer as Manchester continued its celebrations Alex Ferguson followed his now established pattern of making a major transfer move. It was the much speculated purchase of Nottingham Forest's Irish midfielder Roy Keane who

The start of a new era. United celebrate winning the first Premiership trophy and their first Championship since Sir Matt Busby's reign

cost close to £4 million. He made his debut at Wembley against Arsenal in the Charity Shield after going on the club's pre-season warm-up trip to South Africa where they had visited the townships and played in a tournament against their Wembley opponents.

The Wembley curtain-raiser ended 1-1 with Mark Hughes scoring for United and Ian Wright equalising before a penalty shoot-out decided that the shield should once again bear the name of Manchester United as its holders. It was a trophy collected before the season had even started but United wanted more.

Bryan Robson, who was about to commence his final year at Old Trafford, made their aim clear with this statement:

We would dearly love to retain the Championship and there is no reason to believe that we cannot make a good challenge. Over the last two seasons we have the best record in the League. But we also have ambitions to do well in Europe. This club has never won two major trophies in the same season and I feel that would be a tremendous achievement.

United for the double? There was a long road ahead. They

After a Cantona lob from close to the half-way line bounced onto the crossbar and was caught by Chelsea's retreating Russian goalkeeper Dmitri Kharine, the game's only goal came at the opposite end of the field. Kharine's clearance resulted in a shot on United's goal, Schmeichel failed to hold the ball and Gavin Peacock found himself on that score sheet. A similar occurrence, while not in totally identical circumstances, would be reversed the following May when the sides met at Wembley in the FA Cup Final.

Euro exit leads to League form

Before that though was a season filled with drama, joy and sadness for Manchester United. The first disappointment was the failure to get beyond the second round of the European Cup, with defeat under the away goals rule by Galatasaray, the little-known Turkish side, who fought back from two goals down to force a draw at Old Trafford in the first leg of the tie.

Before this United continued their domination of the Premiership with consecutive victories over Arsenal, Swindon, Sheffield Wednesday, Tottenham, Everton and QPR. After 13 games they were 11 points clear of the chasing Norwich, Arsenal, Blackburn and Aston Villa and 20 ahead of their rivals Manchester City, who provided the opposition immediately after the European upset.

It was another televised Sunday game, and the home supporters who had gathered at Maine Road could be forgiven for thinking that they were about to witness a shock. City led 2-0 at half time. Their season had been plagued with demonstrations against chairman Peter Swales and the demands for a change at the top which eventually led to the appointment of Francis Lee. The fact that United were dominating the League in such a fashion was hard to bear for the rival City fans.

Some consolation might come from victory against the 'old enemy' but United were not prepared to lie down. Cantona scored twice during the second period and City fell apart well before Keane scored the winning goal with three minutes left.

An unbeaten run – the Galatasaray scores were 3-3 and 0-0 – had started on 22 September, after a side without Giggs, Cantona, Ince, Parker and Keane lost 2-1 in a League Cup tie at Stoke. It continued for 34 League and Cup fixtures.

Blackburn staged a remarkable challenge and came closest to breaking the sequence on Boxing Day. They led 1-0 at Old Trafford, resisting all United could muster. There was relief for Ferguson and his players when with two minutes remaining Paul Ince scored an equaliser that was just reward for the effort of the afternoon.

After United had beaten Oldham 5-2 at Boundary Park, they began the New Year with a home draw against Leeds. This was

began their defence of their title at Carrow Road, scene of that important victory the previous season, and again came out winners. Ryan Giggs and the veteran Robson each scored with Norwich surprising their audience by facing the Champions with a defensive formation, fielding a sweeper to try to stem any of United's high speed breaks.

United began their season on Sunday, 15 August to meet the demands of television and three days later met Sheffield United in the midweek fixture at Old Trafford. It was Keane's home debut and his two goals in a 3-0 victory thrilled a large crowd.

United saw out August at the top of the table. They had played five games, winning four and drawing at Old Trafford against the revived Newcastle, who had been promoted at the end of the previous season. Then came their first defeat – and one which was to prove significant eight months later. They lost 1-0 at Stamford Bridge against a Chelsea side which was well organised but perhaps a little fortunate.

United introduced a revolutionary new black strip at the start of the 1993-94 season, allowing supporters to follow the fashionable trend of wearing a variety of club colours. It also became fashionable for United to win away from home! Here Roy Keane and Denis Irwin (player's names and squad numbers on shirts were also introduced in the Premiership) celebrate the latter's goal at Southampton which sealed a 3-1 victory. United won 12 away games in retaining the Championship followed by a sensational game at Anfield, where they led 3-0 at one stage thanks to goals from Bruce, Giggs and Irwin, only for Liverpool to fight back and draw 3-3. If United could give away such an advantage in a game, could they also be caught in the Championship they had dominated for so long?

The draw for the Third Round of the FA Cup once again paired United with their namesakes in Sheffield with the tie attracting the attention of BBC television. In it United showed both sides of their character. They won easily but the petulance of Mark Hughes led to him being sent off close to the end after kicking an opponent in anger. He had already been cautioned and the second yellow card brought a one match suspension. The incident also provided TV with evidence it would hold against Ferguson and his players later.

Hughes then scored the only goal of the game as United took their League campaign to Tottenham, three days after drawing at home to Portsmouth in the Coca-Cola (League) Cup.

But before the next fixture, the club was plunged into mourning following the death of Sir Matt.

Sir Matt Busby

Old Trafford was turned into a shrine when Sir Matt Busby died on 20 January 1994, aged 84.

As the news spread supporters came from far and wide to gather at the ground in silent tribute to the man who made their theatre of dreams come alive. It was well before dawn when the first fan arrived to lay a single bunch of flowers on the concrete forecourt beneath the Munich clock memorial, the symbol of the tragic air disaster woven into the history of Manchester United and their distinguished manager who went on to become the President. Before that first day of mourning was over the roped off area below the clock had become a carpet of red and white, as grieving admirers of the grand old man of English football came with flowers and to lay their scarves and flags in his memory. One message summed up the feelings:

You planted the seeds that have made Manchester United the greatest team in the world. Rest in peace Sir Matt, you have left us all in safe hands.

Later all the favours and personal mementoes were gathered up and compressed into bales, a concentration of loving tributes, which will be kept in the club museum.

Sir Matt's funeral procession stopped for a few moments beside Old Trafford, which Martin Edwards believes will be a permanent memorial to his achievements as the architect of today's Manchester United.

'To gauge the life and work of Sir Matt you have only to look at the magnificent stadium and think back to how it was at the end of the war, bombed and derelict,' he said.

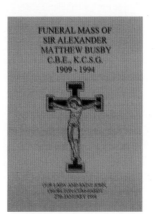

Sir Matt waves goodbye. The man who brought so much glory to Old Trafford died on 20 January 1994 at the age of 84. Football fans everywhere mourned his passing

FUNERAL MASS OF
SIR ALEXANDER
MATTHEW BUSBY
C.B.E., K.C.S.G.
1909 - 1994

OUR LADY AND SAINT JOHN,
CHORLTON CUM HARDY
27th JANUARY 1994

Football goes on

Life and football had to go on, and that Saturday, as the Championship pennant flew at half mast, Old Trafford stood in total silence before the League clash with Everton. There were unfortunate scenes however at Anfield and Ewood Park where Manchester City and Leeds supporters disrespectfully chanted during the one minute silence. Alex Ferguson said before facing the game with Everton:

The result of today's game is irrelevant. I want my players to go out and play the way that Sir Matt would want them to. This game is for his memory and for what he did for football.

His words preceded a display of outstanding skill which remarkably produced only one goal but which had the crowd screaming for more.

Sir Matt's funeral came on the morning after United reached the semi-final of the Coca-Cola Cup by beating Portsmouth 1-0 in a replay they dominated, and three days later they were at Norwich in the FA Cup.

In that game Roy Keane and Eric Cantona scored in a 2-0 win, but Ferguson was angered by comments made on BBC television where slow motion replays were used to highlight an incident involving the Frenchman. He was seen to kick a Norwich player in the back as the two raced for a loose ball and the comments of pundit Jimmy Hill who accused Cantona of vicious play brought a sharp retaliation from the United manager:

Jimmy Hill is a pratt!

Victories followed at QPR, in the first leg of the Coca-Cola Cup semi-final against Sheffield Wednesday, and in the FA Cup away to Wimbledon. United were still top of the Premiership and one game away from the season's first cup final. Talk now was of the treble, a feat yet to be achieved in England.

They reached the Coca-Cola Cup Final following a display

of all out attacking football at Hillsborough, where Sheffield Wednesday were beaten 4-1 (5-1 on aggregate) but the lead in the League was cut to just four points on 5 March when Chelsea visited Old Trafford and won. They became the first side for two years to take six points from United in a season. Once again it was Peacock who scored.

After being drawn away from home for the opening three rounds of their FA Cup campaign United beat Charlton 3-0 at Old Trafford. They paid a hefty price for victory when Peter Schmeichel was sent off for a handling offence outside his area. He would unfortunately miss the Coca-Cola Cup Final.

Disciplinary problems

So began the darkest part of the season when three players were dismissed, one of them on two occasions. Sheffield Wednesday were beaten 5-0 in the Premiership before two away fixtures full of controversy and talking points.

Swindon, the bottom club, bravely fought for a 2-2 draw. Eric Cantona was sent off for stamping on the chest of John Moncur and again this was highlighted by television. Three days later, in another 2-2 draw at Highbury, the Frenchman was again shown the red card after a second bookable offence. This time television came to Cantona's defence showing that the decision was harsh, with the United player the offended rather than the offender. Nevertheless Cantona was suspended for five games and became the target of vicious verbal attacks at away grounds for the remainder of the season.

Schmeichel's suspension meant Les Sealey took over in goal for the Wembley Final, which Aston Villa won 3-1 – and again there was a dismissal. Andrei Kanchelskis received his marching orders for deliberately handling the ball in the last minute and the resulting penalty at least gave Villa the chance to finish the match with what was in reality a flattering scoreline.

Cantona was present for the 1-0 League win over Liverpool at Old Trafford, then missed a 2-0 defeat at Blackburn (now just three points behind), a 3-2 victory over Oldham, and a 1-0 defeat at Wimbledon.

The Frenchman was also unfortunately absent for the FA Cup semi-final against Oldham and its eventual replay.

Against strong opposition from Old Trafford the Football Association decided that the semi-final should be played at Wembley. Oldham were in favour, but after two visits already that season United felt it was asking too much of their supporters to meet the heavy cost of travelling to another game in London.

The game was the turning point of United's season, although at one stage defeat stared them in the face. Goalless it went into extra time and in the 106th minute Oldham's Neil Pointon scored. United fought back throwing the teenage

An understandably angry Eric Cantona walks from the field at Highbury after being sent off for a second bookable offence. Television evidence proved that referee Vic Callow had been harsh in his treatment of the United striker. Six games remained after his ban; five ended in victory and one was drawn. Cantona scored five of his 25 goals during that period

Nicky Butt into the fray to replace Paul Parker and the youngster found himself at the centre of things with only seconds left when he and Robson were part of a move which led to the ball finding its way to Mark Hughes. He scored a brilliant goal with 46 seconds of the 120 minutes to spare.

Oldham were despatched 4-1 at Maine Road as Irwin, Kanchelskis, Robson and Giggs scored. It was to be Robson's last goal for the club and the key to another final. Poor Oldham's season collapsed into relegation.

Although United lost to Wimbledon three days after the win, Blackburn also fell at Southampton leaving the top of the table unchanged as goal difference separated the sides. United had played a game less than their rivals as Cantona returned to face neighbours City at Old Trafford and score twice in a 2-0 win.

The following day Blackburn drew at home to QPR, and when United played Leeds at Elland Road on Wednesday 27 April the 2-0 victory opened a two point head. The scorers that night were Kanchelskis, whose performances were later rewarded with a new five-year contract, and Giggs. Once more the Championship was there for the taking.

United went to Portman Road and beat Ipswich 2-1. By the next evening, Monday, 2 May, the race was over. On the exact date when Aston Villa had lost at home to Oldham the previous year, Blackburn were beaten at Coventry.

The title retained

United were beyond reach and for the first time since the days of the Babes had won back-to-back Championships. They beat Southampton 2-0 as Old Trafford was once again turned into a carnival of colour by 44,705 supporters.

But the Premiership trophy was not presented that night. Instead it was held back until Sunday, 8 May as television once again dictated proceedings. This was the date of the final home game against Coventry, which proved an anti-climax for many of the fans as Alex Ferguson fielded a side which was completely different to his normal line-up.

Peter Schmeichel had been injured at Ipswich and was replaced during that game, and for the final two Premiership fixtures, by Gary Walsh, who had made a remarkable comeback after being transfer listed at the start of the season. He so impressed that he won himself a new contract as the veteran Les Sealey was released.

As they played Coventry, Schmeichel was joined by Ince, Kanchelskis, Hughes, and Giggs on the injured list. With the FA Cup Final six days away, the team included two full debutants in Colin McKee and Gary Neville, plus Bryan Robson making his final appearance. The 0-0 draw saw United end the season eight points clear of the field – but ahead lay more glory.

1990-00

United achieve the double

On Saturday 14 May it came. For the first time United won the elusive League and Cup double, joining Tottenham, Arsenal and Liverpool, the only clubs to achieve that feat this century.

It seemed fate would have a part to play as they faced Chelsea in the final. Remember how earlier in the season Chelsea had beaten United twice? The scorer on each occasion was Gavin Peacock. Remember also how United lost at Stoke in the Coca-Cola Cup? The scorer of both Stoke's goals was Mark Stein. Both played at Wembley!

For the first half Chelsea dominated and, just as that season's result at Stamford Bridge might have hinged on Cantona's shot rebounding from the crossbar when a goal looked certain, Peacock was thwarted in similar style. He seemed destined to score once again but his shot went beyond the reach of Schmeichel, declared fit four days before Wembley, and rebounded to safety.

In the second half United began to play in a way many of their fans expected. Giggs slipped the ball through the legs of Newton and as Irwin ran at goal he was brought down heavily. Cantona's penalty opened the scoring and five minutes later he again struck from the spot after Kanchelskis was pushed over. It was a controversial decision, and Chelsea were finished. Two minutes later Sinclair failed to control the ball, Hughes pounced and made it three-nil as he claimed his fourth goal at Wembley that season.

United celebrate an historic League and Cup double after beating Chelsea 4-0 in the final

Before the game Alex Ferguson had been forced into another heartbreaking decision. Just as in 1990 when Jim Leighton was left out of the replay against Crystal Palace, the manager had told Bryan Robson that he would not be involved against Chelsea. Robson could only look on reluctantly from the wings as substitutes Brian McClair and Lee Sharpe were brought into the game with five minutes remaining.

Ferguson named his side:

Schmeichel, Parker, Bruce, Pallister, Irwin, Kanchelskis, Keane, Ince, Giggs, Cantona, Hughes

McClair was the player who would continue his career at Old Trafford as Robson moved into management and the Scot paid back his manager when he scored the final goal of a 4-0 win. Manchester United had won the double. For Alex Ferguson it was the highlight of a remarkable career. He had won his sixth major trophy in five seasons, but he was still hungry. So was Eric Cantona who after the final revealed that his grasp of English was far better than many had been led to believe: What we have achieved is fantastic, but I hope that we can go on and do even better. Not just the Championship but the European Cup, the FA Cup and perhaps even the Coca-Cola Cup as well. I want us to win everything there is to win.

The new season begins

There was no denying Cantona's contribution to United's success, and he had earned his place in the record books by collecting three successive Championship medals – his first with Leeds in 1992, the others with United in 1993 and 1994. But although his skill was unquestionable, rumbling below the surface was a fiery temperament which would seriously affect United's chances of more success in the season which followed that first-ever double.

No Manchester United manager had won three successive Championships, but Alex Ferguson realised he had a squad capable of achieving that goal. He made only one close-season signing, persuading David May to move from Blackburn for £1.2 million.

Even so, it was Rovers who proved to be his biggest rivals in the 1994-95 campaign.

By this time Bryan Robson had ended his spell at Old Trafford and taken over as player-manager at Middlesbrough, whom he was to guide to the Premier League in his first season. During the summer others had moved too: Michael Phelan to West Brom, Les Sealey to Blackpool and youngsters Colin McKee and Neil Whitworth went to Kilmarnock.

Five players were booked in the Charity Shield and in the opening League game at Old Trafford, Clive Wilson of QPR was sent off after seven minutes, and Paul Parker played only four minutes after coming on as a substitute before he too was sent back to the dressing room.

Newcastle set the pace in the Championship and by October United lay third, seven points adrift, with Blackburn second. Within five days United had to play both the clubs above them.

They won 4-2 at Blackburn in a sensational game which swung on an incident in the 44th minute when Lee Sharpe was barged off the ball as he was about to shoot. Henning Berg was sent off and United were awarded a penalty.

Denis Irwin on international duty during USA 94 fends off Italy's Dino Baggio. Irwin, along with club team-mate Roy Keane, was part of a Republic of Ireland team which sensationally beat Italy, 1-0, in New York. Irwin showed his versatility in the finals, switching from right-back, where he had played most of his international career, to left-back. The Republic was the only team from the British Isles to qualify for the finals, eventually losing to Holland in the second round

By this time 18 games had been played in the League and Blackburn led by one point. United had lost three, at Leeds, Ipswich and Sheffield Wednesday. They had also been knocked out of the Coca-Cola (League) Cup at Newcastle (2–0) and been criticised for using most of their reserve side for the competition.

However they were in confident mood, despite being handicapped by injuries. Lee Sharpe fractured his ankle, Ryan Giggs was sidelined along with Roy Keane and Peter Schmeichel.

By the time the season reached the half-way stage United topped the table, but it was a short stay . . . just six hours! They won 3-2 at Chelsea on Boxing Day; but before many of the travelling supporters who had left at dawn for the 12 noon start were back in Manchester, Blackburn beat City at Maine Road to regain first place in the Premiership.

After United's win at Ewood Park, Blackburn strung together an undefeated run of eleven wins and one draw before the return fixture at Old Trafford. United themselves won seven of their Premiership games in the same period, one of them the 5-0 humiliation of Manchester City at Old Trafford. But they lost at home to Nottingham Forest when Collymore scored a spectacular opening goal.

After the game the player made his ambitions perfectly clear: *Every schoolboy who is interested in football wants to play for the best and when you look around Old Trafford I defy anybody not to be impressed by it.*

The arrival of Cole

Ten days into the New Year Alex Ferguson moved into the transfer market. Not for Collymore, but Andy Cole, the Newcastle United striker, whom he bought for a record £6 million, plus Keith Gillespie, the youngster who had helped knock the Tynesiders off the top of the table some weeks earlier. Cole's debut was against Blackburn and it began as sensationally as his move south. In the opening seconds he was clean through on goal but missed the chance of making a remarkable start to his United career. He said:

I have come to this club to win things and I know that is what is going to happen. I'm not bothered that I didn't score today, because we won. The goals will come later.

United did win, thanks to a superb goal from Eric Cantona. Giggs created it on the left, first losing the ball to Berg then taking it back from him. He crossed from just beyond the edge of the penalty area, Cantona rose at the far post and it seemed the ball was out of reach, but he stretched his body to make perfect contact and head home.

Old Trafford erupted, but it was the final goal they would see from the Frenchman that season. On the night of 25 January 1995 United faced Crystal Palace at Selhurst Park.

Events at Selhurst Park

Football had never seen anything quite like Eric Cantona's kung-fu attack on Crystal Palace supporter Matthew Simmons that night. The 28-year-old French international had been sent off for retaliation five minutes after the interval by referee Alan Wilkie of Chester Le Street. Everyone seemed so stunned that only kit manager Norman Davies reacted, so that Cantona was on his own as he walked towards the dressing room.

The home crowd were naturally jeering and Simmons rushed down to the front of the main stand where he allegedly shouted abuse at Cantona, who clearly heard it, hesitated, moved on again but then obviously changed his mind. He ran towards Simmons and took everyone by surprise by leaping into the air to kick him in the chest. Cantona fell backwards as did Simmons but they were quickly up to start swinging blows at each other.

Peter Schmeichel arrived on the chaotic scene and helped steer Cantona off the field. The player was allowed to travel home with the team that night as the media went into overdrive debating what should be done with him. Television showed the kung-fu kick time after time. The pictures were so unusual that they were transmitted round the world while the tabloid newspapers ran pages of stories and interviews examining the issues. Some said he should be booted out of the country and never allowed to play football in England again. Others wanted to see him given a life ban from the game.

The more balanced *Manchester Evening News* called the next day for an immediate suspension by his club to take the player out of the firing line and give everyone time to think. It was also clearly a police matter as well and eventually after lengthy inquiries and interviews Cantona was charged with common assault, appearing before Croydon magistrates to plead guilty to the offence on 23 March.

United were under pressure from the more hysterical sections of the media to sack the player but they kept their heads and just two days later they announced that he would be suspended until the end of the season and fined the maximum allowed of two weeks wages, amounting to some £20,000. It emerged later that United had been in close touch with the Football Association and had acted decisively in the belief that the FA would later endorse the punishment as appropriate and sufficient.

United knew he would still have to appear in front of an FA disciplinary commission which he duly did a month later when a three-man hearing confounded the club by extending his suspension until 30 September 1995. This meant he would be unable to make a fresh start at the beginning of the following season and that he would in fact be banned for about the first 10 games as well as being forced to miss the pre-season matches. They also fined him a further £10,000.

United decided not to appeal but felt betrayed. The FA pointed out that the men who sat on the commission were

Eric Cantona's extraordinary kung-fu attack on Crystal Palace supporter Matthew Simmons shocked the football world and undoubtedly affected United's title challenge. The Frenchman, sent off for a foul on Palace defender Richard Shaw, reacted violently to abuse apparently hurled at him by Simmons as he left the field. Paul Ince also got involved in the incident, and both were charged with assault. Cantona received 150 hours community service, but Ince was cleared

independent. United felt that they could have given the player a nominal suspension and then wait for the FA hearing to add to it, with the chance that the FA would merely have banned him until the end of the season.

But if United fans had been shocked by the FA it was nothing compared to the stunning verdict from Croydon magistrates, whose chairwoman Mrs Jean Pearch announced:

You have pleaded guilty to common assault and the facts that we have heard show that this is a serious offence. We have heard from your counsel that you deeply regret your actions. We have taken this into account together with your previous good character and your guilty plea. We do feel however that you are a high profile public figure with undoubted gifts and as such you are looked up to by many young people. For this reason the only sentence that is appropriate for this offence is two week's imprisonment forthwith.

United immediately appealed and wiser counsel prevailed at Croydon Crown Court a week later when the judge said that Simmons had indulged in conduct that would 'provoke the most stoic'. The jail sentence was quashed and instead the court ordered Cantona to do 120 hours of community service instead of the lengthy prison term.

Eric, true to form, embarked on a flight of fancy at the Press conference which followed the court case, and said: 'When the seagulls follow the trawler it's because they think sardines will be thrown into the sea.'

The media mostly said they were mystified by this, possibly because they felt he was referring to them as vultures waiting for scraps from the great man. Anyway, Cantona duly completed his order working with 10-year-olds from Salford schools for four hours a day at the United training ground during April and May. He impressed everyone with the responsible and serious way he tackled his commitment and it was even said that year contract before the incident, was granted his wish for a deal which would keep him at the club for a further two seasons.

Hughes missed five games, returning to score against Leeds as United progressed in the FA Cup. They had won at Sheffield United, and beaten Wrexham at Old Trafford before victory over Leeds took them to the quarter-finals.

In the League they beat Villa, where Cole got his first goal, then Manchester City 3-0 at Maine Road, and won 2-0 at Norwich before stumbling to a 1-0 defeat at Everton.

Then came another sensation: Ipswich were beaten 9-0 at Old Trafford. Cole scored five times, Hughes twice and Ince and Keane once each. Although they were still three points adrift of Blackburn at the top, they now had a superior goal difference.

Bad tempered Cup tie

In the FA Cup they beat QPR to go into the semi-finals where fate paired them with Crystal Palace. It took a replay to secure victory and in the second game Roy Keane was sent off after reacting violently to a fierce challenge by Gareth Southgate. Keane kicked out, stamping on Southgate's stomach as he hay on the turf.

Players piled in, Keane and Palace's Darren Patterson were ordered off and the game turned sour. The two were later charged with bringing the game into disrepute.

There had been calls for calmness by the Football Association, who had ruled that the tie should go ahead against the wishes of Crystal Palace. One of their supporters had been killed in an incident outside a Walsall public house prior to the original game, and Palace asked their followers to boycott the replay.

Only 17,987 saw United win comfortably but many claimed it was the cost of tickets which kept some fans away rather than anything else.

Attendances were very much in United's thoughts and a month before the semi-finals, they announced plans for more rebuilding at Old Trafford to increase capacity to 55,300 with a giant grandstand replacing the cantilever building of 1965. Chairman Edwards revealed the plans for the £28 million development but added a footnote for his manager:

Because of the amount of expenditure involved, £9 million to buy the land and £19 million in building costs, it means that we will be restricted in the transfer market for the next two seasons. That is why we invested £6 million in Andy Cole.

Meanwhile big-spending Blackburn continued to lead the chase, but began to stumble as United applied the pressure. United won at Leicester, Rovers drew at Leeds. United drew with Chelsea, Rovers lost to Manchester City at Ewood Park. The nerves were beginning to show. Rovers lost to West Ham,

the youngsters he coached were a key factor in persuading him to stay with Manchester United and sign a new contract.

This was the one big issue remaining. For a long time manager Alex Ferguson felt there would be too many difficulties for Cantona to continue his career in England, not least the hostility of rival fans at away games. Inter Milan hovered in the background confident that they would be able to offer him a new start and make United happy with a £4m fee.

The player, always fall of surprises, delivered a major one on 28 April when he turned his back on Italy to sign a new three-year contract and say that he hoped to stay at Old Trafford for the rest of his career:

'It is a love story. It is something that is very strong for me. The love of the club is the most important weapon in the world. I just couldn't leave. It is something very strong for me.'

In the meantime, Ferguson's plans to play Cole and Cantona together would have to be shelved until October.

Ironically Mark Hughes, seen by many to be surplus to requirements on Cole's arrival, was injured in the League game at Newcastle five days after Cole's transfer. Hughes was on crutches as Cantona was punished, and after rejecting a one-

Top: Andy Cole clutches the match ball after hitting five against Ipswich in March, 1995. The Reds romped to an amazing 9-0 victory

Above: Tempers flare in the FA Cup semi-final replay against Crystal Palace at Villa Park. Roy Keane had stamped on Gareth Southgate in a moment of anger. Keane and Darren Patterson were sent off

1990-00

United won at Coventry. It was neck and neck and by the time the final day of the season arrived and Blackburn were just within reach. Wins for United against Sheffield Wednesday and then Southampton closed the gap to just two points.

Then came one of the most disappointing weeks in the history of Manchester United.

Blackburn clinch title on the last day of the season

Blackburn's closing game was at Anfield, while United were away to West Ham. Victory for United and anything less for Blackburn and the Championship would stay at Old Trafford.

Shearer scored for Blackburn, and West Ham went ahead through Michael Hughes. At half time it seemed all over.

In Liverpool the home side fought back, while in London, United equalised through McClair. It was 1-1 in each game.

The West Ham goal was under siege. They pulled back every player and their goalkeeper Miklosko gave the performance of his life. Efforts from Cole, McClair, Hughes, Sharpe, and Bruce were thwarted and United could not get the second decisive goal. As the final whistle blew at Upton Park, Liverpool were scoring a last minute winner at Anfield.

Blackburn were Champions by a single point, taking the title for the first time in 81 years. So close was the contest that under the old rules of two points for a win and one for a draw United would have won on goal average!

Alex Ferguson congratulated Blackburn and Kenny Dalglish for a remarkable battle, but he also praised the efforts of his own players:

I am really proud of my players, it has been a fantastic effort by them. To amass 88 points in second place is a marvellous performance. They are down on the floor at the moment but they have battled against adversity before and they will bounce back. If you look at our record over the last four years, we have only lost 22 games out of 168 and never finished lower than runners-up and that is remarkable. It takes a good team to beat us and having got to 89 points you cannot deny that Blackburn and Kenny Dalglish have done a great job taking the Championship off us. We at United accepted the spirit of the challenge and congratulate them on their performance.

Six days later the United manager was again gracious in defeat, this time after Everton won the FA Cup.

In an unattractive game in which chances were few and far between, Everton scored the only goal after breaking out of defence, Paul Rideout heading home a rebound from the underside of the crossbar after Graham Stuart thought he had wasted an easier opportunity.

Top: A disconsolate Ryan Giggs troops off after United's 1-0 defeat against Everton in the FA Cup final. Giggs came on as a substitute in the second half, but even he could not light up a scrappy match in which chances were few and far between

United dominated the second half but were thwarted once again by a superb display of goal-keeping, this time from the veteran Neville Southall. Incredibly United were so close to repeating the double, yet had won nothing at senior level.

There was hope for the future with the youngsters winning the FA Youth Cup but there can be no doubting that Manchester United were glad to see the end of the 1994-95 season, a time when the club sailed through turbulent waters . . . with seagulls in their wake.

Transfer surprises

The dust had hardly settled on the Cantona incident when suddenly clouds formed again over Old Trafford at the start of the 1995-96 season.

This time they were real as well as metaphoric. Workers moved in to demolish the North Stand and make way for a giant three-tier structure which would hold 26,500 seated spectators, and controversy filled the air as the transfers of both Paul Ince to Inter Milan, and Mark Hughes to Chelsea, were announced.

There had been speculation that Ince might go, but for Hughes to move was a sensation. Chairman Edwards quickly tried to pacify angered supporters, insisting the players were not being off-loaded to finance the £28 million building project:

We have known for some time that Mark wanted to leave. He has been a great servant and we wish him all the best. As for Paul Ince, we had an offer for him at the end of the season and I put this to the manager. He is responsible for his squad, he is the one who decides who he wants next season. He decided that we have enough cover in midfield and accepted the offer.

Was this Alex Ferguson doing his own demolition, tearing apart his side as vigorously as the crews flattening the cantilever grandstand? The chairman continued:

Only time will tell if it proves to be good business or bad. The manager of Manchester United decides on the squad he wants. All I would say to the fans is that after all the success he has had, we have to have some confidence in the manager's ability. If we were to lift a trophy next year people would say that it was not so bad after all. If however things turn sour they will point to this particular issue as being the start of it.

If Ferguson was reacting like the mad artist slashing his masterpiece he was taking a massive risk. He obviously felt his talented youngsters would succeed, and his decision to sell Ince gave credence to rumours that the player was causing problems in the dressing room. The manager was far from happy with Ince's attitude and his purchase of a car number plate bearing the letters 'GUV' highlighted the problem.

No one knew what lay ahead but some observers felt Edwards was covering himself against disaster when he said it was the

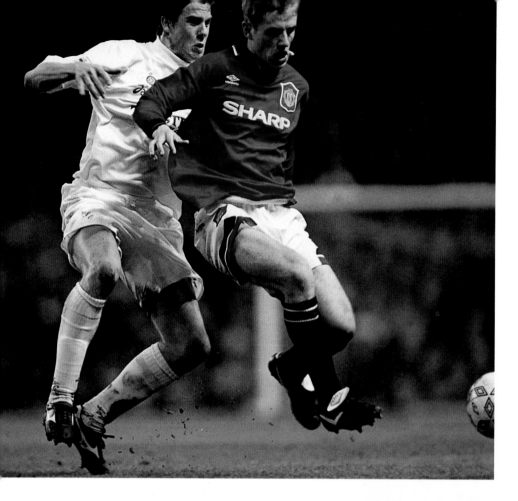

Ince had made a tearful exit hinting that Ferguson was forcing him out. He said:

The only thing I can say is it was a shock. The United fans know that I love them, there will always be a special place for those fans. It was hard for me to make the decision. I was shocked that the decision was made in the first place and here I am.

He may have seemed reluctant to leave, but insiders at Old Trafford claimed he made regular dressing room announcements that one day he would play in Italian football. Had Ferguson called his bluff, or simply had enough of 'The Guv'nor's' ways which could have been a disruptive influence on the younger players? Captain Ferguson wanted a tight ship.

Hughes appeared to have signed a new contract, but did not put pen to paper. His fear was that with Cole an expensive addition to the squad, and the summer announcement by Cantona that he would not be driven out by his ban, there would be little chance of playing many first team games when the Frenchman returned.

The departure of Kanchelskis was prolonged and soured feelings between United and Everton. When the sides met at Goodison in the fifth game of the season, Merseyside saw it as the day of reckoning.

United had recovered from that first defeat and chalked up victories over West Ham and Wimbledon at Old Trafford, followed by a 2-1 win at Blackburn. They were fourth in the table at kick-off and by the end of the game they were lying second.

United won 3-2 but Kanchelskis was put out of action for several weeks as controversy and irony came in one move. After a quarter of an hour the winger fell awkwardly and dislocated a shoulder following a challenge by Lee Sharpe. It was not malicious, but the Everton fans were angered as their new hero was helped from the pitch.

manager who would "stand or fall" by those transfer decisions. The buck stopped with Ferguson, but if the fans were unsettled after seeing two of their favourites depart, there was another shock to come. After weeks of speculation, Andrei Kanchelskis joined Everton. The Ukrainian claimed he could not work with Ferguson and the club was faced with a 'him or me' situation. There could only be one winner, and the player was sold.

It was a surprise. Ferguson had transferred Keith Gillespie, understudy to Kanchehskis, as part of the deal which brought Andy Cole to the club. That, and the fact that the Ukrainian still had four years of his contract to serve, was proof enough that United did not expect the Russian international to defect.

Ferguson made a bid for Tottenham and England winger Darren Anderton, but was rejected, so the supporters were uneasy as the new season began without a major signing. The media hawks were ready, their talons bared, as United faced Aston Villa on the opening day. By half-time they were circling ready for the kill as Villa led 3-0 and after a 3-1 defeat they swooped on Ferguson. with undisguised glee.

"Forget it!" said one headline. "There would be no success for United this season."

"You will never win anything with kids" said television pundit Alan Hansen.

Ferguson felt he could, and replaced his stars with youngsters from his 1992 youth team.

Top: Philip Neville figured in Alex Ferguson's plans for the whole season. He caught the eye of the England manager and was called up for Euro 96

Above: Paul Scholes was a good replacement for Andy Cole, scoring 14 goals in 18 games in the 95–96 season

United crash out of Coca-Cola

As the season progressed, David Beckham, Paul Scholes and the Neville brothers, Gary and Philip, were used on a regular basis. There were signs that United might be able to challenge for a trophy but Europe once again proved a stumbling block.

Later in the season there were celebrations following a ruling by the European Court, when UEFA were forced to change their foreign player restrictions, but, the move came too late to help United in the 1995-96 campaign.

The court ruled that players from EEC countries had to be regarded equally. Scots, Welsh and Irish were no longer classed as foreigners in England as they had been by UEFA since 1991, nor were those from any other member country. Clubs were still restricted to three foreign players, but these were from outside Europe rather than beyond England's borders. The door was

1990-00

The football world waited not knowing what to expect. Those who supported the Frenchman hoped he could pick up where he had left off, those who had screamed for his head wanted him to leap enraged into the crowd again.

With that air of arrogance, Cantona stepped into the spotlight and was an immediate success.

In the months which followed he ignored endless provocation from rival spectators and attempts to rile him on the field, as his influence helped transform the side once again. This was the new improved Cantona, a changed character who walked away from controversy and even played the role of the peacemaker when things became heated.

Cheers greeted the prodigal son on the perfect stage for his much publicised return. United scored in the opening minute. It was not Cantona, but Nicky Butt who grabbed the first goal but the crowd was stunned as they trailed in the second-half after two superb goals from Robbie Fowler. Then in the 70th minute Cantona marked his return in true style. Giggs was pulled down as he ran at goal, Cantona converted the penalty and Old Trafford exploded in noise. The Frenchman celebrated his goal by swinging from a net support and jumping into the crowd to embrace his worshippers. He was back.

Cantona had never been one to say much, his natural shyness and a reluctance to intentionally grab publicity meant that interviews with him were few and far between. There was also the language barrier, although Monsieur Cantona played down his real grasp of English.

After the Selhurst Park incident he had said little. Co-author Tom Tyrrell was possibly the only English journalist to speak on a one-to-one basis with him when he described his reason for staying at Old Trafford and his relationship with the supporters with the words:

"It's a love story . . . a love story."

After this requests for an audience received a polite, "Sorry, but no thank you. I have nothing to say at the moment". In fact things remained that way until the end of the season. Cantona would do his talking on the field of play.

In the Premiership, the gap between United and leaders Newcastle widened as winter set in. Two points separated the sides after United beat Bryan Robson's Middlesbrough at Old Trafford but the difference grew to five following defeat at Arsenal. December was a disaster. It seemed there was little hope of winning the championship. Newcastle were in the driving seat, swept along by a run of victories and urged on by a tidal wave of support.

Roy Keane was sent off against Middlesbrough, his second dismissal of the season following a harsh red card at Blackburn. He served his suspension whilst recovering from a hernia operation; this too was his second of the year. Nicky Butt accumulated 21 disciplinary points and was given a three

opening, but in the 1995-96 UEFA Cup it slammed in United's face, when they lost to the Russian club Rotor Volgograd.

There was little joy in the Coca-Cola (League) Cup where Ferguson followed his pattern of fielding a second string side in the early rounds and paid the penalty.

York City, a struggling side from the Third Division, were the opposition and the first leg at Old Trafford was a disaster. Reserve team goalkeeper Kevin Pilkington was beaten by a deflected shot, then came sensation as United were reduced to ten men when defender Pat McGibbon was sent off. To make matters worse the referee awarded York a penalty because McGibbon had pulled back an opponent in a "professional foul", but television later proved the infringement was outside the area. It mattered little, York scored from the spot kick and a minute later, with United in disarray, made it United 0 York 3. It was one for the record books! The line-up for the second leg was more recognisable, but a 3-1 win was not enough and United made a humiliating exit.

Peter Schmeichel's outstanding ability has earned him the reputation as one of the best goalkeepers in the world. During the UEFA Cup game against Rotor Volgograd, he also proved himself to be the saviour of United's unbeaten home record in European competition, by scoring the most extraordinary goal of the season. With two minutes left and the Russian visitors leading 2-1, Schmeichel headed home a corner to equalise, but United went out on the away goals rule

Cantona returns

Between those games, Eric Cantona returned. His exile ended on 30th September and the first side he faced was Liverpool at Old Trafford the following day.

match ban, Gary Pallister was injured during a 1-1 draw at Nottingham Forest and goalkeeper Schmeichel had to have an operation on an elbow. Added to this, Steve Bruce picked up a hamstring injury, and it was no surprise when form slumped.

Three successive draws were followed by defeats at Leeds and Liverpool, three points from a possible fifteen. As Newcastle led by ten points Ferguson searched for a defender to bridge the gap left by Pallister's absence. Frenchman William Prunier, a friend of Cantona's and a free agent, came on trial and was in the 42,024 Old Trafford crowd as hopes were lifted and Newcastle defeated; Keane gave a superb performance in a 2-0 win and three days later Prunier made his debut against QPR. United won 2-1 and he did enough to be included in the side for the New Year's day game at Tottenham.

It was the last we saw of Prunier who made a swift return to France following a 4-1 defeat, the heaviest United had endured since the Premiership was launched. Ferguson asked him to stay for another trial period, but English football was not for him.

So those early season predictions seemed to have a ring of truth about them; were United destined to fail for a second successive season? The defeat at Tottenham was not the end, however, but the beginning. The side went on an amazing run which started with a somewhat fortunate 2-2 home draw with Sunderland in the FA Cup third round when a Cantona equaliser in the 79th minute kept them in the competition. In the replay, Andy Cole scored a late winner and the show was on the road!

Ten consecutive wins followed as United clawed back Newcastle's lead and reached the quarter finals of the cup. Cantona was in explosive form scoring the only goal at West Ham, two on his media-hyped return to Selhurst Park, scene of his kung-fu attack, and cup goals against Reading in round four, plus a penalty against Manchester City in round five which levelled the scores before Lee Sharpe struck the winner.

Premiership dog-fight

In the league, a 6-0 win at Burnden Park pushed Bolton closer to eventual relegation but boosted United's goal difference as they prepared for the trip to Newcastle. The pressure was now on Kevin Keegan's side as Alex Ferguson predicted:

There's a lot of important games to come up; you cannot place one in front of another. We have to win our games now and we are aware of that. If we win them then that might do the trick. Being there for the last four seasons must give us an advantage.

The confrontation at St James's Park was billed as the championship decider. A Newcastle win would keep them four points ahead with a game in hand, a win for United would close the gap to one point and increase United's psychological advantage.

Newcastle pounded United for the first 45 minutes but

Schmeichel was invincible and the defence held out until half time when Ferguson could impart new instructions. In the 51st minute a touch of Cantona's brilliant finishing silenced the Newcastle support and Tyneside began to fear the worst. A home win over Southampton in the FA Cup earned a semifinal meeting with Chelsea and suddenly with nine league games remaining it became clear that Alex Ferguson's new look side could have another tilt at the double.

The double double? Surely not. To win the championship and the FA Cup in the same season was difficult, to repeat it was virtually impossible. Could those fresh-faced youngsters reach greater heights than Chapman's Huddersfield and Arsenal, the Liverpool teams of Shankly and Paisley, or the United of Sir Matt?

A 1-1 draw at QPR put them top but there was controversy as referee Robbie Hart added four minutes of stoppage time and Cantona scored half way through it. Rangers fans were furious and matters were not made any easier by the Loftus Road scoreboard clock breaking down after an hour. Its blank electronic screen normally signals that 90 minutes have elapsed but it stood that way for half an hour adding confusion to a tense game. One point was of value to United but the loss of two was disastrous to Rangers who were relegated a month later.

Within 48 hours Newcastle were top again, but wins over Arsenal and Tottenham put United in front once more. They reached the Cup final after beating Chelsea 2-1 at Villa Park, and emerged from the Easter games still at the top of the table with wins over Manchester City, another side destined for relegation, and Coventry, hours before Newcastle lost at Blackburn. At Christmas, United had trailed by ten points, after Easter Monday they were six points in front of the Tynesiders and now favourites to lift the championship for a third time in four seasons. The impossible now seemed possible.

The wrong kind of shirts

Then they travelled to Southampton and caused a sensation when the players demanded a change of strip for the second half of the game as they trailed 0-3. They began in a grey outfit which had been launched as the new away kit at the start of the season. Fans took notice that the side had not won a game in these colours and dubbed them unlucky. Footballers are superstitious and few believed Alex Ferguson's claim after the 3-1 defeat that the change had been made because the players had difficulty seeing one another and merged with the crowd.

Defeat meant that the race was wide open again. United beat Leeds 1-0 at Old Trafford after a stirring fight by Howard Wilkinson's players who had been reduced to ten men when goalkeeper Mark Beeney was sent off for palming the ball away

1990-00

outside his penalty area. His replacement, full back Lucas Radebe, a former goalkeeper, played superbly but Ferguson's post-match remarks caused controversy:

> *I am saying this in support of their manager, because he doesn't deserve that (result). What they have been doing for the rest of the season God knows. It will be interesting to see how they perform against Newcastle.*

Psychological warfare? Was this Alex Ferguson challenging Leeds to lift their game against Newcastle the following week, or was he winding up his rivals. For whatever reason Ferguson was genuinely angered.

Kevin Keegan was none too happy either. When they met a week later Newcastle beat Leeds 1-0 and Keegan appeared on television wide-eyed with rage, his voice cracking after the strain of yelling instructions for 90 minutes and lost many admirers as he bleated: "Oh, I hope we beat them, I hope we beat them!".

Premier champions again

The final home game of the season had seen United in championship form and put added pressure on Newcastle as they hammered Nottingham Forest 5-0 at Old Trafford. In the closing six days Newcastle were away to Forest and at home to Tottenham. The ball was back in their court as they went to Nottingham for the game which proved decisive. Peter Beardsley put them ahead, Ian Woan struck a brilliant equaliser and with one game to go United were two points ahead and had a superior goal difference, 35 to 29, a difference of plus six. For Newcastle to win the title, United had to lose their last game, while they had to beat Tottenham at St James's Park.

United's closing fixture? Away to Bryan Robson's Middlesbrough! Football gossip was outrageous in its suggestion that Robson would make it easy for his former club, and in fact Middlesbrough fought like tigers to win the game. They almost scored three times before United took the lead through an unlikely hero. David May, brought into the side at the expense of skipper Steve Bruce, who was relegated to the bench, outjumped all others to head home a corner as the news came through that Newcastle were trailing to Tottenham.

Andy Cole was another left out of the starting line-up as Ferguson handed the striking role to Paul Scholes, as he had against Forest. After 53 minutes the manager made the switch, Cole on, Scholes off, and with his first touch, a clever flick over his shoulder, Cole scored the goal which virtually clinched the championship.

Newcastle pulled level just as Ryan Giggs rammed home a third superb goal after a weaving run. United were champions, their third success in four seasons and as the players danced

Steve Bruce lifts the Premiership trophy for the third time in four years. Newcastle had to win at home to Spurs and United had to lose at Middlesbrough for the Magpies to lift the cup. In the end, Newcastle could only manage a draw and United won at the Riverside. It had been a frustrating year for Bruce who was often injured. At the end of the season he announced that he would be leaving on a free transfer and joining Birmingham City

in celebration after being handed the trophy, chairman Edwards summed up:

> *It was a tense afternoon. Slightly different to last year where we went into the game knowing that if Blackburn won we couldn't win it. Today it was in our own hands. I was a bit nervous at half time, I knew it could still turn round, but once we got the second goal it became comfortable.*

Was this the best championship of the three? He said:

> *Clearly the first championship was important because we had waited so long. It was a tremendous relief but I think today was so good because we were under pressure. At the beginning of the season, having let three very experienced players go, everybody wondered how the youngsters would do. I think that is what is so pleasing about today. They told us we would win nothing with kids . . . I wonder what they are saying now?*

The double double

So the stage was set for Manchester United to write a special page in the history of their club and go for a double double, a feat never before accomplished in English football. This was a golden opportunity for Alex Ferguson and his team.

Perhaps it was the enormity of the opportunity and prize which influenced the manager's tactics, dulled the player's minds and cramped their muscles because the performance never quite lived up to expectations and the display did not match the record book achievement. The purists quibbled afterwards, though that hardly spoiled the enjoyment of the United supporters or diminish the satisfaction of following a team which had broken new ground.

The football at Wembley lacked attacking flair, which came as something of a surprise because in the days leading up to the final everyone had predicted a match which would reveal all the best aspects of the game. Both teams had reputations for playing attractive, creative football and indeed it was a battle between two of the top three teams in the country. On the day itself, though, the defences dominated, and two powerful midfield forces cancelled each other out.

Liverpool, expected to stretch United every inch of the way, were particularly out of touch. The experienced John Barnes had a dismal day and Jamie Redknapp was overshadowed by the driving force of United's Irish dynamo, Roy Keane, voted the man of the match by the BBC. Steve McManaman tried hard with his long penetrating runs but he failed to reach Stan

Top: Eric Cantona scores the only goal of the game in the FA Cup final. The Frenchman hit a superb volley after David James had punched the ball out towards the edge of the penalty area from a David Beckham corner. Alex Ferguson said later: 'It was a quite magnificent goal. Eric showed great composure and such accuracy with the shot... I don't know many players who could have hit the ball the way he did for the goal.'

Collymore and Robbie Fowler up front. Peter Schmeichel in the United goal was rarely troubled, apart from pulling down high crosses.

United were not much better in terms of quality, with the exception perhaps of Ryan Giggs, who burst into action from time to time. Andy Cole was another player who looked a victim of Cup final nerves and he was taken off in the second half to make way for the youngster, Paul Scholes. Eric Cantona also had a relatively quiet afternoon, except that once again he proved to be the complete match winner. He was lurking on the edge of Liverpool's penalty box for a corner at a time when it looked as if the game would need extra time, and fittingly enough, after his marvellous season, he emerged the destroyer of Liverpool's dreams.

The decisive moment of the match came five minutes from the end when David Beckham's corner kick was punched out by David James. The goalkeeper appeared to have cleared the danger because he had got the ball out of the penalty area but he had not legislated for Cantona. The French genius arched his body and met the ball on the volley in the kind of situation which normally sees the shot sail over the goal and into the crowd. This time though there was power and poise behind the blast and the ball flew straight as an arrow past a startled James.

Completing the League and Cup double seemed to make everything worthwhile for Cantona after all the disciplinary troubles of the previous season. His role in United's championship success had seen him voted Player of the Year by the

Footballer Writers Association and after scoring his 19th goal of the season he said:

> Winning the final was important after last season. This is a great moment. I have the highest regard for Alex Ferguson as a man and as a manager. What can I say about the fans? I respect them and I love them and I try to give them the pleasure they need to receive. While I was banned they remembered me during every game even if it was just for 15 seconds. I will never forget that. I am settled in England and will certainly be staying here for the next two years of my contract, even longer than that, who knows?

As the well-travelled and controversial Frenchman led United up to the Royal box to receive the Cup as the team captain in the absence of the injured Steve Bruce, he seemed to have come a long way from the storm-tossed times of his Court case. To his great credit, he had tried to persuade Bruce to lead the team up the steps for the presentation, but the team captain would have none of it and in truth, Cantona had been the team's inspiration in both League and Cup.

Wembley also suggested that the player was more at peace with himself; when an angry Liverpool fan spat at him on the way up for the Cup he contented himself with only glaring at

Ferguson, Cantona and Kidd with the **FA Cup**. United had won an incredible second double in three years, a record for an English club. It was an amazing end to an eventful season for Eric Cantona

the offender. The moment seemed the symbol of his transformation, a remarkable rehabilitation which must surely represent one of Alex Ferguson's shrewdest moves in his management career.

It is impossible to exaggerate Cantona's role in the double double. Not only did he carry the team through March towards the championship, he also scored in nearly every round of the FA Cup and of course it was his goal at Wembley which won

the Cup. It used to be said that when Bryan Robson was acting out his Captain Marvel role that Manchester United were a one-man team, but Cantona has taken over the mantle of the King of Old Trafford, an incredible man and a fantastic footballer.

The fans didn't need telling, of course. The French tricolour made a sea of colour at Wembley and again on the streets of Manchester for the homecoming on the traditional open top bus the following day. The only thing missing at the final was the Marseillaise, though the United fans had their own anthem and there was only one song on their lips. They made it clear that though Keegan was out of sight he was not forgotten. They filled the stadium with a non-stop refrain set to the Monkees' Daydream Believer, deriding the Newcastle manager's efforts.

It was a cruel jibe at the expense of one of their rivals, but fans are generous indeed to one of their own. Two days after the final there was a dinner to mark the retirement of their kit manager and quarter-master, Norman Davies, after 24 years with the club. There was warmth at the dinner also for the manager who had delivered ten trophies in as many years. Completing the double double must have given Alex Ferguson particular satisfaction after the way he had been treated by some of the fans at the start of the season; many thought that it was a time to strengthen the squad rather than strip it of three experienced and influential players. He later explained:

> We had our disappointments this season, like an early departure from the Coca-Cola Cup and a knockout in Europe, but for the most part I always felt we would achieve something. There were doubts in the early days following the departure of three experienced players but I always knew our youngsters would deliver. I didn't know exactly how they would cope with the big games but they had to be given their chance and I am delighted to say that they have shown themselves to be equipped with that final, important factor of temperament.

Alex Ferguson's new deal

The only discordant note was struck when the manager made known his feelings on the subject of a new contract. He indicated that after what he had achieved, he wanted recognition financially as well as a six-year contract to take him up to the age of 60 and retirement in 2002.

Matters came to a head when the *Manchester Evening News* ran a story in the week following the Cup final with a front page banner headline declaring 'Fergie: I'll Quit in Pay Wrangle'. His threat to walk out unless the matter was settled before going on holiday at the weekend seemed to focus minds, for that night agreement was reached for a four-year deal reputed to double his salary to £600,000 a year which with bonuses could reach an annual £1m.

Ferguson said:

It was important to me to get a contract which reflected what I had won and what I was worth. I am delighted with the terms and I can leave for my holiday happy that the issue has been resolved.

The manager returned as England staged the European Championships and United were linked with many players taking part. However it was a second attempt to sign Alan Shearer which made the headlines during the close season.

Shearer added to the speculation while on international duty by saying.

I am flattered to be linked with a club as big and successful as Manchester United.

United were willing to pay a record £10 million for the player who had slipped through their fingers when moving north from Southampton to Ewood Park. Ferguson felt this would be the key to European as well as more domestic success, but Blackburn had other ideas.

Rovers were determined Shearer would not join the club they saw as their biggest rivals and refused to do business with United. Shearer could have his move, but not to Old Trafford.

They accepted Kevin Keegan's world record offer of £15 million and Shearer went home to Newcastle. Martin Edwards did not hide his feelings at the failure to land the England star:

I was disappointed because we had set our stall out to buy Alan. I think circumstances went against us and feel with hindsight we were never going to get him. Blackburn were in the driving seat, he was their player, he had three years of his contract to go, they could dictate whether he came to United or not. I can also understand Newcastle stretching themselves. They have come a long way in a very short space of time. 'They just lost out to us last year and there must have been tremendous disappointment. I think their feeling was that if Manchester United got Shearer then everybody else could forget the championship for the next five years.

Foreign imports

Ferguson was linked with a number of European stars as England enjoyed a summer feast of football, reaching the semi-final of Euro '96 before being beaten by Germany, the eventual winners.

Old Trafford was one of the group venues, and staged the semi-final between France and the Czech Republic. It was the Czech, Karel Poborsky, who caught Fergie's eye and the long haired midfielder was signed for £3.5 million from his club Slavia Prague. He was joined by four other new players before the 1996-97 campaign began. They were Dutchmen Jordi

Cruyff, son of former world star Johan, who had left Barcelona following the dismissal of his father as coach, and goalkeeper Raimond van der Gouw from Vitesse Arnhem. There was a Norwegian duo, defender Ronny Johnsen, signed from Turkish club Besiktas, and young striker Ole Gunnar Solskjaer from Molde.

United were one of many clubs to take advantage of the ruling that players from E.U. countries should no longer be regarded as foreigners. This gave a new look to the Premiership with Italians, Frenchmen, Dutch and Scandinavians joining clubs like Chelsea, Arsenal and Liverpool. Along with Newcastle all were expected to challenge United.

Newcastle, as Premiership runners-up were United's opponents in the Charity Shield and with Shearer and Les Ferdinand leading their attack they were expected to show the champions a thing or two. Newcastle were humiliated 4-0 leaving their fans in stunned silence as United ran rings round them at Wembley. They had their revenge later in the season.

Beckham celebrates his 'wondergoal' against Wimbledon on the first day of the 1996-97 season

Newcastle set the pace

United had a sign of what lay ahead before the new season was a fortnight old. Andy Cole was ruled out with pneumonia, Roy Keane destined for an early knee operation. Not noce throughout the entire campaign would Alex Ferguson field the same side in consecutive games.

They started in spectacular style beating Wimbledon 3-0 at Selhurst Park, the third goal being a remarkable 55-yard shot from inside his own half by David Beckham. The new campaign was only 88 minutes old yet it was hailed as goal of the season!

The first home game, a 2-2 draw against Everton, attracted 54,943 fans. A month later one extra supporter was recorded for the 4-1 win over Nottingham Forest, but by the time Liverpool travelled to Manchester on October 12, all building work on the new North Stand was completed and for the first time over 55,000 supporters sat to watch a game at Old Trafford

By that time Newcastle had established a lead at the top of the league, taking over from Sheffield Wednesday who set the early pace. United were fourth after a 1-0 victory over the Merseysiders boosted hopes, but not the confidence of Eric Cantona:

I forgot that I could play so bad. I am very unhappy, because I am very disapppinted about my performance. If people say I played badly it is true, I realise that myself and I can tell you I am not happy, I am very disappointed.

We got the message, if Cantona was unhappy after beating Liverpool he must have been devastated a week later when United lost 5-0 at Newcastle. Had their bid to retain the title ended?

The goading of the Newcastle supporters was hard to take and United were subjected to another hammering in the press.

It was Alex Ferguson's biggest defeat as a manager and it was understandable that the critics felt United had blown it. Injuries were not helping their cause but were never used as an excuse. Andy Cole, who had recovered from his illness, was finding form in the Reserves, then was struck the cruellest blow.

During a 3-1 win over Liverpool Reserves at Anfield he broke both legs following a challenge by Neil Ruddock and was out of action until Christmas.

Solskjaer was becoming popular with supporters his first five goals coming after 233 minutes of football and just one full appearance. His modesty was outweighed by an honest approach and his way of celebrating a goal, at a time when players competed to be the most outrageous, was true to character. He did little more than open his arms and broaden his ever present smile.

However, the Norwegian could do little to stop the bombshell which struck United in thirteen remarkable days.

After the humiliation of Newcastle they travelled to Southampton and condeded not five, but six goals. The struggling south-coast club beat the reigning champions 6-3. This was followed by the first ever European defeat at Old Trafford, then a 2-1 home upset against Chelsea.

United were seventh in the table and 7-1 to retain the title. Some players may have felt Alex Ferguson was over optimistic when he told them they should take on the bookmakers if they had faith in their own ability!

It was hardly the way to celebrate his ten years in charge, but Alex Ferguson refused to let the slump dampen his spirits.

We aren't in a desperate position. The League can still be won.

A decade at the top

Those were the manager's words – but not on his tenth anniversary. He spoke them on the day he took over from Ron Atkinson, but they were equally apt on November 6, 1996. Ten years on Ferguson did say:

It is a tremendous achievement, ten years as manager of Manchester United. It has been a fantastic experience and hopefully this is the start of another good decade. When I came I never thought that I would still be here ten years on. You never think that way, it is a long time. I was eight-and-a-half years at Aberdeen so eighteen-and-a-half years with two clubs is quite extraordinary. Now I am looking forward to the next ten.

His players paid tribute too. Ryan Giggs a schoolboy when Fergie replaced Atkinson recalled the early years:

He was brilliant with all the lads and took special care of us. He took time out to talk to us and our parents. Ten years on his

Norwegian Ole Gunnar Solskjaer was a huge hit with the fans during 96-97 and ended the season as United's top scorer

will to win is still there and his appetite for the game is the same. I think there is only one place for him and that is here. I don't think he will ever want to leave and I don't think the players will ever want him to either.

Gary Pallister, Ferguson's record signing in 1989 added:
To come to the club and turn the place round like he had to, shows how good a manager he is. It is not just what you see with the first team, the success and the trophies, it goes down through the youth side of things. To bring through the talent we are now seeing in the first team and getting the club to run the way he wanted it to.

It seemed that United's demise, temporary or otherwise, was being enjoyed in certain quarters. Locally, Manchester City fans were able to forget the problems of their own club and poke fun at their illustrious neighbours, while parts of the national media appeared to be under the impression that the season was over for Cantona and Co.

Pallister hit back at the increasing criticism which was coming from people who claimed these were ABU's – football fans who wanted 'Anyone But United' to succeed.

You have to take the rough with the smooth. We have enjoyed six or seven years of being at the top and people saying good things. The jealousy thing is part and parcel of being successful. It is nice to be in the position where you can make people jealous.

United get into their stride

Liverpool edged Newcastle off the top of the table as Christmas approached, United were back to fourth place and beginning to find their feet again. Ferguson had made it clear that once the European Champions' League programme had been completed he would concentrate on the Premiership, and was true to his word.

'December has always proved a very important month. Last year our December form caused us a real headache. It put us so many points behind Newcastle but fortunately we made it up, but we can't take that for granted and a good December would help.'

They went on to beat Sunderland 5-0 at Old Trafford, Nottingham Forest 4-0 away from home and completed their three holiday games by beating Leeds 1-0 in front of 55,256 supporters. United went into the New Year second to Liverpool with Arsenal third.

Set backs continued to plague Ferguson, no sooner had Andy Cole returned as substitute to score at Forest, than Philip Neville was struck down with glandular fever. By the time 1997 began he had used 27 of his squad with senior debuts for teenagers like full-back Michael Clegg and midfielder Michael Appleton.

The manager's New Year message must have sent a shiver down the rest of the Premiership as he made it clear his eyes were set on another year of domination.

This is a big opportunity for us. You cannot lag at this time of the year. We have got to try to be up with them. Last year we gave ourselves a mountain to climb and we just got there. We don't want to be doing that again.

He tried to strengthen his squad but his efforts to land Blackburn's Henning Berg met the same fate as the Shearer bid. David May became the latest player to be hospitalized but made a surprise appearance in the league game at Tottenham four days after he should have had his second hernia operation in a year.

The surgeon had 'flu so rather than wait for him to recover, May trained and faced Spurs for the second time in a week, having taken part in the 2-0 FA Cup Third Round win at Old Trafford on the Sunday before the league encounter in London.

Alex Ferguson spent two weekends in Spain watching Real Betis star Roberto Rios but the cheque book remained firmly shut when the Spaniards asked for a fee of £6 million.

United also lost interest in the FA Cup a little earlier than usual. A remarkable home tie against Wimbledon seemed over when Paul Scholes scored in the 89th minute, but Robbie Earle equalised and the Dons won the replay 1-0.

Between the cup games United played two Premiership matches at Old Trafford, beating Wimbledon then Southampton after conceding the opening goal in both matches. The Wimbledon result took them to the top of the table for the first time since September, and they remained there for the rest of the season.

Schmeichel versus Wright

A 2-1 win at Arsenal sparked off more controversy between the clubs when Ian Wright accused Peter Schmeichel of making racial comments when the keeper responded to a reckless challenge by the England striker. It was the second time the two had been involved in such an incident, the first coming when an Arsenal supporter claimed he had lip read Schmeichel's words in a television close-up during the game at Old Trafford. United's response was to tread water as the Football Association threatened to take action. When it became apparent there would be no criminal prosecution, the FA sent out a letter warning the players about their future behaviour.

Club solicitor and director Maurice Watkins summed up the whole issue by saying:

Peter Schmeichel has never been a racist and never will be.

Defeat at Sunderland came as a setback as the season neared its close, but after a 2-0 win at Everton had opened a six point gap, United were firm favourites to retain their title.

Then they began to struggle. A 3-2 upset against Derby County at Old Trafford was followed by another blow when Schmeichel was injured, missing the European Cup semi-final in Dortmund – and the Premiership game at Blackburn. Raimond van der Gouw was a splendid replacement. Unluckily beaten by a deflection in Germany, he made up for it by being on the winning side at Ewood Park where a 3-2 win threatened Blackburn's Premiership status. This was the club which had snatched the title from United two seasons earlier, without Shearer they were toothless.

With four league games remaining, Ferguson's side was rocked by injuries. Giggs was out of action, Irwin sidelined, May missing, aggrevating an ankle injury while on his first international call up with England.

A trip to Anfield loomed, the game being billed as the

Saint's midfielder Eyal Berkovic scores in the 6-3 thrashing of the champions. The defeat was one of a string of bad results in a thirteen-day period that had many pundits writing off United's championship chances

championship decider and they seemed destined to go to Liverpool without their first choice goalkeeper, an important central defender and the flair of Giggs. Ferguson closed the doors to the training ground as United prepared for the morning encounter at Anfield, but word got out. Schmeichel was training and played. Pallister scored two, and Andy Cole a third as United won 3-1 and found themselves needing four points from as many games to retain the title.

Fixture glut

Those games would be played over a period of eight days between 3 May when they were away to Leicester, and 11 May when West Ham were at Old Trafford. Home games against Middlesbrough and Newcastle were also scheduled for that week and United were again in conflict with the authorites as they tried to extend the season.

Another year, another title

But by Tuesday May 6 the panic was over. United drew at Leicester and at home to Middlesbrough in a game during which half an inch of rain fell. The next evening Liverpool lost to Wimbledon, Newcastle drew at West Ham and United were champions for a fourth time in five seasons.

United did not try to hide their relief that the chase was over. On the night they claimed the title, Alex Ferguson had a gymnasium workout to avoid watching television and knowing the progress of his rivals, Gary Neville and David Beckham went for a walk, and Nicky Butt visited his grandmother then drove home listening to pop music rather than football commentary. David May confessed to wearing the carpets out by pacing his house and Martin Edwards played indoor tennis before saying:

I came off court when there were about fifteen minutes to go in the Newcastle game and Liverpool were losing 2-0. I watched the last few minutes when Shearer nearly did it for them. The feeling inside is one of elation and of relief, particularly with the four games in eight days.

As United's remarkable run continued, Edwards was able to reflect on what Alex Ferguson had achieved since 1990.

We have won four league titles, three FA Cups, the Cup winners' Cup and the League Cup nine major trophies. It really has been a magnificent time, in fact it is the most successful period in Manchester United's history.

For Alex Ferguson there was the satisfaction of seeing his prediction ring true despite the shock results of October and November. Typically he was looking to the future even before the season had ended.

I think that goes without saying that Europe is our aim. Our experience this year has been a good one and it was the type of experience that gives the players the confidence to know that they can do it. I think it will be tough next year but it is always tough. People are saying that we are not good enough to win it again but that is a bit silly. In a league where there is going to be a lot of challengers it is very difficult to imagine that we can't be there. There is going to be a dog-eat-dog situation and we have proved with our experience and the ability of our players that we are equipped for that. We will be there or thereabouts. To say we are not good enough is a bit stupid.

Anyone doubting the manager's view that United's supremacy would continue, needed to have looked no further than Old Trafford on the closing day of the season. United were crowned champions not once but four times. As well as the Premiership, the Reserve side won the Pontin's Premier League, and the A and B teams the First and Second Divisions of the Lancashire League, a clean sweep of every league the club plays in. It was a unique achievement.

However, there was a major shock once the season had ended . . .

Ferguson saw no point in cramming all the games into the final week when there was still time before the FA Cup Final, the traditional end to a season. They fought for all clubs facing fixture congestion after a season filled with blank weekends because of internationals. Even Easter had been disrupted by an England friendly, but Maurice Watkins had to concede defeat:

We asked the Premier League to extend the season and they refused. We wrote to the Football Association and asked them to extend it as we felt they had power within the rules to do that. They disputed that and said it was a matter only within the jurisdiction of the Premier League, so we then took the FA to arbitration on the jurisdiction point. Arbitrator Michael Beloff Q.C. decided the FA had no power of jurisdiction. The merits of the issue haven't been debated, and this is a great pity because we felt there was a lot of merit in the application. We didn't do it just for ourselves, it could have applied to anybody else. We feel that you should not decide the outcome of seasons in a mad panic like that.

Andy Cole celebrates his first and United's third against Liverpool in what was billed as the 'championship decider'. The 3-1 victory meant that United only needed four points from four games to secure another title

Au revoir Cantona

On Sunday 18 May, the day after Chelsea had beaten relegated Middlesbrough in the FA Cup Final, and with speculation growing that Ferguson would add the Brazilian Juninho to his squad, a press conference was called at Old Trafford. Manager Ferguson and chairman Edwards faced the media to break the news:

Manchester United today announced that Eric Cantona has advised the chairman and manager that it is his wish to retire from football with immediate effect.

The shock hit football like a massive tidal wave. Nobody could quite believe such unexpected news. Front and back page headlines told of King Cantona's abdication. Tearful supporters gathered outside the stadium draping shirts and scarves from fences as if in mourning. Martin Edwards said:

I am extremely sorry Eric has arrived at this decision but understand and respect his reasons. Many of us believe Eric has been the catalyst for the most successful period in our history. It has truly been a magical time.

Alex Ferguson's expression said even more than his words.

King Eric abdicates. During his reign United won four Championships and two FA Cups. Never a man to slip into obscurity his departure came as a complete shock, but he had made sure that season that he left as a champion

The Manager knew that life would never be the same without Eric Cantona.

Eric has had a huge impact on the development of our younger players. He has been a model professional in the way he conducted himself and a joy to manage. He is certainly one of the most gifted and dedicated players I have had the pleasure of working with. He leaves with our best wishes and will always be welcome at Old Trafford. He has given us so many wonderful memories.

Eric Cantona's part in the Manchester United story had ended. The Frenchman did not say goodbye in person but left this message for the thousands who worshipped him:

I have played professional football for 13 years which is a long time. I now wish to do other things. I always planned to retire when I was at the top and at Manchester United I have reached the pinnacle of my career. In the last four-and-a-half years I have enjoyed my best football and had a wonderful time. I have had a marvellous relationship with the manager, coach, staff and players and not least the fans. I wish Manchester United even more success in the future.

1990-00

Sheringham replaces Eric

Life without Eric Cantona may have seemed strange, but it would continue and Alex Ferguson was quick to move into the transfer market to find a suitable replacement.

He made a bid for Argentinian striker Gabriel Batistuta, and it seemed at one point that the 28-year-old was willing to leave life in Italy. His wage demands were high and when Fiorentina persuaded him to stay, the deal fell through.

United offered £10 million for Batistuta and made similar unsuccessful bids for two other Serie A players. One was believed to have been for Alessandro Del Piero, star of Juventus, and thorn in United's side during their Champions' League encounters. But eventually Ferguson got his man, and at a third of the price he had been willing to pay.

Tottenham Hotspur and England striker Teddy Sheringharn was the lone summer signing, leaving London to join the reigning champions for £3.5 million:

I have always wanted to play for a club like United. I am delighted to be here. Like any other professional footballer I want to win things and be successful and I have a better chance of doing that here than at any other club in the country.

With those words Sheringham assured United supporters that he would do his best to fill the Cantona void yet, at the same time, upset his former followers at Tottenham. He admitted his one regret was that he never played in the same side as the enigmatic Frenchman. He revealed this as he disclosed that his move north might have come earlier than it did:

I have heard that United tried to sign me three years ago to play me alongside Eric and I would have liked that. I admired him from afar, and I thought he was a great player, but sadly he is not here and life goes on.

Sheringham had a baptism of fire. His first Premiership game was at Tottenham of all places and came a week after he helped United win the Charity Shield.

That victory came after a penalty shoot-out with Chelsea during which he scored. A week later, however, when United were awarded a penalty at White Hart Lane, he took the kick and missed, to the delight of those who baited him from the stands.

I know what it is like to play against United and playing for them is every bit the way the manager said it would be. You know it is going to be a big game, everybody wants to beat Manchester United because they are the best. It is something I am going to have to come to terms with. Coming here is a challenge, but one I am looking forward to.

As the season went on, Sheringham missed two more spot-kicks and was relieved of the responsibility. By the end of the campaign, he was even more aware of the difference between playing for United and any of his previous clubs. Despite his missed penalty United beat Tottenham 2-0 and set off on a run which took them to the top of the table.

Heir to the Cantona throne. Teddy Sheringham could have scored on his debut but missed a penalty against former club Tottenham. Here he celebrates the first of his two goals against Arsenal at Highbury, which put United back in the game until David Platt scored a late winner for the eventual Premiership champions

Pre-season and early injuries

From the start they were handicapped. Ole Gunnar Solskjaer, leading scorer from the 1996-97 season, was injured while playing at Old Trafford in the second of two pre-season friendlies against Inter Milan. The games were arranged as part of the Paul Ince transfer deal and proved costly.

David May was struck down at the San Siro where he ruptured a thigh muscle and both he and Solskjaer missed the opening months of the campaign. The irony of it all was that Ince had by then joined Liverpool, and was playing for United's biggest rivals.

With May now out of contention, Ferguson again turned to the transfer market and bought Henning Berg from Blackburn Rovers in a £5 million move. He made his full debut at Leicester on 23 August after replacing fellow Norwegian Ronny Johnsen when he was injured in the opening home game, a 1-0 win over Southampton.

During the summer, England had been involved in World Cup qualifying games and with David Beckham,

Free-scoring United

Then came two amazing home games which had lasting effects on the opposition.

Barnsley, new boys to the Premiership and enjoying their first spell in the top division, arrived at Old Trafford full of optimism. It was short-lived thanks to a hat-trick from Cole, two goals from Ryan Giggs, and another from Paul Scholes. Karel Poborsky scored the seventh, and his final goal for the club. The Czech Republic international could not win a regular place in the side and amid fears he would not be allowed a new work permit at the end of the season, he moved to Benfica on 29 December.

The defeat added to Barnsley's problems and eventually they were relegated, along with Crystal Palace and Bolton. The three clubs who had won promotion the previous season went down again, an illustration perhaps, of the widening gap between the standard of football in the FA Carling Premiership and the Nationwide League.

A week later United beat Sheffield Wednesday 6-1 at Old Trafford, in a game which signalled the end for manager David Pleat at Hillsborough. He was dismissed two days later to be replaced by former United boss Ron Atkinson, who joined the Yorkshire club for a second time.

At the top of the table the battle was between United, Liverpool, Chelsea and Arsenal. Derby County were the early dark horses and Leeds also pushed hard.

At Christmas more injury problems emerged. Peter Schmeichel was hurt and, with replacement 'keeper Raimond van der Gouw recovering from a cartilage operation, Kevin Pilkington once again found himself in the firing line. He played in the 2-0 Boxing Day win over Everton at Old Trafford and was again in goal at Coventry two days later. This time United lost 2-3, ending a run of six successive League wins which began after a similar upset at Highbury.

Gary Neville and Paul Scholes, regulars in Glenn Hoddle's side, Alex Ferguson decided to approach the new season with caution. England had also taken part in, and won, France's dress rehearsal for the 1998 tournament, Le Tournoi, so when the season began the manager rested his young stars, causing a stir throughout the media.

During the Charity Shield Beckham came on as a substitute and Gary Neville watched from the bench. Neither started the first two games but Beckham played for the last quarter against Southampton and scored the only goal of the night. It was not until the third league game of the season, a trip to Leicester for a goalless draw, that Ferguson used what was considered to be his full strength side.

United made a steady start and were close to the top of the table when they were struck by another injury blow. Playing without Cantona was not as bad as anticipated, but when Roy Keane was badly hurt during the first defeat of the season at Leeds, the odds against retaining the title began to increase.

Keane had been handed the captaincy following Cantona's retirement, and was hurt in a challenge on Alfie Haaland the Leeds midfielder. A cruciate ligament injury ruled him out for the rest of the season and the tabloid press declared, 'No Cantona, no Keane – no chance!'

United tried to prove them wrong. A winning surge saw them open up a four-point gap at the top of the table after beating Crystal Palace at Old Trafford, then fighting back from 2-0 down to draw at Derby County where Andy Cole scored a late equaliser after Sheringham had missed his second penalty of the season.

Above: Victory at Wembley, but as things turned out, it was to be the only trophy United won in the 1997-98 season. Ronny Johnsen (second right) leads the celebrations after United beat Chelsea 4-2 in a penalty shoot-out. The Norwegian defender scored his first goal for the club in the 58th minute to level the game after Mark Hughes put the FA Cup holders in front. United had a 100 per cent performance in the shoot-out with Paul Scholes, Denis Irwin, Roy Keane and Nicky Butt all converting as Peter Schmeichel kept Chelsea at bay

Right: Gary Neville, David Beckham and Roy Keane celebrate victory over Liverpool in December 1997

Poor results give Arsenal hope

The next game was billed as the toughest of the season. The FA Cup campaign began with an away trip to Chelsea, the holders, and it saw an outstanding performance from United. Goals from Beckham (two), Cole (two) and Sheringham gave them an incredible 5-0 lead by the 74th minute after a display of fast, flowing football. Chelsea fought back as United relaxed and the game finished 5-3, but United never hit the peak shown at Stamford Bridge during the rest of the season.

Defeats at Southampton and at home to Leicester, both by a single goal, and a home draw with Bolton gave hope to others. Arsenal set off on a strong run about the same time and the two were on collision course as the finishing post came into sight.

1990-00

Champions' League and the Premiership title.

Form was erratic. The Barnsley games came either side of a 2-0 win at Aston Villa and a similar victory over Derby at Old Trafford. The lead at the top was increased to 12 points thanks to another success at Stamford Bridge, this time when Philip Neville scored his first ever senior goal. It turned out to be the only one of the game.

Arsenal had four games in hand, and were still on their winning streak and when the side returned bruised and battered from its trip to Monaco in the Champions' League, a subsequent 0-2 defeat against a rejuvenated Sheffield Wednesday signalled that all was not well.

The injury crisis hit hard. Schmeichel was missing again, so was Denis Irwin who had missed two months between November and New Year following a career threatening injury

sustained during the win over Feyenoord in Holland, and perhaps most significantly, Ryan Giggs.

The Welshman tore a hamstring during the win over Derby on 21 February, and it was 6 April before he returned. During that spell United played eight games, starting with the Cup replay at Oakwell. They won just two, at Chelsea and at home to Wimbledon but between the two legs of their European quarter-final against Monaco, United earned only one point from three games and that came in a 1-1 draw at West Ham United. They also lost at home to Arsenal in a game billed as the 'championship decider'.

A Marc Overmars goal decided a Saturday morning showdown, but there was an even bigger price to pay for the 0-1 defeat than the three points which gave Arsenal hope; the Gunners still had three games in hand, United's lead was six points, and the injury plague continued with skipper Schmeichel again the victim.

He risked all to venture forward for a late corner in search of

Bolton visited Old Trafford the day after the 40th anniversary of the Munich air disaster, an occasion marked with a Memorial Service at Manchester Cathedral attended by many of the survivors and their families, as well as relatives of those who died. It was a moving time which continued into the Bolton game when wreaths were laid and the 55,156 crowd stood in total silence at four minutes past three, the precise time of the air crash.

The anniversary was also to be marked by a Testimonial Game scheduled for Wednesday, 25 February. United would play against an Eric Cantona European XI and supporters looked forward to seeing the Frenchman for a final time.

However it was not to be. An unexpected FA Cup replay at Barnsley forced the game's cancellation and with Cantona bound for Mexico, on location in his new role as a film actor, it was impossible to plan a new date before the end of the season.

United lost the game at Barnsley and with it their interest in everything but the two biggest prizes, the European

Above: Sheringham puts United 5-0 up in an amazing FA Cup third-round tie at Stamford Bridge. David Beckham opened the scoring with two strikes and Cole got the others. A late rally from Chelsea meant the game ended 5-3

Above, right: Andy Cole struck a golden patch during the first half of the 1997-98 season, scoring eight goals in three games. His 25 goals made him top scorer in all competitions

1990-00

an equaliser, no doubt recalling his famous headed goal against Rotor Volgograd in 1995. However Arsenal won the ball and as Dennis Bergkamp broke from defence, Schmeichel tore a hamstring making a lunging tackle on the Dutchman.

He was ruled out of the return leg against Monaco and with Pallister, Giggs, May, and Keane missing, and Scholes and Gary Neville unable to complete the game because of injury, the European campaign ended in disappointment.

United beat Blackburn Rovers at Ewood Park but drew 1-1 with Liverpool at Old Trafford as the Merseysiders sought revenge for a second successive 3-1 defeat at Anfield earlier in the season. In a game filled with controversy in which Michael Owen was sent off for a reckless challenge on Ronny Johnsen, United threw everything into attack but could not get the winner. Johnsen scored United's goal before being stretchered off

early in the second half. Even against 10 men the defending champions could not manage a second goal and eight days later, after another 1-1 home draw with Newcastle, the race was over.

Arsenal had four games remaining and led the table by a single point as United beat Crystal Palace at Selhurst Park in their 36th Premiership game of the season. Six points would clinch the title for the Londoners and by 3 May, the championship was decided. Arsenal beat Everton 4-0 at Highbury and took the 1998 title thanks to a run of 10 successive victories.

So United turned their thoughts to the 1998-99 season with a determination to regain their Premiership supremacy, plunging into the transfer market to sign Dutch international Jaap Stam for £10.75 million, a world record fee for a defender. Stam tied up the costly move from PSV Eindhoven on Tuesday, 5 May, the day after he had watched his future team mates beat Leeds 3-0 at Old Trafford. In that game Ryan Giggs scored his 50th League goal.

Left: Nicky Butt challenges Crystal Palace's Tomas Brolin during the 3-0 win at Selhurst Park in April. The win narrowed the lead at the top of the Premiership to a single point but afterwards Alex Ferguson appeared ready to concede the title race to Arsenal, who still had two matches in hand

Above: Jaap Stam became the world's most expensive defender at £10.75 million. United bought the Dutchman from PSV Eindhoven. He gave up his share of the massive transfer fee so his move could go through

A rare, trophyless season

The season ended with a 2-0 win at Barnsley two days after the club decided not to renew Brian McClair's contract. The news came as a surprise to many supporters and ended an 11-year association with United. McClair's last appearance was when he came on as a late substitute against Leeds, but unfortunately the Scot failed to score. That truly would have been a fitting ending to a marvellous career.

At Barnsley, Andy Cole scored his 25th goal of the season and took the crown as the Premiership's top scorer in all competitions. Although the season ended with the senior side failing to win any trophies Alex Ferguson pledged his determination to push for success in 1998-99.

The gap between United and Champions Arsenal was finally just a single point but the manager conceded:

Arsenal won it three games ago and good luck to them. They did well, but we will do our best to take the title from them again next season. We are also in Europe once again and it will be our aim to try our best to succeed there as well.

Strengthening the squad

After the disappointments of 1997-98, who could have predicted that the season which followed would be the most successful in the history of Manchester United ?

Certainly between the start in August and a home defeat by Middlesbrough on December 19, there were some glimpses of what was to come, but nothing to suggest United were going beyond all that had been achieved before.

Alex Ferguson spent the summer of 1998 strengthening his squad. He made no secret of his plans to use the World Cup as a market place, but in the end failed to land any of the big name players on show in France '98.

He saw it essential to add new players because of the increased challenge of the Champions' League. Even though entry as runners-up did not have the wholehearted support of many purists, including chairman Edwards, and possibly the manager himself, there would be a determined effort to succeed. More games meant more pressures on the playing staff and Ferguson vowed he would not to be caught out as he had been during the previous season. He knew he needed cover for key positions and firstly his attention turned to midfield.

A £5 million offer was made to French club FC Lens, for their Cameroon international Marc-Vivien Foe. United agreed terms with the player but the unlucky African broke a leg during preparations for the World Cup and eventually the deal was called off. Foe would join West Ham in March of the following year.

Speculation also surrounded Aston Villa striker Dwight Yorke and the first indication this was true came when an £8 million offer was rejected by the Midlands club. Then United made a move for Holland's Patrick Kluivert and again a deal was struck, this time with the club AC Milan. Unlike Foe, Kluivert showed a reluctance to move to Manchester saying he would prefer life in London. He hinted he would join Arsenal, then instead signed for Barcelona !

The names came pouring out of France '98. Argentinians Gabriel Batistuta, and Ariel Ortega, Croatian Davor Suker, there was even a suggestion Alan Shearer might be persuaded to leave his beloved Newcastle, but none of the tabloid newspaper claims solidified.

The World Cup did however have a significant effect on United's season.

During England's game against Argentina in St Etienne, David Beckham was controversially sent-off following a clash with Diego Simeone the Inter Milan midfielder. The United star found himself pilloried by the media and made to shoulder the blame for England's eventual exit when, in his absence they lost the game in a penalty shoot-out.

The new season began with Beckham given Cantona-style treatment by the club with Ned Kelly the security chief acting

Giggs, Yorke and Beckham celebrate Dwight's third goal in consecutive home games against Coventry in September. It was an impressive start to what would prove an incredible first season at United

as a personal bodyguard on visits to away grounds. David Beckham's every touch was booed by opposition supporters, but the player claimed it helped inspire rather than detract and certainly Manchester United fans got behind him more than ever.

There were no new players on view at the kick off other than Stam who made his debut in the side which lost to Arsenal in the Charity Shield. The only other change to the previous campaign was Keane's return after his recovery from his injury with Ferguson claiming:

'That is as good as signing any new player.'

1990-00

Yorke and Blomqvist make debuts

It appeared the attempts to sign Yorke had collapsed but suddenly the deal was on again and Jaap Stam's record fee surpassed as Villa received £12.6 million for their Trinidad and Tobago player.

No sooner had this happened than United accepted a £5 million offer from Tottenham for Solskjaer, but the Norwegian said he preferred life as a squad player at Old Trafford. That was all Alex Ferguson needed to hear and it was fitting fate gave Solskjaer such a crucial part to play in United's glory nine months later.

Ferguson made it clear he wanted to increase his playing staff, not reduce it and added another Scandinavian at the start September. He took his summer spending to a staggering £28 million after the arrival of Sweden's Jesper Blomqvist from Italian club Parma.

Blomqvist made his debut on the day Yorke played his first home game. Both began impressively, with Yorke scoring twice in the 4-1 win over Charlton. Solskjaer got the other two as Ferguson experimented to find the right formation up front.

Eventually it was Yorke and Andy Cole who became the most regular choice and their goals in a 3-0 win at Southampton took United into second place by October.

The Sky bid

It was then matters off the field began to make big news. The club announced it was to be taken over and the Board recommended shareholders to accept a £623 million bid from satellite broadcasting company B-Sky-B.

Supporters were divided in their opinions as to where the buy-out would take the club, and there was an immediate uproar from those opposed to the move, many of whom were not shareholders, simply run-of-the-mill fans.

While there were those who agreed with the official line that the riches of the giant media company would benefit football, independent groups saw it as the end of Manchester United as a traditional football club, and rallied MP's and other influential figures to oppose the move.

Not surprisingly Chairman Edwards faced a hostile reception at the AGM and was accused of 'selling out'.

Rupert Murdoch's connections to B-Sky-B did not help matters and those newspapers not owned by the media magnate came down firmly opposed to the deal. Despite the growing anti-lobby Edwards remained convinced the takeover was the way forward:

When Sky approached us they did so in a friendly manner. They could easily have gone hostile and gone straight to the shareholders and made an offer that the shareholders decided to

accept. They could have gone straight above the Board's head. In this case they came to us and we were able to talk to them and we were able to satisfy ourselves that they were going to leave certain things in place, they were going to look after the existing staff, they had ambitions similar to ourselves, about running the club in the future, and that they were going to put some resource to it. A friendly bid is much better than a hostile bid. There are obligations as directors of a public company which you can't ignore. Even if you wanted to say, 'We don't want

Gary Neville congratulates Roy Keane on his goal against Leeds during a 3-2 win at Old Trafford in November. Keane was an inspirational leader throughout the treble season.

Sky, or A. N. Other. Go away!' you can't just say that as a director of a public company. Your duties are beyond that. I think there has been a lot of misconception. People have just blamed the Board and said they've sold out. We did not seek this sale. We did not go out and say that we want to sell Manchester United. We were approached and once we were approached that put us in a situation that we had to deal with. We believe we have dealt with it in the best possible way by talking it through over several weeks.

And this deal has got very personal. Everybody says Martin Edwards has sold Manchester United. I only own 14 per cent, the institutions own 60 per cent. What they say goes rather than what I say. I am also only one member of a seven man Board.

The Board have collective responsibility for this decision and it was the unanimous decision of the Board that this was put to the shareholders with a recommendation to accept. It was not Martin Edwards's decision in isolation and I would just like to clear that up and take the heat out of that.

But the heat remained until April.

Government blocks deal

It was then the Government intervened, after the takeover had been referred to the Monopolies and Mergers Commission, the Department of Trade and Industry blocked the deal and a stunned Edwards said:

I only look upon it from the point of view of Manchester United for whereas it was a big disappointment, we believed that the backing of Sky made us a lot stronger.

We are not paupers, we have got money and we have done very well over the years, but to take us to that next step we believed that the combination of Manchester United and Sky in unison would have made us much stronger.

The pure logic of the whole thing is that together we were much stronger than we are independently. That doesn't mean that independently we are weak, because we are not, we are still the strongest club financially and probably from a team point of view in England.

We are back to as we were. We are no worse off than we were the day before Sky approached us. Supporters of other clubs are absolutely delighted at what has happened because they could see that the deal would have made us even more powerful. I really cannot see some of the logic in the opposition, I think they have cut of their noses to spite their faces.

The way football is going there will be changes in the next ten years just like there has been in the last. I just want to see Manchester United as the number one football club in the world in terms of reputation and playing ability.

Brian Kidd took charge of the Blackburn hot seat during December '98. He succeeded Roy Hodgson, but despite a brief honeymoon period he couldn't stop their slide into a relegation scrap

Schmeichel's shock decision

During the months of haranguing United rolled steadily onwards but there had also been another major announcement during the winter.

On November 12, Peter Schmeichel revealed his plans to retire from English football saying he wished to end his playing days in a warmer climate. The news stunned many United followers but quickly the names of a possible replacement were bandied about... Mark Bosnich from Aston Villa, Edwin van der Sar of Ajax... Mattias Asper of AIK Stockholm... Fabien Barthez France's World Cup 'keeper who played for Monaco and Luigi Buffon of Parma.

The new goalkeeper would not be brought in until the end of the season but that did not prevent the guessing game getting underway.

Schmeichel knew he faced some emotional months to the end of the season but pledged to do his best to bring more success before standing down.

He had no idea where he would end his playing days:
I have to be honest and say I don't think it would have been fair to the club if I had gone out, before it was properly announced to seek another club, or speak to another club.

The most important thing from me now is to play well and make sure we win trophies this season. It is important for me to be able to concentrate on playing and not all the speculation and whatever else has been going on over the last couple of weeks.

Kidd leaves the fold

United had been beaten just once in the Premiership by the day of Schmeichel's press conference and a week later Sheffield Wednesday joined Arsenal as the second conquerors of Ferguson's side. The only home upset was to come at the hands of Bryan Robson's Middlesbrough but this defeat was followed by another shock, when Brian Kidd accepted an offer to manage Blackburn Rovers.

The assistant-manager left Ferguson's side, breaking up modern day football's most successful partnership. He achieved some success in the early stages of his managerial career with a good run of results that looked to have steadied the boat.

By the time his replacement was appointed United had gone eight more games without defeat. The last of these was a 1-0 victory over Derby County where Steve McClaren spent his last game as deputy to manager Jim Smith.

The relatively unknown McClaren became Ferguson's choice as his new right hand man and took over his post in time to witness a record breaking 8-1 away win at Nottingham Forest.

1990-00

Solskjaer's four seals record win

In that game – against a Forest side managed by Ron Atkinson – Solskjaer came on as a 72nd minute substitute and proceeded to score four times in eleven minutes as United gained a four point lead at the top of the Premiership. It was the biggest away win by any side since the Premier League was launched.

Astonishingly McClaren went on to complete his first season at his new club without seeing United lose!

When he was appointed United were through to the quarter finals of the Champions' Cup and still in the FA Cup and it was understandable there was talk of the elusive treble. The league, FA Cup and European Cup were all within the club's grasp but suggestions they might win all three did not emanate from Ferguson or his players. They simply insisted in true football parlance, that they would take each game as it came.

Cup wins over Middlesbrough and Liverpool, were followed by a quarter final victory over Chelsea. In the Liverpool game an injury time goal by Solskjaer a minute after Yorke scored and equaliser, snatched victory from the Merseysiders and not surprisingly added to United's reputation of playing right up to the final whistle.

Two goals from Yorke, taking him to 26 for the season, won a replay at Stamford Bridge, earning the right to face double chasing rivals Arsenal in the semi-final which also went to a second game.

The goal that won the semi-final for United and 'Goal of the Season' for Ryan Giggs. The following day the papers were asking the question: 'Is This The Best Goal Ever Scored?'. Perhaps a little over-the-top, but nevertheless the sight of Ryan Gigg's powering past the experienced Arsenal defence will live in the memory for a long time to come

Giggs' wondergoal sets up treble

The first at Villa Park, ended goalless and the next encounter three days later summed up the drama which surrounded United's performances for the rest of the season.

Beckham scored after 17 minutes, Bergkamp equalised in the 69th. Then Arsenal were awarded a penalty almost on full-time but Schmeichel saved, and with 109 minutes gone, Ryan Giggs scored an incredible winner.

He ran more than half the length of the field, fending off challenges before shooting high into the net. United were through to the final with what Alex Ferguson claimed as the best FA Cup goal he had seen, and few would argue.

As Chelsea slipped, the title race again became a battle between United and Arsenal with the reigning champions favourites because they had fewer games to play.

The Premiership lead changed hands when United drew at Liverpool and Paul Ince dealt what he thought was the killer blow, by scoring the home side's equaliser in the 89th minute. Ince teased his former followers on a night of even greater disappointment when referee David Elleray's controversial judgement to send off Denis Irwin, for allegedly kicking the ball away, meant the Irishman would be suspended for the FA Cup Final.

With Keane and Scholes already ruled out of the European final it meant United would be handicapped in two of their biggest games.

Ferguson sends friend down

The season headed for an amazing climax, and when Arsenal lost at Leeds things tilted United's way again. Their closing league games were at Blackburn then at home to Tottenham and as always there was a twist to the tale.

Blackburn, the 1995 champions were in deep trouble. They needed to win to keep alive faint hopes of staying in the Premiership. United knew a victory would virtually tie up the title, but the game ended goalless and Brian Kidd's first experience as a top level manager became one of bitter disappointment.

As for United they were left with three games to play, and realised if they could win them all they would achieve more than any British club before them.

A tight finish

Success in the Champions' League (described in detail on pages 204-205) had seen them taking the scalps of Inter Milan and Juventus on the way to the final. That final in Barcelona would be the last game of the season, and everyone at Old Trafford prepared for a dramatic grand finale.

By the closing day of the Premiership campaign, United were in a strong position. For the first time since 1965 they had the chance of clinching the championship in front of their own supporters, but things could not have got off to a worse start. They had to lose or draw with Tottenham to give Arsenal any hope of holding on to the title and went a goal down in the 25th minute.

Those who have followed the club closely knew United never did anything the easy way and went behind to an opportunist goal from Les Ferdinand. With the crowd urging them on they fought back. Beckham scored with a fierce shot from the right wing, and two minutes into the second half, Cole lobbed the ball over the head of Ian Walker in the Tottenham goal to put United ahead.

It stayed that way until the final whistle as the makeshift central defensive pairing of David May and Ronny Johnsen drafted into the side because of injuries to Stam and Berg, held out as Spurs fought for a late equaliser.

Part one of the treble was completed.

United end the century as Champions. It was their fifth Premiership title in seven seasons and Alex Ferguson's tenth major trophy since becoming manager in 1986

1990-00

The double

The second followed six days later when Newcastle were easily beaten in the FA Cup Final.

Stam, who missed three of the last six Premiership games because of an Achilles injury, was left out for the start of the final with May once again playing alongside Johnsen.

The unlucky defender found a unique place in the long history of the competition. May's season had again been plagued by injury and his first taste of the Cup was to play at Wembley. This time he collected a winner's medal having failed to reach the stipulated number of league games to qualify for a Premiership reward the previous weekend.

The hero of the final was another player who had slipped from the spotlight. Injury, and the arrival of Yorke saw Teddy Sheringham slip down the pecking order, but the Londoner had a leading role to play in an epic ending to a remarkable season.

Sheringham took over from Keane after just nine minutes of the final, when the United skipper limped off after being hurt in a double challenge from Dietmar Hamman and Gary Speed. After just 90 seconds Sheringham struck, scoring the first goal from a Scholes pass, then in the second-half reversed roles to set up the second goal and tie up victory.

Even then the season was not over for Sheringham, nor for Solskjaer whose 17 goals from a handful of starts would have made him leading scorer at many other Premiership clubs.

Both came on as substitutes in the Champions' League

Above: The two goal scorers – Teddy Sheringham (left) and Paul Scholes – celebrate United's 2-0 victory over Ruud Gullit's Newcastle in the FA Cup that earned United their third double of the Nineties

Right: From villain to hero. David Beckham started the season under the cloud of his World Cup sending off. He ended the season as the key player in the most successful season an English club has ever had

Final, both scored as Bayern Munich were beaten and the treble was won (see page 204).

The team of the century?

Alex Ferguson had taken his side to new horizons and delighted millions. This was apparent from the rapturous welcome given to the side when it returned on the evening after the final in Barcelona, parading through supporter filled streets on an open topped bus carrying the three precious trophies. It was estimated that around 750,000 Mancunians turned out to greet the players, Alex Ferguson claimed it seemed double that number.

In relaxed mood the manager took the plaudits, yet even as the cheers echoed around the city centre he was thinking of the future. On the day of the homecoming he telephoned Mark Bosnich, now a free agent as his contract with Aston Villa came to an end, and invited him to Old Trafford for talks. On Friday, May 28, Ferguson and the goalkeeper he had at the club as a teenager, agreed terms for a return. Five days later as the manager enjoyed his holiday in France, Bosnich was presented to the media as the man to take over from Schmeichel saying: "Whether I will be good enough to fill his shoes only time will tell, but I'm certainly looking forward to the challenge."

As a new Millennium beckoned Manchester United, unquestionably the team of the Nineties, can also lay claim to being the team of the century. Surely few would deny them that accolade?

1990-00

Manchester United qualified for Europe by virtue of their second place finish in the domestic league. Chairman, Martin Edwards, had originally stated: 'If you allow second-placed teams in, then you are devaluing the competition.' A year later Martin Edwards was more than happy to have allowed his club entry by the back door!

For this was the year they finally emerged from the shadow of the Busby years to win the European crown and celebrate a historic treble grand slam of trophies. Supporters and media were of one mind about the manager... arise Sir Alex Ferguson as they granted him an immediate knighthood to mark his elevation to the ranks of all-time great managers. Ferguson responded by saying simply about his players: "They are today's legends. I said the present squad could only be judged on what they achieved. Now they have achieved, so they are the best, no question about it."

He had every right to be proud of his players because not only did they stage a great rally in the final to beat Bayern Munich 2-1 in Barcelona, they grew in stature as the competition progressed and in the knock-out phase scaled new heights to beat two Italian giants, Inter Milan and Juventus.

Unbeatable United

Firstly, as runners-up in the Premiership, they had to navigate a qualifying round which fell early in the season. They found enough form to beat LKS Lodz 2-0 at Old Trafford and play in a gritty goalless draw in Poland, but the qualifying group, drawn with Barcelona, Bayern Munich and Brondby, they found difficult.

They didn't lose a single game, thus establishing themselves as difficult to beat, but at the same time they only won twice, and those wins were against the Danish part-timers, Brondby, who were whipped 6-2 away and 5-0 in Manchester. All four games involving Barcelona and Bayern were drawn, starting with a highly exciting 3-3 against the Spanish champions at Old Trafford.

It was 3-3 away, too, with Rivaldo snatching the equaliser with a stunning bicycle kick. In between United had drawn 2-2 against Bayern in Germany to find themselves in a shoot-out with Bayern going into their last group game. A 1-1 draw saw the Germans go through as group winners and United stay in the competition as one of the two best runners-up. Again they were in through the back door.

Magic in Milan and Turin

Inter Milan were United's opponents in the quarter-finals. A superb performance gave the Reds a 2-0 win in the first leg at home, with Dwight Yorke scoring twice from Beckham's crosses.

The San Siro was as usual intimidating, but the Reds held their nerve to emerge with a creditable 1-1 draw, Paul Scholes the hero with an 88th minute equaliser after coming on as a substitute. Ferguson said:

"My team has grown in stature. Knocking a big Italian team out of Europe is a major step forward for us and a barometer of our progress. I feel with Inter out of the way we can go all the way to become champions."

They certainly needed all their confidence with Juventus their opponents in the semi-finals and things certainly didn't look too good when the Italians forced a 1-1 draw in the first leg at Old Trafford with the bonus of scoring an away goal. The situation grew even worse in Turin as Filippo Inzaghi gave Juve a two-goal lead in the opening 11 minutes. At least there was time for a comeback and United shrugged off a threatening nightmare to stage an inspired revival that saw Roy Keane lead from the front as captain by storming in to score with a header. Dwight Yorke headed in an equaliser from Andy Cole's cross and the Tobagan international returned the compliment by opening up the way for Cole to notch a memorable 3-2 victory.

Two down, one to go

Now United felt they could take on the world and pulling off a League and FA Cup double simply sent their expectations into orbit as they flew out on Concorde to Barcelona for a final against Bayern Munich. Once again United made a dismal start, defending badly to allow Mario Basler to score with a free kick through their wall after only five minutes. Their response failed to worry the Germans and it seemed as if the absence of Roy Keane and Paul Scholes through suspension would prove costly. David Beckham justified his selection in central midfield, but Ryan Giggs looked out of gear on the right wing, while Jesper Blomqvist, a surprise choice in his place on the left wing, struggled to make an impact. Ferguson later admitted that in the closing stages he had been ready to accept defeat.

"I started to adjust in my mind to the reality of losing the game. I was reminding myself that the important thing in defeat would be to keep my dignity and accept that it was just not our year," he explained.

The story of the final:
Top: Mario Basler curls the ball around the United wall: 1–0 to Bayern in the sixth minute.
Right: Sheringham celebrates his 90th-minute strike: 1–1.
Below: With 3½ minutes of injury time played Solskjaer scores the winner
Bottom, right: Schmeichel lifts the European Cup

Super-subs sink Germans

His players, though, were not ready to accept defeat and in the last few minutes, especially in the injury time allowed by Italian referee Pierluigi Collina, they surged forward to claim an unbelievable 2-1 victory summed up the next day by a Spanish newspaper under the headline which read "Increible" (sic). That's incredible in anyone's language as they went on to explain that it would be "a minute which would pass into history." The clock was already showing 90 minutes when substitute Teddy Sheringham swept in an astonishing equaliser after Giggs had touched on Beckham's corner kick. Goalkeeper Peter Schmeichel had come up into the goalmouth to try to cause confusion and the Germans were in real disarray when United forced another corner three minutes into injury time.

This time it was the inspirational Sheringham heading on

Beckham's kick for the second super-sub, Ole Solskjaer, to lift into the roof of the net. It was a victory for United's never-say-die spirit. It is arguably the most sensational finish at this level in the history of English football and it was impossible not to feel a twinge of sympathy for the Germans after looking to have the game won.

As goalkeeper Peter Schmeichel said after playing his final game for United before seeking pastures new:

"Of course you have to feel a little sorry for Bayern in that situation – but that's the beauty and cruelty of football." Ferguson was not in the mood to feel so sympathetic. *"We were the team trying to attack all the time. Nobody can deny that our team plays with a spirit to attack and will to win. We were prepared to take risks and in football when you are prepared to be like that, you deserve to succeed.*

"We rode our luck in one spell when they hit the post and the bar but towards the end they were tired out. I am so very proud of my players, my family and my heritage.

"This is the greatest moment of my life," he declared.

Happy Birthday Sir Matt

And so it was for the ecstatic United supporters who were convinced that Sir Matt Busby, who would have been celebrating his 90th birthday on the day of the match, had somehow influenced the outcome.

The man hailed as the founding father of United died five years ago but the fact that his birthday fell on the day of the European Cup final seemed somehow appropriate.

Even Ferguson said: "I think Sir Matt must have been kicking for us up there tonight."

A succession of managers tried and failed to conquer Europe but now 31 years later Alex Ferguson has emerged from the shadow cast for so long by the Busby legend.

And so have his players who can now take their place in the club's history free of comparisons with the boys of 1968. Several of the stars of the team that beat Benfica to become the first English club to win the European Cup watched the game in the Nou Camp Stadium as guests of United and they were as thrilled by the success as they were when they celebrated their own triumph.

As Jack Crompton, the coach of the Sixties' team said: "I'm glad Ferguson's players have done it. They have matched what we did and they can now go forward instead of comparisons constantly making them look back over their shoulders."

The Second United Sir

On Saturday June 12, 1999 Manchester United again made headline news when the morning newspapers declared: "Arise Sir Alex !".

It was no major surprise. For weeks there had been speculation Alex Ferguson would follow in the footsteps of his legendary predecessor Sir Matt Busby, and be awarded a knighthood for his services to football. When the Queen's Birthday listings were published this proved correct.

Sir Alex was modest in his acceptance : "This is a great honour for Manchester United, my family and for me," he said. It was the perfect ending to an astonishing season and an ideal start for the manager's testimonial year.

The controversial cup

Within a fortnight United were to make front page news again, this time for a very different reason and a decision which would have repercussions for the rest of the season. They announced their withdrawal from the FA Cup.

It was an unprecedented move and came after the club answered a plea from the Football Association and the government who were represented by the then Minister for Sport, Tony Banks, to take part in a new tournament organised by FIFA.

The Club World Championships were to be held in Brazil in January 2000, but United felt it would be impossible to play in this competition and defend the trophy won only a month earlier.

As winners of the Champions' League, they were to be Europe's main representatives and both the FA and the government felt a rejection might seriously affect England's hopes of staging the 2006 World Cup. Reluctantly United agreed and pulled out of the FA Cup. Immediately they found themselves in the firing line from the media and accused of devaluing football's oldest competition.

Some time later Chairman Martin Edwards revealed that Sports Minister Tony Banks had been the one who urged United to play in South America: "Quite clearly it was put to us that if Manchester United did not compete in the tournament in Brazil, then that would severely damage the chances of England winning the 2006 World Cup bid.

"It was purely on that basis that we withdrew from the FA Cup and agreed to play in Brazil. It was made quite plain to us, that it would severely enhance the chances of the 2006 World Cup bid if we played in Brazil, and it was put even stronger than that, that we could jeopardise England's chances if we didn't."

It was a no-win situation. By pulling out of the FA Cup fingers were pointed at United who were accused of cashing in on the new competition at the expense of tradition. Had they not gone to Brazil, and the World Cup bid went elsewhere fists, not fingers, would no doubt be raised.

Below: Mark Bosnich was the first summer signing of 1999. Mark had already played for the club during the early '90s, but left to join Aston Villa in 1991. His return to Old Trafford was under the Bosman ruling, but injuries meant that Sir Alex would invest £4.5 million in Massimo Taibi. Unfortunately the Italian wouldn't last the season and returned to Italy on loan to Reggina. At the end of the season United signed Fabien Barthez from Monaco in their desperate bid to find the second Peter Schmeichel.

A brace of 'keepers

While this was going on Sir Alex was busy in the transfer market. Because of doubts about the fitness of new man Bosnich who had been out of action following a long injury lay-off with Aston Villa, he bought another goalkeeper, paying £4.5 million for Sicilian Massimo Taibi.

The tall Italian arrived from Serie 'A' club Venezia full of optimism. He was keen to learn English, eager to establish himself in the Premiership and excited at the prospect of following the legendary Peter Schmeichel, however Taibi's passage into England football was far from smooth.

First his UEFA registration missed the deadline for the opening phase of the Champions' League because it was faxed to the Italian FA when the office was closed, then, after a

Keane stays put

It was not the arrival of new players which held the interest of fans as the new millennium approached, but the possible departure of one of the club's existing stars. Uncertainly surrounded the future of Roy Keane whose contract was due to expire at the end of the season. This meant unless he agreed to a new deal, the Republic of Ireland star would be free to walk away from Old Trafford and join another club. No-one knew what would happen with speculation rife that Keane would head for the continent and saw Italian and Spanish clubs ready to lay out the red carpet for such a talent. Keane himself gave few clues. In one interview he hinted everything would be sorted out before Christmas and he would be staying, while in another the vibes were he was ready to turn his back on the Premiership and head for pastures new.

When matters finally reached a conclusion on March 15, and the club joyfully announced the midfielder had agreed a new four-year deal, Keane admitted being undecided right up to the moment of signing. By the time he did put pen to paper

thrilling debut at Liverpool, when his heroics earned a 3-2 win, he began to make costly mistakes.

He played just four games with his final first team appearance coming in a 5-0 humiliation at Stamford Bridge where championship rivals Chelsea began their rout inside the first 30 seconds. Taibi eventually returned to Italy play with Reggina. Schmeichel's was understandably a hard act to follow and the club's two remaining senior 'keepers played musical chairs for the rest of the season. Bosnich made 33 starts, with the veteran Raimond van der Gouw capably filling the gaps in the remaining 22 games.

The Chelsea upset on Sunday, October 3, was United's first Premiership defeat of the season but only two more would follow in 28 league fixtures. They lost at Tottenham and Newcastle and broke new ground in the Premiership, fending off the challenges of a lively young Leeds side, Chelsea, Arsenal and a rejuvenated Liverpool.

The manager's spending in the final season of the 20th century was restricted by the vast investment the club made in building its new training complex at Carrington, and the extensions to the East and West grandstands at Old Trafford, but Sir Alex did bring in two other new players.

Mickael Silvestre, a French Under-21 defender made his debut at Anfield at the same time as Taibi, and Quinton Fortune a young South African, had his first taste of senior football in the 5-1 home win over Newcastle.

Silvestre, had played against United in Inter Milan's European campaign the previous season and cost £4 million, while Fortune's move from Atletico Madrid saw an outlay of £1.5 million.

Top: Andy Cole wrestles his way past Frank Leboeuf and Jes Høgh as the Reds are subjected to a 5–0 mauling at Stamford Bridge.

Above: The £1.5 million signing from Atletico Madrid Quinton Fortune scored on his first Premiership start against Bradford City on Boxing Day.

Right: The protracted contract talks with Roy Keane was a nervy time for United fans, but the conclusion seemed inevitable: the skipper would stay at Old Trafford for four more years.

Middlesbrough beaten again in a 4-3 thriller on Teeside and dark horses Sunderland, who for a time had been among the leaders in their first season back in the Premiership, went down 4-0 as Ole Gunnar Solskjaer struck twice after he earned a rare starting place.

Seven days later the championship was secured by a 3-1 win at Southampton where United's representation in the 15,245 crowd was big enough to make the end of game celebrations worthwhile. The cheers eased some of the pain brought on by a premature exit from the Champions' League three days earlier.

Beckham opened the scoring after just five minutes and United added a second ten minutes later when Francis Benali turned the ball into his own net. Solskjaer – partnering Andy Cole in the attack – tied things up on the half hour and when Southampton scored late in the second half the game was already over.

Van breaks down

Eventual FA Cup winners Chelsea were next to fall beaten 3-2 at Old Trafford as Dutch striker Ruud Van Nistelrooy watched from a seat in the director's box. He was to be the new acquisition for a push for further glories but 24 hours later, after problems with his medical, he returned to Eindhoven and in a bid to attain full fitness ruptured a cruciate knee ligament. The injury halted an £18.5 million deal with PSV but Sir Alex was optimistic that he would sign the player in the summer of 2001 if he has fully recovered from the set-back.

United were heading for their sixth Premiership title in eight seasons and the 13th league championship in the club's history. Whether pending success influenced Keane's decision was never revealed, but it must have played some part. The Irishman became the inspiration behind a run of games which began four days before he signed his contract extension.

Above: Ole Gunnar Solskjaer scores his second goal of four in the 5–1 thrashing of Everton.

Right: Denis Irwin challenges free-scoring Aussie Harry Kewell as the Reds run out 1–0 winners at Elland Road. David O'Leary's young Leeds stars were to prove United's strongest challengers for the Premiership trophy for most of the season.

Formidable Form

The week after a disappointing 1-1 home draw with Liverpool, a Dwight Yorke hat-trick sparked off a 3-1 win over Derby County and the die was cast.

United had stepped into first place in the league on January 29, when a David Beckham strike three minutes from time ended a siege on Middlesbrough's Stretford End goal and were to stay there until the end of the season.

Derby was the beginning. Then came a 2-0 win at Leicester, Bradford City were beaten 4-0 on their own ground a week later and West Ham were humiliated 7-1 in front of a 61,611 crowd at Old Trafford as Paul Scholes scored his first senior hat-trick for the club.

1990-00

Record-breaking season

The Van Nistelrooy fee would have established a new transfer record for the club, but while that was put on hold, other records fell as the season ended in glory. Relegated Watford were beaten 3-2, a 3-1 home win over Tottenham was followed by victory at Villa Park against the other FA Cup finalists who were beaten 1-0 thanks to a Teddy Sheringham goal. Days later the striker signed a new one-year contract.

In a season when the club's share value broke the £1billion barrier, United scored more Premiership goals (97) than the previous best, and secured more points (91) than in any other 38-game campaign.

Old Trafford established a new British average league attendance high of 58,017 bettering that of 1967-68 when 57,758 watched Law, Best and Charlton in action. That record was destined to be short-lived with ground capacity rising to 67,500 at the start of the 2000-2001 season Manchester United will once again head for new horizons.

Above: While the media focused on David Beckham's new haircut the midfielder got on with the more relevant matter of winning the championship. His trademark freekick set United well on course with a 2–0 win away to Leicester City in March 2000.

Right: Déjà vu? Beckham's freekick at Southampton seals the championship for another year, this time by a comfortable margin of 18 points.

EUROPE 2000:
UEFA moved the goalposts

In response to outsiders trying to tempt clubs into a bigger and more lucrative foreign competition, UEFA extended the Champions League by adding a second qualifying group to boost the revenue.

The new structure successfully beat off the predators, but it meant that a club reaching the final would play 17 games and involve a few fixtures in the early stages against smaller clubs with the potential to spring giant-killing shocks.

United got an early warning of the dangers when they opened their campaign against Croatia Zagreb at Old Trafford and found themselves held on their own ground to a 0-0 result. This was not the stuff of reigning European champions but it was difficult because Zagreb had come looking for a draw. They packed their midfield and took no chances, which with a disciplined performance by their defence, saw them frustrate the Reds.

Above: Another domestic season of triumph was celebrated after the Reds 3–1 victory at home to Spurs. The undeniable domination of the Premiership by Sir Alex Ferguson's side is underlined by the fact that it was their sixth title in the eight years of Premiership football.

The trip to Austria the following week brought them up against more underdogs in Sturm Graz, but this time United made their superior ability count. Goals in the first half from Roy Keane, Dwight Yorke and Andy Cole saw them establish a presence in the competition in keeping with their European title.

United first in the first phase

The group was also beginning to take shape with United and Marseille established at the top with two to go through to the second qualifying stage. Winning their next match 2-1 against Marseille at Old Trafford confirmed the rankings, and in fact put United at the top a point ahead of the French team, but not before making their supporters sweat.

Their problems started when Henning Berg slipped and fell in the 40th minute to leave Ibrahima Bakayoko in the clear with only Raimond van der Gouw to beat, which he did with a fierce drive.

1990-00

United were still a goal down 10 minutes from the end, but then, shades of their late revival to win the competition the previous May, they roused themselves to produce two good goals. A free kick from David Beckham was headed back across goal by Jaap Stam for Andy Cole to score with an overhead shot. Paul Scholes ran in the winner to calm the champions' nerves!

It was still proving a bumpy ride, though, with the return against Marseille lost 1-0 to end an unbeaten run of 18 games in the Champions League. Only the fact that Sturm Graz had beaten Zagreb in the other fixture had maintained a gap between the top two and the bottom pair.

Marseille played well and punished United in the 68th minute with a goal from William Gallas to leave the Reds needing a win and a draw from their remaining two games to make sure of qualification.

In fact United qualified in the next match with the final fixture to spare. A 2-1 win in Croatia Zagreb settled it and as Sir Alex Ferguson put it: "Suddenly our position has been transformed with a big black cloud blown away."

David Beckham scored a trademark free kick after half an hour and Roy Keane's goal immediately after the interval settled it with Zagreb's goal not coming until injury time. The last game at home to Sturm Graz found United rather going through the motions until Ole Solskjaer scored after 56 minutes and Roy Keane clinched it 12 minutes later when he fired in a rebound off the bar from Henning Berg. Ivica Vastic scored a penalty, conceded by Ryan Giggs, but too late to stop United emerging group winners with 13 points followed by Marseille on 10, Sturm Gratz six and Croatia Zagreb five.

Above: Beckham, Giggs and Keane congratulate Paul Scholes as United romp to a 3–0 home victory over eventual Champions League finalists Valencia.

Below: Andy Cole outpaces Sturm Graz's Ferdinand Feldhold in the 3–0 victory at the Schwarzenegger stadium.

The Reds fall in Florence

The second phase group saw them lining up against Fiorentina, Valencia and Bordeaux, and it was immediately apparent that the standard had gone up as the Champions returned home from Florence beaten 2-0. It seemed as if the manager's brave words about getting the measure of Italian clubs based on the previous season's successes was so much whistling in the dark. Knocking Juventus and Inter Milan out in the last campaign did not seem to have scared Argentineans Gabriel Batistuta and Abel Balbo as they shot the Florence team to victory.

Keane inspires United

Admittedly United contributed hugely to their own downfall with a failed back-pass by Roy Keane for the first goal. Keane said he was devastated, but he quickly balanced the books in another competition when United set off for Tokyo to play Palmeiras, the South American champions, for the Inter Continental Cup.

United played brilliantly to win 1-0 with a goal scored by Keane after magical play by Ryan Giggs. It must have been a sweet moment for the United skipper.

Keane had a lot on his mind at that point after deliberating for a long time over whether to sign a new four-year contract. He put pen to paper on the afternoon of meeting Valencia at Old Trafford and then scored the opening goal in a 3-0 win to emphasise his value to Manchester United. It was a game United had to win and they did it in style with Ole Solskjaer and Paul Scholes getting the other goals to make everyone feel much more hopeful.

A vintage Bordeaux double

Certainly United were playing much better when the Champions League re-opened in March and they cruised smoothly through 2-0 against Bordeaux at Old Trafford. Giggs was the outstanding player, scoring the first goal and laying on the other for Teddy Sheringham. United were second in their group, one point behind Fiorentina the leaders. The return a week later didn't quite go according to plan when, in the ninth minute, Raimond van der Gouw let a shot from Michel Pavon slip through his hands to aggravate United's problems trying to find a permanent successor for the departed Peter Schmeichel. The goal was a blow but when Bordeaux had Lilian Laslandes sent off after 22 minutes United became more dominant. Goals by Dwight Yorke and Roy Keane in three telling minutes won the game 2-1.

Revenge over Fiorentina

The stage was set now for the visit of Fiorentina and it produced United's best display of the season's European campaign. All the power and precision which had seen them triumph in Europe the previous year flooded back. Gabriel Batistuta scored with a rocket after only 15 minutes but the Champions roared back with goals from Andy Cole, Roy Keane and Dwight Yorke to win 3-1 and have Sir Bobby Charlton purring: "It all came together with every player excelling. It was magic. Even before they had a man sent off, I didn't feel we were in any trouble."

The win put United through to the quarter finals, and again they had emerged from their group with a game to spare. The group programme was completed by a 0-0 draw in Valencia which meant that United finished top of their group on 13 points, three ahead of Valencia, and therefore a top seed. The fancied Fiorentina were left on eight points with just two for Bordeaux.

The first leg in the quarter final took them to Real Madrid and a goalless game which left the United manager angry and already counting the cost of failing to score an away goal.

Sir Alex labelled it the worst big-game display for a long time and criticised the tackling and the possession his team had needlessly frittered away. Only Mark Bosnich was exempt from the criticism and indeed, the fact that United were coming home with at least a draw, was largely due to the excellence of his goalkeeping.

Real shatter dreams

United tried hard to stay upbeat for the second leg and indeed played their hearts out before crashing to a 3-2 defeat which meant they had lost their European crown. It was clear from the

January in the sun

The Champions League then went into its mid-winter break, though United continued to globe-trot by flying out to Brazil in January to take part in the Club World Championship. This was the competition that had forced them to pull out of the FA Cup and in fact it turned out a disaster.

They drew with Necaxa, lost to Vasco da Gama and just managed to win 2-0 against the part-timers of South Melbourne. David Beckham suffered another high profile dismissal and the most satisfaction Sir Alex could draw from the trip was to turn it into a sunshine break for his players.

Above: Solskjaer under pressure from two South Melbourne defenders during the inaugral Club World Championship in Brazil. United failed to qualify from their group with the final being fought out between the country's two representatives, Vasco da Gama and Corinthians.

1990-00

21st minute that it was not going to be their night as Roy Keane, of all players, put through his own goal trying to intercept a cross from Michel Salgado. United charged forward in the second half but Raul scored twice on breakaways in the space of three minutes to give them a mountain to climb. That they attempted the impossible and came close says much for their resilience and powers of recovery. David Beckham pulled a goal back in the 64th minute and Paul Scholes forced it to 3-2 a couple of minutes from the end of normal time.

But as skipper Keane summed up: "You can't concede three goals at home in the quarter-finals of the European Cup against a good team and expect to go through. Going out of Europe is a major disappointment but we have no divine right to win anything. Hopefully we can win the League now and then we can come back into this competition next year and win it."

As the new millennium begins Manchester United could not be in better health. Their unsurpassed level of achievement over the last 10 years has meant that they are the yardstick by which each English club measures its performances. United are not just the most supported and wealthiest club in the world, the name stands for more than that. It encompasses a football heritage that is packed with success, tragedy, characters, innovation and talent.

One hundred and twenty-two years of history has seen domestic and European title triumphs. It has witnessed golden eras under Sir Matt Busby and Sir Alex Ferguson. United have claimed the talents of Duncan Edwards, George Best, Bobby Charlton, Bryan Robson, Eric Cantona, Peter Schmeichel, David Beckham and Roy Keane who have thrilled crowds throughout the world confirming the fans' belief that the are following the greatest club in the world.

Above: Giggs looks on helpless as Real Madrid's Raul scores his side's second goal in their 3–2 victory at Old Trafford. The Spanish side would go on to claim the trophy with Spain having three representatives in the semi-finals.

Right: A disconsolate Paul Scholes and Roy Keane head for the dressing room after United's exit from the Champions League. Euro 2000 awaited Paul Scholes, and Keane was to pick up the PFA and Football writers' Player of the Year awards.

*(left margin, vertical:)* 1990-2000 1990-1991

Date	Opp	V	R	Score												Substitutes
19 Aug	Arsenal	H	W	4–1	Leighton	Duxbury	Blackmore	Bruce1	Phelan	Donaghy	Robson	Webb1	McClair1	Hughes1	Sharpe	Martin for Sharpe
22 Aug	C Palace	A	D	1–1	..	..	..	..	..	..	..1	..	..	..	..	
26 Aug	Derby C	A	L	0–2	..	..	Martin	..	..	Blackmore	..	..	..	..	..	Graham for Martin
30 Aug	Norwich	H	L	0–2	..	..	Blackmore	..	..	Pallister	..	..	..	..	..	Martin for Robson, Robins for Blackmore
9 Sep	Everton	A	L	2–3	..	..	Martin	..	..	..	Donaghy	Blackmore	..1	..	..	Anderson for Duxbury, Beardsmore1 for Martin
16 Sep	Millwall	H	W	5–1	..	Anderson	Donaghy	..	..	..	Robson1	Ince	..	..3	Sharpe1	Duxbury for Ince, Beardsmore for Bruce
23 Sep	Man City	A	L	1–5	..	..	..	Duxbury	..	..	Beardsmore	..	..	..1	Wallace	Sharpe for Beardsmore
14 Oct	Sheffield Wed	H	D	0–0	..	..	..	..	..	..	Robson	..	..	..	..	Martin for Duxbury, Sharpe for Wallace
21 Oct	Coventry	A	W	4–1	..	Donaghy	Martin	Bruce1	..1	..	..	..	..	..2	Sharpe	Duxbury for Ince, Maiorana for Sharpe
28 Oct	Southampton	H	W	2–1	..	..	..	..	..	..	..	..	..2	..	..	Blackmore for Ince
4 Nov	Charlton	A	L	0–2	..	..	..	..	..	..	..	..	..	..	..	Blackmore for Donaghy, Wallace for Sharpe
12 Nov	Nottingham F	H	W	1–0	..	Blackmore	..	..	..	..1	..	..	..	..	Wallace	Sharpe for Wallace
18 Nov	Luton	A	W	3–1	..	..1	..	..	..	..	..	..	..	..1	..1	
25 Nov	Chelsea	H	D	0–0	..	..	..	..	..	..	..	..	..	..	..	Duxbury for Martin, Beardsmore for Wallace
3 Dec	Arsenal	A	L	0–1	..	..	..	..	..	..	..	..	..	..	..	Beardsmore for Blackmore
9 Dec	C Palace	H	L	1–2	..	Beardsmore1	..	..	..	..	..	..	..	Sharpe	..	Hughes for Sharpe, Blackmore for Phelan
16 Dec	Tottenham	H	L	0–1	..	..	Sharpe	..	..	..	..	..	..	Hughes	..	Anderson for Bruce, Blackmore for Beardsmore
23 Dec	Liverpool	A	D	0–0	..	Blackmore	Martin	..	..	..	..	..	..	..	Sharpe	Sharpe for Wallace
26 Dec	Aston V	A	L	0–3	..	Anderson	..	..	..	..	Blackmore	..	..	..	Sharpe	Duxbury for Martin, Robins for Blackmore
30 Dec	Wimbledon	A	D	2–2	..	..	..	..	..	..	..	..	..	..1	Robins1	Sharpe for Ince
1 Jan	Q P R	H	D	0–0	..	..	..	..	..	..	Sharpe	Blackmore	..	..	..	Duxbury for Sharpe, Beardsmore for Blackmore
13 Jan	Derby C	H	L	1–2	..	..	..	..	..	..1	Beardsmore	..	..	..	..	Duxbury for Anderson, Milne for Beardsmore
21 Jan	Norwich	A	L	0–2	..	..	..	..	..	..	Robins	Ince	..	..	Wallace	Blackmore for Phelan, Beardsmore for Ince
3 Feb	Man City	H	D	1–1	..	..	..	Donaghy	..	..	Blackmore1	Duxbury	..	..	..	Beardsmore for Donaghy, Robins for Wallace
10 Feb	Millwall	A	W	2–1	..	..	..	Beardsmore	..	..	..	..	..	..1	..1	Brazil for Anderson, Robins for Blackmore
24 Feb	Chelsea	A	L	0–1	..	..	..	Bruce	..	..	Duxbury	Ince	..	..	..	Donaghy for Anderson, Beardsmore for Duxbury
3 Mar	Luton	H	W	4–1	..	..	..	..	..	..	Robins1	Ince	..	..1	..1	Beardsmore for Wallace
14 Mar	Everton	H	D	0–0	..	Duxbury	..	..	..	..	..	..	..1	..	..	Blackmore for Robins, Beardsmore for Hughes
18 Mar	Liverpool	H	L	*1–2	..	Anderson	..	..	..	..	Blackmore	..	..	..	..	Duxbury for Anderson, Beardsmore for Wallace
21 Mar	Sheffield Wed	A	L	0–1	..	Donaghy	..	..	..	..	Beardsmore	Gibson	..	..	Blackmore	Ince for Blackmore, Wallace for Beardsmore
24 Mar	Southampton	A	W	2–0	..	..	..	..	..	..	Gibson1	Ince	..	..	Wallace	Webb for Gibson, Robins1 for Hughes
31 Mar	Coventry	H	W	3–0	..	..	Gibson	..	..	..	Webb	..	..	..2	..	Martin for Donaghy, Robins1 for Wallace
14 Apr	Q P R	A	W	2–1	Sealey	Ince	Martin	..	..	..	Robson	Webb1	..	..	..	Gibson for Bruce, Robins1 for Hughes
17 Apr	Aston V	H	W	2–0	..	Anderson	Gibson	Robins2	..	..	..	..	..	..	..	Blackmore for Gibson, Beardsmore for Anderson
21 Apr	Tottenham	A	L	1–2	Leighton	Robins	Martin	Bruce1	..	..	..	..	..	..	..	Blackmore for Webb, Beardsmore for Wallace
30 Apr	Wimbledon	H	D	0–0	Bosnich	Anderson	..	..	..	..	Beardsmore	Ince	..	..	Gibson	Wallace for Robins, Blackmore for Gibson
2 May	Nottingham F	A	L	0–4	Leighton	Duxbury	Blackmore	..	..	..	..	Webb	Robins	Robins	Wallace	
5 May	Charlton	H	W	1–0	..	Ince	Martin	..	..	..1	Robson	..	McClair	Hughes	..	

FA Cup

Date	Opp	V	R	Score												Substitutes
7 Jan	N Forest (3)	A	W	1–0	..	Anderson	..	Donaghy	Duxbury	..	Beardsmore	Blackmore	..	..	Robins1	Duxbury for Blackmore
28 Jan	Hereford (4)	A	W	1–0	..	..	..	Donaghy	..	..	Blackmore1	..	..	..	Wallace	Beardsmore for Ince
18 Feb	Newcastle (5)	A	W	3–2	..	..	..	Bruce	Phelan	..	Robins1	Duxbury	..1	..	..1	Ince for Duxbury, Beardsmore for Robins
11 Mar	Sheff Utd (6)	A	W	1–0	..	..	..	..	..	..	..	Ince	..1	..	..	Duxbury for Anderson
8 Apr	Oldham (SF) (at Maine Rd)	N	D	3–3†	..	Martin	Gibson	..	..	..	Robson1	..	..	..	Webb1	Wallace1 for Robins, Robins for Martin
11 Apr	Oldham (SFR) (at Maine Rd)	N	W	2–1	..	Ince	Martin	..	..	..	..	Webb	McClair1	..	Wallace	Gibson for Webb, Robins1 for Martin
12 May	C Palace (F)	N	D	3–3†	..	..	..	..	..	..	..1	..	..	..2	..	Robins for Pallister, Blackmore for Martin
17 May	C Palace (FR)	N	W	1–0	Sealey	..	..1	..	..	..	..	..	..	..	..	

†After extra time

Littlewoods Cup

Date	Opp	V	R	Score												Substitutes
10 Sep	Portsm'th (2)	A	W	3–2	Leighton	Anderson	Donaghy	Beardsmore	..	..	..	Ince2	..	..	..1	Duxbury for Robson, Sharpe for McClair
3 Oct	Portsm'th (2)	H	D	0–0	..	Duxbury	..	Bruce	..	..	..	..	..	..	..	
25 Oct	Tottenham (3)	H	L	0–3	..	Donaghy	Martin	..	..	..	..	..	..	..	Sharpe	Maiorana for Martin

Appearances (goals)

Anderson 23 – Beardsmore 28 (2) – Blackmore 33 (3) – Bosnich 1 – Bruce 43 (3) – Brazil 1 – Donaghy 19 – Duxbury 24 – Gibson 8 (1) – Graham 1 – Hughes 48 (15) – Ince 36 2 – Leighton 45 – Maiorana 2 – Martin 40 (1) – Milne 1 – McClair 48 (8) – Pallister 46 (3) – Phelan 48 (1) – Robins 24 (10) – Robson 27 (4) – Sealey 3 – Sharpe 22 (1) – Wallace 34 (6) – Webb 15 (3) – Own goals 1 – Total 25 players (64)

Football League

	P	W	D	L	F:A	Pts
Liverpool	38	23	10	5	78:37	79 1st
Manchester U	38	13	9	16	46:47	48 13th

SEASON 1990-1991 FOOTBALL LEAGUE (DIVISION 1)

Date	Opp	V	R	Score												Substitutes
25 Aug	Coventry	H	W	2-0	Sealey	Irwin	Donaghy	Bruce1	Phelan	Pallister	Webb1	Ince	McClair	Hughes	Blackmore	Beardsmore for Ince
28 Aug	Leeds	A	D	0-0	..	..	..	..	..	..	..	..	..	..	..	Beardsmore for Donaghy, Robins for Hughes
1 Sep	Sunderland	A	L	1-2	..	..	..	..	..	..	..	..	..	..1	..	Hughes for Robins, Donaghy for Beardsmore
4 Sep	Luton Town	A	W	1-0	..	..	Blackmore	..	..	..	..	..	..	Robins1	Beardsmore	
8 Sep	Q P R	H	W	3-1	..	..	..	..	..	..	..	..	..	..2	..	Beardsmore for Ince, Donaghy for Pallister
16 Sep	Liverpool	A	L	0-4	..	..	..	..	..	..	..	Robins	..	Hughes	Robins	Sharpe for Irwin, Beardsmore for Robins
22 Sep	Southampton	H	W	3-2	..	..	..	Donaghy	..	..	..	Ince	..1	..1	Blackmore1	Hughes for Robins, Martin for Beardsmore
29 Sep	Nottingham F	H	L	0-1	..	..	Blackmore	..	..	..	..	Ince	..	Robins	Beardsmore	Martin for Irwin, Robins for Sharpe
20 Oct	Arsenal	H	L	0-1	..	..	..	Bruce	..	..	..	..	..	..	Sharpe	Wallace for Sharpe
27 Oct	Man City	A	D	3-3	..	..	Martin	..	Blackmore	..	..1	..	..	Hughes1	..	Martin for Wallace
3 Nov	C Palace	H	W	2-0	..	..	Blackmore	..	Phelan	..	..1	..	..	Wallace1	..	Donaghy for Irwin, Wallace for Sharpe
10 Nov	Derby C	A	D	0-0	..	..	..	..	..	..	..	..	..	Hughes	..	Wallace for Irwin
17 Nov	Sheffield Utd	H	W	2-0	..	..	..	..1	..	..	..	..	..	..1	..	Martin for Blackmore, Sharpe for Phelan
25 Nov	Chelsea	H	L	2-3	..	..	..	..	..	..	..	..	..	..1	Wallace1	Martin for Sharpe, Webb for Ince
1 Dec	Everton	A	W	1-0	..	..	..	Donaghy	..	Sharpe1	..	..	..	..	..	Donaghy for Phelan, Robson for Irwin
8 Dec	Leeds	H	D	1-1	..	..	..	Bruce	..	..	..	Webb1	..	..	..	Irwin for Ince, Robson for Sharpe
15 Dec	Coventry	A	D	2-2	..	Blackmore	Sharpe	..	..	..	Webb	Ince	..	..1	..1	Wallace for Blackmore
22 Dec	Wimbledon	A	W	3-1	..	..	Donaghy	..2	..	..	Robson	..	..	..1	Webb	Donaghy for Sharpe, Phelan for Robson
26 Dec	Norwich	H	W	3-0	..	Irwin	Blackmore	..	Webb	..	..	..	..2	..1	Sharpe	Phelan for Webb
29 Dec	Aston V	H	D	1-1	..	..	..	..1	..	..	Webb	..	..	..	..	Martin for Irwin, Robins for Phelan
1 Jan	Tottenham	A	L	1-2	..	..	..	..1	Phelan	..	..	..	..1	..2	..	Robins for Ince, Phelan for Webb
12 Jan	Sunderland	H	W	3-0	..	..	..	..	Webb	..	Robson	..	..	..1	..	Sharpe for Martin, Robins for Beardsmore
19 Jan	Q P R	A	D	1-1	..	..	Martin	..	Phelan1	Donaghy	Beardsmore	Webb	..	..	Blackmore	Wallace for Webb, Martin for Phelan
3 Feb	Liverpool	A	D	1-1	..	..	Blackmore	..1	..	Pallister	Robson	..	..	..	..	Ferguson for Webb, Robins for Robson
28 Feb	Sheffield Utd	A	L	1-2	Walsh	..	Martin	Webb	Donaghy	..	..	Ince	..	Blackmore1	Wallace	Beardsmore for Martin, Giggs for Irwin
2 Mar	Everton	H	L	0-2	Sealey	..	..	..	Ferguson	..	..	Sharpe	..	..	..	Wallace for Blackmore
10 Mar	Chelsea	A	L	2-3	..	Blackmore	..	Donaghy	Phelan	..	Robson	..	..1	Hughes1	Sharpe	Ferguson for Whitworth, Robins for Beardsmore

*(left sidebar:)*

Abbreviations:

Appearances (goals) refer to League games only

Figures shown as 2 etc. refer to goals scored by individual players

* own-goal

Players' names in final column, are substitutes

Date	Opponent	V	R	Score	Team / goalscorers	Substitutions
13 Mar	Southampton	A	D	1-1	.. Whitworth .. .. Beardsmore ..1	Donaghy for Martin
16 Mar	Nottingham F	A	D	1-1	.. Irwin .. Bruce .. .. Robson .. Blackmore1 .. Wallace	Robins1 for Wallace
23 Mar	Luton Town	H	W	4-1	.. .. Blackmore ..2 .. .. .. Wallace McClair1 .. Sharpe	Wratten for Sharpe, Robins for Bruce
2 Apr	Wimbledon	H	W	2-1	Walsh .. Donaghy ..1 .. .. Webb Ince ..1 Blackmore	Robins for Phelan
6 Apr	Aston V	A	D	1-1	Sealey .. .. Robson Webb .. Hughes Sharpe1	McClair1 for Webb
16 Apr	Derby C	H	W	3-1	Bosnich .. .. Webb .. .. ..1 Ince Blackmore1 .. Wallace	Robins for Giggs
4 May	Man City	H	W	1-0	Walsh .. Blackmore .. Phelan .. Donaghy Robson Webb McClair .. Giggs1	Beardsmore for Hughes, Ferguson for Robson
6 May	Arsenal	A	L	1-3	.. .. Phelan .. ..1 Webb Donaghy Ince .. .. Robins	Beardsmore for Pallister, Wratten for Robins
11 May	C Palace	A	L	0-3	.. .. Irwin Donaghy .. .. Pallister Kanchelskis .. Robins Ferguson Wallace	Donaghy for Irwin, Robins for Wallace
20 May	Tottenham	H	D	1-1	Bosnich .. Blackmore .. Phelan .. .. Robson ..1 McClair Hughes	

FA Cup

Date	Opponent	V	R	Score	Team / goalscorers	Substitutions
7 Jan	Q P R (3)	H	W	2-1	Sealey Irwin Blackmore Bruce Phelan Pallister Robson Ince McClair Hughes1 Sharpe	
26 Jan	Bolton (4)	H	W	1-0	.. .. Webb .. ..1 ..	Robins for Phelan
18 Feb	Norwich (5)	A	L	1-2	.. .. Martin .. Blackmore .. .. Ince ..1	Wallace for Martin

European Cupwinners Cup

Date	Opponent	V	R	Score	Team / goalscorers	Substitutions
19 Sep	Pesci Munkas (1)	H	W	2-0	Sealey Irwin Blackmore1 Bruce Phelan Pallister Webb1 Ince McClair Robins Beardsmore	Hughes for Robins, Sharpe for Ince
3 Oct	Pesci Munkas (1)	A	W	1-0	.. Anderson Donaghy .. .. Blackmore ..1 Hughes Martin	Sharpe for Martin
23 Oct	Wrexham (2)	H	W	3-0	.. .. Blackmore Martin ..1 Sharpe ..1 .. Ince .. Wallace	Robins for Wallace, Beardsmore for Ince
7 Dec	Wrexham (2)	A	W	2-0	.. .. Irwin Blackmore ..1 Phelan Robins1	Donaghy for Ince, Martin for McClair
6 Mar	Montpellier (3)	H	D	1-1	.. .. Blackmore Martin Donaghy .. Robson .. ..1 Hughes Sharpe	Wallace for Martin
19 Mar	Montpellier (3)	A	W	2-0	.. .. Irwin Blackmore1 Bruce1 .. .. Martin	Martin for Ince
10 Apr	Legia Warsaw (SF)	A	W	3-1	.. ..1 .. Webb .. ..1 ..1	Donaghy for Phelan
24 Apr	Legia Warsaw (SF)	H	D	1-1	Walsh .. .. Robson Webb 1	Donaghy for Blackmore
15 May	Barcelona (F)	N	W	2-1	Sealey .. .. Ince .. ..2 ..	(at Stadion Feijenoord Rotterdam)

Rumbelows Cup

Date	Opponent	V	R	Score	Team / goalscorers	Substitutions
26 Sep	Halifax (2)	A	W	3-1	Leighton Irwin Blackmore1 Donaghy Phelan Pallister Webb1 Ince McClair1 Hughes Beardsmore	Martin for Ince, Robins for Hughes
10 Oct	Halifax (2)	H	W	2-1	Sealey Anderson .. Bruce1 .. .. .. Irwin .. .. Martin	Wallace for Blackmore, Robins for Irwin
31 Oct	Liverpool (3)	H	W	3-1	.. .. Irwin .. ..1 .. .. Ince 1 Sharpe1	Donaghy for Phelan, Wallace for Hughes
28 Nov	Arsenal (4)	A	W	6-2	.. ..1 .. .. Sharpe3 Robson Webb ..1 Wallace1	Donaghy for Bruce
16 Jan	S'thampton (5)	A	D	1-1	.. .. Donaghy .. .. Robson Webb ..1 Sharpe	Irwin for Webb
23 Jan	S'thampton (5)	H	W	3-2	.. .. Irwin .. ..3 ..	Donaghy for Irwin, Robins for Sharpe
10 Feb	Leeds (SF1)	H	W	2-1	.. .. Martin .. Blackmore .. .. Ince ..1 1	Donaghy for Irwin, Wallace for Martin
24 Feb	Leeds (SF2)	A	W	1-0	.. .. Donaghy Blackmore Webb Phelan .. Robson 1	Martin for Webb
21 Apr	Sheff Wed (F)	N	L	0-1	.. .. Irwin .. Bruce Webb	Phelan for Webb

Appearances (goals)

Anderson 3 (1) – Beardsmore 16 – Blackmore 57 (9) – Bruce 50 (19) – Bosnich 2 – Donaghy 36 – Ferguson 5 – Giggs 2 (1) – Hughes 52 (21) – Ince 47 (3) – Irwin 52 – Kanchelskis 1 – Leighton 1 – Martin 24 – McClair 56 (21) – Pallister 56 (1) – Phelan 51 (1) – Robins 27 (5) – Robson 29 (1) – Sealey 51 – Sharpe 40 (9) – Wallace 29 (4) – Walsh 6 – Webb 47 (5) – Whitworth 1 – Wratten 1

Total 26 players (101)

Football League

	P	W	D	L	F:A	Pts	
Arsenal*	38	24	13	1	74:16	63	1st
Manchester U**	38	16	12	10	56:45	59	6th

*Two points deducted **One point deducted

SEASON 1991-1992 FOOTBALL LEAGUE (DIVISION 1)

Date	Opponent	V	R	Score	Team / goalscorers	Substitutions
17 Aug	Notts Co	H	W	2-0	Schmeichel Irwin Blackmore Bruce Ferguson Parker Robson1 Ince McClair Hughes Kanchelskis	Pallister for Ince, Giggs for Ferguson
21 Aug	Aston V	A	W	1-0	.. ..1 Donaghy .. .. Giggs	Pallister for Irwin, Webb for Blackmore
24 Aug	Everton	A	D	0-0	.. .. Giggs	Blackmore for Ince, Ferguson for Webb
28 Aug	Oldham Ath	H	W	1-0	.. .. Parker Irwin .. Webb Pallister .. .. ..1 Blackmore	Phelan for Bruce, Giggs for Ince
31 Aug	Leeds	H	D	1-1	.. .. Webb 1	Irwin for Phelan
3 Sep	Wimbledon	A	W	2-1	.. .. Donaghy .. Phelan ..1 .. Kanchelskis ..1 .. Giggs1	Blackmore for Kanchelskis, Phelan for Webb
7 Sep	Norwich	H	W	3-0	.. .. Phelan Irwin1 .. Webb .. .. Ince ..	Ince for Kanchelskis
14 Sep	Southampton	A	W	1-0	.. .. Phelan .. .. Ince ..1 ..	Ince for Kanchelskis
21 Sep	Luton Town	H	W	5-0	.. ..1 .. .. .. Blackmore ..1	McClair2 for Blackmore
28 Sep	Tottenham	A	W	2-1	.. .. Kanchelskis .. .. ..1 .. McClair ..1	Blackmore for Kanchelskis
6 Oct	Liverpool	H	D	0-0	.. .. Blackmore	Kanchelskis for Phelan, Donaghy for Ince
19 Oct	Arsenal	H	D	1-1	.. .. Blackmore .. ..1 Webb	Kanchelskis for Webb
26 Oct	Sheffield Wed	A	L	2-3	.. .. Parker .. .. .. Kanchelskis ..2 Blackmore ..	Martin for Bruce
2 Nov	Sheffield Utd	H	W	*2-0	.. .. Blackmore .. .. Donaghy Kanchelskis1 Ince .. Robins	Robson for Ince, Pallister for Giggs
16 Nov	Man City	A	D	0-0	.. .. Irwin Pallister Robson Blackmore .. Hughes	Ince for Webb
23 Nov	West Ham	H	W	2-1	.. ..1 Kanchelskis1 ..1	Blackmore for Parker
30 Nov	C Palace	A	W	3-1	.. ..1 ..1	Blackmore for Irwin
7 Dec	Coventry	H	W	4-0	.. ..1 ..1 .. Ince ..1 ..1	Blackmore for Parker
15 Dec	Chelsea	A	W	3-1	.. .. ..1 ..1 .. Kanchelskis ..1	Blackmore for Giggs
26 Dec	Oldham Ath	A	W	6-3	.. .. ..1 Robson ..2 ..1	Giggs1 for Robson, Blackmore for Irwin
29 Dec	Leeds	A	D	1-1	.. .. ..1 Kanchelskis ..	Donaghy for Kanchelskis, Sharpe for Blackmore
1 Jan	Q P R	H	L	1-4	.. .. Blackmore .. Phelan ..1 .. Sharpe	Giggs for Sharpe
11 Jan	Everton	H	W	1-0	.. .. Kanchelskis .. Giggs	Donaghy for Blackmore
16 Jan	Notts City	A	D	1-1	.. .. Irwin .. .. .. Robins Sharpe	Robins for Giggs, Blackmore1 for Bruce
22 Jun	Aston V	H	W	1-0	.. .. Donaghy .. Hobson ..1 Kanchelskis	Giggs for Ince
1 Feb	Arsenal	A	D	1-1	.. .. Parker Donaghy .. Giggs	Giggs for Ince
6 Feb	Sheffield Wed	H	D	1-1	.. .. Giggs .. ..1 ..1	Phelan for Webb, Sharpe for Giggs
22 Feb	C Palace	H	W	2-0	.. .. Donaghy .. ..2 Kanchelskis	Parker for Robson, Blackmore for Kanchelskis
26 Feb	Chelsea	H	D	1-1	Walsh Donaghy .. Giggs 1	Blackmore for Kanchelskis
29 Feb	Coventry	A	D	0-0	Schmeichel Parker Donaghy .. Kanchelskis .. Giggs	Blackmore for Bruce
14 Mar	Sheffield Utd	A	W	2-1	.. .. .. Bruce Phelan Robson .. Sharpe Kanchelskis	Kanchelskis for Hughes, Giggs for Webb
18 Mar	Nottingham F	A	L	0-1	.. .. Blackmore Webb Phelan .. Hughes Sharpe	Sharpe for Webb
21 Mar	Wimbledon	H	D	0-0	.. .. Kanchelskis .. Giggs	Sharpe for Kanchelskis
28 Mar	Q P R	A	D	0-0	.. .. Donaghy .. Phelan Robson Kanchelskis .. Blackmore	Blackmore for Robson
31 Mar	Norwich	A	W	3-1	.. .. Giggs .. .. Ince2 ..1 Sharpe	Kanchelskis for Blackmore
7 Apr	Man City	H	D	1-1	.. .. Blackmore Giggs1	Webb for Ince
16 Apr	Southampton	H	W	1-0	.. .. Parker Phelan Kanchelskis1 .. Giggs	Kanchelskis for Hughes, Blackmore for Parker
18 Apr	Luton Town	A	D	1-1	.. .. .. Giggs Webb Sharpe1	Hughes for Webb, Donaghy for Kanchelskis
20 Apr	Nottingham F	H	L	1-2	.. .. Blackmore .. Kanchelskis ..1 Giggs Sharpe	Ferguson for Donaghy, Kanchelskis for Blackmore
22 Apr	West Ham	A	L	0-1	.. .. Donaghy Blackmore Giggs .. Hughes	Phelan for Pallister
26 Apr	Liverpool	A	L	0-2	.. .. Kanchelskis Robson Ince .. Giggs	Sharpe for Ince
2 May	Tottenham	H	W	3-1	.. .. Ferguson .. Phelan Donaghy Kanchelskis ..1 ..2	

*Includes own goal

FA Cup

Date	Opponent	V	R	Score	Team / goalscorers	Substitutions
15 Jan	Leeds (3)	A	W	1-0	Schmeichel Parker Irwin Bruce Webb Pallister Kanchelskis Ince McClair Hughes1 Giggs	
27 Jan	S'thampton (4)	A	D	0-0	.. .. Donaghy .. .. Robson .. .. Blackmore	Giggs for Blackmore
5 Feb	S'thampton (4H)	H	D	2-2P	.. ..1 Giggs Kanchelskis	Hughes for Kanchelskis, Sharpe for Donaghy

European Cupwinners Cup

Date	Opponent	V	R	Score	Team / goalscorers	Substitutions
18 Sep	Athinaikos (1)	A	D	0-0	Schmeichel Phelan Irwin Bruce Webb Pallister Robins Ince McClair Hughes Beardsmore	Wallace for Beardsmore
2 Oct	Athinaikos (1)	H	W	2-0†	.. .. Martin .. Kanchelskis .. Robson .. ..1 ..1 Wallace	Robins for Wallace, Beardsmore for Martin
23 Oct	Ath Madrid (2)	A	L	0-3	.. .. Parker Irwin Webb .. .. Phelan	Martin for McClair, Beardsmore for Phelan
6 Nov	Ath Madrid (2)	H	D	1-1	Walsh .. Blackmore .. .. Phelan .. Robins .. ..1 Giggs	Pallister for Robins, Martin for Phelan

European Super Cup Final

Date	Opponent	V	R	Score	Team / goalscorers	Substitutions
19 Nov	Red Star Belgrade	H	W	1-0	Schmeichel Martin Irwin Bruce Webb Pallister Kanchelskis Ince McClair1 Hughes Blackmore	Giggs for Martin

(Final reduced to one game because of Civil War in Yugoslavia)

1990-2000

Rumbelows Cup

Date	Opponent			Score												Substitutes
25 Sep	Cambridge (2)	H	W	3-0	Walsh	Phelan	Irwin	Bruce1	Webb	Pallister	Robson	Ince	McClair1	Hughes	Blackmore	Giggs1 for Webb
9 Oct	Cambridge (2)	A	D	1-1	Wilkinson	Donaghy	..	..	Blackmore	..	..	..	..	..	Martin	Giggs for Martin, Robins for Pallister
30 Oct	Portsmouth (3)	H	W	3-1	Schmeichel	Parker	..	..	Webb	..	Donaghy	Kanchelskis	..	Blackmore	Giggs	Robson1 for Webb, Robins2 for Irwin
4 Dec	Oldham Ath (4)	H	W	2-0	..	..	..	..	..	..	Robson	..1	..1	Hughes	..	Ince for Robson, Blackmore for Giggs
8 Jan	Leeds (5)	A	W	3-1	..	..	Blackmore1	..	..	..	Kanchelskis1	Ince	..	..	..1	Donaghy for Giggs, Sharpe for Kanchelskis
4 Mar	Mid'bro (SF1)	A	D	0-0	..	..	Irwin	Donaghy	..	..	Robson	..	..	..	..	Phelan for Donaghy, Sharpe for Ince
11 Mar	Mid'bro (SF2)	H	W	2-1†	..	..	..	Bruce	..	..	..	..	..	Sharpe1	..1	Robins for Sharpe
12 Apr	Nott F (F)	N	W	1-0	..	..	..	..	Phelan	..	Kanchelskis	..	..	..1	Hughes	Sharpe for Kanchelskis
	(at Wembley)															

†After extra time

Appearances (goals)

Beardsmore 3 – Blackmore 42 (4) – Bruce 50 (6) – Donaghy 26 – Ferguson 4 – Giggs 51 (7) – Hughes 52 (14) – Ince 47 (3) – Irwin 51 (4) – Kanchelskis 42 (8) – Martin 6 – McClair 58 (25) – Pallister 56 (1) – Parker 37 – Phelan 24 – Robins 8 (2) – Robson 38 (5) – Schmeichel 53 – Sharpe 20 (2) – Wallace 2 – Walsh 4 – Webb 44 (3) – Wilkinson 1 – Own goals 1 – **Total 23 players (85)**

Football League

		P	W	D	L	F:A	Pts
Leeds U		42	22	16	4	74:37	82	1st
Manchester U		42	21	15	6	63:33	78	2nd

SEASON 1992-1993 FA PREMIER LEAGUE

Date	Opponent			Score												Substitutes
15 Aug	Sheff Utd	A	L	1-2	Schmeichel	Irwin	Blackmore	Bruce	Ferguson	Pallister	Kanchelskis	Ince	McClair	Hughes1	Giggs	Phelan for Ince, Dublin for Kanchelskis
19 Aug	Everton	H	L	0-3	..	..	..	..	..	..	..	..	..	..	..	Phelan for Ince, Dublin for Giggs
22 Aug	Ipswich	H	D	1-1	..	..1	..	..	..	..	..	Phelan	..	..	..	Webb for Blackmore, Dublin for Kanchelskis
24 Aug	Southampton	A	W	1-0	..	Phelan	Irwin	..	..	..	Dublin1	Ince	..	..	..	
29 Aug	Notts For	A	W	2-0	..	..	..	..	..	..	..	..	..	..1	..1	Blackmore for Phelan, Kanchelskis for Hughes
2 Sep	Crystal Pal	H	W	1-0	..	Blackmore	..	..	..	..	..	..	..	..1	..	Kanchelskis for Dublin
6 Sep	Leeds Utd	H	W	2-0	..	..	..	..1	..	..	Kanchelskis1	..	..	..	..	
12 Sep	Everton	A	W	2-0	..	Irwin	Blackmore	..1	..	..	..	..	..1	..	..	
19 Sep	Tottenham	A	D	1-1	..	..	..	..	..	..	..	..	..	..	..1	Wallace for Kanchelskis
26 Sep	Q P R	H	D	0-0	..	..	..	..	..	..	..	..	..	..	..	Wallace for Kanchelskis
3 Oct	Midds'boro	A	D	1-1	..	..	Phelan	..1	..	..	Blackmore	..	..	..	..	Robson for Hughes, Kanchelskis for Phelan
18 Oct	Liverpool	H	D	2-2	..	Parker	Irwin	..	..	..	Kanchelskis	..	..	..2	..	Blackmore for Kanchelskis
24 Oct	Blackburn	A	D	0-0	..	..	..	..	..	..	Blackmore	..	..	..	..	Kanchelskis for Ferguson
31 Oct	Wimbledon	H	L	0-1	..	..	Blackmore	..	..	..	Kanchelskis	..	..	..	..	Robson for Kanchelskis
7 Nov	Aston Villa	A	L	0-1	..	..	..	..	..	..	Robson	..	Sharpe	..	..	McClair for Ferguson
21 Nov	Oldham Ath	H	W	3-0	..	..	Irwin	..	Sharpe	..	..	..	McClair2	..1	..	Phelan for Irwin, Burt for Ince
28 Nov	Arsenal	A	W	1-0	..	..	..	..	..	..	..	..	..	..1	..	
6 Dec	Man City	H	W	2-1	..	..	..	..	..	..	..	..1	..	..1	..	Cantona for Giggs
12 Dec	Norwich	H	W	1-0	..	..	..	..	..	..	Cantona	..	..	..1	..	
19 Dec	Chelsea	A	D	1-1	..	..	..	..	Phelan	..	..1	..	..	..	Sharpe	Kanchelskis for Phelan
26 Dec	Sheff Wed	A	D	3-3	..	..	..	..	Sharpe	..	..1	..	..2	..	Giggs	Kanchelskis for Giggs
28 Dec	Coventry	H	W	5-0	..	..	..1	..	..1	..	..1	..	..	..1	..1	Kanchelskis for Giggs, Phelan for Bruce
9 Jan	Tottenham	H	W	4-1	..	..1	..1	..	..	..	..1	..	..1	..	..	Kanchelskis for Giggs, Phelan for Ince
18 Jan	Q P R	A	W	3-1	..	..	..	..	..	..	Kanchelskis1	..1	..	..	..1	Phelan for Hughes
27 Jan	Notts For	H	W	2-0	..	..	..	..	..	..	Cantona	..1	..	..1	..	
30 Jan	Ipswich	A	L	1-2	..	..	..	..	..	..	..	..	..1	..	..	Kanchelskis for Sharpe
6 Feb	Sheff Utd	H	W	2-1	..	..	..	..	..	..	..1	..	..1	..	..	Kanchelskis for Giggs
8 Feb	Leeds	A	D	0-0	..	..	..	..	..	..	..	..	..	..	..	Kanchelskis for Giggs
20 Feb	Southampton	H	W	2-1	..	..	..	..	..	..	..	..	..	..	..2	
27 Feb	Midds'boro	H	W	3-0	..	..	..	..1	..	..	..1	..	..	..	..1	
6 Mar	Liverpool	A	W	2-1	..	..	..	..	..	..	Kanchelskis	..	..1	..1	..	
9 Mar	Oldham	A	L	0-1	..	..	..	..	..	..	..	..	..	..	..	Dublin for Kanchelskis
14 Mar	Aston Villa	H	D	1-1	..	..	..	..	..	..	Cantona	..	..	..1	..	
20 Mar	Man City	A	D	1-1	..	..	..	..	..	..	..1	..	..	..	..	
24 Mar	Arsenal	H	D	0-0	..	..	..	..	..	..	..	..	..	..	..	
5 Apr	Norwich	A	W	3-1	..	..	..	..	..	..	..1	..	....	Kanchelskis1	..1	Robson for Kanchelskis
10 Apr	Sheff Wed	H	W	2-1	..	..	..	..2	..	..	..	..	..	Hughes	..	Robson for Parker
12 Apr	Coventry	A	W	1-0	..	..	..1	..	..	..	..	..	..	..	..	Robson for Cantona
17 Apr	Chelsea	H	W	*3-0	..	..	..	..	..	..	..1	..	..	..1	..	Robson for McClair, Kanchelskis for Giggs
21 Apr	Crystal Pal	A	W	2-0	..	..	..	..	Kanchelskis	..	..	..1	..	..1	..	Robson for Kanchelskis
3 May	Blackburn	H	W	3-1	..	..	..	..	Sharpe	..1	..	..1	..	..	..1	Robson for Sharpe, Kanchelskis for McClair
9 May	Wimbledon	A	W	2-1	..	..	..	..	..	..	Robson1	..1	..	..	Cantona	Giggs for Irwin

*Includes own goal

FA Cup

Date	Opponent			Score												Substitutes
5 Jan	Bury (3)	H	W	2-0	Schmeichel	Parker	Irwin	Bruce	Sharpe	Pallister	Cantona	Phelan1	McClair	Hughes	Gillespie1	Robson for McClair, Blackmore for Irwin
23 Jan	Brighton (4)	H	W	1-0	..	..	..	..	..	..	Wallace	Ince	..	Phelan	Giggs1	Gillespie for Wallace
14 Feb	Sheff Utd (5)	A	L	1-2	..	..	..	..	..	..	Kanchelskis	..	..	Hughes	..1	

UEFA Cup

Date	Opponent			Score												Substitutes
16 Sep	Torpedo Moscow (1)	H	D	0-0	Walsh	Irwin	Martin	Bruce	Blackmore	Pallister	Kanchelskis	Webb	McClair	Hughes	Wallace	Neville for Martin
29 Sep	Torpedo Moscow (I)	A	LP	0-0	Schmeichel	..	Phelan	..	Webb	..	Wallace	Ince	..	..	Giggs	Parker for Phelan, Robson tor Wallace

(LP – Lost on penalties)

Coca Cola (League) Cup

Date	Opponent			Score												Substitutes
23 Sep	Brighton (2)	A	D	1-1	Walsh	Irwin	Martin	Bruce	Blackmore	Pallister	Kanchelskis	Ince	McClair	Hughes	Wallace1	Beckham for Kanchelskis
7 Oct	Brighton (2)	H	W	1-0	Schmeichel	Parker	Irwin	..	Kanchelskis	..	Robson	..	..	..1	Giggs	
28 Oct	Aston Villa (3)	A	L	0-1	..	..	..	..	Ferguson	..	Blackmore	..	..	..	..	Kanchelskis for Irwin

Appearances (goals)

Beckham 1 – Blackmore 17 – Bruce 50 (5) – Butt 1 – Cantona 23 (9) – Dublin 7 (1) – Ferguson 16 – Giggs 46 (11) – Gillespie 2 (1) – Hughes 46 (16) – Ince 47 (6) – Irwin 48 (5) – Kanchelskis 30 (3) – McClair 50 (9) – Martin 2 – Neville 1 – Pallister 50 (1) – Parker 37 (1) – Phelan 14 (1) – Robson 17 (1) – Schmeichel 48 – Sharpe 30 (1) – Walsh 2 – Wallace 6 (1) – Webb 4 – Own goals 1 – **Total 25 players (73)**

FA Premier League

		P	W	O	L	F:A	Pts
Manchester U		42	24	12	6	67:31	84	1st

SEASON 1993-1994 FA PREMIER LEAGUE

Date	Opponent			Score												Substitutes
15 Aug	Norwich	A	W	2-0	Schmeichel	Parker	Irwin	Bruce	Kanchelskis	Pallister	Robson1	Ince	Keane	Hughes	Giggs1	
18 Aug	Sheff Utd	H	W	3-0	..	..	..	..	..	..	..	..	..2	..1	..	McClair for Robson
21 Aug	Newcastle	H	D	1-1	..	..	..	..	..	..	..	..	..	..	..1	Sharpe for Parker, McClair for Kanchelskis
23 Aug	Aston Villa	A	W	2-1	..	..	..	..	Sharpe2	..	Kanchelskis	..	..	..	..	
28 Aug	Southampton	A	W	3-1	..	..	..1	..	..1	..	Cantona1	..	..	..	..	McClair for Giggs, Kanchelskis for Keane
1 Sep	West Ham	H	W	3-0	..	..	..	..1	..1	..	..1	..	..	Kanchelskis	..	McClair for Ince, Robson for Kanchelskis
11 Sep	Chelsea	A	L	0-1	..	..	..	..	..	..	..	..	..	Robson	..	McClair for Robson
19 Sep	Arsenal	H	W	1-0	..	..	..	..	..	..	..1	..	..	Hughes	..	McClair for Hughes
25 Sep	Swindon T	H	W	4-2	..	..	..	..	..	..	..	..	..	..2	Kanchelskis1	McClair for Sharpe, Giggs for Kanchelskis
2 Oct	Sheff Wed	A	W	3-2	..	..	..	..	..	..	..	..	..	..2	Giggs1	Kanchelskis for Giggs
16 Oct	Tottenham	H	W	2-1	..	..	..	..	..1	..	..	Robson	..1	..	..	McClair for Robson, Butt for Giggs
23 Oct	Everton	A	W	1-0	..	Martin	..	..	..1	..	..	Ince	McClair	..	Keane	
30 Oct	Q P R	H	W	2-1	..	Parker	..	..	..	Phelan	..1	..	Keane	..1	Giggs	
7 Nov	Man City	A	W	3-2	..	..	..	..	..	Pallister	..2	..	..	..1	Kanchelskis	Giggs for Kanchelskis
20 Nov	Wimbledon	H	W	3-1	..	..	..	..	..1	..	..	..	Robson	..1	..1	Phelan for Robson
24 Nov	Ipswich	H	D	0-0	..	..	..	..	..	..	..	..	..	..	..	Giggs for Kanchelskis, Ferguson for Robson
27 Nov	Coventry	A	W	1-0	..	..	..	..	..	..	..1	..	Ferguson	..	Giggs	
4 Dec	Norwich	H	D	2-2	..	..	..	..	Kanchelskis	..	..	..	McClair1	..	..1	Sharpe for Kanchelskis
7 Dec	Sheff Utd	A	W	3-0	..	..	..	..	Sharpe1	..	..1	..	..	..1	..	Keane for McClair
11 Dec	Newcastle	A	D	1-1	..	..	..	..	..	..	..	..	..1	..	..	Kanchelskis for Hughes, Keane for McClair

Mark Hughes celebrates his goal away to Liverpool as United storm to the first Premiership title.

Date	Opponent			Score														Substitutions
19 Dec	Aston Villa	H	W	3-1	..	..	..	..	..	..	..2	..1	Keane			Kanchelskis		Giggs for Sharpe
26 Dec	Blackburn	H	D	1-1	..	..	..	..	..	..	..1	..			Giggs			McClair for Parker, Ferguson for Hughes
29 Dec	Oldham	A	W	5-2	..	..	..1	..	..1	..	Kanchelskis1	..1					McClair for Cantona, Robson for Ince
1 Jan	Leeds Utd	H	D	0-0	..	..	Robson	..	..	Keane	McClair	..	..					
4 Jan	Liverpool	A	D	3-3	..	..1	..1	Keane	..	Ince			..1					
15 Jan	Tottenham	A	W	1-0	..	..	Kanchelskis	..	..		Keane	Hughes1	..					McClair for Hughes
22 Jan	Everton	H	W	1-0	..	..	..	..	..				..1					
5 Feb	Q P R	A	W	3-2	..	..1	..	..1	..		..1							
26 Feb	West Ham	A	D	2-2	..	..	..	..	..1	McClair	..1	Keane					Dublin for Kanchelskis, Thornley for Irwin
5 Mar	Chelsea	H	L	0-1	..	..	Keane	..	..			Giggs					Robson for McClair, Dublin for Parker
16 Mar	Sheff Wed	H	W	5-0	..	..	Cantona2	..1	Keane	..1							McClair for Giggs, Robson for Kanchelskis
19 Mar	Swindon T	A	D	2-2	..	Keane1	..	..1	McClair	..							
22 Mar	Arsenal	A	D	2-2	..	Sharpe2	..	Keane	..								McClair for Sharpe
30 Mar	Liverpool	H	W	1-0	..	..	..1	Kanchelskis									Giggs for Sharpe, Robson for Cantona
2 Apr	Blackburn	A	L	0-2	..	Kanchelskis	..	Giggs									McClair for Parker
4 Apr	Oldham Ath	H	W	3-2	..	Irwin	Sharpe	..	Kanchelskis	Keane	..	McClair	..1				Dublin1 for McClair
16 Apr	Wimbledon	A	L	0-1	..	Parker	Irwin	..	Sharpe	Robson	..	Keane			Kanchelskis		Sharpe for Robson, Dublin for Parker
23 Apr	Man City	H	W	2-0	..	..	..	Sharpe	Cantona2								Giggs for Sharpe
27 Apr	Leeds Utd	A	W	2-0	..	..	..	Kanchelskis1	..				Giggs1				
1 May	Ipswich	A	W	2-1	..	..	..	..1	..		..1						Sharpe for Giggs, Walsh for Schmeichel
4 May	Southampton	H	W	2-0	Walsh	..	..	Keane	Sharpe	..		Kanchelskis1	..1				
8 May	Coventry	H	D	0-0	..	G Neville	Bruce	..	..	Robson	McKee	Dublin	McClair				Parker for Bruce, Keane for McKee
	FA Cup																	
9 Jan	Sheff Utd (3)	A	W	1-0	Schmeichel	Parker	Irwin	Bruce	Kanchelskis	Pallister	Cantona	Ince	Keane	Hughes1	Giggs		McClair for Hughes
30 Jan	Norwich (4)	A	W	2-0	..	..	..	..	..1		..		..1				
20 Feb	Wimbledon (5)	A	W	3-0	..	..1	..	..	..1	..	..						McClair for Cantona, Dublin for Hughes
12 Mar	Charlton (6)	H	W	3-1	..				..2				..1	..			Sealey for Parker*
10 Apr	Oldham (SF)	N-	D	†1-1	..				Sharpe		Dublin	..	McClair	..1	..		Robson for Dublin, Butt for Parker
13 Apr	Oldham (SFR)	N-	W	4-1	..	..1	..		Kanchelskis1	..	Robson1	..	Keane		..1		Sharpe for Hughes, McClair for Keane
14 May	Chelsea (F)	N+	W	4-0	..	..			..		Cantona2	..	..	..1	..		Sharpe for Irwin, McClair1 for Kanchelskis

* Goalkeeper Schmeichel was sent off with Sealey taking over in goal after Parker was withdrawn.
N+ = Wembley
N- = Maine Road
†Extra time

Coca-Cola (League) Cup

Date	Match	V	R	Score	1	2	3	4	5	6	7	8	9	10	11	Substitutions
22 Sep	Stoke (2)	A	L	1-2	Schmeichel	Martin	Irwin	Phelan	Kanchelskis	Pallister	Robson	Ferguson	McClair	Hughes	Dublin1	Bruce for Phelan, Sharpe for Robson
6 Oct	Stoke (2)	H	W	2-0	..			Bruce	Sharpe1	..	..	Kanchelskis	..	..	Keane	Giggs for Martin
27 Oct	Leicester (3)	..	..	5-1		Phelan	Martin	..2	..	..	..1	..1	..1			Irwin for Pallister, Giggs for Sharpe
30 Nov	Everton (4)	A	W	2-0	..	Parker	Irwin	..	Kanchelskis	..	Cantona	Ince	Robson	..1	Giggs1	Ferguson for Robson
12 Jan	Portsmouth (5)	H	D	2-2							..1	Robson	McClair	..	..	Keane for Hughes, Dublin for McClair
26 Jan	Portsmouth (R)	A	W	1-0								Ince	Keane	McClair1	..1	
13 Feb	Sheff Wed (SF1)	H	W	1-0										Hughes	..1	
2 Mar	Sheff Wed (SF2)	A	W	4-1					..1		Keane	..	McClair1	..2		
27 Mar	Aston V (F)	N	L	1-3	Sealey						Cantona	..	Keane	..1		Sharpe for Giggs, McClair for Bruce

European Cup

Date	Match	V	R	Score	1	2	3	4	5	6	7	8	9	10	11	Substitutions
15 Sep	Honved (1)	A	W	3-2	Schmeichel	Parker	Irwin	Bruce	Sharpe	Pallister	Robson	Ince	Cantona1	Keane2	Giggs	Phelan for Giggs
29 Sep	Honved (1)	H	W	2-1	..			..2	..	..	..	..	..	Hughes		Martin for Irwin, Phelan for Ince
20 Oct	Galatasaray (2)	H	D	*3-3	..	Martin	Sharpe	..:	Keane	..	..1	..	..1	..		Phelan for Robson
3 Nov	Galatasaray (2)	A	D	†0-0	..	Parker	Irwin	..	Sharpe	Phelan	..	..	Keane	..		Dublin for Keane, G Neville for Phelan

*Includes own goal
†Galatasaray won under away goals rule

FA Charity Shield

Date	Match	V	R	Score	1	2	3	4	5	6	7	8	9	10	11	Substitutions
7 Aug	Arsenal (at Wembley)	N	D	1-1P	Schmeichel	Parker	Irwin	Bruce	Kanchelskis	Pallister	Cantona	Ince	Keane	Hughes1	Giggs	Robson for Giggs

P – United won 5-4 on penalties

Appearances (goals)

Bruce 61 (7) – Butt 2 – Cantona 48 (25) – Dublin 11 (2) – Ferguson 5 – Giggs 57 (17) – Hughes 55 (21) – Ince 55 (9) – Irwin 61 (4) – Kanchelskis 46 (10) – Keane 53 (8) – Martin 6 – McClair 25 (6) – McKee 1 – G. Neville 1 – Pallister 60 (1) – Parker 57 – Phelan 7 – Robson 25 (3) – Schmeichel 59 – Sealey 1 – Sharpe 41 (11) – Thornley 1 – Walsh 3 – Own goals 1 – **Total 24 players (125)**

FA Premier League

	P	W	O	L	F:A	Pts	
Manchester U	42	27	11	4	80:38	92	1st

SEASON 1994-1995 FA PREMIER LEAGUE

Date	Opponent	V	R	Score	1	2	3	4	5	6	7	8	9	10	11	Substitutions
20 Aug	Q P R	H	W	2-0	Schmeichel	May	Irwin	Bruce	Sharpe	Pallister	Kanchelskis	Ince	McClair	Hughes	Giggs	Parker for May, Keane for Sharpe
22 Aug	Nottingham F	A	D	1-1	..	..	..	..	..	..	..	1	..	..	..	Keane for Giggs
27 Aug	Tottenham H	A	W	1-0	..	..	..	..	1	..	..	..	..	..	..	
31 Aug	Wimbledon	H	W	3-0	..	..	..	..	..	..	Cantona1	Kanchelskis	..1	..	..1	
11 Sep	Leeds Utd	A	L	1-2	..	..	..	..	Kanchelskis	..	..	Ince	..	..	..	Sharpe for Giggs, Butt for McClair
17 Sep	Liverpool	H	W	2-0	..	..	..	..	Sharpe	..	..	..	Kanchelskis1	..	..	McClair for Hughes
24 Sep	Ipswich Town	A	L	2-3	Walsh	Keane	..	..	..	..	..1	..	McClair	Kanchelskis	..	Butt for McClair, Scholes1 for Sharpe
1 Oct	Everton	H	W	2-0	Schmeichel	May	..	..	..1	..	..	Keane	Hughes	..	Kanchelskis1	McClair for Hughes
8 Oct	Sheff Wed	A	L	0-1	..	Parker	..	..	..	..	Gillespie	..	McClair	..	Keane	May for Parker, Scholes for Gillespie
15 Oct	West Ham	H	W	1-0	..	May	..	..	..	..	Cantona1	..	Kanchelskis	..	Giggs	Butt for May
24 Oct	Blackburn R	H	W	4-2	..	Keane	..	..	..	..	..1	..	Butt	..1	Kanchelskis2	McClair for Butt
29 Oct	Newcastle	H	W	2-0	..	..	..	..	Kanchelskis	..1	..	..	McClair	..	..	Gillespie1 for Giggs
6 Nov	Aston Villa	A	W	2-1	Walsh	..	..	..	Butt	..	..	..1	Scholes	Kanchelskis1	Giggs	McClair for Butt, Gillespie for Scholes
10 Nov	Man City	H	W	5-0	Schmeichel	..	..	..	Kanchelskis3	..	..1	..	McClair	Hughes1	..	Scholes for Giggs
19 Nov	Crystal Pal	H	W	3-0	..	..	G. Neville	..1	May	..1	..	..1	..	..	Davies	Pilkington for Schmeichel, Gillespie for Kanchelskis, Scholes for Davies
26 Nov	Arsenal	A	D	0-0	Walsh	..	..	..	..	..	..	..	..	..	Gillespie	Davies for Gillespie, Butt for Kanchelskis
3 Dec	Norwich City	H	W	1-0	..	..	..	..	..	..	..1	..	..	..	Davies	Butt for Kanchelskis, Gillespie for Davies
10 Dec	Q P R	A	W	3-2	..	..	..	Bruce	Keane1	..	Kanchelskis	..	..	Scholes2	..	Butt for Davies, Gillespie for Neville
17 Dec	Nottingham F	H	L	1-2	..	Keane	..	..	Kanchelskis	..	Cantona1	..	..	Hughes	Giggs	Butt for Giggs, G. Neville for Kanchelskis
26 Dec	Chelsea	A	W	3-2	..	..	..	..	Butt	..	..1	..	..	..1	..1	G. Neville for Ince, Kanchelskis for Butt
28 Dec	Leicester C	H	D	1-1	..	G. Neville	..	..	Kanchelskis1	..	..	Keane	..	..	..	Scholes for Hughes
31 Dec	Southampton	A	D	2-2	..	May	G. Neville	..	Butt1	..1	..	..	..	..	..	Gillespie for McClair
3 Jan	Coventry	H	W	2-0	..	G. Neville	Irwin	..	..	..	..1	..	Scholes1	..	Gillespie	McClair for Keane
15 Jan	Newcastle	A	D	1-1	Schmeichel	Butt	..	..	Sharpe	..	..	McClair	Hughes1	Giggs		Scholes for Hughes, May for Butt
22 Jan	Blackburn R	H	W	1-0	..	Keane	..	..	..	..	..1	Ince	..	Cole	..	Kanchelskis for Sharpe
25 Jan	Crystal Pal	A	D	1-1	..	..	..	May1	..	..	..	..	..	..	..	Kanchelskis for Sharpe
4 Feb	Aston Villa	H	W	1-0	..	G. Neville	..	Bruce	..	..	Scholes	..	..	..1	..	May for Neville, Kanchelskis for Giggs
11 Feb	Man City	A	W	3-0	..	P. Neville	..	..	..	..	Kanchelskis1	..1	..	..1	..	May for Kanchelskis, Scholes for Neville
22 Feb	Norwich City	A	W	2-0	..	Keane	Sharpe	..	Kanchelskis1	..	McClair	..1	Cole	Hughes	..	
25 Feb	Everton	A	L	0-1	..	..	Irwin	..	Sharpe	..	..	..	..	..	..	Kanchelskis for McClair
4 Mar	Ipswich	H	W	9-0	..	..1	..	..	Kanchelskis	..	..	..1	..5	..2	..	Sharpe for Keane, Butt for Bruce
7 Mar	Wimbledon	A	W	1-0	..	G. Neville	..	..1	Sharpe	..	..	..	..	..	..	
15 Mar	Tottenham H	H	D	0-0	..	Irwin	Sharpe	..	Kanchelskis	..	..	..	..	..	..	Butt for McClair
19 Mar	Liverpool	A	L	0-2	..	Keane	Irwin	..	Sharpe	..	Kanchelskis	..	McClair	..	..	Cole for Sharpe, Butt for Keane
22 Mar	Arsenal	H	D	3-0	..	..	..	..	..1	..	..	..1	Cole	..1	..	
2 Apr	Leeds Utd	H	D	0-0	..	G. Neville	..	Keane	Beckham	..	McClair	..	..	..	..	Beckham for Sharpe, Scholes for Hughes
15 Apr	Leicester C	A	W	4-0	..	..	..	Bruce	Sharpe1	..	..	..1	..2	..	Butt	Davies for Beckham, Scholes for Davies
17 Apr	Chelsea	H	D	0-0	..	..	..	..	Beckham	..	..	..	..	..	..	Beckham for Scholes
1 May	Coventry	A	W	3-2	..	..	..	May	Sharpe	..	..	Scholes1	..2	..	..	Beckham for Scholes
7 May	Sheff Wed	H	W	1-0	..	..	..	..	..1	..	..	Ince	..	..	Scholes	P. Neville for May, Butt for Scholes
10 May	Southampton	H	W	2-1	..	..	..	Bruce	..	..	..	..	..1	..	Butt	Scholes for Hughes
14 May	West Ham	A	D	1-1	..	..	..	..	..	..	Keane	..	..	McClair1	..	Hughes for Butt, Scholes for Keane

FA Cup

Date	Opponent	V	R	Score	1	2	3	4	5	6	7	8	9	10	11	12	Substitutions
9 Jan	Sheff Utd (3)	A	W	2-0	Schmeichel	O'Kane	Irwin	Bruce	Butt	Pallister	Cantona1	Keane	McClair	Hughes1	Giggs		Sharpe for O'Kane, Scholes for McClair
28 Jan	Wrexham (4)	H	W	*5-2	..	P. Neville	..2	May	Sharpe	..	..	Keane	Ince	..1	Scholes	..1	Kanchelskis for Keane, Beckham for McClair
19 Feb	Leeds Utd (5)	H	W	3-1	..	Keane	..	Bruce1	..	..	Kanchelskis	..	..1	Hughes1	..		
12 Mar	Q P R (6)	H	W	2-0	..	G. Neville	..1	..	..1	..	..	..	..	..			Keane for Giggs
9 Apr	Crystal Pal (SF)	N-	W	2-2E	..	..	..	..1	Keane	..	•..1	Beckham	..	..	..		Butt for Beckham
12 Apr	Crystal Pal (SFR)	N-	W	2-0	..	..	..	Bruce1	..	..1	Keane	..	..	..	..		McClair for Giggs
20 May	Everton (F)	N+	L	0-1	..	..	..	..	..	..	..	..	..	Butt	..		Giggs for Bruce, Scholes for Sharpe, Giggs for

N-= Villa Park
N+ = Wembley
*= Includes own goal
E = After extra time

Coca-Cola (League) Cup

Date	Opponent	V	R	Score	1	2	3	4	5	6	7	8	9	10	11	Substitutions
Sep 21	Port Vale (2)	A	W	2-1	Walsh	G. Neville	Irwin	Butt	May	Keane	Gillespie	Beckham	McClair	Scholes2	Davies	Sharpe for Butt, O'Kane for Neville
Oct 5	Port Vale (2)	H	W	2-0	..	Casper	O'Kane	..	..1	Pallister	..	..	..1	..		Tomlinson for Gillespie, Neville for Davies
Oct 26	Newcastle (3)	A	L	0-2	..	G. Neville	Irwin	Bruce	Butt	..	..	..	..	..		Sharpe for Irwin, Tomlinson for Sharpe

European Cup (UEFA Champions' League)

Date	Opponent	V	R	Score	1	2	3	4	5	6	7	8	9	10	11	Substitutions
Sep 14	Gothenburg	H	W	4-2	Schmeichel	May	Irwin	Bruce	Sharpe1	Pallister	Kanchelskis1	Ince	Butt	Hughes	Giggs2	Parker for Biggs
Sep 28	Galatasaray	A	D	0-0	..	..	..	Sharpe	..	Butt	..	..	Keane	..	..	
19 Oct	Barcelona	H	D	2-2	..	Parker	Irwin	May	..	..	..	..	..	..1	Sharpe1	Bruce for May, Scholes for Sharpe
2 Nov	Barcelona	A	L	0-4	Walsh	..	..	Bruce	..	..	..	..	..	..	Giggs	Scholes for Giggs
23 Nov	Gothenburg	A	L	1-3	..	May	..	..	Kanchelskis	..	Cantona	..	McClair	..1	Davies	G. Neville for May, Butt for Davies
7 Dec	Galatasaray	H	W	*4-0	..	G. Neville	..	..	Keane1	..	..	Butt	..	Beckham1	..1	

*Includes own goal

FA Charity Shield

Date	Opponent	V	R	Score	1	2	3	4	5	6	7	8	9	10	11	Substitutions
14 Aug	Blackburn R (at Wembley)	N	W	2-0	Schmeichel1	May	Bruce	Pallister	Ince1	McClair	Kanchelskis	Cantona1 (p)	Hughes	Sharpe	Giggs	

Appearances (goals)

Beckham 10 (1) – Bruce 47 (4) – Butt 35 (1) – Cantona 24 (14) – Casper 1 – Cole 18 (12) – Davies 10 (1) – Giggs 39 (4) – Gillespie 10 (1) – Hughes 45 (12) – Ince 47 (6) – Irwin 54 (6) – Kanchelskis 39 (15) – Keane 35 (3) – May 27 (3) – McClair 51 (6) – B. Neville 27 – P. Neville 3 – O'Kane 3 – Pallister 57 (4) – Parker 5 – Pilkington 1 – Scholes 27 (7) – Schmeichel 42 – Sharpe 40 (6) – Tomlinson 2 – Walsh 16 – Own Goals 2 – **Total 27 players (110)**

FA Premier League

	P	W	O	L	F:A	Pts	
Blackburn	42	27	8	7	60:39	69	1st
Manchester U	42	26	10	6	77:26	68	2nd

SEASON 1995-1996 FA PREMIER LEAGUE

Date	Opponent			Score												Notes
19 Aug	Aston Villa	A	L	1-3	Schmeichel	Parker	Irwin		G. Neville	Pallister	Sharpe	Butt		Keane	McClair	Scholes	P. Neville	Beckham1 for P. Neville, Kane for Pallister
23 Aug	West Ham	H	W	2-1	..	G. Neville	..		Bruce	..	..	..		..1		..1	Beckham	Cole for Scholes, Thornley for McClair
26 Aug	Wimbledon	H	W	3-1	..	..	..		..	..	..	..		..2	Cole1	..	..	Giggs for Cole, Davies for Scholes
28 Aug	Blackburn	A	W	2-1	..	..	..		..	..	..1	..		..		..	..1	Giggs for Beckham, Davies for Scholes
9 Sep	Everton	A	W	3-2	..	..	..		..	..	..2	..		..		..	..	Giggs1 for Beckham, Davies for Cole
16 Sep	Bolton	H	W	3-0	..	Parker	P. Neville		..	..	..	..		Cooke	Beckham	..2	Giggs 1	Davies for Cooke
23 Sep	Sheff Wed	A	D	D-0	..		Irwin		..	..	Davies	..		Beckham	McClair	..	..	Cooke for Davies
1 Oct	Liverpool	H	D	2-2	..	G. Neville	P. Neville		..	..	Sharpe	..1		Keane	Cole	Cantona1	..	Scholes for P. Neville, Beckham for Butt
14 Oct	Man City	H	W	1-0	..	..	..		..	..	Beckham	..		..	..	Scholes1	..	Sharpe for Scholes, McClair for Keane
21 Oct	Chelsea	A	W	4-1	..	..	Irwin		..	..	Scholes2	..		..	..	Cantona	..1	McClair1 for Scholes
28 Oct	Middlesbrough	H	W	2-0	..	..	..		..	..1	..	..		..	..	..1	..	McClair for Scholes
4 Nov	Arsenal	A	L	0-1	..	..	..		..	..	..	..		..	..	..	..	Sharpe for Butt, McClair for Irwin, Beckham for Scholes
18 Nov	Southampton	H	W	4-1	..	..	..		..	..	..1	..		Beckham	..1	..	..2	Sharpe for Giggs, McClair for Scholes, P. Neville for Irwin
22 Nov	Coventry	A	W	4-0	..	..	..1		..	..	McClair2	..		..1	..	..		Sharpe for Butt, May for Bruce, P. Neville for G. Neville
27 Nov	Notts For	A	D	1-1	..	..	..		..	..	..	..		..	..	..	..1	Sharpe for Beckham, Scholes for McClair
2 Dec	Chelsea	H	D	1-1	Pilkington	..			..	May	Sharpe	McClair		..1	..	..	Scholes	Cooke for Cole
9 Dec	Sheff Wed	H	D	2-2	..		P. Neville		..	..	..	..		..	..	..2	..	Davies for Scholes, Cooke for Sharpe
17 Dec	Liverpool	A	L	0-2	Schmeichel		Irwin		..	..	..	..		..	..	..	..	Scholes for Cole
24 Dec	Leeds	A	L	1-3	..	Parker	..		..	G. Neville	McClair	Butt		Keane	..	..1	Beckham	May for Parker, Scholes for Beckham, P. Neville for Bruce
27 Dec	Newcastle	H	W	2-0	..	P. Neville	..		May	..	Beckham	..		..1	..1	..	Giggs	McClair for May
30 Dec	Q P R	H	W	2-1	..	..	..		Prunier	..	..	..		..	..1	..	..1	Parker for P. Neville, Sharpe for Beckham, MaClair for Cole
1 Jan	Tottenham	A	L	1-4	..	Parker	P. Neville		..	..	..	..		..	..1	..	..	Pilkington for Schmeichel, Sharpe for P. Neville, McClair for Keane
13 Jan	Aston Villa	H	D	0-0	..	P. Neville	Irwin		Bruce	G. Neville	Sharpe	..		..	..	..	..	Scholes for Sharpe
22 Jan	West Ham	A	W	1-0	..	..	..		..	..	..	..		..	..	..1		Beckham for Cole

The infamous 'Kung Fu' incident at Selhurst Park in January 1994 was the low point in King Eric's amazing United career.

1990-2000

Date	Opponent		Result												Notes
3 Feb	Wimbledon	A W	4-2*	..	..	..				..		..1	..2	..	Beckham for Bruce
10 Feb	Blackburn	H W	1-0	..	..	..	May	Pallister	..1	Beckham	..	..	..	..	
21 Feb	Everton	H W	2-0	..	..	..	Bruce	..		Butt	..1	..	..	..1	Beckham for Sharpe
25 Feb	Bolton	A W	6-0	..	..	..	..1		Beckham1	..1		..1	..	..	Scholes2 for Cantona, McClair for Giggs
4 Mar	Newcastle	A W	1-0	..	..	..		G. Neville	Sharpe		..		..1	..	
16 Mar	Q P R	A D	1-1	..	G. Neville	..		May	Beckham	McClair	..	..	..1		Sharpe for Beckham, Butt for May, Scholes for McClair
20 Mar	Arsenal	H W	1-0	..	..	P. Neville	..	..	Sharpe	Butt	..	..	..	..	Scholes for Cole
24 Mar	Tottenham	H W	1-0	..	..	..	..	..			..	..1	..	..	McClair for Cole, Beckham for P. Neville
8 Apr	Man City	A W	3-2	..	P. Neville	Irwin	..	G. Neville	Beckham	..	..	..1	..1	..1	Sharpe for Cole, May for Bruce
8 Apr	Coventry	H W	1-0	..	Irwin	Sharpe	May	..		McClair	..	..	..1	..	Scholes for Bull, May for Sharpe
13 Apr	Southampton	A L	1-3	..	..	..	Bruce	..	..	Keane	..	..	..	..1	Scholes for Cole
17 Apr	Leeds	H W	1-0	..	P. Neville	..	..	Pallister	..	McClair	..1	..	..	..	May for Bruce, Scholes for McClair, Sharpe for Cole
28 Apr	Notts For	H W	5-0	..	..	..	May	..	..2	Sharpe	..	Scholes1	..1	..1	G. Neville for P. Neville
5 May	Middlesbrough	A W	3-0	..	..	..	..1	..		Butt	..	..	..	..1	Cole1 for Scholes

*Includes own goal

FA Cup

Date	Opponent		Result												Notes
6 Jan	Sunderland (3)	H D	2-2	Pilkington	G. Neville	Irwin	Bruce	Pallister	Beckham	Butt1	Keane	Cole	Cantona1	Giggs	Sharpe for Beckham, P. Neville for G. Neville
16 Jan	Sunderland (3R)	A W	2-1	Schmeichel	Parker	..	..	G. Neville	P. Neville	..	..	..1	..	..	Sharpe for Parker, Scholes1 for Butt
27 Jan	Reading (4)	A W	3-0	..	Irwin	P. Neville	..	Sharpe	..	..	..	..1	..1	..1	Parker1 for P. Neville
18 Feb	Man City (5)	H W	2-1	..	..	..	..	Pallister	..1	..	..	..	..1	..	
11 Mar	Southampton (6)	H W	2-0	..	..	..	..	G. Neville	..1	..	..	..	..1	..	
31 Mar	Chelsea (SF)	N- W	2-1	..	P. Neville	Sharpe	May	..	Beckham2	..	..	..1	..	..	
11 May	Liverpool (F)	N+ W	1-0	..	Irwin	P. Neville	..	Pallister	..	..	..	..	..1	..	Scholes for Cole, G. Neville for Beckham

N- Villa Park N+ Wembley

Coca-Cola (League) Cup

Date	Opponent		Result												Notes
20 Sep	York City (2)	H L	0-3	Pilkington	Parker	Irwin	McGibbon	Pallister	Sharpe	Beckham	P. Neville	McClair	Davies	Giggs	Cooke for P. Neville, Bruce for Davies
3 Oct	York City (2)	A W	1-3	Schmeichel	G. Neville	Sharpe	Bruce	..	Beckham	Cooke1	Scholes2	Cole	Cantona	..	P. Neville for Sharpe, Keane for Cooke

UEFA Cup

12 Sep	Rotor Vol. (1)	A D	0-0	Schmeichel	G. Neville	Irwin	Bruce	Pallister	Sharpe	Butt	Beckham	Keane	Scholes	Giggs	Davies for Keane, Parker for Scholes
26 Sep	Rotor Vol. (2)	H D#	2-2	..1	O'Kane	P. Neville	..	..	..	..	..	..	Cole	..	Scholes1 for O'Kane, Cooke for Beckham

(# Lost on away goals)

Appearances

Beckham 33 (6): Bruce 36 (1): Butt 36 (3): Cantona 38 (19): Cooke 2 (1): Cole 41 (13): Davies 2 (0): Giggs 41 (12): Irwin 39(1): Keane 36 (6): May 13 (1): McClair 13 (3): McGibbon 1 (0) G. Neville 37 (0): P. Neville 29 (0): O'Kane 1 (0): Pallister 29 (1): Parker 7 (1): Pilkington 4 (0): Prunier 2 (0): Schmeichel 45 (1): Scholes 18 (14): Sharpe 29 (6) Own goals 1 **Total 23 players (92)**

FA Premier League

	P	W	O	L	F:A	Pts
Manchester U	38	25	7	6	73:35	82	1st

SEASON 1996-1997 FA PREMIER LEAGUE

Date	Opponent		Result												Notes
17 Aug	Wimbledon	A W	3-0	Schmeichel	Irwin1	P. Neville	May	Pallister	Beckham1	Butt	Keane	Cruyff	Cantona1	Scholes	Johnsen for Butt, McClair for Cantona
21 Aug	Everton	H D	2-2	..	..	..	..	..	..	..	Poborsky	..1	..	Giggs	McClair for Poborsky
25 Aug	Blackburn	H D	2-2	..	..	..	..	..	..	McClair	Johnsen	..1	..	..	G. Neville for P. Neville, Solskjaer1 for May
4 Sep	Derby C	A D	1-1	..	G. Neville	Irwin	..	..	..1	Butt	..	..	..	..	Solskjaer for Cruyff, Scholes for May
7 Sep	Leeds	A W	4-0	..	..	..	..	Johnsen	..	..1	Poborsky1	..	..1	..	Cole for Cruyff, McClair for Beckham Solskjaer for Poborsky
14 Sep	Notts F	H W	4-1	..	..	..	Johnsen	Pallister	..	..	Solskjaer1	..2	..1	..	McClair for Butt, Cole for Solskjaer
21 Sep	Aston Villa	A D	0-0	van der Gouw	..	..	..	..	..	Keane	Cruyff	..	..	..	Cole for Solskjaer, Poborsky for Cruyff
29 Sep	Tottenham	H W	2-0	Schmeichel	..	..	May	..	..	Butt	..	..2	..	..	Cruyff for Giggs, Scholes for Poborsky
12 Oct	Liverpool	H W	1-0	..	..	..	..	Johnsen	..1	..	Poborsky	..	..	Cruyff	Cole for Poborsky, Giggs for Solskjaer
20 Oct	Newcastle	A L	0-5	..	..	..	..	Pallister	..	..	Johnsen	..	..	Poborsky	Cruyff for Solskjaer, McClair for Johnsen, Scholes for Poborsky
26 Oct	Southampton	A L	3-6	..	..	P. Neville	..1	..	..1	Keane	Butt	Scholes1	..	Cruyff	McClair for Butt, Solskjaer for Cruytt
2 Nov	Chelsea	H L	1-2	..	Irwin	..	..1	Johnsen	..	..	..	Solskjaer	..	Solskjaer	Poborsky for Scholes
16 Nov	Arsenal	H W	1-0	..	G. Neville	..	..	..	..	Poborsky	..	..	..	Giggs	
23 Nov	Middlesbrough	A D	2-2	..	Clegg	O'Kane	..1	..	..	Keane1	..	..2	..	Thornley	Cruyff for Thornley, McClair for O'Kane
30 Nov	Leicester	H W	3-1	..	G. Neville	Irwin	..	Pallister	..	..	..2	Cruyff	..	Giggs	Solskjaer1 for Cruyff
6 Dec	West Ham	A D	2-2	..	..	..	..	..	..1	Poborsky	McClair	Solskjaer1	..	..	P. Neville for Poborsky
16 Dec	Sheff Wed	A D	1-1	..	G. Neville	..	..	Johnsen	Butt	Scholes1	..	..	..	Beckham for G. Neville, P. Neville for Johnsen
21 Dec	Sunderland	H W	5-0	..	..	..	..	P. Neville	..	..1	..	..2	..2	McClair for Pallister, Poborsky for Solskjaer, Thornley for Giggs
26 Dec	Notts F	A W	4-0	..	..	..	Johnsen	Beckham1	..1	..	..	..1	..	Cole1 for Solskjaer, McClair for Butt, Poborsky for Giggs
28 Dec	Leeds	H W	1-0	..	..	..	..	..	..	Keane	..	..	..1	..	Butt for Scholes, Cole for Solskjaer
1 Jan	Aston Villa	H D	0-0	..	..	..	..	..	..	..	Butt	..	..	..	Cole for Solskjaer, Scholes for Butt
12 Jan	Tottenham	A W	2-1	..	..	Johnsen	..	Pallister	..1	..	Scholes	..1	..	..	Poborsky for Scholes, Cole for Solskjaer, Casper for Johnsen
18 Jan	Coventry	A W	2-0	..	..	Irwin	Pallister	Johnsen	Poborsky	..	..	..1	..	..1	Casper for Johnsen
29 Jan	Wimbledon	H W	2-1	..	..	..	..	Clegg	Beckham	..	..	..	..	..1	Cole1 for Scholes
1 Feb	Southampton	H W	2-1	..	..	..	..1	..	..	Poborsky	..	..1	..	Cole for Poborsky, Johnsen for Clegg
19 Feb	Arsenal	H W	2-1	..	..	..	Johnsen	Beckham	..	..	..1	Cole1	..	Butt for Poborsky, McClair for Butt
22 Feb	Chelsea	A D	1-1	..	..	..	..	..1	..	McClair	..	..	Cruyff	Cruyff for Giggs, May for Johnsen
1 Mar	Coventry	H W	3-1	..	..	..	May	Pallister	..	Poborsky1	Cole1	..	Cantona	Cruyff	P. Neville for Irwin, McClair for Beckham Johnsen for Giggs
8 Mar	Sunderland	A L	1-2	..	..	..	..	Johnsen	..	..	..	McClair	..	P. Neville	Solskjaer for Poborsky, Cole for Cruyff
15 Mar	Sheff Wed	H W	2-0	..	..	..	..	Pallister	..	Butt	..1	Solskjaer	..	Giggs	Poborsky1 for Cole, Scholes for Solskjaer
22 Mar	Everton	A W	2-0	..	Irwin	P. Neville	..	..	..	..	Keane	..1	..1	..	Johnsen for Pallister, McClair for Beckham
5 Apr	Derby C	H L	2-3	..	G. Neville	..	Pallister	Johnsen	..	..	..	Cole	..1	..	Solskjaer1 for Butt, Irwin for P. Neville, Scholes for Pallister
12 Apr	Blackburn R.	A W	3-2	van der Gouw ..	..	..	..	..	Scholes1	..	..	..1	..1	Solskjaer	Beckham for Scholes
19 Apr	Liverpool	A W	3-1	Schmeichel	..	..	..2	..	Beckham	..	..	..1	..	Scholes	McClair for Scholes
3 May	Leicester	A D	2-2	..	..	..	May	Scholes	..	..	..	..	Solskjaer2	Beckham for Butt, Johnsen for Solskjaer
5 May	Middlesbrough	H D	3-3	..	..1	Irwin	..	Beckham	..1	..	Johnsen	..	..1	Scholes for Johnsen
8 May	Newcastle	H D	0-0	..	..	P. Neville	May	Johnsen	..	..	Poborsky	..	Scholes	McClair for Keane, Solskjaer for Cole
11 May	West Ham	H W	2-0	..	Irwin	..	..	..	..	Butt	Solskjaer	..	..1	Clegg for Irwin, Cruyff1 for Poborsky, McClair for Scholes

FA Charity Shield

Date	Opponent		Result												Notes
11 Aug	Newcastle	N W	4-0	Schmeichel	Irwin	P. Neville	May	Pallister	Beckham1	Butt1	Keane1	Scholes	Cantona1	Giggs	G. Neville for Irwin, Poborsky for Butt, Cruyff for Scholes

European Cup (Champions' League)

Date	Opponent		Result												Notes
11 Sep	Juventus	A L	0-1	Schmeichel	G.Neville	Irwin	Johnsen	Pallister	Butt	Beckham	Poborsky	Cantona	Cruyff	Giggs	McClair for Giggs, Solskjaer for Cruyff, Cole for Poborsky
25 Sep	R.Vienna	H W	2-0	..	..	..	..	..	..	Keane	..1	..	Solskjaer1	..	May for Johnsen, Cole for Solskjaer, Butt for Poborsky
16 Oct	Fenerbahce	A W	2-0	..	..	..	May	Pallister	Butt	..1	Cruyff	..1	..	Johnsen	Poborsky for Cruyff
30 Oct	Fenerbahce	H L	0-1	..	..	..	..	Johnsen	..	..	..	..	Poborsky	Keane	Scholes for Poborsky, Solskjaer for Cruyff P. Neville for G. Neville
20 Nov	Juventus	H L	0-1	..	..	P. Neville	..	..	..	..	Keane	..	Solskjaer	Giggs	McClair for P. Neville, Cruyff for Solskjaer
4 Dec	R.Vienna	A W	2-0	..	..	Irwin	..	Pallister	..	..	..	..	..1	..	McClair for Keane, Poborsky for Butt Casper for G. Neville
5 Mar	F.C. Porto	H W	4-0	-	..	..	..1	..	Johnsen	..	Cole1	..1	..	..1	
19 Mar	F.C. Porto	A D	0-0	..	..	..	..	..	Butt	..	Keane	..	..	Johnsen	Scholes for Solskjaer, Poborsky for Beckham, P. Neville for Irwin
9 Apr	B. Dortmund	A L	0-1	van der Gouw	..	..	Johnsen	..	..	..	..	..	..	Giggs	Cole for Solskjaer, Scholes for Giggs
23 Apr	B. Dortmund	H L	0-1	Schmeichel	..	P. Neville	May	..	..	..	Cole	..	..	Johnson	Giggs for Solskjaer, Scholes for May

Coca-Cola (League) Cup

23 Oct	Swindon (3)	H	W	2-1	van der Gouw	G. Neville	May	Casper	P. Neville	McClair	Appleton	Poborsky1	Keane	Thornley	Scholes1

Davies for Appleton

| 27 Nov | Leicester (4) | A | L | 0-2 | .. | Clegg | | O'Kane | .. | | Cruyff | .. | Keane | .. | |

Cooke for Poborsky, Davies for Thornley
Appleton for O'Kane

FA Cup

| 5 Jan | Tottenham (3) | H | W | 2-0 | Schmeichel | G.Neville | Irwin | May | Johnsen | Beckham1 | Keane | Scholes1 | Cantona | Cole | Giggs |

McClair for Irwin, Solskjaer for Cole

| 25 Jan | Wimbledon (4) | H | D | 1-1 | .. | Clegg | .. | G. Neville | Casper | McClair | .. | ..1 | .. | Poborsky | |

Solskjaer for Poborsky, Cole for McClair

| 4 Feb | Wimbledon (4R) | A | L | 0-1 | .. | G. Neville | .. | Johnsen | Pallister | Beckham | .. | Cole | .. | | |

Solskjaer for Poborsky, McClair for Irwin

(Appearances = games started and does not include substitutions)

Appearances (goals)

Appleton 1 (0) – Beckham 48 (11) – Butt 33 (5) – Cantona (49) (14) – Casper 3 (0) – Clegg 5 (0) – Cole 14 (8) – Cruyff 15 (3) – Giggs 34 (5) – Irwin 40 (1) – Johnsen 37 (0) – Keane 32 (2) – May 38 (4) – McClair 7 (0) – G. Neville 44 (1) – P. Neville 16 (0) – O'Kane 2 (0) – Pallister 35 (3) – Poborsky 22 (4) – van der Gouw 5 (0) – Schmeichel 48 (0) – Scholes 20 (7) – Solskjaer 33 (15); Thornley 3 (0) – Own goals 5 – **Total 24 players (91)**

FA Premier League

	P	W	O	L	F:A	Pts	
Manchester U	38	21	12	5	76:44	75	1st

SEASON 1997-1998 FA PREMIER LEAGUE

10 Aug	Tottenham	A	W	2-1*	Schmeichel	P. Neville	Irwin	Johnsen	Pallister	Keane	Scholes	Butt1	Cruyff	Sheringham	Giggs	Beckham for Scholes
13 Aug	Southampton	H	W	1-0	..	..	..	..	..	..	..	..	..	..	..	Beckham1 for Scholes, Berg for Johnsen
23 Aug	Leicester C	A	D	0-0	..	G. Neville	..	Berg	..	..	Beckham	..	..	..	..	Scholes for Cruyff
27 Aug	Everton	A	W	2-0	..	..	..	..	..	..	..1	..	Scholes	..1	..	Cole for Sheringham
30 Aug	Coventry	H	W	3-0	..	..	P. Neville	..	..	..	..	..	Cole 1	..	..	Poborsky1 for Cole, Irwin for P. Neville
13 Sep	West Ham	H	W	2-1	..	..	..	..	..	..	..1	..	..	Scholes1	..	McClair for Cole, Poborsky for Giggs
20 Sep	Bolton	A	D	0-0	..	..	Irwin	..	..	..	..	..	..	..	Porborsky	P. Neville for Porborsky, Solskjaer for Scholes
24 Sep	Chelsea	H	D	2-2	..	..	..	..	..	..	..	..	..	..1	..	Solskjaer1 for Poborsky, Sheringham for Scholes, Giggs for G. Neville
27 Sep	Leeds	A	L	0-1	..	..	..	..	..	..	..	Scholes	Solskjaer	Sheringham	..	P. Neville for G. Neville, Johnsen for Scholes, Thornley for Poborsky
4 Oct	Crystal Pal	H	W	2-0*	..	..	P. Neville	..	Johnsen	Butt	Scholes	..1	Giggs			Irwin for P. Neville
16 Oct	Derby C	A	D	2-2	..	..	Irwin	..	..	..	Solskjaer	..1	..			Johnsen for Butt, Cole1 for Scholes, P. Neville for Irwin
25 Oct	Barnsley	H	W	7-0	..	..	P. Neville	Curtis	..	Scholes1	..	Cole3	Solskjaer	..2		Cruyff for Scholes, Poborsky1 for Sheringham, Wallwork for Pallister
1 Nov	Sheffield Wed	H	W	6-1	..	..	..	Berg	..	..	..	..2	Sheringham2	Solskjaer2		McClair for Butt, Poborsky for Scholes, Curtis for Berg
9 Nov	Arsenal	A	L	2-3	..	..	..	..	..	..	..	..	..2	Giggs		Johnsen for Pallister, Solskjaer for Giggs
30 Nov	Blackburn R	H	W	4-0*2	..	..	..	..	..	Solskjaer2	Beckham	..	..	..		Johnsen for Butt, Poborsky for Pallister, McClair for Sheringham
6 Dec	Liverpool	A	W	3-1	..	..	..	..	Johnsen	..1	..	..2	..	..		
15 Dec	Aston Villa	H	W	1-0	..	..	..	Johnsen	..	Solskjaer	..	..	..	..1		Thornley for Giggs
21 Dec	Newcastle	A	W	1-0	..	..	..	..	..	Scholes	..	..1	..	..		Solskjaer for Scholes, McClair for Sheringham, Poborsky for Giggs
26 Dec	Everton	H	W	2-0	Pilkington	..	..	Berg1	..	Johnsen	..	..1	Scholes	Solskjaer		Poborsky for Beckham, McClair for Pallister, Curtis for P. Neville
26 Dec	Coventry	A	L	2-3	..	Johnsen	..	Johnsen	..	Solskjaer1	..	Scholes	..	Sheringham1	Giggs	Curtis for Johnsen, Butt for Solskjear
10 Jan	Tottenham	H	W	2-0	Schmeichel	Irwin	Johnsen	..	..	..	..	..	..	..2		
19 Jan	Southampton	A	L	0-1	..	..	..	..	..	..	Butt	..	Scholes	..		McClair for Butt, Nevland for G. Neville
31 Jan	Leicester C	H	L	0-1	..	..	..	..	..	..	..	..	..	..		Berg for Johnsen, Sheringham for Berg, P. Neville for Scholes
7 Feb	Bolton	H	D	1-1	..	..	P. Neville	..	..	Scholes	..1	Sheringham	..			Berg for Sheringham
18 Feb	Aston Villa	A	W	2-0	..	..	Berg	..	McClair	..1	Butt	..	..	..1		P. Neville for McClair
21 Feb	Derby C	H	W	2-0	..	..	..1	..	P. Neville	..	..	..	..	..1		Clegg for Irwin, Cruyff for Cole, McClair for Giggs
28 Feb	Chelsea	A	W	1-0	..	..	..	Johnsen	..	..1	..	..	..	Scholes		Berg for Pallister
7 Mar	Sheffield Wed	A	L	0-2	van der Gouw	..	..	Berg	..	May	..	..	..	Solskjaer		Scholes for Johnsen, Curtis for P. Neville, McClair for Cole
11 Mar	West Ham	A	D	1-1	Schmeichel	..	Irwin	Berg	..	McClair	..	..	..	Scholes1		Thornley for McClair, Curtis for Butt, Solskjaer for Cole
14 Mar	Arsenal	H	L	0-1	..	..	..	..	Curtis	Johnsen	..	P. Neville	..	..		Thornley for Curtis, Solskjaer for P. Neville, May for Johnsen
28 Mar	Wimbledon	H	W	2-0	van der Gouw	..	..	..	May	..1	..	Solskjaer	..1			McClair for Cole, Thornley for Solskjaer
6 Apr	Blackburn R	A	W	3-1	Schmeichel	..	..	P. Neville	Pallister	..	..1	Scholes1	..1	..	Giggs	Butt for Solskjaer
10 Apr	Liverpool	H	D	1-1	..	..	..	..	..	..1	..	Butt	..	Scholes		Thornley for Giggs, May for Johnsen, Sheringham for P. Neville
18 Apr	Newcastle	H	D	1-1	..	..	..	..	..	May	..1	..	..	Sheringham	..	van dur Gouw for Schmeichel, Scholes for Butt, Solskjaer for G. Neville
27 Apr	Crystal Palace	A	W	3-0	..	P. Neville	..	May	..	Scholes1	..	..1	..1	..		Clegg for Irwin
4 May	Leeds	H	W	3-0	van der Gouw	G. Neville	..1	..	..	..	..1	..	..	..	..1	McClair for Sheringham, Brown for May
10 May	Barnsley	A	W	2-0	..	Clegg	Curtis	..	Brown	Berg	Mulryne	..	..1	..1		Higginbotham for Clegg

FA Charity Shield

3 Aug	Chelsea	W+	W	2-2*	Schmeichel	Irwin	P. Neville	Johnsen1	Pallister	Keane	Butt	Scholes	Cole	Sheringham	Giggs	Cruyff for Giggs, Beckham for Sheringham

W+ Wembley
*Won on penalties

European Cup (Champions' League)

17 Sep	Kosice	A	W	3-0	Schmeichel	G. Neville	Irwin1	Berg1	Pallister	Keane	Beckham	Butt	Cole1	Scholes	Poborsky	McClair for Beckham
1 Oct	Juventus	H	W	3-2	..	..	..	Johnsen	..	..	..	..	Solskjaer	Sheringham1	Giggs1	Scholes1 for Butt, P. Neville for Solskjaer
22 Oct	Feyenoord	H	W	2-1	..	..	..1	P. Neville	..	Scholes1	..	Cole	..	..		Solskjaer for Cole
5 Nov	Feyenoord	A	W	3-1	..	..	..	Berg	..	..	..	..3	..	..		P. Neville for Irwin, Poborsky for Scholes, Solskjaer for Cole
26 Nov	Kosice	H	W	3-0*	..	..	P. Neville	..	..	..	..	..1	..1			Solskjaer for Butt, Poborsky for Giggs, Berg for P. Neville
10 Nov	Juventus	A	L	0-1	..	..	..	..	..	Johnsen	..	Poborsky	Solskjaer	..		Cole for Solskjaer, McClair for Poborsky
4 Mar	Monaco	A	D	0-0	..	..	..	..	Irwin	..	..	Butt	Cole	..	Scholes	McClair for Irwin
18 Mar	Monaco	H	D	1-1	van der Gouw	..	..	Solskjaer1	..	..	..	..	..	..		Berg for G. Neville, Clegg for Scholes

Coca-Cola (League) Cup

14 Oct	Ipswich (3)	A	L	0-2	van der Gouw	Curtis	P. Neville	May	Johnsen	Mulryne	McClair	Poborsky	Cole	Cruyff	Thornley	Nevland for Mulryne, Scholes for Thornley, Irwin for Johnsen

FA Cup

4 Jan	Chelsea (3)	A	W	5-3	Schmeichel	G.Neville	Irwin	Johnsen	Pallister	Beckham2	Butt	Scholes	Cole2	Sheringham2	Giggs	Solskjaer for Scholes
24 Jun	Walsall (4)	H	W	5-1	..	P. Neville	..	Johnsen1	Berg	Beckham	McClair	..	..2	Solskjaer2	Thornley	Nevland for Thornley, Mulryne for Scholes
15 Feb	Barnsley (5)	H	D	1-1	..	Clegg	..	Berg	Pallister	Johnsen	..	P. Neville	Nevland	Sheringham1	Giggs	Beckham for Johnsen, Cruyff for Nevland, G. Neville for McClair
25 Feb	Barnsley (5R)	A	L	2-3	..	..	G. Neville	May	..	Beckham	..	..	..	Cole1	Thornley	Sheringham for Nevland, Irwin for McClair, Twiss for Clegg

(Appearances = games started and does not include substitutions)

Appearances (goals)

Beckham 45 (11) – Berg 30 (2) – Brown W 1 (0) – Butt 39 (3) – Clegg 3 (0) – Cole 41 (25) – Cruyff 4 (0) – Curtis 4 (0) – Giggs 36 (9) – Irwin 32 (4) – Johnsen 27 (3) – Keane 10 (2) – May 9 (0) – McClair 6 (0) – Mulryne 2 (0) – G. Neville 44 (0) – P. Neville 33 (1) – Nevland 2 (0) – Pallister 42 (0) – Pilkington 2 (0) – Poborsky 8 (0) – Schmeichel 43 (0) – Scholes 36 (10) – Sheringham 37 (14) – Solskjaer 19 (9) – Thornley 3 (0) – van der Gouw 6 (0) – Own goals 5 – **Total 27 players (100)**

FA Premier League

	P	W	D	L	F:A	Pts	
Arsenal	38	23	9	8	66:33	78	1st
Manchester U	38	23	8	7	73:26	77	2nd

1990-2000

SEASON 1998-1999 FA PREMIER LEAGUE

Date	Opponent	V	R	Score	1	2	3	4	5	6	7	8	9	10	11	Substitutions / Scorers
15 Aug	Leicester	H	D	2-2	Schmeichel	G. Neville	Irwin	Johnsen	Stam	Beckham1	Keane	Butt	Cole	Scholes	Giggs	Sheringham1 for G. Neville, Berg for Stam
22 Aug	West Ham	A	D	0-0	..	..	..	..	..	..	..	..	..	Yorke	..	Sheringham for Cole, P. Neville for G. Neville
9 Sep	Charlton Ath	H	W	4-1	..	..	..	..	Berg	..	..	Scholes	Solskjaer2	..2	Blomqvist	Cole for Solskjaer, Sheringham for Yorke, Berg for Irwin
12 Sep	Coventry	H	W	2-0	..	..	P. Neville	..1	Stam	..	..	..	..	..1	Giggs	Butt for Beckham, Blomqvist for Giggs, Berg for Johnsen
20 Sep	Arsenal	A	L	0-3	..	..	Irwin	Berg	..	..	..	Butt	Blomqvist	..	..	
24 Sep	Liverpool	H	W	2-0	..	..	..1	..	..	..	..	Scholes1	Solskjaer	..	..	Butt for Scholes, Cole for Solskjaer
3 Oct	Southampton	A	W	3-0	van der Gouw	..	..	P. Neville	..	..	..	Butt	Cole1	..1	..	Sheringham for Yorke, Cruyff1 for Blomqvist, Brown for Irwin
17 Oct	Wimbledon	H	W	5-1	..	..	P. Neville	Brown	..	..	..1	Blomqvist	..2	..1	Giggs1	Scholes for Giggs, Cruyff for Beckham, Curtis for P. Neville
24 Oct	Derby	A	D	1-1	Schmeichel	..	..	..	..	..	..	Butt	..	..	..	Cruyff1 for Butt, Blomqvist for Giggs, Scholes for G. Neville
31 Oct	Everton	A	W	*4-1	..	..	Irwin	..	..	..	..	Scholes	..1	..1	Blomqvist1	Irwin for P. Neville
8 Nov	Newcastle	H	D	0-0	..	..	Irwin	..	..	..	..	..	..	..	..	Johnsen for Brown, Butt for Johnsen, Solskjaer for Blomqvist
14 Nov	Blackburn	H	W	3-2	..	..	Curtis	P. Neville	..	..	Scholes2	Butt	..	..1	..	Cruyff for Scholes, Keane for Cruyff, Solskjaer for Blomqvist
21 Nov	Sheff Wed	A	L	1-3	..	..	Irwin	..	..	..	Keane	Scholes	..1	..	..	Butt for Blomqvist, Solskjaer for Keane, Brown for Irwin
29 Nov	Leeds	H	W	3-2	..	..	P. Neville	Brown	..	Scholes	..1	Butt1	..	..	Solskjaer	Sheringham for Scholes, Giggs for Cole, Berg for Stam
5 Dec	Aston Villa	A	D	1-1	..	..	Irwin	..	..	Beckham	..	Scholes1	..	..	Blomqvist	Butt for Cole, Giggs for Blomqvist
12 Dec	Tottenham	A	D	2-2	..	..	P. Neville	Johnsen	..	..	..	Butt	Solskjaer2	Sheringham	Giggs	Cole for Sheringham, Blomqvist for Giggs, Berg for Solskjaer
16 Dec	Chelsea	H	D	1-1	..	..	Irwin	Brown	..	Scholes	..	..	Cole1	Yorke	Blomqvist	Beckham for Yorke, Sheringham for Scholes, Giggs for Blomqvist
19 Dec	Middlesbrough	H	L	2-3	..	..	..	Johnsen	P. Neville	Beckham	..	..1	Scholes	Sheringham	Giggs	Scholes1 for Beckham, Solskjaer for P. Neville
26 Dec	Nottingham F.	H	W	3-0	..	P. Neville	..	..2	Berg	..	..	..	Scholes	..	..1	Blomqvist for Giggs, Solskjaer for Scholes, Greening for Keane
29 Dec	Chelsea	A	D	0-0	..	G. Neville	..	..	Stam	..	..	..	Cole	Scholes	..	Sheringham for Scholes
10 Jan	West Ham	H	W	4-1	van der Gouw	Brown	..	Berg	..	Blomqvist	..	..	..2	Yorke1	..	Johnsen for Brown, Cruyff for Keane, Solskjaer1 for Butt
16 Jan	Leicester	A	W	6-2	Schmeichel	..	..	..	..1	Beckham	..	Blomqvist	..2	..3	..	P. Neville for Brown
31 Jan	Charlton Ath	A	W	1-0	..	G. Neville	..	..	..	..	..	Butt	Solskjaer	..1	..	Scholes for Butt, Solskjaer for Beckham
3 Feb	Derby	H	W	1-0	..	..	..	Johnsen	..	Scholes	..	..	Solskjaer	..1	..	Blomqvist for Giggs
6 Feb	Nottingham F.	A	W	8-1	..	..	P. Neville	..	..	Beckham	..	Scholes	Cole2	..2	Blomqvist	Butt for Blomqvist, Curtis for Keane, Solskjaer4 for Yorke
17 Feb	Arsenal	H	D	1-1	..	..	..	..	..	..	..	Butt	..1	..	..	Giggs for Butt, Scholes for Blomqvist
20 Feb	Coventry	A	W	1-0	..	..	Irwin	..	..	..	..	Scholes	..	..	Giggs1	P. Neville for Yorke, Solskjaer for Cole, Berg for Stam
27 Feb	Southampton	H	W	2-1	..	..	P. Neville	..	Berg	..	Scholes	Butt	Solskjaer	..1	..	Irwin for P. Neville, Cole for Solskjaer, Keane1 for Butt
13 Mar	Newcastle	A	W	2-1	..	..	Irwin	Berg	Stam	..	Keane	Scholes	Cole2	..	..	van der Gouw for Schmeichel, Johnsen for Giggs, P. Neville for Scholes
21 Mar	Everton	H	W	3-1	..	..1	P. Neville	Scholes	..	..1	Johnsen	Butt	..	..	Solskjaer1	Sheringham for Cole, Curtis for Solskjaer, Greening for Beckham
3 Apr	Wimbledon	A	D	1-1	..	..	Irwin	..	..	..1	Keane	Scholes	..	..	Blomqvist	Solskjaer for Blomqvist
17 Apr	Sheff Wed	H	W	3-0	van der Gouw	..	P. Neville	Brown	..	Scholes1	..	Butt	Solskjaer1	Sheringham1	..	Irwin for Blomqvist, May for Stam, Greening for Keane
25 Apr	Leeds	A	D	1-1	Schmeichel	..	Irwin	..	May	Beckham	..	..	Cole1	Yorke	..	Sheringham for Blomqvist, P. Neville for Irwin, Scholes for Beckham
1 May	Aston Villa	H	W	*2-1	..	..	..	Johnsen	..	..1	Scholes	..	Sheringham	..	..	P. Neville for Blomqvist, Brown for May
5 May	Liverpool	A	D	2-2	..	..	..	..	Stam	..	Keane	Cole	..1	..	..	Butt for Cole, P. Neville for Blomqvist
9 May	Middlesbrough	A	W	1-0	..	..	..	May	..	..	..	Sheringham	..1	..	..	Butt for Keane, Cole for Blomqvist, P. Neville for Scholes
12 May	Blackburn	A	D	0-0	..	..	..	Johnsen	..	..	P. Neville	Butt	Cole	..	Giggs	May for Stam, Sheringham for Cole, Scholes for P. Neville
16 May	Tottenham	H	W	2-1	..	..	..	..	May	..1	Keane	Scholes	Sheringham	..	..	Cole1 for Sheringham, P. Neville for Giggs, Butt for Scholes

*includes own goal

FA Cup

Date	Opponent	V	R	Score	1	2	3	4	5	6	7	8	9	10	11	Substitutions / Scorers
3 Jan	Middlesbrough (3)	H	W	3-1	Schmeichel	Brown	Irwin1	Berg	Stam	Giggs1	Keane	Butt	Cole1	Yorke	Blomqvist	Sheringham for Cole, Solskjaer for Blomqvist
24 Jan	Liverpool (4)	H	W	2-1	..	G. Neville	..	..	..	Beckham	..	..	..	..1	Giggs	Solskjaer1 for Irwin, Johnsen for Berg, Scholes for Butt
14 Feb	Fulham (5)	H	W	1-0	..	..	..	..	..	..	..	P. Neville	..	..1	Solskjaer	Johnsen for Cole, Blomqvist for Solskjaer, Greening for Irwin
7 Mar	Chelsea (6)	H	D	0-0	..	..	..	..	..	Brown	..	Keane	P. Neville	Scholes	Blomqvist	Cole for Solskjaer, Sheringham for Blomqvist, Yorke for P. Neville
10 Mar	Chelsea (6R)	A	W	2-0	..	..	..	..	Stam	..	..	Scholes	Cole	Yorke2	Giggs	P. Neville for Cole, Blomqvist for Giggs, Solskjaer for Scholes
11 Apr	Arsenal (SF)	N	D	0-0E	..	..	..	Johnsen	..	..	..	..	..	..	..	P. Neville for Irwin, Scholes for Cole, Solskjaer for Giggs
14 Apr	Arsenal (SFR)	N	W	2-1E	..	..	P. Neville	..	..	..1	..	Butt	Solskjaer	Sheringham	Blomqvist	Giggs1 for Blomqvist, Scholes for Sheringham, Yorke for Solskjaer
22 May	Newcastle (F)	N	W	2-0	..	..	..	..	May	..	..	Scholes1	..	Cole	Giggs	Sheringham1 for Keane, Stam for Scholes, Yorke for Cole

Worthington (League) Cup

Date	Opponent	V	R	Score	1	2	3	4	5	6	7	8	9	10	11	Substitutions / Scorers
28 Oct	Bury (3)	H	W	2-0E	van der Gouw	Clegg	Curtis	May	Berg	Wilson	Mulryne	P. Neville	Solskjaer1	Cruyff	Greening	Nevland1 for Mulryne, Scholes for Wilson, Brown for Clegg
11 Nov	Nottingham F	H	W	2-1	..	..	..	..	..	..	..	Butt	..2	..	..	Wallwork for May
2 Dec	Tottenham	A	L	1-3	..	..	..	Johnsen	..	Greening	P. Neville	..	..	Sheringham1	Giggs	Beckham for Curtis, Blomqvist for Greening, Notman for Butt

European Cup (Champions' League)

Date	Opponent	V	R	Score	1	2	3	4	5	6	7	8	9	10	11	Substitutions / Scorers
12 Aug	LKS Lodz (Qual)	H	W	2-0	Schmeichel	G. Neville	Irwin	Johnsen	Stam	Beckham	Keane	Butt	Cole1	Scholes	Giggs1	Solskjaer for Scholes
26 Aug	LKS Lodz (Qual)	A	D	0-0	..	P. Neville	..	..	..	..	..	..	Sheringham	..	..	Solskjaer for Giggs
16 Sep	Barcelona	H	D	3-3	..	G. Neville	..	Berg	..	..1	..	Yorke	Solskjaer	..1	..1	Butt for Solskjaer, P. Neville for Irwin, Blomqvist for Giggs
30 Sep	Bayern Munich	A	D	2-2	..	..	..	P. Neville	..	..	..	..1	Sheringham	..1	Blomqvist	Cruyff for Blomqvist
21 Oct	Brondby	A	W	6-2	..	..	P. Neville	Brown	..	Blomqvist	..1	..1	Cole1	..	Giggs2	Solskjaer1 for Cole, Cruyff for Giggs, Wilson for Yorke
4 Nov	Brondby	H	W	5-0	..	..	Irwin	P. Neville1	..	Beckham1	..	..1	..1	..1	Blomqvist	Cruyff for Blomqvist, Solskjaer for Cole, Brown for P. Neville
25 Nov	Barcelona	A	D	3-3	..	..	..	Brown	..	..	..	..	..2	..1	..	Butt for Beckham
9 Dec	Bayern Munich	H	D	1-1	..	..	..	..	..	..	..	..	..1	..	Giggs	Butt for Yorke
3 Mar	Inter Milan (QF)	H	W	2-0	..	..	..	Johnsen	..	..	..	..	..2	..	..	Berg for Johnsen, Butt for Scholes
17 Mar	Inter Milan (QF)	A	D	1-1	..	..	..	Berg	..	..	..	..	..	Johnsen	..	Scholes1 for Johnsen, P. Neville for Giggs, Johnsen for Berg
7 Apr	Juventus (SF)	H	D	1-1	..	..	..	..	..	..	..	..	..	Scholes	..1	Johnsen for Berg, Sheringham for Yorke
21 Apr	Juventus (SF)	A	W	3-2	..	..	..	Johnsen	..	..	..	..1	..1	..1	Butt	Blomqvist	Scholes for Blomqvist
26 May	Bayern Munich	N	W	2-1	..	..	..	..	..	..	..	Blomqvist	..	..	Giggs	Solskjaer1 for Blomqvist, Sheringham1 for Cole

Appearances (goals)

Beckham 53 (8) – Berg 11 (0) – Blomqvist 30 (1) – Brown 17 (0) – Butt 33 (2) – Clegg 3 (0) – Cole 42 (24) – Cruyff 2 (2) – Curtis 3 (0) – G.Neville 54 (0) – Giggs 35 (10) – Greening 3 (0) – Irwin 45 (3) – Johnsen 29 (3) – Keane 52 (5) – May 7 (0) – Mulryne 2 (0) – Nevland 0 (1) – P.Neville 30 (1) – Schmeichel 56 (0) – Scholes 33 (11) – Sheringham 11 (5) – Solskjaer 18 (18) –Stam 49 (1) – Van der Gouw 7 (0) – Wilson 2 (0) – Yorke 48 (29). Own goals 5 : Total 26 (starting) players (128)

Own goals 2 – **Total 26 (starting) Players (128)**

FA Premier League

	P	W	D	L	F:A	Pts	
Manchester U	38	22	13	3	80:37	79	1st

SEASON 1999-2000 FA CARLING PREMIERSHIP

Date	Opp	V	Res	1	2	3	4	5	6	7	8	9	10	11	Subs / Notes
8 Aug	Everton	A	D 1-1	Bosnich	P.Neville	Irwin	Berg	Stam	Beckham	Keane	Scholes	Solskjaer	Cole	Yorke 1	Sheringham 1 for G.Neville, Berg for Stam
11 Aug	Sheffield Wed	H	W 4-0	..	..	..	..	..	..	..	..1	Giggs	..1	..1	Butt for Beckham, Sheringham for Yorke, Solskjaer 1 for Giggs
14 Aug	Leeds	H	W 2-0	..	..	..	..	..	..	..	..	..	..	..2	Van der Gouw for Bosnich, Butt for Scholes, Sheringham for Yorke
22 Aug	Arsenal	A	W 2-1	Van der Gouw	..	..	..	..	..	..2	..	..	..	..	
25 Aug	Coventry	A	W 2-1	..	..	..	..	..	..	..	Butt	..	Sheringham	..1	Curtis for P.Neville, Scholes 1 for Butt, Solskjaer for Sheringham
30 Aug	Newcastle	H	W 5-1	..	G.Neville	P.Neville	..	..	..	Scholes	..	..1	..4	..	Sheringham for Beckham, Clegg for P.Neville, fortune for Scholes
11 Sep	Liverpool	A	W **3-2	Taibi	P.Neville	Silvestre	..	..	..	..	..	..1	..	..	Wallwork for Butt, Clegg for P.Neville
18 Sep	Wimbledon	H	D 1-1	..	..	Irwin	..	..	Silvestre	..	Solskjaer	..	Sheringham	..	Cole for Solskjaer, Cruyff 1 for Giggs
25 Sep	Southampton	H	D 3-3	..	..	Irwin	Silvestre	..	Beckham	..	Butt	Solskjaer	..1	..1	
3 Oct	Chelsea	A	L 0-5	Taibi	..	..	..	..	..	..	..	P.Neville	Cole	..	Wilson for Scholes, Sheringham for Cole, Solskjaer for Beckham
16 Oct	Watford	H	W 4-1	Bosnich	..1	P.Neville	Silvestre	..	..	..	..	Giggs	..2	..1	Solskjaer for Cole, Keane for Stam, Greening for Giggs
23 Oct	Tottenham	A	L 1-3	..	..	..	..	..	..	..	Keane	..1	..	..	Solskjaer for Beckham, Greening for Irwin
30 Oct	Aston Villa	H	W 3-0	..	..	..	..	..	..	..1	..1	..	..1	..	Solskjaer for Yorke, Cruyff for Giggs, Wilson for Cole
6 Nov	Leicester	H	W 2-0	Bosnich	P.Neville	Higginbotham	..	..	Scholes	Keane	Giggs	Solskjaer	..2	..	May for Higginbotham, Berg for P.Neville
20 Nov	Derby County	A	W 2-1	..	G.Neville	P.Neville	..	..	Beckham	..	Butt 1	..	..1	..	Berg for Silvestre, Solskjaer for Beckham
4 Dec	Everton	H	W 5-1	..	..	Irwin 1	G.Neville	..	Scholes	..	..	..	Sheringham	Solskjaer 4	Van der Gouw for Bosnich, Cole for Giggs, P.Neville for Silvestre
18 Dec	West Ham	A	W 4-2	Van der Gouw	G.Neville	Irwin	..	..	Beckham	..	Scholes	..2	..	Yorke 2	P.Neville for Irwin, Butt for Beckham
26 Dec	Bradford City	H	W 4-0	Bosnich	P.Neville	..	..	..	..	Scholes	..1	Butt	Fortune 1	Solskjaer	Cole 1 for Sheringham, Yorke 1 for Scholes, Wallwork for Stam
28 Dec	Sunderland	A	D 2-2	..	..	Irwin	..	..	Beckham	..1	..1	Giggs	Cole	Yorke	Sheringham for Irwin, Solskjaer for Beckham, P.Neville for Cole
24 Jan	Arsenal	H	D 1-1	..	..	..	..	..	..1	..	..	..	..	..	Sheringham 1 for Cole, P.Neville for Irwin
29 Jan	Middlesbrough	H	W 1-0	..	..	..	..	..	..	..	..	Sheringham	..	..1	Cole for Sheringham, Scholes for G.Neville, Solskjaer for Irwin
2 Feb	Sheffield Wed	A	W 1-0	..	..	Irwin	..	..	..	..	..	..	..1	..	Scholes for Butt
5 Feb	Coventry City	H	W 3-2	..	..	P.Neville	..	..	..	..	Scholes 1	Solskjaer	..	Cole 1	Butt for Solskjaer, Cruyff for Sheringham
12 Feb	Newcastle	A	L 0-3	..	..	Irwin	..	..	..	..	..	Giggs	..	..	Solskjaer for Sheringham, Butt for Irwin
20 Feb	Leeds	A	W 1-0	..	..	..	P.Neville	..	..	Butt	..	..	Cole 1	Yorke	Sheringham for Yorke
26 Feb	Wimbledon	A	D 2-2	..	..	..	P.Neville	..	Beckham	Butt	Cruyff 1	Sheringham	Cole 1	Yorke	Berg for P.Neville, Solskjaer for Cruyff
4 Mar	Liverpool	H	D 1-1	Van der Gouw	..	Irwin	Stam	Silvestre	..	Keane	Butt	..	Solskjaer 1	Yorke	Cole for Solskjaer, Sheringham for Yorke
11 Mar	Derby County	H	W 3-1	Bosnich	..	P.Neville	Berg	..	..	..	Scholes	Fortune	..	..3	Butt for Fortune, Wallwork for Keane
18 Mar	Leicester	A	W 2-0	..	..	Irwin	Stam	Berg	..1	..	..	Giggs	Cole	..1	Sheringham for Cole, Butt for Giggs
25 Mar	Bradford City	A	W 4-0	..	..	P.Neville	Berg	Silvestre	..1	..	..1	..	..	..2	Solskjaer for Giggs, Wallwork for Keane
1 Apr	West Ham	H	W 7-1	..	..	Irwin 1	Stam	Silvestre	..1	..	..3	Fortune	..1	..	Butt for Keane, Sheringham for Cole, Solskjaer 1 for Scholes
10 Apr	Middlesbrough	A	W 4-3	..	..	..	..	..	Berg	..	..1	Giggs 1	..1	..	Fortune 1 for Giggs, Silvestre for Irwin, Butt for Keane
15 Apr	Sunderland	H	W 4-0	..	..	..	P.Neville	..	Silvestre	Butt 1	..	Fortune	Sheringham	Solskjaer 2	Van der Gouw for Bosnich, Beckham for Scholes, Berg for Stam
22 Apr	Southampton	A	W *3-1	Van der Gouw	..	..	..	..	Beckham 1	..	Butt	Giggs	Cole	..1	Johnsen for Giggs, Yorke for Solskjaer, Sheringham for Cole
24 Apr	Chelsea	H	W 3-2	..	..	..	..	Johnsen	..	..	..	..	Solskjaer 1	Yorke 2	Cruyff for Solskjaer, Berg for G.Neville, Scholes for Keane
29 Apr	Watford	A	W 3-2	..	P.Neville	Berg	..	..	Greening	Butt	Wilson	..1	..	Sheringham	Yorke 1 for Wilson, Cruyff 1 for Wilson, Higginbotham for Johnsen
6 May	Tottenham	H	W 3-1	..	..	..	Stam	Silvestre	Irwin	..	..	Scholes	..1	..1	Berg for Stam, Cruyff for Solskjaer, Greening for Butt
14 May	Aston Villa	A	W 1-0	..	Irwin	Berg	..	Higginbotham	Solskjaer	P.Neville	..	..	Sheringham 1	Yorke	Cruyff for Solskjaer, Wallwork for Higginbotham

*includes own goal
**includes two own goals

FA Charity Shield

Date	Opp	V	Res	1	2	3	4	5	6	7	8	9	10	11	Subs / Notes
1 Aug	Arsenal	W*	L 1-2	Bosnich	Irwin	Berg	Stam	Irwin	Beckham 1	Butt	Scholes	Cruyff	Cole	Yorke	May for Stam, Sheringham for Butt,

*Played at Wembley

European Super Cup

Date	Opp	V	Res	1	2	3	4	5	6	7	8	9	10	11	Subs / Notes
27 Aug	Lazio	M*	L 0-1	Van der Gouw	G.Neville	P.Neville	Berg	Stam	Beckham	Keane	Scholes	Cole	Sheringham	Solskjaer	Cruyff for Beckham, Curtis for Stam,

*played in Monaco

Inter Continental Cup (formerly The World Club championship)

Date	Opp	V	Res	1	2	3	4	5	6	7	8	9	10	11	Subs / Notes
30 Nov	Palmeiras	T*	W 1-0	Bosnich	G.Neville	Irwin	Stam	Silvestre	Beckham	Keane 1	Butt	Giggs	Scholes	Solskjaer	Sheringham for Scholes, Yorke for Solskjaer

*played in Tokyo

European Champions' League

Date	Opp	V	Res	1	2	3	4	5	6	7	8	9	10	11	Subs / Notes
14 Sep	Croatia Zagreb	H	D 0-0	Van der Gouw	Clegg	P.Neville	Berg	Stam	Beckham	Wilson	Scholes	Giggs	Cole	Yorke	Fortune for Clegg, Sheringham for Wilson
22 Sep	Sturm Graz	A	W 3-0	..	Irwin	..	..	..	..	Keane 1	..	Cruyff	..1	..1	Sheringham for Cruyff, Wilson for Keane, Solskjaer for Cole
29 Sep	Marseille	H	W 2-1	..	..	..	..	..	..	Butt	..1	Solskjaer	..1	..	Sheringham for Berg, Clegg for Cole, Fortune for Solskjaer
19 Oct	Marseille	A	L 0-1	Bosnich	..	..	..	..	..	Keane	..	Giggs	..	..	Solskjaer for Berg
27 Oct	Croatia Zagreb	A	W 2-1	..	..	..	..	..	..	..1	..1	..	..	..	Solskjaer for Yorke, Cruyff for Cole, Greening for Scholes
2 Nov	Sturm Graz	H	W 2-1	v	G.Neville	Irwin	..	..	May	Greening	..1	Wilson	..	Solskjaer 1	P.Neville for Wilson, Cruyff for Greening, Higginbotham for May
23 Nov	Fiorentina	A	L 0-2	..	..	..	..	Stam	Beckham	..	Scholes	..	..	Yorke	Sheringham for Cole, P.Neville for Berg, Solskjaer for Yorke
8 Dec	Valencia	H	W 3-0	Van der Gouw	Irwin	P.Neville	Stam	G.Neville	..	..1	..1	..	..	Solskjaer 1	Butt for Scholes, Yorke for Cole
1 Mar	Bordeaux	H	W 2-0	..	G.Neville	Irwin	..	Silvestre	..	..	Butt	..1	..	Sheringham 1	P.Neville for Cole, Solskjaer for Giggs, Fortune for Keane
7 Mar	Bordeaux	A	W 2-1	..	..	..	..	..	..	..1	..	..	..1	Yorke 1	Solskjaer for Irwin
15 Mar	Fiorentina	H	W 3-1	Bosnich	..	..	Berg	Stam	..	..1	Scholes	..	..1	Yorke 1	Cruyff for Solskjaer
21 Mar	Valencia	A	D 0-0	..	..	..	..	..	..	Butt	..	Fortune	Solskjaer	Sheringham	Cruyff for Solskjaer
4 Apr	Real Madrid Q/F	A	D 0-0	..	..	..	..	..	Beckham	..	..	..	Cole	Yorke	Butt for Scholes, Sheringham for Yorke, Silvestre for Irwin
19 Apr	Real Madrid Q/F	H	L 2-3	Van der Gouw	..	..	..	..	..	..1	..	..1	..	..	Sheringham for Berg, Silvestre for Irwin,

FIFA Club World Championships (Brazil)

Date	Opp	V	Res	1	2	3	4	5	6	7	8	9	10	11	Subs / Notes
6 Jan	Necaxa (Mex)	N	D 1-1	Bosnich	G.Neville	Irwin	Stam	Silvestre	Beckham	Keane	Butt	Giggs	Cole	Yorke 1	Solskjaer for Irwin, P.Neville for Butt
8 Jan	Vasco (Brazil)	N	L 1-3	..	..	..	..	..	..	Butt 1	..	P.Neville	Solskjaer	..	Sheringham for Solskjaer, Cruyff for Stam, Fortune for Giggs
11 Jan	S.Melbourne	N	W 2-0	Van der Gouw	P.Neville	Higginbotham	Berg	Wallwork	Greening	Wilson	Cruyff	Fortune 2	Solskjaer	Cole	Beckham for Wilson, Rachubka for Van der Gouw

All games played in Rio de Janerio

Worthington (League) Cup

Date	Opp	V	Res	1	2	3	4	5	6	7	8	9	10	11	Subs / Notes
13 Oct	Aston Villa	A	L 0-3	Bosnich	Clegg	Curtis	O'Shea	Higginbotham	Wallwork	Chadwick	Twiss	Greening	Cruyff	Solskjaer	Healy for Higginbotham, Wellens for Twiss

---

League Appearances (Goals in brackets)

Beckham 43 (8) - Berg 28 (1) - Bosnich 33 (0) - Butt 27 (4) - Chadwick 1 (0) - Clegg 2 (0) - Cole 38 (22) - Cruyff 4 (3) - Curtis 1 (0) - Fortune 6 (4) - G.Neville 33 (0) - Giggs 43 (7) - Greening 4 (0)
Higginbotham 4 (0) - Irwin 40 (3) - Johnsen 2 (0) - Keane 42 (11) - May 1 (0) - O'Shea 1 (0) - P.Neville 33 (0) - Scholes 38 (12) - Sheringham 18 (6) - Silvestre 34 (0) - Solskjaer 22 (15)
Stam 48 (0) - Taibi 4 (0) - Twiss 1 (0) - Van der Gouw 19 (0) - Wallwork 2 (0) - Wilson 4 (0) - Yorke 40 (23). Own goals 3.
Total 31 (starting) players (122).

Position in League Table

	P	W	L	D	F:A	Pts	
Manchester U	38	28	7	3	97:45	91	1st

CHAPTER **10**
THE 21st CENTURY

Apprehension hung over Old Trafford as the 2000–01 season approached. The collapse of the Ruud Van Nistelrooy deal forced the club to change its plans for a plunge in the transfer market although another World star did join the ranks. It was obvious Sir Alex was unhappy with the goalkeeping situation and did not see Mark Bosnich as the long-term replacement for Peter Schmeichel. With Raimond van der Gouw in his 38th year and the unlucky Massimo Taibi transferred back to Italy, the club made a record bid for French World Cup star Fabien Barthez. The extrovert 'keeper had been United's target the previous year but Sir Alex was unable to persuade him to leave the sunshine of Monaco. Twelve months on Barthez had a change of heart and declared he was ready to try his hand in the Premiership.

Signed during the close season, he celebrated the move by adding a European Championship medal to the World Cup honours won in France '98, and once the new campaign got underway became an instant hit. Barthez cost £7.8 million, the highest fee paid for a goalkeeper, but it became apparent from his first game that it was a sound investment. He was a showman, an entertainer and the fans loved him. They enjoyed his eagerness to get involved in the outfield action, although sometimes his sorties upfield must have given his new manager palpitations. His kicking was outstanding and if anything better than Schmeichel's, and this confidence on the ball added another dimension to United's style of play. Defenders would no longer think twice about making a back pass. They would play the ball to the goalkeeper knowing Barthez could cope, and any hesitancy which crept in during Bosnich's short reign quickly disappeared.

Departures

There were no further signings but there was one departure during the summer of 2000, as Jordi Cruyff somewhat reluctantly left to join Spanish club Alaves. He had kept his word and completed his four-year contract, but while Jordi was happy to return to his adopted homeland, his one regret was that he left United feeling he had not been given the chance to prove his real worth to the club. His obvious talent immediately shone through once he returned to La Liga and he played a major part in helping his new club reach the UEFA Cup Final, which they eventually lost to Liverpool in a dramatic match that ended 5–4.

During the early weeks of the campaign Henning Berg also left. He returned to Blackburn Rovers firstly on loan, then later a transfer fee changed hands. The Norwegian teamed up with

Above: United broke the transfer record for a goalkeeper to bring Fabien Barthez to Old Trafford. France's No.1 proved an instant success, particularly with the fans who liked nothing more than seeing his dribbling skills embarass Premiership forwards.

Below: Teddy Sheringham celebrates his hat-trick during a 5–0 romp against Southampton. His 10 goals in eight games were a vital contribution to United's blistering start to the season.

former United youngsters John Curtis and Keith Gillespie and the veteran Mark Hughes at Ewood Park and helped Blackburn win promotion back to the top section.

A solid start

By December, when Berg's move was made permanent, United were firmly a ensconced at the top of the Premiership and heading for another domestic success. They had started steadily. A win and two draws were followed by a 6–0 romp against Bradford City on September 5, which put them briefly on top of the table, then a 3–0 victory over Sunderland who were one of the early pace-setters.

With eight games played there was a new face at the top of the table. Leicester City were surprise leaders and occupied top spot when United visited Filbert Street on October 14. In their previous Premiership game United had lost 1–0 at Arsenal and many experts felt another upset for the reigning champions was on the cards. Those predictions proved totally off the mark, United not only won, but won easily. They beat the home side 3–0 thanks to two goals from a rejuvenated Teddy Sheringham and a late strike from Ole Gunnar Solskjaer, stepping over Leicester to go top of the table where they were to stay for the remainder of the season. Seven successive wins opened up an eight point lead by December 2, and even a surprise 3–3 draw at Charlton and a 1–0 defeat at the hands of Liverpool at Old Trafford did little to distract them.

FA Cup exit

The club played down talk of a repeat of 1999's treble success, and any back page predictions this might happen ended abruptly on Sunday, January 28 in the Fourth Round of the FA Cup.

Following the controversy of the previous season when United withdrew from the competition because of their involvement in the FIFA Club World Championships, they became the obvious focus of attention when drawn away to Fulham in Round Three. The London club was running away with the First Division just as United dominated the Premiership, and the clash of the two league leaders at Craven Cottage made it the tie of the round.

United won 2–1 thanks to a late goal from Sheringham and they were drawn at home to West Ham in the next stage. Having already beaten The Hammers 3–1 three weeks earlier in the league United seemed favourites to go through.

That remained the case until Paolo Di Canio beat United's offside trap and scored the only goal of the game 15 minutes from the end. The Italian ignored the gamesmanship of Barthez who tried to distract him by standing with one arm raised, suggesting play had been stopped for offside, and any chances of a second treble disappeared.

This – and the controversy surrounding the goal which United's defence disputed – led to Gary Neville uncharacteristically lambasting one of the referee's assistants as he left the field at the end of the game. Three months later he was fined £30,000 (later reduced to £7,000 on appeal) and banned for two games for using foul and abusive language.

By the time he served his suspension United were once again champions.

An unassailable lead

By the turn of the year the gap had opened to 11 points with Arsenal their nearest rivals and on January 20, as Barthez chalked up his 15th clean sheet of the season and Aston Villa were beaten 2–0 at Old Trafford, the lead stretched to 15 points.

Shortly before the Villa game Mark Bosnich decided it was time to leave the club for a second time. Pushed down the pecking order by Barthez and the manager's preference of using van der Gouw as back-up he opted for life at Chelsea even though his chances of first team football at Stamford Bridge seemed equally slim.

United sat comfortably at the top of the league as Liverpool, Arsenal, Sunderland and a rejuvenated Leeds, battled it out for second place. Ipswich Town promoted from the First Division the previous season were another of the chasing pack but with four months of the campaign remaining, it seemed to be a case of when, rather than if, United would clinch their third successive championship. With the league campaign going so well and United well place in their Champions League group many fans toyed with idea of another treble.

Above: The new season brought the return of an old adversary and a much cherished derby match. It had been four years since the red and blue halves of Manchester had last met, and the early start did not dampen the atmosphere. It took a classic Beckham free-kick to take home the points from Maine Road.

Right: By January United were firmly in control at the top of the Premiership. Ryan Giggs was back to his best with some scintillating displays of his talent, particularly during the winter away trips to Charlton and Bradford (shown here) .

2000-01

handing over to Joe Fagan before the Merseysiders' third successive championship.

Sir Alex was unquestionably the club's most successful manager, and while he would be too modest to claim it himself, was arguably the best the game had seen.

Earlier in the season he made it clear he intended to carry through his plans of retiring in the summer of 2002. He closed all discussion on the matter when the club announced he would be staying on at Old Trafford in another capacity, and was equally reluctant to speak about his latest personal milestone: "I don't pay much attention to that part I must admit, because I always feel you have got to move on. What we have achieved has been fantastic, and a lot of people have conveniently forgotten how well we have performed to win this championship again."

Responding to the barrage of newspaper criticism which followed United's exit from the Champions' League he added:

Seventh Heaven

On April 14, with five games to spare, they clinched their seventh Premiership title in nine seasons. It was yet another record for Sir Alex and his players with their task completed eight days and one game earlier than the previous season. They did it on the day they fielded the club's oldest debutant, beating Coventry City 4–2 at Old Trafford – a result which helped send Gordon Strachan's club to the First Division.

A few weeks earlier there was a scare when Barthez was injured during the pre-match warm-up for the game against Leicester. With van der Gouw recovering from a knee operation, the manager was forced to turn to 20-year-old stand-in Paul Rachubka who performed well in the 2–0 victory. Feeling it was too big a risk to rely on the youngster as cover for Barthez he then signed former Scottish international Andy Goram from Motherwell.

On the day after his 37th birthday Goram faced Coventry in a game which kicked off at 12 noon. Less than five hours later United were champions. Arsenal were surprisingly beaten 3–0 by Middlesbrough at Highbury and United were beyond reach.

Sir Alex's hat-trick

It meant Sir Alex had become the first manager in the history of English football to lead a club to three successive championships. Before him the legendary Herbert Chapman had seen Huddersfield Town secure the title in 1924 and 1925 then moved to Arsenal before the Yorkshire club won the championship for a third season in a row. At Highbury he was in charge when Arsenal were crowned champions in 1933 and 1934 but died before their third success in 1935. Liverpool's Bob Paisley was another who came close, winning the title in 1982 and 1983, but

Top: Any doubts as to United's claim to the league crown were erradicated with a 6–1 thrashing of the main pretenders, Arsenal, at Old Trafford.

Above: The 37-year-old Andy Goram takes the applause as he faces Coventry in April.

Above, right: A lunging challenge on Manchester City's Alfie Haaland has Keane seeing red in the home derby.

"I suppose it is part and parcel of the modern media that they have slaughtered the team a bit, but that can act as a bit of encouragement to our players next year. You cannot get away from the fact that they won the championship after only losing three games, and had collected 80 points. When you look at the winners of the league titles over the past 20 years you will find that is an exceptional performance. From a personal point of view it doesn't concern me, perhaps when I get older I will be able to reflect on my career but I am not into that at present. The way we have played to win this title has not been forgotten by me or by any of my players. It is a fantastic achievement done by a special bunch of players."

United finally get their man

One of those players was Teddy Sheringham who ended his fourth season at Old Trafford not just taking the crown of the club's top scorer, but by winning the PFA Player of the Year Award and being named Footballer of the Year by the Football Writers' Association. It was to be a triumphant end to his Old Trafford career as he left United to join Spurs on a free transfer. Teddy's move was motivated by a new, but not unexpected, arrival as United broke the British transfer record by finally signing Ruud Van Nistelrooy from PSV Eindhoven.

A year after the original deal collapsed negotiations re-opened and on the day United faced Manchester City at Old Trafford, the Dutch striker was at the club's Trafford Training Centre at Carrington and this time came through the all-important club medical.

On Monday, April 23, United announced they had signed the player for a record £19 million and ended a patient wait by Sir Alex, who had closely monitored the striker's progress as he recovered from cruciate ligament surgery, and eventually made a successful comeback for both PSV and Holland. Facing the media four days after tying up the move, Van Nistelrooy expressed his obvious delight at becoming a

Above: The last home game of the season (a surprising defeat by Derby County) saw the annual ritual of Sir Alex and Roy Keane lifting the Premiership trophy.

Above, right: Patience is a virtue: the season-long saga of the Ruud Van Nistelrooy deal finally came to a close when the Dutch international signed in April for a record £19 million.

Manchester United player. "It feels fantastic to be here. Last year was close but it didn't go through and it was a big disappointment. This is the best thing that has ever happened to me. To give myself the opportunity to come back here was my biggest goal."

Referring to the abortive press conference of the previous year when the media waited at Old Trafford as Van Nistelrooy went home after failing his medical, the young Dutchman said:

"Last year I couldn't be here, when you were all waiting here, I was on the plane home, so my first goal was to fly back and sit here now. Manchester United as a club want to win every trophy there is, every year, because it is one of the best clubs in the world, so the goals at this club are the same as my personal goals. That is why I am happy to come here and I am looking forward to next season."

With a new striker signed, the Premiership's top prize once again tucked away in the trophy cabinet and speculation surrounding the arrival of two more World class players, Manchester United ended another successful campaign. As for Sir Alex Ferguson, his thoughts were firmly focussed achieving a success in 2001–2002 and what is expected to be his final season as manager.

2000-01

The European adventure 2001

There was an urgency in Manchester United's approach to the European challenge in season 2000–01 because Sir Alex Ferguson and his players have set their sights on becoming a great side and they know that the criteria for that distinction is to win the Champions League not once but several times.

With the disappointment of the previous year's quarter-final failure against Real Madrid very much in their minds, they were determined to do better and approached the first group phase involving Anderlecht, Dynamo Kiev and PSV Eindhoven with a zest that was certainly very evident in their opening tie.

A mixed start

Andy Cole led a thrilling charge to score a hat-trick in a 5–1 win against Anderlecht at Old Trafford that took him to 15 goals and a club record in the European Cup ahead of Denis Law. Denis Irwin with a penalty and Teddy Sheringham were the other scorers with the Belgian club replying through Jan Koller.

The emphatic victory and superb football, described by the Anderlecht coach, Aime Anthuenis, as 'something from another planet', filled players and fans with confidence that this time there would be no slip-ups.

The bubble soon burst. A point from a goalless draw in Kiev was acceptable, but a 3–1 defeat against Eindhoven in Holland came as a shock and dropped them from top of the table to third. The manager's gamble of resting David Beckham, Ryan Giggs and Andy Cole on the bench because of a Premiership match at Arsenal at the weekend didn't, with hindsight, look too clever.

Although Paul Scholes had given United an ideal start with a goal after only three minutes, they were swamped by goals from Wilfred Bouma, Mark Van Bommel and Mateja Kezman.

In the more familiar surroundings of Old Trafford for the next game, the Reds took their revenge on the Dutchmen and got back on course with a 3–1 win. Van Bommel equalised a Sheringham opener, but Scholes and Yorke scored late in the game to put their team back at the top of the group.

'Sailing close to the wind'

However, it was becoming clear that United were not travelling well as they crashed to another away defeat, losing 2–1 in Anderlecht. Tomasz Radzinski put United on the rack with two first-half goals and United were lucky to escape so lightly. Irwin raised hopes from the penalty spot but overall United were well beaten and found themselves in the situation of having to win their final group game to qualify for the second stage.

They got through against Kiev at Old Trafford on a Sheringham goal in a 1–0 win but it was a close-run thing. George Demetradze incredibly missed an open goal five

Above: Dwight Yorke latches on to a pass during United's flying start to the Champions League campaign against Anderlecht in September. Andy Cole's hat-trick during the 5–1 rout, gave him the club record for European goals.

minutes from the end that could easily have been an equaliser ... and an early exit from the competition.

The critics were dismissive but Sir Alex Ferguson hit back: "Sometimes football doesn't go strictly to plan, it's the very nature of the game. Naturally I would like to win all our games with flair and a flourish, but some of the time it's about holding your nerve when things are not going right and while I would have much preferred to spare our supporters – not to mention myself – the emotion of sailing so close to the wind against Kiev, I still feel it was a good disciplined performance on our part.

"When you sit back afterwards and analyse the match, Kiev had one chance. Fabien Barthez didn't have a real save to make and in terms of possession and pressure we were way out in front.

"So while there was disappointment that we lacked the sparkle you associate with a Manchester United night in Europe, I was pleased with the concentration and patience we showed. The defensive part pleased me. If we can keep that part of our game we will be OK in the Champions League. Sometimes it is important to get a zero on the board, and even if it comes with a late scare, the message nonetheless goes out.

"Our critics have had a bit of a field day at our expense but the fact is, we are in the next stage now and come the next game I am positive you will see us in better shape. It was the result that mattered. I think we deserved to go through and I am looking forward to giving a better account of ourselves next time out," he declared.

Spanish Stalemate

His players certainly heeded his plea as they ran up a 3–1 win against Panathinaikos at Old Trafford in their opening game in a group that also comprised Valencia and Sturm Gratz. Sheringham put them on the right path with a goal early in the second half. Giorgios Karagounis equalised from a free kick but two goals from Paul Scholes crushed the Greeks.

A 2–0 win in Austria against Sturm Gratz with goals from Scholes and Ryan Giggs not only brought a welcome away win but sent the team into the winter break in the ideal position, topping the group with a maximum six points and everyone feeling much better about their European prospects.

Back-to-back games with Valencia when the competition reopened in February were obviously going to be more searching, but a goalless game for a point in Spain was a reasonable enough result. The opportunity was now there to beat Valencia

Above: United and England midfielder Paul Scholes was on target six times during the European campaign. Vital goals against Panathinaikos (both home and away) helped secure a quarter-final slot for Sir Alex's men.

Below: Wes Brown puts the ball past Barthez in the home tie against Valencia. Two draws for the Spanish side allowed them to progress to the quarter-finals as group winners and give the tougher tie to United.

at Old Trafford and qualify for the quarter-finals with two group games to spare. The mood was good and spirits were high, especially when a dynamic looking Giggs set Andy Cole up to score after only 12 minutes. A recurrence of his hamstring problem put Giggs out of the game shortly after the goal and with him went their best weapon. The team lost its attacking edge and nobody could complain when pressure saw a luckless Wes Brown put through his own goal as he tried to intercept a centre.

A 1–1 draw meant there was no immediate qualification but there seemed nothing to worry about with a two-point lead at the top of the table. With two fixtures remaining after coping with Valencia, the previous year's finalists, it seemed a pretty strong position. Unfortunately they were unable to capitalise and while a 1–1 draw with Panathinaikos in Athens was a respectable result it was not a respectable performance.

The manager and his captain, Roy Keane, both condemned the display and acknowledged that but for the excellent goal-keeping of Fabien Barthez, they could easily have been beaten by a big score. As it was they had to be grateful to Scholes for grabbing an injury-time equaliser to a 25th-minute goal from Giorgios Seitaridis.

Sir Alex was angry enough to put David Beckham, Dwight Yorke, Andy Cole, Wes Brown and Phil Neville on the bench for the final fixture against Sturm Gratz at Old Trafford, and he demanded what he called a top performance. Happily he got it with goals from Nicky Butt, Teddy Sheringham and Roy Keane in a 3–0 win that qualified the Reds for the knockout stage.

He said: "The performance illustrated perfectly where we had been going wrong. Our concentration level had been wayward in our previous attempts for the win that would have moved us into the last eight of the competition with no messing about, but against the Austrians it was quite clear early in the game that there was a resolution and focus to make sure there was no slip-up this time.

"We attacked from the start in a positive fashion and not only qualified in a convincing way but sent out the right message to the other teams left in the competition.

"Of course it would have been nice to have won the group but that was the price we had to pay for letting ourselves down in a couple of the other group games. In actual fact, it might not be a bad thing because as a group runner-up we play the first leg of our quarter-final at home, and our record is good when we have played in Europe in that order. Perhaps fate is taking a hand.

"Obviously the standard goes up another notch because everyone left in has real quality, but again anyone who draws us will also know they are in for a tough tie, especially now that we have reminded everyone that when we concentrate properly we are as good as the next guy.

2000-01

Sour end to the season

Everyone was in good heart again, even when the quarter-final draw paired them with Bayern Munich, a clash offering up the opportunity for the Germans to get their revenge for the way victory had been snatched from their grasp by Manchester United in the 1999 final in Barcelona.

Ferguson was upbeat, and his team responded, at least in the first half of the first leg at Old Trafford when Ryan Giggs was at his mercurial best. The Welsh winger faded, though, and the Bayern captain, Stefan Effenberg increasingly controlled the game until one of their substitutes, Paulo Sergio, scored in the 86th minute for a 1–0 win.

Ferguson said: "Our performance in the first half was a nice balance between making sure we did nothing silly in defence while still taking the game to our opponents in search of a goal or two. At the break I felt we were on the right track and that we could end up with the kind of one-goal win that was my aim.

"Instead, Bayern turned the game round to come out on top with the kind of score with an away goal that I'm sure Ottmar Hitzfeld had in mind. It's easy to criticise our players but you have got to give credit to Bayern for the way they changed their tactics to shut out Andy Cole and Ryan Giggs, the two forward players who had provided most of our threat in the early stages."

Ferguson recalled the way the team had had their backs to the wall against Juventus two years previously in the Champions League semi-final. He said they could draw inspiration from the way they had fought back from being two goals down in Turin to win 3–2.

The magic was missing in Munich though. Giovane Elber and Mehmet Scholl had the German team leading 2–0 at the interval, and though Ryan Giggs pulled a goal back, the match finished with a 2–1 defeat and the roof fell in!

Above: Paulo Sergio's 86th-minute strike stuns Old Trafford. The goal left United a mountain to climb in the second leg.

Above, right: Brazilian striker Giovane Elber breaks United fans' hearts as he wheels away from his 40th-minute goal that put Bayern ahead 2–0 on aggregate. Mehmet Scholl wrapped up the tie and, despite a goal from Ryan Giggs, the Germans were through and on the way to lifting that season's Champions League trophy.

Roy Keane savaged his team-mates as simply not good enough for the European challenge and called for fresh faces. Sir Alex did indeed spend £19m on finally securing Ruud van Nistelrooy from Eindhoven and later made a £24m bid for Juan Veron, Lazio's 26-year-old Argentinian international midfielder. Soon, though, the manager himself was embroiled in bitter dispute with the club over his future, an acrimonious situation which together with the European defeat tended to take the gloss off their 10-point win in the Premiership.

Fans were stunned when Sir Alex suddenly and dramatically announced that he would be leaving the club on completion of his contract at the end of season 2001–02, rather than accepting another role at Old Trafford. There was worse to follow when the papers started to suggest that he might even leave without completing his final year.

Ferguson explained that the club had failed to come up with the right kind of proposal for him to stay on as a global ambassador and that he was bitterly disappointed. Supporters were outraged and bombarded the club's television phone-in programmes with protests. The confrontation was met at first by a deafening silence from the club. Eventually they announced that they had again met with the manager's adviser – his son Jason – and had offered an enhanced package for a consultancy role to follow his retirement as manager in June, 2002. It was thought that the plc board were also offering to upgrade his salary during his final season and Sir Alex set off for his summer holiday in a much happier frame of mind.

United fans are once more looking forward to Sir Alex crowning his final year with a European triumph and see the choice of Hampden Park as the venue for the next final of the Champions League as an appropriate and significant setting in the manager's home city!

SEASON 2000-2001 FA CARLING PREMIERSHIP

Date	Opp	V	R	Score	1	2	3	4	5	6	7	8	9	10	11	Substitutes
20 Aug	Newcastle Utd	H	W	2-0	Barthez	G.Neville	Stam	Johnsen 1	P.Neville	Beckham	Keane	Scholes	Giggs	Cole 1	Sheringham	Yorke for Sheringham, Solskjaer for Cole, Wallwork for Johnsen
22 Aug	Ipswich Town	A	D	1-1	"	"	"	Wallwork	"	" 1	"	"	"	Solskjaer	Yorke	Cole for Solskjaer, Sheringham for Yorke, Silvestre for P.Neville
26 Aug	West Ham	A	D	2-2	"	"	"	Silvestre	"	" 1	"	"	Giggs	Cole 1	Sheringham	Berg for Stam
5 Sep	Bradford City	H	W	6-0	"	"	Wallwork	Johnsen	Silvestre	" 1	Greening	Butt	Fortune 2	" 1	" 2	P.Neville for Johnsen, Scholes for Butt, Solskjaer for Cole
9 Sep	Sunderland	H	W	3-0	"	"	Stam	"	"	"	Scholes 2	"	Giggs	"	" 1	Irwin for Stam, Solskjaer for Cole
16 Sep	Everton	A	W	3-1	"	Irwin	G.Neville	Brown	"	"	"	" 1	" 1	"	" 1	P.Neville for Scholes, Van der Gouw for Barthez, Yorke for Giggs
23 Sep	Chelsea	H	D	3-3	Van der Gouw	"	"	Johnsen	"	" 1	Keane	Scholes 1	"	"	" 1	Butt for Sheringham, Solskjaer for Cole, Brown for Irwin
1 Oct	Arsenal	A	L	0-1	Barthez	"	"	"	"	"	"	"	"	"	"	Yorke for Sheringham, Solskjaer for Giggs, Giggs for Sheringham
14 Oct	Leicester	A	W	3-1	"	Irwin	Brown	"	"	Solskjaer 1	"	Butt	Fortune	Yorke	" 2	Beckham 1 for Keane, Brown for Johnsen
21 Oct	Leeds	H	W	*3-0	"	P.Neville	G.Neville	"	"	"	Scholes	"	"	" 1	Scholes	
28 Oct	Southampton	H	W	5-0	"	Irwin	"	Brown	P.Neville	Beckham	Scholes	"	Giggs	Cole 2	Sheringham3	Yorke for Sheringham, Solskjaer for Cole, Wallwork for G.Neville
4 Nov	Coventry	A	W	2-1	"	"	"	"	"	" 1	Keane	Scholes	"	" 1	"	Yorke for Sheringham, Solskjaer for Scholes
11 Nov	Middlesbrough	H	W	2-1	"	P.Neville	"	"	Silvestre	"	"	"	Butt 1	Yorke	Solskjaer	Sheringham 1 for Solskjaer, Wallwork for Brown, Chadwick for Yorke
18 Nov	Man City	A	W	1-0	"	Irwin	"	"	P.Neville	" 1	"	"	"	"	Sheringham	Giggs for Sheringham
25 Nov	Derby County	A	W	3-0	"	"	"	"	Silvestre	Scholes	"	Butt 1	Chadwick	" 1	" 1	Van der Gouw for Barthez, Solskjaer for Chadwick, Fortune for Giggs
2 Dec	Tottenham	H	W	2-0	"	P.Neville	"	"	"	Beckham	"	"	Scholes 1	"	"	Giggs for Butt, Solskjaer 1 for Yorke
9 Dec	Charlton Ath	A	D	3-3	Van der Gouw	"	"	"	"	"	"	" 1	Giggs 1	Chadwick	Solskjaer 1	Sheringham for Beckham, Scholes for Chadwick, Greening for Keane
17 Dec	Liverpool	H	L	0-1	Barthez	Irwin	"	"	"	"	"	"	"	Scholes	"	Greening for Butt, Chadwick for Irwin
23 Dec	Ipswich Town	H	W	2-0	"	P.Neville	"	"	"	"	"	Fortune	"	"	" 2	Wallwork for Keane, Greening for Beckham, Healy for Giggs
26 Dec	Aston Villa	A	D	1-1	"	Irwin	"	"	"	"	"	Butt	"	"	" 1	P.Neville for Silvestre, Wallwork for Irwin
30 Dec	Newcastle	A	D	1-1	"	P.Neville	"	"	"	" 1	"	"	"	Yorke	"	Scholes for Solskjaer, Wallwork for Silvestre, Chadwick for Butt
1 Jan	West Ham	H	W	*3-1	"	"	"	"	"	"	"	Scholes	"	" 1	" 1	Butt for Scholes, Wallwork for Keane, Greening for Giggs
13 Jan	Bradford City	A	W	3-0	"	Irwin	"	Stam	"	"	"	"	P.Neville	" 1	" 1	Cole for Solskjaer, Brown for Stam, Chadwick 1 for P.Neville
20 Jan	Aston Villa	H	W	2-0	"	"	" 1	"	P.Neville	Greening	"	Butt	"	Sheringham1	"	Cole for Solskjaer, Chadwick for Greening
31 Jan	Sunderland	A	W	1-0	"	G.Neville	Stam	Brown	Silvestre	Beckham	"	Scholes	"	"	Cole 1	Butt for Scholes, P.Neville for Silvestre, Solskjaer for Sheringham
3 Feb	Everton	H	W	*1-0	"	Irwin	"	"	"	"	P.Neville	"	Chadwick	Solskjaer		Sheringham for Chadwick, Giggs for Scholes, Wallwork for Beckham
10 Feb	Chelsea	A	D	1-1	Van der Gouw	G.Neville	"	"	"	"	Keane	"	Giggs	"	" 1	Sheringham 1 for Yorke, Chadwick for Keane
25 Feb	Arsenal	H	W	6-1	Barthez	"	"	"	"	"	" 1	"	Butt	" 1	Yorke 3	Yorke for Sheringham, Chadwick 1 for Butt
3 Mar	Leeds	A	D	1-1	"	"	"	"	Irwin	"	P.Neville	"	"	"	Sheringham	Yorke 1 for Greening, Chadwick for Butt, Silvestre 1 for P.Neville
17 Mar	Leicester	H	W	2-0	"	Rachubka	Irwin	"	G.Neville	P.Neville	Greening	Keane	"	"	"	Scholes for Butt, Silvestre for Irwin, Chadwick for Sheringham
31 Mar	Liverpool	A	L	0-2	Barthez	"	Brown	"	"	Beckham	"	Butt	Giggs	Sheringham	Yorke	Scholes for Butt, Silvestre for Irwin, Chadwick for Sheringham
10 Apr	Charlton Ath	H	W	2-1	"	"	"	"	Silvestre	Scholes	"	"	"	Cole 1	"	Sheringham for Butt, P.Neville for Irwin, Solskjaer 1 for Yorke
14 Apr	Coventry	H	W	4-2	Goram	G.Neville	Stam	Brown	"	" 1	"	"	" 1	"	" 2	Beckham for Butt, Van der Gouw for Goram, Solskjaer for Cole
21 Apr	Man City	H	D	1-1	Barthez	Brown	G.Neville	Stam	P.Neville	Beckham	"	Scholes	Chadwick	Sheringham1	Solskjaer	Butt for Scholes, Giggs for Chadwick, Silvestre for Brown
28 Apr	Middlesbrough	A	W	2-0	Van der Gouw	"	Stam	Johnsen	" 1	" 1	Stewart	Butt	Fortune	Sheringham	Solskjaer	Cole for Solskjaer, Giggs for Fortune, Chadwick for Stewart
5 May	Derby County	H	L	0-1	Barthez	Irwin	Wallwork	"	"	"	"	"	Chadwick	"	Cole	Giggs for Stewart, Van der Gouw for Barthez
13 May	Southampton	A	L	1-2	Goram	"	Brown	"	"	Chadwick	"	Wallwork	Fortune	Giggs 1	Yorke	Van der Gouw for Goram, May for Wallwork
19 May	Tottenham	A	L	1-3	Van der Gouw	"	May	"	Silvestre	Butt	Scholes 1	P.Neville	Giggs	Sheringham	Cole	Djordjic for Irwin

* includes own goal

European Champions' League

Date	Opp	V	R	Score	1	2	3	4	5	6	7	8	9	10	11	Substitutes
13 Sep	Anderlecht	H	W	5-1	Barthez	Irwin 1	G.Neville	Johnsen	Silvestre	Beckham	Keane	Scholes	Giggs	Cole 3	Sheringham1	P.Neville for Irwin, Yorke for Cole, Solskjaer for Giggs
19 Sep	Dynamo Kiev	A	D	0-0	Van der Gouw	"	"	"	"	"	"	Butt	"	"	Yorke	Sheringham for Yorke, Solskjaer for Cole
26 Sep	PSV Eindhoven	A	L	1-3	"	P.Neville	"	Brown	"	Greening	"	"	Scholes 1	Solskjaer	"	Beckham for Greening, Giggs for Scholes, Wallwork for Silvestre
18 Oct	PSV Eindhoven	H	W	3-1	Barthez	Irwin	"	Johnsen	"	Beckham	"	Scholes 1	Giggs	Cole	Sheringham1	Butt for Beckham, Yorke 1 for Sheringham, Brown for Irwin
24 Oct	Anderlecht	A	L	1-2	"	" 1	"	"	"	"	"	"	"	"	Yorke	Solskjaer for Irwin, Brown for Silvestre
8 Nov	Dynamo Kiev	H	W	1-0	"	"	"	Brown	P.Neville	"	"	Butt	"	"	Sheringham1	Yorke for Sheringham, Fortune for Giggs, Silvestre for Fortune
21 Nov	Panathinaikos	H	W	3-1	"	P.Neville	"	"	"	Silvestre	"	"	Scholes 2	Yorke	" 1	
6 Dec	Sturm Graz	A	W	2-0	"	Irwin	"	"	"	"	"	"	"	" 1	" 1	Giggs 1 for Butt, P.Neville for Irwin, Solskjaer for Yorke
14 Feb	Valencia	A	D	0-0	"	G.Neville	Stam	"	"	"	"	Scholes	Giggs	Cole	"	Butt for Beckham, Solskjaer for Cole
20 Feb	Valencia	H	D	1-1	"	"	"	"	"	"	"	"	"	" 1	"	Butt for Giggs, Solskjaer for Sheringham
7 Mar	Panathinaikos	A	D	1-1	"	"	"	"	"	"	"	" 1	P.Neville	"	Yorke	Sheringham for P.Neville, Solskjaer for Cole, Chadwick for Silvestre
13 Mar	Sturm Graz	H	W	3-0	"	Irwin	G.Neville	Stam	"	Chadwick	" 1	"	Butt 1	Solskjaer	Sheringham	Greening for Scholes
3 Apr	Bayern Munich	H	L	0-1	"	G.Neville	Stam	Brown	"	Beckham	"	"	Giggs	"	Cole	Yorke for Beckham
18 Apr	Bayern Munich	A	L	1-2	"	"	"	"	"	Butt	"	"	Giggs 1	Yorke		Sheringham for Yorke, Solskjaer for Butt, Chadwick for Brown

FA Cup

Date	Opp	V	R	Score	1	2	3	4	5	6	7	8	9	10	11	Substitutes
Jan 8	Fulham	A	W	2-1	Van der Gouw	G.Neville	Brown	Silvestre	P.Neville	Beckham	Keane	Butt	Giggs	Solskjaer	Yorke	Sheringham 1 for Yorke, Wallwork for Butt, Chadwick for Beckham
Jan 28	West Ham	H	L	0-1	Barthez	Irwin	G.Neville	Stam	Silvestre	"	"	"	"	Cole	Sheringham	Yorke for Butt, Solskjaer for Irwin

Worthington (League) Cup

Date	Opp	V	R	Score	1	2	3	4	5	6	7	8	9	10	11	Substitutes
Oct 31	Watford	A	W	3-0	Van der Gouw	Clegg	O'Shea	Brown	P.Neville	Chadwick	Greening	Wallwork	Fortune	Solskjaer 2	Yorke 1	Stewart for Wallwork, Rachubka for Fortune
Nov 28	Sunderland	A	L	1-2	"	"	"	Johnsen	"	"	"	"	"	"	" 1	Stewart for Johnsen, Healy for Chadwick, Webber for Wallwork

FA Charity Shield

Date	Opp	V	R	Score	1	2	3	4	5	6	7	8	9	10	11	Substitutes
Aug 13	Chelsea	W+L		0-2	Barthez	G.Neville	Johnsen	Silvestre	Irwin	Beckham	Keane	Scholes	Giggs	Solskjaer	Sheringham	Yorke for Sheringham, Stam for Silvestre, Cole for Solskjaer,

Abbreviations:

Appearances (goals) refer to League games only

Figures shown as 2 etc. refer to goals scored by individual players

* own-goal

Players' names in final column, are substitutes

League Appearances (Goals in brackets)

Barthez 43 (0) - Beckham 42 (9) - Brown 37 (0) - Butt 35 (4) - Chadwick 9 (2) - Cole 25 (13) - Fortune 8 (2) - G.Neville 49 (1) - Giggs 35 (7) - Goram 2 (0) - Greening 6 (0) - Irwin 27 (2) - Johnsen 16 (1) - Keane 43 (3) - May 1 (0) - O'Shea 2 (0) - P.Neville 30 (0) - Rachubka 1 (0) - Scholes 40 (12) - Sheringham 32 (21) - Silvestre 41 (1) - Solskjaer 25 (13) - Stam 22 (0) - Stewart 3 (0) - Van der Gouw 10 (0) - Wallwork 6 (0) - Yorke 25 (12) - Own goals 3 - **Total 27 (starting) players (107)**

FA Premier League

	P	W	L	D	F:A	Pts	
Manchester U	38	24	8	6	79:31	80	1st